The Scope and Structure of Civil Codes

IUS GENTIUM

COMPARATIVE PERSPECTIVES ON LAW AND JUSTICE

VOLUME 32

For further volumes:
http://www.springer.com/series/7888

Julio César Rivera
Editor

The Scope and Structure of Civil Codes

Springer

Editor
Julio César Rivera
Faculty of Law
Universidad de Buenos Aires
and Universidad de San Andrés
Buenos Aires, Argentina

ISSN 1534-6781 ISSN 2214-9902 (electronic)
ISBN 978-94-007-7941-9 ISBN 978-94-007-7942-6 (eBook)
DOI 10.1007/978-94-007-7942-6
Springer Dordrecht Heidelberg New York London

Library of Congress Control Number: 2014930754

Printed on acid-free paper

Springer is part of Springer Science+Business Media (www.springer.com)

Preface

This work has its genesis in the Second Thematic Congress of the International Academy of Comparative Law, held in Taiwan in May 2012.

The subject matter of this Congress was "Codification", and the subject of the panel regarding the civil codes was: "*The scope and structure of civil codes. The inclusion of commercial law, family law, labor law, consumer law*".

The essays that make up this volume are based on the National Reports presented in the panel, but are not necessarily identical, for the subthemes have been reformulated; considerations, arguments and conclusions from the debates that took place at the Congress were incorporated and minor or accessory details that may not result interesting for the audience were suppressed.

Hence, the comparatist paper *The Scope and Structure of Civil Codes* opening this volume is not a mere reproduction of the General Report presented at the Congress, but it is a re-elaboration written in light of the essays from all the collaborators. Nevertheless, the essay makes reference to the National Reports, specifically for countries that did not present contributions for this volume. The National Reports will be published by Taiwan University.

An original work has been shaped from this material seeking to respond questions ranging from the philosophical, political or economic justification for legislation under the form of civil codes, to essentially practical matters such as the content of contemporary codes and their relation with the rest of the national and supranational legal frameworks.

The comparatist analysis allows to envision that countries often offer similar and on occasions totally diverse solutions to the same problems; and yet this is not an impediment to begin by noting a conclusion: the announced death of the codes has not occurred, and on the contrary its survival is seen in the countries that adopted codification as a method of legislative expression during the nineteenth and twentieth centuries, as well as in the growing interest it attracts in countries that are getting closer to world markets. Furthermore, even countries whose tradition and peculiar legal culture do not adhere to the codification method use alternative methods that result in an approximation to that product, the code, that has quite accurately been qualified as one of the most important fruits of the human spirit.

Buenos Aires, Argentina Julio César Rivera

Acknowledgements

As editor of this volume, I am grateful to each and every author of the works that are included herein. Particularly I am obliged to acknowledge Prof. Maxeiner's contribution, whose initiative made possible the support from Springer publishing.

Further, I would like to express my gratitude to Laura Piedrahita, a lawyer who has been for years collaborating with my research works, and whose excellent performance in the English language allows me to overcome the shortcomings in that field.

Likewise I must acknowledge the support of Eleonara Bianchi, lawyer and public translator in English, who also revised my papers before and after the Taiwan Congress.

And fundamentally, I would like to manifest my appreciation to the International Academy of Comparative Law for having honored me with the responsibility of performing as General Reporter for the panel that explored the theme developed in this book.

Contents

Part I
A Comparative Approach to the Scope and Structure of Civil Codes

Chapter 1
The Scope and Structure of Civil Codes. Relations with Commercial Law, Family Law, Consumer Law and Private International Law. A Comparative Approach

Julio César Rivera

Abstract In May 2012, the International Academy of Comparative Law held in Taiwan the Second Intermediate Thematic Congress with the general theme "Codification". Naturally, one of the topics was the codification of civil law, which included the history of codification in each participating country and its evolution, the current status of the codification method, and the role of the civil code and its relation with constitutional, international and other branches to which civil law is closely linked.

Therefore, the National Reports included as an introduction a general overview of the legislation on private law, with a description of the historical, economic, political, and social context in which such codes were enacted and the description of their original contents. Following, they outlined the evolution of codification, comprising the processes of "decodification" and "recodification"; the current status of the method of codification of private law, the relation of the civil codes with other branches of law such as private international law, consumer law and its consolidation or separation from commercial law or family law. The National Reports also informed about the relation between the codes and constitutional law and supranational law, which is a relevant chapter in the evolution of the role of the codes in the various nations; they also referred to current processes to update the codes and concluded by covering the role and present status of civil codification.

This material was supplemented with Reports from countries not familiar with the private law codification tradition, such as those belonging to the common law tradition. In these cases, the National Reports examined the status of legislation in the areas that are commonly covered by the civil codes in the civil law countries (e.g. contracts, family) as well as attempts to codify certain areas of the law.

J.C. Rivera (✉)
Prof. Faculty of Law, Universidad de Buenos Aires
and Universidad de San Andrés, Buenos Aires, Argentina
e-mail: juliocesar@rivera.com.ar

J.C. Rivera (ed.), *The Scope and Structure of Civil Codes*, Ius Gentium: Comparative Perspectives on Law and Justice 32, DOI 10.1007/978-94-007-7942-6_1,

As is the practice in the Congresses of the International Academy of Comparative Law, the General Report included a comparative analysis of all the contributions made by the countries. This paper has been prepared on the basis of such General Report and we have divided it into two parts: the first covers the reasons for codification, the criteria behind its expansion, and its current status despite the decodification processes which took place especially during the twentieth century. The second part covers the contents of the current civil codes and its relation to constitutional law and supranational law, as well as with the various areas of what in the civil law family is known as private law (commercial law, family law, consumer law, and private international law).

Keywords Civil codes • Private law • Codification • Decodification • Recodification • Civil codes relations with other branches of law

1.1 First Part. The Codification Era. Origin and Expansion of the Method. Decodification and Recodification of Private Law

1.1.1 Introduction. Codification. Origin, Importance and Reasons

1.1.1.1 Origin. The Expansion of the Method. Influence of the Napoleonic Code

Causes of the codification movement. Castán Tobeñas states that in general the codification movement has been the effect of three causes: (1) the philosophical and legal doctrines of the eighteenth century, mainly represented by the Natural Law School, which, based on the idea of the existence of an ideal and universal Law revealed by human reason, aimed at a legislation inspired in rationalist principles and translated into concrete formulas; (2) The French Revolution which, having destroyed all the past political institutions, and affirming the new principles of freedom and equality of citizens, urged the reconstruction of the whole public and private Law; (3) The formation of the new modern nations that needed to be reinforced by the territorial unity of the Law.[1]

Later codification was consolidated as an effect of the French Revolution; afterwards, it rapidly developed as a result of the Napoleonic Code (1804) which has had a remarkable diffusion and influence on the codification of countries of the most

[1] Castán Tobeñas, José, *Derecho Civil Español Común y Foral*, tomo Primero, volumen Primero, 12ª edición, revised by José Luis De los Mozos, Reus, Madrid, 1984, ps. 214/215.

diverse cultural and legal traditions[2]; and, finally, codification became an instrument for the affirmation of national identity.[3]

1.1.2 Reasons for the Expansion of Codification

The reasons for the expansion of codification as a method of legislative expression are varied and may differ from country to country.[4]

In Europe, it is known that Napoleon himself took his code to the countries he occupied, but it is true that once the imperialistic adventure was over, the codification process did not end.[5] As it occurred in other continents – particularly in Latin America – the codification process was observed not only as a rational expression of an up to then dispersed legislation hard to understand, overcome by new social and economic realities, but as an instrument for national cohesion[6] and for the exercise of state monopoly in the creation of laws. As a result, the countries in occidental Europe either enacted their own civil and commercial codes during the nineteenth century, or, plainly and simply, maintained the Napoleonic Code with

[2] V. Vogel, Louis, "Le monde des Codes civils"; Kerameus, Konstantinos, "L'influence du Code Civil en Europe centrale et orientale"; Jahel, Selim, "Code civil et codification dans les pays du monde árabe"; Goré, Marie, "L'influence du Code Civil en Amérique du Nord"; Wald, Arnoldo, "L'influence du Code Civil en Amérique latine"; Hoshino, Eiichi, "L'influence du Code Civil au Japon"; all in *1804–2004. Le Code Civil. Un passé. Un présent. Un avenir*, Université Panthéon-Assas (Paris II), Dalloz, Paris, 2004. The subject was already widely covered in the centenary of the Napoleonic Code: v. *Le Code Civil – 1804–1904, Livre du Centenaire*, reedición, Dalloz, Paris, 2004.

[3] The 1811 Austrian Civil Code has also been influential in the codification process; even the Argentine Civil Code has adopted a few rules from that Austrian Code.

[4] It is said that: "The undeniable influence of the Napoleonic Code in nineteenth century is a mixture of complex phenomena, where the strength of weapons and ideas, the case of profound "reception" and of superficial adoption of the French model, the progressive signals of decline and the persistence of an image are all mixed": Halpérin, Jean-Louis, "Deux cents ans de rayonnement du *Code Civil des Français*", en *Codes et Codification*, Les Cahiers de Droit, volume 42, nº 1 y 2, March–June 2005, Faculté de Droit Université Laval, Quebec, ps. 229 y ss.

[5] Furthermore, in some countries the Napoleonic Code did not only survive but the recipient proved to be more faithful to the original text than France itself; it was the case of Belgium.

[6] A very well-known Spanish publication reads: "The *historical and political* aim of the Spanish codification was to unify as substantially as possible our national Law, still affected by the breakdown caused during the Spanish *Reconquista*": Castán Tobeñas, ob. cit., lug. cit., p. 260. In Argentina, one of the greatest nineteenth century constitutionalists considered the Code to be a serious contradiction with the federal regime adopted for the organization of the State. (Alberdi, Juan José, *Obras Completas*, volume VII, Bs. As., 1887, ps. 80). But the Civil Code was also regarded as an extraordinary element for national cohesion that permitted to overcome outdated, disperse and chaotic legislation; it allowed for the development of local legal literature and the modernization of the teaching method, which in many areas solved the problems of *Derecho Castellano* and Spanish-American law (*Derecho Indiano*). Thereby, obstacles to the disposition of property were eliminated, such as censuses, ecclesiastical benefits, and linkages; equality among sons was established with the abolition of the right of primogeniture; and by giving sons the quality of forced heirs, the division of property was facilitated.

minor changes; even in Germany the discussion over codification itself and the Napoleonic Code gathered authors such as SAVIGNY, HEGEL, MARX and VON STEIN.[7]

In Latin America, the codification process was seen as a way to become independent from Spanish-American law (*Derecho Indiano*), name given to the law enacted in the metropolis – Spain – to be enforced in the Indies (America); and as the affirmation of their national identity and political independence. It also coincided with the philosophical ideas of the Creole intellectuals and politicians of the time, resulting in every constitution of Latin American countries including provisions for the enactment of Codes, tendency which continued to progress throughout the nineteenth century.[8] The adhesion of these codes to the Romano-Germanic family was a natural consequence due to the education received by the jurists of the time on the foundations of Roman Law and the Seven Divisions of Law of Alfonso X, the Learned (*Siete Partidas*) – which were applied in the times of colonies and even survived on certain matters after the independence. The Napoleonic Code was a source of inspiration for many subjects, partly due to its strong Roman influence, especially in the sphere of contract law and obligations[9]; the American codifiers – as many jurists in all latitudes – have many times unknowingly reproduced the rules of Roman Law, since they have done it through intermediaries such as DOMAT, POTHIER and the Napoleonic Code.[10]

However, the identification of national independence and codification is not exclusive of Latin American countries; likewise, Greece – independent from the Ottoman Empire in 1821 – embarked into the codification of the national civil law as the first revolutionaries (1821) agreed on a clause in the Constitution which envisaged the enactment of a Civil Code to be passed by the "*most distinguished wise and virtuous Greeks*". Eventually in the face of the vicissitudes of history, the Civil Code was finally enacted in 1940 and enforced in 1946, 124 years after the commencement of the debate.

---

[7] HALPÉRIN, ob. cit., explains how, once the Napoleonic invasions ceased, the Code falls into an object of condemnation, it is abandoned in many States in which it had been adopted, but the most remarkable issue is the Code's resistance to the hostile forces inflicted against it, which contributes to its survival in many places such as the Netherlands, Geneva, and a few Italian States; or to local codes being passed taking it as a model: Parma, Kingdom of the two Sicilies; and it is still upheld by citizens of places near France, Renania and Jura Bernés: ob. cit., ps. 236/237.

[8] The first Code of all Latin American countries is the Haiti's Code (1825); the State of Oaxaca enacted its Civil Code in 1827 and Bolivia codified its civil law in 1830 (Santa Cruz Code), but the main codes in the area are the Chilean Code (1855) of strong influence on the codes of other American countries (Ecuador, Colombia, Venezuela and some Central American Countries) and Argentina (1869) which also had influence on, for example, the Uruguayan Civil Code and was plainly and simply adopted by Paraguay.

[9] V. GAUTIER, PIERRE-YVES, "Sous le Code Civil des Français: Rome (l'origine du droit des contrats)", en *1804–2004. Le Code Civil...*, quoted, p. 51.

[10] GAUTIER is expressive on the point when he states: "*...il ne faut pas oublier Labéon, Celse, Martine, Africanus, Proculus et Sabinus, Javolenus, Julien, Pomponius et tant d'autres; tous ces noms sont tombés dans la poussière des millénaires, mais les juristes de 2004, lorsqu'ils cherchent une règle dans le code civil ou un ouvrage moderne, utilisent encoré leurs idées souvent sans le savoir*": ob. cit., p. 53.

Czechoslovakia gained its independence as a result of the fall of the Austro-Hungarian Empire and the 1811 Austrian Civil Code remained in force long after for the country was not institutionally prepared for the independence. And even though the idea of amending the Austrian code soon gained force and was indeed embodied in the 1937 Draft, the reform could not come into force due to the German invasion and the Second World War.

On some occasions, the codification process enabled the maintenance of the cultural profiles of political institutions, which had lost independence throughout the course of history as they were absorbed by States which as a whole belonged to another cultural and legal tradition. Indeed, in Quebec and Louisiana, the codification of the civil law can be clearly explained by their bonds with French culture and law; their incorporation to Canada and the United States did not force them to give up the idea of codification; thus, the Civil Code reflects – especially in the case of Quebec – an obvious identification with the feeling of belonging to a nation[11] and to a cultural and legal tradition. The peculiar inclusion of these two models in the frame of countries with uncodified law will be subject of analysis in this paper owing to the excellent essays from these jurisdictions comprising this volume.

As in the case of Turkey, codification has also been the result of highly revolutionary processes carrying deep social transformations. The essay written by Ergun Özsunay illustrates this rigorously. And as the essay from the Czech Republic suggests, to a certain extent, this is what happened in countries that separated from communism since 1989.

Another codification case is given by a colonial authority imposing a Code. That was what occurred in Macau, where the Portuguese Civil Code was in force for many years, though, as it will be also illustrated, coexisting with the culture, institutions and the law of the Chinese people, which makes it a very interesting case of study.

And finally in the case of Japan, it may be argued that codification was necessary to sustain modernization and Westernization; in this sense, the Japanese Civil Code was the result of the acceptance of Western civilization.[12]

1.1.2.1 The Continuance of Codification in the Early Twentieth Century

To sum up, the nineteenth century was the codification century of civil law and the model most demanded was the French. The twentieth century began under the influence of the German Civil Code and a few years later, the Code of Obligations

[11] The character of "Nation" of Quebec has recently been expressly acknowledged by Canada, to be more exact on 27th November 2006 the House of Commons in Canada passed a motion introduced by the Prime Minister Stephen Harper stating that: "Que cette Chambre reconnaisse que les Québécoises et les Québécois forment une nation au sein d'un Canada uni." / "That this House recognizes that the Québécois form a nation within a united Canada."

[12] See Professor Ishikawa's essay.

of Switzerland. The German Code influenced many codes of the twentieth century, such as the Brazilian Civil Code of 1916, the Greek Code of 1940,[13] as well as the Japanese Code of 1896,[14] the Portuguese Code of 1966 and, through it, Macau's Code.[15] In addition, it should be emphasized that the German dogmatic approach influenced the replacement of the Italian Code by its 1942 Code.[16]

Moreover, the Swiss Code of Obligations was adopted by Turkey with minor changes as a way to modernize and occidentalize the law in the emerging State. The Civil Code in force in Taiwan from 25th October 1945 was inspired in the German Civil Code and the Swiss Code of Obligations.[17]

1.1.2.2 The Importance of the Civil Codification

During the nineteenth century a statement by a French professor gained popularity: "I don't teach Civil Law. I teach the Civil Code". Years later, Dean Carbonnier described the Napoleonic Code as "the civil constitution of the French people", expression repeated by many others with a slight change when they say it is "the economic constitution of the French people". Many years later, specifically in 1968, when the Argentine Civil Code Reform Law was passed, the Minister and distinguished Professor of Civil Law Guillermo Borda stated that "*at the risk of being considered heretical, I am tempted to say that the Civil Code is more important than the National Constitution itself, because the Constitution is more distant to people's daily lives than the Civil Code, which, otherwise, is all around people all the time, being the weather under which people move and has a decisive influence on the orientation and formation of a society*". This paragraph was reproduced in the Message for the Introduction of the Unified Code Project in 1998.

Thus, the Civil Code constituted the main source of civil law – almost exclusive – and many times was attributed a value equivalent to that of a Constitution.

---

[13] In force since 1946.

[14] Professor Ishikawa explains that the Civil Code is a product of comparative law and notes it was influenced by the French Civil Code – through the "Boissonade Draft" – and the First and Second drafts of the German Civil Code.

[15] The essay about codification in Portugal written by Prof. Dário Moura Vicente describes the influence of the Portuguese Civil Code of 1966 in Africa.

[16] The essay written by the distinguished comparatist Professor Roberto Sacco is eloquent when it states that "*the civil code is the product of Italy's adhesion to the German categories and concepts. The practical rules are always French (…), but the concepts are German …*".

[17] The Civil Code of Taiwan is the Civil Code promulgated by the Nationalist Government of China during the period 1929–1931. However, at that time, Taiwan was still under Japanese rule, the Civil Code of the Republic of China did not come into effect in Taiwan until October 25, 1945.

1.1.2.3 The Content of the Nineteenth Century Codes

The Codes of the nineteenth century basically followed the structure of the Napoleonic Code. Therefore, it included the rules about the person – which in the French Code started with the concept of nationality –, the family that was directly related to the person[18]; property or patrimonial rights which entailed contracts, obligations arising from contracts and wrongful acts; real property rights; and succession law.

The criteria behind the structuring of the nineteenth-century codification can be in general terms described as follows:

(i) The absolute nature of the property right;
(ii) The absolute value of the pledged word, which gave the contract a compulsory force as if it were the law in itself;
(iii) Family Law conceived from the idea of an indissoluble marriage.

The person was regarded as the subject of family and patrimonial legal relations, and for that reason, references to the person's individual rights were scarce.

This notion of civil law restricted in the end to the person and their patrimony would be broadened. Pursuant to this, the civil codes included the general law of the person (from the Swiss Civil Code) and the Italian Civil Code incorporated labor law.

1.1.2.4 Partial Conclusions

To sum up the reasons for the expansion of the codification method, we can say that:

- The nineteenth century showcased the expansion of the codification method;
- The reasons for this expansion are many and varied: the rationalization of a dispersed legislation; the regulation of new social and economic realities; the National cohesion and the exercise of the state monopoly in the creation of laws;
- The Napoleonic Code had a decisive influence in the expansion of the method serving as a source for many codes of European and Latin American countries as well as countries in other continents;
- The codification process was not restricted to civil law, but it also extended to commercial and other branches of law;
- The Civil Codes of the nineteenth century contained the regulation of the typical market institutions: contracts and property – which included then succession upon death –, but also regulations over natural persons, artificial persons, and family;
- As of the beginning of the twentieth century, the German and Swiss Codes of Obligations reflected a more modern methodology than the Napoleonic Code and served as a source of inspiration to new Codes and the reforms of the existing ones.

[18] Thus, Book I of the Civil Code of Argentina is called "Of the Person", is divided into two sections, the first of which named "Of the Person in General" and the second "Of the personal rights in family relations".

1.1.3 A Code, Multiple Codes. The Issue in Federal States

The phenomenon of federal States and codification presents several models that must be considered before regarding the object and structure of the Codes. Evidently, a Civil Code which rules a whole State (Switzerland, Germany, Argentina) differs from a Civil Code only applicable to a province or local state (the civil code of Oaxaca or any other Mexican state).

Furthermore, we will also identify states where, even though there is a single civil code, there are rules of private law which collect particularities for certain provinces, regions or other minor political entities.

1.1.3.1 Federal States with Unified Substantive Law

As mentioned above, the codification boom had various reasons; one was the aim of having a single legislation in the States that at the same time could monopolize the law making process.

This was a relatively easy objective to be attained in the unitary countries such as France. But, it was – and it is still – much more complex in the federal states and, in general, in those in which the political entities within the same State maintain – generally due to particular historical reasons – a certain legislative autonomy.

This has given rise to the development of two completely different models.

On the one hand, States have unified the civil legislation, in such a way that there is a single Code valid and enforceable in all the political entities of the National State, even when those entities still retain a certain degree of constitutionally recognized autonomy.

Therefore, in federal states like Germany, Switzerland, Brazil and Argentina there is a single Civil Code for the whole State. This, notwithstanding the fact that in many particular states preexisting the National State there could have been local codes in force, like in Bevier and Prussia which is Germany nowadays; in some cantons of the Helvetic confederation, such as Vaud and Geneva.[19]

In Argentina, the 1853 Constitution, which was strongly inspired in the United States Constitution, recognizes the Provinces as entities legally and historically preceding the National State, which is formed by a pact among them resulting in its creation. Delegating to the Federal Congress the power to pass a single Civil Code, and the Commercial, Criminal and Mining codes, was seen as enabling national cohesion.

---

[19] One particular case is the one of Poland, which 1791 Constitution set forth the enactment of a civil code as well as a criminal code, but what happened was that during the existence of the Polish – Lithuanian State foreign codes were in force in different parts of the country; so, according to the region, the Austrian Code, the Napoleonic Code, and the Prussian Code, later replaced by the BGB's, were applicable. Only after the First World War, Poland undertook the task of codifying all the country, which resulted in the 1933 Code of Obligations and 1934 Commercial Code.

1.1.3.2 Federal States with Local Substantive Law

The second model is given by federal countries which have assigned their states or provinces the authority to enact their own Codes or civil legislation. In this area, the most remarkable case is that of Mexico in which the states are constitutionally empowered to pass their own civil codes; while the Commercial Code is enacted by the Federal Congress and, therefore, it is the one for the whole federation. It is widely known that the system tends to be rather inefficient due to the possibility of conflict with respect to the applicable substantive law to the legal relations of private law.

Also, in the United States, each State of the Federation has its own substantive law, but there is no national code for the whole Federation. The Uniform Commercial Code – similar to a code of national enforceability – is a legal body applicable in the states which incorporate it as local law. And, the Restatements are private works that have importance, but they cannot be compared with a code of general enforceability for the whole country. Local regulations, uniform laws, model laws, federal statutes governing certain matters make an extremely complex puzzle and, in the end, not very efficient, as Professor Maxeiner points out in the title of his essay: "Costs of no Codes".

1.1.3.3 Spain

In some countries, where private law is codified in order to be applicable to the whole State, there still may be some local arrangements.

The most obvious example is that of the Kingdom of Spain, where owing to historical reasons originated in the *Reconquista* period, certain territories were granted some prerogatives known as "*fueros*"[20] (Charters) which are currently retained.[21] So, Navarra, Aragón, Cataluña and other territories have regimes of regional law, some of which have enacted their own codes, such as the Cataluña Civil Code (2004) and the 2011 Regional Law Code of Aragón. The essay of Professor García Cantero describes the relation of these regional law systems with the whole Spanish legal system.

---

[20] The territory of the Iberian Peninsula was invaded by Muslims coming from Africa in the year 711. What is named the *Reconquista* was completed by the year 1492, year in which the Catholic Monarchs – Isabel of Castile and Ferdinand of Aragón – took control of Granada. In this long period of almost eight centuries, certain principalities and kingdoms were granted "fueros" (charters) which are currently retained.

[21] The 1978 Constitution sets forth in its section 149 that the State has the exclusive jurisdiction over the commercial, criminal and procedural legislation, as well as the civil legislation; however such exclusivity exists *"Notwithstanding the Autonomous Communities' rights of conservation, modification and development of the civil, regional law codes or special laws, where they exist. In any case, the rules related to the application and enforceability of legal statutes, legal-civil relationships as to the forms of marriage, the organization of registries and public instruments, basis of contractual relationships, statutes to resolve conflict of laws and the definition of the sources of the law with regard, in this last case, to regional laws or special laws."*

1.1.3.4 Partial Conclusions

The aforementioned suggests that those countries taking steps towards codification should bear in mind that:

- On the one hand, a system with a civil code of general enforceability in the entire territory is much more efficient than a system in which multiple codes or statutes of limited territorial enforceability coexist.
- However, so long as historical, political, ethnic and geographic reasons impose respectable particularities, such codes may coexist rather reasonably, though they should define the limits within which each general or particular statute shall rule.

1.1.4 "Uncodified" Models

Although the codification model was indeed very much followed in the nineteenth century by countries in all latitudes, there is still an important part of the world that failed to adhere to codification; thus, it is worth pointing out that a significant percentage of the world population lives in countries of an undeniable political and economic weight that have no codes, or, at least, they lack a civil code or a commercial code like the one Portalis and his colleagues bequeathed to humanity.

Under this important category, two different models may be identified which have not followed the codification idea, but, at the same time, belong to different legal families: such models are the Scandinavian and the common law.

1.1.4.1 Scandinavian Countries

Scandinavian countries are generally classified under the Romano-Germanic family. In this way, the essay written by the Finnish Prof. Teemu Juutilainen and the Norwegian National Report presented at the Taiwan Congress state that both legal systems are "*part of the Nordic (less precisely: Scandinavian) legal community, together with Sweden, Denmark, and Iceland*", and referring to the classification of this group the Finnish essay appeals to the opinion of René David by stating: "*René David and John E.C. Brierley include Finnish and the other Nordic legal systems in the Romano-Germanic legal family. as a secondary grouping, alongside Latin, Germanic, and Latin American laws, and so on*". Even if the relation between the Nordic system and the Continental European system seems undeniable, the truth is that these countries did not follow the codification tradition.

The conclusion on this matter can be found in the Finnish essay when it explains that: *"Other parts, notably when it comes to general principles of law, are uncodified and expected to remain so. To be sure, a comprehensive codification of the "general part" of private law would be at odds with the Nordic tradition"*.

1.1.4.2 Common Law: The United States Case

Common law is broadly speaking judge-made law with different features in the United States and England that have been extensively studied by doctrine.[22] Codification is then completely outside the tradition of this legal family; however, in the United States, the subject has been the topic of much doctrinal and political intense debate for a very long time; and, nowadays there exists a legislative body known as Code – Uniform Commercial Code – which deserves a detailed analysis.

Today, Private Law, including the topics of this essay, contract law, commercial law, consumer law, and family law, is principally the law of 50 separate states; and state law, with the lone exception of Louisiana, is uncodified law.

The complex legislative system added to the other sources, in particular the legal precedents, makes it extremely difficult to understand the private law in the United States.

Afterwards, we will see how, during the twentieth century, the idea of a comprehensive codification of private law is practically not discussed, and even in a lesser degree at a national level; but the complexities we refer to have caused some private institutions to work very hard to issue documents that could make current law applicable. All this has given rise to documents like the *restatements* and model or uniform laws that were adopted in some cases as local law by the States, such as the case of the Uniform Commercial Code.

1.1.4.3 The Scotland Case

Scotland is classified as a mixed legal system but not codified – as the essay written by the Scottish Professor Elspeth Reid illustrates –, in which features of the civil law and the common law traditions combine. Scottish Law presents a mixture not just in terms of the rules themselves, but also in terms of processes of legal reasoning. The style of legal reasoning is strongly rooted in the common law, in that it is inductive, moving from the specific case to general principle, rather than deductive, starting from general principle and moving to the specific case. But while case-law is very important, there is also a strong conceptualist tradition, and if there is no obvious answer in the case-law or in statute, the Scottish courts will readily look at the texts of classic jurists of high authority, the Scottish "institutional" writers which are regarded as important sources of law, as noted above. Whatever the historical significance attributed to its components, a mixed system is deeply embedded in modern Scottish law.

Thus, the Scotland Act 1998 established the Scottish Parliament and devolved legislative competence in areas of private law that were within the competence of

[22] DAVID, RENÉ – JAUFFRET-SPINOSI, CAMILLE, *Les grands système de droit contemporains*, Dalloz, 11e édition, Paris, 2002, p. 265, state: "Le droit anglais, issu des procédures de la common law, est encore essentiellement un droit jurisprudentiel...".

the Westminster Parliament; but still Scotland has no Civil Code as such, though certain discrete areas of the law are governed by a comprehensive statute, or series of statues.

Although Scotland is far from the codification tradition, there have been various initiatives in recent years directed at codification. The draft prepared by McGregor had no success, but was a project undertaken in order to provide a starting point for negotiations in developing a common European Contract Law. From that time, both Scotland and England have participated in such European initiatives, but with separate representatives from north and south of the border.

1.1.4.4 Codes in Force in the Framework of Uncodified Models: The Quebec, Louisiana and Puerto Rico Cases

Canada and the United States share the characteristics that they are both federal states, belong to the common law system, recognize to their Provinces or States certain autonomy in the matter of private law and both are absent from national or provincial codes. But, they also have a very special circumstance in common: there is in both countries a Province or State that since the nineteenth century has had its own Civil Code with a clear French inspiration. We are making reference to the Canadian Province of Quebec and the State of Louisiana in the United States.

The essay of Andrés Parise, about the Louisana's experience, begins by stating: "*Louisiana is the only U.S. state that is considered to be a member of the [Romano-Germanic] family. It is the only state with a civil code that originally followed the tenets of nineteenth-century continental European codes*".

The process of codification starts at the beginning of the nineteenth century and Louisiana has its first Civil Code in 1825; revised in 1870.

As for the "*structure and content of nineteenth-century civil codes in Louisiana was pretty much in harmony with that of other contemporaneous codification endeavors. The structure in Louisiana followed the model provided by the Code Napoléon, and a similar situation took place with other civil codes in the Latin American countries.*"

It is obvious that "*Louisiana has been an isolated "Civil Law island" partially surrounded by a "sea of Common Law"*", but "*…the content of the Louisiana Civil Code presents interesting features: it is applicable in a mixed jurisdiction, and it is drafted in English language. Louisiana, considered by many a mixed jurisdiction, combines aspects of common- and civil-law*".[23]

Quebec reality does not differ so much. Originally conquered by France, it was then incorporated to Canada, which was part of the British Empire, though maintaining its mother tongue and its law, affiliated to the Romano-Germanic family.

---

[23] Puerto Rico can also be described as a mixed legal system highly influenced by special American styled statutes, especially with regard to administrative and commercial rules of law. But, as in Quebec, "the Code is now a symbol as being Puerto Rican". See the essay written by Prof. Muñoz.

Thus, in 1866 the Civil Code of Lower Canada was enacted and it recognized the Napoleonic Code as its main source. Of course, it is worth mentioning that, as is the case in Louisiana, Quebec is also a mixed jurisdiction given that procedural law, the judicial system and many statutes in the matter of commercial law are based on the common law; notwithstanding the foregoing, the Quebecer report for the Taiwan Congress notes that: "*Still, in everything that concerns patrimonial relationship within the provincial jurisdiction, the civilian and Romano-Germanic concepts rule and reasoning methodology apply*".

Puerto Rico, is today, "as codified as possible under the circumstances".[24] Puerto Rico was a country member of the continental European culture until it was annexed to the United States as a result of the Spanish – USA war. But the substitution of Spanish public law – constitutional and administrative law and organization – with American rules and statutes, the virtual suppression of the Commercial Code due to the adoption of many special commercial statutes copied from the United States, and the adoption of United States models of judicial administration and procedure changed the perspective. American case law quickly developed and by 1938 legal studies became U.S. patterned, with students entering law schools after completion of any one of a series of university studies and learning the law, at least public, procedural and commercial law through the case method. Private non-commercial law, however, remained codified and since the early 1970s a renewed source of pride and revival, despite efforts to adopt a new and modernized Civil Code, proved fruitless. The Civil Code has been modernized through special statutes, especially in matters of Family Law, which at times have amended the Code and at times complemented it.

1.1.5 The "Decodification" Era

1.1.5.1 What Is the "Decodification Era"

As we have noted the twentieth century commenced with the coming into effect of the BGB (German Civil Code) and a few years later, with the Swiss Code of obligations, promptly taken on by Turkey. Furthermore, some North African countries adopted civil codes following European models, especially the French one.[25]

---

[24] See Muñiz Argüelles' essay.

[25] In North African countries, French law has been combined with Islamic law, especially in family law matters and law of the persons; however, it still has great influence as in the case of the 1975 Algeria Civil Code and 1948 Egypt, copied then by Libya; and on the civil law of countries like Morocco and the Tunisian Republic: Tetley, William, "Mixed Jurisdictions: common law vs. civil law (codified and uncodified)", 4 Uniform L. Rev. (N.S.) 1999-3, 591–619.

However, jurists commented on the existence of a decodification process; NATALINO IRTI and his famous publication "The Decodification Era" paved the way for it.[26]

Professor Rodolfo Sacco summarizes IRTI's ideas on the subject by saying: "*The civil code has lost its monopoly… [it] has lost its central place to the constitution, administrative law, and labor law and shares its role with a number of small laws that speak a language and adopt their concepts*" Moreover, the decodification process seems even more critical in the sphere of commercial law.

The different essays included in this book are eloquent on this issue.

The Argentine essay points out that the 1869 Civil Code, in force as from 1871, has been subject to some revisions; the most relevant one in 1968. But, dozens of laws on relevant matters pertaining to private law have been passed and are in force outside the scope of the Civil and Commercial Codes. In a number of cases, what was simply done was "removing" from the code institutions in it such as: company law, bankruptcy, insurance, maritime transport, and so on.

In France, as it is universally known, the Napoleonic Code applies, but it has been revised in many opportunities, in general terms, to incorporate innovative topics; for example, those related to the protection of privacy; bioethics and the liability for manufactured products.

Spanish Prof. García Cantero also recognizes the existence of a decodification process. But also shows the existence of an inverse process given that certain special rules detached, even ideologically, from the Civil Code have to some extent, returned to it. This is the case of the lease contract and rural rental contracts. Anyway, there are other laws in force outside the scope of the Civil Code.

Even though Portugal has enacted a new Civil Code in 1966, Prof. Moura in his Portuguese essay says: "*To a certain extent, a phenomenon of de-codification has thus also occurred in Portugal, by virtue of which Civil Law now comprises many rules not included in the Civil Code*".

The essay from the Czech Republic, written by Professor David Elischer, Ondřej Frinta and Monika Pauknerová, states that this country also "*has experienced a significant process of decodification…*"

However, the decodification process does not exhaust in the cases in which certain matters "separate from" the Civil Code or the Commercial Code to be regulated by special laws, which constitute "legislative microsystems"; or in that certain new matters are treated by special laws which are not incorporated to any code.[27] As the essays from France, Italy and Argentina point out, the Code must coexist with other sources even of a higher hierarchy – like the Constitution, the supranational law and the community law – from which subjective rights arise, the

[26] IRTI, NATALINO, *La edad de la decodificación*, translated by Luis Rojo Ajuria, Barcelona, 1992; German scholars – as JOSEPH ESSER and FRIEDRICH KÜBLER – have also announced the end of the code's era: cited by SCHMIDT, KARSTEN. "Il Codice Commerciale Tedesco: dal declino alla recodificazione", *Rivista di Diritto Civile*, Cedam, Padova, 1999.

[27] In Argentina, the trust, leasing and credit card are subjects never covered by the Commercial Code and from their origin were treated in special laws.

fulfillment of which individuals may demand either at national or supranational levels. We will go back to this subject later.

1.1.6 The "Recodification" Era

1.1.6.1 Overestimation of the "Decodification"

Despite the announcement of the "death" of the Codes, a significant trend of opinion makes an accurate distinction between the aging of the Codes and the codification method. It is beyond doubt that the nineteenth-century codes aged as a result of the accelerated social changes of the twentieth century. And, this aging process is even more evident in the case of relations originated in the creation of supranational communities not even envisaged by the authors of such Codes.

But this does not mean abdicating the method because codification is a systematic demand of law.[28] And codification should be conceived not as an immovable target, but, as a living process, an essentially dynamic set in which new laws are constantly being incorporated and outdated ones displaced; thus, demanding a permanent revision. Indeed, it seems that there can be no doubt that the codification method is still in practice and that, according to DE LOS MOZOS, the "decodification era" is *now fortunately overcome.* This is evidenced by the process which doctrine has referred to as "recodification" and which actually encloses diverse factors. On the one hand, countries with a codification tradition which have totally or partially rewritten their codes. On the other hand, countries which, by mid twentieth-century, did not have civil or commercial codes, but have been incorporating them in the recent years as a way to adapt to the market economy, ratify their national identity or simply to improve the quality of expression of their legal systems.

1.1.6.2 Recodification in Countries with a Codification Tradition

As mentioned above, many countries that drafted their civil codes in the nineteenth century have totally or partially rewritten them in the twentieth century or even in the few years of the twenty-first century. It was Professor Sacco who affirmed in a 1983 publication that, as events have developed, it looks as if legislators have forgotten we are in the decodification era, "*due to the fact that in the last half century forty new Civil Codes have been promulgated*".[29] And, since this remarkable contribution of the distinguished Italian jurist many more reforms have followed:

---

[28] SCHMIDT, op. cit.

[29] SACCO, RODOLFO, "Codificare, modo superato di legiferare?", *Rivista di Diritto Civile,* Cedam, Padova, 1983.

the Dutch reform, the Codes of Quebec, Peru and Paraguay, the German reform and the draft or revision of codes in numerous countries which began to incorporate to the market economy upon the dissolution of the Soviet Union, such as the Russian Federation, Lithuania, Estonia, the Czech Republic and so on.

It can be pointed out that a milestone in this process was the draft of the 1942 Italian Civil Code, which served as a model to the renovation of the Latin American legislations, especially the Bolivian Code in 1975, the Peruvian Code in 1984 and the Paraguayan Code in 1985; also, the Argentine reform in 1968.

Portugal has replaced the old Civil Code for the new Civil Code in 1966; but, Portugal also has: the Companies Code, the Copyright and Related Rights Code, the Industrial Property Code, the Labour Code, the Insolvency Code, the Code of Civil Registry, and the Code of Securities.

Quebec's recodification has been relevant. The new code has been in force since 1st January 1994 and has become the source of inspiration in other countries for the revision of their own codes.[30]

On the other hand, the codification tendency was evident in France; about 70 codes can now be found on the French Government's official legal website. Some of these codes are nothing more than ordinary, normal length statutes. However, if it is evident in many branches of the law, it is different in the field of the Civil Law, where even though many limited reforms concerning parts of the Code were enacted, "a global reform of the Code is not on the agenda".[31] In the same way, the whole process of updating the Civil Code has been chaotic in Belgium.[32]

1.1.6.3 The Situation in Former Socialist Countries: Estonia, Poland and the Czech Republic

Another aspect of the recodification process of private law was seen in the countries that after the Second World War were left under soviet influence – such as Poland, Czecho-Slovakia or Hungary – or were directly a part of the URSS, such as Estonia, Lithuania and Latvia. After the disappearance of the Soviet Union, they changed their economic system radically, and the Baltic countries regained their political independence. This required arduous work to rebuild a private law system adapted to the new political circumstances and economic system.

This is all very thoroughly explained in Irene Kull's essay about Estonia Republic, which refers to how private law in Estonia has been restructured in different periods to pave the way to the recognition of private property and economic freedom. This permitted their opening to the influence of the law from Western Europe, though not

[30] For example, in Argentina it has been the source of numerous solutions proposed by the 1998 Project; on the subject s. Rivera, Julio César, "Le projet de code civil pour la République argentine", *Les Cahiers de Droit*, (Quebec, Canada), vol. 46, nº 1–2, mars/juin 2005, ps. 295 y ss.

[31] Borghetti, Jean Sebastien, "French Law".

[32] Heirbaut, D. and Storme, M. E., "Private Law Codifications in Belgium".

following the codification method beyond the existence of a Commercial Code, the characteristics of which will be later discussed.[33]

The situation in the Czech Republic is alike: although the 1964 Civil Code was amended on many occasions, it is significantly stigmatised due to its socialist origin. Moreover, after so many amendments, the text of the Code was absent from any conception and appeared to be completely unsatisfactory. In consequence, the 1964 Civil Code was finally replaced by a new Civil Code in effect since 1st January 2012, and was completed with the Business Corporation Act and the Private International Act.

1.1.6.4 The Situation in the Countries Outside the Scope of the Codification Method

We have already transcribed the Finnish essay where it explains: "*Other parts, notably when it comes to general principles of law, are uncodified and expected to remain so. To be sure, a comprehensive codification of the "general part" of private law would be at odds with the Nordic tradition*".

Some traits of this can also be seen in the Scottish essay. Even though the McGregor Project failed to receive much support, the potential codification at a European level aroused interest. Additionally, the United States follows a tendency to consolidate some branches of private law through crossed channels: model laws, uniform laws and restatements.

And, finally, among the common law countries, Israel has a Civil Code Project under development.

1.1.6.5 Decodification and Recodification in the Field of Commercial Law

The decodification and recodification of the Commercial Law will be treated again *infra* n° 7.1 and following.

---

[33] In other countries that were part of the socialist area, there may still be some statutes in force from the time of the soviet influence; but were strongly reformed. Thus, in Poland, the 1964 civil and commercial codes are still in force. But "*...from 1990 the changes of both codes are numerous and frequent. At first, already in 1990 the provisions connected with the previous economic system were eliminated from the civil code, while the provisions important for free market economy were introduced (for example general provisions on securities). The changes were timing at:*

- *adjustment to the new economic and political system defined by the Constitution of 1997*
- *adjustment to international obligations*
- *adjustment to European law, especially important in the period prior to Polish accessions to EU on May 1, 2004 (National report presented at the Taiwan Congress)*".

1.1.6.6 Partial Conclusions

- The decodification process was a consequence of the aging of the Codes; but it did not imply the abandonment of the codification method as rational expression of the law;
- The evidence of the survival of the codification method is the recodification process, which includes the renovation of the old Codes of the nineteenth century and the new Codes enacted by countries incorporated to the free market economy

1.2 Second Part. The Content of the Codes and Their Relation with Other Branches of the Law

As noted before the civil codes of the nineteenth century referred to the persons and their family relations; the typical market institutions: the property and the contract,[34] which led to the regulation of all real rights over a person's property or third parties' property as well as the regulation of the contractual obligations and obligations resulting from wrongful acts; and, to the succession of legal relations and situations.

Still, in many countries, codification was not limited to civil law, but, following the French model, it was completed drafting a commercial code.[35] In this section we will consider the relation between the Civil Code and the Commercial Code in its origins and its evolution to these days.

1.2.1 The Civil Code and Commercial Law

As noted before, the codification process did not stop nor did it restrict to civil law only. Regarded as the maximum legislative expression, it spread into many areas of law and to the sphere of private law, especially the mercantile branch of the law.

The initial model was the French Commercial Code of 1807, followed by many others, like the Portuguese (1833, replaced in 1888), Italian (1865, rewritten in 1882), the 1859 Spanish Code,[36] made applicable to Puerto Rico[37]; the German

[34] Galgano, Francesco, "Interpretación del contrato y lex mercatoria", *Revista de Derecho Comparado* (Santa Fe – Buenos Aires), 2001.

[35] Outside the scope of private law, codification generally extended to criminal law and procedural law.

[36] Revised in 1885.

[37] The Commercial Code of Spain is applicable in Puerto Rico from 1886. It was readopted in 1932, but many parts are not in force because some matters are part of the federal system of the United States, as Bankruptcy and Maritime Law.

Commercial Code in 1897, and many Latin American countries' codes such as Argentina (1859 for the Buenos Aires State and 1862 as a National code), Venezuela (enacted in 1919, revised in 1955), Uruguay, Brazil, Peru, Colombia, Bolivia, etc.. These Commercial Codes conceived commercial law on a subjective basis: the merchant, subject who develops his profession by performing commercial acts; and on an objective basis: the acts of commerce, of which the most common is the exchange of personal property (or goods).

The commercial codes of the nineteenth century generally governed the regulation of commercial contracts – which resulted in an overlap of provisions with the civil codes, given that there were two regulations over the same type of contract – either executed by merchants or not –, companies, bankruptcies and maritime law.[38]

This commercial law was the law of a class or profession. It was mainly the law of merchants, which was even applied to the unilaterally mercantile relations.[39] Moreover, as the commercial codes of the nineteenth century did not comprise general rules on contracts nor a general theory of the obligations, it was common that the Civil Code be subsidiarily applicable to solve those matters not expressly provided for in the mercantile law[40] – underlying criteria applicable nowadays in most countries.

1.2.1.1 Decodification in the Field of Commercial Law

Commercial codes have been most seriously affected by the decodification process. In this regard, the French essay points out: "*...the* code de commerce *terribly suffered from decodification. In the 1980s, the situation had come to a point where this Code had nearly become an empty shell. Most areas of commercial law were regulated outside the code de commerce. There was a major Act on company law, another on insolvency law, etc...*". Also, the Belgium case clearly illustrates this point; the code was subjected to multiple revisions during the nineteenth century; the national essay describes the process as follows: "*The need of new texts was so*

[38] Such is the example of the Venezuelan Code which is divided into three books, the first for the law of merchants, commercial contracts, commercial companies, credit instruments; the second for maritime law and the third for bankruptcies.

[39] Argentine Commercial Code, Section 7°: "Should one act be deemed commercial by one of the parties, all the participants become, to such extent, subjected to mercantile law ..."

[40] The Argentine Commercial Code expressly states in its Section 1° Preliminary Title: "*To all the cases that are not specially governed by this Code, the provisions of the Civil Code shall apply*". The French report explains: "*The* code civil *was never intended to cover commercial law, since it was always understood that it should be complemented by a commercial code. Nevertheless, many rules of commercial law can only be read in connection to the code civil. This is especially true of contracts. The basic rules on contracts are set by the code civil and the rules on various commercial contracts which may be found in the code de commerce only come to supplement or, on certain points, correct the code civil rules. This is also true, though to a lesser extent, for company law, since "société" is seen as a contract by the code civil and the basic rules on companies are set in the code civil*". In Germany the Commercial Code of 1897 had the purpose to adequate the commercial law regulated by the ADHGB of 1861, to the Civil Code adopted in 1896: Schmidt, ob. cit.

urgent, that the legislator very soon gave up the idea of one new Code. Instead, the old Code remained, but its parts were replaced piecemeal throughout the second half of the nineteenth century, so that only four of the original articles survived into the twentieth century".

Likewise, the Argentine essay states that bankruptcy law, companies, insurances, warrants, pledge, and other matters disappeared from the Commercial Code and today are regulated in particular statutes. The panorama is very similar in Portugal; the essay from this country states that "*many Commercial Law issues are regulated by special statutes. This is the case, for example, of corporations... securities... industrial property... and insolvency...*".[41]

As for Belgium, the essay written by D. Heirbaut and M. E. Storme states that "*In 1988 Belgium woke out of its lethargy in the field of commercial law. The country's deficient legislation enabled a foreign company to lay the hands on the Société Générale de Belgique, a holding which controlled a great part of the Belgian economy. Suddenly, the legislator became more active, with for example new statutes on bankruptcy and reorganization (1997) or a new code of companies (1999). The new statutes are not always innovative (e.g. the code of companies). If they are, the innovations are not always successful. For example, a 2009 statute has already replaced the 1997 legislation. However, what they all have in common is that they are no longer part of the commercial code. The latter has also lost articles to the new code of private international law (2004). The underlying idea this time is that the Commercial has been robbed of so many topics, that one more will not matter. In fact, as of now, only the status of the merchants and the law of the sea are still in the commercial code*".

Similar considerations appear in Venezuela, where maritime law, insurance, cooperative associations and trust are legislated in legal bodies separated from the Code; and also in Japan.[42]

In a few cases, the code survives, but the political and economic changes in the country turn it void of efficacy in substantial matters. Such is the case in Poland, where, although the provisions of the Commercial Code concerning companies remained in force, they regained their full practical meaning only after the political breakthrough of 1989.

---

[41] The same essay from Portugal says: "A code unique *approach, such as the one that prevailed in the Swiss, Italian, Dutch and Brazilian Civil Codes (which also comprise rules on several Commercial Law issues), has thus been rejected by the Portuguese legislators. The basic reason for this is that, according to the traditional view prevailing in Portugal, Civil Law is the common core of Private Law, whilst Commercial Law is seen as a special branch of Private Law, dealing with relationships arising from acts of trade and with the specific needs of trade. The latter should accordingly remain outside the scope of the Civil Code*".

[42] Prof. Ishikawa in his essay states that "*...some books of the Commercial Code have been transferred to special laws, corresponding to the rapid changes in the rules and orders of commercial transactions. The law of commercial paper (Book IV) was transferred to the Act on Bills (1932) and to the Act on Check (1933); the company law (Book II) to the Companies Act of 2005; and the insurance law (Chapter 10 of the Book III) to the Insurance Act of 2008. The Commercial Code has substantially lost its original content, with matters of great importance instead being addressed through special laws.*"

1.2.1.2 The Recodification of Commercial Law. What Commercial Law Is

Legislation in the matter of commercial law is faced nowadays with important uncertainties. In a few words, the matters are: Is there a need to have a commercial code separated from the civil code or is it appropriate that a civil code be at the same time a commercial code, like the 1942 Italian Code? And, if a commercial code exists, what is the scope of this code, what is the core of the codified commercial law?; the status of the merchant as in nineteenth century; the "acts of commerce", the enterprise, the external effects of the enterprise as Karsten Schmidt proposes[43]; the market private law, as is suggested in Spain[44] or if this "core" does not exist and the commercial code will remain a mere compilation of different matters such as companies, partnerships, bankruptcy, insurance, transport, etc., without a systematic approach.

It can be said that there are some different models: on the one hand, France has recodified its commercial law; on the other hand, the 1942 Italian Code incorporated commercial law with the subsequent disappearance of the Commercial Code, which never existed in Switzerland or in the countries which followed the Swiss Code of Obligations.

We will first see the content of the "new" commercial codes, but distinguishing different cases: the recodification process in countries with a long codification tradition (Sect. 1.2.1.3); codification in countries incorporated to the market economy (Sect. 1.2.1.4); the particular case of Macau (Sect. 1.2.1.5). After that, we will expose the experience of countries where civil and commercial law are unified (Sect. 1.2.1.6. and following).

1.2.1.3 The "New" Commercial Codes

In the last few years, "new" commercial codes have come to light. They responded to different causes and have diverse methodologies and contents.

It is appropriate to start by pointing out that in some countries the name "code" has been used to identify what is in fact a mere compilation.

France is one example where, as already mentioned, by the 1980s, the Commercial Code was reduced to an "empty shell", and was forced to recodify the matter having a new Commercial Code come into force in 2001.

However, the essay about French Law points out that "*This new Code is actually rather a compilation of statutes on different subjects: company law, insolvency law, credit instruments, business practices, various commercial contracts, etc. Thanks to this new Code, however, the greater part of commercial law can now again be found in one same book*".

In this regard, it may be argued that the French Code resembles a compilation of regulations on different subjects more than a rationally developed Code because

43 Schmidt, ob. cit.

44 V. Rojo, Ángel, *El Código Mercantil*, Otrosí, Madrid, n° 12, oct./dec.. 2012, ps. 17.

"*It is now very difficult to identify where the 'core' of commercial law lies*" In effect: as was said before, "merchant'" statute has no reason today when the subject of the business activity seems to be "the company", nor the regulation of the acts of commerce, given that the concept of "commerce" has a scope that goes beyond the limited framework of the exchange of movables; thus, primary activities such as – agriculture or livestock – or activities of extraction – like mining – and construction are carried out by commercial companies – many times transnational – with business and commercial criteria incomprehensible under the concepts of the codes of the nineteenth century.

And, therefore, the existence of a new Commercial Code does not affect the relation with the Civil Code. Accordingly Prof. Borghetti states: "*Besides, it is clear that links between civil law (and thus the* Code Civil*) on the one hand, and some specialised branches of commercial law, on the other hand, tend to grow thinner. Nevertheless, civil law remains the source of the basic rules on property law and the law of obligations, as well as an essential toolbox*".

Another body named code, but which as a matter of fact is not a code, is the Estonia Commercial Code[45] (1995) which does not contain rules on transactions but only rules on different kind of commercial corporations. Even, business transactions are regulated in the Law of Obligations Act, and there are a big number of special statutes concerning commercial matters.

1.2.1.4 The Codification of Commercial Law in Countries Incorporated to the Market Economy

The Czech Republic is a good example to illustrate this group of legislations. The essay from this country points out on this regard: "*Fundamental changes to Czechoslovak business law came about after November 1989, when the democratic system was reinstated, changes were made to Czechoslovak legislation resulting from the transition of the society to political pluralism and a market economy, and the environment for private business was established. In a very short period of time, the Commercial Code, No. 513/1991 Sb., was prepared and passed; it was intended to replace, in particular, the former socialist Economic Code No. 109/1964 Sb., regulating relations between socialist organisations (i.e. enterprises), and the International Trade Code, No. 101/1963 Sb., oriented towards international trade relations*".

Finally, the Commercial Code of the Czech Republic has disappeared because the new Civil Code repealed it. The drafters of the new Civil Code, considering the purpose of private law re-codification, opted for the monistic concept of the law of obligations as a reasonable and functional system. The monistic concept is based upon the principle of the uniform and integrated law of obligations, which is encompassed in the Civil Code and is used as a general legal regulation in the whole of

[45] *Commercial Code* (äriseadustik), passed 15.02.1995, entry into force 01.09.1995. Available in English: https://www.riigiteataja.ee/tutvustus.html?m=3

private law. But, on the other hand, there is a Business Corporation Act contemporary to the Civil Code, and some specific statutes remain in force: insolvency, insurance, accountancy, laws regulating securities, Act on Collective Investment, Act on Transactions in the Capital Market, etc. Other important laws cover specific types of company and other entities, such as state enterprises, as well as laws implementing European legislation, namely Act No. 627/2004 Sb., on the European Company, Act No. 360/2004 Sb., on the European Economic Interest Grouping, and Act No. 307/2006 Sb., on the European Cooperative Society.

1.2.1.5 The Recodification of Commercial Law in Asia: The Macau Case

One case of recodification of mercantile law, less known to the occidental jurists, is that of Macau, which in 1999 replaced its old 1888 code. This new code had revisions in 2000 and 2009. Its content is really extensive; it covers the contemporary phenomenon of commerce, the central role acquired by the company; it regulates the most important commercial contracts and practically there are no typically mercantile matters left outside the Code, except for bankruptcy – is ruled by the Procedural Code –, maritime law and intellectual property. Contrary to the French and Estonian Commercial Codes, this Macau Code does not appear as a mere compilation of laws on different subjects with no significant connection, but it is structured as a real code, with a general part and special parts all related to each other. As is the case in many other places, the civil law is of supplementary application, but the essay of Macau states: "*if the situation is of commercial nature and the Commercial Code does not provide for a direct solution the interpreter should first seek an analogous situation in the code itself and only if none can be found can he resort to the Civil Code, as long as the potentially applicable rules of this law do not contravene any principle of commercial law*".

1.2.1.6 The Unification of Civil and Commercial Legislation

The model opposed to recodification is the enactment of a single code, which was pursued by Switzerland with its Code of Obligations[46] and a few years later by Italy. Prof. Sacco justifies the method adopted in 1942 arguing that the discrepancies between civil and commercial law giving rise to separate codification in the twentieth century have disappeared, specially those which made commercial law the law of the merchants, with institutions that sometimes could not adapt to the more rational institutions of civil law; like the *de facto* association which did not fit in the notion of legal act, nor the bill of exchange to the idea of consideration as an

[46] The Taiwan report states that this country has followed the Swiss model and argues that is why they do not have a Commercial Code.

essential element of any contract; and, thus, their controversies had to be resolved by experts more than by doctorate judges. All this disappeared by the end of the twentieth century; Professor Sacco notes that "*the new commercial law professor has the same educational background as his civil colleague, he can discuss with him and formulate the rules of law on the very same basis (…) And having reached this point, why drafting two codes?*"

Nevertheless, the unification of civil and commercial legislation was not complete because the Navigation Code, the Bankruptcy Law (*Legge falimentare*) and special laws on the most relevant credit instruments continued to exist as separate bodies.

The Italian model has been followed by a few countries. In Argentina, the Commercial Code still exists, but in 1987 a Civil Code reform had been projected involving the derogation of the Commercial Code[47]; also in 1998 there was a single Code project that was never treated by Congress. Currently, a commission has developed a new project which undertakes the draft of a single Code and thus the disappearance of the Commercial Code.[48] It should be noted that the proposal to unify the codes dates back to many years as it has been encouraged since 1940.[49] Anyway, numerous laws regulating mercantile institutions will survive; such as company, bankruptcy, navigation, bill of exchange, check and insurance law. As mentioned earlier, the Czech Republic has also opted for the monistic system.

1.2.1.7 The Special Case of the United States UCC

A model different from the former ones is the United States model. The following paragraphs have been extracted from the essay written by Professor Maxeiner.

The Uniform Commercial Code comes as close as any American private law legislation both to being a code and to being national, but really it is a *uniform law* proposed for adoption. It was drafted in the 1940s as a joint product of the Uniform Law Commission and the American Law Institute. The first Official Text was presented for adoption in 1951, but was adopted by only one state, Pennsylvania. It was reformulated and the 1962 Official Text was the first that was widely adopted. Forty-nine of 50 states adopted the entire code with only a few variations.

The UCC is not limited in its application to merchants. It governs all persons, and consists of ten articles: (1) General Provisions, (2) Sales of Goods, (2A) Leases of Goods, (3) Negotiable Instruments, (4) Bank Deposits, (4A) Funds Transfers, (5) Letters of Credit, (6) Bulk Transfers and Bulk Sales (repealed), (7) Warehouse Receipts, Bills of Lading and Other Documents of Title, (8) Investment Securities, and (9) Secured Transactions. It thus brings together all of the basic aspects of commercial transactions of the day.

---

[47] The reform was passed by the National Congress, but was vetoed by the Executive Power.

[48] In Latin America, Peru had its single Code in 1984 and Paraguay in 1987.

[49] In this year, the first Argentine Congress of Commercial Law was held and unification was advised. Doctrine has consistently endorsed this unification tendency, with only few exceptions.

Other commercial laws exist, with different relations with the UCC. For example, the UCC covers commercial papers and warranties for goods; however, these matters are also covered in important separate legislation, including the Magnuson-Moss Warranty – Federal Trade Commission Act (1975), 15 U.S.C. §§ 2301 *et seq*. The UCC makes clear that it does not preempt the field. Section 1-103(b) states that "unless displaced" by particular provisions of the UCC, the "principles of law and equity ... supplement" the Code.

In the United States, the only state of Romano-Germanic tradition, Louisiana, resisted adoption of the Uniform Commercial Code, but now has largely capitulated to it. Exceptions are found in Articles 2 (sales) and 6 (bulk sales) of the UCC. In revising the Louisiana Civil Code, Article 2 was considered, and some ideas from it were introduced into the Louisiana text. In making those changes the legislature declared it had adopted "whatever provisions were thought useful, regardless of the source, yet [adapted] the language of those provisions to fit the civilian mould and the plan of the Louisiana Civil Code. The result is a modern sales scheme that fits well in Louisiana's civil law tradition while at the same time adequately serving the personal and commercial needs of Louisiana citizens." And Puerto Rico, also a country of Romano-Germanic tradition, has adopted the UCC, but with exceptions; Article 2 (sales) and Article 2A (lease) were not adopted because they are inconsistent with the system of the Civil Code.

1.2.1.8 The Commercial Law in Uncodified Law Countries

Regardless of the United States case we have just discussed, in other countries outside the codification tradition, such as the Scandinavian countries and Israel, commercial law is scattered in different laws and codification is not considered. Israel does not even contemplate that the Civil Code Project could contain laws on typical commercial matters such as corporation law, the law of bankruptcy, and negotiable instruments.

1.2.1.9 Partial Conclusions

It is very difficult to draw a conclusion on this matter, because the first issue is to determine what commercial law is today, and there are many possible answers to this question.[50] Hence, the attitude adopted by each country depends on the answer chosen by legislators and scholars resulting in diverse approaches to the codification of commercial law.

[50] Following the same rationale, the essay from Japan states: "...*the Commercial Code provides the special rules for merchants or commercial acts, but nowadays it seems doubtful whether the concepts of merchants and commercial acts are significant enough to* implement *special regulations. For example, according to case law, a credit association cannot be a merchant, but a bank is*".

1.2.2 The Civil Code and Family Law

In doctrine, some authors have favored the separation of family law from civil law, explaining that the former governs extra-patrimonial relations, has its own principles and is closer to public law than to the core of patrimonial law.[51] However, this thesis failed to have much impact on this area of legislation; usually the civil code contains the essential parts of family law (Spain,[52] France, Italy, Turkey, Greece and in the Czech Republic in the 2012 Civil Code).

In Estonia, as we have seen, there is not "one" civil code, there are *"five separate laws which have been enacted at different times as separate laws but functioning as codified legal acts*". One of these is the Family Act adopted in 1995 which was rewritten and adopted as a new act in 2010.

Furthermore, certain matters can be separately legislated as is the case of Macau.[53] In Taiwan *"formally speaking, family law refers to provisions in the Civil Code Part IV Family. However, family law also refers to laws and regulations governing domestic relations or family chief-member relations and the rights and obligations arising wherefrom*"; as the *Children Welfare Act, Juvenile Welfare Act, Domestic Violence Prevention Act, Law Governing the Application of Laws to Civil Matters Involving Foreign Elements, Nationality Act, Household Registration Act, Naming Act, Code of Civil Procedure, Non-contentious Matter Law, the customary law, jurisprudence, case law and legal interpretations are all major sources of family law…other special laws or jurisprudence governing domestic relations and*

---

[51] This idea was promotes by Cicu in the earlier twentieth century.

[52] Even is the same in Puerto Rico.

[53] In this jurisdiction, family law is comprised in Book IV of the Civil Code, but certain areas pertaining to family law are legislated in other codified bodies or not. According to the essay "…the fundamental rights and duties of Macao residents are part of Macao Basic Law (MBL)". "The freedom of marriage of Macao residents and their right to form and raise a family freely shall be protected by law. The legitimate rights and interests of women shall be protected by the Macao Special Administrative Region. The minors, the aged and the disabled shall be taken care of and protected by the Macao Special Administrative Region" (article 38). Still according to MBL (article 40), in what Family Law is concerned, the provisions of International Covenant on Civil and Political Rights (*Pacto Internacional sobre os Direitos Civis e Políticos*) and International Covenant on Economic, Social and Cultural Rights (*Pacto Internacional sobre os Direitos Económicos, Sociais e Culturais*) shall remain in force and shall be implemented through the laws of the MSAR. Codified legislation with significance for Family Law, other than the Civil Code, is as follows: Civil Registry Code (*Código do Registro Civil*), approved by *Decreto-Lei n.° 59/00/M, de 18 de Outubro*; Civil Procedure Code (*Código de Processo Civil*), approved by *Decreto-Lei n.° 55/99/M, de 8 de Outubro*. Among the non codified legislation we would still mention the following: Family Policy Basis Law (*Lei de Bases da Política Familiar, Lei n° 6/94/M, de 1 de Agosto*); Educational and Social Protection Régime of Minor's Jurisdiction (*Regime Educativo e de Protecção Social de Jurisdição de Menores*, regulated by the *Decreto-Lei n° 65/99/M, de 25 de Outubro*).

family matters[54] *are substantial family law, namely, the family law in broad sense. Those provisions are scattered in different laws.*[55]

In Argentina, the case has been the "decodification-recodification" of family law. Shortly after the enactment of the Civil Code, a civil matrimony law was passed (1888); by the end of the twentieth century, the first adoption law and other statutes with strong influence on family law were sanctioned. But, once democracy was reinstated in 1983, an integral revision of this branch of the law was undertaken, introducing significant changes like divorce, equality between spouses in the exercise of parental rights, new provisions on adoption, etc.; and this revision was attained by incorporating the new solutions to the Civil Code. The same has recently occurred regarding marriage between persons of the same sex: the reform was made "in" the Civil Code itself. Thus, what remains out of the scope of the Civil Code is the law for the Protection of Children and Adolescents' Rights which incorporates the International Convention to domestic law. Also, some rules about reproductive health are in a separate statute.

A singular case, which we have mentioned in this essay, is the Quebec Civil Code, which contains family law almost in its entirety, with the exception of divorce, because "*under the Canadian Constitution, regulation of divorce in within the jurisdiction or the central government and it is indeed regulated by the Canadian Divorce Act, which is applicable to all Canadian provinces and territories*".[56]

Regardless of this trend, which is proper of the countries with a long codification tradition, we can refer to many cases in which the regulation of the main issues within family law has been separated from the Civil Code.

One case of separation of family law from the Civil Code is that of Poland, because since 1959 there is a Family Code, "*based on a joined Polish and Czechoslovakian project. At that time were running the works on the preparation of the draft of Civil Code. Up to 1962 several drafts were proposed. Especially heated discussions concentrated on three general problems concerning the Civil Code:*

- *whether the code should regulate the issues connected with economic turnover (at that period it meant the turnover between nationalized units)*
- *whether the code should regulate the issues connected with family law*
- *whether the code should regulate the issues connected with labor law*

Final decisions concerning these problems were taken by the politicians. The first question was answered positively, while the second and third negatively. Thus, finally the provisions concerning family and guardianship were gathered in a separate code, the Family and Guardianship Code, which was issued in the same year when the civil code (1964).[57]

[54] Article 1, Civil Code provides: "...if there is no applicable act for a civil case, the case shall be decided according to customs. If there is no such custom, the case shall be decided according to the jurisprudence."

[55] National Report of Taiwan presented in the Taiwan Congress.

[56] National Report presented at the Congress of Taiwan.

[57] National report presented before the Taiwan Congress.

In Latin America, Bolivia has had a Family Code since August 26th 1977; and other Family Codes exist in Cuba (1985), El Salvador (1983), Costa Rica (1974), and Panama (1994); Peru (Infancy and Adolescence Code, 2000); Colombia (Infancy and Adolescence Code). The Spanish report points out that in Cataluña there was a family code, but it was derogated when the new Civil Code of its Autonomy was sanctioned.

In uncodified law countries, family law sometimes appears regulated in one single law, as is the case of Croatia and its Family Act[58]; or in separate laws or statutes. For example, in Norway, the main acts are Marriage Act, Children Act and Adoption Act. Similar is the case in Finland.

We must make reference to the countries in which there is more than one system of family law; under this category we will find those countries Professor David called systems "tied to religion" and certain federal countries where diverse provincial legislations coexist.

These systems "tied to religion" have a regulation of family law rooted in sacred texts or religious texts prior to the existence of civil law. So, in Israel, "*Issues of marriage and divorce are governed by religious laws, which are not an integral part of Israeli private law*", and "*the religious communities – Muslims, Christians, and Jews – enjoyed autonomous jurisdiction that included separate tribunals, each applying its own religious law*". Then, "*the current Bill (of the civil code) does not deal with marriage or divorce, and there is no plan to include these issues within the ambit of the Code*".

Finally in the United States the situation is as well complex because, even though there has been an attempt to the unification or uniformity of certain matters, "*family law, is principally law of fifty separate states*".

As we have pointed out, there have been attempts to uniform family law at least in certain essential matters. Thus, the Uniform Law Commission proposed in 1970 a Uniform Marriage and Divorce Act, revised as the Model Marriage and Divorce Act, but just six states – large in area but not so large in population – have adopted it (Arizona, Colorado, Georgia, Minnesota, Montana and Washington). That 1970 Act was the closest that the Uniform Law Commission has come to a single code solution for family law.

We may conclude this section noting that there is almost universal coincidence in the fact that even though the method to enforce its reform varies from country to country, family law is one of the fields that has experienced a deeper transformation in its roots and rules during the twentieth century and so far the current century. Thus, from Japan's abandonment of the patriarchal family after the World War to the recognition of same sex marriages in Spain, Argentina, Canada, Island, Sweden, Norway, the Netherlands, New Zealand, France, Uruguay, Denmark and Finland, a

---

[58] We refer to the 2003 Family Act which comprises the regulation of almost all the areas of this branch of law; the National Report presented at the Taiwan Congress points out "*...it provides for marriage, relations between parents and children, adoption, custody, maintenance, property, relations of spouses and common law partners...Obligations Act applies to family relations only subsidiary, unless it is provided differently in the provisions of the Family Acts*".

family model absolutely different from that provided in the nineteenth century codes is evident. And, even more significant is the fact that there is a radical change in the pillars over which the whole subject is built: while in the nineteenth and even the twentieth century codes, family law was built over mandatory legal regulations and the margin for autonomy was minimal, today there is a clear inversion of that idea, as there is a growing margin for the autonomous formation of the family and the relations among its members.

1.2.3 The Civil Code and Consumer Law

Over the past few decades, out of all the branches of law, consumer law has developed most significantly,[59] and has started to define itself as a virtually autonomous branch from a legislative, doctrinal and didactical point of view.[60]

Now; as difficult as it may be to find a generalized trend on the legislative method used for commercial and family law, in the field of consumer law, it is clearly settled that, even in those countries with a codification tradition, its regulation is generally outside the scope of the civil codes.

It appears this is caused by the fact that consumer law regulation is usually scattered in more than one law or statute, covering subjects pertaining to civil law – such as contracts with consumers and product liability –, administrative law – organization of institutions for the protection and education of consumers –, and procedural law – collective actions, consumer arbitration systems –. Indeed, in a large economic scale, there is supranational regulation to which national States have to adapt.[61]

One model of this kind of legislation is that of Spain, where the 1984 Consumers and Users Protection Law has given rise to abundant special legislation. Another example could be that of Japan, where the system of consumer law comprises a number of special laws covering private law and administrative law.

Of course, this is also the case in those countries where civil law is not codified. Thus, in the Scandinavian countries, Israel, Scotland and the United States consumer law is scattered in various laws each addressing specific matters.

The latter indicates a trend also followed in other countries, which is that parallel to laws addressing matters pertaining to the consumer, there are other laws that rule general matters but which outline specific rules applicable in the event the

---

[59] Prof. Borghetti points out: "*The development of consumer law over the last decades has been a major phenomenon in France, like in many other countries*".

[60] However, ideas on this matter are far from being unanimous. Prof. Deliyanni-Dimitrakou points out on this topic that "*In contrast to commercial law, consumer protection law is not unanimously recognized by Greek legal scholars as an autonomous branch of law*".

[61] Again, Deliyanni-Dimitrakou emphasizes: "*The core legislation in this area is Law 2251/1994, as modified by the Law 3587/2007, which transposed into national law all EU directives on consumer protection that existed at the time of its enactment*".

legal relations under such laws affect the consumer. For example, in Finland, the Electricity Market Act (1995), Insurance Contracts Act (1994) and Interests Act (1982).

This way to legislate generates several inconveniences, affecting in particular the relation between consumer regulations and the general rules of the civil code, for example in the matter of contracts or civil liability.[62]

In response to this scattered and, thus, rather anarchical legislation, some attempts to systematize the display of consumer law have stemmed and some currents of action in this direction may be observed.

On the one hand, some countries have opted to incorporate certain parts of consumer law to the Civil Code. It is known that the revision of the German Code (BGB) was effected by means of a law passed by the Federal Parliament on 11th October 2001 which came into force on January 1st 2002. This law is known as the "law for the modernization of the law of obligations" and among various reforms undertaken, it incorporated to the Code some of the most important European Directives related to consumer protection, distance contracts, warranties in the purchase and sale agreements of consumer assets, default in commercial relations and electronic commerce. The Czech Republic, inspired by the German BGB, opted for integration and implemented most European directives related to consumer protection directly into the Civil Code.[63]

Prof. Parise informing about the Louisiana Civil Code, states that "[P]rotection of consumer rights is welcomed in the Louisiana Civil Code. For example, consumers can seek for protection in the warranty against redhibitory defects that is included in Chapter 9, Title 7, Book III of the Louisiana Civil Code. Defects are redhibitory when the buyer would have not bought the thing had he known of the defect or paid a lesser price for it. Additional codified tools for consumer protection can be found in the law of obligations (*i.e.,* article 1758) and in the law of torts (*i.e.,* article 2315) of the Louisiana Civil Code"; however, consumer protection "has grown significantly in the Louisiana Revised Statutes, resulting in an example of decodification".

In Quebec, over a strong debate, consumer law was left outside the 1994 Civil Code,[64] "*...however, a number of articles in the Civil Code of Quebec refer directly to consumers*".

But, other countries have plainly and simply opted for the codification of consumer law. In line with it, we find countries with a long-standing codification tradition like France.

[62] This is pointed out by Hernández Breton and Madrid Martínez in the Venezuelan essay, but the idea is applicable to other countries.

[63] However, the Czech legislature has not incorporated all aspects of consumer law into the Civil Code 2012. In addition, there is a special law implementing the public law aspects of consumer protection.

[64] The National Report from Quebec states: " *that it was felt that the consumer's law deals mostly with detailed and specific provisions which are mostly of a regulatory nature and do not fit with the more principles and general approach of a civil code*".

France has adopted a Consumer Code (*code de la consommation*) (1993) in which most rules pertaining to consumer protection are gathered. Prof. Borghetti, in his essay about French Law, describes: "*The existence of a separate code for consumer law has contributed to consumer law and civil law remaining quite separate from each other. Consumer law is still considered in France by most civil lawyers as not belonging to civil law*", but at the same time there is no systematic approach to consumer law, probably because it is, in general terms, originated in European Union Directives which separately deal with diverse topics or matters absent from a systematic perspective.

In Italy, as we anticipated, there is also a *Codice del Consumo* (2005), which coexists with some rules on the protection of the weak contracting party under the *Codice Civile*.

In Portugal, Consumer Law issues are currently regulated by a number of special statutes, the most important of which is Law no. 24/96, of 31 July 1996 (Consumer Protection Law). But the idea of codification is present; a *Draft Consumer Code*, which to some extent reflected the influence of the Brazilian Consumer Code, was published in Portugal in 2006 "*...but it has so far not been enacted*".

On the other hand, Taiwan has regulated consumer law in a law separate from the Code which bears with it a relation of special law to general law. This is outlined by the national report of Taiwan "*...the Consumer Protection Act and the Civil Code are two separate laws. However, in substance, Consumer Protection Act stipulates special provisions regarding the specific matters relating to the signing of contracts between consumers and enterprises. The establishment, effectiveness, performance and elimination of the contracts are not provided in the Consumer Protection Act, and such issues shall be governed by the relevant provisions in the Civil Code Part I General Principles and the Civil Code Part II Obligations*", and "*it is in effect in a general-special law relationship with the Civil Code in application*".

Finally, in Argentina, there is a consumer protection law which stipulates provisions applicable to contracts with consumers, administrative and procedural rules. But, it is important to emphasize that the Civil Code Draft under development intends to incorporate the rules on consumer contracts to the Civil Code. The "Preamble" for the Draft notes there are diverse tendencies in comparative law regarding the appropriate methodology for the regulation of consumer law, and it is further noted that Germany, Quebec and other countries have included rules on the subject in their civil codes. Professor Medina's essay explains the solution adopted by the Civil Code Draft in Argentina.

1.2.4 The Civil Code and Private International Law

Private International Law legislation recognizes internal sources and external or international ones (conventions, treaties, so on).

The civil codes of the nineteenth century included rules on private international law, many times in an initial or introductory chapter to the civil code itself; such is the case of the 1889 Spanish Civil Code and the Argentine Civil Code; afterwards, in the twentieth century, the 1942 Italian Civil Code.

Some codes still maintain in their essence rules of private international law. Among them, we can mention the Quebec Civil Code, which includes a Book on the rules pertaining to this matter. The National Report describes: *"This last book is a major innovation and codifies a number of rules concerning conflicts of law (incapacities, marriage, separation from bed and board, civil union, filiation, alimony), the status of property, the status of obligations, the international jurisdiction of Quebec authorities and the recognition and enforcement of foreign decisions and jurisdiction of foreign authorities*".

In the same perspective we find the Dutch Civil Code; in which the most recent addition is Book 10 on Private International Law, which entered into force on 1st January 2012. And in Greece the Civil Code "*...contains also private international law provisions (PIL) which are included in Arts 4-33. These Articles have governed private law relations with foreign elements since the GCC entered into force, and have not been subjected to significant reforms. The only exceptions are the provisions governing family relations with foreign elements which were affected by the successive reforms of the fourth GCC book, on Family Law*".[65]

However, there is also a tendency to withdraw Private International Law from the civil codes and concentrate it on special laws or codes. This is illustrated by the very well-known case of Switzerland; it also occurred in Italy where the law passed on 31st May 1995, nº 218 (Reform of the Italian International Private Law System) derogated the corresponding articles under the Civil Code and entirely ruled the subject, including regulations from the 1980 Rome Convention on the Law Applicable to Contractual Obligations.

In Belgium, Private International Law had its own code in 2004, though it would be more accurate to call it a "mini-code".

The same system was followed by Venezuela, where the Act on Private International Law came into effect on 6th February 1999 and replaced almost all rules of Private International Law contained in the Civil Code and other codes.

Argentina, on its part, has the Civil Code as its main internal source, though with provisions which are rudimentary today and are in need of an urgent renovation. To that effect, the 1998 Civil Code Project stipulated an integral regulation of Private International Law; when the Draft lost political endorsement and it was clear it would not be passed, the Book of Private International Law was proposed as a separate Code of Private International Law, but the attempt was unsuccessful. Finally, the Civil Code Draft currently under development will also contain an entire regulation of Private International Law.

In other countries, private international law legislation has always been separated from the Civil Code. Indeed, the paper from the Czech Republic outlines that "Private international law has traditionally been regulated autonomously by a special legal act; formerly by the Act Concerning Private International Law and the

[65] Deliyanni-Dimitrakou, Christina, "The Greek Civil Code Facing the Process of Decodification and Recodification of Law".

Rules of Procedure Relating Thereto 1963, and, with effect from 1 January 2014, by the Act on Private International Law".[66]

Regarding those countries of an uncodified tradition, Israel portrays an interesting case. Prof. Zamir in his essay outlines that "*Subject to significant exceptions, private international law is governed in Israel by judge-made law, heavily influenced by the English Common Law...*", but, "*The Bill of the Civil Code... does not contain a chapter on private international law. However, the Bill's introduction indicates that such a chapter should be integrated into the Civil Code at a later stage*".

1.2.5 The Role of the Civil Code in Relation to Other National or Supranational Sources of Positive Law

Previous Congresses held by the International Academy of Comparative Law have discussed the influence of constitutional law on civil law (Utrecht, 2006). It is more and more evident, considering the contributions comprising this volume, that the description of the Code as a "civil constitution" or "economic constitution" seems to equate the role of both of them, while one seems to lose effect. Constitutional supremacy means recognizing the Constitution as a source of subjective rights which the inhabitants of a country are entitled to invoke before a court of law or other authorities, without the need of a law to effect or rule them. And, legal courts may regard inferior laws as ineffective, among them the Codes, when the solutions provided by them are inconsistent with constitutional principles.[67]

---

[66] The new PIL Act thus includes relevant conflict-of-law and/or international procedure rules concerning not only the classical parts of private international law, that is, personal, family and succession law and rights *in rem*, but also rules on bills of exchange, promissory notes and cheques, securities, insolvency, and arbitration. It consists of nine parts: (1) General provisions, (2) General provisions of international civil procedure, (3) General provisions of private international law, (4) Provisions for individual types of private law relations (capacity, legal acts, agency, statute of limitation, family law, registered partnership and similar relationships, rights *in rem*, succession law, intellectual property law, securities and other instruments, obligations), (5) Legal assistance in contacts with foreign countries, (6) Insolvency procedure, (7) Arbitration, and (8) Transitional and final provisions. The general part of the Act, including definitions of such terms as classification, evasion of law, overriding mandatory rules, preliminary questions, etc., may also be treated as new.

[67] The evolution on this field in France is noticeable. Professor Borghetti's essay is highly illustrative in this regard. Specifically it points: "*...a 2009 constitutional reform, which came into force in 2010. Constitutional review by the Conseil constitutionnel of a parliamentary law already in force is now possible, if it is argued that this law violates a right or freedom granted by the Constitution. This possibility has actually proven extremely successful and hundreds of claims regarding the constitutionality of existing laws and statutes have been raised over the last two years. This, of course, has a major impact on civil law and the Code civil. The Code is not anymore the highest rule in its field. It actually took French lawyers some time to realise that constitutional law and constitutional review were bound to have an impact on civil law. In that respect, they certainly laid behind their colleagues in other legal systems, especially in Europe (in Italy, for example) and South America. Things have changed, however. It is now clear that*

Even in the common law countries the Constitution is recognized as a source of implicit civil liberties.[68]

Additionally, it should be emphasized that in certain civil law matters – such as the law of persons and family – a protective net of international sources covers the rights of certain subjects: women, children and the people with disabilities. The States undertake to acknowledge and guarantee the validity and enforceability of certain basic rights and this engagement requires adapting their internal law, including the Civil Code.

Furthermore, the validity of communitarian regulations – subject matter of another session in the Comparative Law Congress held in Taiwan –, should also be noted, as the States must incorporate it to their internal law and in the case of certain matters like consumer law, civil liability for manufactured products and so on, such regulations outline very clear orientations and, thus, leave their mark on the national legislations.

1.3 Conclusions

1.3.1 Prevalence of the Codification Method

There seems to be no doubt that codification is still prevailing as a means of legislative expression, especially in the sphere of civil law. Those countries that in the twentieth century embarked in the codification of their civil law have still remained faithful to it, even if their nineteenth century codes have become outdated and, thus, are continuously being revised by means of legislative reforms or, simply, by the coming into effect of new codes.

These countries were followed by many others that enacted their civil codes in the last few years, as is the case of those countries which, after the implosion of the Soviet Union, have joined the market economy. Likewise, it should be noted that some common law countries consider codification as a short – term objective, like Israel.

---

constitutional law, and more precisely the individual rights secured by the Constitution, do have a major impact on civil law. All branches of civil law are concerned: the personal status and family law, of course, but also property law and the law of obligations. The right of ownership (droit de propriété), for example, which is described by the Code civil as an absolute right (article 544), and which is actually protected by the Constitution, must be reconciled with other constitutional rights.

[68] The Australian report presented at the Taiwan Congress states: "... in recent years the High Court of Australia...has recognized certain freedoms as implicit or in implied by the Constitution, which have had an indirect impact on private law by curtailing certain common law principles..."

And, finally, it seems appropriate to observe carefully the open debate over supranational codification in the sphere of patrimonial law – especially contracts – as is taking place in the European Union or even in Latin America.[69]

1.3.2 Loss of the Central Role of the Civil Code

The prevalence of the codification method does not prevent us from seeing, at least in the sphere of the civil law – like Professor Sacco says – that the Civil Code has lost its monopoly, its central position to the Constitution, administrative law, labor law; now it must share its role with laws that speak another language and deal with different concepts.

Therefore, the main topic is not whether there will be codes in the twenty-first century, but which content they will have, as well as their relation with other areas of private law and their mode of expression.

1.3.3 The Prevailing Content of the Civil Codes

Pursuant to the essays included in this book and the National Reports presented at the Taiwan Congress, it seems clear that the Civil Codes still contain the law of contracts and obligations, in some cases with the inclusion of a general theory of the act of law ("*negozio giuridico*", "*acto o negocio jurídico*", "*acte juridique*"), real property rights – property and its subcategories – and succession law. It must also be noted that the Code coexists with other laws governing certain special contracts or aspects of civil liability (liability for traffic accidents, liability for products, etc.).

In addition, it appears that as the law of persons and family law are part of the Civil Code the enforceability of independent family codes is decreasing.

---

[69] Though less known than the European initiative, in Latin America there have been supranational codification projects on the law of contracts. The so called Alfa Group presented in 2000 the first part of a project for a Latin American Code of Contracts. Doctrine has intensively debated on the matter; see.: Dreyzin de Klor, Adriana – Lloveras, María Emilia, "Bases para un Código latinoamericano tipo del contrato (parte general)", *Rev. de Derecho Privado y Comunitario*, Bs. As. – Santa Fe, nº 20; Fueyo Laneri, Fernando, "Proyecto de Código Único de las Obligaciones y de los Contratos para los países de origen latino", *Rev. Jurídica de San Isidro* (Argentina) 1982-11; Schipani, Sandro, "Codificación de los principios generales del derecho latinoamericano" in *Diez años del Código Civil peruano. Balance y perspectivas*, Lima, 1995; Garro, Alejandro M., "Armonización y unificación del derecho privado en América Latina: esfuerzos, tendencias y realidades", Roma, 1992. The advantage Latin America has to undertake a supranational codification is that all the countries belong to the same legal family and linguistic community; on this see Catalano, Pietro, "Sistemas Jurídicos. Sistemas jurídicos latinoamericanos y derecho romano", *Rev. Gral. de Derecho y Jurisprudencia* – Madrid – 1982-161.

However, in some cases, there is evidence of a certain decodification of the law of persons and family law, because there are certain issues being ruled by statutes separated from the Code (adoption, domestic violence, matrimony or same-sex couples, etc.)

1.3.4 Possible Extension to Commercial Law

Even if evidence seems to show that the content of the civil codes is abridged, has no pretention to embrace all private law, is subordinated to the Constitution and supranational rules and must coexist with specific local statutes, there is no clear tendency regarding commercial law.

On the one hand, there are recodification processes on commercial law, of which the French is the most notorious but not the only; and where the UCC in force in the United States may also be included.

On the other hand, many countries have done without a Commercial Code and thus without a differentiation between civil and commercial contracts and obligations, or without a regulation of the merchant's statute. But, even in these countries, the codes coexist with a number of special statutes comprising extremely relevant areas, such as company law, bankruptcy law, insurance, banking and negotiable instrument or titles of credit.

It is clear that this is a highly relevant issue in current discussion; first of all, it will be necessary to define commercial law and, then, the content of a commercial code. In the debate it must also be analyzed whether it will be a real code or a compilation of statutes on diverse matters such as companies, bankruptcy, negotiable instruments, and insurance.

1.3.5 Consumer Law

One of the branches of the law which has had a major development over the past few decades is consumer law. This has led to the existence of a complex web of regulations on the matter due to the fact that there are supranational provisions and multiple local regulations either on subjects pertaining to civil law, such as contracts entered into by consumers with their multiple characteristics, or on administrative law, procedural law (collective actions), tax law, and so on.

With regard to the role of the Civil Code in the matter of consumer law, different criteria can be observed; while some countries have decided to incorporate at least the rules on contracts with consumers, other countries have practically done without the Code on this matter except for some rules pertaining to the protection of the contracting parties with inferior bargaining power.

This is also a matter open to diverse models, the efficiency of which can be extensively debated.

1.3.6 Private International Law

There is no defined trend on this topic either. While some countries have removed private international law from their codes almost in entirely – such is the case of Switzerland, among others – many other countries still maintain in their codes general provisions and few rules on contracts and obligations. Countries applying this last method had the necessity to multiply the regulations on private international law, as they had to repeat them in areas like company law, bankruptcy law and sometimes in laws governing certain family relations (minors, matrimony).

1.3.7 Effects on the Civil Code and Its Functions

Pursuant to the abovementioned, it may be concluded that Codes nowadays have no pretention to cover everything. They must coexist with other sources of positive private law, some with superior hierarchy to which they have to adapt – the Constitution, international conventions, and communitarian law; and with national microsystems to which there is generally a relation of general law to special law.

However, the Code still remains the seat to the general concepts (the person, the contract, civil liability, real property law, the means to transfer legal obligations and subjective rights, etc.), which makes the Code the setting of all the special legislation and at the same time – recalling GIORGIO CIAN's clever expression – the connective tissue linking all the special laws and making them intelligible.[70]

Therefore, the Code is the regulation of what is included in it and at the same time the *lingua franca* of all private law scattered in special laws which remain outside codification for diverse reasons.

[70] CIAN, GIORGIO, "Il diritto civile come diritto privato commune", *Rivista di Diritto Civile, Cedam, Padova,* 1989.

Part II
Essays on Civil Law Codification from Around the World

Chapter 2
Argentina on the Eve of a New Civil and Commercial Code

Graciela Medina

Abstract This paper originates in the report submitted to the Intermediate Congress of the International Academy of Comparative Law, which took place in Taiwan in May 2012 under the heading "Scope and Structure of the Civil Codes". However, this is in fact a different paper because in between the preparation of such paper and today, Argentina has decisively advanced towards the enactment of a new Civil and Commercial Code. Hence, this paper will mainly refer to the presentation of the Civil and Commercial Code Draft which will probably have been passed by Congress by the time this book gets to the readers.

The first few pages will be covering introductory matters to focus then our analysis on the Draft and we will respond the suggested topics from this perspective.

Keywords Argentina • Civil Code • Civil and Commercial Code Draft • Codification • Recodification • Unification

2.1 Introduction

This paper originates in the report submitted to the Intermediate Congress of the International Academy of Comparative Law, which took place in Taiwan in May 2012 under the heading "Scope and Structure of the Civil Codes". However, this is in fact a different paper because in between the preparation of such paper and today, Argentina has decisively advanced towards the enactment of a new Civil and Commercial Code. Hence, this paper will mainly refer to the presentation of the Civil and Commercial Code Draft which will probably have been passed by Congress by the time this book gets to the readers.

The first few pages will be covering introductory matters to focus then our analysis on the Draft and we will respond the suggested topics from this perspective.

G. Medina (✉)
Civil Law, Law School of the University of Buenos Aires, Buenos Aires, Argentina
e-mail: graciela@gracielamedina.com

J.C. Rivera (ed.), *The Scope and Structure of Civil Codes*, Ius Gentium: Comparative Perspectives on Law and Justice 32, DOI 10.1007/978-94-007-7942-6_2,

2.2 History of Codification

2.2.1 Political Organization in Argentina

The territory of what is Argentina nowadays was discovered and inhabited by the Spaniards in the sixteenth century.[1]

At the beginning of the nineteenth century, more specifically in 1810, an emancipation movement originated which ended in the declaration of independence from Spain in 1816. The national organization process was consolidated in 1853 with the enactment of the Constitution; however, it was in 1860 that the National State adopted the features it has maintained up to these days.[2]

In 1853, the Constitution which created the Argentine Confederation was enacted, but the Province of Buenos Aires did not agree to its incorporation and remained separated from the Confederation and it was the State of Buenos Aires until the Constitutional Reform in 1860. As a result of this reform, the term Confederation was no longer used and Argentina began to be organized as a Federal State. Such 1853/60 Constitution is the one in force nowadays, though with a number of revisions, which we will make reference to later in this paper.

The 1853 Constitution organizes a representative and federal republic, basically inspired in the model of the United States Constitution, though recent research focuses on the influence the 1812 Cadiz Constitution could have had.

The constitutional organization in Argentina is based on the division of three branches of power.

The Executive Branch is in the hands of the President vested with major authority in political decisions.

The Legislative Branch with a bicameral legislature divided into the House of Representatives and the Senate.

The Judicial Branch presided over by the Supreme Court of Justice, regarded as the ultimate interpreter of the Constitution; constitutionality control is diffused owing to the fact that all judges are vested with authority to check the constitutionality of statutes and administrative acts, and it is within the authority of the Supreme Court to monitor the constitutionality of the judgments rendered by any other federal or local court.

Today in Argentina there exist 23 provincial states and the Autonomous City of Buenos Aires; each of which also has a three branch power system. That is to say,

---

[1] Buenos Aires was first founded in 1536 and Santiago del Estero in 1550. The land was only partially occupied by the original inhabitants of scarce population and of a highly primitive nature. It was part of the Viceroyalty of Peru until August 1st 1776 when the Viceroyalty of Rio de la Plata was created.

[2] In 1853 the Constitution which creates the Argentine Confederation is enacted, but the Province of Buenos Aires does not incorporate to it and remains separated from the Confederation as the State of Buenos Aires until the 1860 Constitutional Reform. As a result of this Reform, the term Confederation is no longer used and Argentina organizes as a Federal State.

each province – and the Autonomous City – has an Executive, a Legislature and a Judiciary independent from the federal authority.

The relation between the "provinces" and the Federal State may be summarized as follows:

- The National State acknowledges the provinces as entities legally and historically preceding the creation of the Federal State.
- The provinces delegate some of their authority to the National State.
- The provinces retain all the powers other than those delegated to the federal government.
- The National Constitution clearly outlines which powers the provinces are to delegate to the Federal Congress.

One of the powers delegated by the Provinces to the Federal Congress is the authority to draft the civil, commercial, criminal and mining codes.[3]

Therefore, in Argentina, despite its federal organization, the provincial states have delegated to the Federal Congress the authority to enact its substantive codes. This is one of the most remarkable differences between the Argentine Constitution and the United States of the Mexican Constitution.

It is important to note that the Argentine Constitution – like the American Constitution – is of a highly liberal spirit in that it acknowledges an absolute equality status to foreigners, the freedom of religion, freedom of press, respect for private property and freedom of commerce and the principle of individual autonomy.

The Argentine Constitution was subjected to many revisions, the most relevant in 1957 and 1994. The latter gave international treaties a hierarchy superior to laws, attributed constitutional hierarchy to a number of human rights treaties listed under article 75, section 22, and included competition law, consumer protection and the conservation of the environment within its constitutional safeguards.

2.2.2 Civil Code

2.2.2.1 Standing in the Contemporary Legal Families

The Civil Code of the Argentine Republic is a member of the Romano-Germanic family according to the classification of Rene David.

The Civil Code was enacted on September 29th 1869, and it has been in force since January 1st 1871.

The Civil Code was drafted by Dalmacio Vélez Sarsfield, not only a jurist but a true statesman, who stood out as Minister of the Executive on a number of occasions and for valuable contributions during his public life.[4]

---

[3] Article 67, section 11 of the original text; article 75, section 12 of the text reformed in 1994.

[4] V. Rescigno, Pietro, Dalmacio Vélez Sarsfield codificatore, en Dalmacio Vélez Sarsfield e il diritto latinoamericano, a cura di Sandro Schipani, Atti del congreso Internazionale, Roma, march 1986, page 27.

2.2.2.2 Sources

The author of the Argentine Civil Code used five relevant sources in the draft of the code.

The first source was Roman Law, not only legislated law but that which stem from the treatise authors as well. Thus, our codifier continually quotes authors in his notes[5] such as Vinnio, Heinecio, Cujas and the Romanic authors of that time, like Maynz, Mackeldey, Molitor, Ortolan and specially Savigny.

The second source was the applicable law in force at the time and with which Vélez Sarsfield was very familiar due to his practical experience as a lawyer. This applicable law contained numerous and complex statutes, such as the Seven-Part Code (*Libro de las VII Partidas*) which in *Indies* was the effective applicable law–laws specifically enacted for its application in *Indies* – which gave rise to what was known as "patriot law", which was in fact the law enacted by the Provinces during the national organizational stage.

Other sources were the foreign codes and the doctrine arising from them; mainly the Napoleon's Code and its commentators. Among them, Vélez repeatedly quotes the German Zachariae, his Alsatian followers Aubry and Rau, as well as Troplong, Toullier, Demolombe, Duranton, Marcadé, Merlín, Mourlon and the Belgian Laurent. Also, Pothier is frequently quoted, especially in the sphere of obligations and contracts.

The fourth source accounted by Vélez was Freitas' *Esboco*, draft of a Civil Code in Brazil. Freitas was characterized by a particularly balanced spirit in legal matters and very progressive ideas. He was the main source of inspiration for Vélez Sarsfield in the book "Of the Persons".

A fifth group was comprised by other codes, such as the Bavarian Code, the Chilean Code of Andrés Bello, the Civil Code Draft for Spain of García Goyena, Acevedo's Draft for the Oriental Republic of Uruguay, the 1811 Austrian Code; and further doctrinal works less quoted such as those of Story, Gregorio López, to name but a few. Vélez also worked with codes of German States, such as Sajonia, Wurtenberg and the abovementioned Bavaria.

Additionally, many other codes, many of which were almost an exact copy of the Napoleon's Code, have served as sources of the Argentine Civil Code such as the Sardinia Code, the Codes of Tuscany, Parma, the two Sicilies, Holland, the Louisiana Code, the Vaud Code, the State of New York Code and even the 1865 Italian Code.

The sources used in the draft of the Civil Code show that the legislator was clearly familiar with the comparative law of that time.

---

[5] All editions of the Argentine Civil Code have a special feature: they include the notes that Vélez wrote as he advanced on the texts; in such notes he included the authors or legal bodies he consulted and were his sources, pointing out similarities and differences with them; and on some occasions he justified the draft as an article of the Code. Although the notes have not been passed by the Federal Congress, they are regarded as a valuable tool in the interpretation of the Code.

The knowledge of comparative law enabled Vélez to draft a code which succeeded in merging the law applicable in Argentina at that time with the innovations demanded by a plan or project of country endorsed by his generation, and with the necessary modernization of the institutions in force.

2.2.2.3 The Commercial Code

The history of legislation in Argentina reveals a curious feature, which is that the Commercial Code was enacted before the Civil Code. As it has already been pointed out, between 1853 and 1860 the State of Buenos Aires was separated from the Argentine Confederation. In this period and in this independent State the enactment of a Commercial Code was prompted, which draft was commissioned to a Uruguayan jurist, Eduardo Acevedo and Dalmacio Vélez Sarsfield himself. Their draft became the Commercial Code of the State of Buenos Aires in 1859. Having the State of Buenos Aires been incorporated as part of the Argentine Republic with the constitutional reform of 1860, such Code became the National Commercial Code in 1862.

2.2.2.4 Content of the Civil Code. Governing Principles

The Argentine Civil Code begins with two preliminary titles: "Of the Laws" and "Of the methods to count the intervals of the Law."

From the titles, it breaks down into four Books.

Book I is entitled "Of the Persons", and deals with persons in general in the first section, and "the personal rights in the family relations" in the second section; this Book legislates on marriage, divorce, filiation, parental rights and duties, guardianship and curatorship.

Book II is named "Of the personal rights in the civil relations" and it regulates obligations, events and acts of law and contracts, and civil liability.

Book III governs real estate rights and Book IV is called "Of the real and personal rights: Common Provisions", and it comprises in rem rights, succession, preemption and prescription.

The Argentine Civil Code, like other codes of the time, was founded on the following principles:

(i) the absolute respect for the pledged word and the unquestionable enforceability of the contractual bond
(ii) liability for negligence
(iii) the patrimony unit
(iv) the absolute nature of the ownership right
(v) the family law relying on indissoluble marriage, obviously between different-sex couples.
(vi) the incapacity of the married woman.
(vii) parental rights and duties in charge of the father.

2.3 The Decodification Process

2.3.1 Introduction

During the twentieth century, a number of matters of the Civil Law separated from its common backbone. Among them, we find labor law, agricultural law and consumer law.

Notwithstanding this, a few matters which had not been incorporated to the Civil Code were legislated outside the Code, such as name, adoption, property registry and even civil matrimony, even when such laws are deemed to integrate or form part of the Civil Code.

In the past few years, this trend accelerated and we will continuously see that many institutions have been legislated outside the Civil Code, prompting the creation of real microsystems.

2.3.2 Reforms to the Civil Code

The rationalistic concept of a "code" under which all law is to be laid down opposes to the reality of constant social, ideological, political and economic changes which prompt the continuous adjustment of texts, which is achieved by means of case law or legislative revisions.

I will detail below the most relevant revisions of the Civil Code by diving them into stages:

2.3.2.1 First Stage

The first stage comprises the period from the enactment of the Civil Code until 1968, when the Code was updated by special laws regulating new issues or modifying existing institutions.

(a) Civil Matrimony Law:
On November 12th 1888, Law 2393 of Civil Matrimony was passed which superseded the matrimonial regime of the Civil Code. This was a necessary reform owing to the fact that the system of the Civil Code excluded non-Catholics from the possibility of the celebration of marriage.
This Law was then modified in 1968, by Law 17.711, and replaced by Law 23.515, enacted on June 8th 1987, and finally revised by Law 26.618 in 2010 which permits marriage between people of the same sex.

(b) Law of the Civil Rights of Women
Law 11.357, passed on September 14th 1926, considerably broadened the civil capacity of the married woman.

The capacity and the rights of women have extended to civil equality with men and to the elimination of all kinds of discrimination.

(c) Adoption Law:
Our Code failed to regulate adoption, which was incorporated by Law 13.252, today replaced by Law 19.134, which was revised by Law 24779 modified by Law 26.618 in 2010 to permit adoption by same-sex couples.

(d) Horizontal Property Law:
The codifier had prohibited the horizontal division of property (article 2617). This was derogated by Law 13.512, passed on September 30th 1948, which is still applicable.

(e) Law for the sale of land in lots and in installments:
Law 14.005, enacted on September 30th 1950, regulated the sale in installments of pieces of land, with the aim of protecting the purchasers who were on many occasions the victims of unfair acts. This Law is still in force with the revisions introduced by Law 23.266.

(f) Law on Children born in or out of wedlock:
Law 14.367 of October 11th 1954 introduced substantial reforms to the regime of Family and Succession Law when it partially abolished the difference between children born in or out of wedlock. Nowadays, children have the same status under the law (law 23.264).

(g) Land Registry and Prescription of real estate property:
Law 14.159 of October 3rd 1952 outlined regulations on the Land Registry and ruled that the acquisition of real estate property through prescription would be subjected to a court procedure. It is substantially in force.

(h) Regime of minors and the family:
Law 14.394 of December 30th 1954 introduced major reforms in the matter of the legal capacity to celebrate marriage and presumption of death from absence or disappearance.

It also incorporated the "homestead exception", property which cannot be foreclosed for debts incurred subsequent to the coming into effect of this exemption.

Although it was not part of the draft submitted by the Executive to the Congress, this Law included divorce (article 31) for the first time in the history of the national legislation. The validity of this text was suspended (decree law 4070/56), and then reinstated by Law 23.515 which ruled again this form of marriage dissolution.

2.3.2.2 Second Stage. The 1968 Revision: Law 17.711

In 1968, the Argentine Civil Code was partially revised by Law 17.711 which modified about 200 articles of the Code. Nevertheless, its importance does not lie in the number of articles, but in the change of perspective of the Code, which is reflected in some of the institutions incorporated to it.

Thus, it is worth mentioning that law 17711 incorporated to the Code:

- the abuse of law (article 1071);
- fraud in the inducement (article 954);
- the principle of good faith as a rule for the interpretation of contracts (article 1198);
- the unforeseeability rule (article 1198);
- the limitation to the absolute nature of the ownership right (articles 2512, 2513);
- extended compensation for moral distress in civil liability either contractual (article 522) or extra contractual (article 1078);
- the possibility to reduce the compensation in torts (article 1069);
- vicarious liability in civil wrongs caused by the act of things (article 1113);
- joint and several liability of joint tortfeasors (article 1109, 2nd paragraph.);
- equitable compensation for the victim of an involuntary act (article 907);
- automatic default in payment as a rule in obligations with a term certain (article 509);
- forfeiture clauses implied in contracts (article 1204);
- registration in real estate registries as public notice for the conveyance of real estate rights in property (article 2505);
- protection of the third party in good faith, sub-purchasing real or personal property rights in the event the transaction is void (article 1051);
- the protection of the purchaser with a preliminary sales contract (articles 1185 bis and 2355);
- attainment of the age of majority at 21 years old (article. 126);
- emancipation of minors at the age of 18 years old (article 131);
- extension of the capacity of the minor who works (article 128);
- divorce (personal separation), by mutual agreement (article 67 bis of the Civil Matrimony Law);
- modification of the order of succession (articles 3569 bis, 3571, 3573, 3576, 3576 bis, 3581, 3585, 3586);
- presumption of acceptance of the inheritance by the heirs with the right of inventory (article 3363).

The preceding enumeration is a clear illustration of the relevance of the reform, which changed the pillars of the nineteenth century codification as follows:

- Limitation to the absolute nature of the principle *pacta sunt servanda*, with the admission of the unforeseeability rule, fraud in the inducement and the abuse of law, all corollaries of the general principle of the good faith which is expressly set forth;
- Limitation to the absolute nature of the ownership right, by abridging the powers of proprietors;
- Change in the regime of civil liability by admitting the vicarious liability, the redress of moral distress in a broader extent and joint and several liability of joint tortfeasors.
- Adoption of solutions which respond to a dynamic concept of patrimony, such as automatic default in payment and the forfeiture clause implied in contracts;

Law 17.711 represented a significant breakthrough in our civil legislation, a modernization of the law which allows us to state that as of 1968 there has been a new Civil Code, which, without abandoning the protection of freedom, has adopted a less individualistic perspective and a more accentuated solidarity aspect in comparison with the original Civil Code.[6]

2.3.2.3 Third Stage

The third stage comprises the period between the laws passed as from 1968 to today. The most relevant laws will be mentioned as follows:

(a) Real Estate Registry:
Law 17.711 had provided in its article 2505 the registration in real estate registries as public notice for the conveyance of real estate rights in property. A few days later, Law 17.801 was enacted, which was the National Law of the Real Estate Registry.

(b) Name of natural persons:
The isolated provisions existing on this matter were replaced by Law 18.248, which ruled the subject on its entirety. This Law has been subjected to subsequent partial revisions, the most relevant being the reform introduced by Law 26.618 which governs the family name of homosexual couples.

(c) Adoption:
The up-to-then in force law was replaced by Law 19.134, enacted on June 3rd 1971. Afterwards, such text was superseded by Law 24.779 which incorporated the adoption regime in between articles 311 and 340 of the Civil Code.
In 2010, Law 26.618 reformed adoption and permits that children be adopted by same – sex married couples.

(d) Prehorizontality:
Law 19.724, named Prehorizontality Law was passed on July 6th 1972.

(e) Non-Profit Organizations:
The Non-Profit Organizations Law, which fills a void in the Code, has been in force since September 25th 1975, under number 19.836.

(f) National Land Registry:
The National Land Registry Law has the number 20.440 and was passed on June 5th 1973.

(g) Right of habitation of the surviving spouse:
Law 20.793 incorporated article 3573 bis to the Civil Code which established the in rem right of habitation of the surviving spouse.

(h) Right to privacy:
Law 20.889 had attempted to regulate for the first time the right to privacy, by means of the incorporation of article 32 bis, but there existed a defect in its enactment, as both legislative chambers had voted on different texts. Therefore,

---

[6] V. Casiello, Juan José, "Memorando la reforma civil de 1968", LL 28.11.08.

by means of Law 21.173 of September 30th 1975, article 1071 bis of the Civil Code was finally enacted.

(i) Adjustment clauses in mortgages and pledges:
Law 21.309 set forth a system for the public notice of adjustment clauses in mortgages and pledges with registry. It was enacted and promulgated on May 7th 1976. It was derogated by the Convertibility Law 23.928. Convertibility had no further effect as of January 6th 2002 when Law 25.561 was passed for such purpose, though this has not prompted the reappearance of the adjustment clauses; as it was already explained, Law 23.928 is still in force and it expressly prohibits the use of these adjustment clauses.

(j) Transplants:
Law 21.541 constitutes the first national regime on the transplant of organs; passed on March 18th 1977, it was partially revised by Law 23.464, enacted on October 30th 1986. Nowadays, Law 24.193 is in force.

(k) Marks and signals:
The regime of marks and signals, used as a way to identify small and large cattle, omitted by the Civil Code and gathered in rural codes, became incorporated to national legislation by means of law 22.939 of October 6th 1983.

(l) Blood Law:
Law 22.990 called Blood Law and passed on November 20th 1983 constitutes an extensive text of 100 articles which governs different aspects in the use of human blood.

(m) Filiation and Parental Rights and Duties:
One of the most relevant reforms as from the 1968 reform is that effected by Law 23.264, passed by the National Congress on September 25th 1985.

It is especially relevant in the matter of filiation, as it recognizes the absolute equality between children born in or out of wedlock and parental rights and duties which are to be exercised equally by both parents.

In addition, it introduced reforms in other matters such as capacity, domicile, to name but a few.

(n) Civil Matrimony:
Another important revision of our Family Law originates in Law 23.515, which replaced the 2393 Civil Matrimony Law.

Among other multiple modifications, it is important to bear in mind that this regime reinstates divorce, which had been suspended as of 1956.

(o) Pact of San Jose, Costa Rica:
Law 23.054, passed on March 19th 1984, ratifies the American Convention on Human Rights, generally referred to as Pact of San Jose, Costa Rica.

By its incorporation to internal law, it has had direct influence on many matters, especially on those related to the rights of personality.

(p) Convention on the Elimination of all Forms of Discrimination against Women (CEDAW):
Law 23.179 ratified the Convention on the Elimination of all Forms of Discrimination against Women (CEDAW), passed by resolution 34/180 of the General Assembly of the United Nations.

(q) Law of *fideicomiso* or trust and leasing:
Law 24.441 generally referred to as the construction financing law, represents one of the most relevant advances in the Argentine legislation in the last few years. This is due to the fact that it incorporated the trust agreement, which permits the creation of a separate patrimony which cannot be reached by creditors of neither of the two parties; and the leasing, a very much used contract in the contemporary economy. Also, a few reforms were made to the Civil Code on the matter of assignment of claims. The regulation of the leasing contract made by Law 24.441 has been replaced by that of Law 25248, now in effect.

(r) Law of Forest Surface
Law 25.509, passed in November 2001, incorporated the in rem right of forest surface with the intention of facilitating and promoting forestation activities.

(s) Sexual health and responsible procreation
Despite criticism from reactionary sectors, Law 25673 was enacted on October 30th 2002 which created the National Program of Sexual Health and Responsible Procreation. It integrates to Law 26.150 of Sexual Education (National Program of Integral Sexual Education) and Law 26.130, Regime for Surgical Contraceptive Operations.
Many provinces have passed legislation on the matter within the scope of their constitutional jurisdictional authority[7];

(t) Protection of children and adolescents
Law 26.061 of Integral Protection of Children and Adolescents represents a significant advance not only in their protection but in the recognition of their rights and the exercise of such rights by themselves. Argentina has also ratified the Convention on the Rights of the Child (Law 23849 of 1990). Like in the case of the Convention on the Elimination of all Forms of Discrimination against Women, this Convention on the Rights of the Child has constitutional hierarchy as from the reform of the supreme law in 1994 (article 75, section 22).

(u) Integral protection of women
On April 14th 2009 Law 26.485 on the Integral Protection of Women was enacted. This Law completes the anti-discriminatory policy with respect to women and is directed to their effective protection against all kind of violence women are subjected to in contemporary societies.

(v) Civil Registry
In September 2008, Law 26.413 was enacted, which sets forth the organization of the Registry of Civil Status and Capacity of Persons, both within the jurisdiction of the Autonomous City of Buenos Aires and in the Provinces. Article 95 of Law 26.413 derogated decree 8204/63.

(w) Law 26618 of equal marriage passed in 2010.
This Law permits the marriage of persons of the same sex with the same effects of the marriage between people of different sex.

[7] V. Rosales, Pablo O. – Villaverde, María Silvia, *Salud Sexual y Procreación Responsable*, Bs. As., 2009.

2.3.3 Decodification of the Commercial Code

Having read the abovementioned sections, it can be concluded that the codified civil law has experienced a process of permanent transformation, both inside and outside the Code. However, the decodification process has had a major impact on the Commercial Code, as there is hardly anything left from the 1859/62 Code substantially modified in 1889.

Bankruptcy Law was detached from the original Commercial Code (four laws from the enactment of the code in 1889: Law 4156, Law 11719, Law 19551–reformed by law 22917–and Law 24522, reformed twice in 2002–Laws 25563 and 25589–and again in 2011).

Also, the regulation of companies, bill of exchange, promissory note, check, navigation and insurance was removed from the Commercial Code.

In addition, many institutions which had not been originally covered by the Code were then legislated, such as: customs warrant, warrant, pledge with registry, stock exchange and markets, agricultural pledge, mixed economy entities, cooperatives, the Companies' Board (IGJ), negotiable obligations, mutual funds, financial entities, and so on.

Another new topic is that pertaining to the air transportation which gave rise to the Aeronautic Code, independent from the Civil Code. And, maritime law is governed by the General Maritime Law, incorporated to the Commercial Code.

A number of rules surviving the Commercial Code, like that in Article 7 which states that unilaterally commercial acts are governed by the Commercial Code, have lost importance due to the fact that when such acts are undertaken with consumers, they will be subject to the regulations of the special law; thus, only the general regulation of the typical contracts in the Commercial Code will be applicable to such acts with consumers as long as it does not contradict the provisions of the consumer protection law.

2.3.4 Acknowledgment of Other Sources as Further Decodification

As Professor Rivera has pointed out on many other occasions, the decodification process does not end in the reforms to the Code or in a number of matters detached from the Civil or the Commercial Code to be regulated by special laws. However, beyond all these factors, it is true that the Code has to co-exist with other sources of an even superior hierarchy – such as the Constitution, supranational law, communitarian law – out of which subjective rights arise, the fulfillment of which individuals may be entitled to claim before national or supranational instances.[8]

---

[8] Rivera, Julio César, "Codificación, descodificación, recodificación", not published, to appear in Revista de Derecho privado y Comunitario.

2.3.4.1 The Constitution as a Source of Subjective Rights

For a long time, jurists have noticed that the Constitution is a source of statutes which could have a direct efficacy and not only pragmatic. In Argentina, the role of the Supreme Court was extremely valuable for this concept to be understood when 50 years ago in two extraordinary judgments, "Siri" and "Kot", our Supreme Court set forth that individuals were entitled to claim the enforcement of the rights acknowledged by the Constitution without the need of an inferior statute to regulate the exercise of such rights.

On the other hand, it has also been outlined that many matters of private law are in the National Constitution, a few from its enactment, others from the 1994 reform. This is what is known as "constitutionalization of the civil law."

2.3.4.2 Supranational Law

Since 1983, Argentina has embarked on a process to incorporate human rights to supranational law. This was effected by the 1994 constitutional reform in section 22 of article 75.[9]

The impact of supranational law when it became incorporated to the Constitution by the 1994 reform has been appropriately pointed out by the Supreme Court in recent decisions. In the "Arriola" case, the Supreme Court has stated as follows:

> "...*One of the basic principles of all the institutional scaffolding prompting the Constitutional Convention in 1994 was to incorporate the international treaties on human rights on par with the National Constitution (article 75, section 22). Therefore, the 1994 constitutional reform recognized the importance of an international system of human rights and did not restrict to the principle of unrestrained sovereignty of the nations ... This historical event has deeply modified the constitutional perspective in many aspects ...*" .[10] And,

---

[9] Article 75 (22) "*To approve or reject treaties concluded with other nations and international organizations, and concordats with the Holy See. Treaties and concordats have a higher hierarchy than laws.*

The American Declaration of the Rights and Duties of Man; the Universal Declaration of Human Rights; the American Convention on Human Rights; the International Pact on Economic, Social and Cultural Rights; the International Pact on Civil and Political Rights and its empowering Protocol; the Convention on the Prevention and Punishment of Genocide; the International Convention on the Elimination of all Forms of Racial Discrimination; the Convention on the Elimination of all Forms of Discrimination against Woman; the Convention against Torture and other Cruel, Inhuman or Degrading Treatments or Punishments; the Convention on the Rights of the Child; in the full force of their provisions, they have constitutional hierarchy, do no repeal any section of the First Part of this Constitution and are to be understood as complementing the rights and guarantees recognized herein. They shall only be denounced, in such event, by the National Executive Power after the approval of two-thirds of all the members of each House.

In order to attain constitutional hierarchy, the other treaties and conventions on human rights shall require the vote of two-thirds of all the members of each House, after their approval by Congress."

[10] CSN, Arriola, 25.8.09; in Zaffaroni's vote in this same case Estrada was quoted: "... article 19 clearly separates law and individual morality, making a distinction, once and forever, between the State that imposes a morality and that which respects the moral freedom of the individual; the first he calls "pagan and socialist" and the second "Christian and liberal"".

in the same decision, the Court emphasized: "*...the hierarchy granted to the international treaties has had, on occasions, the virtue of ratifying the protection of rights and safeguards already provided for in our Magna Charta of 1853; in other cases, it has strengthened them, and in other cases it has raised further proclamations or has defined their extent with more detail and precision.*"

2.3.4.3 Supreme Court's Precedents

In Argentina, case law as a source of law is practically not questioned. Beyond all theoretical debates aroused by this topic, it is true that no lawyer, professor, judge or law student could be oblivious to the decisions of the Supreme Court.

This is due to the fact that it is very frequent for courts to base their decisions on precedents rendered by other courts. And, it is also attributed to the fact that the work of courts has been relevant in the transformation of the civil law.

For many decades, the judgments which were better known and quoted were those rendered by the civil courts of the City of Buenos Aires.

Notwithstanding this, a few Supreme Court decisions have had a decisive influence on central aspects of private law.

However, since 1983 and also as a result of the Constitution being regarded as another source of private law and the incorporation of Argentina to the map of supranational law on human rights, it is the Supreme Court's precedents that begin to have a leading role.

And, it is important to mention that this Supreme Court has had the virtue of reinstating and ratifying the liberal spirit of the 1853 Constitution.

This is what the Court did in the judgment rendered on the case "Asociación Lucha por la Identidad Travesti Transexual" (Association for the Fight of Transvestite Transsexual Identity) – in November 2006 – in which the Court set a number of paramount outlines.

As for the liberal and democratic ideas of the Constitution, the Court – referring to the "Portillo" precedent and even improving it – said:

> *The definite reinstatement of the democratic and republican ideals constitutionalists laid down in 1853 and deepened in 1994 calls for a national unity in freedom, but not for uniformity or homogeneity. The sense of democratic and liberal equality is the right to be different, but it cannot be confused with the "equalization" which is a totalitarian concept. Article 19 of the National Constitution, combined with all safeguards and rights recognized by the Constitution, undoubtedly illustrates the concern constitutionalists had to respect the autonomy of consciousness as an essence of the person – and, therefore, the diversity of thoughts and values – and not to force citizens to a uniformity which fails to be in line with the* ***liberal political philosophy that inspires our Fundamental Statute****.* (third paragraph of whereases; emphasis added)[11]

It is important to mention that what was being discussed was the possibility of either granting or not authorization to a civil association in the framework of the

[11] CSN, "Asociación Lucha por la Identidad Travesti – Transexual c. Inspección General de Justicia", 21.11.06, Fallos 329:5266.

general law. It is the requirement of the Civil Code that associations have a "common weal" aim. The Court construed this requirement in the light of the liberal spirit of the Constitution.

2.3.4.4 Conclusion

To some extent, what has happened is what the Italian jurist Natalino Irti anticipated: "*On the one hand, the Code has lost all constitutional value due to the fact that all political and civil freedoms, the property right, the private economic initiative, are all safeguarded by the Constitution, that is to say, by statutes of a superior hierarchy (…) To these safeguards, there is nothing the Civil Code could add as it was deprived of the protection role it assumed in the XIXth century and it is daily undermined by special laws.*"

2.4 Current Status of the Codification

Private Law in Argentina is still codified law. But, as we have already pointed out, the civil code and the commercial code are no longer the exclusive sources in such matters. Both Codes have to co-exist with sources of a superior hierarchy, such as the Constitution and the international treaties; with legislative microsystems which comprise numerous and relevant matters (name of persons, companies, bankruptcy, insurance, property registry, etc.); and with case law which has an extraordinary value due to the fact that it has permitted that the structures and principles of patrimonial and family private law be renewed by means of judges' decisions.

All this process which resulted in the codes losing their central and almost exclusive role prompted changes – as we have already anticipated – in the fundamental principles on which the nineteenth century codification relied. Thus,

- the family founded on indissoluble marriage has given place to multiple forms of family[12];
- as of the coming into effect of divorce, matrimonial and extra matrimonial families are given equal status;
- the principle of contractual freedom still continues to be the basis of the contractual system, though it recognizes multiple limitations, most in force nowadays, such as: the unforeseeability rule, fraud in the inducement, the abuse of law, consumer protection, control of general provisions, special regulation of adhesion contracts; which have extended to commercial law;
- civil liability may see negligence as its backbone, but big sectors have been invaded by objective factors of attribution of liability, so in practice negligence becomes a residual factor;

[12] The subject was dealt with in the International Congress of Family Law held in Mendoza in 1998.

- the right of ownership has limits set forth by the same code, significantly accentuated since the revision in 1968.
- the principle of patrimony unit has been replaced by the recognition of the possibility that a natural or legal person may be holder of more than one patrimony; this has been ratified by the incorporation of the *fideicomiso* or trust to Argentine law by means of Law 24441, inspired in the Anglo-Saxon trust;
- Women have equal rights to men and parental rights and duties are to be exercised by both parents equally.
- Different-sex couples are no longer a requirement for the celebration of marriage as of 2010 when homosexual matrimony began to be admitted.

2.5 The Recodification. 2012 Draft of the Civil Code

We agree with Professor Rivera that a transformation of the private law legislation is essential. Even though some areas – such as family law – have been deeply modified, there are others like real estate, succession and private international law which have been subjected to very few changes since the enactment of the Civil Code. Indeed, the significant influence of the constitutionalization of private and supranational law demands the adaptation of the inferior legislation.

For that purpose, Argentina has seen in the past 25 years many attempts to recodify private law. We could mention the following drafts:

- The 1987 Unification Draft; it was enacted by Congress but vetoed by the National Executive Power.
- Civil Code Draft prepared by the Executive Power by Decree 468/92
- Draft submitted by a Parliamentary Commission known as the 1993 Draft;
- Draft of the Civil Code unified with the Commercial Code in 1998.

Finally, in 2010, the President of the Argentine Republic commissioned three jurists to prepare a Civil Code Draft unified with the Commercial Code.

These jurists have invited 90 people to cooperate in the draft of the reform of the Code dividing them into sub Commissions who were requested the draft of a first proposal on a specific part of the Civil Code and on the basis of the following premises:

- Adequacy to the Constitution and to the participation in the MERCOSUR
- Reception and regulation of human rights, so that the codes will be, out of all the sources, the one closer to the protection of the person.
- Protection of the weak and respect for the contractual freedom between people with the same bargaining power
- Reformulation of the contractual principles, informatization processes and the circulation of assets.
- Recognition of the new forms of property.
- Definition of a balanced system of civil liability

- Strengthening of the family.
- Respect for minorities.
- Acknowledgment of the cultural identity of the aborigine populations
- Procedure to facilitate cultural integration by means of internal legislation

The Civil and Commercial Code Draft was presented in 2012 and after a revision of the original text by the Executive, it was directed to the National Congress. A bicameral commission was formed which has heard in public hearings social organizations and individuals interested in expressing their opinions to the Congress. The report of the bicameral Commission is expected to be released during the first months in 2013 and from that point the prompt enactment of the new Civil and Commercial Code of the Argentine Republic.

Given this new reality, the recommended topics will be dealt with in the context of the Civil and Commercial Code Draft.

2.6 Commercial Law

2.6.1 Commercial Law in Codification

The Argentine Commercial Code, like many others of the nineteenth century, considered commercial law as the law of merchants, individuals whose profession is the exercise of commerce and commercial acts.

Under Argentine legislation, like in many other countries, civil law is of supplementary application in the scope of commercial law. However, the connections between both branches of law have significantly strengthened.

Over the twentieth century, the diffusion of massive contractual forms and the relevance attained by business associations changed the relation that Civil and Commercial Law had during the nineteenth century. Today it is possible to observe a commercialization of civil law and a civilization of commercial law.

2.6.1.1 The "Commercialization" of Civil Law

On the one hand, Commercial Law has expanded in comparison with Civil Law, resulting in a phenomenon that authors refer to as the commercialization of Civil Law, strengthened by the social-economic transformation known as industrial revolution. Technological innovations enable the introduction of machines to the productive process making mass industrial production technically possible, which contributes to both an increase in job productivity and a reduction of production costs. Demographic development and urban concentration have both given rise to a huge availability of the workforce. Galgano, with his peculiar ideological tone, states that in this era of the industrial revolution, it is no longer possible to make a distinction between relations relevant and relations indifferent to the mercantile class and this is the reason to explain why this strong influence of commercial law takes place, which has led Argentina to look for the unification of its Civil Law and Commercial Law for more than 50 years.

2.6.1.2 The "Civilization" of Commercial Law

But, at the same time, Civil Law has had influence on Commercial law through its civil institutions. The protection of the weaker party to a contract, the protection of consumers in general subjected to commercial regulations under provisions like Article 7 of the Argentine Commercial Code, and undoubtedly the event that the general theory of obligations does not appear anywhere but in the Civil Code, have evidenced the influence of the Civil Law on Commercial Law.

2.6.1.3 Tendency to Unification

The drafts for the reform of the Argentine Civil Code we have referred to recommended a legislative unification of the civil and commercial codes similar to that of the Swiss Code of Obligations of 1911 and the 1942 Italian Civil Code.

The recommended unification does not mean the disappearance of the commercial law, or the loss of its didactic, doctrinal or scientific autonomy; but it involves recognizing that provisions in common to all patrimonial private law should be elaborated.

Such unification is grounded on the following reasons:

- the existence of a commercial law of subjective orientation with the merchant at its center is absent from real substance; this is a classic conception of the commercial law, largely superseded by others;
- the reason for a commercial law of objective orientation sustained in the existence of certain acts which are commercial by nature has been lost forever;
- in fact the concept of *commerce* as a means to the exchange of movables is extremely narrow and unsuitable given the current reality; otherwise, all productive activities form part of the current idea of commerce;
- there is no ontological distinction in the essential concepts of patrimonial law (obligation, contract, in rem right) whether they are expressed in Civil Law or in Commercial Law;
- there are certain law fields that have become unified (bankruptcy) and others have done so by default (companies, due to the use of the corporation (*sociedad anónima*) for all kind of activities and given the virtual disappearance of the Civil Code corporation (*sociedad* civil);
- commercial law is today the law of companies, of the economy, of business, according to the many expressions used by doctrine and it is formed by a fluctuating mass of matters such as competition law, industrial property law, law of companies and business groups, company reorganization, bankruptcy law, distribution, and so on. These are matters which are not contemplated in what is left of the Commercial Code, but under special legislation.

Thus, the 1998 Civil Code Draft and the 2012 Draft recommend a single Code of Private Law in the body of the Civil Code, with the corresponding derogation of the Commercial Code.

2.6.1.4 Commercial Law in the 2012 Draft

Regardless of the intention of the jurists in charge of the preparation of the Draft, it is important to mention that there exists in the Draft a virtual absorption of the commercial law by the general law. In this sense, we could refer to the absence of rules on a subject proper of the commercial law, the merchant, the business enterprise. Also, there are no rules on the Public Registry of Commerce and the terms "commerce", "commercial" or similar words have almost disappeared. Additionally, the law of business associations – which survives in a separate body – is now called "General Law of Companies". That is the reason why some authors have recently referred to the "blurring of commercial law".[13]

From a different perspective, institutions which are typical of commercial law are incorporated to the Code; for example, securities and contracts like leasing, franchise, trust and banking.

However, it is important to note that the unification of the codes does not mean that the microsystems typical of the commercial law will disappear. Therefore, upon the enactment of the new Civil and Commercial Code, the law of business associations will survive under its new name, as well as the bankruptcy law, insurance law, the multimodal transport law, credit cards law, the aeronautic code and hundreds of other statutes that regulate specific institutions. Notwithstanding the Vienna Convention on the international sale of goods which has been ratified by the Argentine State and is part of its domestic law.

2.6.2 Consumer Protection Law

In Argentina, like in many other countries, consumer law is ruled by means of a special law, independent from both codes of private law.

However, this does not mean that the consumer protection law is completely autonomous, but – on the contrary – it integrates to all the body of laws in general and to the Civil Code in particular, either when it introduces new regulations applicable to the acts or contracts these regulations rule, or when it imposes solutions to matters which, partially or totally, cannot be solved by the rules of the general law.

The title of this section resembles that of article 3 of Law 24.240 in its drafting by Law 26.361. Given its importance, we transcribe this article: "*Article 3°*:

[13] Junyent Bas, Francisco, "La "difuminación" de la comercialidad en el Proyecto de Código Civil y Comercial y la necesidad de una relectura completa. A propósito del nuevo rol de la empresa y el quehacer mercantil", *Rev. Derecho Comercial, del Consumidor y de la Empresa*, LL, Octubre 2012, ps. 3–28.

Consumer Relation. Integration to Statutes. Preeminence. The consumer relation is the legal bond between the supplier and the consumer or user. The provisions under this law are integrated to the general laws and special laws applicable to consumer relations.... In case of doubt regarding the interpretation of the principles set forth by this Law, the provision more favorable to the consumer shall prevail."

The law transcribed envisages its integration to the Civil Code and other regimes and the preeminence of the Consumer Protection Law over other legal rules comprised by the Civil Code. But, should there exist any clash between a general law rule and another provision which protects the consumer, the latter will prevail. Therefore, the legal regime arising from the Consumer Protection Law will not only *supplement* but also *modify* or *derogate*, even partially, the statutes pertaining to other legal spheres applicable to the consumer relation taken into consideration.

2.6.2.1 Consumer Protection Law in the 2012 Draft of the Civil and Commercial Code

The status of consumer law will see a substantial change with the enactment of the Civil and Commercial Code of the Argentine Republic, as it contains regulations on the consumer protection law which shall be construed and applied in relation to the special regulation.

The bases for the Civil and Commercial Code Draft justify the inclusion of regulations of consumer protection law, though initially recognizing that it is a debated topic and that in comparative law there exist many models: that which keeps separate regulations (followed in Italy, Spain, by the Draft to Reform the French Civil Code in the Law of Obligations and Prescription, directed by Professor Pierre Catalá and submitted to the Ministry of Justice in 2005, and in all the Mercosur States (Brazil, Paraguay, Uruguay and Venezuela) as well as in all the Associated States (Bolivia, Chile, Peru, Ecuador and Colombia). And, the model followed by the 2002 reform of the German Civil Code which incorporated a number of statutes specifically applicable to consumer law as well as the Québec Civil Code which also included provisions pertaining to the consumer contracts and adhesion contracts.

The bases for the Draft state as follows: "In the Argentine legal system, the constitutional status of consumer protection law should be born in mind as well as the broad application of these statues to the legal cases and the opinion of the majority of the doctrine. Following these guidelines, it is necessary not only to advance to the unification of the civil and commercial contracts, but also to incorporate consumer contracts."

The bases for the Civil and Commercial Code Draft assume that "The breadth of the regulatory subject matter poses difficulties as for the distinctions and the way in which they are presented" and after ruling out various possible methods, they conclude by stating that "consumer contracts are to be regulated taking into consideration that they are not another special type of contract (for example, sale contracts), but a fragment of the general type of contracts, which has influence on the special types (for example, consumer sale contract), thus the need to incorporate its regulation to the general part.

This solution is in line with the National Constitution under which the consumer is the subject of fundamental rights, as well as with the special legislation and the extensive case law and doctrine on the matter.

It becomes necessary, then, to regulate the civil contracts and the commercial and consumer contracts, making reference to the general type of consumer contract."

For all these reasons, the Draft recommends including in the Civil Code a series of general principles for the protection of the consumer which will act as a "minimum protection", which – according to the Bases of the Draft – "has important effects:

(a) In the matter of regulation, this means there are no obstacles for a special law to establish superior conditions.
(b) That no special law dealing with similar aspects could derogate such minimum protection without affecting the system. The Code, like any other law, may be modified, but it is much more difficult to do this than it can be done with respect to any other special law. Therefore, such "minimum" will act as solid protection.
(c) The benefit as for the coherence of the system is to be considered as well because there are general rules on prescription, termination, civil liability, contracts in the Civil Code which supplement the special legislation displaying a common normative language.
(d) In the field of interpretation, a "dialogue of sources" is defined, by virtue of which the Code recovers a central role in the interaction with the other sources.

The interpreter of a special law will refer to the Code for the common language of what is not regulated in the special law and, also, to determine the minimum levels of protection in accordance with the interpretation principle more favorable to the consumer.

From this perspective, an integration of the legal system is bought about on a different-level scale comprised by: (a) fundamental rights recognized by the National Constitution; (b) the general principles and rules of minimum protection and the common language of the Code, (c) the existing detailed regulation under the special legislation. The first two levels are stable, whereas the third is flexible and adjustable to the changing circumstances of uses and practices."

2.6.3 Family Law

The basic institutions of family law have always been regulated by the Civil Code. Notwithstanding this, the first significant reform of the Code was the enactment of the law of civil matrimony, Law 2393, on 12th November 1888, though it was regarded as part of the Code.

Unlike other countries in Latin America, there is no Family Code in Argentina and there has never been an idea to have one.

As already pointed out in this paper, family law has been deeply modified in the past years. The laws for the protection of children and adolescents, for the integral protection of women, of equal marriage, of genre equality, etc., in addition to other reforms which were consolidated in the past 15 years of the twentieth century (parental rights and duties, divorce, adoption, etc.) have radically changed the family law which has practically no resemblance to the original regulation of the Civil Code. Such process will be finally consolidated with the enactment of the 2012 Civil and Commercial Code due to the fact that, as we will see in the following paragraph, such Draft envisages relevant modifications in this field.

2.6.3.1 Family Law in the 2012 Civil and Commercial Code Draft

The Draft, which is currently subject to debate in the National Congress, follows the traditional criteria, that is to say, it comprises family law and its main institutions within the body of the Code. It is important to note that even though this branch of the law is the one that has been subjected to major reforms since 1983, and specifically in the last few years with the incorporation of the equal marriage law and the law for the rights of children and adolescents, the Draft deepens its transformation.

In this sense, we could point out the regulation of cohabitation; assisted conception techniques which include third party assisted conception; post mortem fertilization; filiation resulting from assisted conception which is known as conception willingness; divorce without cause; retirement compensatory plans inspired in the French and Spanish Law; adoption which is again regulated within the Code; marriage between same sex couples; rules relating to the blended families are also provided for. And, even though Argentina – as has already been explained – is a federal state in which procedural laws are within the jurisdiction of the provinces, the Civil Code Draft regulates a family procedure on the basis of principles of oral and efficient proceedings.

2.6.4 Private International Law and the Civil Code

The Civil and Commercial Code Draft contains the regulation of private international law of an internal source. As it is pointed out by one of the authors[14] of this chapter of the Draft, the methodology followed is that of the Civil Code of Québec, the German Civil Code and the Civil Code of Peru. The Dutch Civil Code could be

[14] Uzal, María Elsa, "Breve panorama de la reforma del derecho internacional privado", in Rivera, Julio C. (dir.) – Medina, Graciela (coord.), *Comentarios al Proyecto de Código Civil y Comercial de 2012*, Abeledo Perrot, Bs. As., 2012, p. 1233.

added to this list in which Book X devoted to this matter came into effect on January 1st 2012.

It should be noted that the Civil Code had rules of private international law in its Preliminary Title and in a number of topics (contracts, succession) and that there existed in the past drafts of private international law codes following the Swiss model, which were not passed by Congress, though they became a source of inspiration for the concrete solutions proposed in the 2012 Draft.

The Title of Private International Law comprises the regulation of a number of matters but it has not addressed the issues ruled by special statutes. Thus, this Title will have to co-exist with the provisions of private international law in the law of companies, bankruptcy law, maritime law, in the trademarks and intellectual property law, insurance law and the aeronautic code.

The Title commences with a series of "general provisions", covers the international jurisdiction and then contains a Special Part divided into 16 sections (persons, matrimony, cohabitation, alimony and child support, filiation, adoption, parental responsibility, international restitution of children, successions, form of legal acts, contracts, consumer contracts, civil liability, securities, civil liability and prescription).

Professor Uzal points out that the Draft relies on the study of the sources of comparative law, which is evidenced in the solutions given, on the previous analysis of a number of codes and statutes of private international law, either the most modern ones or the classical ones, as well as on domestic or foreign drafts.[15]

2.7 Conclusions

As we have already mentioned, the transformation of the private law legislation is of paramount importance. Even though some areas – such as family law – have been subjected to significant changes, there are others such as real estate law, succession law and private international law which had very few adjustments since the Civil Code was enacted. On the other hand, the remarkable influence of the constitutionalization of private law and supranational law calls for the adaptation of the inferior legislation.

Therefore, all the recodification process is admirable.

As for the content of the Code, the Commission has followed criteria which are in general acceptable.

The unification of the civil and commercial code is agreed by the majority of the national doctrine and it was the 1987 Draft and 1998 Draft which paved the way in this direction. It has the Italian and Dutch legislation as precedent. Anyway, we should point out that the commercial law appears with minimum references in the draft, because other than the regulation of securities and some contracts recently

[15] Uzal, ob. cit., p. 1235.

regarded as commercial, there is no reference to the merchant's regulations, the business enterprise is not regarded as subject of mercantile legal relations and there is no mercantile registration discipline. In relation to the other matters, the unification is partial as all the special statutes survive such as those referring to companies – with some modifications – bankruptcy, insurance, credit card, maritime law and the aeronautic code, etc.

The introduction of regulations on consumer law also follows the German model; as we have seen, other civil codes have incorporated a few rules on the subject which form the basis of the consumer protection system.

Family law is still within the Code, following our legislative tradition. Both a modernization of family law and its adjustment to the supranational rules are intended. Regardless of the way this is carried out, in my view inappropriate, from the methodological perspective the decision is unquestionable.

The inclusion of private international law in the Code is also a solution with solid precedents in comparative law; the recent example of Holland is relevant. This contributes to a significant evolution in the study of the matter.

Therefore, we can conclude that the recodification proposed follows generally accepted guidelines, with solid precedents in comparative law, which will mean a modernization of concepts in many matters claimed for a long time by the Argentine society. All this, notwithstanding the reasonable controversy that may arise over some of the proposals individually considered.

Chapter 3
Private Law Codifications in Belgium

Dirk Heirbaut and Matthias E. Storme

Abstract As Belgium received its codifications from Napoleon, this chapter does not focus on the history of these codifications but on the history of private law since these codifications. It tells the story of the lack of recodification (except for civil procedure) and the updating of private law inside or outside the code and tries to explain why new rules were placed inside or outside. It further discusses shortly the role new legislation and case law have played in the process of adapting private law. Specific sections are devoted to the fate of a separate commercial code and the question of codification of consumer law.

Keywords Belgium Civil Code • Codification • Private law • Decodification • Current role of the Civil Code

3.1 Introduction: Belgium Received Its Codifications from Napoleon

In 1795 the Southern Netherlands, today's Belgium, became a part of France. Consequently, all of the Napoleonic codifications, including his 1804 Civil Code also were promulgated in Belgium. As such this is not so remarkable, as Napoleon imposed his law in many other European countries. Belgium, however, is different in that it still has the French Civil Code with all it entailed, like, for example a separate Commercial Code. In fact, Belgium is more faithful to the French Civil Code

D. Heirbaut (✉)
Department of Legal Theory and Legal History, Universiteit Gent, Ghent, Belgium
e-mail: dirk.heirbaut@ugent.be

M.E. Storme
Institute for Commercial and Insolvency Law, Katholieke Universiteit Leuven Law School, Flanders, Belgium
e-mail: matthias@storme.be

J.C. Rivera (ed.), *The Scope and Structure of Civil Codes*, Ius Gentium: Comparative Perspectives on Law and Justice 32, DOI 10.1007/978-94-007-7942-6_3,

than France itself. In 2004 the Belgian version had preserved more articles of the original than the French one. Moreover, in Belgium the official version is still the 1807 Code Napoleon, whereas France had changed the Code after the fall of Napoleon to reflect the political changes. Although Belgium became independent from France – and also lost its emperor – in 1815 (and separated from the Netherlands in 1830), the official text of the Code continued to talk of an emperor, the empire, France and Frenchmen until a clean-up operation of 1950 finally adapted the text.

3.2 The Survival of the French Civil Code in Belgium

3.2.1 The Great Influence of France on the Law of the Southern Netherlands Before 1795

The French annexation in 1795 led to the abolition of all the old laws and the imposition of French law in the so-called Code Merlin. Nevertheless, it would be going too far to state that the French suddenly introduced a completely unfamiliar law. In fact, from the thirteenth century on the main foreign influence was French. The county of Flanders, which was a French fief in the Middle Ages, generally was the first in taking over French innovations which spread from there to the rest of the Low Countries. The French model was particularly important for the so-called homologations of the customs. These official redactions of the customary law of a city or a region started in France in the fifteenth century, when Frenchmen, the dukes of Burgundy, were the princes of the Low Countries. They copied this method of law making from France, but most homologations date from the sixteenth century thanks to the emperor Charles V, their Habsburg successor and the process of homologation continued until the early seventeenth century. Whereas the principle of the homologation of customary law was French, the contents were based on local customs. As such, the homologations can be seen as precursors of the later codifications, though they were different in many ways. They were not so much legislation, as custom turned into legislation. Moreover, the systematic structure that is typical of a modern Code was lacking in them. Many of the homologated customs are not very impressive in comparison with, for example, the Napoleonic Civil Code. An exception is the Antwerp customs of the sixteenth and early seventeenth centuries. There are four successive texts of Antwerp law, which gradually became more elaborate.

In general however, the contents of the homologated customs of the Southern Netherlands were very similar to those of their Northern French counterparts. Add to this the growing influence of France over the centuries and it becomes clear that the imposition of France law in 1795 was less radical than one would, at first, assume. French annexation only accelerated an on-going process. Moreover, in many cases, the law of the French Civil Code corresponded to the most common practice in the Southern Netherlands. For example, in matrimonial property law, the 1804 Civil Code opted for a community of movables and acquisitions, which was already the most popular system in the Southern Netherlands anyway. If the

'Belgians' had unified their private law themselves, they would in all likelihood have ended up with the same rule. Thus, in 1795 the problem of the 'Belgians' was not so much the French nature of their new laws, but rather the truly revolutionary character of parts thereof, like some aspects of the new law of succession or the new possibility of having a divorce. Resistance against the radical ideas of the Revolution, however, was also rather common in France. Napoleon by eliminating the excesses of the Revolution from his Civil Code did much to reconcile Frenchmen and Belgians to the 'new' law, which in many ways turned back to old patterns. In some parts of the Southern Netherlands, mainly the *département de l'Escaut* and the *département de la Lys* (today: the Belgian provinces of Eastern Flanders and Western Flanders) family law had been rather progressive, awarding more rights to married women and children born out of wedlock. The Civil Code also abolished the rights of widows or widowers to their partner's inheritance, which had been very extensive. The old law of the Southern Netherlands had also been much better in regulating mortgages and registering property transfers than Napoleonic law. These and a few other minor points aside, the new French law corresponded rather well to the old law of the Southern Netherlands.

3.2.2 The Failure of Projects of Reform After the French Era

The 1804 French civil Code in its form of the 1807 Code Napoleon is still the law of the land in Belgium in spite of several failed efforts to replace it with another Code. The first of these is rather special in that it did not so much fail, but rather in that failed only in Belgium. In 1815 the North and the South of the Low Countries, which had gone apart at the end of the sixteenth century, once again became one country, the United Kingdom of the Netherlands. The Dutch had been working on their own codifications since the end of the eighteenth century, but finally had to accept Napoleonic law after an annexation in 1813. As soon as they regained their independence, they started the work on a new civil Code. Due to some strange twists of history the draft of a civil Code which parliament finally accepted, was not written by the Dutchman Joan Melchior Kemper as originally had been planned, but by the Belgian Pierre Thomas Nicolaï. Another of these ironies of history then led to this draft replacing the 1804 Civil Code in the Netherlands (in a slightly amended version), but not in Belgium. The new Code was to come into force in 1831, but by then Belgium had already become independent. Only two parts of the new Code, the statutes on long-term leases and on building rights had already become law in Belgium in 1825, because the French Civil Code did not contain anything about them.

The constitution of the new state had a final article that, *inter alia*, called for new national codifications, to be written as soon as possible. In reality, nothing happened. It took until 1841 before the minister of justice appointed a commission and its work only resulted in an 1851 statute dealing with mortgages and the registration of property transfers, a particular weakness of the French civil Code. In 1879, however, the minister of justice charged François Laurent with writing a new Code. Laurent, Belgium's greatest lawyer at that (and any other) time had become frustrated with the current law and had therefore asked for this new charge His draft Code is a splendid piece of work in many ways which combines erudition with a very pragmatic attitude. It failed to become law in spite of its many qualities. First of all, Laurent, a radical liberal (in the European sense), hated the Catholic Church with a passion and saw his Code as a weapon against its growing power. Unfortunately, he did not manage to finish his draft before the catholic party came to power in 1884. Even if he would have, it is doubtful that it could have become law. Laurent had a very progressive attitude in family law and even his liberal friends did not approve of a project that gave, for example more rights to married women. The Catholics appointed a new commission, which produced some texts, and thereafter faded into obscurity. There have been several calls for a new civil Code since the 1960s and at the occasion of the bicentennial of the Napoleonic civil Code in 2004 some politicians made proposals for a new civil Code, or at least a general revision of family law. Nothing came of them because of the general standstill of political life in Belgium between 2007 and 2011. It remains to be seen what will happen in the future. For reasons that will be explained below, the new proposals concerned family law.

The only Code that was really replaced by a new one was the Code of Civil procedure of 1809, replaced in 1967 by the Judiciary Code. It also incorporated the Statutes on Judicial Organisation and many other specific statutes, and it was not a mere coordination of existing rules but contained some real reforms. One could also mention the recodification of company law in 1999 (replacing part of the Commercial Code) and the first codification of international private law in 2004.

3.2.3 The Constant Updating of the Civil Code

3.2.3.1 In General

The French Civil Code has not just survived because new codes failed to see the light, but also because, so far, it has served the interests of Belgium, or rather its jurists, quite well. In the nineteenth century a new Code was not to their liking. Any new Code would have meant a retraining. It would also have amounted to cutting off the links with France, whereas using the French Code gave Belgium a tremendous advantage. The country did not need to invest itself in legal literature or creative case law. It only had to copy French solutions and could as such have a free ride. The latter for a long time may also be taken literally. Belgium, originally, did not protect the copyright of French publications, so that Brussels editors could print pirated editions of French law books at a cheaper price. This was no longer possible in the second half of the nineteenth century, but French law books remained popular and until the 1950s the great French treatises of private law were just as popular as those of leading native authors, like Laurent and De Page.

French and Belgian law have grown gradually apart because the modernisation of society made changes inevitable. The whole process of updating the Civil has been very chaotic in Belgium. In general, the preference has been for subjects that originally were in the Code in 1804 to remain in them and for others to be regulated outside them. However, there are many exceptions to this. It can even happen, as was the case with a part of marriage law, that the legislator took something out of the Code and later put it in again. Commercial editors are not much better. For example, in the nineteenth century they published in 1825 statutes on long-term leases (*emphyteusis*) and building rights (*superficies*) as titles of the Civil Code, but they no longer do so today. The fact that a new text is in the form of a statute with its own numbering has never stopped the Belgian legislator from integrating it as such in the Code. Thus, new parts either have their own numbering and stand out because of that, or have somehow been integrated into the original, though once again without any consistency. For example, new numbers can take several forms, e.g. 212a, 577-2, 377quinquies or 388bis, b. The current version of the Civil Code does not deserve to get any prizes for its beauty and one can only wonder what its original framers would think of the horrible creature the Belgian legislator has made of it. Chaotic though the updating may be, it has ensured that the Civil Code in Belgium has remained a living document.

3.2.3.2 Contrast Between Patrimonial Law on the One Hand and Family Law

There is a contrast between patrimonial law on the one hand and family law (including the law of succession and the law of married property) on the other. Patrimonial law in the Civil Code has remained stable and it still sticks, to a large extent, with the original 1804 text. Family law is its opposite with many titles having been completely replaced. Changes in the late nineteenth and early twentieth centuries were rather limited and hesitant. The first major change of the Napoleonic model happened in 1940 with a new adoption law. The process of amending the family law of the civil Code accelerated from the 1970s and continues until the present day. Its last major feat is a new law in 2007. Compared to the revolutions in family law, patrimonial law was a fortress of stability, with only a few major changes, like the abolition of the title on imprisonment for debt in the nineteenth century and the 1851 Act on mortgages and registration of transfers of real property.

An explanation for this difference is not that patrimonial law has not seen any changes. However, these took place outside the Code because they were different from the revolutions in family law. There, the old and the new are in a complete contradiction and cannot live together. For example, either a married woman is her husband's first subject or she is his equal. She cannot be both at the same time. Thus, in order for a change in family law to be effective, it has to abolish the old law, so that it is impossible to have both the old law in the Code and the new in a separate statute. In patrimonial law, however, old and new can coexist, because the new rules complement the old. Therefore, the old law of the Code has remained intact and the new rules have their own statutes. There are exceptions, where new rules of patrimonial law contradict the original spirit of the Code. For example, the legislator has given more protection to lessors of some types of real property, like farmland, the main residence of the lessor and commercial buildings. The statutes on these types of leases are part of the Civil Code, though with their own numbering. A special case is private international law, which received its own Code in 2004.

3.2.3.3 Language Versions

A special update of the Civil Code was the enactment of an authentic Dutch translation in 1961. The original 1804 text was French. Official translations in Dutch (actually presented as so-called Flemish, because there were other Dutch translations for the Netherlands) were available, but they were not authentic and had no legal value in court. Throughout most of the nineteenth century this did not matter much. Dutch may have been the language of the people in Flanders who formed the majority of the Belgians, but lawyers all over the country preferred French. The rise of the Flemish Movement also led to a call for law in Dutch. This resulted in new statutes having an authentic text in Dutch also from 1898 on, and to the obligation to use Dutch in the Flemish courts from 1935. The Civil Code however predated all this, so that the only authentic version of it remained the French one until parliament approved a Dutch translation in 1961 and awarded it the same position as the French original. Flemish lawyers nowadays work with a text in their own language. The codes have gradually been translated also in a German version (German being an official minority language in Belgium), which does however not enjoy the same status as the Dutch and French versions.

3.2.4 The State of Legislation in and Codification of Civil Law Today

3.2.4.1 Overview of the Situation in the Various Branches of Private Law

As a result of this development, the Civil Code still contains many of the core subjects of civil law, but certainly not all of them. Next to it, there is a mass of hundreds of special statutes dealing with other aspects of private law ("decodification"). Some of them are very old, many others fairly young.

As to *family law*, the bulk of it is in the Civil Code, unless the legislator has put it in the "Judiciary Code" because he considered it connected to specific procedures.

The *law of persons* is basically found in the Civil Code, except those aspects considered being more public law. But there are many special statutes, as e.g. in matters of privacy, funerals, etc....

A big part of *property law* is in the Civil Code, including the specific rules for apartment rights and other forms of co-ownership, most easements or servitudes (other are found in the Rural Code of Oct 7, 1886 and a number of specific statutes); most special proprietary security rights however are regulated by separate statutes, such as the Act on Agricultural loans and pledges (April 15, 1884), the Act on the Enterprise Pledge of October 25, 1919, the Security rights in financial Assets (Collateral) Act of December 15, 2004 (revised 2011); the Act on Derelicted Goods of February 21, 1983, etc. A Draft fundamentally reforming the security rights in movables (to a large extent based on a first draft by a commission chaired by prof. E. Dirix) was submitted to the federal Parliament in 2012 and will most probably be enacted early 2013.

Intellectual property law is found exclusively in specific statutes, some of them Benelux Statutes (Design rights and Trademarks now integrated in a single Benelux instrument of February 25, 2005), some Belgian statutes (Copyright Act of June 30, 1994; Patent Act of March 24, 1984; Databases Act of August 30, 1998, Domain names Act of June 26, 2003; Anti-Piracy Act of May 15, 2007, many of them evidently influenced by EU Directives.

The law on matrimonial agreements, successions, wills and donations (*patrimonial family law*, in the French tradition including the law on donations) is to a large extent in the Civil Code. There are a few special statutes on succession law ("small inheritances" Act of May 16, 1900, "agricultural inheritances" Act of August 29, 1988, etc.).

Most of *general contract law* is in the Civil Code, apart from e-commerce (Acts of July 9, 2001 and March 11, 2003). The same is true for most "classical" contracts such as sale, barter, lease, service contracts (although only a few rules, mainly dealing with construction contracts, most specific rules are in specific statutes), mandate, loan, deposit, suretyship, etc. Specific statutes deal *inter alia* with the sale of unfinished houses (Act of July 9, 1971) (for other specific contracts, see *infra* commercial law and consumer law). *Labour law* is entirely outside the Civil Code and fragmented over many specific statutes.

As to *Tort law*, the civil Code contains only a few basic rules, most rules on strict liability are in specific statutes (e.g. Product Liability Act of February 25, 1991; Statutes dealing with liability for Fire, Oil Pollution, Nuclear Energy etc.), as are a myriad of duties which in case of violation may give rise to fault liability. It must however be said that Belgian tort law – just like French tort law – is in essence based on the few general clauses in the Civil Code (Art. 1382 ff.), which have been developed largely by case law.

The law on *non-profit organisations* (associations and foundations) is almost entirely found in an Act of June 27, 1921 (rewritten in 2002).

Finally, International Private Law (including International Civil Procedure) has been codified in a 2004 Code, containing virtually all relevant rules (except the EU Regulations, which are self-standing and thus not repeated in the Code, and some other international instruments).

3.2.4.2 Some Factors Leading to Complexity and Decodification

The presence of numerous specific statutes is to some extent the result of the enormous power in fact of the Executive (government) and of the internal structure of the Executive (division of competences between the Ministries, such as Justice,

Trade, Consumer Affairs, Labour, Transport, Energy, etc.), each Department usually having also its own advisory councils and similar institutions – see also some further information on this *infra*.

The complexity of private law is enhanced by the fact that even in this part of the law many European and international instruments form part of domestic law, either as such (ratified Conventions, EU Regulations, etc.) or after implementation (EU Directives). Thus, Belgium has e.g. ratified the CISG (International sales), the Unidroit Convention on international Factoring, many Transport Law Conventions, etc.; the Geneva Uniform Law on bills of exchange 1930 has been inserted in the Commercial Code (see *infra*) and the Geneva Uniform Law for Cheque 1961 was introduced as such in 1961; the law on Arbitration was largely copied from the European and Uncitral Model Law, etc.

3.2.5 Sources of Civil Law Today

As to the sources of law, the few provisions dealing with them have not changed since 1804 … ! – and basically do not give any official status to other sources than legislation, except for the interpretation of contracts (art. 1135 CC refers to customs and equity in this respect). But the reality has changed enormously, and the real meaning of many provisions, especially older ones, cannot be grasped without a thorough knowledge of case law. A trained lawyer will read in the provision the meaning case law has given to it (as the French say: "*la jurisprudence forme corps avec la loi*"), even if that meaning is exactly the opposite of the literal meaning of the text (a typical example is the actual meaning of art. 1142 Civil Code, which literally says that in case of an obligation to do or not to do, the remedy is damages and not specific performance; according to case law it means that the principal remedy is specific performance, unless specific performance cannot be granted because of impossibility, disproportionality or the personal character of the performance). In that sense, the "decodification" of much of private law is maybe as much the result of case law than of the fragmentation of the rules by the legislator over many statutes.

Further, the understanding of civil law has been influenced strongly by the doctrine of authors. Most doctrine uses a systematic approach that is rather different from the Code Napoleon and more in line with the German science of law as developed in the nineteenth and twentieth century (even if the German influence was more indirect than direct). Thus, the concept of juridical act is absent from the Code (and only marginally present even in contemporary in legislation), but the basic concept of patrimonial law also in Belgian doctrine since the twentieth century.

Finally, case law will predominantly classify statutory rules as either the rule or the exception, and give a restrictive interpretation to the latter. In many cases, it is still the code civil that is considered to be the "common law" in relation to which derogatory specific statutes have to be interpreted restrictively (a kind of hidden continuation of the pre-codification maxim "*statute stricte sunt interpretanda*"). A typical example is the case law on termination of sole distributorship contracts: a specific statute of 1961 on their termination provides that they can be terminated by one of the parties either in case of gross non-performance of the other party or with a reasonable period of time; the Court of cassation decided that this statute does not prevent the parties from stipulating an express resolutory clause (termination clause) deviating from it, as an application of the common law of contract (Cass. 19 April 1979).

3.2.6 Constitutional Rules and Fundamental Rights

Another important recent development was the introduction of constitutional review, more precisely judicial review of statutes by the Constitutional Court, either directly or by way of preliminary ruling. This has fundamentally affected also many rules of private law, even in such classical fields as the law on suretyship, bankruptcy law, law on prescription (limitation of actions). As to international law: insofar as ratified or recognised by Belgium, it has priority over domestic law.

The main element of constitutional and international law which has really affected private law, is probably not so much the effect of substantive fundamental rights, but the requirement that legislative rules cannot discriminate, i.e. not treat comparable situations differently without justification. As to the effect of substantive fundamental rights in private law, it is under debate – some authors would simply apply them horizontally, whereas other authors only accept that they are an element of interpretation of the rules of civil law themselves; still authors consider the reference to fundamental rights in private law is purely rhetorical and rarely changing anything in substance.

3.2.7 Regional Law

The devolution of powers to the Regions and Autonomous Communities and the transformation of Belgium from a centralised or unitary state in a federal state with strongly centrifugal dynamics on the other hand (started in 1970, but continuing until today), have until now strongly affected public law, but not private law. Regional private law is thus a marginal phenomenon, except in some matters as housing and sale and transfer of property in land, environmental liability, contracts with schools, funerals, placement service contracts and some other service contracts, etc.

3.3 The Commercial Code: Undisputed, but Reduced to a Shadow

3.3.1 No Debate on the Existence of a Separate Commercial Code

A major difference between Belgium and some other countries is that the country has never had a real debate on the necessity of a separate commercial law. This is very remarkable as one of its great specialists, Simon Fredericq, wrote a Ph.D. on the integration of commercial law into private law. Drafters of new civil codes, like Laurent, so far have not thought to question the existence of a separate commercial law. In general, the legislator has refrained from legislation that would have chipped away at the division between private law and commercial law. For example, instead of expanding the concept of bankruptcy to others than merchants, parliament introduced a separate system of 'collective debt settlement' in 1998. Whereas a separate commercial law has no real opponents, it has its institutional defenders in the commercial courts. The Southern Netherlands originally had no commercial courts, which were an innovation of the French occupation around 1800. During the reunion with the Netherlands the plan was to abolish the separate commercial courts. In the Netherlands this happened in 1838, but in Belgium this was prevented by the 1830 revolution and independence. In the 1960s, the drafters of the new Judicial Code, Charles Van Reepinghen and Ernest Krings wanted to abolish the commercial and the labour courts, because their work could just as well be done one general court at the level of first instance. In fact, many districts did not have a commercial or labour court, proving that these courts could indeed be missed. Resistance by the unions saved the labour courts and also guaranteed the survival of the commercial courts. The result was even that there is now a commercial court in every district. This means that the defenders of a separate commercial law are nowadays even better entrenched in their own courts than in the past.

One of their main arguments has been the idea of a *lex mercatoria*, a special merchant law, which existed in the past. Historical research has shown that the *lex mercatoria* in the sense of a separate European-wide merchant law that originated in the Middle Ages is a myth. For Belgium the arguments against a historical merchant law are even stronger. The country had neither commercial courts nor great commercial legislation before the French era. They were unknown not just in rustic places, but also in Bruges, a major trading centre of the middle ages, and Antwerp, Europe's main commercial hub in the sixteenth century. Antwerp developed a lot of law for commerce, but this was the work of the ordinary courts and it was never seen as being separate from the rest of Antwerp law. Nevertheless, the myth of a *lex mercatoria* which justifies the existence of a commercial law, commercial courts and a commercial Code caught on in Belgium and still has its believers. A young legal historian, Dave de Ruysscher, is doing his best to debunk the myth, but it is too convenient for the merchants who want to have their own courts and the judges staffing them to be successful.

On the other hand, commercial law has since the codification always been separate, but never really autonomous. Commercial law needs civil law, as it consists of additional rules or derogatory rules, but it has no law of obligations or property law of its own. There is no autonomous legislation on commercial sales as distinguished from the "common" civil law on sales (at least in the internal law; the CISG (Vienna Convention) is an autonomous law for international commercial sales), no autonomous legislation on commercial mandate contracts, etc.; the rules on bankruptcy deviate from the general rules on *concursus creditorum*, but they presuppose such a set of general rules in civil law, the rules on pledges differ, but there is no autonomous set of rules on commercial pledges, etc. Some authors have argued in favour of a full autonomy of commercial law (e.g. Van Ryn & Heenen), but this has never been the dominant doctrine in Belgium.

3.3.2 A Death by Neglect May Be Expected

Once again, a new draft commercial Code was written during the union with the Netherlands, which became law in the Netherlands in 1838, but not in Belgium because of its independence. If possible, the merchants loved France even more than the jurists and did not complain about the existing Code. The 1831 constitution called for new codes and in particular for a new legislation on bankruptcy, companies, imprisonment for debt and insurance. The legislator only revised the part of the code that dealt with bankruptcy in 1851, because it was too harsh. Thereafter, a process started of constant revision and innovation of commercial law. Belgium was the second in the world to industrialize and its great attention for commercial law in the second half contributed to that. Only the rich could vote for parliament and only the even richer could be elected to it. Stimulating economic growth by good legislation was one way for the latter to make their own fortunes grow. Before the introduction of universal, though still unequal, male suffrage in 1893, only Catholics and liberals held seats in parliament. In spite of their quarrels about religion, they had one common view on the economic development of the country, co-operating over party lines.

The unity of vision and purpose in parliament did not lead to a coherent process of revision. The need of new texts was so urgent, that the legislator very soon gave up the idea of one new Code. Instead, the old Code remained, but its parts were replaced piecemeal throughout the second half of the nineteenth century, so that only four of the original articles survived into the twentieth century. Because speed was of the essence, each new part received its own numbering and co-ordination with other parts of the Code was, at best, an afterthought. Moreover, the legislator called little for the original contents of the Code. Some subjects that had a place in the original Code, fall out of it during the revision. New subjects could have their own statute (like the cheque) or were integrated into in the Code (like transport by rail) without any general principle guiding the over-all process. In defence of this haphazard method, one can only say that anything else would have been impossible in Belgium at that time. The field of company law, for example, was so dynamic that drafting commissions had to write three new versions of it during this period. The first one was never enacted, because it was already out-dated by the time it was finished. The second and third were, in 1873 and in 1886 respectively, but already in 1893 the minister of justice appointed a commission for yet another revision. Moreover, the ultimate goal of the politicians was economic growth, not a perfect Code and, in that, they did not fail. By 1914 the GNP of tiny Belgium ranked fifth in the world.

After the early 1890s the constant revision of the commercial Code came to a halt. Any vision on the place and importance of commercial law for economic growth disappeared and the Belgian legislation consisted mainly of reactions to crisis of the 1930s or foreign influences, before World War II, France and international treaties, thereafter, also the Benelux and European directives. If the new legislation concerned new fields, the new statutes, in general remained, apart from the Code. Subjects that were already there could also disappear from it. There was no master plan concerning the commercial Code as a whole. The general idea was that this was superfluous, because national legislation was on the way out and Europe would take care of commercial law. The upshot was an out-dated and chaotic commercial law.

In 1988 Belgium woke out of its lethargy in the field of commercial law. The country's deficient legislation enabled a foreign company to lay the hands on the *Société Générale de Belgique*, a holding that controlled a great part of the Belgian economy. Suddenly, the legislator became more active, with for example new statutes on bankruptcy (Bankruptcy Act of August 8, 1997) and judicial reorganization (1997) or a new Code of companies (1999). The new statutes are not always innovative (e.g. the Code of companies). If they are, the innovations are not always successful. For example, a 2009 statute on Judicial Reorganisation of Enterprises of January 31, 2009 has already replaced the 1997 legislation. However, what they all have in common is that they are no longer part of the commercial Code. The latter has also lost articles to the new Code of private international law (2004). The underlying idea this time is that the Commercial Code has been robbed of so many topics, that one more will not matter. In fact, as of now, only the status of the merchants and the law of the sea are still in the commercial Code. A number of special statutes are formally also included in the Code (in the place of the provisions of the original Commercial Code replaced by them), but they have their own numbering and have therefore in practice to be cited as separate Statutes (the Statutes on Commercial Pledges, on Commission Contracts, on Bills of Exchange and Promissory Notes, on Maritime Insurance Contracts). The law of the sea will disappear very soon from the Code, as a new draft Code of the law of the sea is ready. After its enactment, a mercy killing of the commercial Code may be unavoidable. An added reason for that will be a second draft codification, finished in 2009, but still waiting to become law[1]; this

[1] By the time this volume is printed part of the project was passed into law. For a current text of the project please visit http://economie.fgov.be/fr/spf/codification_legislation_economique/#.UpiysdKLJY5. Accessed 29 August 2013.

draft Code of economic law is almost the opposite of the commercial Code. It wants to unite a lot of the existing economic legislation in one text. Expressly excluded, however, are subjects like bankruptcy or the status of the merchants, not because anyone doubts that such topics belong to the new Code, but because of an institutional problem. The minister of justice is responsible for them, whereas the new Code is the product of an initiative of the Minister of Economic Affairs ... Thus, the coming birth of the Code of economic law will not automatically result in the demise of the old commercial Code. The institutional division also explains why the new law of the sea will have its Code. Belgium may only have a small stretch of land near the North Sea, but that seems to justify a separate ministerial competence and thus a separate Code.

Unless the draft of an Economic Code would become law, most of commercial law is thus now found in specific statutes. The draft would integrate, apart from a lot of Economic Regulation (including *inter alia* the Antitrust Act of June 10, 2006), commercial statutes such as the Termination of distributorship contracts (Act of July 27, 1961), the Commercial Agency Act (Act of June 2, 1995 implementing an EU Directive); the Precontractual duties in Franchising Act (Act of December 19, 2005), the Copyright Act and Patent Act (supra), the Late Payments Act (Act of August 2, 2002) and parts of the Trade Practices and Consumer Protection Act (infra). Some other important commercial statutes existing today, not integrated in the Draft, are the Payment Services Act (Act of December 10, 2009, *inter alia* implementing the EU SEPA-Directive) and the statutes on Insurance Law (for transport insurance still the old Act of 1874, for other contracts the Act of June 25, 1992) and Transport law. The Government has introduced part of the Draft in Parliament late 2012, but only a very small part, consisting basically only of the rules on Product Normalisation and Product Quality.

3.4 Consumer Law: A Stepchild

Consumer protection has its own statute, which is integrated neither in the Civil Code, nor in the Commercial Code; nor will it be part of the new Code of economic law. Once again, the reason is institutional. Consumer protection is a separate ministerial competence and it may end up with the Minister who is responsible for Economic Affairs, but also with one of his colleagues (At the start of 2012 the same minister is responsible for Economic Affairs, Consumer Protection and the North Sea. The combination is due to the personal interests of the current officeholder. For example, the North Sea is in the list, because the minister himself comes from a coastal city).

The 1804 Civil Code contained no specific consumer law, though several of its rules, for example some rules on the contract of sale, ensured some protection of the consumer. Administrative regulations, mostly at the local level, from the Napoleonic era can also be seen as embryonic consumer law. After independence the goal was economic liberty, so that many of these regulations disappeared. Moreover, Belgium became a paradise for cartels. Special legislation in the 1930s even foresaw the possibility of making a cartel generally binding if the majority of enterprises in a sector took part in it. Consumer protection was mostly limited to regulations of prices or special legislation after the two world wars. A 1971 statute on trade practices claimed to also benefit the consumers. Its main goal was to protect small shopkeepers against supermarkets and the interests of the consumers were sometimes sacrificed to satisfy the former. Moreover, anti-cartel legislation was a paper tiger.

In the 1990s the growing attention for consumer law as a separate field of study, the action of consumer organizations and European influence contributed to several changes. The legislator established an anti-cartel authority in 1991 that has since proven its effectiveness. Parliament enacted a new law on trade practices in that same year and by adding the information and protection of the consumer in the title clearly indicated its willingness to put the consumer and the small shopkeeper on a par. Moreover, consumer protection became a separate ministerial competence of its own in the federal government, soon to become very popular because it guarantees its minister a lot of media time.

Nevertheless, consumer law still has not fully established itself. In the academic world many of the older professors remain very sceptical about it. Moreover, the legislator still is not very clear about his goals. True, in 2010 a new statute on trade practices and consumer protection abolished some rules that protected the small shopkeeper at the detriment of the consumer, but not all of them. Moreover, European law, not a Belgian willingness to protect the consumer led to the 2010 statute. It is hard to see how consumer law can fully establish itself in Belgium as long as it does not have a statute of its own and remains mixed up with the conflicting goal of protecting the small shopkeeper.

Also, the dominant doctrine considers consumer law not as a fully autonomous branch of law, but rather like commercial law as a set of additional and derogatory rules. There is no general theory of consumer contracts in dominant doctrine: the common doctrine of contracts is the basis for consumer contracts, too, although many rules of contract law are either made mandatory (thus deviating from the principle of party autonomy) or replaced by stricter rules in consumer contracts. It must be said that Belgian law has in many cases maintained stricter rules than the European ones (providing for a higher level of consumer protection, "gold plating"), the consumer organisations being politically influential, and Belgium is therefore an opponent of "full" (instead of minimum) harmonisation of consumer law in the EU.

There are additional grounds why an autonomous code of consumer law is problematic, such as the fact that it becomes increasingly difficult to determine its precise scope. Thus, in our contemporary society, the distinction between private and professional use of an increasing number of goods and services is problematic. Secondly, Belgian law traditionally distinguishes the liberal professions (outside commercial law) from business persons, whereas European consumer law does not (and the Belgian Constitutional Court has judged the distinction in general unconstitutional – decision No. 55/2011 of 6 April 2011). Thirdly, Belgian law often protects non-profit organizations as consumers, whereas in European law there are generally not protected as consumers.

Consumer law is further complicated by the fact that is increasingly difficult to determine in this field in the EU member states what is governed by national law and what by European law, because of the overlapping competence of both levels and the doctrine of full or useful effect (leading to a spill-over of elements of uniform law in the non-harmonized parts of consumer law and even further).

3.5 Final Remark

Let us finish with a general remark on the role of codified law in contemporary legal development. Our experience teaches us that in a domain where there is a central text which is imperfect, legal science keeps that part of the law a living law. When there is no central text in a field of law, the effect depends on the alternative texts available outside that field. Thus, the absence of a common text in private law on a European law is one of the causes of the loss of influence of private law; lawyers then seek ground in common texts outside private law such as human rights conventions, and the result is that private law is flooded by so-called human rights. Many lawyers seem to be irresistibly attracted to central texts and lost without them. If that's the case, it is an important task for the other lawyers to provide central texts for private law as such. We cannot leave private law in the hands of those who believe it can be reduced to a few universal principles.

Chapter 4
Codification in China: The Special Case of Macau

Augusto Teixeira Garcia, Dan Wei, Paula Nunes Correia, and Tong Io Cheng

Abstract This essay entitled **Codification in China**: **the special case of Macau** is a result of a national report, or preferably a regional report, prepared by a team of four law professors of the University of Macau, to be presented at the IACL Conference held in Taiwan, in May 2012. Being the main issue the Codification of Private Law in Macau, Civil Law (or general Private Law) and Commercial Law are, for such reason, the main targets. Although non-codified, Labor Law and Consumer Law are also part of the theme. Family Law, even though not separately codified, is also highlighted, mainly due to its recognized "institutional" nature and susceptibility to transformations occurred within the society. Finally, the unique situation of Macau, as a Special Administrative Region of China, with its particular relevance in every field – namely political, economic, social, cultural and of course legal – is duly emphasized as well.

Keywords Legal pluralism • Macau Basic Law • Macau Civil Code • Commercial law codification

Authors: Augusto Teixeira Garcia, Dan Wei, Paula Nunes Correia and Tong Io Cheng. The report prepared for the Conference in Taiwan and subsequently the present essay also counted with the cooperation of Chan Ka Man and Yang Meng, post-graduate students of the Faculty of Law of the University of Macau.

A.T. Garcia (✉) • T.I. Cheng
Faculty of Law, University of Macau, Taipa, Macau
e-mail: ATG@umac.mo

D. Wei
Institute for Advanced Legal Studies of the Faculty of Law,
University of Macau, Taipa, Macau
e-mail: danwei@umac.mo

P.N. Correia
Centre for Law Studies of the Faculty of Law, University of Macau, Taipa, Macau

Bachelor of Law in Portuguese Language Programme, University of Macau, Taipa, Macau

J.C. Rivera (ed.), *The Scope and Structure of Civil Codes*, Ius Gentium: Comparative Perspectives on Law and Justice 32, DOI 10.1007/978-94-007-7942-6_4,

4.1 Macau Special Administrative Region of People's Republic of China

Macau, just like Hong Kong, is a Special Administrative Region (SAR) of People's Republic of China (PRC).

According to the Chinese Constitution (PRCC), special administrative regions enjoy a "high level of autonomy" from the Central Government (article 31). The People's National Assembly (PNA), in harmony with the principle "One Country, Two Systems",[1] approved the establishment of Macau Special Administrative Region (MSAR), directly subordinated to the People's Central Government and endowed with a basic law. Macau Basic Law (MBL),[2] "a constitutional document elaborated by the People's National Assembly, which is the supreme organ of politic power in People's Republic of China",[3] defines the applicable system to the Special Administrative Region, conferring executive, legislative[4] and independent judicial powers, including that of final adjudication. Such autonomy does not apply to issues concerning defense and external relations (MBL, articles 2, 11, 12, 13 and 14). Furthermore, in MSAR the socialist system and policy are not applicable: the capitalist system and the previously existing way of life remain unmodified for 50 years (article 5 of MBL, which establishes a fundamental principle of maintenance of Macau's way of life, with various and relevant consequences, namely the principle of the continuity of the legal system, basically unaltered.)[5]

Therefore, in accordance with these principles and the Basic Law, Macau legal system is guaranteed to be in force in the territory for 50 years.[6]

Macau Basic Law, as well as the Codes of Macau, were prepared during the designated "transition period", which went from 1988, sometime after the Joint

[1] Deng Xiaoping was the one who firstly coined the expression "one country, two systems", in January 1982. Later, in December of the same year, "a new Constitution of the PRC was enacted" (Albert Chan, "The concept of 'one country, two systems' and its application to Hong Kong", *Boletim da Faculdade de Direito, Universidade de Macau*, VI, no. 13, 2002, page 123). Article 31 of PRCC "contemplates the establishment of special administrative regions of the PRC, which may practice social systems different from other parts of China" (Albert Chan, "The concept", page 123). The Sino-Portuguese Joint Declaration, signed in 1987, regulated the implementation of the principle to the future Special Administrative Region of Macau.

[2] Approved by the PNA in March 31, 1993, to be in force in December 20, 1999.

[3] Ieong Van Chong, "A Lei Básica da RAEM e a concretização do princípio 'um país, dois sistemas' ", *Boletim da Faculdade de Direito, Universidade de Macau*, V, no. 12, 2001, page 98.

[4] The laws enacted by the Legislative Assembly of MSAR, as well as the regulations adopted by the Government of MSAR, shall not contradict the Basic Law.

[5] Paulo Cardinal, "A questão da continuidade dos instrumentos de Direito Internacional aplicáveis a Macau", *Boletim da Faculdade de Direito, Universidade de Macau*, V, no. 11, 2001, page 94. Ieong Van Chong refers to this principle as the "principle of maintenance of stability and prosperity", one of the five fundamental principles of the Basic Law, according to the author, being the other four the "principle of sovereignty", the "principle of high degree of autonomy", the "principle of progressive development of democracy" and the "combination of the principles of flexibility and standardization" ("A Lei Básica da RAEM", 99–101).

[6] Counted from the moment when MBL came into force, of course.

Declaration was signed by the People's Republic of China and Portugal back in April 1987, until the return of the territory to Chinese sovereignty in December 20, 1999.

Macau was governed by Portugal for over four centuries: although a Portuguese colony, Macau gained later the status of Chinese territory under Portuguese administration.[7] Portuguese sovereignty was also, inevitably, expressed through the laws officially enforceable in the territory.

Thus, the fundamental recognition of the principle "One Country, Two Systems" (OCTS) also reflects the recognition of different law systems valid in one same sovereign state. The OCTS, according to Albert Chan, "is not a federal system because there is nothing in the national constitution, which provides for a formal division of power between the national government and the provincial, municipal and SAR governments. (...) All in all, the Basic Law establishes in the SAR political, legal, social and economic systems that are very different from those in force in Mainland China. Hence the expression 'one country, two systems'. (...) Both the OCTS model and the federal model mentioned above are models of autonomy. The strength of the OCTS model is that the degree of autonomy enjoyed by the SAR is in fact much higher than that enjoyed by member states of federal states."[8] Being so, having in consideration the essence of the OCTS principle which also implies the recognition of different legal systems simultaneously in force in Mainland China (Chinese legal system), in Hong Kong Special Administrative Region (Hong Kong legal system, part of the Common Law family) and in Macau Special Administrative Region (Macau legal system, a Civil Law structure), one may rather refer to a "one country, two systems, three legal orders" principle.

4.2 Codification of Private Law: Brief History

Prior to the present Civil Code, Macau was governed by the Portuguese Civil Code dated from 1966 (still in force in Portugal, by the way), enforceable in the territory since 1967 (*Portaria no. 22869*).

The first Portuguese Civil Code, the designated *Código de Seabra* dated from 1867, was extended to Macau as well (*Decreto Régio de 18 de Novembro de 1869*).

Very briefly, the 1966 Portuguese Civil Code is clearly influenced by the *BGB*, therefore follows the Savigny plan. Otherwise, its ancestor, the Portuguese Civil Code dated from 1867, in spite of being influenced by the *Code Napoléon*, "uses an original systematization" departing from man as a subject of rights. The *Código de Seabra* also suffers the influence of the Austrian Code and the Prussian "Allgemeines Landrecht".

---

[7] This legal status of Macau was recognized by the Portuguese Constitution of 1976 and stipulated by the Organic Statute of Macau.

[8] Albert Chan, "The concept", 126–127, 133–134.

Despite the mentioned extensibility of the Portuguese Codes to Macau, it is important to note that many local usages and customs, mainly in family, succession and commercial issues, were preserved. As a matter of fact, the above cited *Decreto Régio* in 1869 determined the preservation of the Chinese usages and customs in Macau in certain cases [article 8.°, § 1.°, b)]. In 1909, a Code on the usages and customs of the Chinese of Macau was approved (*Decreto de 17 de Junho*). Nonetheless, other usages and customs could be applied beyond the usages and customs established in the 1909 Code. There was a Counsel formed by six Chinese with the mission to help the judge to determine which usages and customs were applicable. The 1909 Code was in force until 1948. However, marriages that had been celebrated in Macau, following the Chinese usages and customs and until May 1, 1987,[9] in the terms of the law then in force, could have been registered at the civil registry office, if authorized by the registrar, until November 1, 2000.[10] Though, this delay has in fact been extended up until presently, as it has also been provided that such delay may be prolonged by dispatch from the Director of the Justice's Office.[11]

The Civil Code of Macau was enacted in August 3, 1999, to be in force in October 1, 1999 (decree-law no. 39/99/M). However, its enforceability was later postponed to November 1, 1999 (decree-law no. 48/99/M).

The Civil Code of Macau was enacted in a very particular political, sociological and economic context. Actually, this Code was prepared to respond to the specific needs of the Macanese people during a limited period of time, 50 years, in view of Macau's return to Chinese sovereignty, which happened in December 20, 1999, although granting the continuity with the previous *status quo*. Therefore, until 2049 the previous capitalist system and way of life shall remain unchanged (MBL, article 5).

In what Labor Law is concerned, labor contract is typified in Book I, Title II, Chapter VI of the Civil Code (article 1079). The Code determines the submission of labor contract to special legislation (article 1079, paragraph 2). Among the latter, and within special Private Law, we would highlight the following: the general regime on labor relationships (*Lei das Relações de Trabalho, Lei no. 7/2008*); the regime on non-resident workers contracts (*Lei da contratação de trabalhadores não residentes, Lei no. 21/2009*); the regime on labor accident (*Lei no. 40/95/M*).

As mentioned before, Macau is a Civil Law system. Moreover, ours is also a generally codified law. With regard to Obligations Law, Property Law, Family Law

[9] Until the moment the previous Code of Civil Registry, approved by the Decree-Law 14/87/M, March 16, came into force.

[10] Article 5, paragraph 1 of the Decree-Law 59/99/M, October 18, which approved the Code of Civil Registry of Macau.

[11] Article 5, paragraph 2 of the Decree-Law 59/99/M. Provided that the matrimony in accordance with the Chinese usages and customs was celebrated until May 1, 1987, of course. Actually, such matrimonies are still being recognized by official dispatch, once no special law has yet been adopted. See Sou Kin Fong, "Casamento segundo os Usos e Costumes Chineses", in *Contribuições Jurídicas sobre a União de Facto e Direitos sobre a Terra em Macau e Moçambique, Universidade de Macau*, 2011, 41–45.

and Succession Law (i.e., general or common Private Law, or Civil Law if one prefers) they are mainly codified in the Civil Code (*Código Civil*). In what special Private Law is concerned, the same applies to our Commercial Code (*Código Comercial*) with reference to Commercial Law. Otherwise, Labor Law is not codified, such as Consumer's Law.

Taking into consideration that Commercial Law and Consumer's Law will be developed later on, we will mainly restrict, at this point, to Civil Law (or general private law).

Civil Law is essentially codified in our Civil Code (*Código Civil*), as already stated. Although beyond Private Law, we cannot omit our Civil Procedure Code (*Código de Processo Civil*), our Civil Registry Code (*Código do Registo Civil*), our Real Estate Registry Code (*Código do Registo Predial*) and our Notary Code (*Código do Notariado*). Other than the codes, we do have non-codified legislation on various Civil/Private Law issues, such as: the regime on author's rights and other connected rights (*Regime Jurídico do Direito de Autor e Direitos Conexos*); the regime on general contractual provisions (*Regime Jurídico das Cláusulas Contratuais Gerais*); the special regime on minors' protection (*Regime Educativo e de Protecção Social de Jurisdição de Menores*); the Land Law legislation (*Lei de Terras*). With a particular importance for Macau, we must still mention that, in spite of being typified in our Civil Code, contracts on gambling and betting are regulated in special legislation. *Lei no. 16/2001*, contains the regime on gambling in casinos; *Lei no. 5/2004*, regulates the credit concession for gambling and betting in casinos.

Finally, with regard to Private International Law, conflict norms are included in our Civil Code (Book I, General Part, Title I, Chapter III, article 13–62).

4.3 Actual Status of Codification

4.3.1 Contents of the Macau Civil Code

The very first article of our Civil Code establishes that written laws are immediate sources of law (article 1, paragraph 1). The same article (paragraph 3) determines that international conventions applicable in Macau prevail over ordinary written laws. Uses are only taken into consideration when a written law determines so, provided that they are not against the good faith principles (article 2). Courts are allowed to decide according to equity as long as a written legal disposition accepts it, or in certain terms when there is an agreement between the parties (article 3).

Judicial decisions, custom and doctrine or legal theory are not (formally) recognized sources of law.

We do not have Contract Codes, or Obligations Codes, or Family Codes. Issues on Contract Law, Obligation Law or Family Law are essentially contained in the Civil Code, or in the Commercial Code in what Contract Law is concerned.

Following the "Savigny plan", within the Roman-Germanic or Civil Law model, our Civil Code, just like its ancestor, the Portuguese Civil Code dated from 1966, on its turn inspired in the *BGB*, is divided (like the Roman *Pandectas* or *Digesto*) into five books: Book 1 – General part; Book 2 – Law of Obligations; Book 3 – Property Law; Book 4 – Family Law; Book 5 – Law of Succession.

Book 1, or General part, comprehends two titles: in the first title, chapters 1 and 2 are on sources, enforceability, interpretation and application of law, both applicable to Private and Public Law, while chapter 3 is on Private International Law conflicts; the second title, based on the concept of juridical relationship (as the whole Code, by the way), is divided according to the four elements of the juridical relationship – persons, object, juridical facts and warranty – being applicable in general to the four different species of civil juridical relationships which are especially regulated in the four following Books of the Code, that is obligation, property, family and succession juridical relationships.

Therefore, the remaining four Books form, altogether, the Special part of the Code corresponding, each of them, to one of the different species of civil juridical relationship. Moreover, and except for the third Book on Property Law, each of the other three Books comprehends one first part with general regulations on the juridical relationship especially concerned, as well as one special part containing special regulations on the concerned relationship.

Hence, Book 2, on Obligations Law, contains one first title on obligations in general, as well as one second title on contracts in special. This second part of the second Book contains the regulation on 14 typified contracts.

In Book 3, on Property Law, due to the special features of our property right (*mütter recht*) and the remaining real rights, there is a different organization: its first title is on possession, its second title is on property right and the other three titles are on *iura in re aliena*, on the so called *direitos reais de gozo*, or "limited property rights".

Book 4, on Family Law, also starts with general regulations applicable to the family juridical relationships in general, followed by the regulation, in particular, of marriage, affiliation, adoption and alimony.

In Book 5, on Succession Law, its first title is also dedicated to succession in general, followed by the regulation of succession in special, either legal succession, or voluntary succession by means of a will or testament (taking into account that a contract on succession is, in principle, void).

4.3.2 Commercial Law

There is a Commercial Code in Macau enacted in 1999 by Decree-Law no. 40/99/M, of 3 August, in force since the 1st November 1999. The first Portuguese Commercial Code has been enacted in 1833[12] and basically followed the model of the French

[12] Approved by the Decree of 18 September of 1833 and entered in force on 14 January 1834. See António Menezes Cordeiro, *Manual de Direito Comercial*, 2nd ed. (Coimbra: Almedina, 2007), 88 ff.

Commercial Code. Soon it attracted major criticism[13] and was replaced in 1888[14] by the enactment of the new Commercial Code. Contrary to the former one, this last Commercial Code was enacted in Macau and has been in force until late 1999, when it was replaced by the new Commercial Code.[15]

Starting in the nineteenth century some of the original contents of the Commercial Code (e.g., bankruptcy, commercial registrar, bill of exchange) have been repealed and displaced from the Commercial Code into autonomous laws (*decodification*). In what relates to company law the major modification refers to the enactment of Law of 11 April 1901 (known as *Lei das Sociedades por Quotas*),[16] which introduced in the Portuguese legal system the private limited liability company, based in the German law of private limited companies (*Gesetz betreffend die Gesellschaft mit beschränkter Haftung – GmbH – 20.4.1892*).[17] Contrary to what happened in Portugal, many of the laws related with commercial matters, both before and after the 25 April 1974, were not extended to Macau, therefore a gap between the two legal jurisdictions was created that kept growing.

If we consider the Commercial Code of 1888 and the LSQ we have a synopsis of the Macau commercial law and its roots as of 1999. As a matter of fact if the Commercial Code of 1833 was a direct offspring of the French Commercial Code, the Commercial Code of 1888, although the basic notion was still the "acte de commerce", has had as its main source the Italian Commercial Code of 1882,[18] and thus has been influenced both by French and Italian legal theory. LSQ on the other hand followed the German model of the private limited liability company, the *GmbHG* of 1892, opening the door of the Portuguese commercial law to the influence of the German legal theory.[19]

As said during the so called localization process, the Commercial Code of 1888 has gone under a profound reform that concluded in the enactment of the new Commercial Code, which has come into force on 1st November 1999.

---

[13] Menezes Cordeiro, *Manual*, 92 ff.

[14] The Code was approved by the (*Carta de Lei*) Law of 28 June 1888, and entered in force on 1 January 1889.

[15] Enacted by Decree-Law no. 40/99/M, of 3 August, published in BOM (Macau Official Gazette) 31/1999, of 3 August, to become in force on the 1st October 1999, which was deferred to the 1st November 1999 by Decree-Law no. 48/99/M, of 27 September, published in BOM 39/1999, of 27 September as amended by Law no. 6/2000, of 26 April, published in BOM 17/200, of 27 de April, and by Law no. 16/2009, of 28 July, published in BOM 32/2009, of 10 August.

[16] From now on LSQ.

[17] A. Ferrer Correia, *Lições de Direito Comercial*, Reprint (Lisboa: Lex, 1994) page 34.

[18] It was also influenced by the Spanish Commercial Code of 1885 (Menezes Cordeiro, *Manual*, page 96). Nevertheless Spanish legal theory has no relevant influence in Portuguese legal theory and the authors kept their allegiance with the French and now also, and mostly, Italian legal theory. This last influence is quite obvious in one of the most important legal works on the Commercial Code of 1888, the Commentary on the Commercial Code by Luís da Cunha Gonçalves, *Comentário ao Código Comercial Portuguez*, 3 vols. (Lisboa, 1916, 1918).

[19] Erik Jayme, *100 Jahre BGB und die lusophonen Länder*. Translated by M. Malheiros, *Revista da Ordem dos Advogados* 57, (vol. II, 1997).

The Commercial Code is divided in four books: Book I which title is "The exercise of a commercial enterprise in general", is the general part of the code and rules the acquisition of the merchant or entrepreneur condition, special obligations of entrepreneurs, representation in the exercise of the enterprise, liability arising from the exercise of the enterprise, which contains a chapter for product liability, negotiation of the enterprise (e.g., sale, lease) and a basic set of rules on competition law and a comprehensive set of rules on unfair competition; Book II is named "Exercise of a collective enterprise and co-operation in the exercise of an enterprise" and contains company law, which previews the four common types of companies in Civil Law countries, unlimited liability companies, limited liability "partnerships", private limited companies and joint stock companies, and other association or cooperation contracts, e.g. Economic Interest Grouping, association in participation (association en participation, stile *Gesellschaft*) and consortium contract; Book III contains the discipline of a long list of special commercial contracts, those we could call the classic commercial contracts, e.g., commission contract, carriage contract, commercial pledge contract, but also those so called modern contracts, e.g., franchising, leasing, factoring, independent guarantee, etc. and is named "External activity of an enterprise"; finally Book IV which title is "Negotiable Instruments", contains a general discipline for negotiable instruments and the discipline of Bill of Exchange, Promissory Notes and Checks as resulting from the Geneva Conventions.[20]

The Commercial Code brought back to its rules of trade related matters that have been out of it, either because they were dislocated or because they have never been within the code, aimed at putting back in the natural place of the system matters related with the legal discipline of commerce, following a path that Karsten Schmidt, considering the situation in Germany since the mid 1980s, named of re-codification of commercial law.[21,22]

[20] The Geneva Conventions on Bill of Exchange and Promissory Notes and on Checks has been entered into force in Macau in the late fifties after Portugal withdraw the reservation it has made to its enforcement in the then called Ultramarine Provinces, the former colonies. The discipline of these conventions has been transported to the new Commercial Code, as such, since the People's Republic of China has informed the UN Secretary-General of the maintenance of their application in Macau, after 1999: that is after PRC resumed the administration of Macau.

[21] Karsten Schmidt, *Handelsrecht*, 5th ed. revised (Colónia/Berlim/ Bona/Munique: Carl Heymanns Verlag, 1999) page 46.

[22] "Il Codice Commerciale tedesco: dal declino alla ri-codificazione (riflessini sulla riforma del HGB)", *Rivista di Diritto Civile* 711–724 (XLV, no. 6, 1999, Parte Prima). The expression re-codification comes as challenge to the opposite idea of *decodificazione*, of Natalino Irti [*L'età della decodificazione*, Milão, 1979; this A. ("L'età della decodificazione" vent'anni dopo, in *Rivista e società*, 1999, page 193) seems to have reformulated his ideas, according to Diego Corapi, "L'unificazione parziale del codice di commercio e del codice civile in Brazile", *Rivista di Diritto Commerciale*, 802, footnote 1 (no. 11–12, 2002)]; this book *di dimensioni piccole, ma di grande peso* (idem, ibidem), has raised the reaction of Zweigert-Puttfarken, *Allegemeines und Besonderes zur Kodifikation*, in Festschrift Zajtay, 568 ff (1982), *apud* K. Schmidt, *Handelsrecht*, page 712, and footnote 4; and of K. Schmidt, *Die Zukunft der Kodifikationsidee* (1985).

An interesting note of the Commercial Code of Macau is that it included institutes of Common Law origin. One of the main criticisms that were voiced time and again in business circles was that there were in comparison to Hong Kong few alternatives to create guarantees. Having this into consideration the legislator, also taking into account the evolution pretended to Macau economy, decided to introduce the floating charge (articles 928–941), based on the discipline of the floating hypothec of the Civil Code of Quebec. In Civil Law countries a guarantee over the business itself as a whole takes the form of a pledge (e.g., the French law of 1909 on the *nantissement du fonds de commerce*). Also this type of guarantee has been included in the Commercial Code under the name of "*Penhor de empresa*", "Pledge of Enterprise", in articles 144–152. Offering two similar legal instruments aimed at solving identical problems it can be said that the law promotes an unnecessary hybridism, but it was intention of the legislator to suit the interested parties according to their own background in order that they could use legal tools familiar to their origin. And if criticism can be aimed at the law for this maybe it can be said in its defense that to the law it is not to decide what is or what is not scientifically correct, but rather to solve in the most efficient way the problems that business needs present. The pragmatism of the law may be adequate in a place like Macau where different legal traditions, mainly Civil and Common Law traditions, with elements of Chinese tradition, are in a continuous competition. The hybridism of the law, in this particular, is no more than the reflection of the hybridism of Macau itself, which has always been a revolving door between East and West: Macau is *Janus*.

The Commercial Code mainly deals with the private aspects of the legal commercial relations (private commercial law). Which means that public legal aspects of the same questions are ruled by specific laws. Therefore although the discipline of the insurance contract is contained in the Commercial Code, the insurance activity is ruled by several laws, being the most important the Decree-Law no. 27/97/M, of 30th September 1997, entered into force on 1st September 1999. The same can be said of banking contracts that although some of them are ruled in the Commercial Code banking activity as such is regulated in Decree-Law no. 32/M/99, of 5th July. Also the most important industry in Macau, gaming industry, is ruled by Law no. 16/2001. Bankruptcy rules are to be found in the Civil Procedure Code, enacted by Decree-Law no. 55/99/M, of 8 October 1999, as special civil process "liquidation in the benefit of creditors", sections 1043 through 1184. Bankruptcy only applies to entrepreneurs; for the non-entrepreneurs there is an insolvency procedure, although similar but simpler. Maritime law is not included in the Commercial Code but rather in a special law, the Maritime Commerce Ordinance (*Regime Jurídico do Comércio Marítimo*), which was enacted by Decree-Law no. 109/99/M, of 13 December 1999. Intellectual Property Law is divided in two laws: the Industrial Property Code (*Regime Jurídico da Propriedade Industrial*), enacted by Decree-Law no. 97/99/M, of 13 December 1999 and the Copyright Law (*Regime do Direito de Autor e Direitos Conexos*), enacted by Decree-Law no. 43/99/M, of 16 August 1999, that came into force on the 1st October 1999. Contrary to what is the traditional division and contents of the old European commercial codes, matters related with commercial registration[23] were not included in the Macau's Commercial Code. The commercial registration is governed by the so called Commercial Registration Code, enacted by Decree-Law no. 56/99/M, of 7 October 1999, entered in force on 1st November 1999, modified by Law no. 5/2000, of 26th April 2000. There is no law on trust.

In what concerns the relations between the Civil Code and the Commercial Code it is understood that the former encapsulates the general law, therefore it is applicable to all private matters where there is no special rule. Since the Commercial Code is construed as a set of special rules in face of the Civil Code, this will cover the commercial matters only if the Commercial Code does not offer a solution. However in commercial matters before resorting to the Civil Code it is necessary to take into consideration section 4 of the Commercial Code. According to this section, if the situation is of commercial nature and the Commercial Code does not provide for a direct solution, the interpreter should first seek an analogous situation in the code itself and only if none can be found can he resort to the Civil Code, as long as the potentially applicable rules of this law do not contravene any principle of commercial law.

4.4 Consumer Law: Relationship with the Civil and the Commercial Codes

In Macau, Consumer Law is normally perceived as a special branch of economic law.[24] Consumer protection can be achieved by different areas of legal devices, namely, private law, administrative law, criminal law and procedural law. From the perspective of private law, the protection measures are not attached exclusively to the Law no. 12/88/M, of June 13 on Consumer Protection. Consumer Law is a special legislation outside the Civil Code and the Commercial Code. Generally speaking, the relationship between the Civil Code and Consumer Law is the one between special law and general law in consumer relations. While Consumer Law deals with the issues in a more synthesized way, the Civil Code and the Commercial Code contain relatively broad and detailed provisions with respect to the quality of products and services, prevention and compensation for injuries, commercial practices and various contractual protections. The two Codes address civil liability for manufacturers, producers and sellers and define unfair and abusive commercial practices.

---

[23] Commercial registry was contained in the Commercial Code of 1888, but in the late fifties it was revoked with the enactment of an independent law the Commercial Registry Code (Decree no. 42644) and the Commercial Registry Regulation (Decree n.º 42645), both of 1959, that have been extended to Macau by Order no. 22139, of 29 July 1966, and gazetted together with the extension Order in BO Macau no. 35, of 27 August 1966.

[24] Chou Kam Chon, "Consumer Protection Law of Macau" and Fan Jianhong, "Introduction to Macau Economic Law", in *New Commentary on Macau Law* (in Chinese), Liu Gaolong and Zhao Guoqiang, eds., (Macau: Macau Foundation, 2005), 281–286 and 143–147.

Taking into account that Law on General Contractual Clauses is not made to apply only to consumers and there is no typical consumer contract being regulated and incorporated by Consumer Law of Macau, one cannot come across any confrontation or discrepancy in legal norms between Consumer Law and Civil Code.

It is recognized worldwide that the perceptions and notions underpinning Civil Code and Consumer Law are very different. Conventionally, contract law was rooted and developed aiming to prevent the State from interfering and controlling private freedom and equality to establish and carry on trade and business. Nonetheless, Consumer Law can be said to be based on "social task of private law", with an objective to remedy the "exaggerated individualism and formalistic concept of freedom and equality".[25] Therefore, "freedom of contract" and "party autonomy" are not the best rules in consumer contracts. In addition to define the notion of "consumer" and the notion of "consumer contract", in the private law area, the main devices of Consumer Law are the imposition of the duty of information of the entrepreneur, the right of revocation of the consumer and the establishment of mandatory rules of law or contract regimes.[26] So far, such law tools have not been granted and implemented in Consumer Law in Macau. In this sense, the provisions and the consumer's basic rights enshrined in the Law no. 12/88/M, of June 13 on Consumer Protection are very difficult to be effectuated. Some modern and new types of consumer relations (for instance, sale of consumer goods, distance selling, package travel, e-commerce and credit card, etc.) have not been regulated yet in Macau and consumers have to depend on Civil Code and Commercial Code in concrete consumer relation. In case that a consumer understands standard terms in a way different from the entrepreneur's interpretations, it will not be easy for the consumer to defend his rights in judicial actions based on the available legal rules. For the time being, in many cases, the relationship between Consumer Law and Civil Code of Macau can be described as a relation of "passive-conflict", in other words, neither Consumer Law nor Civil Code is able to provide an effective protection for consumers.

Considering that the quantity of legislation pieces on Consumer Law of Macau is still very limited, and for consumer relations the genuine legislation overturning the classical paradigms of contract law such as "party autonomy" and "*pacta sunt servanda*" does not exist in Macau, it can be said that at present there are not collisions between the existing Consumer Law and Civil Code. However, along of the constant improvement of Consumer Law legislation in the foreseeable future, how to systematize different rules and approaches of Consumer Law and harmonize with Civil Code will be an inevitable question. Macau legislature has to reflect on the social function of private law as well as the thinking and values to be incorporated into Consumer Law in the future.

---

[25] Zweigert, Konrad and Hein Kötz, *An Introduction to Comparative Law*, 3rd Edition, 1996, translated by Tony Weir, page 148; Reinhard Zimmermann, 2005, 161–1622, David W. Oughton, *Consumer Law Texts, Cases & Materials*, Blackstone Press Limited, 1991, 14–17.

[26] See, for instance, provisions in German *BGB*, Japanese Law of Consumer Contract (2000) and the Brazilian Consumer Protection Code (Law no. 8078/90).

Since 1988 when the first Consumer Law (Law no. 12/88/M of June 13 on Consumer Protection) was enacted, Macau's Consumer Law has been developed to a certain extent. As for contractual protection, the Law no. 17/92/M of September 28 on General Contractual Clauses is the most relevant legal device which prevents unfair and abusive clauses from being included in business-to-consumer contracts. The two laws and other pieces of legislation of Consumer Law are not included in Civil Code of Macau. Despite some recent development, the effectiveness of Consumer Law of Macau is not very strong and its influence on the general theory of contract is not remarkable. In recent years, the literature on consumer contract remains to be insufficient and there are not many scholarly debates about the need to provide consumers with special protection with special rules of interpretation of standard terms. Due to peculiar socio-economic factors, Macau's legislature has always tended to depend on free market's operation and to avoid governmental intervention in private relations.

However, after the transfer of sovereignty to China, the city has become no. 1 of profitability in global gambling destinations by gaming revenue as well as a tourism and leisure destination for millions of consumers worldwide. In pace of the societal development and the growth of the consumer market, classical paradigms of contract law have long ceased to reflect reality. Macau is no exception. It has been argued that modern advertising methods misinform rather than inform the consumers[27]; as a consequence, consumers are at the risk of making unfavorable decisions. Nevertheless, traditional principles such as "party autonomy" and "*pacta sunt servanda*" cannot reduce the risk and restore the balance of power in contracting. Without recognizing information obligations and withdrawal rights in consumer contracts as legitimate tools for consumers, Consumer Law will not turn to be effective. In this sense, the Consumer Law of Macau has to respond to new challenges. There is an urgent need for scholars, practitioners and legislators of Macau to rethink about the underlying assumptions of conventional private law, the new trend of private law and the direction of Macau Consumer Law.

If Macau draftsmen of the legislation are aware that to draft Consumer Law on the agenda is a general trend in many jurisdictions, then the next challenge is to find new legal measures and approaches.[28] Is there any good reason to deal with the general clauses of commercial contracts at a separate place? Will codification promote the coherence of the Consumer Law? More radically, how to insert and integrate the Consumer Law into the intricate fabric of the Civil Code? All these are not merely formalistic issues, but ones involve many theoretical supports and perceptions. Unfortunately, we cannot provide any solutions at this moment. But one thing is certain: Macau Consumer Law should provide minimum standards to passive

[27] David W. Oughton, 1991, page 14, "The adviser only tells the consumer what he wants the consumer to hear and the other facts which might be relevant to a prudent shopping decision tend to be omitted".

[28] European Law, as an example, is confronted with the question of coordinating general contract law and consumer contract law. See Christian Twigg-Flesner, ed., *European Union Private Law*, (Cambridge: Cambridge University Press, 2010), 131 ff.

consumer protection in all distance contracts, contracts negotiated in Macau by local or non-local people or when the advertisings or the offers are made in Macau.

4.5 Family Law

As previously stated, Family Law is part of the Civil Code,[29] of its fourth Book to be precise. Nonetheless, we recall that some important Family Law matters are not regulated in the Civil Code, but separately, in other codified and non-codified legislation. Here are the most relevant sources of Family Law, and thus beyond the limits of private law.

To begin with, the fundamental rights and duties of Macau residents are part of Macau Basic Law (MBL). "The freedom of marriage of Macau residents and their right to form and raise a family freely[30] shall be protected by law. The legitimate rights and interests of women shall be protected by the Macau Special Administrative Region. The minors, the aged and the disabled shall be taken care of and protected by the Macau Special Administrative Region" (article 38).

Still according to MBL (article 40), in what Family Law is concerned, the provisions of International Covenant on Civil and Political Rights (*Pacto Internacional sobre os Direitos Civis e Políticos*) and International Covenant on Economic, Social and Cultural Rights (*Pacto Internacional sobre os Direitos Económicos, Sociais e Culturais*) shall remain in force and shall be implemented through the laws of the MSAR.

Codified legislation with significance for Family Law, other than the Civil Code, is as follows: Civil Registry Code (*Código do Registo Civil*), approved by *Decreto-Lei no. 59/00/M, de 18 de Outubro*; Civil Procedure Code (*Código de Processo Civil*), approved by *Decreto-Lei no. 55/99/M, de 8 de Outubro*.

Among the non-codified legislation we would still mention the following: Family Policy Basis Law (*Lei de Bases da Política Familiar, Lei no. 6/94/M, de 1 de Agosto*); Educational and Social Protection Régime of Minor's Jurisdiction (*Regime Educativo e de Protecção Social de Jurisdição de Menores*, regulated by the *Decreto-Lei no. 65/99/M, de 25 de Outubro*).

The most important modifications brought into the 1999 Macau Civil Code were, not surprisingly, in Family Law. Briefly, here are the matters concerned and the main reformations: models of marriage – limited to one only model, that is, marriage according to the civil law; marriage procedure – simplification, in general; matrimonial assets regime – adoption of the participation in acquests regime with regard to the supplementary legal assets regime; matrimonial conventions – admission of post-nuptial conventions (together with pre-nuptial conventions) and therefore abolishment of the principle of the immutability of the assets regime; spouses'

[29] Unlike Chinese Family Law, where we can find a Marriage Law and an Adoption Law, along with a Law of Succession.

[30] This is a fundamental right. Therefore, the Chinese "one child policy" does not stand for Macau.

debts – more protection for the non-debtor spouse in case of debts of exclusive responsibility; separation from bed and board or legal separation – abolishment; divorce – decrease in the delays required with regard to divorce by litigation due to rupture of life in common (for instance, the duration of a *de facto* separation as grounds for divorce was decreased from 6 to 2 years), as well as the adoption of a registry divorce, side by side with a judicial divorce, whenever there is mutual consent for divorce and no minor children involved; affiliation – reinforcement of the biologist principle in what its establishment is concerned, somehow compensated by some concession to social parenthood, as well as the introduction of regulation, even though very limited, on medically assisted procreation; adoption – limited to one only model, resulting from the abolishment of the previously designated "restrict adoption"; *de facto* union – regulation, although according to a "minimum juridical environment", in the words of the lawmaker, that is, cautious and limited to indispensable ruling; alimony – alimony obligation generally improved, namely in accordance to some of the previously mentioned amendments.

4.6 Relationships Between the Civil Code and the Basic Law and Treaties

Macau Basic Law is described as the "mini-constitution" of Macau, as it regulates fundamental rights and duties of the residents, political structure and authorities. Furthermore, Macau has its own legal and economic system, which implies that policies introduced and legislations enacted in China will not have any effects over Macau.

Such a new legal framework created by the Basic Law shall of course generate doubts in the first stage of its implementation. The first doubt among others is perhaps the relation between the National Constitution of PRC and the Basic Law.

Legislative basis of Basic Law comes from the National Constitution and is enacted in accordance with the provisions of the latter, thus is regulated by the Constitution.[31] It should be known that the Chinese Constitution has legal force over Macau through medium of the Basic Law. They differ from one another in many aspects, so it is not proper to call the Basic Law or even equalize it with the Constitution. In general, the origin of legislative legitimacy of the Basic Law comes from the National Constitution.

Noted that the Basic Law is a national law, it has its legal force and effects not just within the special administrative regions, and also among other provinces and regions of China which they have to respect and comply with it, too. It requires both Macau and other provinces of China to obey it. Regarding its special and extraordinary legal force and as a national law, it means although other provinces could still

[31] See Lok Wai Kin, "One Country, Two Systems of the Chinese Constitution – Discussion to relations of power between the Central and Special Administrative Regions", in *One Country, Two Systems and Execution of the Macau SAR Basic Law*, GuanDong Printing Press, 2009, 13–14.

make their own regional regulations or other regulatory documents to complement or harmony with their execution of regimes like Macau (the legislature can enact laws to implement and define in details in area of practice and execution of policies issued by Central Government), they should never enact regulations contravened with provisions of the Basic Law. This can be easily understood to be a consequential outcome for being a national law.

Nonetheless, though considered a national law, the dignity of Basic Law is not parallel to other national laws enacted for the ruling of affairs within the boundaries of mainland China. By elaborating a comparison between legal force of the Basic Law and other national laws, it is easy to come to a conclusion: the Basic Law is regarded as a special national law. Its classification is done because of several key factors: the scope of application and its suppressing effect over other national laws with contraventions to the Basic Law. Firstly, it is nationwide applicable for the sake of its legislative organ that enacted it – National People's Congress, thus local legislature of Macau, the Legislative Council, has no power to alter, amend or suspend provisions of the Basic Law even for benefits of Macau's economy or society. This does not provide a legitimate basis for the Legislative Council to make any alteration or amendments, in fact, it is forbidden to do so. These issues are all reserved and to be done by the National People's Congress, therefore it shows the Basic Law is not just a regional law, but a national one. Secondly, based on its reserved legislative power,[32] the National People's Congress had stated in the Basic Law the concrete policies and regimes to be practiced after the handover of Macau in 1999. With establishment of institutions and introduction of policies differed from those in operation in China, the context of the Basic Law forces it to be a special legislation, in turn ensures its effects to dominate in Macau's legal order and even reject other constitutional documents to come into effect in Macau. This is due to the basic concept of legal theory: special legislations are superior to ordinary ones.[33]

Hence, the Basic Law is granted a supreme status among legislations in Macau's legal order, and thus leads the directions of evolution and orientation of various significant areas in Macau, such as economy, society and external affairs.

---

[32] See Article 31 of the National Constitution of People's Republic of China, this article reads: *The State may establish special administrative regions when necessary. The systems to be instituted in special administrative regions shall be prescribed by law enacted by the National People's Congress in the light of specific conditions.* From official website of the National People's Congress: http://www.npc.gov.cn/englishnpc/Constitution/2007-11/15/content_1372963.htm. Also see Article 8, no. 3 of the Legislation Law of the People's Republic of China, this article reads: *only national law can be enacted in respect of matters relating to autonomy system of ethnic regions, system of special administrative region, and system of autonomy at the basic level.* From official website of the Central People's Government of the people's republic of China: http://www.gov.cn/test/2005-08/13/content_22423.htm

[33] See *Commentaries on Contemporary Macau Law*, Vol. 1, Macau Foundation, 2005, page 51. It discussed further on the Basic Law's supreme power of authority in the Macau Special Administrative Region, and in two aspects pointing out the Basic Law is a national law and also the supreme in Macau SAR.

The Legal Hierarchy was developed in classical legal science. It mainly refers to relations among various forms of law.[34] It results the following consequence: laws in lower-levels cannot contradict or go against those in higher-levels.

In fact, it is a consequence of logics if considered to which legislative organs they are enacted, their context materials and applicable areas. To minimize controversy in this respect, some measures may be taken in the legislative level.[35]

Generally speaking, the problem of Legal Hierarchy is a synthesis of observance to the existing forms of laws by placing them in orders according to their force over the legal order. This is usually expressed in a pyramid form or triangular figure, in which the higher-level legislations are put in the tip while those lower-levels put in the bottom part. They are arranged in decreasing order corresponding to their legal forces: the higher the legal force, the higher it is placed in the hierarchy, and vice-versa.

After discussing status of the Basic Law, we are about to relate on its interaction with public international law and ordinary laws. It is evident that a legal order is not only composed of a constitutional document, but also with many other regulatory acts in various forms (they can be international conventions, treaties, agreements, internal ordinary laws, etc.).

The Legal Hierarchy can be established by comparing the limits of legislative authority or legislative power. Therefore, in the case of Basic Law, as discussed above, it is enacted by the National People's Congress, and is considered to be a special national law.

It is the Basic Law that laid out the whole framework of the normative order in Macau, while other regulatory documents fill in the detail. Basic Law and legal diploma in other levels together form an integrated legal structure which provides the citizens with behavioral criterion.[36] In Macau, it is mainly the Legislative Council that amends codes and enacts separated legislations so as to give response to social needs in time, yet it is the Government that is entitled to propose a bill.

There is no difficulty to see that the Basic Law stands in a higher hierarchy in relation to any other ordinary laws, including the Civil Code. The more controversial case is the hierarchy of international law, which once became the subject matter of legal dispute in the Macau Courts.

Based on general theory of international law, there is possibility for countries, organizations or entities to be qualified as the subject, and only with this quality, it can participate and be a party in international legal relation, exercise rights and bear

[34] See João de Castro Mendes, *Introdução ao estudo do Direito*, Lisboa, 1984, 95 ff.

[35] Just take the examples of Macau and China. In Macau, there is the "*Regime jurídico de enquadramento das fontes normativas internas*", *Lei no. 13/2009* , that is the legislation law stating on the contents to be regulated by law, independent administrative regulations and complement administrative regulations, approved on 14th July of 2009 by the Macau SAR Legislative Council; also see the Legislation Law of the People's Republic of China that is approved by the 3rd Congress of the National People's Congress on 15th March of 2000, and it also aims at similar functions like the above.

[36] See Tong Io Cheng, "The origin of Dominium and the Legitimacy of the Continuity of its System: an Interpretation of the Individual Property Protection in the Macau basic Law", *Academic Journal of One Country Two Systems*, no. 4, 2010, page 57.

responsibility (but qualification of subject of international law is not the issue to be discussed here). What is significant here is the statue of these international treaties and conventions negotiated and signed in internal legal system. This is *ex facto* quite apparent to reach a conclusion. It can be divided into four situations:

(a) International treaties or conventions had already come into effect before the handover of Macau, and these were all extended to apply in Macau by ordinances or ordinations promulgated by the Republic of Portugal, thus it suggested that the agent (sujeito) signing all these treaties was Portugal;
(b) When contracting international treaties of defense, foreign affairs or matters that Macau does not have any deciding power (these have been prescribed in the Basic Law), thus it is the Central Government of China that can decide and take action to negotiate in this case, and the treaties must be applied to Macau because it is lack of jurisdiction or deciding power in those areas;
(c) When contracting international conventions of other areas, such as society, culture, etc. by the Central Government of China, the central government will depend on Macau's situations and needs, and after seeking the views of Macau government, then decides if the convention is applied to Macau or not; and
(d) Contracting international agreements of certain aspects that Macau, on its own, is authorized to join international organization and agreements in the name of "Macau, China".

For the first circumstance, since it is not Macau who directly joins those international conventions, instead, the subject of those relations is Portugal. For this case, the Basic Law has already given the solution in accordance with Article 138, stated that they will continue to implement in local legal order. The Central Government only needs to do some appropriate arrangements to notify continuation of effects of those conventions in Macau. But before this, the Foreign Affairs of the Central Government will have to verify criteria if the international law is against sovereignty of China or contravene the Basic Law.

With regard to the second situation, this is a natural consequence of logics since it is beyond jurisdiction owned by Macau with accordance of Article 14 and 19 of the Basic Law.

Concerning the third situation, in accordance with first part of Article 138 of the Basic Law, the subject is the Central Government and the extension of applying those treaties or agreements depends on decisions made by the Central, thus in this case, Macau does not have much influence in the decision-making process, but only providing its own review.

With reference to the fourth condition, this is prescribed in the Article 136 of the Basic Law and stated plainly in which areas Macau can join international treaties on its own.

From all the above, among the first three situations the subject falls on the Central Government of China. Frankly speaking, Macau does not have much room to interfere during the process, and the most important is the quality of subject. As all those are signed and approved by the Central, the local legislature has no power or authority to alter or repeal application of international law. As a matter of course, the international law has a higher ranking than ordinary laws. Only in the last case, Macau signs and contracts in its own name as an independent signatory, but noted that this power is authorized and based on the Basic Law in terms of Article 136 of the Basic Law.

Eventually, the Legal Hierarchy could be done after the above discussions on their respective field: the Basic Law is certainly located at the top level, public international law in the middle level whereas the Civil Code, part of ordinary laws, is placed at the bottom in this case.

The Basic Law gives a legitimate basis to enact or impose ordinary laws, but it is not the source of private law. Noted that the provisions in the Basic Law are abstract and general, they are not suitable to apply directly to discipline civil legal relations in daily lives which it might be too general and not technical[37] enough to modulate behaviors of beings.[38] But those rights stated in the constitution play an important role in opposing the government or "authoritative power", enabling fundamental rights of people will not be violated or infringed by exercise of public authority, especially fundamental rights, freedom and protection. They are the bases for residents and set a bottom line where the public authority can never stride across.

Civil law is just one of the components of the private law, and in its own is not able to form a whole, integrated private law. Private law simply regulates relations that each person, both natural and legal one, can join as a party, thus it is related to the whole community.[39] There are still other components in the private law system, such as commercial law and other independent legislations (those are not able or appropriate to be included in the Civil Code).[40]

In Macau, for influences of the Basic Law on the Civil Code, actually it is mostly distinctive before the resumption of exercise of sovereignty and at that time, a temporary council[41] was set up in order to follow and take charge of enactment of the Civil Code, the Civil Procedure Code and the Commercial Code. Thus, this council had aimed to moderate institutions and innovate provisions in the Civil Code corresponding to current needs from society.

Due to higher and stronger legal force imposed by public international law, ordinary laws have to obey and adopt regulations from international treaties, conventions or agreements if necessary.

---

[37] See Wang Tez Chien, *General Theory of Civil Law*, Series of Study in Civil Law, Peking University Press, 2009, page 39.

[38] Here includes both categories of natural person (*pessoa singular*) and legal person (*pessoa colectiva*).

[39] See Karl Larenz, *General Theory of German Civil Law*, translated in Chinese version, Law Press, China, 2007, page 9.

[40] There are so many examples in the Continental Family, especially after codification, some regulations or laws are not suitable to add into the code which may disturb or even destroy logics of system. In Macau, it has labor law (some scholars say that part of it belongs to private law, other part is public law), commercial law and many other legislations.

[41] See Annex concerning on reform of the Civil Code – Initial Planning, official website of the Legislative Council: http://al.gov.mo/lei/codigo/civil/po/4.htm

It is somehow compatible for cooperation of public international law and the Civil Code within legal orders, especially in cases involving members of European Union (EU),[42] they show a great example in this case. Take as an example the Republic of Portugal, as a member of the EU, the EU treaties and directives are also applicable in internal legal order. Besides, Portugal has expressly prescribed that general or common international law is a part of Portuguese law.[43] Since international law signifies a relative unification of rules and principles where persons of different countries or other subjects of private law can contract under the same terms and conditions, they could make use of the same set of instruments. Therefore, enables more efficient and rapid business transactions and encourages exchange of information and progress of globalization. More conclusion of a treaty can do good to global trade, intercommunications, cultural and other exchange of ideas.

On the contrary, it brings side-effects to internal legal system under total adoption of public international law, particularly when it causes conflicts or inconveniences to social progress. That is the conclusion of treaties may not bring benefits and even do harm to the countries, at the same time hinder it from evolution because it fails to adapt to environmental changes easily. Take an example, if a country signs a treaty without any reserves, which means it accepts all the provisions written and its internal ordinary law has to obey all these. Sometimes, it might cause conflicts with internal legislations, however, the contracting party has no way to choose since it has to obey the treaty completely (*pacta sunt servanda*).[44] It implies there is no room for them to alter or repeal application of part of the treaty, however, in various cases this would retard progress of the country. A good example is the *Geneva Uniform Law* adopted in Macau. This is a convention applied to Macau since its publication on official bulletin on 8th February, 1960, and it stated the interest rate of checks, bill of exchange and promissory notes is fixed at 6 %. Nevertheless, in virtue of rapid economic progress and inflation, the current legal interest rate

---

[42] Internal legislations of members of European Union (EU) have to obey the directives issued by the EU as they have some common and mutual systems which have to be regulated by the EU, but not individual country.

[43] See the Constitution of the Republic of Portugal, concerning the international law, reads:
Artigo 8.º
(Direito internacional)

1. *As normas e os princípios de direito internacional geral ou comum fazem parte integrante do direito português.*
2. *As normas constantes de convenções internacionais regularmente ratificadas ou aprovadas vigoram na ordem interna após a sua publicação oficial e enquanto vincularem internacionalmente o Estado Português.*
3. *As normas emanadas dos órgãos competentes das organizações internacionais de que Portugal seja parte vigoram directamente na ordem interna, desde que tal se encontre estabelecido nos respectivos tratados constitutivos.*
4. *As disposições dos tratados que regem a União Europeia e as normas emanadas das suas instituições, no exercício das respectivas competências, são aplicáveis na ordem interna, nos termos definidos pelo direito da União, com respeito pelos princípios fundamentais do Estado de direito democrático.*

[44] Stated Article 26, Section 1 observance of Treaties, Part 3 of Vienna Convention on the Law of Treaties, done at Vienna on 23 May 1969, reads: *every treaty in force is binding upon the parties to it and must be performed by them in good faith.*

increases to 9.75 %.[45] But because of intrinsic binding force of the convention, the legislature can find no way to make amendments, and if it is desperate to alter the respective interest rate, the only method it can do is to terminate the treaty or withdraw from it: in conformity with the provisions of the treaty, or at any time by consent of all the parties after consultation with the other contracting States, in terms of Article 54 of Vienna Convention on the Law of Treaties. Therefore, it leads to a long-winded, complicated and not economical process which none of the parties is willing to choose.

4.7 Conclusions

The reform of Civil Code in Macau was done under the context of the handover of Macau from Portugal to PRC, in 1999. In the preparatory period, both PRC and Portugal have recognized the importance of a stable legal order in the future SAR, and therefore a series of measures were taken to assure such an order. Justification of the works done could be seen in an opinion drawn by the then Portuguese Government about the Civil Code, the Civil Procedure Code and the Commercial Code (*Parecer no. 2/99 da Comissão Eventual destinada a acompanhar e participar na elaboração dos projectos relativos aos Códigos Civil, Processual Civil e Comercial*). It mentioned various reasons for the desperate need to revise the institutions adopted in the Civil Code:

(a) Only a short period of time was remained until resumption of exercise of sovereignty, at the same time, after consideration of dimension of the code;
(b) Neither moderations nor alterations were done since the promulgation of the code in Macau, as a result, it hardly matched the current needs and social lives;
(c) Give response to the Joint Declaration was one of its purposes and were anticipated to reach, so as to protect those deep-rooted values from current legal system; and
(d) Building up its own legal system with reserve of antecedent experiences, resulted in a more precise and decisive guidance to behaviors.

By nature, the Macau Civil Code can be seen as a product of legal transplant from the Portuguese's,[46] thus there are of course cultural aspects to be considered whenever there is a chance for reform. On the other hand, for a code promulgated for more than 30 years, it must be modified in some points in order to respond to

[45] See the Administrative Order, no. 29/2006, promulgated on 6th July, 2006 which repealed the previous administrative order, no. 9/2002 and increased the legal interest rate from 6 to 9.75 %.

[46] See Tong Io Cheng and Wu Yanni, "Legal Culture and Legal Transplants", *ISAIDAT Law Review*, Volume 1, Issue 2, 633–637. Detailed exposition of the process of legal transplant of Portuguese law in Macau can be seen in this paper, especially how the Portuguese law "*rooted*" to form a unique legal order after eventual combination with the original existing traditional legal culture in its colonized cities.

current social needs. After all, it is for the first time in history Macau has been given the chance to mode its future Civil Code with a focus on its local interest. In this context, we can see why the Coordinator of the Project, Luís Miguel Urbano, referred the following in the brief statement of reason in the Macau Civil Code: "*it was not to create a new code from nothing, (…) while the raw materials have been provided and are in good condition*". Besides, he mentioned that "*radical changes signify a loss of experiences accumulated in application of civil law*". "*In reality, this reform had just cancelled or amended those lagged regimes.*"[47]

As a final remark, a distinction between Chinese law and law in China is advisable: if the former remains, so far, non-codified, with regard to the latter Macau legal order is definitely supported by codes.

[47] See the Macau Civil Code, Portuguese version, Macau Government Printing Bureau, 1999, VIII–IX.

Chapter 5
Recodification of Private Law in the Czech Republic

David Elischer, Ondřej Frinta, and Monika Pauknerová

Abstract The chapter brings a general overview of legislation on private law in the Czech Republic, notably with respect to the Civil Code, Business Corporations Act, Labour Code, and Private International Law Act. Attention is paid not only to the legal history of codification and decodification of private law in the Czech Republic up to the present, but also, and in particular, to the recent radical reforms and complete re-codification of private law, notably to the new Civil Code, effective as from 1 January 2014. The general overview of legislation governing private law starts with the description of legal sources, including European Union law and international treaties, and continues with the introduction into the rather dynamic history of civil codes and other sources of private law in the Czech Republic. The authors tried to focus on the starting points and main features of the completely new recodified legislation, the major axis of which is a human being and his or her interests, predominantly individual in the private law sphere.

Keywords Private law • Czech Republic • Codification • Recodification of private law • Decodification of private law • Recodification in former socialist countries

This essay was drafted with the support of the Research Programme of Charles University in Prague "Prvouk 05".

D. Elischer • O. Frinta • M. Pauknerová (✉)
Department of Commercial Law, Faculty of Law, Charles University Prague, Prague, Czech Republic
e-mail: elischer@prf.cuni.cz; frinta@prf.cuni.cz; pauknero@prf.cuni.cz

J.C. Rivera (ed.), *The Scope and Structure of Civil Codes*, Ius Gentium: Comparative Perspectives on Law and Justice 32, DOI 10.1007/978-94-007-7942-6_5,

5.1 Brief Introduction – History of Codification and Recodification of Private Law up to the Present

Czech law, that is, the law applicable within today's Czech Republic, historically belonged to the so-called Austrian family of continental law.[1] Austrian law, primarily the General Civil Code of 1811 (ABGB) and the Commercial Code of 1863, was incorporated into the Czechoslovak legal order after the establishment of independent Czechoslovakia in 1918; as such, it applied in its essence until 1950, when Civil Code No. 141/1950 Sb. (Sb. – Collection of Laws) came into effect. That Civil Code was soon replaced by the Civil Code, No. 40/1964 Sb. as a result of an extensive socialist codification pursued in the mid-1960s; the latter Code ceased to be effective on 31 December 2013. Although the Civil Code 1964 was amended on many occasions, it is significantly stigmatised due to its socialist origin. Moreover, after so many amendments, the text of the Code was lacking any conception and appeared to be completely unsatisfactory.

Apparently, the whole field of private law, including those areas omitted by the existing Civil Code but which logically relate to it – in particular family law and commercial law – was in rather urgent need of new codification which has been discussed in the Czech Republic since the early 1990s.[2] Finally, the process of the complete re-codification of Czech private law has now been accomplished. New laws, which are closely linked to one another, or even interwoven, will become effective on 1 January 2014; these are the Civil Code, No. 89/2011 Sb., the Business Corporations Act, No. 90/2012 Sb., and the Private International Law Act, No. 91/2012 Sb. The process of adopting the new codification was rather difficult, accompanied by harsh intellectual discussions or even December disputes regarding their overall conception, primarily with respect to the new Civil Code and regarding the sources to be used and to find inspiration in. The results attained will be assessed from various perspectives for a long time: the new laws are built upon clear ideological foundations and leading ideas corresponding to Central European traditions. At the same time, however, there is no clear accord as to whether all positive aspects of former legislation have been absorbed by the new laws in order to preserve certain legal continuity, or whether, on the other hand, some time-proven and well-established institutions have been disregarded to no effect. What is absolutely unpredictable is whether and how the new codification, introducing some revolutionary changes, would be accepted by the legal public, in particular by the judiciary; whether judges would be brave enough to follow new principles stipulated in new provisions having, in the first years, practically no backing in case law.

[1] Knapp, V. *Velké právní systémy* (Great Legal Systems), Prague: C.H. Beck 1996, p. 118. Sometimes the Austrian and Swiss families of law are conceived to be part of the German legal family; see, for example, Koch, H., Magnus, U., Winkler von Mohrenfels, P. *Internationales Privatrecht und Rechtsvergleichung*, Munich: C.H. Beck 1989, p. 196.

[2] For details see, in English, Pauknerová, M. *Codification of Czech Private Law in the Middle and on the Outskirts of Europe*, Liber Amicorum Valentinas Mikelenas, Justitia, Vilnius 2008 (2009), p. 239.

Moreover, the three new laws should not be generally evaluated as one whole. Each of them possesses specific features not only in its substance but also in its legislative background, the link to EU law and to global or at least European trends. In any case, however, we may arrive at the conclusion that the results of the new Czech private law codification will contribute to the formation of new European Private Law, in particular if we observe the "respect for ... the different legal systems and traditions", as declared by the Treaty on the Functioning of the European Union.[3]

5.2 General Overview of Legislation on Private Law in the Czech Republic

5.2.1 General Overview of Private Law in the Czech Republic

In the Czech Republic the body of law is divided into two main branches in the same way as in other countries belonging to the continental legal system. These branches are private law and public law. However, this division is not absolute and should not be overemphasized in particular for two reasons. Firstly, there is an influence of *acquis* of the European Union law on legislation in the Czech Republic with the result that elements and methods of private and public law are influencing each other more than in the past.[4] This phenomenon is more general and can be traced in other countries of Europe. The second reason is specific for the Czech Republic as a post-communist country. Legal theory based on Marxism-Leninism denied the distinction between these two main branches of law. Although that theory was rejected after the political, social and economic changes of November 1989, relics of that era and theory can be traced even today.

Describing private law legislation in the Czech Republic, it is necessary to distinguish legislation from the perspective of its legal force. The following types of legislation are relevant:

(a) Constitutional acts, which are the source of law of the highest level of legal force, namely the Constitution of the Czech Republic, No. 1/1993 Sb., as amended (Constitution), and the Charter of Fundamental Rights and Freedoms, No. 2/1993 Sb., as amended (Charter). These contain provisions which have fundamental significance for the branch of private law. This is the reason why the Constitution and the Charter are taken as a source of private law.

[3] See Art. 67(1) of the Treaty on the Functioning of the European Union.

[4] Compare the decision of the Constitutional Court of the Czech Republic, published under No. 78/2001 Sb.: "*Even though the legal system of the Czech Republic is based on the dualism of public and private law, this division of laws into two large areas, proceeding from classical Roman law, cannot be treated as a dogma, but as taking account of modern tendencies of development in laws and also the laws of the European Communities. Private and public law are not separated by "the Great Wall of China" in the present. The elements of private and public law are blending more often and in a narrower way; they combine together mutually and intensively.*"

(b) Acts, which are sometimes referred to as "ordinary acts".[5] Codes also belong to this category. The reason is that the legal force of a Code is at the same level as that of other acts. The difference between a Code and other acts does not subsist in its legal force, but in the scope of regulation. Codes regulate comprehensive and complex parts of the legal system (or its particular sub-systems), whereas other acts focus on particular issues.

The core of private law legislation consists of the Civil Code of 2012 including the area of family law, the Business Corporations Act and the Labour Code.

Intellectual property rights are covered by several laws. The Copyright Act, No. 121/2000 Sb., as amended, implements the relevant legislation of the European Union and regulates the rights of an author to his or her work and rights related to copyright.[6] Industrial property rights, as the other part of intellectual property are again governed by particular acts. The rules of private international law are included in the new Act on Private International Law (the Private International Law Act). There are other laws, regulating particular issues, which are also considered as a source of private law. The following laws should be mentioned in this context: the Act on Liability for Damage Caused by a Defective Product, No. 59/1998 Sb., and the Act on Bills of Exchange, Promissory Notes and Cheques, No. 191/1950 Sb.

(c) Legislation having legal force lower than acts passed by Parliament is adopted within limits set out by relevant acts. The purpose of this legislation is only to implement and execute acts, not to enact and regulate rights and duties of persons. It is recognized that the Government of the Czech Republic may adopt Government Decrees based upon acts adopted and does not need express authorization to be stated in the text of a respective act. On the other hand, ministries and other state and local authorities are allowed to adopt implementing legislation only when expressly authorized to do so in relevant acts.
(d) In addition, legal rules are included in international treaties; should there be a conflict between an international treaty and a concrete law, the international treaty takes preference.[7] International treaties are important in private international law, business law and family law, while their role is rather limited in the sphere of public law.
(e) The European Union law should be mentioned in this context; it includes both substantive rules of private law and conflict-of-law rules. European Regulations are legal instruments which are directly applicable in the Czech Republic as of the date of accession of the Czech Republic to the EU (1 May 2004). As an EU Member State the Czech Republic is obliged to implement the respective European Directives relevant for European private (international) law.

---

[5] This concept is not used in legislation; it is used only in theory and sometimes in the reasoning of decisions of the Constitutional Court of the Czech Republic. The purpose of this concept is to underline the difference between constitutional acts and acts with a lower level of legal force.

[6] E.g. the rights of a performer to his or her artistic performance, the right of a producer of an audiovisual fixation, to his or her fixation, etc.

[7] Art. No. 10 of the Constitution of the Czech Republic.

5.2.2 *The Civil Code, the Business Corporations Act and the Labour Code*

As mentioned above, the area of private law is covered by more than one law. These are the Civil Code 2012, the Business Corporations Act 2012, and the Labour Code 2006. The area of family law was originally governed by the Family Act; this law was not labelled as a code despite the fact that the regulation was quite complex. However, the Civil Code 2012 also covers the area of family law and as such repealed the Family Act.

The Civil Code, adopted in 1964, was effective until 31 December 2013. It was amended many times, particularly after 1989. The Civil Code 1964 was composed of nine parts: Part One – General Provisions; Part Two – Rights Related to Things (Rights in Rem)[8]; Part Six – Liability for damage and unjust enrichment; Part Seven – Inheritance law; Part Eight – The law of obligations (containing two large groups of provisions, namely general provisions for obligations and provisions for individual types of contracts); and Part Nine – Final, transitional and repealing provisions.

The new Civil Code adopted in 2012 is composed of five parts:

Part One – General Part. This part encompasses provisions with the highest level of universality. There is a list of basic principles of private law and provisions for natural persons (their legal personality and capacity to perform legal acts) and legal entities. In general, the Civil Code 2012 is based on the fictional theory of legal entities, which means that legal entities (organized bodies with legal personality) are declared as legal entities by the law. Other general issues are enacted, such as legal conduct, representation, statutory limitation of actions. Definitions of some general concepts are provided, such as close persons, division of things into corporeal and incorporeal,[9] movable and immovable, computation of time along with the beginning and end of time-limits.

Part Two – Family Law (described below), including community property of spouses.[10]

Part Three – Absolute Property Rights (rights *in rem*). This part starts with provisions for possession and ownership rights, followed by provisions for co-ownership. It provides for rights to another person's thing (*iura in re aliena*).

[8] Parts Three through Five were repealed; this situation existed till the end of 2013.

[9] This is one of the most important changes between the Civil Code 1964 and the Civil Code 2012. The former defined only corporeal things, but the latter adopted the conception of incorporeal things well known in the Civil Code 1811.

[10] There are crucial differences in Czech law between the institution of co-ownership and community property of spouses. Firstly, community property can arise only between spouses. Secondly, the co-owner (co-ownership) is an owner of an abstract ("ideal") share of the thing; however, each spouse (community property) is an owner of the whole thing (there is no share whether abstract or real), but s/he is restricted in his/her ownership by the same right of the other spouse.

This includes easements (restriction of the owner of real estate in favour of another person), lien, the right of retention, and inheritance law.

Part Four – Relative Property Rights (the law of obligations). This part is subdivided into three larger groups of provisions. The first group contains general provisions for obligations with respect to their formation,[11] modification, securing and discharge. The second group deals with individual types of contracts (purchase contract, donation contract, contract for work done, loan, borrowing, lease, mandate, bailment, lodging, carriage, etc.). The third group contains provisions regulating liability for damage and unjust enrichment.

Part Five – Final, transitional and repealing provisions.

As indicated above, the Business Corporations Act regulates the legal position of legal entities formed for the purpose of business; the Labour Code enacts primarily legal relationships arising from dependent work carried out by employees for their employers (Sec. 1 of the Labour Code).

There are interlinks among the codes. The Business Corporations Act stipulates in its Sec. 3 (1), that provisions of the Civil Code will be used only when this is expressly stipulated in the Business Corporations Act.

The relationship between the Labour Code 2006 and the Civil Code 1964 was originally based on the principle of delegation. The intention was that the Civil Code 1964 would be used only in cases when expressly permitted by respective provisions of the Labour Code. This was strongly criticized as a really inadequate solution which had not been used or tried in any other legal system, and it could have triggered a lot of problems. It was the Constitutional Court of the Czech Republic which eventually repealed this provision (Sec. 4 of the Labour Code).[12] The consequence is that the relationship between the Labour Code and the Civil Code 2012 will be treated as is usual, i.e. the Civil Code 2012 will play a subsidiary role in all situations where the provisions of the Labour Code turn to be insufficient to solve an issue.

To sum up, the law of the Czech Republic does not encompass separate bodies, like "Contract Codes" or "Obligations Codes" or "Books", covering particular branches of private law. It is just the Civil Code 2012 (as a single law), which is taken as a general (universal) code for the whole private law, despite the fact that some parts of this (business corporations and labour law) are not included in the Civil Code and are enacted by a separate code and act respectively.

---

[11] It should be mentioned that it is necessary to distinguish the concept of the "formation of obligations" from the concept of the "formation of a contract". The latter means an offer and its acceptance, which together give rise to a contract; but this is only one of several ways to form or create an obligation.

[12] The decision was published under No. 116/2008 Sb.

5.3 The Civil Code

5.3.1 Political, Sociological and Economic Context of Enactment of the Civil Code

When the totalitarian regime collapsed in 1989, Czechoslovakia claimed allegiance to the democratic legacy of the Czechoslovak Republic founded in 1918. Totalitarian ideology was rejected and replaced by ideas of liberal democracy and rule of law. It was clear that the law as a whole needed a thorough depuration of totalitarian relics. Initially, this meant the depuration of the Civil Code 1964; but it was clear quite soon, that in the future there would be a need for a completely new civil code. An explanation follows below on how entirely different the socialist Civil Code 1964 was. Two proposals of a new civil law of the 1990s were not adopted. Finally, at the end of that decade, consent was reached over the concept of a new private law. Preparatory work on a third draft started in 2001, when the basis of the code was agreed upon by the Government of the Czech Republic. The draft of the Civil Code 2012 was finalized in 2011; it was adopted by Parliament and later officially promulgated, i.e. published in the Collection of Laws under No. 89/2012 Sb.[13] The main idea was to enact a civil code such as would be fully comparable with standard civil codes in Europe (as is, for example, *Code Civil* in France, or the Civil Code 1811 still in force in Austria). In accordance with general ideas of liberal democracy and rule of law, the Civil Code 2012 is based on two fundamental principles. The first principle is respect to the liberty of every individual person; it is accompanied with a second principle that every person is basically fully responsible for one's behaviour. From a systematic point of view, the Civil Code 2012 starts with a fundamental idea that there are three key institutions to be regulated in private law: the family, ownership, and the contract. It is then not surprising that the Civil Code 2012 is mostly inspired by the Civil Code 1811 (and in its revised draft from 1937) and standard civil codes of Europe (Austria, Germany, France, the Netherlands, etc.).

5.3.2 Prior Civil Codes

In chronological order, the first Civil Code was the General Civil Code of Austria, No. 946/1811 Sb., enacted in 1811 (the Civil Code 1811). The geographical region of the so-called "Czech lands[14]" was a part of the Austro-Hungarian Empire until 1918.

[13] The number of the new Civil Code is not a coincidence. It should remind us of the year 1989, when the totalitarian regime collapsed. The number symbolizes the breakup with socialistic laws.

[14] This includes Bohemia, Moravia and Czech Silesia. In the Middle Ages, these areas were more or less extensive in comparison to the borders of the modern age Czechoslovakia.

In that year,[15] Czechoslovakia declared its independence from the Austro-Hungarian Empire and started its independent existence as a sovereign state composed of two main nations – Czechs and Slovaks.[16] Despite the fact that there was an effort by Czechs to become independent of the Empire as early as before World War I, the creation of a new state was a consequence of the total collapse of the Austro-Hungarian Empire after World War I, and, as such, it was not methodically planned and prepared long before it happened. The point is that, at the moment of the creation of the new state, there was no individual legal system prepared and available. As a solution, the legal system of the Austro-Hungarian Empire was resumed as a legal order of the newly created Czechoslovakia.[17] From the perspective of private law, this meant that in one state there were two systems of private law in force. In the Czech part of the Republic (Bohemia, Moravia and Czech Silesia), the Civil Code 1811 was in force even after 1918. In the Slovak part (Slovakia), private law was not codified.[18] It was clear that such a situation should be changed. As Czechoslovakia stabilized, the first amendments of the Civil Code 1811 were made, and these amending Acts were also in force in the Slovak part of the Republic.

Such an approach was only provisional. There were two opinions on the further development of private law: (a) to enact a new Civil Code or (b) to revise the Civil Code 1811. Eventually, the second opinion prevailed and a proposal of the revised Civil Code was submitted to Parliament in 1937. However, the draft was not enacted because of the invasion by Nazi Germany and World War II.

As mentioned before, after World War II Czechoslovakia changed its political orientation from a liberal democracy to Communist totalitarian ideology. After 1948 the Communist Party pronounced a so-called "Two-Year Plan for Law" (1949–1950) intending to codify and adapt the legal system to the new political and economic situation and to approximate it to the legal system of the Union of Soviet Socialist Republics. The goal was to simplify the legal system. This simplification had two ideological reasons: the first was that a society developing itself towards socialism did not need a detailed legal system; the second premise was that simplified law would be easier for people to understand.

The first outcome of this "Two-Year Plan" was the codification of family law, enacted as the Family Act, No. 265/1949 Sb., followed by the Civil Code, No. 141/1950 Sb., in force from 1 January 1951. Despite the idea of simplification

---

[15] On 28 October 1918.

[16] The newly born state was composed of the historical regions of Bohemia, Moravia, Czech Silesia, Slovakia and the eastern part of Carpathian Ruthenia. This is the reason why that state was really multinational: apart from Czechs and Slovaks, there were other nations as well, namely Germans (the western part of the new state), Hungarians (the southern part of Slovakia), Ruthenians (the eastern part of the new state), Jews and Poles (Czech Silesia).

[17] This happened by so called "Reception Act" (No. 11/1918 Sb.); the resumption had, of course, some exceptions.

[18] In that part of Czechoslovakia, the main sources of private law were legal customs (which were written down in *Tripartitum opus iuris consuetudinarii inlycti Regni Hungariae partiumque adnexarium* by a land judge, Štefan Verböci, in 1514). In addition, there were also some acts regulating particular private law issues.

and despite inspiration from the law of the Soviet Union (namely its conception of ownership), the system and terminology of that Civil Code was not as distant from traditional European civil codes as was the later Civil Code 1964. The Civil Code 1950 was in force until 31 March 1964; 1 April 1964 was the date of force of the Civil Code 1964.

It is crucial to emphasize that the Civil Code 1964 was enacted under circumstances, which were totally different from those applicable today in all aspects mentioned – political, sociological and economic. After World War II Czechoslovakia found itself in the zone of influence of the Soviet Union. After 1948 Czechoslovakia changed its political orientation from a liberal democracy to the Communist totalitarian ideology based on the principles of Marxism-Leninism. The main goal of that ideology – the creation of a totalitarian, single-party state,[19] was realized in Czechoslovakia after the elections and coup d'état in 1948. This historical development naturally influenced the development of law and jurisprudence. The impact upon law culminated only in the 1960s. The most obvious demonstration of ideological orientation was the adopting of a new Constitution (No. 100/1960 Sb.), which proclaimed that "*socialism in our country has achieved victory*". That idea had an impact upon the area of private law in three respects.

The first aspect was a total change in the conception of how to regulate the branch of private law.[20] The intention was to deconstruct the complex system of private law, to repudiate the idea of a central and universal Code, which should be replaced by a number of specialized Codes and acts.[21] The second aspect was to manipulate the parties (persons) to private law relationships with a large number of mandatory rules, without any possibility for using the autonomy of their will in individual circumstances. This allowed for numerous eruptions of public law into private relationships. The third aspect is a change of terminology. The original wording of the Civil Code 1964 used concepts different from both the national and European tradition.[22] The purpose of this was to demonstrate that this Code had nothing in common with the previous era.[23]

In fact, the Civil Code 1964 was reduced to being a consumers' protection code. This was in accordance with the economic context of that era. The most significant characteristic for the economy in states of this kind was central planning for all

[19] Ian Adams, *Political Ideology Today*. Manchester: Manchester University Press, 1993, p. 201.

[20] To be more precise – how to regulate the area of law, which was called private law before WWII.

[21] Family law was even taken out of the Civil Code adopted in 1950. What is significant for totalitarian ideologies is that they focus first on the most private area of life inside family.

[22] Just a few examples for demonstration: the term "natural person" was replaced by the term "citizen", the term "legal entity" by the term "socialist organisation" and even the part of the Civil Code entitled "Particular types of contracts" was replaced with the term "Services". The last change is not only a change of terminology but a change of the whole concept. A citizen did not enter into a contract with a socialist organisation but was only provided with its services in order to satisfy his/her material needs.

[23] Eliáš, K. –Zuklínová, M. *Principy a východiska pro nový kodex soukromého práva* (*Principles and Background of a New Code of Private Law, in Czech*). Praha: Linde Praha, a. s., 2001, pp. 91–94.

branches of the economy; there were no (private) undertakings. The regulation of ownership was strongly affected by this fact. Three kinds of ownership were distinguished: (1) socialist social ownership (persons were the state and cooperatives), (2) personal ownership (objects were things for the personal use of citizens), and (3) private ownership, which was treated as a relic of the previous era and was restricted. The most protected ownership was the first one.

To sum up, the Civil Code 1964, in its original wording, was adopted in the totally different political situation of the totalitarian state, which affected all aspects of life – social and economic.

In November 1989 the totalitarian regime collapsed. Czechoslovakia claimed allegiance to the democratic legacy of the Czechoslovak Republic, founded in 1918; totalitarian ideology was rejected and replaced by the ideas of liberal democracy. It was clear that the law as a whole needed a thorough depuration of totalitarian relics. This was also the case for the Civil Code 1964; its extensive amendment, abolishing the most apparent totalitarian relics, was adopted in 1991 (Act No. 509/1991 Sb.).

In order to make this explanation complete, it should be added that Czechoslovakia was turned into a federation of the Czech Socialist Republic and the Slovak Socialist Republic in 1968–1969. However, the Civil Code 1964 was in force in both parts of the newly created federation with private law remaining uniform. Czechoslovakia ended its existence as a federal state on 31 December 1992. The Czech Republic and the Slovak Republic continued their existence as separate sovereign states beginning 1 January 1993.[24] While in the Slovak Republics, the Civil Code 1964 has remained in force till today, in the Czech Republic it was repealed by the Civil Code 2012.

5.3.3 The Civil Code of the Czech Republic and Legal Families

It emerges from the discussion about the Civil Code 1811 that the real roots of Czechoslovak jurisprudence and law were very strongly subject to the influence of Austrian private law, and the Czech Civil Code belongs to the Roman-Germanic subgroup of Western legal systems. The influence of the law of the Soviet Union was strong during the Communist era of the Czechoslovak state (1948–1989). As suggested earlier, although its most apparent relics were abolished after 1989, some of them can still be traced even today. Generally speaking, the development after 1989 has shifted Czech private law back to the traditional Roman-Germanic subgroup of Western law without interrupting its links with Austrian private law.

[24] It is often said that Czechoslovakia was "split" into two new states. As was demonstrated above, this is a simplification and not precise, because both the Czech and the Slovak Republics existed as states inside the Czechoslovak federation; it was only the federal state that ceased to exist on 31 December 1992. This being so, the Czech and the Slovak Republics commenced their existence as sovereign states on 1 January 1993.

5.3.4 Sources in the Civil Code of the Czech Republic

The Civil Code does not recognize any parallel sources of law regulating the same matters as those governed by the Civil Code itself. There are no legal customs as a source of private law in the Czech Republic. However, the Civil Code 2012 often refers to "good morals" (proper morality). This is a set of ethical rules applied in the exercise of rights and the performance of duties. But the system of good morals is not a source of law existing independently of the Civil Code 2012. This system of ethical rules is only referred to by the Civil Code 2012 to be used in relevant situations anticipated by the law.

5.4 Relationships Between the Civil Code and the Constitution, Treaties, and Private International Law

5.4.1 The Constitution and the Civil Code

According to the Constitution of the Czech Republic, the Czech Republic is a sovereign, unified, democratic, and law-abiding state, founded upon the principles of respect for the rights and freedoms of the individual and citizen (Article 1). The power of the state can be exercised only in cases and within the limits described by law, and by the means set out by the law (Article 3). Part of the constitutional order of the Czech Republic is the Charter of Fundamental Rights and Freedoms (Article 3). Fundamental rights and freedoms are under the protection of the judiciary (Article 4).

It follows from what has been mentioned that the Constitution is the basis and the cornerstone for the scope of the whole of Czech legislation. The bases of the rights of individuals are laid down in the Charter of Fundamental Rights and Freedoms. Of particular importance is the principle that all citizens may do what is not prohibited by law, and nobody may be compelled to do what is not imposed upon him by law (Article 2 paragraph 4 of the Constitution). The judicial body responsible for the protection of constitutionality is the Constitutional Court (Article 83); the Court ensures that the "common" legislation is in conformity with the Constitution.

5.4.2 Private Law and International Treaties

The Czech Republic is party to a number of international treaties, both multilateral and bilateral. Apart from treaties of a public law nature, the Czech Republic is a contracting party to international conventions aimed at the unification of private law, such as conventions on the international sale of goods, international transport, intellectual property, conventions adopted by the Hague Conference on Private

International Law, as well as conventions concerning international procedural law, both international litigation and arbitration.

The general solution regarding the preferential application of international treaties is laid down in the amended Article 10 of the Constitution, under which promulgated treaties, to the ratification of which Parliament has given its consent and by which the Czech Republic is bound, form a part of the legal order; if a treaty provides something other than that which a statute provides, the treaty applies. This means that an international convention complying with Article 10 of the Czech Constitution, i.e. having consent of the Parliament to ratification and being officially promulgated in the Collection of International Treaties, takes precedence over respective provisions of the Czech domestic law. The requirement of the publication of conventions in the Collection of International Treaties applies in general.[25]

Czech constitutional law, as amended by Constitutional Act No. 395/2001 Sb., is based on the rule that the Czech Republic observes its obligations resulting from international law (see Article 1 paragraph 2 of the Constitution, as amended). This means that, in conformity with Article 10 of the Constitution, as amended, the relationship between international treaties and domestic law in general rather corresponds to the monistic scheme (interrelationship of national and international law).[26] This represents a significant change, indicating the general preference in application of all fully ratified international treaties which are officially promulgated – that is published in the Collection of International Treaties.

The relationship between provisions contained in international treaties and national law, as well as potential conflicts between international treaties, is quite complicated in itself; but the complexity may be multiplied in cases where European Union law is involved. What is particularly meant here are two articles of the Czech Constitution: Article 10, stipulating the primacy of ratified and promulgated international treaties over Czech law, and Article 10a, the so-called "integration clause", under which treaties may transfer certain powers and competences of Czech authorities to international institutions and organisations. These two provisions and their interrelationship, particularly the scope of applicability of Article 10a, are not uniformly understood in Czech legal literature.[27]

---

[25] For details with respect to the Hague Conventions see Pauknerová, M. *Conflict of laws conventions and their reception – Czech Republic*, in Jorge Sánchez Cordero (ed.), *The Impact of Uniform Law in National Law. Limits and Possibilities*, Instítuto de investigaciones jurídicas, México 2010, pp. 299–304.

[26] See Čepelka, Č. and Šturma, P. *Mezinárodní právo veřejné* (Public International Law, in Czech), (Prague: C.H. Beck, 2008), p. 199 with further references.

[27] For details see Pauknerová, M. *International Conventions and Community Law: Harmony and Conflicts, in Nuovi strumenti del diritto internazionale privato. New instruments of private international law – Liber Fausto Pocar* – Giuffrè Editore, Milano 2009, p. 793.

5.4.3 Civil Code and Private International Law

Private international law has traditionally been regulated autonomously by a special legal act; formerly by the Act Concerning Private International Law and the Rules of Procedure Relating Thereto 1963,[28] and, with effect from 1 January 2014, by the Act on Private International Law. In private international law, unlike in civil law, legal continuity prevails: both private international law acts are a follow-up to the first Act Concerning Private International and Interregional Law and the Legal Status of Aliens in the Sphere of Private Law of 1948, inspired by the so-called Vienna Draft of 1913, widely recognized as an outstanding work.[29] The Private International Law Act 1963 (PIL Act) was divided into two main parts: the first part covered provisions dealing with the conflict of laws and the legal status of aliens; the second part covered international procedural law. Despite the fact that some private international law rules were also incorporated in other acts (e.g., in the Commercial Code, in the Act on Bills of Exchange, Promissory Notes and Cheques, etc.), the Private International Law Act 1963 was the main source of regulation in this respect.

Changes introduced by the new PIL Act are far from being as substantial and revolutionary as are those in the new Civil Code. The main reason for this difference is that conflict-of-law rules are considered to be neutral, and therefore more resistant with respect to the governing political and social system: the Act of 1963 was a standard European codification of private international law. The new Private International Law Act is primarily a reaction to the new Civil Code 2012, particularly with respect to legal terminology and certain brand new institutions. What should be considered essential is that it reflects new trends in private international law in general, and in changing the connecting factor of nationality to that of habitual residence, as regards personal, family and succession law in particular. The intention of the legislature was to unify all laws related to private international law in one piece of legislation. The new PIL Act thus includes relevant conflict-of-law and/or international procedure rules concerning not only the classical parts of private international law, that is, personal, family and succession law and rights *in rem*, but also rules on bills of exchange, promissory notes and cheques, securities, insolvency, and arbitration. It consists of nine parts: (1) General provisions, (2) General provisions of international civil procedure, (3) General provisions of private international law, (4) Provisions for individual types of private law relations (capacity, legal acts, agency, statute of limitation, family law, registered partnership and similar relationships, rights *in rem*, succession law, intellectual property law, securities and other instruments, obligations), (5) Legal assistance in contacts with foreign countries, (6) Insolvency procedure, (7) Arbitration, and (8) Transitional and final

[28] For details see M. Pauknerová, *Private International Law in the Czech Republic*, International Encyclopaedia of Laws, 2nd ed., Kluwer Law International 2011.

[29] See in particular F. Korkisch, *Das neue internationale Privatrecht der Tschechoslowakei*, RabelsZ (1952): pp. 410–450, with further references.

provisions. The general part of the Act, including definitions of such terms as classification, evasion of law, overriding mandatory rules, preliminary questions, etc., may also be treated as new.

Obviously, the concept of private international law, both in legislation, and in the academic approach, has been traditionally broad.[30] The scope of private international law includes: (a) conflict-of-law rules, which are the nucleus of private international law; (b) the direct rules of substantive law, the sources of which are mostly international conventions (i.e. uniform substantive rules); exceptionally such rules form a part of domestic law; these rules are directly applicable to relations with an international element – that is they will be used without the previous application of conflict rules; (c) rules governing the legal status of aliens; and (d) rules of international procedure law. Codification in the new Private International Law Act lays down rules of international civil procedure, conflict-of-law rules and rules governing the legal status of aliens, as they correspond to the tradition of Czech law. The combination of these three areas into one piece of legislation has proved to be successful, although the route to the uniform and autonomous Private International Law Act was not simple at all.

5.5 Content of the Civil Code

5.5.1 The Original Contents of the Civil Code 1964 – Legal Context

The Civil Code 1964 broadly reflected the idea of the "winning socialism" and consequently differed very much from similar codifications not only within the continental European legal family: but even within the socialist countries in Central and Eastern Europe it was special.[31] During that period, the distinction of private/public law was abolished as a "bourgeois anachronism" not only in the practical sense but also theoretically; it was replaced with the single socialist law. That law was actually public law, leaning towards public law methods of regulation which facilitated state intervention in the private sphere of citizens. The most important legal institutions of civil law were state socialist ownership (in the domain of rights *in rem*), and the central economic plan (in the domain of obligations). It should be noted that

[30] See in particular, Kučera, Z. *Mezinárodní právo soukromé* (Private international law, in Czech), 7 ed., Doplněk and Aleš Čeněk, Brno Plzeň 2009; see also Pauknerová, *Private International Law, Czech Republic*, p. 23 et seq., with further references.

[31] In comparison with the Hungarian and Polish civil codes, the Czech Code of 1964 seemed to be the most orthodox in the way it applied the principles of the new socialist law. The Polish and Hungarian civil codes, in the sphere of the law of obligations, were much more tolerant vis-à-vis private ownership and small business activities.

there was a strict hierarchy among the different forms of ownership, and only state socialist ownership was the most protected under the former legal system.[32]

Legislation concerning economic relationships was removed from the Civil Code 1964 and incorporated into a special "Economic Code", No. 109/1964 Sb. The Civil Code 1964 was thus conceived purely and simply as a code of consumer law in the socialist context. Civil legislation focused only on proprietary relationships and largely neglected other aspects of private life. The accent upon physical substance resulted in obvious underestimation of personal rights and things related to personal status.

Another very negative trend was the idea of simplifying most traditional legal institutions. That effort led to the abolition of many classical legal concepts and institutions, such as "possession", "positive prescription", "easements", "purchase", "rent", "tenancy", "neighbourhood rights", "legacy", "disinheritance", etc. Even the classical term "obligation" was replaced by the expression "service", so as to be allegedly closer to the popular understanding of such institutions.[33] This tendency was part of a generally shared idea of law declining and finally being extinguished, based on the thesis that law will not be needed at all in a developed socialist society. Shortly after its conception this idea revealed itself to be completely mistaken and erroneous; but unfortunately it damaged Czech civil law and private law as such irreversibly.

Czech civil law, with regard to all political and ideological resources, shifted away from the European conventional tradition of civil codification and became a simple instrument for the direction of the society.

5.5.2 New Content Incorporated into the Civil Code 1964

After the restoration of a pluralistic democracy and market economy in 1989, the Civil Code 1964 revealed itself to be completely unfit and unusable for the forthcoming period, in spite of several modifications (namely that modification introduced by Act No. 131/1982 Sb.) trying to resume traditional civil law institutions which had been eliminated in the original wording of the Civil Code 1964. It was necessary to prepare and adopt a new Civil Code; but, because of a shortage of time, it was decided to incorporate only fundamental provisional amendments to the original Civil Code 1964 so that the basic systemic and material deformations of valid civil law legislation could be removed.

[32] One of the earliest changes made in the very beginning of the whole legal transformation process was abolishing such differentiation among the several forms of ownership. The Czech Constitution proclaimed the unity of property law, restored equality among different owners and introduced the principle of equal protection of property law, no matter who the owner is.

[33] "Person" was replaced with "participant or citizen"; "proper morals" were replaced by "the rules of socialist common life"; "obligation" by "service", "legal entity" by "organisation", etc.

To summarize the approach, the aim was to clear away ideological aspects and to restore the private law method of regulation in all spheres of personal and property relationships. The fundamental amendment (Act No. 509/1991 Sb.) struck the civil law corpus deeply since it changed its very conception by cancelling the International Trade Code and the Economic Code. Another principal change followed immediately with the adoption of the Commercial Code. During the application of both new laws it emerged that the legislative work on the new Commercial Code and the new amendment of the Civil Code were insufficiently coordinated to such an extent that a lot of duplications appeared.

In order to form a comprehensive view of the new contents incorporated into the Civil Code 1964, different parts of that Civil Code were subject to examination. The General Part (Part I), the part related to civil liability and unjust enrichment (Part VI) and the part concerning succession (Part VII) remained valid with only minor modifications. The other parts were essentially rebuilt, particularly Part II dealing with *iura in rem* (property rights) – especially the institution of ownership. Part III, dealing with so-called personal use of an apartment, other premises and land, Part IV, concerning "services", and Part V, regarding the rights and duties resulting from other legal acts, were completely repealed; instead of "services", the restored concept of "obligation" was re-introduced and incorporated into a new and more extensive Part VIII, which was rather unsystematically put at the very end of the amended Civil Code 1964. In the following period several amendments were adopted to modify the Civil Code 1964; but the fact remained obvious that even the amended Civil Code could be nothing more than merely a temporary solution.

5.5.3 Process of "Decodification"

The Czech Republic had experienced a significant process of decodification. The biggest inconvenience of Czech private law subsisted in the existence of so-called "complex regulations", which treated the institutions of private law independently of civil law. This meant there were many separate legal enactments outside the Civil Code 1964, which provided for different legal conceptions applicable to similar situations.

Traditionally, Czechoslovakia had, as a result of Soviet doctrinal influence, an autonomous Labour Code applicable to legal relationships arising from employment. After more than 40 years of its being applied, the Czech legislature decided to replace it by a new code. In 2006 the Czech Republic adopted a new Labour Code. Unfortunately, it appeared to be a product of rather bad legislative coordination. The new Labour Code 2006 completely denied any reasonable link with, or connection to, the Civil Code. It closed itself up into an impenetrable barrier and tried to regulate all obligations autonomously, with no regard to the Civil Code as the main enactment of private law. At first the Civil Code provisions might be used only exceptionally, i.e. if the Labour Code expressly provided so. The principle of pure delegation was chosen instead of the principle of general subsidiarity.

One of the main deplorable consequences was petrification of the undesirable duplicity of institutions relating to obligations. A group of deputies unsatisfied with the new Labour Code applied to the Constitutional Court of the Czech Republic for re-examination of certain provisions due to their alleged constitutional inconformity. After deliberation, the Constitutional Court quite openly declared that the principle of delegation which the Labour Code was based on was contradictory to the constitutionally guaranteed principle of legal certainty.[34] After that decision, the subsidiary application of the Civil Code in employment relationships became possible.

The Commercial Code codified obligations rather extensively, and, as a result, it regulated many institutions relating to obligations. Nevertheless, considering the purpose of private law re-codification, the drafters of the Civil Code 2012 opted for the monistic concept of the law of obligations as a reasonable and functional system. The monistic concept is based upon the principle of the uniform and integrated law of obligations, which is encompassed in the Civil Code and is used as a general legal regulation in the whole of private law.

5.6 The Civil Code and Business Law

5.6.1 Brief History and Current Legislation

Within the Czech system of law business law is considered to be a part of private law; as such it forms a subdivision of civil law. It should be noted that many rules of business law are of a public law nature (regulation of entrepreneurial activities and trade law, the Commercial Register, accountancy, insolvency, competition, etc.) and often create only a framework for application of private law. Fundamental changes to Czechoslovak business law came about after November 1989, when the democratic system was reinstated, changes were made to Czechoslovak legislation resulting from the transition of the society to political pluralism and a market economy, and the environment for private business was established. In a very short period of time, the Commercial Code, No. 513/1991 Sb., was prepared and passed; it was intended to replace, in particular, the former socialist Economic Code No. 109/1964 Sb., regulating relations between socialist organisations (i.e. enterprises), and the International Trade Code, No. 101/1963 Sb., oriented towards international trade relations. Within the re-codification of the private law process, the 1991 Commercial Code was repealed by the new Civil Code 2012 and partially replaced by the Business Corporations Act, with effect from 1 January 2014.

---

[34] See the Constitutional Court's Decision No. Pl. ÚS 83/06 of 12 March 2008 which touched directly, and in a significant manner, on the very conception of the new Labour Code.

The Commercial Code 1991 was broadly conceived; it regulated the status of entrepreneurs, commercial companies, business obligations and some other relations connected with business activities. Section 1 (2) of the Code was crucial for the determination of the sources of business law; it stipulated that legal relations falling within the scope of the Commercial Code were subject to the provisions of that Code. In case it proved impossible to resolve certain issues under that Code, they should be resolved in accordance with the provisions of civil law. As a result, the main source of business law was the Commercial Code. If a particular issue could not be resolved under the Code, civil law rules should be applied, in particular the Civil Code and some related acts of a civil law nature, such as Act No. 72/1994 Sb., on the ownership of flats, or Act No. 116/1990 Sb., on the lease and sublease of non-residential premises. Therefore the Civil Code was subsidiary to the Commercial Code. Where no civil law provision was applicable, trade usage could be applied. In the absence of usage, business relations should be resolved in conformity with the principles upon which the Commercial Code was based. It is obvious that such principles included the autonomy of will in contractual relations, the equality of parties to commercial transactions, the protection of a weaker party, etc.

The new Business Corporations Act, as is suggested by its name, has reduced its scope to the regulation of business entities; as a result, the issue of the relationship between the Act and the new Civil Code 2012 is essentially non-existent since the complex area of obligations has been incorporated directly into the new Civil Code.[35] Many other laws mentioned above were repealed by the new Civil Code.

5.6.2 The Content of the Business Corporations Act and Other Relevant Business Legislation

The new Business Corporations Act is applicable to business companies and cooperatives. It is composed of two parts: (1) Business Corporations (general provisions, unlimited company, limited partnership company, limited liability company, joint-stock company, cooperative), and (2) Common and Transitional Provisions. The remaining issues comprised in the 1991 Commercial Code were either included in the new Civil Code (commercial obligations in particular, but also commercial agency, business enterprise, proxy, etc.) or are regulated separately (e.g. the Czech register of companies, called the Commercial Register). The protection of economic competition has been, and will be a subject-matter of a special law (Act No. 143/2001 Sb., on the protection of competition), while unfair competition rules were included in the Civil Code 2012. The general regulation of persons in the Civil Code 2012 lays down some common principles related to business companies, originally comprised in the Commercial Code1991. The Business Corporations Act

[35] An exception is Sec. 3 of the new Act which stipulates that the Civil Code rules on associations are applicable to Business Corporations.

fully respects the sovereign position of the Civil Code 2012; the primary intention was to prevent any duplicity of the institutions of civil law and business law. The duplicity instituted by the former Civil Code and the Commercial Code represents a problem which Czech legal practice must face even today. The Business Corporations Act appears to be a modern codification of company law, which has incorporated relevant European Union law and reflects the general global trends in the regulation of business entities. Its principles closely follow those in the Civil Code 2012.

There are other laws governing various issues within business law, such as insurance (Insurance Act No. 277/2009 Sb.), insolvency (Insolvency Act No. 182/2006 Sb.), accountancy (Act No. 563/1991 Sb., on Accountancy), laws regulating securities (Act No. 189/2004 Sb., on Collective Investment, Act No. 256/2004 Sb. on Transactions in the Capital Market), etc. Other important laws concern specific types of company and other entities, such as state enterprises (Act. No. 77/1997 Sb., on a State Enterprise), transformation of companies (Transformation Act No. 125/2008 Sb.), as well as laws implementing European legislation, namely Act No. 627/2004 Sb., on the European Company, Act No. 360/2004 Sb., on the European Economic Interest Grouping, and Act No. 307/2006 Sb., on the European Cooperative Society.

This outline clearly suggests that the alteration of the legislative regulation of business law has been radical. Several special laws were repealed (e.g. the Insurance Contract Act, the Securities Act) and their substance incorporated in the Civil Code 2012. The unification of obligations and some other important issues of business law in one piece of legislation is a positive step forward; on the other hand, the rules for some specific practical types of contract, such as an exclusive sales contract, were not included in the Civil Code 2012. It should also be noted that the Civil Code 2012 did not identify other types of contracts which are quite frequent in practice, such as franchising, lease-purchase or factoring. The legal practice will have to adapt to this failure.

5.7 Consumer Law

5.7.1 Consumer Law and Consumer Contracts Included in the Civil Code

Consumer protection and the legal reflection of consumer law as such have been topical and important aspects of modern private law codification. Consumer law is perceived more and more as a relatively compact subdivision of private law. The question remains how national legislation should take this fact into consideration. Two principal approaches to consumer law have been employed within European legal systems. The first solution is to somehow integrate consumer protection into the existing civil codifications. This is the case of Germany, the Netherlands, Slovakia and the Czech Civil Code 1964, as well as the new one (2012). The Czech Republic, inspired by German BGB, opted for integration and implemented most European directives related to consumer protection directly into the Civil Code (with exceptions indicated below).[36]

However, the Czech legislature has not incorporated all aspects of consumer law into the Civil Code 2012. In addition, there is a special law implementing the public law aspects of consumer protection. The Civil Code 2012 in its Chapter 4, entitled "Provisions on contracts concluded with the consumer", deals with the following issues: unfair terms in consumer contracts, consumer protection in the case of contracts negotiated outside business premises, consumer protection in the case of distant contracts, the protection of acquirers regarding certain aspects of time-share contracts. Further issues concerning certain aspects of sale and warranty regarding consumer goods and package travel are regulated in another place of the Civil Code 2012, namely in its obligation part. All other aspects – especially consumer credit/loan matters, the general framework of activities in favour of consumers (consumer protection associations), false advertising matters, labelling and advertising matters of food products, misleading advertising, including comparative advertising, price indication matters in products offered to consumers, general safety of products and products which place health and safety of consumers in danger – are governed by a special law containing regulatory and administrative provisions so as to keep the Civil Code 2012 free from public law regulation.[37]

Another possible approach that can be found in many European systems (France, Spain, Italy, Belgium, Luxembourg, Austria, Finland, Latvia, Lithuania, etc.) is to pass a special law which would cover consumer law as a whole. Both private and public aspects of consumer protection are placed altogether in one regulatory act.

There is no general theory of consumer contracts in Czech jurisprudence. The Civil Code 2012 provides for the concept of a consumer contract in Section 1810. According to this provision a consumer contract may be a purchase contract, contract for work, or any other contract stipulated within the Civil Code provided that the contracting parties are the consumer, on the one hand, and the supplier (provider), on the other. Generally speaking, the consumer is a person acting, buying and using services for his/her own use; his/her conduct does not have any business character. Each person could be a consumer as well as an entrepreneur; the distinctive mark between the conduct of either one is primarily the aim and purpose of their legal acting.

---

[36] The Dutch model seems more sophisticated in this context, as it tries to incorporate European consumer protection directives continuously and rigorously into the Dutch Civil Code in such a way that it does not concentrate all issues in one place but always amends relevant articles and paragraphs.

[37] In particular: Act No. 634/1992 Sb., the Consumer Protection Act; Act No. 59/1998 Sb., the Product Liability Act; Act No. 321/2001 Sb., the Consumer Credit Act; Act No. 145/2010 Sb., the General Safety Product Act.

5.7.2 Relationship Between the Civil Code and Consumer Law

The Civil Code 2012 fulfils the role of general legislation, which is subsidiary to other special acts which may have an impact upon private law relationships. The predominant part of consumer law is an integral part of the Civil Code, so it is applied as the Civil Code itself. The other aspects of a public law nature mentioned above are governed by special legislation which is primarily applied if it concerns the determined situation, and the Civil Code 2012 is applied subsidiarily.

5.8 The Civil Code and Family Law

5.8.1 Historical Development

Family law is a specific part of private law. In jurisprudence across Europe and in Czech jurisprudence, it is treated as a relatively autonomous part of private law, no matter if enacted in a civil code, or in a separate code or act. From the historical perspective, it should be mentioned that family law was (and in Austria still is) a part of the Civil Code of 1811. The Family Act 1949 has been mentioned above.[38] This Act was replaced with the Family Act 1963, which came into force on 1 April 1964 (the same day as the Civil Code 1964 did).

It should be explained why the Family Act has not been referred to as a "Code" in Czech law. The issue is connected with the scope of family law. The scope of family law is usually defined by setting three types of mutual relationships: (a) between spouses, (b) between parents and children (and other relatives), (c) arising from foster care.[39] Another perspective, also maintained by Czech jurisprudence, suggests there are three other relationships distinguished within a family (and particularly between spouses): (a) relations of an exclusively personal nature, (b) relations of a solely property nature, (c) relations of a nature combining both types.

After 1948, when the reconstruction of law due to new political and economic circumstances started, family law was the first to be focused on. The reasons were ideological: relationships within the family have been stable and traditionally developed, so that part of law would not have to be subject to many changes. The objective of a newly prepared Family Act 1949 was to enact family law, which would be considered to be new socialist law, remaining stable in the future and requiring no

[38] It is interesting, that there was an intensive international cooperation between Czechoslovakia and Poland during the preparatory works. As an outcome, laws with quite identical wording were adopted in both countries. See Józef Piątowski St. (red.), *System prawa rodzinnego i opiekuńczego* (*The System of Family and Guardianship Law*). Część 1. Wrocław: Zakład Narodowy im. Ossolińskich – Wydawnictwo, 1985, p. 8.

[39] In a broad sense of this word, as every kind of substitute for family care.

amendments. On the other hand, property law (particularly the conception of ownership) was exposed to changes as the society was officially approaching socialism and subsequently communism. These ideas resulted in the decision that corresponding parts of the Civil Code of 1811 should be repealed and replaced with the new Family Act 1949. Such an approach was quite common in "people's democracy" states in Middle and Eastern Europe during the 1940s and 1950s. The Family Act 1949 governed marriage (including mutual property relationships of the husband and wife), divorce, mutual rights and duties of parents and children and tutorship.[40] Although this Act covered the whole scope of family law, it was not called a "Code". There was no provision for the relationship between the Family Act 1949 and the Civil Code 1950.[41] Despite the political situation, the Family Act 1949 was a real milestone in the development of Czechoslovak family law. Old family patterns were replaced with new ones: husband and wife were now taken as equal in their marriage,[42] the distinction between legitimate and illegitimate children was abolished, the only way to enter into marriage was before a state authority (no longer before the authority of a Church).

During the codification of private law in the 1960s, the first intention was to just amend the Family Act 1949. But in the end a new act was adopted. The content of the Family Act 1963 was quite identical when compared to its predecessor from 1949. The most important change was made to provisions for property relationships between spouses. They were shifted to the Civil Code 1964, and therefore not governed by the Family Act 1963. That approach resulted from the idea that all property relationships should be regulated by the Civil Code 1964. Bearing this in mind, it is no surprise that the new Family Act was not labelled a "Code" as an important issue – property – was missing. The second important change can be seen in the (re) establishing of the relationship between civil law and family law. Section 104 of the Family Act 1963 stipulated that the provisions of the Civil Code 1964 would apply unless something else was stipulated by the Family Act 1963. This means that the idea of the (total) isolation of family law as a separate branch of law was overcome and the supportive role of civil law and of the Civil Code 1964 (as a universal code) was admitted.

After several amendments of the Family Act 1963, before it was repealed by the Civil Code 2012, the content of this Act was as follows:

---

[40] Tutorship is understood here as an institution substituting for family care, where a tutor is put in the place of parents, as a person taking care for a child (but the tutor is not obliged to provide the care personally) and primarily to act as a legal representative of the child (instead of his or her parents). For details see Section 78 and subs. of the Family Act 1949.

[41] However, this was not surprising if we bear in mind that the Civil Code 1811 ought to be repealed in the next few months and the new Civil Code 1950 was not yet adopted by the time the Family Act 1949 was published.

[42] The husband and wife were considered equal in both their mutual relationship and in their common relationship towards their children. In other words, the ancient supremacy of father (*patria potestas*) was abolished.

Part One: Marriage.[43] Part Two: Relationships between parents and children (parental responsibility,[44] measures for upbringing, foster care,[45] determination of parenthood,[46] adoption, tutorship and curatorship[47]). Part Three: Maintenance duty. Part Four: Final provisions.

In conclusion, it can be stated that the only important issue missing was the arrangement for the property regime of spouses, which was included in the Civil Code 1964. Although Section 104 of the Family Act 1963 refers to the Civil Code 1964 with respect to matters not enacted by the Family Act 1963, the application of provisions of the Civil Code 1964 in issues generally regulated by the Family Act 1963 was really rare.[48]

5.8.2 Family Law in the Civil Code 2012

As has been mentioned, family law is enacted in the second part of the Civil Code 2012 (immediately after the general provisions). This should indicate the importance and significance of family law in the Civil Code 2012. Despite the fact that the Civil Code 2012 is generally inspired by the Civil Code 1811 and by civil codes enacted in Western Europe, the area of family law was inspired primarily by the Family Act 1963. Most provisions for family law in the Civil Code 2012 were taken from the Family Act 1963 (and adequately reformulated); more changes were made only in provisions for adoption and parental responsibility. This can be explained by the fact that family relationships cannot be subject to an "overnight revolution" in law, as they develop very slowly and relatively independently of the legislature's intents and wishes. Another reason for legal continuity in this area of law can be seen in that the Family Act 1963, and even the Family Act 1949, contained a

---

[43] Act No. 234/1992 Sb. was adopted to demonstrate the rejection of a totalitarian attitude to family law; spouses became free to decide whether they wish to enter into marriage before the authority of the state or before the authority of a Church.

[44] A set of legal rules and duties of parents concerning the proper upbringing of a child, his or her legal representation and administration of the child's property (Sec. 31 of Family Act 1963).

[45] Foster parents are obliged to take care of the child personally, but they are not legal representatives as tutors are.

[46] The mother is the woman, who gave birth to the child. Paternity is based on one of three legal presumptions.

[47] The institution of the tutor was explained above; the curator is established for a particular issue (e.g. for the representation of a child when dealing with rights or duties against his or her parents, for the administration of a child's property instead of the parents, etc.).

[48] For example, the institution of the determination of paternity by the common consent of the mother and the man stating he is the father of the child is generally regulated by the Family Act 1963. The provisions of the Civil Code 1964 could be used in a case when one of the consenting parents was affected by a mental disorder at the moment of articulating his or her consent. This situation would rarely occur in practice, as the representative of a registering authority will refuse to record the consent when finding the parent in such a mental condition.

concept of family law based on modern principles (equality of spouses in marriage, no distinction between legitimate and illegitimate children, substitute care of children, etc.). Having these reasons in mind, it is not surprising that there was no need for many changes in the Civil Code 2012 (or even discontinuity with the Family Act 1963).

The structure of this part in the Civil Code 2012 is similar to the structure of the Family Act. Title One contains provisions for marriage (creation, invalidity and non-existence, rights and duties between spouses, property issues – community property of spouses,[49] termination by death and divorce). Title Two enacts kinship and relationship in law (determination of parenthood, adoption, rights and duties between parents and children). Title Three governs tutorship, curatorship and foster care. Part Two of the Civil Code 2012 contains 320 provisions on family law in total.

In conclusion it can be stated that provisions regulating family law in the Civil Code 2012 are based on a deeply rooted concept of modern family law in the Czech Republic.

5.9 Reforming Civil Code – A New Czech Civil Code (2012)

Even though the main insufficiencies and defects were mitigated by the fundamental amendment in 1991, many imperfections and inconsistencies mentioned above persisted and were hardly to eradicate as they were spread all over the Civil Code 1964. Since 1991, the Civil Code 1964 was amended 30 times, but there was no deeper modification of its ideological basis, no rectification of its unsuitable and inappropriate conception. The first real attempt to proceed with re-codification was made very early – before 1993, at the very beginning of our social, economic and political transformation. That draft, as well as the second project in 1996, was not completed for various reasons, particularly political.[50]

However, the Czech Republic went on passionately discussing the third draft, proposed by two professors of law,[51] which finally became the new Civil Code 2012. The work on it started in 2000 and was submitted to expert and professional review. The reason for such a procedure was to subject the draft to a critical analysis and to obtain remarks and observations which might be finally incorporated into the Code. The academic and scientific circles were widely included into this debate. The Code

[49] As was mentioned above, this was not enacted in the Family Act 1963, but in the Civil Code 1964. In the Civil Code 2012 relevant provisions were moved from property rights into family law.

[50] The first draft of a new Civil Code existing for a very short time was introduced for discussion in 1992. The work on its articulated version ceased soon after the termination of the Czechoslovak Federation and the splitting of both republics into independent states. The second draft published in 1996 was based upon the conception of largely concentrated private law. With regard to governmental changes operating afterwards, there was no political will to support such a draft any longer.

[51] Prof. JUDr. Karel Eliáš, University of Western Bohemia in Pilsen, and Doc. JUDr. Michaela Zuklínová, Charles University in Prague.

itself is supplemented by two other laws, the Act on Private International Law, which regulates relations with foreign elements, and the Business Corporations Act.

The Civil Code 2012 tries to return civil law back into the European continental tradition and to make it conform to the European Civil Code standards. The basic aim is to wholly restore the idea of private and public law duality. It implies a definite and consequent turnover from the Marxist-Leninist concept of the legal system and its functions, whose relics were still resisting, and adopts a way oriented towards the idea of private law in the sense of the European intellectual legacy.

The primary inspiring source for the Civil Code 2012 was the Government draft of a Civil Code from the pre-war period.[52] That draft, originally published in 1937, was intended to modernize and revise the Austrian ABGB which was valid on the territory of Czechoslovakia until 1950. Obviously, such an inspiration, however important, had to be subject to substantial revision and critical evaluation, particularly due to its age. Finally, the authors of the Civil Code 2012 based their work upon three main intellectual resources: (1) a critical analysis of the development of private law valid and effective in our territory since the nineteenth century; (2) the principal national Civil Codes of European countries, particularly Austria, Switzerland, Germany, Italy, the Netherlands and Poland. The latest codifications in Québec and Russia were taken into account. French, Spanish, Belgian and Portuguese Civil Codes were also considered; and (3) international treaties and EU legislation. European soft law papers and drafts, such as the Principles of European Contract Law,[53] the Principles of European Tort Law,[54] the Common Frame of Reference,[55] Code européen des contrats[56] (prepared by the academic group led by Professor Gandolfi), etc., apparently served as inspiration.

---

[52] The so-called "First Czechoslovak Republic" was created in 1918 at the very end of the First World War after the disintegration of the former Austro-Hungarian Monarchy.

[53] The document, entitled the Principles of European Contract Law (PECL), was published by the Lando Commission established for contract law in 1995. The main aim of PECL has been to create the legal basis for any future European code of contract law; as such it served, to a certain extent, as an inspiration for the Draft Common Frame of Reference.

[54] The area of tort law is represented (in addition to non-contractual parts contained in the DCFR) by a more substantial document, namely the "Principles of European Tort Law" (PETL). These principles are valuable material in the field of tort "soft law" at two levels: first, they represent a typical picture of the European legal culture in tort law; second, the case-law of some European countries has determined that PETL serve as the reference basis for certain considerations in the reasoning of judgments. For more details on the role and significance of PETL for Czech tort law see Elischer, D.: *Pojetí škody, resp. újmy v aktuálních dokumentech evropského deliktního "soft law"* (*Conception of loss/harm in the recent documents on European tort "soft law"*), Právník, No. 4/2011, pp. 378–399.

[55] See Draft Common Frame of Reference (DCFR), prepared by the Study Group on a European Civil Code and the Research Group on EC Private Law (Acquis Group) and edited by Christian von Bar, Eric Clive and Hans Schulte-Nölke: http://ec.europa.eu/justice/contract/files/european-private-law_en.pdf

[56] The Academy of European Private Lawyers (Gandolfi Group) was formed by a public act in Pavia in 1992 with the intention of preparing the draft of a "European Contract Code". For more details see http://www.accademiagiusprivatistieuropei.it/

The main principles upon which the Civil Code 2012 is built may be expressed by the following triad: conventionalism, discontinuity, and integration. The crucial ambition of the Civil Code 2012 is to be conventional vis-à-vis the standard European legislation originating from Roman law, but, at the same time, to respect the legal thinking tradition of Central Europe. This point is relatively well accepted and widely shared in the Czech Republic. In this context, many legal institutions commonly known within the European legal family are introduced into the Civil Code 2012 (such as inheritance contract, privileged testament, assignment of contract,[57] purchase on trial,[58] etc.). The second point is much more controversial. The discontinuity might be considered as something inopportune, unwelcome and completely unacceptable. Such a negative opinion was emphasized by the Czech legal practice. Judges, lawyers, notaries, executors and other legal professionals expressed their concern regarding such a legal rupture and were trying to push their own proposals through in order to participate in the preparation of the draft. These concerns, expressed by part of the legal community, have accompanied the new Code along its whole legislative journey from its adoption to the date of effect.

Philosophically stated, the Civil Code 2012 seeks to achieve the ideals of Europeanism and humanism. The major axis of the whole instrument is a human being and his or her interests, which are predominantly individual in the private law sphere. It is the end of preferring any kind of collectivism and of giving a higher protection to collective interests, which approach seemed to be inappropriate for a standard private law codification.

According to this anthropological approach and from a systematic point of view, the first part of the Civil Code 2012 deals with the legal status of a person as an individual and with his or her personal rights. The second part focuses on the legal regulation of an individual's family and family law related questions; the third part concentrates on an individual's property during his or her life or after his or her death. The last part of the Code concerns the law of obligations, i.e. it contains legal enactment of an individual's legal relationships with others arising either from their contractual activity or from tort responsibility. The human being is in the centre of the lawmaker's view from the very beginning to the end of the Code.

Legal entities and their legal regulation are, naturally, included in the Civil Code 2012. The regulation of legal entities is relatively extensive and is conceived as general enactment applicable subsidiarily to all artificial legal persons in the Czech Republic.

In the context of discussions on the system of values and general legal principles which are supposed to be determinant for the Civil Code 2012, one of the key battles was fought over whether the principle of equality in legal relationships, or the

[57] For more details on the new institution of assignment of contract see Elischer, D: *Cese smlouvy jako nový institut českého soukromého práva, několik úvah k obecné úpravě postoupení smlouvy* (*Assignment of contract as a new institution of Czech private law, several remarks on the general provisions related to assignment of contract*). Aspi, Právní Fórum No 5/2007, pp. 162–172.

[58] See Elischer, D.: *Koupě na zkoušku v mezinárodním srovnání*: *Návrat do civilního korpusu aneb východiska a možnosti českého zákonodárce de lege ferenda* (*Purchase on trial in international comparison*: *Comeback to the Civil Code or the resources and the potential of the Czech legislature de lege ferenda*), Právní Fórum 6/2008, pp. 257–262.

principle of private autonomy, should be the leading principle of a new codification of private law. The drafters strongly believed that the determinant principle of civil law is the principle of private autonomy. They argued that there could hardly ever be equality between individuals and legal entities. The latter are created by individuals and serving their interests; positive law can, but need not, acknowledge them as holders of rights and duties.

In order to improve the legislative quality of succession law the drafters proposed entirely new legislation representing a real breaking through with respect to the provisions of the Civil Code 1964. The Civil Code 2012 includes over 230 sections concerning succession law, which is eight times as many as in the previous code. Naturally, the quantity is not a decisive element, but it at least shows the legislator's deeper interest. This domain was mostly inspired by legislation in France, Switzerland, Germany, Austria, Spain, Italy and the Netherlands; for example, the Civil Code 2012 introduces into Czech law the special institution of a succession agreement[59] or a privileged testament.[60]

What was seen as one of the most convincing arguments against the passage of the Civil Code 2012 was the enormous legal uncertainty which necessarily accompanies the adoption of such regulation. This uncertainty, resulting from different and varying interpretations, undoubtedly creates a great deal of controversy which can be solved only by courts until the disputed items are definitely clarified and uniformly interpreted by the Supreme Court and possibly commented on by legal scholars. It has constantly been pointed out that it may take even several decades for courts and the legal doctrine to study and to properly interpret thousands of new sections and provisions. During that time judicial decisions in the same cases would not be uniform, and therefore the consequences of civil proceedings would become unpredictable for all parties concerned. This particularly applies to all new concepts and restored institutions; however, the same problems may occur with respect to institutions subject to essential rewording and redefining by the legislature. For example, the issue of compensation for damage to health and satisfaction of immaterial aspects of harm to health would be significantly affected since the Civil Code 2012 has intentionally derogated from the existing standardization of non-pecuniary losses.

5.10 Current Importance of the Civil Code

The adoption of the Civil Code 2012 is a significant turning point in the development of private law in the Czech Republic. The last relics of the socialist conception of private law have been removed and replaced by the Code built upon a traditional understanding of private law in West European countries. However, the radical

---

[59] A succession contract as a bilateral legal act providing a possibility to establish a contractual relationship between the testator and any other person concerning the testator's property is regulated in Sections 1582 et seq. of the Civil Code 2012.

[60] See Sec. 1542 et seq. of the Civil Code 2012.

change would be, from the very beginning, highly demanding for both legal theory and practice. The task for theory would primarily be to elaborate on institutions not yet existing in Czech private law (or existing more than 60 years ago) and to make them comprehensible for a wider legal public. Legal practitioners would be required to change some of their modes of construction and mental patterns and procedures. The role of case law would substantially increase and the judgments of courts would be carefully evaluated and observed by the legal practice.

The role played by the Civil Code 2012 in the Czech Republic is apparent from the whole paper. To sum everything up and by way of conclusion, the Civil Code 2012 is the basic legislative instrument of Czech civil law as well as a universal source of private law in the Czech Republic.

Chapter 6
Codification of Private Law in Estonia

Irene Kull

Abstract Estonia as a state had a chance to develop its legal system for the first time only in the twentieth century. The civil law reform starting from 1991 was politically influenced by the resolution of Estonian Parliament from 1992, which stated that new laws should follow the laws and codes which were in force before 1940. In practice, this meant that legal acts from the first period of independence were to be studied and, if possible, followed. That decision was one of the main dominants in the choosing of the system and method of the codification and models for establishing Estonia's own civil law system. Estonian Civil Code consists of five separate laws which have been enacted at different times as separate laws but functioning as one codification. These five laws are the General Part of Civil Code Act, the Property Law Act, the Law of Obligations Act, the Law of Succession Act and the Family Law Act. As Estonian private law is based on the unitary concept of regulation of legal relations in the civil law field, there are no commercial or consumer codes. Estonian Constitution contains a detailed catalogue of fundamental rights and freedoms and is characterised as being more liberalistic and individual by nature in comparison to many other Western constitutions. Future of the codification of private law regimes in Europe may be put into the context of following problems: the need for a national private law codifications and choice between monistic and dualistic systems in implementation of EU consumer law. In conclusion Estonian private law system which was basically initiated with a blank slate, with no predetermined authorities, meant a unique opportunity to realise number of harmonisation ideas that are under the discussion today in Europe.

Keywords Estonia Civil Code • Recodification in former socialist countries • Private law codification • Civil code relations with other branches of law

---

This paper is written also as a part of the grant project GOIEO 9301.

I. Kull (✉)
Professor of Civil Law, University of Tartu, Tartu, Estonia
e-mail: irene.kull@ut.ee

J.C. Rivera (ed.), *The Scope and Structure of Civil Codes*, Ius Gentium: Comparative Perspectives on Law and Justice 32, DOI 10.1007/978-94-007-7942-6_6,

6.1 Introduction

Estonia gained its independence for the first time in 1918, in 1940 it was occupied by the Soviet Union and again in 1944 after the retreat of the German occupation forces. Estonia regained its independence in 1991. Only then the opportunity to codify private law emerged for Estonia. Codification of Estonian private law means firstly replacing soviet legal system with new legislation to establish private law system of an independent country after changing politico-economic order. Today, when the main reforms in different areas of law have already been finalised and creation of systematic bases of written law have been completed, the codification should concentrate on practical application of legal acts and impact of regulation. New areas have been defined where the legislation is yet to be harmonised and systematised. To understand Estonian private law system and special features of codification processes this paper will start from the historical development of private law regime in Estonia. In the following sections the general description of the Estonian private law system and content of civil code acts will be given. Further sections will be dedicated to the relationship between the civil code acts and the Constitution and to the future of the codification and Estonian private law.

6.2 History of Codification of Estonian Private Law System

6.2.1 Introduction

Estonia as a state had a chance to develop its legal system for the first time only in the twentieth century. Various regimes have attempted to create a uniform legislative system out of the existing one and it has been a continuous feature in the legal history of Estonia.[1] However, on the territory of Estonia there have only been two prior civil codes: Baltic Private Law Code from 1865 and Soviet Civil Code from 1965. Codification of private law starting from 1991 was completed in 2002 when all five laws as parts of the non-codified civil code were adapted and came into force.

[1] Marju Luts, "Integration as Reception: University of Tartu Faculty of Law Case in 19th Century," *Juridica International* 3 (1998): 130–141; Marju Luts-Sootak, "Die baltischen Privatrechte in den Händen der russischen Reichsjustiz," in *Rechtsprechung in Osteuropa. Studien zum 19. und frühen 20. Jahrhundert. (Rechtskulturen des modernen Osteuropa. Traditionen und Transfers)*, Studien zur europäischen Rechtsgeschichte. Veröffentlichungen des Max-Planck-Instituts für europäische Rechtsgeschichte (Frankfurt am Main: Vittorio Klostermann, 2012): 267–375; Harri Mikk, "Zur Reform des Zivilrechts in Estland," *Jahrbuch für Ostrecht* 42 (München, 2001): 31–52; Marju Luts-Sootak, "Die estnishe Privatrechtsreform zwishen den Vorbildern aus der Geschichte, aus Deutchland und aus der europäischen Zukunft," in *Deutch-Estnische Rechtsvergleichung und Europa*, eds. Sven I. Oksaar and Niels von Redecker, Studien des Instituts für Ostrecht München 50, (Frankfurt am Main: Peter Lang Europäischer Verlag der Wissenschaften, 2004), 51–68.

Civil law on the territory of modern Estonian Republic, previously part of the Baltic Provinces of the Russian Empire, was until 1865 regulated by many different legal acts. Friedrich Georg von Bunge being professor of provincial law of the University of Tartu from 1831 to 1842, drafted the first codification – Baltic Private Law Code (BPLC), part of which ("Est-, Liv- und Curlaendische Privatrecht") was in force on the territory of Estonia from 1 January 1865 to 1940. The Baltic Private Law Code appears to be by its content a bulk of legal rules based on the legal pluralism which was the main feature in western law at that time. His work did not contain general principles, but rather, was as casuistic and detailed collection of applicable law as possible.[2] This code was also a result of the first law reform of the second half of the nineteenth century on the territory of Estonia toward the modernisation of the law. Only then the basic features of the modern western legal culture and traditions started to develop and constitute as the basics of Estonian law to date.[3] BPLC was based on the pandect system, containing the general part, property law, family law, law of succession and law of obligations parts, and can be classified as a civil code of Germanic legal family.

The process of modernisation of civil law began during the first independency starting from 1920 and was nearly completed before the Soviet takeover in 1940. The draft Civil Code from 1940, preparations of which started already in 1920, was never formally enacted.[4] It was largely influenced by Germanic civil codes like German, Swiss and Austrian Civil Code[5] and followed the traditions of pandect civil codes.[6]

During the second legal reform carried out in the years 1940 and 1944–1945, the legal system based on private property and private autonomy was replaced by the soviet legal system based on the nationalisation and the collective and state owned property. The Civil Code of Russian Federation from 1922 was in force on the

[2] About the Baltic Private Law Code see Marju Luts, "Private Law of the Baltic Provinces as a Patriotic Act," *Juridica International* 5 (2000): 157–167.

[3] About the medieval past and influences of German private law on codification and development of Estonian modern private law statutes see Marju Luts-Sootak, "Die neue estnische Privatrechtskodifikation zwischen Geschichte und Zukunft von Europa," *Die Kodifikation und die Juristen, Rättshistoriska studier* 23 (Stockholm: The Olin Foundation for Legal History, 2008): 133–156.

[4] Dietrich A. Loeber, "Kontinuität im Zivilrecht nach Wiederherstellung staatlicher Unabhängigkeit – Zu den Zivilgesetzbüchern von Lettland (1937), Estland (1993) und Litauen (2000)," Aufbruch nach Europa: 75 Jahre Max-Planck-Institut für Privatrecht, ed. Jürgen Basedow (Tübingen: Mohr Siebeck, 2001), 943. See also Henn-Jüri Uibopuu, "Der "Svodzakonov" der Republic Estland – eine vergessene Kodifikation," in Sowjetsystem und Ostrecht (Berlin: Duncker & Humblot, 1985), 504–527.

[5] About the influence of Austrian Civil Code see Irene Kull, "Impact of the Austrian Civil Code 1811 on the Estonian Civil Law," in *200 Jahre ABGB-Ausstrahlungen. Die Bedeutung der Kodifikation für andere Staaten und andere Rechtskulturen*, eds. Michael Geistlinger, Rudolf Mosler and Johannes M. Rainer (Wien: Manzsche Verlags- und Universitätsbuchhandlung, 2012), 265–274.

[6] Priidu Pärna, "Legal Reform in Estonia," *International Journal of Legal Information* 33, Issue 2 (2005): 220.

territory of the Estonia till January 1965, when the Soviet Civil Code of Estonian Republic came into force. The legislative system imposed on the territory of the Estonian Soviet Socialist Republic was based on the general principles adopted by the central government and the possibility to develop its own legislative system was very limited.[7]

Soviet Civil Code was a mixture of legal systems by content, adopting rules from the French Civil Code but also from the German Civil Code. Soviet Civil Code consisted of the following parts: general part, law of ownership, law of obligations, intellectual property law, patent law, law of inheritance and international private law. There was no differentiation between private and public law in the Soviet legal system. Family law was regulated by a separate Marriage and Family Law Code (1970), labour law by Labour Law (1973) and land law by Land Law Code (1970). Socialist economy was based on a completely different concept of property and the legal relations emerging from it. State was the main owner of the land and the means of production, allocating the economic unities (state enterprises etc.) only for management, not for full use and disposal. Some forms of collective, cooperative and communal property were installed. Because of that property law, contract and company law played a very minor role in the economic relations. The principles of autonomy and other principles of free economy were not known. Estonian civil laws during the Soviet occupation were drafted and adopted with the strong influence of Soviet legal system and legal culture, which influenced legal thinking and understanding of law for a long time even after the regaining independence. Without legal science and legal literature in the Estonian language, the old system of legal education did not give any expertise in drafting legal acts in a new political and economic situation. Therefore the main actors in drafting new laws were very young lawyers who had had a possibility to study abroad for very short time at that time.

6.2.2 Codification of Private Law After Regaining Independence in 1991

After regaining independence in 20 August 1991 after 51 years of Soviet occupation, the drafting and establishment of all the necessary new laws became the primary task for an independent Estonia.[8] Civil law reforms and enactment of the different civil law statutes took place in the situation of political, economic and

[7] See Norbert Reich, "Law and Civil Justice in the New EU Countries," in *The Institutional Framework of European Private Law*, ed. Fabrizio Cafaggi (Oxford: Oxford University Press, 2006), 275.

[8] Paul Varul, "Creation of New Estonian Private Law," *European Review of Private Law* 16 (2008): 98; Martin Käerdi, "Die Neukodifikation des Privatrechts der Baltischen Staaten in vergleichender Sicht," in *Zivilrechtsreform im Baltikum*, ed. Helmut Heiss (Tübingen: Mohr Siebeck, 2006), 19–25.

social revolution.[9] Estonia had to take over western principles of ownership, legal personality and restricted autonomy after having lost these during the period of Soviet dominance. The main bases for new private law system was the Constitution passed in June 1992.[10]

The new laws can be divided into two basic categories – reform laws of the transitional period and permanent e.g. "regular" laws for further developments. Primary task – changing the ownership relations in the society was based on the one of the most important reform laws – Land Reform Act, adapted on 17 October 1991, followed by the Privatisation Act on 17th June 1993 and Agricultural Reform Ac. The second most important step was the legislation which establishes the basic principles of company law as a very important prerequisite to the privatization of land and state enterprises. Enterprise Act and Statute of Public Limited Company were adopted already in 1989, but the general system of companies was established by the Commercial Code adopted in 1995.[11]

Economic reforms were the most essential task for the transitional period at the beginning of the 1990s to develop modern society based on market economy. The economic situation was already deteriorating in Estonia in 1990 and 1991 and in 1999 Estonia experienced its worst year economically since it regained independence in 1991. However, Estonia joined the WTO in November 1999 and with assistance from the European Union, the World Bank and the Nordic Investment Bank, Estonia completed most of its preparations for the European Union membership by the end of 2002. The economic situation improved significantly after 2002 and made the entering into European Union from 1 May 2004 possible.

Taking into account the political situation and preparations for the future independency already at the end of 1990s, the drafting of the new private law system can be divided into the preparatory period 1988–1991 when the main goal was the preparation of laws necessary for reforms and creation of preconditions for new private law, the period of decisions and choices 1992–1993, when in the process of finding models for future legislation the Germanic family was chosen as the main source for drafting new laws and the period of implementation of earlier decisions and choices 1994–2002, during which the majority of private law legislation ("civil code" and other important legal acts in the field of private law) was drafted and came into force.[12]

[9] Norbert Reich, "Transformation of Contract Law and Civil Justice in the New EU Member Countries – The Example of the Baltic States, Hungary and Poland," *Penn State International Law Review* 3 (2005): 587–623.

[10] The Constitution of the Republic of Estonia, passed 28.06.1992, entry into force 03.07.1992. Available in English: http://www.legaltext.ee/et/andmebaas/tekst.asp?loc=text&dok=X0000K2&keel=en&pg=1&ptyyp=RT&tyyp=X&query=p%F5hiseadus

[11] Agricultural Reform Act (from 11 March 1992), Principles of Ownership Reform Act (from 13 June 1991), Enterprise Act (from 17 November 1989), Statute of Public Limited Company (from 22 November 1989), Commercial Code (from 15 February 1995). Texts of the legal acts are available in English: http://www.legaltext.ee

[12] Paul Varul, "Legal Policy Decisions and Choices in the Creation of New Private Law in Estonia," *Juridica International* 15 (2000): 105.

The civil law reform was politically influenced mainly by the resolution of Estonian Parliament from 1992, which stated that new laws should follow the laws and codes which were in force before 1940.[13] In practice, this meant that legal acts from the first period of independence were to be studied and, if possible, followed.[14] That decision was one of the main dominants in the choosing of the system and method of the codification and models for establishing Estonia's own civil law system. From one perspective, it was a clear and understandable choice to not use Soviet legislation (which was partly still in force at that time) as the basis for the new draft statutes, but in reality the draft Civil Code from 1940 was of no significance in the new legislative process.

Taking into account real possibilities and targets the decision was made in favour of step-by-step codification of civil law, starting with the most urgent subjects.[15] The extensive legal reform at the legislative level began with great intensity: in 9 years, all five parts of civil code – Property Law Act (1993), General Part of Civil Code Act (1994), Family Law Act (1995), Succession Law Act (1997) and Law of Obligations Act (2002) – were adapted.[16] For the court system, this period was the most difficult as practitioners were not supplied with commentaries, textbooks or other sources.[17] That period was as characterised as 'revolutionary fever' and Estonia as an experimental field in Europe or "Estonians experiment with themselves".[18]

Despite the historical justification of following Germanic legal traditions in the private law reforms, the impossibility of mere reintroduction of the old draft statutes from 1940s became evident. Different options were discussed and considered thoroughly, but it was concluded from the beginning that one legal family has to be chosen as a model for the entire private law system to avoid eclecticism, while examples and solutions from other legal families (and also model laws) should be considered in drafting the different subcomponents of legal system.[19] For a country with the aim of codification and modification of obsolete fundamental principles in the legal system, the rapid legal development and re-codification of private law in Eastern and also in Western Europe played an important role in searching for new

---

[13] Resolution of the Riigikogu (Estonian Parliament) concerning the continuity of legislation. Riigi Teataja (State Gazette) 1992, 52, 651 (in Estonian).

[14] Irene Kull, "Reform of Contract Law in Estonia: Influences of Harmonisation of European Private Law," *Juridica International* 14 (2008): 122.

[15] See Priidu Pärna, "The Law of Property Act – Cornerstone of the Civil Law Reform," *Juridica International* 6 (2001): 89–101.

[16] Today, three laws have been redrafted and new versions have been adopted: General Part of Civil Code Act, Family Law Act and Succession Law Act. See more in Sect. 6.3.2.

[17] The first commentary on the Law of Obligations Act was published only in 2006. Paul Varul et al., Võlaõigusseadus. I, Üldosa: kommenteeritud väljaanne (Law of Obligations Act. I, General Part: Commented edition) (Tallinn: Juura, 2006), in Estonian. Following commented editions of the Law of Obligations Act were published in 2007 (II) and in 2009 (III).

[18] Marju Luts, "The certainty/stronghold of law, the world of yesterday and today's weather," speech on the celebration of 90 years of the Supreme Court of Estonia, 14.01.2010. See: http://www.riigikohus.ee/vfs/927/Marju_Luts-Sootak_ENG.pdf

[19] Martin Käerdi, "Estonia and the new civil law," in *Regional Private Laws & Codification in Europe*, eds. Hector MacQueen et al. (Cambridge: Cambridge University Press, 2003), 250.

legislative models and the best solutions. Decisions made by politicians and persons responsible for the drafting process were influenced by overall developments in European countries, requirements provided to the national law by the European Union legislation and also the idea of the European Civil Code influenced.[20]

In conclusion, main sources for drafting Estonian "civil code" acts were the German Civil Code, Swiss Code of Obligations, Civil Code of Netherland and Civil Code of Austria. In addition, European model laws (Principle of European Contract Law and UNIDROIT Principles of International Commercial Contracts[21]) and international conventions like Vienna United Nations Convention on Contracts for the International Sale of Goods from 1980[22] and others were widely followed.[23] However, each and every part of the Estonian "civil code" was drafted under the influence of different models.

6.3 Status of Codification

6.3.1 General Characteristics of Estonian Private Law System

K. Zweigert and H. Kötz divided all legal systems into legal families on the bases of historical background and development of the legal system, its predominant and characteristic mode of legal thinking, distinctive institutions, the kind of legal sources it acknowledges and the way it handles them and its ideology.[24] Taking Germanic legal family as the basis for the Estonian private law system does not imply the copying of German law, but means more guidance and bases for the legal regulation. However, it is interesting to see that the mode of thinking of Estonian lawyers in 1992 was closer to the Romanistic legal family, while historical background influenced the choice toward the Germanic system. Today the style of Estonian lawyers is more abstract and based on general principles of private law.

Every legal system is characterised by certain specific legal institutions, whereas their existence is dependent on each other. An important choice that triggered many

---

[20] See Irene Kull, "Effect of Harmonisation of European Civil Law on Development of Estonian Law of Obligations," *Juridica International* 3 (1998): 98–102.

[21] Part I of the Principles of European Contract Law (PECL) was published in 1995 and available during the preparation of drafts of Law of Obligations and a new General Part of Civil Code Acts. Revised version from 2000, Parts II and III were published in 2003 and had no influence to the drafting process. UNIDROIT Principles of International Commercial Contracts (UPICC) were published in 1994 and were widely used in preparation of the draft of General Part of Civil Code Act and Law of Obligations Act.

[22] Estonia became a member of the United Nations Convention on Contracts for the International Sale of Goods (CISG) on 20th September 1993.

[23] See Villu Kõve, "Applicable Law in the Light of Modern Law of Obligations and Bases for the Preparation of the Law of Obligations Act," *Juridica International* 6 (2001): 36.

[24] Konrad Zweigert and Hein Kötz, An Introduction to Comparative Law, (Oxford, New York: Clarendon Press, 1998), 67–72.

of the following preferences was the selection of a so-called strong land register maintained by courts where all real rights concerning real estate are recorded. A strong land register requires the application of the abstraction principle (*Abstraktionsprinzip*), by which the voidness of an obligation contract does not in itself render a disposal contract or real right contract void. A strong land register in turn should ensure legal certainty and contribute to economic development and stability. The application of the abstraction principle to real property in turn caused it to be applied to movable property and claims, which attributes our private law an important characteristic of the Germanic family of law. The choice of the abstraction principle as an important principle of private law caused the establishment of the unfair enrichment institute as it exists in Germany. In Estonia, an entry in the land register has been accorded as negative disclosure effect (Art. 561 para 2 of the LPA), as well as positive disclosure effect (Art. 561 para. 1 of the LPA) which mean that Estonia belongs to an intermediate group of countries that allow the owner to reclaim a thing from a possessor in good faith if it was removed from the owner's possession against said owner's will.[25] However, Estonian property law and related provisions in the Constitution protect the market-economy grounds of society at times more emphatically than do its Western European counterparts and raises theoretical discussions about the constitutionality of the regulation of good faith acquisition of ownership.[26]

Legal sources of Estonian private law are laws and customs (Art. 1 para. 2 of the GPCCA). The concept of "law" has to be interpreted narrowly meaning that sources of law are only legal acts adopted by the Estonian Parliament. Constitution as the most important legal act in the hierarchy of legal acts cannot be applied directly in private law matters despite the opposite practice in the first years of independency. Court decisions do not have functions of precedent which means that courts shall not follow the decisions of higher courts (but in fact they often follow), still, court practice, particularly judgements of the Supreme Court play an important role in developing law and filling gaps. Although the main emphasis remains on statutory law, it can still be said that the legal practice of the highest court does play an important role as the source of Estonian law.

GPCCA or the 'private-law constitution' of the Estonian private law system provides a whole range of rules for understanding law, providing in addition to the definition of sources of law also rules on interpretation of acts (Art. 3 of the GPCCA) and meaning of principle of analogy (Art. 4 of the GPCCA). However, provisions consisting of interpretation canons in the GPCCA do not cover all elements in the 'catalogue' of classical interpretation methods. As Estonia is a member of the EU, the courts are also under the obligation to interpret and adapt the law in conformity with the basic principles and court practice of EU.

Finally, taking into account the political, social and economic situation existing during the adoption of the "civil code" acts, the impact of these circumstances to the content and system of legislation is evident. Firstly, the legal acts contain numerous

[25] In general this group includes Germany, Austria, France, and Switzerland.

[26] About the constitutional problems and discussions in Estonian legal literature see Priit Kama, "Evaluation of the Constitutionality of Good-Faith Acquisition," *Juridica International* 19 (2012): 23–31.

legal definitions. The attempt to formulate legal terms becomes apparent in all areas of law, not only in private law. Secondly, Estonian legislation stands out by the detailed and didactic nature of regulation. To a certain extent it is caused by the pursuit of change of the transitional society and lack of experience. Thirdly, traditions in jurisprudence and practice are not yet mature, but evolving rapidly. Estonian Supreme Court practice serves much of what belongs to the tradition of legal dogmatic elsewhere.

Today the legal acts forming the Estonian "civil code" are functioning as a unitary codification without the need to incorporate new laws or to decodify the already existing legal acts. The reason for the relative success of Estonia since the start of the transitional period beside the proximity of Nordic markets, location between Eastern and Western Europe, competitive cost structure and highly skilled labour force was certainly the modern legislation. Today the most important developments influencing the entire process of formation[27] of Estonian private law system were and still are based on the new possibilities of digital technology.

6.3.2 The Estonian "Civil Code"

Estonian civil code consists of five separate laws which have been enacted at different times as separate laws but functioning as one codification. These five laws are the General Part of Civil Code Act,[28] the Property Law Act,[29] the Law of Obligations Act,[30] the Law of Succession Act[31] and the Family Law Act.[32] Here the International Private Law Act[33] has to be mentioned also as a part of private law system.[34]

---

[27] About the legislative policy of the Estonian government see Guidelines for Development of Legislative Policy until 2018, Annex to Resolution to Riigikogu, available in English: http://www.just.ee/orb.aw/class=file/action=preview/id=55852/GuidlinesforDevelopmentofLegislativePolicyuntil2018.pdf

[28] General Part of Civil Code Act (*tsiviilseadustiku üldosa seadus*) entered into force in 01.01.1994, revised version of the Act was passed 27.03.2002, entered into force 01.07.2002. Available in English: https://www.riigiteataja.ee/tutvustus.html?m=3

[29] Property Law Act (*asjaõigusseadus*), adapted on 09.06.1993, entered into force in 01.12.1993. Available in English: https://www.riigiteataja.ee/tutvustus.html?m=3

[30] Law of Obligations Act (*võlaõigusseadus*), entered into force in 1.07.2002. Available in English: https://www.riigiteataja.ee/tutvustus.html?m=3

[31] Law of Succession Act (*pärimisseadus*), entered into force 01.01.1997, new law was entered into force in 01.01.2009. Available in English: https://www.riigiteataja.ee/tutvustus.html?m=3

[32] Family Law Act (*perekonnaseadus*), entered into force in 1.01.1995; new law was entered into force in 1.07.2010. Available in English: https://www.riigiteataja.ee/tutvustus.html?m=3

[33] Private International Law Act (rahvusvahelise eraõiguse seadus), passed 27 March 2002, entered into force 1 July 2002. Available in English: https://www.riigiteataja.ee/tutvustus.html?m=3

[34] In the field of property law the most important legal acts are Land Register Act (passed 01.12.1993), Restrictions on Acquisition of Immovables Act (passed 12.02.2003), Immovables Expropriation Act (passed 12.02.2003), Commercial Pledges Act (passed 01.01.1997), Apartment Ownership Act (passed 01.07.2001), Law of Maritime Property Act (passed 1.07.1998). In the field of law of obligations Merchant Shipping Act (passed 1.10.2002) and Debt Restructuring Law (passed 17.11.2010). Available in English: https://www.riigiteataja.ee/tutvustus.html?m=3

As Estonian private law is based on the unitary concept of regulation of legal relations in the civil law field, there are no commercial or consumer codes. Legal act called Commercial Code[35] (1995) does not contain rules on transactions but only rules on different kind of commercial corporations.[36] The Commercial Code is functioning only together with other parts of "civil code" being subject to principles of foundation, rules on internal relations between the organs and bodies of the legal person, principles on management, representation and transactions provided for in GPCCA and rules on transactions provided for in the LOA.

General Part of Civil Code Act (GPCCA) was adopted in 1994 and replaced by a new version of the law from 2002. GPCCA can be described as a legal act covering the rules belonging to the general parts of typical pandect civil codes. The law consist of rules about the general principles of civil law, persons, things, transactions, representation, conditions, dates and terms, execution of rights and prescription. The GPCCA follows mainly the main doctrines borrowed from German law and Swiss Law. Some concepts like mistake and fraud are drafted on the bases of rules from UNIDROIT Principles of International Commercial Contracts and Principles of European Contract Law.

Property Law Act (PLA) is based mainly on the main concepts and provisions of German Civil Code. The Property Law Act from 1993 introduced the German system of transfer based in a real agreement and delivery of possession. All property rights based on the principle of *numerus clausus*.[37] There is a unitary concept of ownership which means that various entitlements arising from the right of ownership pass to the transferee at one moment in time. The system of transfer of ownership is based on the delivery of the object. The real agreement is separated from the underlying obligation (Art. 6 of the GPCCA). The transfer of ownership is abstract, the validity of the transfer is not contingent upon the existence of a valid causa from which the obligation to transfer the ownership arises.[38] Property Law Act provides rules on possession, movable and immovable property ownership, restrictions on immovable property ownership, servitudes (among others usufruct), real encumbrances, right of superficies, right of pre-emption, pledge (possessory, registered security over movables, pledge of rights, mortgage) and rules on land register.

Law of Obligations Act (LOA) consists of a general part dealing with problems common to all obligations, consumer contracts, conclusion of contracts, performance of contracts, breach and remedies, damages, termination, guarantee and suretyship, rules on standard terms. The special part of the law consists of rules addressing various types of contracts, the law of extra-contractual relations like

---

[35] Commercial Code (äriseadustik), passed 15.02.1995, entry into force 01.09.1995. Available in English: https://www.riigiteataja.ee/tutvustus.html?m=3

[36] See Andres Vutt, "Harmonisation of Estonian Company Law: Pre-conditions in Existing Law," *Juridica International* 2 (1997): 100–102.

[37] Kaupo Paal, "The numerus clausus Principle and the Type Restriction – Influence and Expression of These Principles. Demonstrated in the Area of Common Ownership and Servitudes," *Juridica International* 19 (2012): 32–39.

[38] Kama, "Evaluation of the Constitutionality of Good-Faith Acquisition," 23–31.

delicts, unjustified enrichment, actions taken without authority and public promises to pay. In the special part modern contracts are also regulated such as leasing, franchising and factoring, contracts of settlement, brokerage, agency, and insurance, as well as contracts for medical services, transportation, electronic payment instrument, etc. The preparation of the draft of Law of Obligations Act was based on three civil codes: the German BGB (taking into consideration the reform proposals made by the Commission for the Revision of the Law of Obligations, BGB-KE),[39] the Swiss Law of Obligations[40] and the Dutch Civil Code.[41] These legal acts were chosen because they were already being used as the foundation for the reform of other legal acts in private law, and because these were the closest to Estonian legal system and traditions. Besides this, the German Commercial Code and Insurance Contract Act played important roles, as well as other German laws regulating issues surrounding the law of obligations. Other models examined in the course of drafting include the Italian Civil Code, the new Russian Civil Code (1995), legal acts of the American State of Louisiana, the Canadian province of Quebec, the Scandinavian countries (Sweden, Finland and Denmark, especially concerning contracts for the sale of goods and compensation for damage), the Czech Commercial Code and the Japanese Civil Code.[42] All these sources were studied and used mainly on the bases of comparison of rules, but also by taking into account contextual aspects of legal regulation.

Family Law Act (FLA) from 1995 was rewritten and adopted as a new law in 2010. Family Law Act is based on German Civil Code and on the principle that a marriage is contracted between a man and a woman. The act consist of rules on invalidity of marriage, matrimonial cohabitation and rights and obligations of spouses, proprietary relations of spouses based on the general joint ownership and freedom to choose between types of proprietary systems provided by law, termination of marriage, rights and obligations arising from blood relationship, obligation to provide maintenance arising from filiation, legal relationship between parents and children, custody over person, custody and guardianship. The past 15 years brought radical changes in the rights of the spouses and children, among which the right to regulate the proprietary relationship changed the most. Today the freedom of contract of spouses is limited to the right to choose from among three matrimonial property regimes stipulated by law. Despite the many positive developments in regulation of proprietary relations, the new Family Law Act has been heavily criticised because of lack of coherency and unclear basic principles.[43] The main topic of the discussions

---

[39] Abschlussbericht der Kommission zur Überarbeitung des Schuldrechts, 1992.

[40] Bundesgesetz vom 30. März 1911 betreffend die Ergänzung des Schweizerischen Zivilgesetzbuches (Fünfter Teil: Obligationenrecht).

[41] Burgerlijk Wetboek (New Dutch Civil Code), reformed in 1992.

[42] See Kõve, "Applicable Law in the Light of Modern Law of Obligations and Bases for the Preparation of the Law of Obligations Act," 36.

[43] Liis Hallik, "Regulation of Proprietary Relations between Spouses in the New Family Law Act: Toward Better Regulation by Means of Private Autonomy?," *Juridica International* 17 (2010): 161–166.

today is mainly the scope of the obligations of the state in guaranteeing solidarity between the spouses and ensuring protection for the more vulnerable spouse.

First version of Succession Law Act (SLA) from 1997 was drafted mainly under the influence of the draft Civil Code from 1940 and was not entirely free of the standpoints of Soviet succession law. The drafters of law took the position that the law of succession, like the law of property, should remain relatively static.[44] For example, the choice was made in favour of the acceptance system as it was described as historically more inherent in Estonia – already BPLC was based on that system, draft Civil Code from 1940 intended to use it and such was the regulation in the soviet civil code.[45] In the second version of the Succession Law Act from 2009 the system of inheritance was changed to the renunciation system, also functions of the executor of the will, rules on transfer of rights and obligations of bequeather and legal consequences of inventory of the estate and obligations related to the estate were specified and amended to provide legal security.[46] Today the Succession Law Act provides rules on will, succession contract, subsequent successor, legacy, rules on testamentary obligations, reciprocal will of spouses, compulsory portion, succession process and succession register.

6.3.3 Labour Law

After restoration of independence, the drafting of new labour laws began in order to replace the corresponding parts of the soviet Labour Code and to elaborate modern labour law which is in accordance with European standards and principles. In 1996, most of the essential labour legislation was adopted and at that stage there was an idea to prepare uniform labour code.[47] For a long time, labour law was predominantly public law, the state determined all the compulsory terms of employment and relations between the employee and employer were based on the order or directive by which a person was hired.[48]

After 1992 when the Employment Contracts Act was adopted, the employment contract based on the free will of two parties and it became the primary bases of

[44] The law of succession contained in the 1940 draft Civil Code was largely influenced by the German Civil Code, also by the Swiss, Austrian and Italian Civil Codes. A great deal was also borrowed from the Baltic Private Law Code (BPLC). See Urve Liin, "Laws of Succession in Europe and Estonia: How We Got to Where We Are and Where We Should Be Heading," *Juridica International* 6 (2001): 114–124.

[45] Urve Liin, "On Reform of Estonian Succession Law," *Juridica International* 3 (1998): 105–109.

[46] About the succession law reforms see Paul Varul and Urve Liin, "Two Reforms of the Estonian Law of Succession," in *Private law: past, present and future. Liber Amicorum Valentinas Mikelenas*, ed. V. Mizaras, (Vilnius: Justitia, 2008), 301–310.

[47] See Gaabriel Tavits, "Scope of Application of Estonian Labour Legislation," *Juridica International* 1 (1996): 114–125.

[48] Labour law was dominantly public law already during the first independency period 1918–1940.

employment relationships. The Public Service Act entered into force on 1 January 1996 and it stood for the continuous tendency of Estonian labour law to move towards private law. In addition, Estonia re-associated with the ILO in 1992 which broadened its activities in the sphere of international labour law and improved Estonian labour legislation in the light of international standards. In the years 1992 to 1996, Estonia ratified seven ILO Conventions which concern protection of employees' fundamental rights.[49] At that time, the main discussion in the society was about the options to adopt uniform Labour Code or regulate labour contracts by the law of obligations acts and other labour law issues by separate Acts.[50]

Discussions about the nature of labour law and its position in the legal system were on-going debate for many years.[51] The main fear was that the application of civil law principles to labour relations will bring uncertainty and weaken the protection of the interests of the employees. Private law was in the beginning of this century understood as total freedom of contract without any restrictions.[52]

Today one may say that employment contracts are bound to the general principles under law of obligations even if they are technically outside of the Law of Obligations Act.[53] Provisions concerning the protection of employees are e.g. working time and rest period, holiday or regulating the status of an employee in a work relationship as a whole which belong to the public law provisions. The main legislative acts governing the legal aspect of individual employment relationships are the Employment Contracts Act[54] and Collective Agreements Act.[55]

In 2010 labour law modernisation was carried out to bring greater flexibility to the labour market. There was also a need to revise the principles of payment of unemployment benefits, unemployment insurance compensation, expansion of the range of people eligible for benefits, and establishment of schemes facilitating access to lifelong learning. There are no long traditions of negotiating collective employment agreements at the level of the enterprises which mean that mandatory legal regulation plays bigger role in comparison to other European countries. In the nearest future there are no plans to codify labour law into one legislative act.

---

[49] See Merle Muda, "Improving Estonian Labour Legislation on Integration with Europe," *Juridica International* 1 (1996): 109–114.

[50] Merle Muda, "Application of International Labour Standards in the Regulation of Employment Relationships in Estonia," *Juridica International* 2 (1997): 112–118; Gaabriel Tavits, "The Nature and Formation of Labour Law," *Juridica International*, 2 (1997): 103–111.

[51] About the codification of labour law see Gaabriel Tavits, "The Position of Labour Law in the Private Law System. The Past, Present and Future of Estonian Labour Law," *Juridica International* 5 (2000): 124–134.

[52] Gaabriel Tavits, "Why Do We Fear Civil Law in Labour Law?" *Juridica International* 6 (2001): 142–151.

[53] Article 1 paragraph 1 of the LOA provides that the provisions of the General Part of this Act apply to all contracts, including employment contracts. See also Gaabriel Tavits, "Indispensability of the Law of Obligations in Employment Relationships: Problems in Application of the Law of Obligations to Employment Relationships in Estonia," *Juridica International* 10 (2005): 71–78.

[54] Employment Contracts Act, passed on 17 December 2008, entry into force 1 July 2009. Available in English: https://www.riigiteataja.ee/tutvustus.html?m=3

[55] Collective Agreement Act, passed on 14 April 1993, entry into force 16 May1993. Available in English: https://www.riigiteataja.ee/tutvustus.html?m=3

6.4 Consumer Law

Political and legal link to the European *acquis* by Europe Agreement from 1995 influenced significantly the process of drafting of consumer law. The most difficult task was the implementation of EU consumer law into the legal acts of "civil code". From the very beginning, the drafters attempted to not merely copy the rules of the EU literally, but to incorporate them into the rest of the system and creatively harmonise the directives in order to avoid possible conflicts upon the application of Estonian national law. Estonia decided to include all EU directives into the acts of civil code. That decision has certainly had positive consequences in many ways.

Firstly, it allows us to build up a system of private law based on the same general principles, terminology and methods. Secondly, the rules transferred from consumer law directives and other *acquis* remained *lex specialis* even if some of consumer law rules were made part of the general contract law.

Today in Estonia the rights of consumers are regulated in detail by ordinary legislation. Consumer law in Estonia consists of a variety of legal rules, which are concentrated for the most part in two statutes: Consumer Protection Act[56] and the Law of Obligations Act. The latter consists of regulations pertaining to various types of consumer contracts. Section 3 of the Consumer Protection Act enumerates six fundamental consumer rights: the right to obtain goods and services which meet the requirements and are harmless; the right to the protection of consumer's health and safety; the right to appropriate information; the right to claim damages; the right to advice and assistance; and the right to be heard. The Consumer Protection Act consists of mainly public law rules and refers to the Law of Obligations Act in questions concerning private law matters like transactions or civil law remedies. It is distinctive of the Estonian private law system that the full set of remedies is gathered together in the general part of the LOA.[57]

Consumer protection in Estonia operates appropriately, and protection at a higher level is not actualised.[58] Estonia has fulfilled its duty of high-level protection of consumers by enacting specific consumer laws (which are strongly influenced by EU law) and, when necessary, modifying them over the course of time. The conformity of the consumer protection legislation with the Constitution is ensured by Article 139 of the Constitution, which states that the Chancellor of Justice shall review the legislation of the legislative and executive powers and of local governments for conformance with the Constitution.

---

[56] Consumer Protection Act, passed 11.02.2004, entry into force 15.04.2004, partially 01.05.2004, consolidated act – entry into force 12.12.2007. Available in English: https://www.riigiteataja.ee/tutvustus.html?m=3

[57] See Margus Kingisepp, "The European Consumer Sales Directive – the Impact on Estonian Law," *Juridica International* 14 (2008): 219–227.

[58] See Margus Kingisepp, "The Constitutional Approach to Basic Consumer Rights," *Juridica International* 19 (2012): 49–58.

6.5 Private International Law and Relationship Between the Civil Code Acts and Treaties

In order to ascertain the domestic validity of treaties, a rule of recognition can be found in the Constitution of Estonia. Article 3 paragraph 1 of the Constitution provides that generally recognised principles and rules of international law are an inseparable part of the Estonian legal system and Article 123 paragraph 2 of the Constitution explains that if laws or other legislation of Estonia are in conflict with international treaties ratified by the Parliament, the rules of the international treaty shall apply. Articles 15 and 152 of the Constitution enable the courts not to apply or appeal any law or other legislation that is in conflict with the Constitution. The legislation does not refer to the opportunity of courts to refuse to apply or repeal any domestic legal act due to its conflict with a rule of international law. Nevertheless, the Constitutional Review Chamber of the Supreme Court has detected conflicts between domestic legislation and treaties binding on Estonia, but not all references to the treaties (or any other rules of international law) in the judgements have carried merely the meaning of *obiter dictum*. Supreme Court examines the correctness of the interpretation of substantive law. Consequently, on the basis of the wording of Article 123 paragraph 2 of the Constitution and the enforcement and implementation practice of treaties, we may claim that Estonia's approach to treaties (at least those enforced by the Parliament) is monist.

The enforcement laws of treaties also serve as the incorporation acts thereof, as a result of and by virtue of the rule of recognition found in Article 123 paragraph 2 of the Constitution. Constitution refers to the general principles and rules of international law which are, according to that provision, an inseparable part of the Estonian legal system. Treaties binding on Estonia, generally recognised rules of international customary law, general principles of international law can be used in interpretation of Estonian laws and they are all valid as a part of the Estonian domestic law.

In the situations where the provisions of Estonian domestic law conflict with the provisions found in the international treaties ratified by the Parliament or with the general principles of international law, the latter should be applied (as provided by the constitution itself). This issue has not been raised (and probably will not rise) with regard to the substantive private law provisions since Estonia has not concluded many international treaties harmonizing substantive private law (with the exception of CISG and CMR[59]) and since the domestic rules are usually drafted in the light of the international treaties Estonia has ratified (for example CISG provisions were taken as an example when drafting LOA provisions on offer-acceptance and legal remedies). However, there are some treaties on private international law and international civil procedure (namely – the bilateral and trilateral treaties on legal aid concluded with the neighbouring states of Estonia at the beginning of the regained independence), which differ considerably from the domestic Private International

[59] Convention on the Contract for the International Carriage of Goods by Road. 19 May 1956.

Law Act and rules on civil procedure. It was mentioned in the literature that these treaties do not provide for renvoi as does the Estonian Private International Law Act. Taking into account the principle of primacy of the international treaties over the domestic law acts, the courts cannot apply Private International Law or Code of Civil Procedure rules when the legal aid treaties would otherwise be applicable, regardless of the problems that the lack of such provisions in the legal aid treaties may pose for the Estonian political order (due to the lack of public policy exception in the legal aid treaties) or for the need to determine the law most closely connected with the dispute (due to the lack of any provision of renvoi in these treaties).

6.6 Relationship Between the Civil Code Acts and the Constitution

Estonian Constitution contains a detailed catalogue of fundamental rights and freedoms and is characterised as being more liberalistic and individual by nature in comparison to many other Western constitutions.[60] Constitution should be applied as source for legal acts and application of general principles. In private law, a court has to take into account the rules of private law, the intrinsic logic and purpose of the provisions and the underlying system of values, and on this basis weigh the need to protect the various interests under the specific circumstances of the case.[61]

Fundamental rights are not directly applicable in private law, especially in contract law, where private law itself contains the principles corresponding to the purposes and substance of these rights. At the same time courts have a right to declare the legislation of general application to be in conflict with the Constitution and to be revised by the chamber of constitutional review of the Supreme Court. Principles of Estonian private law were largely adopted from German private law that rests on the ideas of social state and protection of the weaker party. Today the principles of liberal market economy seem to be sometimes more influential in comparison to the ideas of social state. Court decisions demonstrate the effect of principles of private autonomy and freedom of contract rather than apply arguments of social justice.[62] The catalogue of fundamental rights that follows not only the principle of the freedom of contract, but also the principle of protecting the weaker party, and can be

---

[60] Katrin Saaremäel-Stoilov, "Liberal Communitarian Interpretation of Social and Equality Rights: A Balanced Approach?," *Juridica International* 11, (2006): 90.

[61] Irene Kull, "Principle of Good Faith and Constitutional Values in Contract Law," *Juridica International* 6 (2002): 142–149; Mari Ann Simovart, "The Standard of Reasonableness in the Estonian Law of Obligations," in *Development of Estonian Contract and Company Law in the Context of the Harmonized EU Law I*, ed. Irene Kull (Tartu: Tartu Ülikooli Kirjastus, 2007), 65–86.

[62] Irene Kull, "Unfair Contracts of Suretyship – a Question about the Horizontal Effect of Fundamental Rights or about the Application of Contract Law Principles," *Juridica International* 12 (2007): 36–45.

exercised via the indirect horizontal effect with the help of private law principles (principles of good faith and fair dealing,[63] good morals, reasonableness, freedom of contract *etc.*).

6.7 Future of the Codification and Estonian Private Law

Future of the codification of private law regimes in Europe may be put into the context of following problems: the need for a national private law codifications and choice between monistic and dualistic systems in implementation of EU consumer law.[64] Movements to harmonise or unify European private law started at the same time that Central and Eastern European countries had a chance to create their new national codes and codify private law. During these processes developments and achievements in harmonising European private law and EU legislation in private law matters were available and widely used in the codification of national legal systems.[65] Today the idea of harmonisation of national private laws has lost its previous attraction and seems to not be the main goal for the EU anymore.

The turning point in harmonisation processes was the proposal made by European Commission in 2011 for an adaption of Common European Sales Law[66] for B2C and B2B contracts. Reason for proposal not to use directive setting up minimum standards of a non-optional European contract law was that it would not be appropriate since it would not achieve the level of legal certainty and the necessary degree of uniformity to decrease the transaction costs. New single uniform set of contract law rules with the same meaning and interpretation in all Member States harmonises the contract laws of the Member States not by requiring amendments to the pre-existing national contract law, but by creating within each Member State's national law a second contract law regime for contracts within its scope. This second regime should be identical throughout the Union and exist alongside the pre-existing rules of national contract law.[67]

---

[63] For example Constitutional obligation to observe the law and freedoms in exercising his or her rights and in fulfilling his or her duties (Art. 19 para. 2 of the Constitution) is specified in the Article 138 paragraph 2 of the GPCCA: "A right shall not be exercised in an unlawful manner or with the objective to cause damage to another person" and Article 6 of the LOA: "(1) Obligees and obligors shall act in good faith in their relations with one another. (2) Nothing arising from law, a usage or a transaction shall be applied to an obligation if it is contrary to the principle of good faith."

[64] Lajos Vékàs, "Models in Central-Eastern European Codes," in *The Architecture of European Codes and Contract Law*, eds. Stefan Grundmann and Martin Schauer (The Netherlands: Kluwer Law International, 2006), 120–127.

[65] Irene Kull, "European and Estonian Law of Obligations – Transposition of Law or Mutual Influence?" *Juridica International* 9 (2004): 32–44.

[66] The European Commission has made a proposal for a Common European Sales Law, Brussels, 11.10.2011, COM(2011) 635 final.

[67] Ibid., p. 9.

Thus, after completing private law reforms and codification of the most important fields of private law, national private law systems have to choose between two possibilities – to develop and modify national private law in the purpose of having more influence on European private law developments or rely on the developments in EU private law as a "second legal regime" which will replace part of the national law.

Estonia made a choice in favour of monistic system of private law and the survey of key issues such as the concept of breach, specific performance, and compensation for delivery of non-conforming goods gives evidence of a substantial harmonising of Estonian law with generally accepted principles and modern concepts of European private law.[68] From the beginning of codification of Estonian private law the basic principle was that EU private law should be transferred into the system of private law to ensure the integrity of the existing system and avoid unnecessary problems in delimiting the application of the different branches of private law and relevant general principles on consumer contracts. Today the monistic interpretation of applicability of private law rules on commercial, private and consumer legal relations is still the main policy of Estonian legislator.[69] However, the incorporation of EU consumer law into the Estonian civil code acts became more complicated due to the need to hold internal coherence of the private law system established by codification.

6.8 Conclusions

Estonian private law system was basically initiated with a blank slate, with no predetermined authorities, which meant a unique opportunity to realise all those unification and harmonisation ideas that most of Europe itself can only dream of. Due to time limits no significant attention has been paid to issues such as the social consequences of borrowing foreign rules, their impact on the formation of legal culture or difficulties in finding a fair balance between different interests in the society. Estonian private law can be still found in the laws, but due to the rising court

[68] Kalev Saare, Karin Sein and Mari Ann Simovart, "The Buyer's Free Choice Between Termination and Avoidance of a Sales Contract," *Juridica International* 15 (2008): 43–53; Piia Kalamees, "Hierarchy of Buyer's Remedies in Case of Lack of Conformity of the Goods," *Juridica International* 18 (2011): 63–72.

[69] For example, LOA was very strongly and directly influenced by international sources of commercial law like CISG. There was an impact on the Law of Obligations and also on the General Part of Civil Code Act where CISG forms the basis not only for the sales contract chapter but has also been an important source for drafting the general provisions like formation of contracts, breach of contract, exemption from liability, remedies, prescription, expression of intention and juridical acts. See also Paul Varul, "CISG: a Source of Inspiration for the Estonian law of Obligations," *Uniform Law Review* 8 (2003): 209. See also: Franco Ferrari, "The CISG and its Impact on National Legal Systems – General Report," in *The CISG and its Impact on National Legal Systems*, ed. Franco Ferrari (Munich: Walter de Gruyter, 2008), 475–474; Karin Sein and Irene Kull, "Die Bedeutung des UN-Kaufrechts im estnishen Recht," *Internationales Handelsrecht* 4 (2005): 138 ff. Peter Schlechtriem, "Basic Structures and General Concepts of the CISG as Models for a Harmonisation of the Law of Obligations," *Juridica International* 10 (2005): 27–34.

practice and decision of the Estonian Supreme Court[70] to allow the use of foreign law and legal practice in interpretation and application of the provisions borrowed from other similar legal systems if there are no Estonian court practice, the court practice will play a more important role in developing law.

Bibliography

Dietrich Loeber A (2001) Kontinuität im Zivilrecht nach Wiederherstellung staatlicher Unabhängigkeit – Zu den Zivilgesetzbüchern von Lettland (1937), Estland (1993) und Litauen (2000). In: Jürgen B (ed) Aufbruch nach Europa: 75 Jahre Max-Planck-Institut für Privatrecht. Mohr Siebeck, Tübingen, pp 943–954

Ferrari F (2008) The CISG and its impact on national legal systems – general report. In: Ferrari F (ed) The CISG and its impact on national legal systems. Walter de Gruyter, Munich, pp 413–480

Hallik L (2010) Regulation of proprietary relations between spouses in the new family law act: toward better regulation by means of private autonomy? Juridica Int 17:161–166

Heiss H (2001) Vom EU-zum gesamteruopäischen Privatrecht? – Privatrechtsharmonisierung in der sich erweiternden Union. In: Basedow J (ed) Aufbruch nach Europa: 75 Jahre Max-Planck-Institut für Privatrecht. Mohr Siebeck, Tübingen, pp 132–133

Käerdi M (2003) Estonia and the new civil law. In: MacQueen H et al (eds) Regional private laws & codification in Europe. Cambridge University Press, Cambridge, pp 250–259

Käerdi M (2006) Die Neukodifikation des Privatrechts der Baltischen Staaten in vergleichender Sicht. In: Heiss H (ed) Zivilrechtsreform im Baltikum. Mohr Siebeck, Tübingen, pp 19–25

Kalamees P (2011) Hierarchy of buyer's remedies in case of lack of conformity of the goods. Juridica Int 18:63–72

Kama P (2012) Evaluation of the constitutionality of good-faith acquisition. Juridica Int 19:23–31

Kingisepp M (2008) The European consumer sales directive – the impact on Estonian law. Juridica Int 14:219–227

Kingisepp M (2012) The constitutional approach to basic consumer rights. Juridica Int 19:49–58

Kõve V (2001) Applicable law in the light of modern law of obligations and bases for the preparation of the Law of Obligations Act. Juridica Int 6:30–37

Kõve V (2008) Draft common frame of reference and Estonian Law of Obligations Act: similarities and differences in the system of contractual liability. Juridica Int 14:199–208

Kull I (1998) Effect of harmonisation of European civil law on development of Estonian law of obligations. Juridica Int 3:98–102

Kull I (2002) Principle of good faith and constitutional values in contract law. Juridica Int 6:142–149

Kull I (2004) European and Estonian law of obligations – transposition of law or mutual influence? Juridica Int 9:32–44

Kull I (2007) Unfair contracts of suretyship – a question about the horizontal effect of fundamental rights or about the application of contract law principles. Juridica Int 12:36–45

[70] Foreign law can be used by Estonian courts if in Estonian law the provision has never been applied, there is a parallel or analogous provision or relevant court practice in other legal systems, the model state's legal system and court practice is similar to that in Estonia. Judgments of the Civil Chamber of the Estonian Supreme Court from February 11, 2003 in the civil case No. 3-2-1-9-03, December 21, 2004 (civil case No. 3-2-1-145-04), December 9, 2008 (civil case No. 3-2-1-103-08) and October 12, 2011 (civil case No. 3-2-1-90-11).

Kull I (2008) Reform of contract law in Estonia: influences of harmonisation of European private law. Juridica Int 14:122–129

Kull I (2012) Impact of the Austrian Civil Code 1811 on the Estonian civil law. In: Geistlinger M, Mosler R, Rainer JM (eds) 200 Jahre ABGB-Ausstrahlungen. Die Bedeutung der Kodifikation für andere Staaten und andere Rechtskulturen. Manzsche Verlags- und Universitätsbuchhandlung, Wien, pp 265–274

Liin U (1998) On reform of Estonian succession law. Juridica Int 3:105–109

Liin U (2001) Laws of succession in Europe and Estonia: how we got to where we are and where we should be heading. Juridica Int 6:114–124

Luts M (1998) Integration as reception: University of Tartu Faculty of Law Case in 19th century. Juridica Int 3:130–141

Luts M (2000) Private law of the Baltic Provinces as a Patriotic Act. Juridica Int 5:157–167

Luts M (2001) Textbook of Pandects or new style of legislation in Estonia? Juridica Int 6:152–158

Luts M (2010) The certainty/stronghold of law, the world of yesterday and today's weather. Speech on the celebration of 90 years of the Supreme Court of Estonia, 14 Jan 2010. See: http://www.riigikohus.ee/vfs/927/Marju_Luts-Sootak_ENG.pdf

Luts-Sootak M (2004). Die estnishe Privatrechtsreform zwishen den Vorbildern aus der Geschichte, aus Deutchland und aus der europäischen Zukunft. In: Oksaar SI, von Redecker N (eds) Deutch-Estnische Rechtsvergleichung und Europa. Studien des Instituts für Ostrecht München 50. Peter Lang Europäischer Verlag der Wissenschaften, Frankfurt am Main, pp 51–68

Luts-Sootak M (2008) Die neue estnische Privatrechtskodifikation zwischen Geschichte und Zukunft von Europa. Die Kodifikation und die Juristen, Rättshistoriska studier 23. The Olin Foundation for Legal History, Stockholm, pp 133–156

Luts-Sootak M (2012) Die baltischen Privatrechte in den Händen der russischen Reichsjustiz. In: Rechtsprechung in Osteuropa. Studien zum 19. und frühen 20. Jahrhundert. (Rechtskulturen des modernen Osteuropa. Traditionen und Transfers), Studien zur europäischen Rechtsgeschichte. Veröffentlichungen des Max-Planck-Instituts für europäische Rechtsgeschichte. Vittorio Klostermann, Frankfurt am Main, pp 267–375

Mikk H (2001) Zur Reform des Zivilrechts in Estland. Jahrbuch für Ostrecht 42:31–52 (München)

Muda M (1996) Improving Estonian labour legislation on integration with Europe. Juridica Int 1:109–114

Muda M (1997) Application of international labour standards in the regulation of employment relationships in Estonia. Juridica Int 2:112–118

Paal K (2012) The numerus clausus principle and the type restriction – influence and expression of these principles. Demonstrated in the area of common ownership and servitudes. Juridica Int 19:32–39

Pärna P (2001) The Law of Property Act – cornerstone of the civil law reform. Juridica Int 6:89–101

Pärna P (2005) Legal reform in Estonia. Int J Leg Inf 33(2):219–223

Reich N (2005) Transformation of contract law and civil justice in the new EU member countries – the example of the Baltic States, Hungary and Poland. Penn State Int Law Rev 3:587–623

Reich N (2006) Law and civil justice in the new EU countries. In: Cafaggi F (ed) The institutional framework of European private law. Oxford University Press, Oxford, pp 271–302

Saare K, Sein K, Simovart MA (2008) The buyer's free choice between termination and avoidance of a sales contract. Juridica Int 15:43–53

Saaremäel-Stoilov K (2006) Liberal communitarian interpretation of social and equality rights: a balanced approach? Juridica Int 11:85–92

Schlechtriem P (2005) Basic structures and general concepts of the CISG as models for a harmonisation of the law of obligations. Juridica Int 10:27–34

Sein K, Kull I (2005) Die Bedeutung des UN-Kaufrechts im estnishen Recht. Int Handelsrecht 4:138–142

Simovart MA (2007) The standard of reasonableness in the Estonian law of obligations. In: Kull I (ed) Development of Estonian contract and company law in the context of the harmonized EU law I. Tartu Ülikooli Kirjastus, Tartu, pp 65–86

Tavits G (1996) Scope of application of Estonian labour legislation. Juridica Int 1:114–125
Tavits G (1997) The nature and formation of labour law. Juridica Int 2:103–111
Tavits G (2000) The position of labour law in the private law system. The past, present and future of Estonian labour law. Juridica Int 5:124–134
Tavits G (2001) Why do we fear civil law in labour law? Juridica Int 6:142–151
Tavits G (2005) Indispensability of the law of obligations in employment relationships: problems in application of the law of obligations to employment relationships in Estonia. Juridica Int 10:71–78
Uibopuu H-J (1985) Der "Svodzakonov" der Republic Estland – eine vergessene Kodifikation. In: Sowjetsystem und Ostrecht. Duncker & Humblot, Berlin, pp 504–527
Varul P (2000) Legal policy decisions and choices in the creation of new private law in Estonia. Juridica Int 15:104–118
Varul P (2003) CISG: a source of inspiration for the Estonian law of obligations. Uniform Law Rev 8:209–210
Varul P (2008) Creation of new Estonian private law. Eur Rev Priv Law 16:95–109
Varul P, Liin U (2008) Two reforms of the Estonian law of succession. In: Mizaras V (ed) Private law: past, present and future. Liber Amicorum Valentinas Mikelenas. Justitia, Vilnius, pp 301–310
Varul P et al (2006) Võlaõigusseadus. I, Üldosa: kommenteeritud väljaanne. Law of Obligations Act. I, General Part: Commented edition. Juura, Tallinn
Vékàs L (2006) Models in Central-Eastern European codes. In: Grundmann S, Schauer M (eds) The architecture of European codes and contract law. Kluwer Law International, Alphen aan den Rijn, pp 120–127
Vutt A (1997) Harmonisation of Estonian company law: pre-conditions in existing law. Juridica Int 2:100–102
Zweigert K, Kötz H (1998) An introduction to comparative law. Clarendon, Oxford

Chapter 7
Finnish Private Law: Statutory System Without a Civil Code

Teemu Juutilainen

Abstract Finland counts as a civil law jurisdiction, but Finnish private law is not based on a comprehensive civil code. As in the other Nordic countries, codification of private law has taken place in the form of statutes, that is, various individual acts. General principles and other contents of the "general part" of private law are largely uncodified and will most likely remain so. The absence of a civil code and a comprehensive statutory general part leaves the system of private law open-ended, which accounts for several aspects of the Finnish overall approach to private law. These concern interpretation and application of law, the relative weight of different sources of law, the role of legal science, and the openness of law to external influence. Despite the absence of a civil code, Finnish lawyers perceive domestic private law as a systematic whole, a doctrinal structure. Systematisation is entrusted to legal science, rather than predetermined by legislation.

Keywords Finland • Nordic countries • Private law • Civil law • Statutory law • Systematisation • Uncodified models

T. Juutilainen (✉)
Faculty of Law, Centre of Excellence in European Law and Polity (Finland), University of Helsinki, Helsinki, Finland
e-mail: teemu.juutilainen@helsinki.fi

J.C. Rivera (ed.), *The Scope and Structure of Civil Codes*, Ius Gentium: Comparative Perspectives on Law and Justice 32, DOI 10.1007/978-94-007-7942-6_7,

7.1 Overview of Private Law

7.1.1 Implications of the Absence of a Civil Code

Finnish law is a statutory system.[1] Legislation is strongly emphasised as the primary source of law, and application of written law is regarded as the paradigmatic model for legal decision-making. In these respects, Finnish law follows the Continental European tradition. However, legal-culturally Finland is first and foremost a part of the Nordic (less precisely: Scandinavian) legal community, together with Sweden, Norway, Denmark, and Iceland. Thus, many general characteristics of Finnish law are shared by the other Nordic legal systems.[2]

As opposed to the Continental European tradition, Finnish private law is not based on a comprehensive civil code. That is, with respect to the organisation of law, Finland has no equivalent, say, to the French *Code Civil*, the German *Bürgerliches Gesetzbuch*, or the Dutch *Burgerlijk Wetboek*. As discussed below, certain parts of Finnish private law are codified in various individual acts. Other parts, notably when it comes to general principles of law, are uncodified and expected to remain so. To be sure, a comprehensive codification of the "general part" of private law would be at odds with the Nordic tradition.[3]

This open-ended structure has shaped certain aspects of the Finnish overall approach to private law. First, legal norms of a general nature are thought to exist

---

[1] In this chapter, references to statutes are given with their respective numbers in the Statutes of Finland, for example, the Contracts Act (228/1929). The latter part of the number indicates the year when the statute was published, which is usually also the year of enactment. Most of the statutes referred to have been amended several times, but the numbers do not reveal amendments. The statutes can be found in their original form as well as in their amended and consolidated form, indicating the dates of amendment, in the Finlex data bank (http://www.finlex.fi/en/). While Finnish statutes are official only in the Finnish and Swedish languages, the data bank provides unofficial translations in other languages, mostly in English. These translations, when available, have been used in the present chapter. The text has greatly benefited from comments by Katri Havu and Janne Kaisto (University of Helsinki, Faculty of Law) and language editing by Christopher Goddard (Riga Graduate School of Law).

[2] Thomas Wilhelmsson, *Critical Studies in Private Law: A Treatise on Need-Rational Principles in Modern Law* (Dordrecht: Kluwer Academic Publishers, 1992), 15–17. See Ulf Bernitz, "What is Scandinavian Law? Concept, Characteristics, Future", in *Scandinavian Studies in Law*, vol. 50, ed. Peter Wahlgren (Stockholm: Stockholm Institute for Scandinavian Law, 2007), 17–20. For reasons of geography and history, Finnish law is more similar to Swedish law than the laws of the other Nordic countries. Finland was a part of the Kingdom of Sweden from the thirteenth century to 1809. Nevertheless, significant differences exist even between Finland and Sweden. For example, see Johanna Niemi-Kiesiläinen, "Comparing Finland and Sweden: The Structure of Legal Argument", in *Nordic Law – Between Tradition and Dynamism*, eds. Jaakko Husa, Kimmo Nuotio, and Heikki Pihlajamäki (Antwerp: Intersentia, 2007). Niemi-Kiesiläinen compares these legal systems with respect to the theory of legal sources and legal argumentation.

[3] Wilhelmsson, *Critical Studies*, 17–18. See Bernitz, "Scandinavian Law", 20–22; Aulis Aarnio, "Introduction", in *An Introduction to Finnish Law*, 2nd ed., ed. Juha Pöyhönen (Helsinki: Talentum Media, 2002), 12–13.

even without a statutory "general part". These norms can be developed by doctrine, and then applied by courts. Moreover, particular existing rules can be applied by way of analogy.[4] Indeed, due to the central role of legislation and the absence of a comprehensive civil code, the "inductive" method of constructing general principles on the basis of analogies from pieces of legislation has become natural. Hence, it is relatively common to ask whether given provisions express a general principle, despite their limited scope.[5]

Second, in the absence of a comprehensive civil code, other accepted sources have gained more significance. This holds true for the application of individual acts and the construction of general principles alike. Considerable weight is placed on *travaux préparatoires* as well as legal practice, especially precedents of the Supreme Court. Also noteworthy is the weight of so-called "real arguments", that is, substantive arguments concerning the expected consequences of a decision. These arguments are often associated with Scandinavian Legal Realism and its emphasis on legal science as a form of social engineering. The breakthrough of social engineering and the strengthening of the position of "real arguments" in private-law research took place in Finland in the 1940s, which is later than in other Nordic countries.[6] Notwithstanding the fact that private-law research eventually came to adopt many methodological tenets of Scandinavian Legal Realism,[7] the realist impact on Finnish law in general remained rather modest.[8]

Third, legal science has relatively great latitude, and authority, in building theoretical structures of law. Arguably, this would be less so if these structures were predefined in a comprehensive civil code or other statutory "general part".[9] If theoretical structures of law are understood as concepts and principles, this role of legal science can be illustrated by paradigm shifts that occurred in Finnish private-law research in the course of the twentieth century. Without going into too much detail, reference can be made to two schools of thought, namely, analytical and post-analytical.

---

[4] Jan M. Smits, "Nordic Law in a European Context: Some Comparative Observations", in Husa, Nuotio, and Pihlajamäki, *Nordic Law*, 62–63. Smits suggests that reasoning by analogy may be more common in Nordic countries than in jurisdictions with comprehensive civil codes.

[5] Wilhelmsson, *Critical Studies*, 18. Generally on interpretation and gap-filling in Finnish law, see Aulis Aarnio, "Statutory Interpretation in Finland", in *Interpreting Statutes: A Comparative Study*, eds. D. Neil MacCormick and Robert S. Summers (Aldershot: Dartmouth, 1991), 131–44.

[6] Wilhelmsson, *Critical Studies*, 18–19.

[7] Markku Helin, *Lainoppi ja metafysiikka: Tutkimus skandinaavisen oikeusrealismin tieteenkuvasta ja sen vaikutuksesta Suomen siviilioikeuden tutkimuksessa vuosina 1920–1960* (Vammala: Suomalainen Lakimiesyhdistys, 1988), 423–25.

[8] Toni Malminen, "So You Thought Transplanting Law is Easy? Fear of Scandinavian Legal Realism in Finland, 1918–1965", in Husa, Nuotio, and Pihlajamäki, *Nordic Law*, 82–87. Malminen's main explanation for this is the legacy of the Finnish Civil War of 1918, and in particular the ideology of the winning "Whites", which was the side of the propertied class. Scandinavian Legal Realism was often suspected of being socialist ideology in a legal disguise.

[9] Wilhelmsson, *Critical Studies*, 19–20.

A grand project of the analytical school was to break up "lump" concepts, which *Begriffsjurisprudenz* ("conceptual jurisprudence") had used for deductive purposes, into more refined "relational" or "functional" concepts. The aim of this exercise was to clear space for new kinds of research questions, to be then answered by argumentation based on positive law. Post-analytical scholars approve the heuristic role that the analytical school assigned to concepts, but fill the opened argumentative space differently; that is, these scholars emphasise application of principles. The focus of their doctrinal work is on principles rather than concepts, and the work is often explicitly tied in with its societal context (the welfare state).[10]

Fourth, an open-ended structure is likely to be more open to external influence than a comprehensive civil code. Avenues for that influence are legislative co-operation, conventions, doctrine, and court practice. Legislative co-operation between the Nordic countries was lively in the twentieth century. In several instances, the different countries enacted, as normal national legislation, acts that share not only almost the same content, but also the same section-by-section structure.[11] The potential of conventions can be exemplified by the United Nations Convention on Contracts for the International Sale of Goods (CISG), which has strongly influenced Nordic acts on the sale of goods, including the Finnish Sale of Goods Act (355/1987).[12] As for doctrine, references to foreign legal materials are well accepted. Thus, import of dogmatic constructions and arguments takes place. Courts do not generally cite foreign legal material when deciding a case on Finnish law, but such material may have *de facto* weight. In most cases, courts are influenced by foreign legal material indirectly through legal doctrine.[13]

---

[10] Kaarlo Tuori, *Oikeuden ratio ja voluntas* (Helsinki: WSOYpro, 2007), 216–18. See Niemi-Kiesiläinen, "Comparing Finland and Sweden", 95–97. Some post-analytical studies are representative of "alternative" or "critical" legal dogmatics. On these approaches, see Jaakko Husa, Kimmo Nuotio, and Heikki Pihlajamäki, "Nordic Law – Between Tradition and Dynamism", in Husa, Nuotio, and Pihlajamäki, *Nordic Law*, 35; Wilhelmsson, *Critical Studies*, 4–11.

[11] Thomas Wilhelmsson, "Harmonization of Private Law Rules – a Finnish Perspective", in *The Finnish National Reports to the XIIIth Congress of the International Academy of Comparative Law, Montréal 19–24 August 1990*, eds. Kaarina Buure-Hägglund, Heikki E.S. Mattila, and Karla Kilpeläinen (Helsinki: Institutum Iurisprudentiae Comparativae Universitatis Helsingiensis, 1990), 1–7, 11. Examples of Finnish acts with close counterparts in the other Nordic countries include the Contracts Act (228/1929), the Promissory Notes Act (622/1947), the Act on Gift Promises (625/1947), and the Sale of Goods Act (355/1987). See Stig Strömholm, "General Features of Swedish Law", in *Swedish Legal System*, ed. Michael Bogdan (Stockholm: Norstedts Juridik, 2010), 12–13; Severin Blomstrand, "Nordic Co-operation on Legislation in the Field of Private Law", in *Scandinavian Studies in Law*, vol. 39, ed. Peter Wahlgren (Stockholm: Stockholm Institute for Scandinavian Law, 2000); Jan Hellner, "Unification of Law in Scandinavia", *The American Journal of Comparative Law* 16, no. 1–2 (1968).

[12] For example, the "control liability" defined in Article 79 of the CISG, which had previously been unknown in Finnish law, was adopted in the act, and has later spread to other parts of Finnish contract law as well. On this, see Wilhelmsson, "Harmonization of Private Law", 9–10.

[13] Ibid., 11–17. Particularly in doctrine, legal material from other Nordic countries has a special position. In some cases, its weight is almost comparable to domestic sources. The influence of German law was strong until the Second World War. Since then, a shift has occurred towards Anglo-American law. See Husa, Nuotio, and Pihlajamäki, "Nordic Law", 20–21.

In relation to the matter of external influence, an additional point can be made concerning the Europeanisation of private law. As a Member State of the European Union, Finland is subject to its legislation. A common topic among private-law scholars in Member States is the fragmentary effect of European Union legislation on national systems of private law. This effect is mainly perceived as a problem caused by directives,[14] the type of legislative act that requires Member States to achieve a particular result, but leaves the choice of form and methods to the national authorities.[15] In Finland, and in other Member States without a general civil code, the problem of fragmentation is almost entirely about the substantive content of private law. By contrast, in Member States with a general civil code, the problem comes with an additional layer, namely, the question whether directives should be implemented within or outside the civil code.

Professor Jan Smits sums up the Dutch discussion on this point as follows: "there is no easy way out of the dilemma posed by the Europeanization of private law: a coherent implementation inside the Civil Code is never fully possible, whereas implementation outside the Code would damage the idea of the Code as a complete and consistent whole."[16] Of course, it would go too far to argue that an open-ended structure of private law is better equipped than a comprehensive civil code to function in the context of a transnational multi-level system like the European Union. Still, to a Finnish private lawyer, who has no "code idea" to be concerned about,[17] the question of within or outside of the civil code may give a feeling of a pseudo-problem.

7.1.2 Main Sources of Private Law

In Finnish legal science, the sources of law have been sorted into groups on the basis of their stating grounds and binding force. The stating grounds refer to the distinction between authoritative and substantive sources of law. Authoritative sources derive their importance from the social position of the institution from which they originate, whereas substantive sources derive theirs from the perceived significance of their content. Binding force determines how difficult it is for the interpreter to set aside the source of law in question. The distinction between strongly binding, weakly binding, and permitted sources is used for this purpose. The interpreter may deviate from a strongly binding source only exceptionally. Deviating from a weakly binding source is allowed, but such a decision is considered as properly made only if the interpreter gives solid reasons for the deviation. Permitted sources may be

[14] See Jan Smits, "Dutch Report: Coherence and Fragmentation of Private Law", *European Review of Private Law* 20, no. 1 (2012): 157–60.

[15] Article 288 of the Treaty on the Functioning of the European Union.

[16] Smits, "Dutch Report", 163.

[17] As elaborated in Sect. 7.1.3 below, Finnish private law is perceived as a systematic whole despite the absence of a general civil code.

used in interpretation, and it is not necessary to give special reasons for doing or not doing so.[18]

Authoritative strongly binding sources are written law. Authoritative weakly binding sources are *travaux préparatoires* and court decisions (precedents). Authoritative permitted sources are works of legal science. Substantive strongly binding sources are established custom. Substantive permitted sources form an open-ended category, including general principles of law, morality, and factual arguments ("real arguments").[19]

The status of written law and established custom as strongly binding sources is stated in Chapter 1 Section 11 of the Code of Judicial Procedure (4/1734):

> A judge shall carefully examine the true purpose and grounds for the law and render judgment accordingly, and not following his own opinions against the law. In the absence of statutory law, the custom of the land, if not unreasonable, shall also be his guide.

Established custom is of very limited importance in practice. National statutes form the following hierarchy (from highest to lowest): Constitution > act ("ordinary law") > decree > decision of the Council of Ministers > decision of a Ministry > other authoritative instructions. A lower-level statute may only be given if it can be based on an entitling or justifying provision in a higher-level statute. According to Chapter 6 of the Constitution of Finland (731/1999), the power to enact acts belongs to the Parliament and to the President (the former passes the contents of acts and the latter confirms them), and issuing decrees may be a function of the President, the Council of Ministers, or a Ministry.[20]

Section 107 of the Constitution concerns the hierarchy of national statutes with respect to their application:

> If a provision in a decree or another statute of a lower level than an act is in conflict with the Constitution or another act, it shall not be applied by a court of law or by any other public authority.

A significant part of private law legislation is non-mandatory, which means that contracting parties are free to agree on deviations from the obligations or procedures set by law. This is the case, for example, with the Sale of Goods Act (355/1987). In addition, some areas of private law remain wholly or largely unregulated. Building contracts provide an example of this. While building contracts are subject to the general Contracts Act (228/1929), which is fragmentary and partly outdated, no special legislation exists on this type of contract.[21] Consequently, disputes concerning these contracts may have to be considered in the light of the contract itself,

---

[18] Pekka Timonen, "Sources of Law and Material on the Sources of Law", in Pöyhönen, *Introduction to Finnish Law*, 24–25; Aulis Aarnio, *Laintulkinnan teoria*: *Yleisen oikeustieteen oppikirja* (Porvoo: WSOY, 1989), 218–22.

[19] Timonen, "Sources of Law", 25; Aarnio, *Laintulkinnan teoria*, 218–47.

[20] Timonen, "Sources of Law", 26.

[21] However, the Consumer Protection Act (38/1978) includes a chapter on the sale of building elements (installation-ready construction parts) and construction contracts.

possible private sources of norms (for example standard terms), earlier court decisions, and the general doctrine of contract law.[22]

Travaux préparatoires are said to express the legislator's meaning, and to derive their authority as a source of law from the Parliament. Although many of these documents are produced outside the Parliament (for example in the relevant Ministry), their importance is based on the idea that the Parliament has processed them. They contain information on the purposes of the new enactment and its relationship to existing legislation. Essential material in legal interpretation might be, for example, government proposals that include detailed grounds for each section and subsection of the proposed enactment. The most important group of *travaux préparatoires* are printed parliamentary documents, that is, government proposals, reports of the Parliamentary Committees, and statements given and suggestions accepted during the plenary session of the Parliament. Significant or politically sensitive enactments are often prepared in committees and task groups. Their reports may also become significant in interpretation.[23] In practice, the more recent the enactment is, the more significant the *travaux préparatoires* are in its interpretation. However, they should not be seen as an exhaustive source or a basis for conclusions *e contrario*. That is, the fact that a certain interpretive option is not mentioned does not usually justify the conclusion that the option is meant to be excluded.[24]

Of court decisions, the most important as sources of law are those of the Supreme Court and the Supreme Administrative Court. The decisions of these courts are called precedents. Although precedents are not legally binding sources, they are very important in practice. It is a task of these two courts to unify and guide court practice, and they admit cases partly on the basis of the importance that the legal question is assumed to have when it comes to deciding other similar cases. In view of the limited number of cases processed by the Supreme Courts, decisions of lower courts may become significant sources of law as well. In addition, special courts (such as the Market Court) and boards (such as the Consumer Disputes Board) produce important legal source material.[25]

The position of legal science as a source of law derives from its function to research (that is, to systematise and interpret) the content of the legal system. With respect to its own object of research, legal science is an authoritative institution.[26] Yet, in an interpretive situation, the weight of proposals by legal science should only depend on how convincing they are as to their substance.[27]

Substantive permitted sources are in practice clearly more important than their classification as "less than weakly binding sources" might suggest. The more room

[22] Timonen, "Sources of Law", 26.

[23] Ibid., 28.

[24] Jarno Tepora, *Johdatus esineoikeuden perusteisiin* (Helsinki: Helsingin yliopiston oikeustieteellinen tiedekunta, 2008), 7.

[25] Timonen, "Sources of Law", 29.

[26] Ibid., 30.

[27] Tepora, *Johdatus esineoikeuden perusteisiin*, 8–9.

for interpretation and the more alternative outcomes the case at hand involves, the more a good judge considers these sources, even without being formally obliged to do so. The sources are solely substantive, and often derive their importance from ideas of justice and morality, as perceived in the interpretive situation under consideration. General principles as a source of law may concern, for example, legal certainty, equality before the law, and fairness. Morality in this context refers primarily to general arguments of justice and public consciousness of what is just. Factual arguments, then, involve assessment of expected consequences when choosing between interpretive options.[28]

The above description focuses on domestic sources of law. However, a complete picture would require inclusion of European Union law, which has been binding on Finland since it became a Member State in 1995. The European Union has no direct and general competence to legislate in the field of private law, but measures adopted in the context of specific European Union policies, relating above all to creation of the internal market, have included private law elements. In some cases, the principal treaties, particularly the Treaty on the Functioning of the European Union, have a direct impact on private law. This is most notable in competition law. In most cases, though, the impact comes through secondary legislation, that is, directives or regulations. Directives have to be implemented in national law, whereas regulations are binding as such. An example of a field that has been heavily influenced by the European Union is consumer law. The Court of Justice of the European Union plays an important interpretive role.[29]

7.1.3 System of Private Law

From a structural viewpoint, Finnish lawyers perceive domestic law in the Continental European manner as a systematic whole. That is, despite the absence of a general civil code, the law is thought to form a doctrinal structure.[30] Finnish accounts of the systematisation of law often begin with the distinction between the legal order and the legal system. The legal order is the entirety of valid legal norms at a given moment, whereas the legal system is the result of systematisation efforts by legal science. Systematisation efforts involve, above all, organising legal norm material into fields of law. It is commonly thought that the general doctrines of a field of law are decisive for its existence and identity, that is, its concepts, principles, and theories. In other words, in addition to a specific regulatory object, a field of law

---

[28] Timonen, "Sources of Law", 30.

[29] Christian Twigg-Flesner, "Introduction: Key Features of European Union Private Law", in *The Cambridge Companion to European Union Private Law*, ed. Christian Twigg-Flesner (Cambridge: Cambridge University Press, 2010), 1–3.

[30] Wilhelmsson, *Critical Studies*, 19.

needs concepts that structure its normative material, principles that condense its normative contents, and theories that combine concepts and principles.[31]

Legislation does not predetermine the systematisation of Finnish private law. The task of system building is largely entrusted to legal science. To be sure, systematisations created by legal science change over time. Furthermore, different scholars may have differing views as to how the system should be built, at least when it comes to details. However, the following outline of the fields of private law is well established and generally accepted.

Finnish private law is first divided into two parts, namely, general private law (or "civil law") and special private law (or "economic law"). General private law consists of the law of persons, patrimonial law (here, "patrimonial" refers to a person's property in general), family law, and inheritance law. Special private law, which is not the main concern of this chapter, includes commercial law, labour law, and environmental law. Patrimonial law, then, consists of the law of obligations, property law, and the law of intellectual property.[32]

Two different ways of thinking affect the present division between the law of obligations and property law. According to the older and perhaps somewhat old-fashioned view, the law of obligations concerns rights to receive something from another person, whereas property law concerns rights in physical things (literally, the Finnish word for property law, *esineoikeus*, means "the law of things"). The newer view maintains that both fields of law concern relations between persons, yet different kinds of relations. While the law of obligations deals with relations between contracting parties, or other relations *inter partes*, property law deals with relations *ultra partes*, that is, relations between a contracting party and a third party. According to the newer way of thinking, property law is about questions of third-party protection in the exchange of rights, and its objects are not confined to rights in physical things.[33] For example, with respect to assignment of claims, the relation between assignor and assignee would belong to the law of obligations, whereas potential relations between the assignee and the assignor's creditors and between the assignee and a competing assignee (double assignment) would belong to property law.

Generally, the greater the detail of systematisation, the greater the differences between divisions suggested by different scholars. The law of obligations is further systematised in two somewhat overlapping ways. On the one hand, its field is divided into a general part and a special part. The general part includes legal norms and doctrines common for all obligations, whereas the special part deals with

[31] Tuori, *Oikeuden ratio ja voluntas*, 105–10; Lars Björne, *Oikeusjärjestelmän kehityksestä* (Vammala: Suomalainen Lakimiesyhdistys, 1979), 1–3. Differing views have been presented on the prospects of creating coherence within a field of law by developing general doctrines. See Thomas Wilhelmsson, "Yleiset opit ja pienet kertomukset ennakoitavuuden ja yhdenvertaisuuden näkökulmasta", *Lakimies* 102, no. 2 (2004): 203–7.

[32] Janne Kaisto and Tapani Lohi, *Johdatus varallisuusoikeuteen* (Helsinki: Talentum, 2008), 16–18; Tepora, *Johdatus esineoikeuden perusteisiin*, 12–13.

[33] Kaisto and Lohi, *Johdatus varallisuusoikeuteen*, 22–24; Tepora, *Johdatus esineoikeuden perusteisiin*, 13–16.

specific types of obligations. When it comes to details, different scholars have drawn the line differently. Nonetheless, the general part is usually thought to include the content (correct fulfilment), sanctions, alteration and cessation of obligations. The special part, then, is usually related to the different types of contracts and other dispositions, debts, and means of payment. The refund of benefit by unjust enrichment is in most cases dealt with in the special part, but it has been considered to fit into the general part, too.[34] On the other hand, the law of obligations is divided into the fields of contract law, the law of compensation for (non-contractual) damages, and the refund of benefit by unjust enrichment.[35] Section 7.4.3 below gives a picture of the subfields of property law. The law of intellectual property, which is the third field of patrimonial law, is divided into two main fields, namely, copyright and industrial rights (for example patents and trademarks).[36]

7.2 Historical Context

7.2.1 Explanations for the Absence of a Civil Code

Legal history offers some plausible explanations for the absence of comprehensive civil codes in the Nordic countries. The explanations have been developed by contrasting the situation in the Nordic countries with the legal, social and political reasons for the emergence of codifications elsewhere in Europe during the same period.

At least three factors account for the codification movement. First, codifications were aimed at remedying the abundance of competing legal sources. Continental European legal systems had become extremely complex in the early modern period. Roman law had absorbed canon law, customary law, and the *lex mercatoria*. Local princes and cities had been issuing their own statutes. Complicated legal doctrines were needed to determine the relation between the different sources. On top of all this had grown an immense mesh of privileges. Second, codifications were seen as tools for modernising societies and changing social structures. In this sense, codifications provided national lawgivers with an easier and more effective way to steer the course of their nations. In contrast to *ius commune*, which had been above all a product of academe, codifications could easily be changed according to political will. Courts and citizens could follow codifications more easily than the old law. Importantly, judiciaries also had to follow the codified law. Third, codifications could serve nationalist purposes. Indeed, national codifications could be seen as important as national languages or literature.[37]

---

[34] Erkki Aurejärvi and Mika Hemmo, *Velvoiteoikeuden oppikirja*, 3rd ed. (Helsinki: Edita, 2007), 7–9.

[35] Heikki Halila and Mika Hemmo, *Sopimustyypit*, 2nd ed. (Helsinki: Talentum, 2008), 2.

[36] Pirkko-Liisa Haarmann, *Immateriaalioikeus*, 4th ed. (Helsinki: Talentum, 2006), 3–4.

[37] Husa, Nuotio, and Pihlajamäki, "Nordic Law", 18–19.

The Nordic countries were never burdened by such an abundance of legal sources. The legal landscape and the social structure were relatively simple. Separate city laws, manorial law, and local princely legislation were unknown. The content of customary law was not clearly established, partly because it remained unwritten. Canon law had ceased to exist as a separate body of law after the Lutheran Reformation. Most importantly, *ius commune* was never received as the subsidiary body of law; the number of trained lawyers was simply too small for full reception.[38]

All this left ample space for the so-called proto-codifications, namely, *Danske Lov* of 1683 (Denmark), *Norske Lov* of 1687 (Norway), and the Swedish Law of the Realm of 1734. These collections of laws are called proto-codifications because they were, unlike the Prussian *Allgemeines Landsrecht* and the French *Code Civil*, and others, not products of the scientific environment of natural law and conceptual jurisprudence. Although they were not codifications in the modern sense, they served similar needs. Furthermore, as Denmark-Norway and Sweden-Finland came to resemble typical nation states in the nineteenth century, the proto-codifications were already national in character.[39]

In sum, because of the fewness of competing legal sources, the existence of proto-codifications, and the absence of Roman law to be cleared out the way, nineteenth century Nordic societies felt no need for modern codifications. As the century advanced and the Nordic countries began to compile their laws and practices in statutory form, statutory law as such, even without the form of codification, could cater for the modernisation needs of these societies.[40]

7.2.2 Closest Counterpart to a Civil Code: The Law of 1734

Finland has never had a general civil code in the modern sense of the term. The closest historical counterpart is the Swedish Law of the Realm of 1734 ("the Law of 1734").[41] Until 1809, Finland was the eastern half of the Kingdom of Sweden, thereafter an autonomous part of the Russian Empire, and declared independence in 1917.[42] The first five of the nine codes (or "beams", as they were named; in Swedish: *balk*) of the Law of 1734 concern private law, namely, marriage, inheritance, real property, building, and trade. This law did not deal with abstract legal institutions and their effects. Instead, it was built by the casuistic method, and thus provided

---

[38] Ibid., 19.

[39] Ibid. See Ditlev Tamm, "The Nordic Legal Tradition in European Context – Roman Law and the Nordic Countries", in *Nordisk identitet: Nordisk rätt i europeisk gemenskap*, ed. Pia Letto-Vanamo (Helsingfors: Institutet för internationell ekonomisk rätt vid Helsingfors universitet, 1998), 22–24.

[40] Husa, Nuotio, and Pihlajamäki, "Nordic Law", 19–20.

[41] See the remarks on this and the other so-called proto-codifications in Sect. 7.2.1 above.

[42] On codification attempts during the Russian Era, see Sect. 7.12 below.

rules for concretely described situations.[43] Some of its original provisions (in the codes of building, trade, and judicial procedure) are still in force in Finland, but most of them are of very little practical importance.[44] Legal historians tend to emphasise the significance of this law as a carrier of legal tradition.[45]

7.3 Comparative Classifications

René David and John E.C. Brierley include Finnish and the other Nordic legal systems in the Romano-Germanic legal family. They admit, though, that the diversity within this legal family may necessitate secondary groupings. In their view, Nordic (Scandinavian) laws could be recognised as a secondary grouping, alongside Latin, Germanic, and Latin American laws, and so on. However, they do not seem to seriously pursue this idea. While they discuss certain particular features of Nordic laws, such as the absence of modern codifications, these legal systems generally merge into their account of the Romano-Germanic legal family.[46]

A more detailed, and today arguably more influential, classification is presented by Konrad Zweigert and Hein Kötz. They remark that the Nordic legal systems expose difficulties with the usual implicit assumption that the Western legal systems belong either to the common law or to the civil law. According to them, Nordic laws cannot be allocated to the common law because their development has been quite independent of English law and because they display few, if any, indications of the common law, such as the typical methods of finding law and the strong emphasis on judicial decisions in important areas of private law. They have doubts about allocating Nordic laws to the civil law either, due to the fact that Roman law has played a relatively modest role in the legal development of the Nordic countries, and because of the absence of comprehensive civil codes. Nevertheless, they conclude that Nordic laws belong to the civil law, but "by reason of their close interrelationship and their common 'stylistic' hallmarks, they must undoubtedly be admitted to form a special legal family, alongside the Romanistic and German legal families".[47]

Zweigert and Kötz's view comes close to the prevailing opinion, which is also shared by Nordic jurists. The prevailing opinion is that the Nordic legal systems form a separate legal family distinct not only from the common law but also from the civil law, in spite of the considerable Continental European influence. A typical

---

[43] Jukka Kekkonen, "Suomen oikeuskulttuurin suuri linja 1898–1998", in *Suomen oikeuskulttuurin suuri linja: Suomalainen Lakimiesyhdistys 100 vuotta* (Helsinki: Suomalainen Lakimiesyhdistys, 1998), 19.

[44] An exception to "very little practical importance" is mentioned in Sect. 7.4.3 below.

[45] Kekkonen, "Suomen oikeuskulttuurin suuri linja", 18–19.

[46] David and Brierley, *Major Legal Systems in the World Today: An Introduction to the Comparative Study of Law*, 3rd ed. (London: Stevens & Sons, 1985), 34, 112–13.

[47] Zweigert and Kötz, *An Introduction to Comparative Law*, 3rd ed., trans. Tony Weir (Oxford: Oxford University Press, 1998), 277.

justification for this opinion is the long and continuing Nordic legal tradition which, to name some of its reputed characteristics, attaches relatively little importance to legal formalities and construction of large theoretical systems, and avoids undue conceptualism. It is often suggested that the absence of comprehensive civil codes contributes to an atmosphere of concrete and pragmatic thinking, as opposed to the more abstract and systematic thinking of Continental Europe.[48]

7.4 Patrimonial Law Legislation

7.4.1 Contract Law

The great bulk of Finnish contract law legislation is contract-type specific. The most important exception is the Contracts Act (228/1929),[49] which is a general act on concluding contracts, authorisation to conclude contracts, and invalidity and adjustment of contracts.[50] No general legislation exists on other central matters such as the content of contractual obligations, breach of contract, and contractual remedies. Contracts unregulated by legislation are subject to relatively uniform general principles. However, the content of general principles varies according to the following distinctions: standard-term contracts and individually negotiated contracts, consumer contracts and contracts between businesses, and transactions and long-term contracts. General principles also complement regulation of those contract types that are subject to special legislation, unless the relevant legislation provides otherwise.[51]

Since the end of the 1980s, contract law legislation has remarkably expanded. As a consequence, the position of written law as a source of contract law has strengthened. Examples of this legislation include the Sale of Goods Act (355/1987), the Act on Commercial Representatives and Salesmen (417/1992), the Act on the Regulation of Contract Terms between Entrepreneurs (1062/1993), the Act on

[48] Tamm, "Nordic Legal Tradition", 17. For discussion of Nordic laws against the backdrop of methodological questions of comparative classifications, see Husa, Nuotio, and Pihlajamäki, "Nordic Law", 2–10. For a critical "outsider's view" of the alleged pragmatism of Nordic laws, see Smits, "Nordic Law", 61–63.

[49] A more accurate translation would be "Act on Juridical Acts in the Field of Patrimonial Law". Some provisions of the act seem to represent the view that the concept of contract is an instance of the concept of juridical act.

[50] See Christina Ramberg, "The Hidden Secrets of Scandinavian Contract Law", in Wahlgren, *Scandinavian Studies in Law*, vol. 50, 250. According to Ramberg, the Nordic contracts acts, one of which is the Finnish Contracts Act, are fragmentary and unable to address modern contractual problems. In Finland, a committee report on the need to reform the Contracts Act was published in 1990. However, the project was then halted, partly because wishes were expressed that the reform should be undertaken as Nordic co-operation. On this, see Mika Hemmo, *Sopimusoikeus I*, 2nd ed. (Helsinki: Talentum, 2003), 39–40.

[51] Hemmo, *Sopimusoikeus I*, 28–37.

Residential Leases (481/1995), the Act on the Lease of Business Premises (482/1995), the Housing Transactions Act (843/1994), the Insurance Contracts Act (543/1994), the Package Travel Act (1079/1994), the Code of Real Estate (540/1995), the Payment Services Act (290/2010), the Act on Guaranties and Third-Party Pledges (361/1999), the Act on Real Estate and Housing Agency Services (1074/2000), and the Employment Contracts Act (55/2001).[52]

7.4.2 The Law of Compensation for (Non-contractual) Damages

The general act regulating compensation for non-contractual damages is the Tort Liability Act (412/1974). In matters unregulated by this act, such as causality and unforeseeable damages, the case law of the Supreme Court is of particular importance.[53]

Special legislation is common in this field. Examples include the Employment Accidents Insurance Act (608/1948), the Traffic Insurance Act (279/1959), the Nuclear Liability Act (484/1972), the Act on Compensation for Crime Damage (1204/2005), the Act on Compensation from State Funds for the Arrest or Detention of an Innocent Person (422/1974), the Patient Damages Act (585/1986), the Occupational Disease Act (1343/1988), the Product Liability Act (694/1990), the Act on Compensation for Damage Caused by Ordnance to a Civilian (1213/1990), the Act on Compensation for Environmental Damage (737/1994), the Environmental Damage Insurance Act (81/1998), the Rail Traffic Liability Act (113/1999).[54]

7.4.3 Property Law

The law of real property is largely covered by the Code of Real Estate (540/1995). The code includes provisions on sale and transfer of real property, the registration system,[55] registration of title and special rights, and real estate liens and mortgages. It has been discussed whether the principles and rules of this code could be generalised within the field of property law, that is, whether they could be applied beyond the law of real property. Other central statutes in the law of real property are the

---

[52] Ibid., 38–39. Some of these acts replaced previous regulation on the same subject matter.

[53] Mika Hemmo, *Vahingonkorvausoikeus*, 2nd ed. (Helsinki: WSOYpro, 2006), 15.

[54] Ibid., 15–16. Some of these acts are insurance-based or other special non-fault compensation systems.

[55] A country-wide real estate register is maintained in accordance with the Real Estate Register Act (392/1985).

Real Estate Register Act (392/1985), the Real Estate Formation Act (554/1995), and the Land Use and Building Act (132/1999).[56]

No general legislation or provisions exist on ownership, except the Act on Certain Co-ownership Relations (180/1958). Besides real property, registration legislation exists on book-entry securities: the Act on the Book-Entry System (826/1991) and the Act on Book-Entry Accounts (827/1991). In addition, legislation on industrial rights, such as patents and trademarks, includes provisions on registration of these rights. Registration also plays a role with respect to certain non-possessory security rights over movable property (mortgages). Legislation exists on mortgages over aircraft, vessels, and certain kinds of cars, albeit that the respective acts have long needed reform. The Enterprise Mortgage Act (634/1984) enables businesses to use their tangible movables and intangibles as "floating" security for credit. No general legislation exists on rights to use and rights of severance, but special legislation has been enacted on leases: the Act on Residential Leases (481/1995), the Act on the Lease of Business Premises (482/1995), and the Act on the Lease of Land (258/1966). Some provisions of the archaic and casuistic "Trade Code" of the Law of 1734 still apply to matters of movable property. For example, good faith acquisition is based on these provisions. The Promissory Notes Act (622/1947) regulates the transfer and pledge of negotiable and ordinary promissory notes, and applies to receivables by way of analogy. Furthermore, many provisions relevant to substantive property law are found in insolvency legislation.[57]

7.5 Commercial Law Legislation

Finland does not have a commercial code in the sense of a comprehensive codification. Still, a field of law called commercial law exists. Its systematic place is in special private law (see Sect. 7.1.3 above), and its subfields are rather heterogeneous. The central subfields are the law of business organisations, market law, and consumer law. Sometimes, especially in university curricula, the law of intellectual property is also included in commercial law.

Many matters of a commercial nature, such as specific types of commercial contracts, negotiable instruments, means of payment, and security rights (security for credit) are traditionally dealt with in the relevant fields of general private law (patrimonial law). As a matter of fact, one of the common characteristics between the Nordic legal systems is that no sharp distinction exists between civil law and commercial law.[58]

Central statutes in the law of business organisations are the Partnerships Act (389/1988), the Act on European Economic Interest Grouping (1299/1994), the

---

[56] Tepora, *Johdatus esineoikeuden perusteisiin*, 3–4.

[57] Ibid., 4–6.

[58] Tamm, "Nordic Legal Tradition", 17.

Limited Liability Companies Act (624/2006), the Act on European Company (742/2004), the Co-operatives Act (1488/2001), and the Act on European Cooperative Society (906/2006). In market law, central statutes of general application are the Competition Act (948/2011), the Unfair Business Practices Act (1061/1978), and the Act on the Right to Practice a Trade (122/1919). Additionally, market law includes sector-specific legislation on, for example, energy markets, communications, postal services, transport, financial services and insurance.[59] Consumer law is discussed in more detail in the following section.

7.6 Consumer Law Legislation

7.6.1 Overview

Finnish consumer law legislation consists of several statutes. In recent years, this field has been heavily influenced by European law. It has been estimated that at least three fourths of the provisions are based on European Union legislation.[60]

The core statute of the field is the Consumer Protection Act (38/1978). In its present form, the act includes provisions on its scope of application, which largely define the scope of consumer law in general, as well as chapters on regulation of marketing, regulation of contract terms, adjustment and interpretation of a contract, sale of consumer goods, door-to-door selling and distance selling, distance selling of financial services and instruments, consumer credit, certain consumer service contracts, sale of building elements (installation-ready construction parts) and construction contracts, and time-share and long-term holiday products. Other consumer legislation includes the Act on Real Estate and Housing Agency Services (1074/2000), the Housing Transactions Act (843/1994), the Package Travel Act (1079/1994), the Consumer Safety Act (920/2011), and the Product Liability Act (694/1990). Additionally, decrees have been issued that specify some acts.

The following statutes concern the consumer authorities: the Act on the Consumer Agency (1056/1998), the Act on the Consumer Disputes Board (8/2007), the Act on Financial and Debt Counselling (713/2000), the Market Court Act (1527/2001), the Act on Certain Procedures before the Market Court (1528/2001), and the Act on Class Actions (444/2007).

In addition, certain statutes of a general nature contain special provisions concerning consumer relations. Examples include the Electricity Market Act (386/1995), the Insurance Contracts Act (543/1994), and the Interests Act (633/1982).

---

[59] Pentti Mäkinen et al., *Markkinaoikeuden perusteet*, 2nd ed. (Helsinki: Talentum, 2006).

[60] Tuula Ämmälä, *Suomen kuluttajaoikeus* (Helsinki: Talentum, 2006), 1.

7.6.2 *Consumer Contracts*

Consumer contracts are concluded between a business (entrepreneur) and a consumer. These contracts concern consumer goods or services, that is, "goods, services and other merchandise and benefits that are offered to natural persons or which such persons acquire, to an essential extent, for their private households" (Consumer Protection Act, Chapter 1 Section 3).

Consumer contracts do not belong to the traditional systematisation of contract law, which is based on recognition of different contract types. In that respect, the concept of the consumer contract can be said to have a fragmenting effect on the traditional system. On the one hand, the concept of the consumer contract splits traditional contract types into two parts. For example, instead of speaking of sales contracts as a unitary type, consumer sales have to be distinguished from "ordinary" sales. On the other hand, the concept of the consumer contract includes several traditional contract types: consumer sales, consumer services, and so on. It should be also noted that the significance of the concept of the consumer contract is not limited to the scope of application of the Consumer Protection Act. That is, the concept plays a role in general doctrines of contract law and the law of obligations (see Sect. 7.6.3 below).[61]

The Consumer Protection Act includes some general provisions that concern all consumer contracts. These are found in Chapter 3 on regulation of contract terms, according to which a business may be enjoined from using a contract term which is to be deemed unreasonable from the point of view of consumers, and in Chapter 4 on adjustment and interpretation of a contract. Additionally, the provision of Chapter 10 Section 5 of the Code of Judicial Procedure (4/1734), which concerns jurisdiction as to claims based on consumer protection legislation, concerns all consumer contracts. However, the main part of the more specific regulation concerns specific types of consumer contracts. A common feature of the special provisions on consumer contracts is that they are usually mandatory. For example, Chapter 5 (Sale of Consumer Goods) Section 2 of the Consumer Protection Act prescribes: "A contract term differing from the provisions of this chapter to the detriment of the buyer shall be void unless otherwise provided below." That is, deviations from the provisions are allowed if they improve the consumer's position. Similar examples are Section 3(2) of the Insurance Contracts Act and Section 25a(1) of the Electricity Market Act.[62]

The general aim of regulation of consumer contracts, which holds true for consumer law as a whole, is to improve the consumer's position in relation to the entrepreneur, who is generally assumed to be the stronger party both in terms of bargaining power and information. Because this regulation is based on the formal

---

[61] Thomas Wilhelmsson, "Kuluttajasopimukset", in *Encyclopædia Iuridica Fennica I*: *Varallisuus- ja yritysoikeus*, eds. Heikki E.S. Mattila et al. (Helsinki: Suomalainen Lakimiesyhdistys, 1994), 377–78.

[62] Ibid., 379–80; Halila and Hemmo, *Sopimustyypit*, 5.

statuses of consumer and business, the protection it offers is sometimes criticised for over- and under-inclusiveness, that is, of having too little regard for the contracting parties' actual need for protection.[63]

7.6.3 *Relationship Between General Contract Law and Consumer Contract Law*

In the wake of consumer legislation, consumer law, with its strong public law elements, has emerged as a field separate from general private law. The same can be said about the relationship between consumer contract law and general contract law. This can also be seen in matters unregulated by legislation. It is considered clear that general principles of contract law and the law of obligations may be applied differently depending on whether the issue at hand concerns a relation between a consumer and a business or a relation between businesses.[64]

However, this separateness is only relative. That is, many provisions of general contract law legislation, such as the Contracts Act, apply to consumer contracts and other contracts alike, as *lex generalis*. As regards consumer sales, the provisions of Chapter 5 of the Consumer Protection Act have been squared with those of the general Sale of Goods Act. The provisions of Chapter 5 of the Consumer Protection Act are the primary source as *lex specialis*. Additionally, Section 29 of the same chapter explicitly states that the provisions of the Sale of Goods Act apply to a sale referred to in the chapter, unless otherwise provided in the Consumer Protection Act. The section includes a list of provisions of the Sale of Goods Act which do not apply at all to consumer sales.[65]

It has also been argued that isolation of consumer contract law from general contract law would be undesirable. According to this view, consumer contract law provides important impulses to the development of general contract law. Regulation of marketing liability in the Sale of Goods Act has been referred to as an example of these impulses because the provisions of the Consumer Protection Act served as one

[63] See Halila and Hemmo, *Sopimustyypit*, 5–8. They remark that consumer protection is not the only instance of weaker-party protection in Finnish contract law. For example, according to Section 3(2) of Insurance Contracts Act, the mandatory provisions protect not only the consumer but also "another natural person or legal person that in terms of the nature and scope of its business or other activities or other circumstances can be compared to a consumer". In addition, the Act on Residential Leases (481/1995) protects the lessee as the weaker party irrespective of whether the lessor is an entrepreneur, and the substantive provisions of the Hire-Purchase Act (91/1966) seem to be based on the view of the buyer as the weaker party. Perhaps the most obvious example, however, concerns employment contracts.

[64] Thomas Wilhelmsson, "Kuluttajaoikeus", in *Encyclopædia Iuridica Fennica I: Varallisuus- ja yritysoikeus*, eds. Heikki E.S. Mattila et al. (Helsinki: Suomalainen Lakimiesyhdistys, 1994), 359; Wilhelmsson, "Kuluttajasopimukset", 377–78.

[65] See Wilhelmsson, "Kuluttajaoikeus", 359; Ämmälä, *Suomen kuluttajaoikeus*, 37–67.

of its models.[66] Furthermore, it has been argued that some provisions of Chapter 8 of the Consumer Protection Act on certain consumer services (repair and manufacture) may also become applicable in relations between businesses by way of analogy or as general principles of the law of obligations.[67] In conclusion, the influence between consumer contract law and general contract law seems to go both ways.

7.7 Labour Law Legislation

Most labour law can be divided into three subfields, namely, employment contract law, the law of collective agreements (collective bargaining) and employee participation, and the law of occupational safety and health.[68] The core statute of employment contract law is the Employment Contracts Act (55/2001). This regulates, among other things, employer and employee obligations, family leave, lay-offs, termination and cancellation of employment contracts, invalidity of employment contracts and unreasonable terms, international aspects of employment contracts, and liability for damages. Employment contracts are also regulated in the Seafarers' Employment Contracts Act (756/2011) and the Act on the Employment of Household Workers (951/1977). Additionally, the provisions on apprenticeship in the Act on Occupational Training (630/1998) can be included in employment contract law.[69]

Central statutes in the law of collective agreements and employee participation are the Collective Agreements Act (436/1946),[70] the Act on Collective Agreements for State Civil Servants (664/1970), the Act on Collective Agreements for Local Government Officials (669/1970), the Act on Confirmation of the General Applicability of Collective Agreements (56/2001), the Mediation in Labour Disputes Act (420/1962), the Act on the Labour Court (646/1974), the Act on Co-operation within Undertakings (334/2007), the Act on Personnel Funds (934/2010), and the Act on Personnel Representation in the Administration of Undertakings (725/1990).[71] In the law of occupational safety and health, central

[66] Wilhelmsson, "Kuluttajaoikeus", 359.

[67] Halila and Hemmo, *Sopimustyypit*, 94.

[68] Kari-Pekka Tiitinen, *Työoikeuden pääasiat* (Helsinki: Helsingin yliopiston oikeustieteellinen tiedekunta, 2005), 1. See Niklas Bruun, "Labour Law and Non-discrimination Law", in Pöyhönen, *Introduction to Finnish Law*, 175–76. An example of a statute that may be difficult to fit into these categories is the Act on the Right in Employee Inventions (656/1967).

[69] Tiitinen, *Työoikeuden pääasiat*, 10–11.

[70] An important contact point between the law of collective agreements and (individual) employment contract law is the principle of the general applicability of collective agreements. That is, as provided by Section 7 of the Employment Contracts Act, even employers who are not members of an employer organisation and not a party to any collective agreement are still obliged in certain cases to follow the relevant collective agreement. See Bruun, "Labour Law", 183–84.

[71] Tiitinen, *Työoikeuden pääasiat*, 132–58.

statutes include the Occupational Safety and Health Act (738/2002), the Radiation Act (592/1991), the Occupational Health Care Act (1383/2001), the Young Workers' Act (998/1993), the Working Hours Act (605/1996), and the Annual Holidays Act (162/2005).[72]

Furthermore, labour law has important intersections with non-discrimination law and social security law. The issue of discrimination is addressed in Section 6 of the Constitution of Finland (731/1999),[73] and further concretised in the Employment Contracts Act and the Act on Equality between Women and Men (609/1986).[74] Social security law is often considered to include both employment related and general social security law. Employment related social security law includes legislation on accident insurance, employment pension, wage guarantee in the case of employer insolvency, and unemployment benefits.[75]

7.8 Family and Inheritance Law Legislation

Family law, which encompasses several statutes, is divided into the subfields of child law, name law, guardianship law, and relationship law. Inheritance law consists of statutory succession law and testament law (the law of wills).[76]

In child law, central statutes are the Paternity Act (700/1975), the Act on Assisted Fertility Treatments (1237/2006), the Act on Legal-Genetic Paternity Test (378/2005), the Adoption Act (153/1985), the Child Custody and Right of Access Act (361/1983), the Act on the Execution of a Decision on Child Custody and Right of Access (619/1996), the Act on Child Maintenance (704/1975), the Maintenance Support Act (580/2008), and the Child Welfare Act (417/2007). The core statute of name law is the Names Act (694/1985). In guardianship law, central statutes are the Guardianship Services Act (442/1999), the Act on the Arrangement of Guardianship Services (575/2008), and the Continuing Power of Attorney Act (648/2007). Central statutes in relationship law are the Marriage Act (234/1929), which applies to couples of the opposite sex, the Act on Registered Partnerships (950/2001), which applies to same-sex couples, and the Act on the Dissolution of the Household of Cohabiting Partners (26/2011). As for inheritance law, the core statute is the Code of Inheritance (40/1965), which covers statutory succession law and testament law alike.

---

[72] Ibid., 158–82.

[73] When it comes to protection of union activities, Section 13 of the Constitution, on freedom of assembly and freedom of association, is relevant.

[74] Bruun, "Labour Law", 204–10.

[75] Tiitinen, *Työoikeuden pääasiat*, 1.

[76] Urpo Kangas, *Perhe- ja perintöoikeuden alkeet* (Helsinki: Helsingin yliopiston oikeustieteellinen tiedekunta, 2006), 3–7.

7.9 Regional Private Law Legislation: Åland

Finland is a unitary state and, generally speaking, a unitary jurisdiction with respect to private law legislation. That is, as a starting point, the same private law applies in all parts of the country. The only exceptions stem from the autonomous status of the Region of Åland. The region is located in the Åland Islands, an archipelago in the Baltic Sea, at the entrance to the Gulf of Bothnia. The Åland Islands are demilitarised, and the region is monolingually Swedish-speaking. The population is approximately 28,000 people.

The region's autonomous status includes competence to enact regional legislation in matters specified in Section 18 of the Act on the Autonomy of Åland (1144/1991). Of these matters, at least the following may directly concern or touch upon private law:

> 7) building and planning, adjoining properties, housing; 8) the appropriation of real property and of special rights required for public use in exchange for full compensation ... 9) tenancy and rent regulation, lease of land; 10) the protection of nature and the environment, the recreational use of nature, water law; 11) prehistoric relics and the protection of buildings and artifacts with cultural or historical value; 12) health care and medical treatment ... 14) education, apprenticeship, culture, sport and youth work; the archive, library and museum service ... 15) farming and forestry, the regulation of agricultural production ... 16) hunting and fishing, the registration of fishing vessels and the regulation of fishing industry ... 18) the maintenance of the productive capacity of the farmlands, forests and fishing waters; the duty to transfer, in exchange for full compensation, unutilised or partially utilised farmland or fishing water into the possession of another person to be used for these purposes, for a fixed period; 19) the right to prospect for, lay claim to and utilise mineral finds; 20) the postal service and the right to broadcast by radio or cable in Åland ... 21) roads and canals, road traffic, railway traffic, boat traffic, the local shipping lanes; 22) trade ... 27) other matters deemed to be within the legislative power of Åland in accordance with the principles underlying this Act.[77]

To give but one example, which directly concerns contract law, the region has enacted an act on the lease of apartments and other premises, *hyreslag för landskapet Åland* (1999: 19). By contrast, Section 27 of the Act on the Autonomy of Åland includes a list of matters in which legislative competence belongs to the State of Finland. The list includes, among other things, the following matters:

> 6) surname and forename, guardianship, the declaration of the legal death of a person; 7) marriage and family relations, the juridical status of children, adoption and inheritance ... 8) associations and foundations, companies and other private corporations, the keeping of accounts; 9) the nation-wide general preconditions on the right of foreigners and foreign corporations to own and possess real property and shares of stock and to practice trade; 10) copyright, patent, copyright of design and trademark, unfair business practices, promotion of competition, consumer protection; 11) insurance contracts; 12) foreign trade; 13) merchant shipping and shipping lanes; 14) aviation ... 16) the formation and registration of pieces of real property and connected duties; 17) mineral finds and mining ... 21) labour law ... 40) telecommunications ... 41) the other matters under private law not specifically mentioned in this section, unless the matters relate directly to an area of legislation within

[77] Exceptions to the listed matters are omitted.

> the competence of Åland according to this Act; 42) other matters that are deemed to be within the legislative power of the State according to the principles underlying this Act.[78]

Another aspect of the region's autonomous status, which clearly has implications for private law, is the so-called right of domicile, regulated in Chapter 2 of the Act on the Autonomy of Åland. The right of domicile is a form of regional citizenship, introduced with a view to protecting the local culture and Swedish language as well as keeping the land in Ålandic ownership. The right of domicile can be acquired by birth or application. Acquisition by application normally requires that the applicant, who must be a Finnish citizen, has lived in Åland for at least 5 years, and has a satisfactory command of the Swedish language. Persons without the right of domicile are subject to restrictions on the right to acquire real property and the right to practice a trade. The former restrictions are laid down in the Act on the Acquisition of Real Property in Åland (3/1975), and the latter restrictions in regional legislation.[79]

In conclusion, the instances where the autonomous status of the Region of Åland may concern private law are limited and rather disjointed. They do not form a coherent whole, let alone being able to create a complete system of private law. The general framework and great bulk of private law applied in Åland is the same as in mainland Finland.

7.10 Private International Law Legislation

At present, Finnish private international law is largely based on European Union legislation. The core of this field consists of the Regulation (EC) 593/2008 on the law applicable to contractual obligations (Rome I) and the Regulation (EC) 864/2007 on the law applicable to non-contractual obligations (Rome II), which provide uniform conflict rules.[80] Both regulations are applied universally in the sense that the law specified by the regulation will be applied whether or not it is the law of a European Union Member State.

Conflict rules and other private international law regulation on specific types of contracts are also found in individual domestic acts. Examples include the Act on the Law Applicable to Certain Insurance Contracts of International Character (91/1993), the Maritime Act (674/1994), the Act on Negotiable Promissory Notes (242/1932), the Act on Cheques (244/1932), the Act on the Law Applicable to Sale

[78] Again, exceptions are omitted.

[79] *Åland in the European Union* (Helsinki: Europe Information, Ministry for Foreign Affairs of Finland, 2005), 14–15.

[80] Depending on the definition of private international law followed, Regulation (EC) 44/2001 on jurisdiction and the recognition and enforcement of judgments in civil and commercial matters ("Brussels I") may also be mentioned, as well as Regulation (EC) 2201/2003 concerning jurisdiction and the recognition and enforcement of judgments in matrimonial matters and the matters of parental responsibility ("Brussels IIA").

of Goods of International Character (387/1964), the Consumer Protection Act (38/1978), and the Posted Workers Act (1146/1999).[81]

Before the Rome II Regulation entered into force, Finnish conflict rules on non-contractual obligations were unwritten and ambiguous.[82] This is still largely the case for conflict rules on property law matters.[83] The unwritten general rule for rights in immovable and tangible movable property is the *lex rei sitae* rule. An open question is the law applicable to third-party effectiveness of an assignment of claims.

Finnish international family law was quite thoroughly reformed in 2002. The new provisions are found in Part V of the Marriage Act (234/1929) and Chapter 26 of the Code of Inheritance (40/1965).[84]

7.11 Private Law Legislation, the National Constitution, and Public International Law

7.11.1 Relationship Between Private Law and the Constitution

The relationship between private law legislation and the Constitution of Finland (731/1999) is too complicated a topic to be thoroughly discussed in this chapter. Therefore, suffice to mention just some of their contact points. These can be found in legislative work, application of law by courts, and systematisation efforts by legal science.

First and foremost, private law legislation, like legislation in general, must be enacted in accordance with the Constitution. The rules on enactment of legislation are included in Chapter 6 of the Constitution. If the legislation to be enacted restricts a fundamental right (Chapter 2 of the Constitution), the following list of preconditions compiled by the Constitutional Law Committee of the Parliament has to be fulfilled: the restriction has to be enacted by an act (not a lower-level statute), the scope of the restriction and its limits have to be exact, the grounds for the restriction have to be acceptable (pressing societal need), the core of the fundamental right in question has to remain untouched, the restriction has to be proportionate, "protection under the law" in accordance with Section 21 of the Constitution has to be available, and Finland's international human rights obligations have to be adhered to. According to Section 22 of the Constitution, the public authorities shall guarantee the observance of fundamental rights and human rights. This provision seems to set

[81] See Ulla Liukkunen, "Recent Private International Law Codifications", in *Studies on the Finnish Legal System*: *Finnish Reports to the 18th Congress of the International Academy of Comparative Law (IACL) Washington D.C. 25th July – August 1st 2010*, ed. Erkki J. Hollo (Edilex database, Edita, 2011), 131–32, http://www.edilex.fi/lakikirjasto/8059.pdf

[82] Ibid.

[83] For one exception, see Section 5a(4) of the Act on Book-Entry Accounts (827/1991).

[84] See Tuulikki Mikkola, *Kansainvälinen avioliitto- ja jäämistöoikeus* (Helsinki: WSOYpro, 2009), 53–61.

some requirements as to the content of private law legislation. For example, it has been argued that when it comes to fundamental rights of a personal and economic nature, one of the most central means of protection is compensation for damage.[85]

In the application of law by courts, Section 106 of the Constitution may also become relevant with respect to private law legislation. According to this section, if applying a provision of an act would be in evident conflict with the Constitution, the court has to give primacy to the Constitution. The requirement of an "evident conflict" underlines the exceptionality of these situations.[86]

Furthermore, private law legislation may be touched by the requirement of fundamental-right conforming interpretation. This relates to the horizontal effect of fundamental rights, that is, the effect between private parties. In this respect, the starting point of the Finnish system of fundamental rights is the so-called indirect horizontal effect, which means that the effect of fundamental rights between private parties takes place primarily through ordinary legislation. When applying legislation, courts have to choose the outcome alternative which best promotes realisation of fundamental rights. Thus, fundamental rights provide arguments and supplementary aspects for adjudication that applies ordinary legislation.[87] However, it is common that in a dispute both parties are able to invoke their "own" fundamental rights. For example, in a damages case, the claimant may rely on the right to personal integrity (Section 7), the right to privacy (Section 10), or protection of property (Section 15), whereas the defendant may rely on the right to work and the freedom to engage in commercial activity (Section 18), or freedom of expression (Section 12). Since the Constitution includes no order of priority as to fundamental rights, the court has to weigh the parties' arguments. Generally, arguments that concern the core of a fundamental right weigh more.[88]

In legal science, Professor Juha Pöyhönen (Karhu) has outlined a theoretical resystematisation of Finnish private law (patrimonial law) in accordance with fundamental rights. Instead of the mere concept of freedom, which has been the core of the traditional system, the new system would be founded on the entire system of fundamental rights.[89]

7.11.2 Relationship Between Private Law and Treaties

Finland adheres to the so-called dualist theory, which perceives national law and international law as separate systems. Therefore, the provisions of treaties or other international obligations are not formally considered as a part of the Finnish internal

---

[85] See Päivi Tiilikka, *Sananvapaus ja yksilön suoja: Lehtiartikkelin aiheuttaman kärsimyksen korvaaminen* (Helsinki: WSOYpro, 2007), 146–59.

[86] Ibid., 160–62.

[87] Ibid., 162–65.

[88] Hemmo, *Vahingonkorvausoikeus*, 16–17. See Tiilikka, *Sananvapaus ja yksilön suoja*, 165–69.

[89] Pöyhönen, *Uusi varallisuusoikeus*, 2nd ed. (Helsinki: Talentum, 2003).

legal system until they have been implemented into it, that is, until they have been brought into force.[90] Before implementation, an international obligation would not, as a rule, be applied by Finnish courts or other authorities, nor would it affect the rights or obligations of a person within Finland's jurisdiction. Section 95(1) of the Constitution prescribes as follows: "The provisions of treaties and other international obligations, in so far as they are of a legislative nature, are brought into force by an act. Otherwise, international obligations are brought into force by a decree." Implemented international obligations occupy the same hierarchical position as Finnish domestic legislation, and they will be applied similarly.[91]

In practice, implementation is usually achieved by so-called blanket acts or decrees, which merely state that the treaty in question is brought into force, and the text of the treaty is annexed to the act or decree.[92] As regards norm conflicts between implemented treaties or between an implemented treaty and ordinary national legislation, the prevailing view (already formed before the present Constitution was enacted) has been that the norm-hierarchical level of an implemented treaty follows the norm-hierarchical level of its implementing enactment. Then, the usual principles of *lex superior*, *lex posterior*, and *lex specialis* can be applied. However, these principles should not be taken too rigidly. It has been suggested as a strong presumption that the legislator cannot have meant a binding international obligation to be derogated (for which Finland could become liable). Conflicts can, and should, usually be avoided by way of harmonising interpretation.[93]

7.12 Codification Attempts and Prospects

Comprehensive codification of law, including private law, was attempted in Finland in a project that began seriously in 1835. At that time (between separation from the Kingdom of Sweden in 1809 and the declaration of independence in 1917), Finland was an autonomous Grand Principality ("Grand Duchy") of the Russian Empire. The project was an offshoot of Russian efforts, directed by Mikhail Speransky, that had resulted in the *Svod Zakonov Rossiskoj Imperii* codification of 1832.[94]

---

[90] European Union membership entails exceptions to this. See Sect. 7.1.2 above.

[91] *Valtiosopimusopas*: *Kansainvälisten ja EU-sopimusten valmistelua ja voimaansaattamista koskevat ohjeet* (Ulkoasiainministeriö, 2012 – ennakkoversio, päivitetty maaliskuussa 2012), 6, 70–71. As for treaties concluded by or in the context of the European Union, see ibid., 7–15, 80–81.

[92] Kari Hakapää, *Uusi kansainvälinen oikeus*, 3rd ed. (Helsinki: Talentum, 2010), 22. Hakapää notes that the use of blanket acts and decrees does not represent dualism in its pure form, but is rather somewhere between dualism and monism.

[93] Allan Rosas, "Kansainvälinen normisto ja Suomen oikeusjärjestelmä", in *Kansainvälinen normisto Suomen oikeusjärjestelmässä*, eds. Allan Rosas and Catarina Krause (Helsinki: Lakimiesliiton Kustannus, 1993), 20.

[94] Kekkonen, "Suomen oikeuskulttuurin suuri linja", 24.

Finnish law was to be codified according to the Russian model. From the Russian authorities' viewpoint, this project was about rationalisation, essentially for Finland's own good. Unlike later Russian policies towards the Grand Principality of Finland, it was not motivated by Russian nationalism and Pan-Slavism. Nevertheless, Finns perceived the Russian measures as a policy of oppression.[95]

The project faced firm opposition in Finland, and was eventually rejected. However, the Finnish response was not unanimous.[96] Proponents of codification saw a chance to reform out-dated legislation, and to organise the large body of existing norms in a more manageable way. Opponents claimed that codification would discontinue the Swedish-Finnish legal tradition, stir confusion in legal practice, and open the door for Russification of Finnish law. Finally, the opposing arguments convinced the Russians to set the project aside "for the time being".[97] The stability of the Grand Principality was regarded as more important than codification and unification.[98] Codification plans were resumed on some later occasions, but they never led to concrete results.[99]

Apparently, enactment of a comprehensive civil code has not been planned or seriously discussed in Finland during its independence. In 1948, Frederik Vinding Kruse, a Danish professor, presented his own proposal for a Nordic Civil Code.[100] However, as Professor Ulf Bernitz states, "this project was hardly taken seriously".[101] Recently, Finnish scholars have participated in discussions on the need for and feasibility of a European Civil Code.[102]

---

[95] Osmo Jussila, *Suomen perustuslait venäläisten ja suomalaisten tulkintojen mukaan 1808–1863* (Helsinki: Suomen Historiallinen Seura, 1969), 196–97.

[96] It should be noted that even though the aims and general framework of the project were imposed by the Russians, the detailed plans were drafted in Helsinki. The work commenced with a plan by Carl Evert Ekelund, Professor of Roman and Russian law at the Imperial Alexander University of Finland (renamed in 1917 as the University of Helsinki). In this plan, the second of the two main parts concerned civil law. See Jussila, *Suomen perustuslait*, 195–96.

[97] Kekkonen, "Suomen oikeuskulttuurin suuri linja", 24–25. Kekkonen remarks that the debate has some parallels with the German Thibaut–Savigny controversy.

[98] Jussila, *Suomen perustuslait*, 204–8.

[99] Matti Klinge, *Keisarin Suomi*, trans. Marketta Klinge (Espoo: Schildts, 1997), 295–96.

[100] Fr. Vinding Kruse, *En nordisk lovbog*: *Udkast til en fælles borgerlig lovbog for Danmark, Finland, Island, Norge og Sverrig* (København: Centraltrykkeriet, 1948).

[101] Bernitz, "Scandinavian Law", 20.

[102] For a culmination of the discussions, see Christian von Bar and Eric Clive, eds., *Principles, Definitions and Model Rules of European Private Law*: *Draft Common Frame of Reference (DCFR)*, vols. I–VI (Oxford: Oxford University Press, 2010). Despite being essentially an academic undertaking, the DCFR resembles a civil code. In addition to a book entitled "General provisions", it includes six books on the law of obligations and three books on property law.

Chapter 8
French Law

Jean-Sébastien Borghetti

Abstract The Code Civil has enjoyed a very special status in French law since 1804. This is due to the matters it covers and to the intrinsic qualities of its provisions, but also to its political and symbolic significance. Over the last decades, however, this status has been increasingly challenged by the development of supra-legislative rules and a strong 'decodification' movement, resulting in ever growing areas of private law being regulated outside the Code. The legislator has reacted by reforming parts of the *Code Civil*, mostly in the field of personal status and family law. However, what is generally regarded as the heart of the *Code Civil*, i.e. property law and the law of obligations, has remained to a large extent unchanged since 1804. Most lawyers agree that a reform of these parts of the Code is now overdue, but it not so easy to alter a national monument! A reform of the law of obligations in the *Code Civil* is now on the agenda, but its precise contents are not yet known and expectations among French lawyers are running high.

Keywords France • Code Civil • Decodification • Reform • Constitution • European Convention of Human Rights

8.1 Introduction

Codes and codification are familiar to French law.[1] The leading role of France in the history of codification is well known. Between 1804 and 1811, Napoleon, as part of his building the country anew after the French Revolution, had five codes drafted

[1] For an excellent introduction to French law, in English, see John Bell, Sophie Boyron and Simon Whittaker, *Principles of French Law* (2nd ed., Oxford: Oxford University Press, 2008).

J.-S. Borghetti (✉)
Professor of Private Law, Université Panthéon-Assas Paris (France), Paris, France
e-mail: Jean-Sebastien.Borghetti@u-paris2.fr

J.C. Rivera (ed.), *The Scope and Structure of Civil Codes*, Ius Gentium: Comparative Perspectives on Law and Justice 32, DOI 10.1007/978-94-007-7942-6_8,

and put into application: the *Code Civil* (Civil Code), of course (1804), but also the *Code de commerce* (Commercial Code), the *Code de procédure civile* (Civil Procedure Code), the *Code penal* (Penal Code) and the *Code d'instruction criminelle* (Criminal Procedure Code). There had already been some attempts at codifying the law in other European countries in the preceding decades (Bavaria, Prussia, Austria), but the Napoleonic codification was to be the starting point of a new legal tradition and it set a model, which has remained influential up to this day.

Codification completely changed the face of French law.[2] Before the French Revolution, there actually was no such thing as French law in the actual sense of the term. Each province in the kingdom of France had its own customary law; in some fields, there also existed rules adopted under the King's authority, which applied to the whole kingdom; and, Roman law, in the form of *jus commune*, as well as canon law, i.e. the law of the Catholic Church, also played a role. Codification therefore really created French law, by unifying the legal traditions of the various provinces and severing this new legal system from the two major transnational legal systems: Roman law and canon law.

French codification marked the birth of a truly national legal system in Continental Europe. It also established a link between political modernity, national independence and the possession by a Nation of its own legal codes. This was especially true of the Civil Code[3]: it was not only a practical tool for citizens and lawyers, but also became a symbol of political modernity and national prestige.[4] It is therefore no surprise if many countries, in Europe, America and elsewhere, were eager to have their own civil code after France had set this example.

Needless to say, France itself has been deeply impregnated by the Napoleonic codification.[5] The *Code Civil*, undoubtedly the masterwork of this codification, has enjoyed a unique status and remarkable longevity since 1804 (2). Yet, the practical role of the *Code Civil* is being affected by the extension and increasing autonomy of

---

[2] On the history of French civil law, see Jean-Philippe Lévy and André Castaldo, *Histoire du droit civil* (Paris: Dalloz, 2002).

[3] A translation into English of the *Code Civil*, as well as of some other major French codes, can be found on the official legal website of the French government: http://www.legifrance.gouv.fr

[4] The contents of the Napoleonic *Code Civil* were of course also very important in that respect. Whether it be in the field of property law or of personal and family law, the Code turned its back on the former feudal and stratified society, by recognising the equality of all citizens in civil matters (with some exceptions regarding married women) and establishing new types of property rights, more adapted to a merchant and capitalist society. For these reasons, and because it came from the land of the Great Revolution, the *Code Civil* became a symbol and an object of desire for political liberals in many parts of the Western world – as well as an object of hatred for many political conservatives!

[5] It goes without saying that codification turned France into a country of 'written law' (as opposed to judge-made law). This has weighed all the more heavily on French legal culture, as a very strict view of the role of judges and case law prevailed until recently in legal discourse: it used to be said that judges should only be 'the mouth of the law', i.e. apply the rules set by the legislator, and should therefore not create new rules or even adapt existing ones. The fact that this principle has long been proved false by judicial practice has not significantly modified the traditional view, according to which France is a written law country.

other branches of the law (3). These developments bear heavily on the issue of the Civil Code reform (4), which now stands on the French Government's agenda, and what exactly the future of the *Code Civil* will be is an open question (5).

8.2 The Special Status of the *Code Civil*

Codes are rather common in France. There were already five of them in 1811, a number that remained unchanged during about a century. A couple of new codes, including the *Code du travail* (Labour Code) were drafted in the first half of the twentieth century. It is after World War II that codification received a new impulsion.[6] Starting in the post-war years, with moments of acceleration and others of lesser activity, tens of new codes have been drafted over the last 60 years or so, and a few have been rewritten. About 70 codes can now be found on the French Government official legal website[7]! Some of these codes are actually little more than ordinary, normal length statutes. Nevertheless, this great number of codes testifies to the French ambition of gathering the various rules and regulations pertaining to specific subjects in books, called codes, in order to make them more easily accessible.

The *Code Civil* is therefore not remarkable in that it is a code. Yet, it can be described as unique (Sect. 8.2.1); but this uniqueness does not prevent its authority from being challenged (Sect. 8.2.2).

8.2.1 The Uniqueness of the Code Civil

The *Code Civil* is unique first of all because there has only been one civil code in France since 1804. This is true both from a material and a formal point of view (Sect. 8.2.1.1). Besides, the *Code Civil* has had a political and symbolic importance reaching far beyond that of an ordinary code (Sect. 8.2.1.2).

8.2.1.1 The Material and Formal Uniqueness of the Code Civil

From a material point of view, the *Code Civil* has always been the only code in France to cover the field of civil law. In contrast to other countries, such as Switzerland for example, France does not have and never had a civil code for, say, family and property law, and a distinct code for the law of obligations. All the traditional branches of civil law have always been gathered and regulated in the *Code Civil*: personal status and family law (part I), property law (part II) and the law of obligations (part III), with its various branches (contracts, torts, securities, etc.).

---

[6] B. Oppetit, *Essai sur la codification* (Paris: Presses universitaires de France, 1998).

[7] http://www.legifrance.gouv.fr

The origins of the rules contained in the *Code Civil* are diverse. In the field of personal status and family law, the Code strikes a compromise between the traditions of the French provinces before the Revolution. It also contains distinctive new features, which are a direct result of the latter, such as the principle of civil equality. In the field of property law, the code creates a new concept of ownership (*propriété*), which did not exist in pre-revolutionary French customary law. In the field of the law of obligations, the code draws heavily on the *jus commune*, or more precisely on the French version of it, as synthesised in the seventeenth century by Domat and in the eighteenth by Pothier.[8]

The *Code Civil* is also unique from a 'formal' point of view. That is: there has never been another Civil Code in France than the *Code Napoléon*.[9] As shall be seen, parts of the *Code Civil* have been modified and even completely changed, sometimes several times, since 1804. But some other parts have remained practically unaltered. More importantly, the Code, taken as a whole, has never been officially changed, renewed or replaced, as has been the case for example in Italy, in Québec or in the Netherlands. Even though significant portions of it have been modified over the time, it is therefore the one and same code that applies since more than 200 years.

Besides, France being a strongly united and centralised State, it has never been disputed that there could only be one national *Code Civil*, and that no province or region should have its own code. This actually does not exclude the existence of specific rules applying to specific territories, even in the field of civil law[10]: but there is no other civil code than the Napoleonic *Code Civil* that applies in France.

8.2.1.2 The Political and Symbolic Importance of the Code Civil

Jean Carbonnier, one of the greatest twentieth century civil lawyers in France, once described the *Code Civil* as the "civil constitution of France" (*la constitution civile de la France*). He thus outlined the stability of the *Code Civil*, which sharply contrasts with the constitutional instability of France between the Revolution and the 1960s. In little more than 150 years, France was subjected to more than ten different constitutional regimes: two empires, two monarchies, five republics, and a few other more 'exotic' ones. Needless to say, constitutional law has not been very firm legal ground over the last 200 years! In contrast to this political and constitutional instability, the *Code Civil* became the symbol of legal continuity. It more or less embodied France's legal identity, at times when what should have been the more basic

[8] As is well known, many provisions of the Code Civil on the law of obligations are actually cut and paste from either Domat (1625–1696) or, more often, Pothier (1699–1772).

[9] This has been its official name up to this day, even if the Government and Parliament seem to ignore it.

[10] This is true for some overseas territories. A few specific rules also apply, in mainland France, to Alsace and Moselle, as a result of these *départements* having belonged to Germany between 1870 and 1918.

norms (i.e. constitutional ones) proved to be hopelessly unstable, and to a certain extent, unreliable.

Of course, the *Code Civil* was able to play this political role because it possesses intrinsic qualities, most of which are well known. One of them, which should not be underrated, is that it is written in a very elegant language, typical of late eighteenth-century French. This makes the *Code Civil* not only a legal tool, but also a part of France's cultural and literary heritage. Some articles of the Code are (or should be) known by heart by many lawyers, because they are important, of course, but also because the way in which they are written makes them easy to remember – a bit like proverbs.[11] The qualities of the Code, however, are not only literary ones. The rules it sets, at least in the field of the law of obligations, have proved sufficiently robust to adapt to changing circumstances; and God knows how much the social, economic and political context has evolved in France, like in all other Western countries, over the last two centuries! This does not mean that the *Code Civil*, including its part on the law of obligations, should not be reformed. But even if one admits that reform of some aspects of the Code is overdue, the mere fact that French lawyers and French society have been able to function until now in a reasonably satisfying way with such antique rules is a proof of their quality. It must also be said that the very style of the Code has contributed to its longevity. The fact that most rules are stated in rather general terms and leave it to judges to specify the details of their application[12] is indeed a factor of flexibility and adaptability, which has made it possible for the same rules to apply over such a long and chaotic period: while the Code sets a canvass, judges have the possibility and the liberty to adapt their solutions to the changing circumstances, within that general frame.

Whatever these qualities, however, the uniqueness and the precedence of the *Code Civil* have been challenged recently by the emergence of superior rules.

8.2.2 The Challenge Set to the Code Civil by the Emergence of Superior Rules

The special status of the Code Civil has been altered by the increasing practical importance of constitutional (Sect. 8.2.2.1) and international norms (Sect. 8.2.2.2) over the last decades.

[11] One thinks of course, first of all, of article 1134, which provides that contracts are binding onto the parties: "*Les conventions légalement formées tiennent lieu de loi à ceux qui les ont faites.*" But one could also mention articles 544, 1382 or 2279 (now 2276).

[12] This, of course, makes the theory according to which judge should only be the mouth of the law an illusion, at least in the field of civil law.

8.2.2.1 The Increasing Importance of Constitutional Rules

As has been said, French constitutional law used to be an area of great instability. Things have however changed since 1958, when the Fifth Republic was instituted, under which the country still leaves. The Constitution of the Fifth Republic has been modified several times over the last 50 years, but France nevertheless lives nowadays in a time of reasonable constitutional stability. What more, the Constitution of the Fifth Republic introduced the constitutional review of parliamentary laws. Until 1958, courts and government authorities were bound to apply laws adopted by Parliament, even if they infringed the Constitution. The courts were not allowed to control the conformity of laws and statutes to the Constitution. As a result, the Constitution had little impact on the legal system, at least in the field of private law. This has now changed. Since 1958, a special court, the *Conseil constitutionnel* (Constitutional Court), is in charge of reviewing the conformity of parliamentary laws to the Constitution. Until recently, however, constitutional review of parliamentary laws could only be carried out in the interval between the vote of the law by Parliament and its coming into force. In other words, only preliminary constitutional review was possible. As this review was furthermore not compulsory, this meant that laws and statutes could still come into force and be applied, which violated the Constitution. This was changed by a 2009 constitutional reform, which came into force in 2010. Constitutional review by the *Conseil constitutionnel* of a parliamentary law already in force is now possible,[13] if it is argued that this law violates a right or freedom granted by the Constitution.[14] This possibility has actually proven extremely successful and hundreds of claims regarding the constitutionality of existing laws and statutes have been raised over the last 2 years.

This, of course, has a major impact on civil law and the *Code Civil*. The Code is not anymore the highest rule in its field. It actually took French lawyers some time to realise that constitutional law and constitutional review were bound to have an impact on civil law. In that respect, they certainly laid behind their colleagues in other legal systems, especially in Europe (in Italy, for example) and South America. Things have changed, however. It is now clear that constitutional law, and more precisely the individual rights secured by the Constitution, do have a major impact on civil law. All branches of civil law are concerned: the personal status and family law, of course, but also property law and the law of obligations. The right of ownership (*droit de propriété*), for example, which is described by the *Code Civil* as an absolute right (article 544), and which is actually protected by the Constitution, must be reconciled with other constitutional rights. Even the law of obligations is

---

[13] For more details on constitutional review, see Pascale Deumier, *Introduction générale au droit* (Paris: LGDJ, 2011), 299–304.

[14] The French Constitution of 1958 contains no Bill of rights or equivalent. It makes a reference to the 1789 *Déclaration des droits de l'homme et du citoyen*, however, and in 1971 the *Conseil constitutionnel* ruled that the Declaration was in fact part of the Constitution. Nowadays, the impact of the Constitution on civil law is mostly, though not exclusively, that of the *Déclaration*.

affected: liability for fault or freedom of contract, for example, have been the subject of decisions by the *Conseil constitutionnel*.[15]

It is now clear that the *Code Civil* is not any more the ultimate authority in the field of civil law. Constitutional rules and rights have precedence over the rules and rights it sets. Quite often, actually, the Constitution, or the interpretation of it given by the *Conseil constitutionnel*, comforts the *Code Civil* solutions. But this confirmation of the Code is also a dispossession, since the ultimate justification and source of the rule lay no more in the Code, but in the Constitution. This impact of the latter remains of course limited, as many civil law rules have apparently little to do with rights guaranteed by the Constitution; but the matters affected by the latter keep increasing in numbers. The insistence of our society on fundamental rights, and its deep aspiration to equality, are potentially disruptive of the whole field of civil law, and there are only few rules, which, in the long term, should remain totally immune to constitutional scrutiny.

8.2.2.2 The Increasing Importance of International Law

The French Constitution of 1958 did not only ascertain the importance of the Constitution in the French legal order. It also recognised the precedence of international rules over national ones.[16] Two sets of international rules are of special relevance: the law of the European Union (Union law – Sect. 8.2.2.2.1), and the law of the European Convention on Human Rights (ECHR – Sect. 8.2.2.2.2).

8.2.2.2.1 Union Law

Union law constitutes nowadays a massive set of rules, reaching out through the greater part of the member States' legal systems, including of course France's. The European Union has been little concerned with general civil law until now, though, concentrating itself on matters more directly connected with economic issues. Yet, the impact of Union law on civil law and the *Code Civil* is not negligible.

First of all, a heavy body of Union legislation concerns itself with consumer law. France has made the choice to keep consumer law apart from civil law and the *Code Civil*, by drafting a separate *Code de la consommation* (Consumer Code).[17] This apparently preserves the autonomy of the Civil Code. But the price for this is that the latter has been deprived of something very important in practice, i.e. the setting of rules pertaining to the protection of consumers.

A second field in which Union law has had an important, and also more direct, impact on the *Code Civil* is product liability. As is well known, the European Union

---

[15] See *Les Nouveaux cahiers du Conseil constitutionnel*, n. 31, 2011: "Le Conseil constitutionnel et le droit des biens et des obligations".

[16] Article 55 of the Constitution.

[17] See below Sect. 8.2.2.2.

(then called the European Economic Community) adopted in 1985 a directive on the subject.[18] This directive was transposed in France, with some delay, in 1998, and integrated into the Code Civil (articles 1386-1 to 1386-18).[19] As a result, part of the Code is now Union law and cannot therefore be modified by the French legislator. Formally speaking, product liability has been made a part of the *Code Civil*, but from a substantial point of view it is an alien element.

The impact of Union law on civil law and the *Code Civil* is bound to increase in the coming years. Of special relevance in that respect is the European Commission's ambition to create a European law of contract. The precise features and status of such a European contract law are still unclear – and heavily disputed in academic circles. If it comes to life, however, it will have a tremendous impact on the *Code Civil*. Even if this European contract law only takes the form of an optional instrument, as is often predicted, the *Code Civil* risks being deprived of its 'monopoly' on an essential part of civil law. The importance of such an evolution, should it take place, hardly needs to be underlined.

Union law and its impact on French law naturally reach far beyond civil law and the *Code Civil*. It is the autonomy of the Member States' legal systems, which is globally at stake in the process of European unification. But in so far as the *Code Civil* is a symbol of France's legal identity and autonomy, the way in which it is affected by Union law is of specific relevance. This also applies to the relation of the *Code Civil* to ECHR law.

8.2.2.2.2 ECHR Law

France is a party to the ECHR. As has been said, the Constitution gives precedence to ECHR rules over national rules. This precedence is guaranteed both by national courts, which are bound to disregard a national law or statute if it conflicts with an ECHR rule, and by the European Court of Human Rights, which may fine France when a public authority or court has violated a right granted by the ECHR.

The impact of the ECHR on French law has been extremely strong since the 1990s, all the more so as the European Court of Human Rights has a very extensive interpretation of the ECHR, which makes the latter reach far beyond what its drafters had contemplated. As is the case with constitutionally guaranteed rights (which quite often overlap with those stated in the ECHR), all fields of civil law are concerned by the Convention: personal status law, family law, property law, the law of obligations.[20] One used to believe that the latter could remain to a large extent unaf-

---

[18] Council Directive 85/374/EEC of 25 July 1985 on the approximation of the laws, regulations and administrative provisions of the Member States concerning liability for defective products, *Official Journal L* 210, 7.8.1985, 29–33.

[19] See Jean-Sébastien Borghetti, *La responsabilité du fait des produits. Étude de droit comparé* (Paris: LGDJ, 2004), 507–508.

[20] On the incidence of the ECHR on French civil law generally, see Anne Debet, *L'Influence de la convention européenne des droits de l'homme sur le droit civil* (Paris: Dalloz, 2002).

fected, as the Convention was considered to have only a vertical effect, i.e. between the States and their citizens, as opposed to a horizontal effect, i.e. between the citizens themselves. In that perspective, contracts and conventions between private persons would have remained outside the field of application of the Convention. However, both the European Court of Human Rights and French courts are developing the horizontal effect of the Convention, which therefore has a growing impact on private contracts.[21] The question of the extent to which private contracts should respect basic rights as set out by the ECHR or other instruments is actually a very complicated but also fascinating question. In any case, what is clear is that the *Code Civil* and the rules it sets are now superseded by the ECHR, which may not positively dictate new civil law rules, but certainly sets a limit to the autonomy of the *Code Civil* and national civil law.

8.3 The Relation of the Code Civil to Various Branches of the Law

The contents of the *Code Civil* have remained remarkably stable over the last 200 years. Given the development of the legal system, however, the importance of the Code in respect to various branches of the law has been modified. This is true for civil law (Sect. 8.3.1), and even more so for other branches of the law (Sect. 8.3.2).

8.3.1 The Code Civil and Civil Law

The *Code Civil*, in its initial version, was divided into three parts: persons (*les personnes*, i.e. the law of personal status and family law), goods (*les biens*, i.e. property law) and obligations.[22] These three parts have remained until today. Recently, however, securities law has been taken out of the third part and turned into an autonomous fourth part; but this is no change in the substance of the Code.[23] The matters the Code deals with have therefore remained the same for 200 years.[24]

---

[21] See e.g. European Court of Human Rights, 13 July 2004, *Pla and Puncernau v. Andorre*, req. 69498/01.

[22] The actual title of the third part of the *Code Civil* is "Des différentes manières dont on acquiert la propriété" (Of the different ways through which ownership is acquired). It has long been acknowledged, however, that this title is not adequate and does not really express the contents of this part, which deals mostly with the law of obligations, but also with the law of inheritance and patrimonial relations between spouses (which is the reason why 'obligations' could not be chosen as a title in the first place).

[23] The code also contains (since 2004) a very short fifth part dealing with the rules specific to Mayotte, a small French overseas territory with a special status.

[24] At one time, the rules regarding the acquisition of the French nationality had been brought out of the *Code Civil* and made the subject of a code of their own (*Code de la nationalité française*), but they are again to be found in the *Code Civil* since 1993.

In contrast to what happened in other countries, no part of civil law, like for example family law, has been voluntarily brought out of the Code. Some new matters have even been introduced into the code. In 1970, the right of privacy was recognised.[25] Provisions on bioethics were introduced in 1994.[26] And in the field of tort law, provisions on product liability were adopted in 1998, following the above-mentioned European directive.

Yet, the whole of civil law is not anymore to be found in the *Code Civil*, as this used to be (almost) the case when the Code was adopted. One reason for that is the fact that the courts have refined the rules of the Code and sometimes created new ones. These new rules have therefore emerged at the margin of the Code, where they still lie. To a certain extent, however, such a phenomenon is inevitable and, besides, these new rules still have a strong link to the Code, since they are more or less extensions of it.

Of more significance to our subject is the fact that the legislator has created new rules in the field of civil law, but without integrating them into the *Code Civil*. This is especially true in the field of the law of obligations and of property law. One good example is the 1985 law on the compensation of traffic accidents. This statute is, to a large extent, a tort law statute; yet, it has not be integrated into the Code, with the result that what may be in practice the most important rule in the field of tort law is not in the *Code Civil*. Another very important Parliamentary law, which has not been integrated into the Code, even though it clearly deals with civil law, is the 1989 law on housing leases (*baux d'habitation*). Quite a few other examples could be found, for example in the field of property law, where some recent developments, like the possibility to create a separate range of assets (*patrimoine d'affectation*) for business purposes have taken place outside the Code, even though they are of paramount importance from a theoretical point of view.[27]

If the contents of the Code have apparently been preserved, the truth is therefore that, even within the field of the civil law, the Code's importance has weakened. It undoubtedly remains the heart and core of civil law, but important developments have taken place outside it and it does not contain any more the whole of civil law. This evolution, however, has not been the result of a voluntary 'decodification'. If the legislator did not integrate some important new laws or rules into the Code, it is not out of a deliberate intention to empty the Code of its substance: it was rather for the sake of (apparent) facility. Integrating new rules and concepts into the Code probably appeared too complicated. The quality of the Code, its systematic organisation, its reputation also, made it difficult to build important new developments into it. Such a difficult task as the systematic reorganisation of the Code should only be carried out within the frame of a general reform of the *Code Civil*, or so it often said. But such a reform, as we shall see,

[25] Article 9.

[26] Articles 16 ff.

[27] One could also mention the 1965 statute on the collective ownership of buildings, which has not been integrated into the Code.

is all the more arduous, as the developments that have taken place outside the Code are more important.

8.3.2 The Code Civil and Other Branches of Law

The *Code Civil* was never intended to cover the whole field of substantial private law. As early as 1806, the Commercial Code (*Code de commerce*) was adopted, which purported to regulate commercial law. At that time, however, civil and commercial law together encompassed the most of substantial private law. This of course, is not true anymore. Even though commercial law has tremendously developed itself (Sect. 8.3.2.1), other branches have emerged: consumer law, of course (Sect. 8.3.2.2), but other ones as well (Sect. 8.3.2.3).

8.3.2.1 The Code Civil and Commercial Law

The *Code Civil* was never intended to cover commercial law, since it was always understood that it was to be complemented by a Commercial Code.[28] Nevertheless, many rules of commercial law can only be read in connection to the *Code Civil.* This is especially true of contracts. The basic rules on contracts are set by the *Code Civil* and the rules on various commercial contracts that may be found in the *Code de commerce* only come to supplement or, on certain points, correct the *Code Civil* rules. This is also true, though to a lesser extent, of company law (*droit des sociétés*), since 'société' is seen as a contract by the *Code Civil*, which contains the basic rules on companies (art. 1832 ff.).

The balance between the *Code Civil* and the *Code de commerce* has long been upset, however. The first reason for it is that the *Code de commerce* terribly suffered from decodification. In the 1980s, the situation had come to a point where this Code had nearly become an empty shell. Most areas of commercial law were regulated outside the *Code de commerce*. There was a major Act on company law, another on insolvency law, etc. The decision was finally taken to redraft the *Code de commerce* and a new one came into force in 2001. This new Code is actually rather a compilation of statutes on different subjects: company law, insolvency law, credit instruments, business practices, various commercial contracts, etc. Thanks to this new Code, however, the greater part of commercial law can now again be found in one same book.

But some branches have separated from commercial law. This is true of banking and financial markets law, which is now the subject of a specific code, the Monetary and Financial Code (*Code monétaire et financier*). Insurance law, which may be regarded in some countries as part of commercial law, is also seen as distinct from

[28] See esp. article 1107 of the Civil Code.

commercial law, with a specific code devoted to it: the Insurance Code (*Code des assurances*).

Commercial law, this ever-expanding field, is also the best example of the tendency of the various law branches to subdivide again and again. It is now very difficult to identify where the 'core' of commercial law lies. Besides, it is clear that links between civil law (and thus the *Code Civil*) on the one hand, and some specialised branches of commercial law, on the other hand, tend to grow thinner. Nevertheless, civil law remains the source of the basic rules on property law and the law of obligations, as well as an essential toolbox.

8.3.2.2 The Code Civil and Consumer Law

The development of consumer law over the last decades has been a major phenomenon in France, like in many other countries. And like these countries, France has been faced with the choice whether or not to insert consumer law rules into civil law and into the *Civil Code*. Some countries, like Germany, have made the choice of such an insertion, with the main European consumer law directives[29] being transposed into the Civil Code.[30] France, on the contrary, decided to leave consumer law outside civil law and the *Code Civil*. It even adopted in 1993 a Consumer Code (*Code de la consommation*), in which most rules pertaining to consumer protection are gathered.

The existence of a separate code for consumer law has contributed to consumer law and civil law remaining quite separate from each other. Consumer law is still considered in France by most civil lawyers as not belonging to civil law. As a result, systematic study of consumer law is not very widespread. More surprisingly, no systematic theory of consumer contracts has yet emerged in France. This may partly be due to the fact that the approach taken by the Consumer Code, which basically mirrors that of the European Union directives, is not really a systematic one. As a matter of fact, these directives purport to regulate specific contracts (credit contracts or insurance contract, e.g.), or contracts concluded in specific circumstances (contracts concluded outside business locations, e.g.), or specific aspects of consumer contracts (unfair contract terms, e.g.). So far, however, the European legislator has not taken a truly systematic approach to consumer law; and the divide between consumer law and civil law in France has prevented French doctrine from filling this gap. Of course, specific rules pertaining to consumer contracts are mentioned when 'general' contract law is studied; yet consumer law very often remains a kind of inelegant appendix which must be dealt with, but is rather frowned at.

---

[29] Consumer protection is a competence of the European Union and the Union has adopted many directives in that field. The result of it, is that the greater part of consumer protection law in the Member States is actually made of European Union rules.

[30] This choice was made when Germany reformed its law of obligations in 2001.

8.3.2.3 The Code Civil and Yet Other Branches of Law

If the relation of civil law and the *Code Civil* to commercial law and consumer law is of paramount importance, other branches of law have emerged out of civil law and can now be considered as autonomous.

It must be reminded, first of all, that there exists in French law a sharp divide between private and public law. Things were not that clear when the *Code Civil* was adopted, however. It is in the second half of the nineteenth century that public law clearly detached itself from private law, when courts decided that the rules of the *Code Civil* were not adapted for deciding cases in which the State was involved. Thus, interestingly, administrative law (*droit administratif*) was born in France out of an explicit refusal to apply the *Code Civil* to certain matters.

The separation from civil law and from the *Code Civil* has also taken place within the field of private law. The best example is probably labour law (*droit du travail*). In 1804, the whole of labour law consisted in two articles of the *Code Civil.*[31] Quite quickly, however, new and special rules appeared, which now form a massive body of law, clearly distinct from civil law and the *Code Civil.*[32] More recently, other branches, like building law (*droit de la construction*) have developed and are gaining increasing autonomy.[33]

The legislator has therefore not deliberately trimmed the *Code Civil*'s contents. But the mere fact that these contents have remained stable means that the relative importance of the Code within the legal system has diminished, it not shrunk. If the Code's hold on the law of persons and family law has remained very strong, the same is not true of property law and the law of obligations. Many operations and situations, which substantially belong to these parts of law, are now regulated outside the code. Yet, the *Code Civil* still contains basic rules, which are used in all fields of law. What is a contract?, what are its basic conditions of validity?, what are the basic rules of liability for fault?, what are the basic operations through which an obligation can be transferred?, what is property/ownership?, etc.: all these questions are answered by and in the *Code Civil*. The Code therefore remains a central piece, and probably THE central piece, of the French private law system. This makes the issue of its reform all the more difficult.

8.4 Reforming the Code Civil

The *Code Civil* has never been globally reformed since 1804. Talks about such a reform started as early as the beginning of the twentieth century, however. When the first centenary of the Code was celebrated in 1904, the opinion was forcefully expressed, especially by Raymond Saleilles, one of the greatest French lawyers of

[31] Articles 1780 and 1781.

[32] The adoption of the Labour Code (*Code du travail*) started in 1910.

[33] There now exists a *Code de la construction et de l'habitation*.

the time, that the Code should be reformed in order to adapt to the new times. Besides, in the context of the then strong rivalry between France and Germany, the adoption of the German civil code (*bürgerliches Gesetzbuch*, or BGB), a few years before, sounded like a challenge.[34] The German code naturally appeared more modern[35] and set an example that some wished to follow. In the end, however, no real reform project of the French *Code Civil* was initiated at the time. After the First World War, Italian and French lawyers drafted the project of a common code of contracts and obligations, which, if adopted, would have reformed a central part of the *Code Civil*. The project was stillborn, however, at least on the French side.[36] Later, immediately after the Second World War, the French government appointed a commission, with the task of drafting a new *Code Civil*. The commission met until 1964, but no new legislation came out of its efforts.[37] Since that time, there has been no project in France to reform the *Code Civil* globally. The possibility of drafting a new Civil Code, as has been made for example in the Netherlands or in Québec, has not been seriously contemplated, neither by the Government or Legislator nor by the academia.

If a global reform of the Code is not on the agenda, however, limited reforms, concerning parts of the Code, have proliferated since the 1960s. This has been especially true in the field of personal status and family law (Sect. 8.4.1). Reforming the code is more difficult when it comes to property law and the law of obligations, but things are now changing in that field as well (Sect. 8.4.2).

8.4.1 Personal Status and Family Law

The original rules on personal status and family law, in the first part of the *Code Civil*, were the product of their time. They had a strongly patriarchal flavour, which would be totally unacceptable nowadays. The social dimension of these branches of law is actually such that is has long been accepted that the rules of the *Code Civil* could and should be modified from time to time in order to reflect the changes in French society. Some modifications were actually adopted as early as the nineteenth century.[38] The greatest and most ambitious reform, however, took place in the 1960s and at the beginning of the 1970s, when most aspects of personal status and family law were reformed one after the other under the lead of Jean Carbonnier, one of France's greatest civil lawyers in the twentieth century. These reforms, although they were sharply criticised

---

[34] As is well known, the BGB was adopted in 1896 and came into force in 1900.

[35] Even though it was also criticised by some authors in Germany for having left aside difficult questions raised by the contemporary social situation.

[36] But the project was a major source of inspiration for the new Italian Civil Code adopted of 1942.

[37] The Commission was established in June 1945 and presided by Léon Julliot de la Morandière, a distinguished civil lawyer.

[38] Divorce, for example, which was possible under the 1804 *Code Civil*, was suppressed in 1814 and reintroduced into the Code in 1886 only.

by some people because of their (mildly) liberal orientation, especially in the field of divorce and family law, were also considered at the time as examples of legislative masterwork. The quality of the new texts put them on a par with the standard set by the *Code Civil* in 1804 and many believed that they would last decades. But what had not been foreseen was the extraordinary speed at which society would keep changing.

As a matter of fact, as early as the 1970s, new changes were made in the first part of the *Code Civil.* And things have accelerated since the 1990s. Same-sex partnerships were introduced in 1999, the rules regarding the transmission of family names were changed in 2002, divorce was reformed again in 2004, the rules on filiation were modified in 2005, those on the incapacity of natural persons in 2007, provisions on bioethics have been revised regularly since 1994 and lastly in 2011, same-sex marriage and adoption for homosexual couples are to adopted in 2013... It would hardly be an exaggeration to describe the first part of the *Code Civil* as being in a state of permanent reform, or at least modification. It is now widely acknowledged that, regrettable though it may be, rules in the field of personal status and family law have a limited life expectancy. Reforms of the *Code Civil* in that field are therefore regarded as normal, rather than exceptional. The new provisions of the Code are usually very different from the original ones. Elegant and rather general formulations have been replaced, in many cases, by lengthy, technical, and sometimes rather clumsy texts. It is not sure, however, if the legislative style of the early nineteenth century could still be used today.

8.4.2 Property Law and the Law of Obligations

Until recently, property law and the law of obligations had undergone few modifications, usually of limited scope. Change is accelerating, though, and the reform of the inner sanctum of the *Code Civil,* i.e. the general part of the law of obligations, is now on the agenda (Sect. 8.4.2.1). Future prospects are less clear as far as property law is concerned (Sect. 8.4.2.2).

8.4.2.1 Reforming the Law of Obligations

As has already been said, a great part of the law of obligations is now outside the *Code Civil,* if only because many specific contracts are regulated in other branches of the law than civil law (labour contracts by labour law, intellectual property contracts by intellectual property law, etc.) In the *Code Civil* can be found the general rules on obligations, the general rules on contracts, the rules on certain specific contracts (sale, mandate, etc.), most rules on tort law, the rules on '*quasi-contrats*' (i.e. *negotiorum gestio*, restitutions and unjust enrichment), the rules on securities law and the rules on prescription. A vast majority of these rules had remained unchanged from 1804 until very recently. A few modifications had been made here and there, but they were really marginal.[39] Things have been changing since 2004, however.[40]

This was the year when the 200th birthday of the Code Civil was celebrated. A group of French scholars, led by professor Pierre Catala, seized the occasion of this celebration to launch a reform project of those parts of the Civil Code dedicated to the 'general' law of obligations (i.e. general rules on obligations, general rules on contracts, tort law, and *quasi-contrats*) and the law of prescription. This was a purely academic project, which had not been commissioned by the Government or any official body. But the promoters of the project were able to 'surf' on the celebration wave and to rely on a declaration by the then French President, according to which time was ripe for a reform of the *Code Civil*. The project was finally officially presented to the Minister of Justice in September 2005, under the name of *Avant-projet de réforme du droit des obligations et de la prescription* ('First draft for a reform of the law of obligations and prescription').[41] It is usually called *Projet Catala*, however, after the name of its main promoter.

---

[39] The single most important modification in the third part of the code had been the above-mentioned introduction of the provisions on product liability in 1998.

[40] Two years before, however, in 2002, a commission was set up by the ministry of Justice in order to translate into French law a 1999 European directive on the sale of consumer goods. In Germany, the translation of this directive was the occasion of the big *Schuldrechtsreform* (reform of the law of obligations) of 2001. In France, nothing as grand was contemplated. At that time, reforming the whole law of obligations was not regarded as an option. However, some wanted to seize the opportunity of this new directive to reform the law of guarantees in the contract of sales in general, and not just in consumer sales. The commission which had been set up by the ministry therefore suggested that the whole law of guarantees in the contract of sales be redesigned along the lines of the directive. The idea was to turn the regime set up by the Directive into the common law of guarantees in the contract of sales (consumer and professional sales alike), and to get rid of the current system of guarantees in '*Code Civil*' sales, which is extremely complicated. But this suggestion met with fierce criticism. Business circles, first of all, were opposed to the reform, as they are to nearly all reforms modifying the rules in the field of civil law. Besides, some lawyers opposed the suggested reform because they refused that the law of sales be based on European law. Their argument was that if the French law of sales, and not just the law of consumer sales, was based on EU law, France would not be free to amend this piece of legislation and thus the Parliament would relinquish its power over part of the Civil Code. Whatever the truth of this argument, the fact is that the proposal made by the commission was cast away and no real reform of the law of sales was carried out. The 1999 Directive was finally translated in 2005 into the Consumer Code, not the Civil Code, and the new consumer sale guarantees have simply been added to the existing ones provided for in the *Code Civil*. This first limited attempt at reforming the French law of obligations was therefore a failure. In the end, there was no reform, but only the piling up of a new regime on top the existing ones, and outside de *Code Civil*.

[41] P. Catala, ed., *Avant-projet de réforme du droit des obligations et de la prescription* (Paris: La Documentation française, 2005). An English translation of the *Projet* can be found in Stefan Vogenauer, John Cartwright and Simon Whittaker, ed., *Reforming the French Law of Obligations, Comparative Reflections on the Avant-projet de réforme du droit des obligations et de la prescription ('the Avant-projet Catala')* (Oxford: Hart Publishing, 2009).

This *Projet* was translated in several languages and attracted considerable attention, both in France and abroad. It also stimulated other members of the French academia. A second reform project was launched under the direction of another professor, François Terré, and is generally called *Projet Terré*. The two first parts of this second project, on general contract law and on tort law, were published in 2009[42] and 2011,[43] and the third part, on the general rules on obligations and *quasi-contrats*, is now finished and about to be published.

These doctrinal initiatives have prompted the legislator and the Government to enter into a reform process of the law of obligations. In 2006, the Government passed a reform of part of the of securities, which had remained practically unchanged since 1804.[44] Two years later, Parliament, on its own initiative, voted a general reform of the law of prescription.[45] Interestingly, the contents of both these reforms were not based on the doctrinal reform projects: securities were never a part of these projects in the first place; as for the law of prescription, it was covered by the *Projet Catala*, but the reform adopted by Parliament runs along quite different lines. Yet, it is quite clear that these doctrinal reforms projects have played a decisive role in bringing the reform of the law of obligations on the agenda.

The question now is whether the other aspects of the law of obligations contained in the *Code Civil* are going to be reformed. This looks likely for the general part of contract law. The French ministry of justice is working on the subject since 2007 at least. A third draft has been completed in 2011, whose content has not been made public yet, but which is presumably based on a large extent on the Catala and the Terré projects. Besides, the ministry has produced a first reform draft on the general rules on obligations and *quasi-contrats*, which was circulated and commented on by lawyers and business organisations. A second draft is now said to be in preparation. As for tort law, it is said that the ministry has prepared a first reform draft, which has however not yet been made public. If these various drafts are brought together, the ministry will have a project covering the greater part of the law of obligations. The question now is: will the Government have the political will to set a reform of the law of obligations through? Their intentions are not yet known, but expectations among French lawyers are running high. Should this reform finally take place, the only remaining sections of the original *Code Civil* in the third part of the Code would be the ones on specific contracts.[46]

---

[42] F. Terré, ed., *Pour une réforme du droit des contrats* (Paris: Dalloz, 2009).

[43] F. Terré, ed., *Pour une réforme du droit de la responsabilité civile* (Paris: Dalloz, 2011).

[44] *Ordonnance du 21 avril 2006*. The text only deals with *sûretés réelles*, and not with *sûretés personnelles*. This text also separated securities law from the rest of the law of obligations and brought it into a newly created fourth part of the *Code Civil*.

[45] *Loi du 17 juin 2008*.

[46] The sections on *sûretés personnelles* have not been reformed either. But they now stand in the recently created fourth part, dealing with the law of securities.

8.4.2.2 Reforming Property Law

Some small parts of property law have been reformed over time. Provisions on collective ownership (*indivision*), in particular, have been amended several times.[47] Until recently, however, there had been no talk of reforming the whole of property law. But the reforming zeal, which has manifested itself in the field of the law of obligations since 2005, has finally spilled over into property law. A reform draft covering most of property law was written under the authority of *Association Henri Capitant des amis de la culture juridique française* and made public in 2008.[48] This is a purely doctrinal project, however, and nothing indicates that either the Government or Parliament is contemplating a reform of property law in the near future.

At the intersection of family law, property law and the law of obligations, inheritance law (which is dealt with in the third part of the *Code Civil*) was reformed in 2006. Although several provisions had already been modified since 1804, this has been the single biggest reform in that field. This reform had been made necessary by the evolution of society and family structures.

As for the rules on patrimonial relations between spouses (*régimes matrimoniaux*), which also stand at the intersection of family law, property law and the law of obligations, and which together with inheritance law form what French lawyers call patrimonial family law (*droit patrimonial de la famille*), they had undergone a thorough reform in the 1960s, as part of the wider reform of personal status and family law. Several smaller modifications have been made since.

8.5 Conclusion: The Importance of the Code Civil Today

The *Code Civil* does not any more reign supreme in the field of civil law. Quite independently from the question of its reform and of its contents, the Code is no more the ultimate authority in civil law matters. There may not (yet) be another coherent body of civil law rules challenging it, but constitutional and internationally guaranteed rights have a growing impact on civil law. Whether they confirm the rules of the *Code Civil*, limit or even contradict them, it is now undisputed that they have precedence over the Code. The Code is therefore not any more a fully autonomous body of law. It must be interpreted and applied in the light of and in accordance with these superior rules. Civil law has entered the fundamental rights' era. In the French context, one should probably not speak of a constitutional civil law, in the sense of a specific body of law within the field of civil law. It is rather the whole of civil law which is being affected (though at varying degrees, depending on the areas concerned),

[47] A special statute was also adopted in 1965 on the subject of collective ownership of buildings. It has remained outside the Code up to this day.

[48] *Propositions de l'Association Henri Capitant pour une réforme du droit des biens* (Paris: Litec, 2009). The draft was written by a commission chaired by professor Hugues Périnet-Marquet.

and which now cannot be considered independently from the Constitution and the ECHR. Civil law used to be dealt with at one level only: that of the *Code Civil*. Today, the *Code Civil* is still standing, but there is a higher level looming over it. This is a change of status for the Code. It is also a challenge for civil lawyers and *Code Civil* specialists, who were used to a rather simple, one-level, system, and who must now learn to play on two or three keyboards at a time.

The on-going reform of the *Code Civil*, which is now reaching the heart of the law of obligations, will not change that state of things. This reform is nevertheless a great challenge. Admittedly, whatever its contents, the *Code Civil* is bound to remain at the heart of French civil and private law. But the better its provisions, the greater its ability to radiate over the French legal system and abroad. It is therefore to be hoped that the expected reform of the law of obligations will make that part of law more legible and will give lawyers an efficient tool to adapt to a changing world.

Chapter 9
The Greek Civil Code Facing the Process of Decodification and Recodification of Law

Christina Deliyanni-Dimitrakou

Abstract This chapter is dedicated to the basic features of the Greek Civil Code and to the alterations to its image under the influence of two contrasting tendencies: on the one hand, of the phenomenon of decodification, which emerges through the regulation of legal issues that traditionally belonged to the scope of Civil Law through laws entirely disparate from the Civil Code. On the other hand, there is the tendency of recodification, which is expressed through the consecutive reforms of the past 30 years to the text of the Greek Civil Code. Following the presentation of the evolution of the Greek Civil Code through history and of its content, as well as its relation to the Constitution, to international treaties and EU law, the impact of the two aforementioned phenomena on its structure and content shall be outlined. Emphasis will be given to the decodification and to the consequent autonomy of Commercial and Labour law from the text of the Civil Code, to the emergence of the semi-autonomous area of Consumer Law, as well as to the modernization of Family Law which has been linked to the process of recodification.

Keywords Greece • Codification • Decodification • Recodification • History of Greek Civil Code Constitution • International treaties • EU Law • Consumer Law • Family Law

9.1 Introduction

The modern Greek legal system was formed after the Greek Revolution of 1821, i.e. the uprising against the Turks, and the foundation of the Modern Greek state in 1830. As the Greek Revolution of 1821 was not only a liberation movement, but also a social and political revolution deeply rooted in the ideological and

C. Deliyanni-Dimitrakou (✉)
School of Law, Aristotle University Thessaloniki, Chiou 5, GR 55236 Panorama, Greece
e-mail: chdel@law.auth.gr

J.C. Rivera (ed.), *The Scope and Structure of Civil Codes*, Ius Gentium: Comparative Perspectives on Law and Justice 32, DOI 10.1007/978-94-007-7942-6_9,

philosophical ideals of the Enlightenment (Theocharides 1971; Dimaras 1985; Kitromilides 1996), it was inevitable that the codification of law, which was one of the main goals of the Enlightenment, keenly preoccupied Greek legal scholars and the lawmakers of the revolutionary and post-revolutionary era (Svolos 1935; Michaelides-Nouaros 1988; Vlachos 1991; Papachristou 1975; idem 1991).

Therefore, it is not coincidental that the first revolutionary assembly in Epidaurus (1821) decided to include a clause in the first revolutionary constitution which established, "the laws of our ever-memorable Christian Emperors" (i.e. the Byzantine Emperors), as the official law of the modern Greek state, that would be in effect until the drafting of a modern Civil Code by a committee consisting of the "most distinguished, wise and virtuous Greeks (Pantazopoulos 1948; idem 1945, 1952). This decision was crucial for the development of Greek law in general and for the subsequent evolution of the Greek Civil Code in particular. Thirteen years later, the new Greek state had a new Commercial Code, a Criminal Code, a Code of Civil Procedure and a Code of Criminal Procedure. However, the Greek Civil Code was adopted very late, in 1940, and entered into force even later, in 1946, i.e. 124 years after its adoption was discussed for the first time. But, before we present the structure and content of this Code let us have a look at its historical evolution, in order to better illuminate its foreign influences and its ideological background.

9.2 Historical Underpinnings, Socio-political Background and General Characteristics of the Code

9.2.1 Historical Evolution

Five years after the Constitution of 1822, a new one, the Constitution of Troizena recommended that all future codes should be influenced by French legislation, and especially by the French Civil Code, which was considered to be a perfect example of codification in its time. This explicit reference to the French codification was fully justified, not only by the liberal and democratic character of the latter as a product of the French revolution. It was also the result of the discourse among the French-educated members of the so-called Greek bourgeoisie, who embraced democratic ideas and advocated the introduction of modern legislation in Greece that would respond better to the needs of the renascent nation (Michaelides-Nouaros 1988; Vlachos 1991; Papachristou 1975; Papantoniou 1976; Vrellis 1990; Deliyanni-Dimitrakou 1996). Therefore, it is not an accident that both the Penal Code and the Code of Criminal Procedure, adopted by the first Governor of Greece, Ioannis Kapodistrias (1827–1831), took as their model the respective French Codes while the Greek Code of Commerce which came into force in 1827 was nothing more than a faithful translation of the French Commercial Code of 1807, which had been already applied as customary law in pre-revolutionary Greece (Yannopoulos 2008). Alongside this French influence, one can observe also in Greece a parallel English influence due to the dissemination of Jeremy Bentham's utilitarian theories, which were in line with the rational and liberal spirit of the Greek revolution of 1821 (Zepos 1976; Kotsiris 1994; Hatzis 2001). Apart from this link, G. Bentham had been associated also with the classical Greek scholar and thinker of Enlightenment A. Koraïs. Both wrote commentaries on the first Greek Constitution (Kitromelides 1985, 34). This influence, however, was undermined by the debate concerning the sources of the future Greek Civil Code, which divided the representatives of the emerging Greek bourgeoisie, on the one hand, who supported the introduction of the French Civil Code, and the representatives of the conservative faction of land-owners, on the other hand, who advocated the implementation of Byzantine Roman Law (Papachristou 1975; Papantoniou 1976).

Yet the Governor Kapodistrias, as well as King Otto, who came to power after the assassination of the former, gave the lead in the second of these trends. He favored, in other words, the revival of Byzantine Roman Law. Governor J. Kapodistrias particularly designated the corpus of Byzantine law as the source of Greek Civil Law (1928) and King Otto's viceroy Georg Ludwig Von Maurer followed a completely different policy to that prescribed by the Troizena Constitution of 1827 (Papantoniou 1976; Hatzis 2001). As Maurer was an adherent of the Historical School of Jurisprudence, he believed that the new civil law had to reflect the customary law and the spirit of the Greek people ('Volksgeist') as set out in the current interpretations of the Byzantine Laws (Pantazopoulos 1966–1969; Stathopoulos 1992). He ordered, therefore, the collection and study of local customs, a project which was abandoned in July 1835, after his resignation from the regency council (Stathopoulos 1992). Seven months later, King Otto announced the commencement of the process for the elaboration of Civil Law, with the enactment of the decree of 23 February 1835, which declared that "the civil laws of the Byzantine emperors contained in the Hexabiblos of Harmenopoulos (Pantazopoulos 1952) shall remain in force until the promulgation of the Civil Code, whose drafting we have already ordered, and that customs, sanctioned by uninterrupted use or by judicial decisions, shall have the force of law wherever they prevail" (Pantazopoulos 1958). This decree was the cornerstone for the edifice of the civil law in Greece since the regime that it introduced, though short-termed and transitional, in the end remained in force for a period of no less than 111 years (Deliyannis 1996; Hatzis 2001).

According to the spirit of its drafters, the aforementioned Decree did not refer to the Hexabiblos of Harmenopoulos in an exclusive manner. The reference to this compilation by this Decree was indicative, given the fact that it was a mere collection of Byzantine laws, a simple compilation of selected fragments of Basilica and of the most accessible imperial Novels, circulating in very few copies and therefore difficult to use. For all these reasons, the Greek courts adopted a broad interpretation of the Decree of 23 February 1835 that led to the introduction of the Roman Law, *in globo*, in Greece, as it was received in Germany and applied by the German Pandect School (Pantazopoulos 1958; Michailides-Nouaros 1959). It is therefore no accident that Greek legal thought, which had been oriented almost exclusively towards France, became increasingly oriented towards Germany (Vrellis 1990; Deliyanni-Dimitrakou 1996; Troianos and Velissaropoulou-Karakosta 1997, 354–357). Moreover, the enactment of the German Civil Code (hereinafter BGB) during the late nineteenth century enhanced the opportunities for an enlarged influence of German Law in Greece, because it offered a new model of codification (Vrellis 1990). Nevertheless, the Greek jurists had already begun to treat with a certain caution the reception of foreign legal texts – as such – for three reasons. Firstly, the Pandects Roman Law, as elaborated by the German Pandect School and introduced in Greece through the Decree of 23 February 1823, was already complemented during this long transitional period by the jurisprudence of the Greek courts, as well as by a special statutory law (Litzeropoulos 1932). Secondly, the territorial enlargement of Greece through the liberation of significant territories from the Turks had added to the complex statutory mosaic of Greek civil affairs not only three local codes which were already in force in the Ionian Islands, the island of Samos and the island of Crete, but also the Israelite and Muslim Family Laws as personal laws of the relevant minorities (Ast. Georgiades 1996). And thirdly, because the circulation of several new projects of civil law codifications in Europe had already expanded the range of the foreign legal influences on the Greek legislator (Deliyanni-Dimitrakou 1997b).

In the meanwhile, efforts to elaborate the Civil Code continued at a breathless pace in Greece. During the long transition period, and until 1930, a dozen committees succeeded each other in this work (Introductory Report of the Greek Civil Code of 1945, 1946). A draft Civil Code of 1887 based on French, Italian and Saxon models, was not adopted, partly because of constitutional difficulties (Triantaphyllopoulos 1937; Zepos 1946). After another attempt failed in 1922, a new five-member drafting committee was appointed to the task in 1930. This committee published a series of drafts up to 1937, and in the following year Professor G. Balis of Athens was appointed to co-ordinate them. In 1938, the dictator Ioannis Metaxas decided to complete the final text of the Code and asked G. Balis to organize and revise the drafts (Gazis 1996; Hatzis 2001). As a result, the final text of the Code was ready at the end of 1939 and in 1940 was adopted by the Greek state with the Law 2250/1940 which fixed the first July of 1941 as the day of it enforcement. But the new Code never actually came into force because Greece was occupied by the Nazis in April of 1941. After the liberation (October 1944), a new committee was set up to revise the Code all over again, because it had been enacted during the Metaxas dictatorship (Maridakis 1946; Triantaphyllopoulos 1946). This revised version was put into force in February 23 of 1945 under the title "Greek Civil Code" but was replaced again by the 1940 Code, which was to take effect retroactively from February 23 of 1946, thus 111 years after the enactment of the Royal Decree of 23 February 1835! Under the law introducing the Code, all local preexisting Codes and personal laws were abrogated, with the exception of the Muslim law which continues even now to govern family and inheritance affairs of the members of the Muslim minority living in the area of Thrace (Grammatikaki-Alexiou et al. 2002, 48). For the last 60 years, the Civil Code 1940/1946 has been the main source of Greek civil law – and for many scholars, the most important source of Greek law.

But for reasons that will be presented in the following sections of this paper, the Greek Civil Code had been the object of many criticisms both positive and negative before its enactment and during the early years of its implementation (Zepos 1967; Valticos 1947; Matzoufas 1954; idem 1956; Maridakis 1959; Sakkelaropoulos 1944;

Simantiras 1967; Tambacopoulos 1940; Litzeropoulos 1956; Makris 1945; Dimakis 1946; Manessis 1946). For these reasons it is necessary, in order to form an objective appreciation, to examine the external style of the Code, as expressed in its writing methods and techniques, as well as its socio-political background.

9.2.2 The External Style of the Code

As far as the external style of the Code is concerned, it must be mentioned again that the drafting Committee of 1930 had decided to follow the method of the German Civil Code (Ministry of Justice 1930, 1936). Therefore, the Greek Code was and is until now divided into five Books which reflect the traditional classification of the civil law that had long been used in Greece under the inspiration of the German Pandect School. The style of the German Code has also been followed in both the internal system of the subdivisions of the Books as well as the order of the provisions included in each of them.

In contrast, as far as the style of the writing of the Code is concerned, it was decided in 1930 to seek simplification and clarity, to limit the number of articles strictly to the necessary, to eliminate references from one article to another and to keep a distance from foreign patterns and especially from the model of the German Civil Code, which was known for its abstractness and its excessive casuistry (Ministry of Justice 1930, 1936). But although the authors of the Code made many efforts to endow it with greater simplicity, they failed to eliminate the structural defaults of the German model. Therefore, the Greek Civil Code has been criticized for the inadmissible abstraction and excessive splitting of the rules governing the law of obligations (general regulation of the obligation, general provisions on non-performance, special rules on contracts in general, then rules of bilateral contacts and finally an unjustified casuistry about special contacts) (Valticos 1947; Makris 1945). Another example of inadmissible casuistry due to the influence of the German Civil Code is also the one that refers to the rules of the law of torts. Particularly, despite the adoption by the Drafting and Revision Committees of two general clauses (Art. 914 and 919 of the Greek Civil Code) based on the model of articles 41 par. 1 and 2 Swiss Code of Obligations and reflecting the spirit of Article 1382 of the French Civil Code, one can find in the relevant chapter of the Code a number of provisions regulating specific torts (Deliyannis 1996).

9.2.3 Complaints of a Sociopolitical Nature Against the Code and Their Mitigation

But the main complaint against the Code was of a sociopolitical nature. The Code was specifically criticized for the disadvantage of expressing foreign laws, including the German law, a feature which could not be adapted to the collective consciousness of the nation (Pantazopoulos 1958; Makris 1945). In addition, it was argued that the law introduced by the Code was outdated and completely unsuited to the needs of postwar Greek society. Alongside these arguments is necessary to add that the Code had not been approved by the representatives of the people and was divorced from the popular consciousness as expressed by the customs in force. Nevertheless, it is necessary to underline that all this criticism responded only partially to the reality.

9.2.3.1 The Eclectic Character of the Code

There is no doubt that the men drafting the Code had to choose between two solutions: the introduction of a new law, on the one hand, and the simple systematic gathering of the rules of positive law already in force, on the other. They decided finally on an intermediate solution. As we see from the early work of the Drafting and Revision Committees of 1930, the decision was taken to move to a codification of the rules that already existed and to proceed to the elaboration of new rules, exceptionally, only when the circumstances made it necessary (Drafting and the Revision Committees at their meetings on November 11 and December 17, 1930, 14; *Project of the Civil Code-General Principles*, 8–10, Valticos 1947; Deliyannis 1996). It is true that during the preparation of the various books of the Code, certain deviations from the above mentioned guideline were made. But Professor Balis, who was responsible for the final drafting of the Code, later eliminated all these deviations. He even abandoned in other branches of Civil Law, such as Family Law, a number of innovations that the needs of social life rendered necessary. Thus, despite its external appearance and the content of many of its rules, which are reminiscent of the German Code, the Greek Civil Code of 1940 (GCC) was in principle a systematic collection of the earlier law, formed by the influence of jurisprudence and doctrine, and supplemented by the new legislation (Litzeropoulos 1956; Daskarolis 1996; Dacoronia 2003). Some very important new provisions, however, were also involved, which gave to the Code a progressive character and a dynamism that permitted it to revive itself during the 60 years of its implementation. And despite a few shortcomings and the obsolescence of some of its regulations, the new Code did the Greek legal world the great service of liberating it from the confusion arising from the sources of Roman Law and the full submission to the Pandect German doctrine (Deliyannis 1996).

Thus, although the new Greek Code contains provisions that are similar to those of other European codifications and especially of the German and Swiss Civil Codes, this is not the result of an uncritical imitation. All these common rules are the expression of "the common legal fund of the European People" (Michaelides-Nouaros 1958, 8; Deliyanni-Dimitrakou 1997a, 126–127; idem 1997b). Namely of a common core of legal convictions, conceptions and institutions which has its roots in a complex web of factors, such as e.g.: the predominance in Europe of a common morality based on Christianity, humanism and classical ancient Greek philosophy; the common economic infrastructure and the common social and cultural ties of the

European societies; the influence of Roman and Canon law on modern European legal thought and the common background of legal concepts, categories and constructions that derive from this influence. It is therefore this common legal heritage that permits us to explain the similarities between the Greek Civil Code and the Codes of the other European countries and it is also the same heritage that excludes the classification of the former within the family of Germanic group (Zweigert and Kötz 1992, 160). As we have already emphasized, the authors of the Greek Civil Code had used the comparative eclectic method, drawing on both the laws of the Germanic group and those of the French group, and using the common progress of European legal science. Consequently, it is not a coincidence that a significant number of theorists describe both the Greek Civil Code and the Greek legal system as mixed legal phenomena within the wider Romano-Germanic Legal Family (Michaelides-Nouaros 1958; Deliyanni-Dimitrakou 1997a, 77–78).

9.2.3.2 Mitigation of the Complaints Underlying the Non-conformity of the Code with the Requirements of the National Social Consciousness

Let us now examine the complaints related to the lack of approval of the Code by the House of Representatives (Maridakis 1946) and the discrepancy of its contents from the legal conscience of the Greek people, as expressed through the customary law that had evolved during the Turkish occupation (Pantazopoulos 1958). As far as the first complaint is concerned, it must be observed that the elaboration of the final drafting of the Code as well its promulgation in 1940 bear a certain number of abnormalities. On the other hand, however, the need to have a code ending the uncertainty of law that prevailed before was recognized unanimously as a very serious counterargument, that finally managed to outweigh all these objections.

Finally, regarding the alleged failure to take into consideration the customary law, it was underlined firstly that the very content of such a law is not always progressive and secondly that in post-revolutionary Greece there had never existed a customary law of general application (Michaelides-Nouaros 1959). Moreover, in most of the cases where general rules such as those referring to the principles of good faith, the protection of the weaker party and contractual freedom were already to be traced in the local customs, the same regulations also existed in the Code as elements of the common legal heritage of the European countries, as we have mentioned above.

It is true that in the discussion initiated in Greece just after World War II, voices were raised against the immediate implementation of the Code, arguing that it would be better to wait for the crystallization of the new ideas, which were still under formation. However, there were many theorists who wisely replied, firstly, that the renewal of the positive law is not necessarily related to changes in its content through legislative intervention (Maridakis 1944). Secondly, that the aforementioned renewal depends more on the flexibility of the positive law, which facilitates the interpretation of its rules by the courts. According to this view, the

Greek Civil code is imbued with such flexibility because it contains a great number of abstract notions and general formulas which allow its renewal through the interpretation of its rules by the judiciary (Ap. Georgiades 1996).

9.3 Relationships Between the Civil Code with the Constitution and Trieaties

9.3.1 General Observations

The Greek Civil Code recognizes in the first of its articles two distinct sources of law: legislation, i.e. the statutes enacted by the State, and custom. Customary law has nowadays an extremely limited application in Greece, owing to the superiority, both quantitative and qualitative, of the statute law – which is more clear and certain than custom. A third source of law is recognized in the Greek legal order: a) "the general accepted rules of international law" (Art. 28 par. 1 of the Greek Constitution) and b) the rules of EU law that have been adopted by the Member States. Generally recognized rules of international law are basically the rules of international customary law (sometime derived from international conventions that are not ratified (Ioannou et al. 1991, 113). International conventions do not constitute a separate source of law. This is due to the dualistic approach to the relationship between international conventional law and national law that had been adopted by Art. 28 par. 1 of the Greek Constitution, providing that international treaties acquire legal force in the Greek legal order only if they are ratified by statute. Contrary to the tradition of the Anglo-American legal systems, the courts' jurisprudence does not constitute a source of law in the Greek legal system. Nevertheless, judicial decisions as well as legal writings are commonly taken into account by the Greek courts and Greek legal theory in interpretation of the positive law (Ap. Georgiades 2002; Litzeropoulos 1980).

9.3.2 Civil Code and Constitution

9.3.2.1 The Supremacy of the Constitution Over Ordinary Legislation

In the Greek legal system the Constitution is not amended or replaced through the common procedure used for the replacement or amendment of ordinary legislation. It enjoys therefore a high formal power that gives to its provisions precedence over all other legislation. In consequence of this supremacy, ordinary legislation should at least not contravene the principles enshrined in the Constitution. But the Greek courts do not have the power to deprive the law which they reject as unconstitutional of its force as is the case for example with the German Constitutional Court or recently with the French Conseil Constitutionel (Drago 2008). The only power they have is to abstain from applying the unconstitutional provision in the specific case which they are hearing (Skouris and Venizelos 1985; Spiliotopoulos 1983).

The constitutional review of legislation is a very sensitive issue because the Greek Constitution of 1975, like all modern Constitutions, does not regulate only questions related to the political regime and the organization of the state, but also contains general principles deriving from its provisions concerning human rights. Therefore, it is very interesting to examine whether the aforementioned principles regulate directly the relationships between private parties, or impose guidelines binding exclusively on the national legislator.

9.3.2.2 The Horizontal Effect of Constitutional Provisions Concerning Fundamental Rights in the Relations Between Private Parties

The Greek constitutional amendment of 2001 gave an answer to this question in a new sub-paragraph added to Art. 24 § 1 of the Greek Constitution, stating that "These rights also apply to the relationship between individuals wherever appropriate." It should however be noted that the theoretical debate about the relationship between fundamental rights and private law started in Greece much earlier, specifically in the mid 1970s when the Constitution of 1975 came into force. Greek legal theorists decided then to introduce the German theory of Drittwirkung (Markesinis 2001) in order to determine this relationship (Kalomiris 1969, 47; Korsos 1973).

More particularly the problem that preoccupied Greek legal scholars was not so much whether fundamental rights should bind individuals in their private relationships. It was mainly the manner, degree and extent to which this influence should be exercised in practice (Iliopoulou-Straga 1990; Akrivopoulou 2007). Between the disciples of the indirect Drittwirkung which argued that constitutional rights must penetrate indirectly into private relationships through general clauses and abstract legal concepts of civil law (Korsos 1973; Dagtoglou 1982; Spyridakis 1985, 73; Deliyannis 1981; idem 1997) and the proponents of the direct Drittwirkung, on the other part, which argued that constitutional rights should bind individuals in a direct manner, generating obligations for them (Katranis 1978; Dimitropoulos 1981; Kassimatis 1981) a third opinion rejected the transplantation of the notion of Drittwirkung into Greek legal system underlying the differences that separate the liberal character of Greek Constitution from the corresponding German one (Manitakis 1991; idem 1992). According this opinion, public freedoms are not only moral commitments. They operate also as rules of public order which penetrate private law relationships through the clauses of civil law, making the use of the legal construction of the Drittwirkung unnecessary.

But outside this theoretical controversy it must be recognized that the reception of the Drittwirkung in Greek legal order was unnecessary for another reason. Namely, because of the diffused character of the judicial review of constitutional matters, which allowed the Greek courts not only to meet the constitutional provisions guaranteeing fundamental rights, as public policy rules, but also to implement them in private relationships without any reference to the mechanisms of direct or indirect Drittwirkung (Manitakis 1991). According to the view that prevails nowadays in Greek scholarship (Chrysogonos 2006; Katrougalos 2001; Papanikolaou 2006; Ch. Akrivopoulou 2007) and case law (AP 2159/2007 (www.areiospagos.gr) the Art. 25 par. 1 of the Greek Constitution ensures the horizontal effect of all human rights regardless of their distinction into civil, political and social, and whether they are regulated by the Constitution or other international or supranational texts. Certainly, this provision does not specify the way in which human rights should be applied to private relationships. This issue however, depends on how the rule embodied in each of these rights is formulated and should be decided by the judge *in concreto*.

From the above considerations it can be concluded that the Greek courts must interpret the provisions of positive law in a manner that is compatible with the Constitution, and in particular with the constitutional provisions concerning fundamental rights. This kind of interpretation, which tends to examine civil law and in particular the Civil Code in the light of the Constitution, is not new. It was established years ago by the Supreme Constitutional Court of Germany and it has been applied more and more frequently in Greek jurisprudence (Ap. Georgiades 2002, 69; Stamatis 1999, 292; Papanikolaou 2000, no 261).

9.3.3 Civil Code and International Treaties

The 1975 Constitution has taken a very positive attitude towards international law. Apart from the fact that it recognizes in Art. 28 par. 1 of the Greek Const. the generally accepted rules of international law as a source of law, it lays down also in this provision that the generally accepted rules of international law, as well as the international treaties ratified by statute and coming into force under their respective conditions, shall prevail over any contrary statutory provision. In the interpretation given to this provision, it is unanimously accepted that the term «legislative provisions» includes only the provisions of ordinary legislation and not constitutional provisions (Vegleris 1977; Ioannou et al. 1991, 189–192). Thus, according the hierarchy of Greek legal rules, the 'generally accepted rules of international law and the international treaties ratified by Greece', rank between the Constitution and ordinary legislation. This means that in case of conflict of an international agreement with the rules of the Constitution, the latter shall prevail.

But in reality the chances of such a conflict are small because the Greek courts tend to align the content of the Constitution with the requirements of the international treaties ratified by Greece. The European Convention on Human Rights is very often the cause of such an alignment, since it not only protects human rights but is also equipped with an international judicial mechanism, the European Court of Human Rights, to guarantee application of its provisions.

In line with the general policy adopted by the courts in most European countries, Greek jurisprudence very often invoques the provisions of the ECHR as a hermeneutic criterion in interpreting the provisions of ordinary legislation. We see therefore a tendency for Greek courts to rely on Art. 6 of the Convention establishing the right to a fair trial (Kroustalakis 2002; Chrysogonos 2001), and on Article 1 § 1 of the First Protocol of the ECHR, requiring respect for property rights (Drossos 1997; Manitakis 2008). Regarding the use of this hermeneutic criterion, one could repeat the thoughts outlined above regarding the interpretation of law as consistent with the Constitution. The same observation can be made as far as for the horizontal application of the Convention's provisions to interpersonal relationships. This is why it is specifically acknowledged: firstly that violations caused by individuals, that could have been avoided by the adoption of appropriate measures by the State, can qualify as state violations – as far as the ECHR is concerned; and secondly, that the provisions of the Convention can be applied to relations between individuals, but only if they are deemed to be appropriate.

9.3.4 Civil Code and EU Law

9.3.4.1 General Characteristics of EU Law

By virtue of Art. 28 of the Greek Constitution, EU law is regarded as a source of law in the Greek legal order. A key feature of EU law is its autonomy in relation to both international law and the national laws of Member States. This characteristic is shaped by the case law of the ECJ, which very early on considered as a basic element of European Community law the fact that it is produced within a new autonomous legal order, one which has real powers stemming from the limitation of the sovereignty of the Member States (Sachpekidou 2011, 482). A result of the autonomous character of the EU law is its greater efficiency, achieved through the recognition of the primacy, the direct applicability and the direct effect of its acts.

9.3.4.2 Supremacy in Relation to National Laws

Using the criterion of the autonomous nature of Community law, the ECJ has established from its inception the principle of the absolute primacy of Community over national laws. However, the majority of the Greek courts have not recognized this criterion. They have preferred, in other words, to base the supremacy of founding Treaties and secondary Community legislation adopted prior to the accession of Greece to the European Communities on Art. 28 par. 1 of the Greek Const. (Sachpekidou 2011, 482; Christianos 2008; Papadopoulou 2009, 387) while as regards secondary EU Law adopted subsequently, the supremacy thereof is usually founded on Art. 28 par. 2 of the Greek Const. Controversy has also raged within Greek legal theory and praxis on the extent of this primacy, and in particular whether or not it includes constitutional provisions within its scope. While some court decisions have recognized the absolute priority of Community law over national legislation as a whole, including the Constitution, the majority of the Greek courts and in particular the Council of State and the Supreme Court on civil and penal matters (Areios Pagos) have only accepted the priority of Community law over ordinary legislation, declining to take sides on the issue of the relationship of the former to the Constitution. Certainly, for a long period of time the possibility of a conflict between Community law and the Constitution seemed impossible (Sachpekidou 2011). Nevertheless, a fierce such conflict arose during the decade 2000–2010, when the constitutional revision of 2001 added to Art. 14 of the Greek Constitution a new paragraph which established absolute incompatibility between major shareholdings in the media and major state procurement contracts. The aforementioned constitutional provision, as well its executive statute of 2002, ran counter to earlier European Community Directives regulating public contracts for services and projects (Directive 93/37 EEC). Following a preliminary question posed to the ECJ by the plenary session of the Council of State (OlStE 3670/2006, *ToS* 2007, 547) the former confirmed this incompatibility very clearly. It avoided, however, relying on the hierarchical supremacy of EU law, invoking only the violation of a principle common to both legal orders, i.e. the principle of proportionality (Papadopoulou 2009, 387).

9.4 The Contents of the Code

The Greek Civil Code comprises 2035 articles divided into five books (General Principles, Law of Obligations, Property Law, Family Law and Law of Succession).

General Principles The first of its books, titled General Principles ('*Yenikes Arches*') follows the deductive style of the German Civil Code (BGB) It gathers together provisions on natural and legal persons; capacity to hold rights and to enter into judicial acts; formal and substantive validity of judicial acts; representation and authority; consent and ratification; terms and conditions; prescription and pre-emption; abuse of rights; self-help and self-defence. A common characteristic of all these provisions is their breadth and unlimited scope of application. Indeed, unless displaced or contradicted by more specific rules, the general principles included in the first book are applicable throughout the Civil Code, and for that matter, the entire realm of civil law, including commercial law. But, although the systematization attempted in this book helps to avoid repetitions and promotes efficiency and consistency, it can become problematic for practitioners of law who are not accustomed to the civil law tradition, because in many cases rules regulating or affecting a given transaction, for example a sale of a chattel, are placed not only in the first book but also in different parts of the GCC, depending on their relative generality or specificity. Each of this group of articles presupposes the existence of the other and this interdependence should not be overlooked by lawyers handling such cases.

Law of Obligations The second book of the GCC, the Law of Obligations ('Enohikon Dikaion') is based on the model of the BGB, but also has many national and specifically Byzantine legal influences (Christodoulou 2008).

The book contains 40 chapters. Although they are not formally divided into groups, the first 12 chapters deal with the general principles of the Law of Obligations, applicable to all forms of obligations which are regulated more specifically elsewhere and which form the General Law of Obligations ('Yenikon Enohicon Dikaion') The remaining 28 chapters, which are called the 'Special Law of Obligations' ('Eidikon Enohikon Dikaion'), cover specific contracts such as donations, sales, leases, partnerships, production contracts, employment contracts, surety, loans, etc., and also *negotium gestio*, law of restitution and law of torts. The second book of the GCC regulates the specific types of these contracts in a sequence that does not have the character of a logical arrangement. A systematic arrangement, preferred by several legal scholars, would be to group the different categories of particular contracts according to their economic function. But the authors of the GCC did not choose to do this. Besides, no exhaustive list of all possible types of contractual agreements can be made. Nor does the validity of any contract depend on its correspondence to any of the recognizable categories. The underlying principle in the Law of Obligations is the principle of contractual freedom that permits private parties to construct all kinds of obligations as their interests and needs require.

Property Law The third book of the GCC is called Property Law ('Empragmaton Dikaion') and contains eleven chapters. The substance of the articles of these chapters (Arts 947-1345 GCC) is derived from the Roman tradition, the indigenous Greek variations that were developed in the nineteenth century, and certain modern civil codes. The influence of the French, German and Swiss Civil Codes is particularly evident. In Greece, as in most Civil Law jurisdictions, the number of real rights is limited (*numerus clausus*). In contrast to the Law of Obligations, parties cannot create new or different rights of property unless otherwise provided by law. According to Art. 973 GCC the real rights that the parties can acquire are: ownership, personal and real servitudes, pledges and mortgages. Possession and detention are *sui generis* rights, neither real nor personal. The only case in which the parties have discretion in the formation of a property right is in personal servitudes (Art. 1188 GCC). The creation of a real right is a real transaction, and as such it is subject to the rule of temporal priority. Real rights may be subject to a term or a condition. When a real right is extinguished with retroactive effect, all real rights granted by the holder of that right are also extinguished in the absence of contrary provision of law.

Transfer of real rights in movable property is regulated in Greece on the basis of the German model. The GCC requires more particularly for its realization, in addition to the delivery of possession of the thing, the conclusion of two separate contracts, one real and the other personal. It qualifies, moreover, the first of these contracts as abstract – in the sense that it does not subject its validity to the validity of the personal contract. In, contrast, the GCC partially follows the German model as regards the transfer of real rights in immovable property. While it requires the conclusion of two contracts: a real and a personal, it does not confer an abstract character on the real contract, considering it void whenever the personal contract which constitutes its cause is void. But, apart from the conclusion of the two contracts, the GCC requires, as does its German model, for the transfer of real rights in immovable property, the registration of the real contract in the public records according to the traditional system established by Arts. 1192-1208 GCC. However this system only partially satisfies the requirement of public recording of acts involving immovable property, because the public records merely show the existence of an act and fall short of certifying its validity. Therefore, the Greek legislator has introduced a new system, a 'National Land Registry' which provides legal, technical and other pertinent information on all immovable property (Kousoulas 2001). Nevertheless, the transition from the traditional system of registration to the new one has not yet been implemented all over the country.

The last two chapters of Book III of the GCC, consisting of Articles 1209-1345, deal with real security rights: pledge and real mortgage. It is necessary to stress that the Code's system of pledging movables (tangible or intangible) as proprietary security has not been very useful in practice because it requires respectively, under Articles 1213 and 1248, that when a movable tangible thing is pledged, possession must be transferred to the creditor and when a claim is pledged, it is necessary to notify the debtor.[1] The GCC provides furthermore the device of fictitious pledge that does not involve delivery of the possession of the moveable to the creditor. But this last device was until recently not implemented by the Greek legislator. Law 2844/2000, which regulated for the first time in Greece the fictitious pledge, provides in Article 3 a system for recording of the pledge agreement in a public registry (Karibali-Tsiptsiou 2003; Koutsouradis 2002). However this special legislation, which applies only to professional and company-related security, has not been incorporated so far in the GCC.

Family Law The fourth book of the GCC, Family Law ('Oikogeneiakon Dikaion'), contains 18 chapters, which deal with engagement, marriage and divorce, relations between parents and children, and the legal effects of parenthood, adoption, guardianship of minors and of imprisoned persons, the representation of absent persons, and judicial supervision. The particular flavour of this book results not only from Greek tradition but also from the Greek Orthodox Church. Therefore its provisions reflected until recently the outdated patriarchal perceptions of the division of roles between spouses, according to which the husband and father is the head of the family and the exclusive bearer of paternal power over children, while the wife must obey her husband, running the household and educating the children. However all these attitudes were eliminated in the beginning of the 1980s, when the first legislative revision of Family Law took place in the form of Law 1329/1983, which implemented in civil law the constitutional requirement of equality between men and women. The aforementioned Law brought a partial modernization of the fourth book of GCC concerning Family Law, which was

[1] Because of these provisions two fundamental requirements of the borrower are not satisfied: firstly his will to keep the transaction secret. And, secondly, his need to keep possession of the thing in order to continue his professional activity with it.

subsequently complemented by a series of newer laws which attempted to adapt Greek family law to the new requirements set by both socio-economic developments and progress in the area of biotechnology.

Law of succession The Greek Law of Succession – 'Klironomikon Dikaion' – has its origins in ancient Greek law. Indeed, several of its basic concepts – such as testate and intestate succession, legacy, or the institution of the executor of a will – are found in Attic inheritance law, while subsequent developments in this field were the contribution of the Romano-Byzantine Law. The authors of the GCC gathered all this material in the fifth Book, entitled Law of Succession, enriching it by means of comparative law with new institutions, and thereby leading to its improvement and modernization.

The fifth book of the GCC on inheritance law is divided into 20 chapters, dealing with intestate and testamentary succession. They designate methods by which successors other than heirs are established. These include legacy, fideicommissum, modus and donation in contemplation of death. The book also contains provisions covering disinheritance and the relations of the heir with co-heirs and third parties. Law 1329/1983, which amended the fourth book of the GCC concerning Family Law in order to align it with the constitutional requirement of the equality of men and women, brought a number of amendments to the Law of Succession in order to assure the preservation and the systematic unity of the GCC. It is nevertheless necessary to emphasize that the task of the legislator dealing with the Law of Succession is very delicate, because he is called on to balance the conflicting interests of the deceased, his family and other relatives, the state and any creditors. All these factors, combined with the influence of the Pandects, gave the fifth book of the GCC a highly technical and formal character.

International Private Law The GCC does not contain only substantive law provisions. It contains also private international law provisions (PIL) which are included in Arts 4-33. These Articles have governed private law relations with foreign elements since the GCC entered into force, and have not been subjected to significant reforms. The only exceptions are the provisions governing family relations with foreign elements which were affected by the successive reforms of the fourth GCC book, on Family Law. More particularly, Law 1250/1982 on civil marriage, Law 1329/1983 on implementation of the principle of gender equality in private law relations, and Law 2447/1996 on adoption and other related matters, contained a significant number of PIL which replaced the corresponding provisions of the GCC.

The PIL provisions of the GCC are not the product of rough-and-ready, uncritical, legal transplants. They constitute rather the result of eclectic borrowings, introduced after an extensive use of comparative law. Most of these provisions are conflict-of-law rules, the only exceptions being Art 4 GCC establishing the equality of civil rights of Greek and foreign citizens, and Arts 21-31 GCC, which regulate questions relating to nationality. There are also two PIL provisions of the GCC which regulate general questions: Art 32 GCC, on the one hand, which prohibits renvoi, and Art 33 GCC, on the other hand, which introduces the *ordre public* exception.

In respect of the general methodology followed by the GCC in PIL matters, it should be noted that neither escape chances nor 'soft' connecting factors are used by the relevant provisions (Vassilakakis 2010). However, Article 31 GCC refers to the country an individual is more closely connected to. But this provision is not a conflict-of-law rule. It constitutes a conflict-of-nationality rule, determining the applicable law according to the relevant conflict-of-law rule, as far as nationality is retained by the latter as connecting factor. The GCC also provides a single choice-of-law rule for the law applicable to contracts (Art 25 GCC) as well as a single choice-of-law rule for the law applicable to torts (Art 26 GCC). In contrast, in Family Law matters it uses more than one choice-of-law rule (Arts 13-24 GCC). As Greek Law is nowadays widely affected by EU Law, Rome I and Rome II Regulations play a dominant role in the determination of applicable law in contractual and tort relations. Therefore, Articles 25 and 26 GCC are applicable only to the issues which do not fall under the scope of the aforementioned Regulations.

The conflict-of-law rules of the GCC are not content or result oriented, but Greek courts do sometimes pursue a result-oriented solution by using the "ordre public" exception, whose interference leads to the application of Greek Law. This strategy is mainly followed in the field of family law, owing to the court's intention to apply domestic law – either because its content seems to comply better with the result achieved on the merits of the case, or because they want to avoid the difficult task of determining the content of foreign law (Vassilakakis 2010).

Conflict-of-law rules providing for the alternative application of one of the listed laws are a rarity in GCC. The only example to be mentioned is Art 11 GCC concerning the applicable law on the form of contracts, which provides that "a juridical act shall be formally valid if its form is in conformity with the form provisions of the law governing the substance of the act, or of the law of the place where the act has been concluded, or of the national law of all the parties to the act.

There is no direct reference to the concept of "règles d'application immediate", in the GCC. In any case, Greek courts rarely use this term in connection with mandatory rules without making a clear distinction between them. The only unilateral PIL rule included in the GCC is Art 9 providing the application of Greek law in cases in which an alien carrying out a legal transaction in Greece is capable of proceeding therewith according to Greek Law, but not so capable under her/his national law (Vassilakakis 2010).

Ordre public exception (Art 33 GCC) is applied in a rather defensive and moderate way by the Greek courts. They set aside a foreign law designated by a choice-of-law rule only exceptionally, if it is manifestly contrary to the fundamental principles of Greek legal order. In contrast, the *ordre public* exception is more often invoked when the recognition and enforcement of foreign judgments are at stake (Vassilakakis 2010).

9.5 The Process of Decodification and Its Reasons

9.5.1 Generalities

With the introduction of the GCC the previous legislation concerning civil law matters was repealed and expired (Ladas 2009, § 2, no 8). But there are some texts and provisions of this legislation that remained in force even after the introduction of the GCC, working alongside the latter. Nowadays, the aforementioned legislation regulates a plethora of issues relating to: civil and commercial leases, insurance contracts, urban law, intellectual property, individual and collective employment relationships, chattel mortgage and registration, responsibility for risk, accidents at work, competition and consumer protection, etc. (Ladas 2009, § 2, nos 24–29).

Moreover, it should be emphasized that the purposes of this legislation have been expanded dramatically during the last few years because of the new needs created by recent socio-economic and scientific developments as well as by the effects of globalization and economic integration. There appears therefore in Greece, as in other civil law countries (Murillo 2001; Ap. Georgiades 1998), a shift towards the decodification which has been manifested through the creation, alongside the civil code, of a variety of heterogeneous areas of statutory law which follow their own methodological and ideological orientation. These new areas of statutory law are not merely a supplement to the GCC that complete or clarify its provisions. They rather break up the original unity and consistency of the Code – creating a plurality of legislative microsystems.

Two main factors have led to the decodification of the GCC: firstly the need for the regulation of the novel contractual forms of the modern economy. And secondly, the need to implement the various EU Directives regulating issues of civil law.

9.5.2 Regulation of New Contractual Forms in the Modern Economy

The complexities of modern financial life; the rapid evolution of technology; the flourishing of international trade – all these developments have enabled transactional practice to create new forms of contracts designed primarily to meet the needs of business. More specifically, new ways of funding and of exploiting tangible and intangible assets have developed and under freedom of contract, new types of contracts such as leasing, factoring, franchising, time sharing, sponsoring, consulting, management etc. have been born (Ap. Georgiades 1998).

These new contractual forms are not regulated by the GCC. They are subject in principle to the general provisions of the Law of Obligations concerning contractual relations, while many of the rules governing them are derived from their own content. It constitutes in other words what is known in international trade as *lex mercatoria*.

But beyond these autonomous or semi-autonomous regulations, there are also specific laws which govern these new contractual forms.[2] A common feature of these laws is that they are written in a piecemeal fashion without an adequate alignment with the general law of contracts established by the GCC. Often the exceptions to the general law of contracts provided by for these new contractual forms could apply also to ordinary contracts. This piecemeal legislation not only creates disharmony, but it also multiplies the possible instances of unequal treatment of similar situations.

9.5.3 The Enactment of Laws Incorporating European Union Directives on Civil Law Matters

The Directives for harmonization issued to date by the European Union do not seem to have a direct impact on the general principles of the civil law of the member states, although many Directives regulate matters belonging to the Law of Obligations (contract law), such as for example unfair terms (Council Directive 93/13 CEE), the responsibility of the producer of defective products (Council Directive 85/374/EEC) door to door sales (Directive 97/7 EEC of May 1977), or package holiday contracts (Council Directive 2011/83/EU). In general, it has to be noted that the European Community and now the European Union did and does not opt for the entire harmonisation of the civil law of the member states, not even for the entire harmonization of their contract laws, but has been contented with a case-by-case regulation of certain types of contracts belonging mainly in the area of specific contracts (special part of the Law of Obligations), thus avoiding the harmonisation of rules concerning the general part of the Law of Obligations (Directive 97/7 EEC of May 1977). Also the interest of the European Union in the harmonisation of Real Property Law -with the exception, perhaps, of the law of real securities claims – of Family Law, and of the Law of Succession, is justifiably very limited to non-existent, as the corresponding provisions are not directly linked to the function of the European market and free competition (Ap. Georgiades 1994; Stathopoulos et al. 1995; Dacoronia 2003).

As far as Greece is concerned, most of the Directives regulating civil law matters have become internal law. Among the Greek Laws on civil law matters which have an European origin we can specifically mention Law 2251/994, as amended by Law 3587/2007, on consumer protection (regulating producer protection on defective products, protection against abusive clauses, the law on the protection of consumers in the case of door to door sales) and Law 2472/1997 on the protection of the individual against the unlawful processing of his personal data. The European origin of the provisions of the aforementioned national laws obliges the courts,

[2] See e.g. Law 1652/1986 on contract of time sharing; Law 1665/1986 on leasing- 1905/1990 on factoring forfeiting; Law 1969/1991 as replaced by Law 3283/2004 for Collective Investment Organizations in Movables.

when interpreting those provisions, to take into consideration the principles of European Union law, according to which national laws of European origin are interpreted in such a way as to attain the goals of the European Union regulations.

9.6 Civil Code, Autonomous Legal Branches and Semi-autonomous Legal Fields

9.6.1 Generalities

In Greece, as in other countries of the Romano-Germanic legal family, other autonomous branches of law, such as commercial and labour law, emerged from early on alongside civil law. There are however branches of law which have not yet been unanimously recognized as autonomous in relation to civil law, even though they are governed by special legislation and are influenced – beyond civil law – by various areas of private and public law. Consumer Protection Law belongs to the latter category.

9.6.2 Civil Law and Commercial Law

Commercial law constitutes in Greece a special branch of Private Law, regulated by special legislation which governs the relations of traders and commercial transactions. As already mentioned, the Napoleonic Code of Commerce of 1807, which had been applied as customary law in Greece even before its independence from the Ottomans, was introduced officially after the creation of the modern Greek state by virtue of the Royal Decree of April 19/May 1/1835. Since then, the Greek Law on Commerce has undergone many amendments, so that actually only a few Articles of Book I ('of Commerce in General') still remain in force, while Books II and II were replaced in 1878 and 1958 respectively. Since the original enactment of the Greek Law of Commerce, several attempts have been made to revise it, which however remain to date incomplete (Rokkas 1999). In 1981 a draft of a new Commercial Code was submitted to the Minister of Justice. The draft was revisited twice, in 1991 and 1996, but it has never been enacted by the Parliament.

At present, Civil and Commercial Law have a relationship of general rule to special rule (Rokkas 1999). Firstly, the rules of Civil Law contained in its first three books (General Principles, Law of Obligations and Property Law) contain general rules on the entire private law and consequently, on commercial law. Commercial law rules, however, are special rules and therefore do not apply generally, i.e. they apply only to commercial contractual relations, irrespective of whether the contracting parties are traders or not. In fact, owing to the aforementioned relationship of general rule to special rule, Civil Law applies complementarily to commercial relations.

Therefore, commercial relations are governed by two basic categories of legal rules: rules of Civil and Commercial Law. As special rules, the latter have priority over and override the general rules of civil law, which apply, as previously noted, complementarily in cases where commercial legislation presents lacunae. On the other hand, as commercial law is *lex specialis*, it does not apply complementarily to the civil law relations. Nevertheless, its analogous application cannot be excluded, provided that the conditions for analogy are met (Rokkas 1999).

Of the subsequent commercial laws, there are some that are generic in the sense that they contain general provisions relating to a very large circle of trade relations, while others are specific and related to a narrower circle of such relations. The most important of these laws are those of the first group that replaced or removed parts of the Greek Law of Commerce of 1835 and which form the basis of the particular branches of commercial law. We could mention here: Law 2190/1920 on Stock Corporations, Law 3190/1955 on Closed Corporations, the Code of Private Maritime Law, Law 5325/1955 on Bills of Exchange and Promissory Notes, Law 5960/1933 on Checks, the Stock Markets legislation, the laws on International Road and Rail Freight, the Aviation Code, Law 146/1914 on Unfair Competition, Law 3959/2011on the Protection of Free Competition, Law 2239/1994 on Trademarks, Law 1733/1987 on Transfer of Technology, Inventions and Technological Innovations governing patents, Law 2251/1944 on Consumer Orotection and Law 3588/2007 on bunkramptcy code.

9.6.3 Civil Law and Consumer Law

In contrast to Commercial Law, Consumer Protection Law is not unanimously recognized by Greek legal scholars as an autonomous branch of law. The core legislation in this area is Law 2251/1994, as modified by Law 3587/2007, which transposed into national law all EU directives on consumer protection that existed at the time of its enactment. One of the novelties in this law that distinguishes it from the majority of similar laws in European countries is the broad content it attributes to the notion of "consumer", i.e. the fact that in Art. 1 par. 4 it identifies consumers not only as persons that use products or services for reasons other than professional, but also as persons for whom products and services offered on the market are intended and persons that use such products or services as final recipients (Alexandridou 1996; idem 2006; Perakis 2009; Karakostas 2008). On the other hand, Law 2251/1994 also contains, apart from the above general definition of consumers, special definitions that identify consumers as persons acting beyond their professional capacity. It thus frequently happens that the same person is categorized as a consumer for one consumption activity and a non-consumer for a similar one. Given these anomalies, the broadening of the notion of consumers introduced by this law and the coexistence of the broadened version of this notion with narrower legal definitions of the same have rendered necessary a deeper investigation of the nature of consumer law and its position in the overall system of civil law (Dellios 2001, 119).

Greek legal scholars had already debated the matter before the entry into force of Law 2251/1994. Based on the results of a critical approach to law, some scholars had already noted by the end of the 1980s that the adherence of civil law to the formal equality of contracting parties impeded it from perceiving the socioeconomic inequality between suppliers and consumers, so that the latter could enjoy effective legal protection (Douvlis 1980; Pampoukis 1985; Kazakos 1987). In this view, Consumer Protection Law should declare its independence from classic Civil Law and either be categorized under Economic Law or under a new branch of law, the law of socially weak groups, designed to protect the interests of workers, employed persons and consumers (Kazakos 1987, 30).

These rather absolute views were gradually abandoned in the Greek legal order during the 1990s: not only because Law 2251/1994 broadened the notion of the consumer, but also because legal scholars in Greece and abroad realized that inequality in transactions is not merely due to the different economic power of the contracting parties but also due to several other factual circumstances which are simply amplified in the context of consumer sales.

In particular a theoretical approach used the element of economic inequality between consumers and suppliers not to exclude but to locate the idea of consumer protection in the principles of civil law. According to one of its representatives, the consumer protection principle is a fundamental expression of the old Civil Law principle of favour to the debtor, which refers solely to the protection of the weakest contracting party, whether this is the debtor or the creditor (Stathopoulos 2004, 32). Thus, consumer protection law which concretizes the above principle is not a particular branch of law that is separate from traditional branches. On the contrary, almost all branches of law, i.e. private, public, criminal, procedural law, contain legal rules that are protective of consumers (Stathopoulos 2004, 32). Nevertheless, this does not deter the collection and classification of protective legal rules from individual branches under a "Consumer Law" system. Irrespective of this classification though, as the principle of consumer protection remains a general principle of law that is enforced through special provisions, the interpretation of all individual legal branches should pursue the fulfillment of this principle (Stathopoulos 2004, 32).

It has nonetheless been ascertained that the admission of a general principle of protection of consumers as the weakest contracting party is not strong enough to counter the oppositions emerging from the fact that modern consumer law is not always equally protective of everyone, as well as from the fact that the same law 2251/1994 restricts the initial broad definition of the notion of "consumers" in its individual chapters. Based on this fact, another representative of Greek legal theory tried to determine the relationship between Consumer Law and Civil Law, having regard to the positions of the revised version of the German systemic theory (Dellios 2001, 174).

Based on the results of the above theory, the said academic claimed that the aim of the consumer provisions is not the protection of a category of persons, but the protection of each person that finds itself in certain situations that are known to private law and require legal protection. "Situations that are worthy of protection" are in particular those that arise whenever the right of conventional self-determination of the person as well as its legitimate expectations and legal interests are jeopardized (Dellios 2001, 174). Exactly because any subject of law can be found in such situations, their particular regulation by consumer law does not contravene the Civil Code system. Quite to the contrary, the said provision belongs by nature to Civil Law, if one accepts a global perception, which classifies Civil Law under the general part of Private Law and commercial and Labour Law under the special part of this branch (Dellios 2001, 174).

In this view, the commercial-law approach to Consumer Law differs from the respective civil-law approach in two aspects (Perakis 2009, 30). Firstly, Consumer Law is considered to be market law in the eyes of Commercial Law. Consumers are classified in the overall chain of movement of goods and services in large volume, whereas their protection is combined with other forms of intervention, such as the law of unfair and free competition. A second feature of the commercial-law approach is that it recognizes the effectiveness of legal rules as a measure of good legal regulation. In other words, that it takes into account not only the benefit, but also the cost incurred by these rules. As a matter of fact, the stronger or the broader the legal protection of the consumer is, the higher the cost is for the company, for society but also for consumers too, as they have to bear this cost through the increase in prices or by higher interest rates. In view of these two diversifications, the commercial-law approach to consumer law favours the maintenance of this branch's autonomy within civil law. In other words, it counters the reservation about its classification under civil law, while it accepts with great caution the expansion of its protection to all contracting parties.

9.6.4 Civil Code and Labour Law

In contrast with Consumer Law, Labour Law gained very early its independence from the Civil Law. Initially Labour Law constituted a complex of special regulatory provisions within Civil Law. Nevertheless, it came through its evolution to be dominated by a particular nature, to derive from disparate sources and avail itself of its own methods of interpretation and have separate aims. Due to the aforementioned development, Labour Law was considered to be an autonomous branch of law (Koukiades 2005, 57) a fact that was also recognized in article 38 of the Introductory law to the Greek Civil Code. In particular, this last provision stipulates that "all laws and decrees on collective employment agreements or other special laws on individual employment contracts remain in force even after the introduction of the Civil Code".

The recognition of the autonomy of Labour Law impacted also on the interpretation of its legal rules. According to the prevailing opinion in Greek legal theory, lacunae in labour legislation should be filled by mutatis mutandis application of the other rules of labour law, as they constitute a set of legal rules that are in close interrelation to each other (Koukiades 2005, 64). Resorting to the legal rules of civil law is only permissible when no solutions are available within the frame of labour law rules. Thus, the application of civil law to employment relations is only of a subsidiary nature.

9.7 The Code's Revisions and the Idea of Recodification

9.7.1 Preliminary Observations

However, the proliferation of specific legislation moving away from the Code causes confusion and uncertainty about the applicable law and reinforces the idea of the re-codification i.e. of a revision of the Code having as a scope the incorporation of special legislation on its current system. Unlike the Netherlands (Verschraegen 2006) Quebec and many Latin American countries (Murillo 2001), Greece has not yet made a global revision of its Civil Code. It has preferred, in other words, as far as this issue is concerned, to adopt the policy of piecemeal revisions followed by European countries such as France, Germany, Switzerland, Italy, Belgium and Spain (Murillo 2001). But unlike what happened in these countries, the revisions of the GCC were until the late 1990s limited in scope, with the exception of the major revision of the fourth book concerning Family Law as well as of the other chapters of the Code that have been introduced by Laws 1250/1982 and 1329/1983 concerning respectively the recognition of civil marriage and the implementation of the constitutional principle of the equality of man and women and the liberalization of divorce and parenthood.

However, it should be noted that the tendency of the Greek legislature to move to broader reforms of the Civil Code had been manifestly stronger in the last decade, not only because during this period a series of laws were enacted, aiming to promote even further the modernization of Family Law, but also because for the first time in Greek legal history a revision of the narrow core of the Code was effected, i.e. the provisions that belong to the second book of the Code, concerning the Law of Obligations.

9.7.2 The Limited-Scope Revision of the Law of Obligations

As has been already mentioned, the Greek legislator chose a system prevailing in a great number of European countries according to which contract law and consumer contract law exist in parallel. But although the aforementioned model worked harmoniously in Greece for a certain period of time, the enactment of Directive 99/44 EC on certain aspects of the sale of consumer goods and associated guarantees (Directive 1999/44/EC) unsettled this equilibrium, because it introduced in the area of sales a number of rules whose philosophy differed significantly from those of the corresponding provisions of the GCC. Between the two solutions, i.e. either adopting a specific text for the transposition of the directive or integrating its provisions into the sales chapter of the CC, the Greek legislator has decided, like its German counterpart, in favor of the second option (Alexandridou 2006). But in contrast to what has happened in Germany, where the implementation of Directive 99/44 led to a comprehensive revision of the second book of the BGB concerning the Law of

Obligations, the Greek legislator chose the so-called 'small solution', e.g. the amendment of the sales provisions of the Civil Code.

The first basic reform of Law 3041/2002 concerns the conversion of what was up till then the 'warranty liability' of the vendor – for defects of the thing or lack of agreed qualities – into full contractual liability, like the liability for non-performance because of impossibility of performance, or defaults of the debtor, or legal defect etc. Thus, the new Art. 534 GCC imposes an additional obligation on the vendor to deliver the thing with the agreed qualities and without defect, irrespectively of whether the later is specified or determined in kind. In line with this new obligation of the vendor, the new Art. 540 GCC provides the right of the purchaser to seek the repair of the thing in parallel with its earlier rights of the replacement of the thing, reduction of the purchase price and reversal (today rescission) of the sale. Another important innovation of Law 3041/2002 is that it replaced the term 'right of reversal' of the sale used by the earlier law by the term 'right of rescission' of the sale that is used in cases of breach of contractual obligations according to the general law of contracts (Papanikolaou and others 2003, 142; Kornilakis 2005, 94; Stathopoulos 2004, 218).

9.7.3 Law Reforms in the Area of Family Law

But the most significant revisions of the Greek Civil Code were those concerning its fourth chapter on Family Law. The aims of these reforms were first to adapt the provisions of the aforementioned chapter to the profound changes undergone by family relationships, as a result of sociopolitical and economic developments and progress in biotechnology and biomedicine. And, secondly, to harmonize these provisions with fundamental principles of the Greek legal order enshrined in its Constitution and by international treaties, such as respect for human dignity and the personality of the individual, and the protection of gender equality.

9.7.3.1 Recognition of Civil Marriage, Implementation of Spouse's and Parents Equality, Liberalization of Divorce, Protection of Minors Personality

During the years 1982 and 1983 there took place in Greece the first revision of Family Law – carried out in two stages. As a first stage Law 1250/1982 reduced the church influence on family relationships, both through the recognition of civil (registered) marriage as an optional form of marriage and the abolition of a great number of matrimonial impediments (Koutsouradis 1983). As a second stage, Law 1329/1983 concerned the application of the constitutional principle of the equality of men and women to Civil Law (Deliyannis 1986; Koumantos 1982–1983; idem 1984, 1989–1990; Kounougeri-Manoledaki 2008, vol. I; Grammatikaki-Alexiou 2008, 179).

The drafting committee of this Law was charged with making broader reforms, that involved most of the family institutions: minimum age of marriage (18 years for both sexes) combined with the lowering of the age of maturity in general, personal relations between spouses and matrimonial property regime, divorce, filiations and status of children born out of wedlock, relationship between parents and children. The only questions left outside the reform were the adoption and guardianship of minors and other incapable persons which were, as we will see, the subject of the subsequent Family Law reform which took place in 1996.

9.7.3.2 Reforms in the Area of Adoption, Guardianship of Minors, Guardianship of Interdicted Persons and Judicial Supervision

Thirteen years after the enactment of Law 1329/1983, Law 2447/1996 (Deliyannis 1996; idem 1998) came into force in Greece in order to fill the gaps of the former. To renew, in other words, the law of adoption and to implement radical reforms in outdated institutions such as guardianship of minors, guardianship of interdicted persons and judicial supervision.

Prior to Law 2447/1996 (Fountedaki 1998; Androuridakis-Dimitradis 2009, 98; Spyridakis 1997) adoption was governed by Arts. 1568-1588 GCC, Legal Decree 610/1970 and the European Convention on the Adoption of Children, ratified by Law 1049/1980. Law 2447/1996 does not only codify the existing provisions in a coherent set of rules included in Art. 1542-1588 GCC. It also brought major reforms in order to ensure the harmonization of these rules with the modern approach to adoption and to permit them to protect in an effective manner the child's best interests.

Also of extreme importance is the contribution of Law 2447/1996 to the organization of the guardianship of minors (Arts 1589-1654 GCC) (Kounougeri-Manoledaki 2008, vol. II, 367; Pantelidou 2007; Androuridakis-Dimitradis 2009, 119). and their with foster families. But the most important innovation of the Law 2447/1996 is that it established the institution of judicial assistance in order to ensure the protection of adults (Deliyannis 1997). The novelty of the institution is that in cases of physical disability, only the disabled person has the right to apply for judicial assistance. The judicial assistance is therefore formed as a family law institution and only if there is a special need is institutional assistance chosen. Law 2247/1996 has also modernized the anachronistic institutions of guardianship of interdicted persons and of judicial supervision regulated previously by the GCC. The new flexible regime introduced by the aforementioned Law respects the personality of the person who needs protection. It should however be noted that these provisions seem today outdated if one takes into account the UN Convention for Persons with Disabilities, ratified recently by the EU which places an obligation on the State to recognize persons with disabilities as individuals before the law, possessing legal capacity, including the capacity to act, on an equal basis with others (Degener 2010).

9.7.3.3 Regulation of Juridical Problems Arising from the Use of Methods of Artificial Human Reproduction

At the beginning of 2000 significant reform took place in Greece to address the social, ethical and legal problems arising from the use of methods of artificial human reproduction (Kounougeri-Manoledaki 2008, vol. II, 1; Papachristou 2005, 199; Agallopoulou 2011; idem 2004, 33; Fountedaki 2007). This reform has been realized through Law 3089/2002, which is incorporated almost in its entirety into the GCC According to the new provisions incorporated by the Law 3089/2002 into the special chapter of the GCC dedicated to medically assisted human reproduction (Arts 1445-1460) all the practiced methods of assisted reproduction are permitted by the law. Married and unmarried couples as well as single women have the right to use medically assisted methods in order to procreate. Moreover, medically assisted reproduction is even permitted *post mortem* and the same holds true for the reproduction by the way of the intervention of a surrogate mother. But the preconditions required for the last two cases are stricter. Law 3089/2002 was complemented by Law 3305/2005, which deals with the application of assisted reproduction technologies (ART). This law clarifies the provisions of Law 3089/2002 by giving them a biomedical dimension (Kounougeri-Manoledaki 2005; Karasis 2005; Kotzabassi 2006).

9.7.3.4 The Incidence of Laws on Domestic Violence and Cohabitation Pacts Between Partners of Different Sex in the GCC Provisions Concerning Family Law

Furthermore, more recently two additional laws regarding family relations have been enacted in Greece: Law 3500/2006 on domestic violence, and Law 3719/2008, entitled "Revision of the law relating to the family, the child, the society and other provisions", representing the first attempts to regulate these areas. Although these Laws have not been incorporated into the GCC and thus have not revised in a profound manner its family law provisions, they have brought however piecemeal change to some of them.

Law 3500/2006 does not aim to reform Family Law. Its primary purpose is to protect by means of Penal Law the weaker members of the family against domestic violence. The only influence of this Law on the Family Law provisions of the GCC is the fact that it included domestic violence among the grounds mentioned by Art. 1439 GCC whose existence creates a rebuttable presumption of an irretrievable breakdown of conjugal life unbearable for the plaintiff in actions for divorce. By contrast, Law 3719/2008 touched upon hardcore Family Law issues because it regulated for the first time in Greece cohabitation agreements between partners of the opposite sex.

9.8 Final Conclusion

The above analysis has shown that Greek Civil Law has already entered on a process of recodification. But, in contrast to what has happened in other European countries, this process remains uncoordinated and uneven in Greece. Indeed, while the Family Law book of the GCC has been subjected to several amendments modernizing its content, the revision of the other books of the same Code has been marginal and superficial. The only exception is the legislative intervention in the field of the Law of Obligation, which took place at the beginning of the last decade – on the occasion of the implementation of Directive 1999/44 EC. Certainly in countries such as Germany the implementation of the same Directive triggered a comprehensive reform of the general part of the Law of Obligations. In Greece, by contrast, the aforementioned implementation was substantiated through revision of Arts 332, 334 and 534 et seq GCC. But although this moderate solution was preferred by the Greek legislator, the idea of a comprehensive reform of the Law of Obligation has been mooted in Greece – discussed on several occasions by Greek legal scholars who emphasized the need for a thorough review of the relationship between the special and the general provisions of the second book of the GCC.

In their opinion, the attempts to draw general rules from the legal regulations concerning special contracts as well as the effort to develop a uniform contract law, are nowadays perfectly legitimate and realistic goals in Greece. Indeed, the frequent, useful, but uncoordinated attempts of legislators to regulate the various contractual forms of the modern economy necessitates not only the harmonization of all these regulations but also the drawing up of general legal rules emanating from the latter. This move from a scattered civil law legislation to a general reform of the second book of the GCC concerning the Law of Obligations should include, beyond the legislation governing the new conventional forms of the modern economy, a set of rules that will lead to the following reforms:

- Firstly, to the unification of the distinct forms of abnormal development of obligation provided for by the GCC into a uniform formula with the title "breach of contractual obligations" which will allow variations only where needed.
- Secondly, to the unification of the different devices designed to subvert the contract (annulment, rescission, withdrawing, termination notice of standing contracts) with the maintaining of differentiations (i.e. real and personal effect, effect *ex nun* and *ex tunc* etc.) where they are justified by circumstances.
- Thirdly, to the recognition of the termination notice as a general device leading to the termination of standing contracts when serious compelling reasons require this.
- And fourth, the enlargement of the moral prejudice restitution in order to include within its scope certain cases of breach of contractual duties.

Moreover, all these proposed amendments of the second book of the Code could be accompanied by some additional legislative measures that would aim: to integrate into the Code the existing legislation on the liability of the producer for defective products, to introduce into its text a general clause recognizing the liability for risk, to regulate the transfer of fiduciary property and to insert into the third book of the Code concerning Property Law the legislation on fictitious pledges and on the National Land Registry, to align the provisions regulating the institution of judicial assistance with the requirements of the UN Convention on the Rights of Persons with Disabilities and to regulate finally, within the fourth and fifth books, cohabitation agreements between individuals of the same or opposite sex and their effects on personal, matrimonial and inheritance matters. Thanks to these amendments, the GCC will acquire a more modern character that will enable it to respond successfully to contemporary social and economic needs. But until this radical reform of the Greek Civil Code took place, the process of recodification will continue to coexist with that of decodification in the framework of Greek Civil Law.

Bibliography

Agallopoulou P (2004) Medically assisted human reproduction. Int Fam Law:33

Agallopoulou P (2009) Greek Law on cohabitation. Int Fam Law:86

Agallopoulou P (2011) Assisted reproduction techniques and anonymity under Greek law. In: Feuillet-Leger B, Orfali K, Callus T (eds) Who is my genetic parent? Donor anonymity and assisted reproduction: a-cross-cultural perspective. Brullant, Bruxelles, pp 189–198

Akrivopoulou C (2007) Chapter 5: Greece: Drittwirkung and taking private law seriously in the application of constitutional rights. In: Oliver D, Fedtke J (eds) Human rights and the private sphere, a comparative study. Routledge, New York, p 157

Alexandridou E (1996) Consumer protection law. Sakkoulas Publications, Thessaloniki (in Greek)

Alexandridou E (2006) The Greek consumer law. In: Grundmann S, Shauer M (eds) The architecture of European codes and contract law. Kluwer International, Alphen aan den Rijn, p 220

Alexandridou E (ed) (2008) Consumer protection law, commentary of the Law 2251/1994, as it has been modified by the Law 3587/2008. Nomiki Vivliothiki, Athens (in Greek)

Androuridakis-Dimitradis I (2009) Greece. In: Pintens W (ed) International encyclopedia for family and succession law – supp. 46. Kluwer Law International BV, Alphen an den Rijn

Christianos VA (2008) The application of community law in Greece, Chapter 4. In: Kerameus K, Kozyris P (eds) Introduction to Greek law, 3rd edn. Kluwer Law International, Alphen aan den Rijn, pp 64–77

Christodoulou PC (2008) The law of Obligations, Chapter 6. In: Kerameus K, Kozyris P (eds) Introduction to Greek law, 3rd edn. Kluwer Law International, Alphen aan den Rijn, pp 103–152

Chrysogonos K (2001) The incorporation of the European convention of human rights into the National Legal Order. Ant. Sakkoulas Publications, Athens/Komotini

Chrysogonos C (2006) Individual and social rights, 3rd edn (in Greek)

Dacoronia E (2003) The development of Greek civil law: from its Roman Byzantine origins to its contemporary European orientation. Eur Rev Priv Law 5:661

Dagtoglou PD (1982) The Drittwirkung of individual rights (especially freedom of will and sex equality). Nomiko Vima 32:785 (in Greek)

Daskarolis G (1996) The ten first years of the civil code. Kritiki Epitheorissi 1:203 (in Greek)

Degener T (2010) Die UN-Behindertenrechtskonvention. Grundlage für eine inklusive Menschenrechtstheorie. Vereinte Nations 58: 57

Deliyanni-Dimitrakou C (1996) Comparative law and Greek judicial practice. Kritiki Epitheorissi:99 (in Greek)

Deliyanni-Dimitrakou C (1997a) Introduction to comparative law, Thessaloniki (in Greek).

Deliyanni-Dimitrakou C (1997b) Uses and misuses of comparative law by the Greek Legislator. Hellenic Review of European Law:173 (in Greek)
Deliyannis I (1981) L'influence de la Constitution hellénique sur le droit des personne et de la famille. Journées de la Société de la Législation Comparée:594
Deliyannis I (1986) Les grandes lignes de la reforme de la famille hellénique, Revue Hellénique de Droit International:811
Deliyannis J (1996) La cinquantenaire du Code Civil. Revue Hellénique de Droit International:2
Deliyannis I (1997) Judicial assistance. Sakkoulas Publications, Thessaloniki
Deliyannis I (1998) Inherent characteristics and subsequent adventures of the recent family law reform, Union of Civil Lawyers (ed) The recent reform on family law (Law 2447/1996), Athens (in Greek)
Dellios G (2001) Consumers protection and the system of private law, vol I. Sakkoulas Publications, Thessaloniki (in Greek)
Dimakis K (1946) The problem of the Greek civil code, Athens, (in Greek)
Dimaras KT (1985) Greek enlightenment, 4th edn. Ermis, Athens (in Greek)
Dimitropoulos A (1981) The constitutional protection of human being from private power, a contribution to the problem of 'Dritwirkung'. Ant. Sakkoulas Publications, Athens/Komotini (in Greek)
Douvlis B (1980) Elements for the creation of an autonomous consumer protection law. Epitheorisi Emporikou Dikaiou 30:186 (in Greek)
Drago G (2008) Exception d'inconstitutionnalité. Prolégomènes d'une pratique contentieuse. JCP, G 49, I.217: 13
Drossos I (1997) The protection of property under the European convention on human rights. Nomiki Vivliothiki, Athens (in Greek)
Fountedaki K (1998) Adoption: prerequisites, procedure, contest. A study on the law of adoption after the law 1447/1996. Sakkoulas Publications, Thessaloniki (in Greek)
Fountedaki K (2007) Medical assisted procreation and civil medical responsibility. Sakkoulas Publications, Athens/Thessaloniki (in Greek)
Gazis A (1996) The drafting of the civil code, 3.1 Kritiki Epitheorissi: 11 (in Greek)
Georgiades Ap (1994) The harmonization of private law in Europe. Nomiko Vima 32:321 (in Greek)
Georgiades Ap (1996) The import of the civil code in the renewal of the law, 3.1 KritE: 131 (in Greek)
Georgiades Ap (1998) New contractual forms of modern economy, 4th edn. Ant. Sakkoula, Athens/Komotini (in Greek)
Georgiades Ap (2002) General principles of civil law, 3rd edn. Athens/Komotini
Georgiades Ast. (1996) The civil code 'Jubilee'. Harmenopoulos 50:809
Grammatikaki-Alexiou A, Papassiopi- Passia Z, Vasilakakis E (2002) International private law, 3rd edn. Sakkoulas Publications, Athens/Thessaloniki (in Greek)
Grammatikaki-Alexiou A (2008) Family law. In: Kerameus K, Kozyris PJ (eds) Introduction to Greek law, Chapter 9. Kluwer/Sakkoulas, Athens, pp 179–199
Hatzis AN (2001) An introduction to Greek contract law. Glob Jurist Top 1:1
Iliopoulou-Straga J (1990) The Drittwirkung of individual and social rights of the constitution 1975. Ant. Sakkoula Publications, Athens/Komotini (in Greek)
Ioannou K, Economides K, Rozakis C, Fatouros A (1991) International public law, vol 2, Relations between international and municipal law. Ant. Sakkoulas Publications, Athens/Komotini (in Greek)
Kalomiris D (1969) Labour law. General principles. Tzaka Publications, Athens (in Greek)
Karakostas I (2008) Consumer protection law, Law 2251/1994, as it has been amended by the Law 3587/2008. Nomiki Vivliothiki, Athens (in Greek)
Karasis M (2005) The new law on the application of medically assisted procreation methods. Harmenopoulos 49:829 (in Greek)
Karibali-Tsiptsiou Y (2003) Property and trust law in Hellas. In: Verbeke A, Sagert V (eds) International encyclopaedia for property and trust. Kluwer Law International BV, Alphen an den Rijn
Kassimatis G (1981) The problem of the Drittwirkung of civil and social rights, To Syntagma:1 (in Greek)

Katranis A (1978) The theory of Dritwirkung of human rights (The German teaching and the possibility of its application under the Greek Constitution of 1975), To Syntagma:237 (in Greek)

Katrougalos G (2001) Legal and political meaning of the Revision of Article 25 Greek Constitution, Dikaiomata tou Anthropou:468 (in Greek)

Kazakos A (1987) Civil Law, market economy and consumers protection. Sakkoulas Publications, Thessaloniki (in Greek)

Kitromelides P (1985) Jeremy Bentham and Adamantios Korais. Bentham News 9:34

Kitromilides P (1996) New Greek enlightenment. The political and social idealism. Cultural Foundation of the National Bank of Greece, Athens (in Greek)

Kornilakis P (2005) Special part of the law of obligations. Sakkoulas Publications, Athens/Thessaloniki (in Greek)

Korsos D (1973) The individual rights in private law. In: Kaiser JH, Caemmerer E, Kegel G, Müller-Freienfels W (eds) Festschrift für Pan. J. Zepos anlässlich seines 65. Geburtstages. Freiburg, Köln: Katsikalis, Athens, p 175 (in Greek)

Kotsiris L (1994) The jurist Jeremy Bentham. Harmenopoulos 48:1013 (in Greek)

Kotzabasi A (2000) Anonymity of the sperm donor in artificial insemination as a legal and moral question. Harmenopoulos:710

Kotzabassi A (2006) The right to procreation. In: Genethlion Ap. Georgiades, Stathopoulos M, Beis K, Doris F, Karakostas I (eds). Ant. N. Sakkoulas Publications, Athens/Komotini, p 396 (in Greek)

Koukiades I (2005) Labour Law, individual labour relations and the law of flexibility, 3rd edn. Sakkoulas Publications, Athens/Thessaloniki (in Greek)

Koumantos G (1982–1983) Le nouveau droit de la famille en Grèce, Revue Hellénique de Droit International. 14:35–36

Koumantos G (1989–1990) Towards a freedom from discrimination. J Fam Law 25:137

Kounougeri-Manoledaki E (2005) Artificial insemination and family law, 2nd edn. Sakkoulas Publications, Athens/Thessaloniki (in Greek)

Kounougeri-Manoledaki E (2008) Family law, vols I, II, 4th edn. Sakkoulas Publications, Athens/Thessaloniki (in Greek)

Kousoulas C (2001) The law relating to the land registry. Sakkoulas Publications, Athens/Thessaloniki (in Greek)

Koutsouradis A (1983) Das Neue Griechische Eheschliessungrecht: Kritische Darstellung einer Reform. Zeitischrift für das gesamte Familienrecht 30:851

Koutsouradis A (2002) Present and future of real personal security. Revue Hellınique de Droit International:49

Kroustalakis E (2002) The European convention of human rights: keystone for the Rejuvenation of case law. In: Ktistakis (ed) The influence of the European convention of human rights on the application and interpretation of the Greek Law. Athens/Komotini, p 85 (in Greek)

Ladas P (2009) General principles of civil law, vols I, II. Sakkoulas Publications, Athens/Thessaloniki

Litzeropoulos A (1932) The case law in its role as a factor in creation of private law, Thessaloniki. Reprinted 2000. Ant. Sakkoulas Publications (in Greek)

Litzeropoulos A (1956) The ten first years of the Civil Code. Nomiko Vima:230 (in Greek)

Litzeropoulos A (1980) Greek report. In: Les réactions de la doctrine à la création du droit par le juges. I Droit Civil et Rural. Travaux de l'Association Henri Capitant (Journées italiennes). Economica, Paris, pp 105–116

Makris T (1945) On the problem of the civil code, critical observations on the codification. Archeio Idiotikou Dikaiou 10:472 (in Greek)

Manessis A (1946) The social impact of the civil code (in Greek). Social Rev: 341

Manitakis A (1991) Drittwirkung: a Superfluous for Greek Legal Order Concept, Annals of the Foundation Marangopoulou. Ant. Sakkoulas Publications, Athens/Komotini, p 290 (in Greek)

Manitakis A (1992) The impact of the constitution in Private Legal Relations. In: NOMOS-Acta Legalia Quotannis Edita A Schola Jurisprudentiae, Charistia Ioanni Deliyanni, 4th part. 247. (in Greek)

Manitakis A (2008) Interrelationship between the judicial review of the constitutionality of laws and the judicial review of the conventionality of laws under the light of the European Convention

of Human Rights: the paradigm of personal rights. In: Nikas N (ed) The civil trial in the light of the case Laws of the European court of justice and the European court of human rights. Sakkoulas Publications, Athens/Thessaloniki, pp 111–136 (in Greek)
Maridakis (1944) The Ministry of Justice deliberation on Civil Code. Themis:108
Maridakis G (1946) The Greek Civil Code of 1945. Neon Dikeon 2:130 (in Greek)
Maridakis G (1959) La tradition européenne du code civil héllénique. In: L'Europa e il Diritto Romano: Studi in Memoria de Paolo Koschaker, vol II, pp 157–179
Markesinis B (2001) The applicability of human rights between individuals under German Constitutional Law. In: Idem, always the same path, 176. Oxford University Press, Oxford
Matzoufas G (1954) Das griechische ZGB und seine theoretischen Grundlagen, Athens
Matzoufas G (1956) Uber griechisches Privatrecht, Athens
Michaelides-Nouaros G (1958) Les systèmes juridiques des peuples européens, Athènes
Michaelides-Nouaros G (1959) Popular law and official law in legal life. In: Volume in Honour C. Triantafyllopoulos, 164. Athens. Reprinted in Law and social conscience. Eight studies of sociology and philosophy of law, ed. G. Michaelides-Nouaros, G. 1972, pp 164–190. Athens (in Greek)
Michaelides-Nouaros G (1988) The influence of the ideas of the French revolution on modern Greek private law. Nomiko Vima 36:1 (in Greek)
Ministry of Justice (ed) (1930) Plan on the project of the civil code
Ministry of Justice (ed) (1936) Project of the civil code-general principles
Murillo ML (2001) The evolution of the codification in the civil law legal systems: towards decodification and recodification. Transnatl Law Policy 1:1
Pampoukis K (1985) General transactions terms and consumers protection. Harmenopoulos 39:445 (in Greek)
Pantazopoulos N (1945) The civil code and "National Law":-reflections on clash between "Scholarly" and "Popular" tradition in law, Athens. Reprinted in Annals of the Faculty of Law and Economic Sciences, Aristotle University Thessaloniki. 1986. vol 19, fasc. 4:437 (in Greek)
Pantazopoulos N (1948) From scholarly tradition to the civil code, Athens (in Greek)
Pantazopoulos N (1952) Konstantinos Harmenopoulos: Law keeper und Judge of Thessaloniki. In Volume edited by The Faculty of Law and Economics of the Aristotle University of Thessaloniki in Commemoration of 600 years since the Publication of the Hexabible: 516 (in Greek)
Pantazopoulos N (1958) "Popular" and "Scholarly" influences on the law of revolution, Athens. Reprinted in Annals of the Faculty of Law and Economic Sciences of the Aristotle University of Thessaloniki, 1986, vol 19, fasc. 4: 3 (in Greek)
Pantazopoulos N (1966–1969) The turn of the Hellenic Legislation to European models: Georg Ludwig von Maurer. In: Studies in Honour H. Kyriakopoulos, Annals of the Faculty of Law and Economics of the Aristotle University of Thessaloniki, vol E A '-B', 1345. Thessaloniki (in Greek)
Pantelidou R (2007) Guardianship of minors. Ant. Sakkoulas Publications, Athens/Thessaloniki (in Greek)
Papachristou A (1975) La réception des droits privés étrangers comme phénomène de sociologie juridique. L.G.D.J, Paris
Papachristou A (1991) The French civil code in Greece. In: NOMOS-Acta Legalia Quotannis Edita A Schola Jurisprudentiae, Charistia Ioanni Deliyanni, Second Part, 133 Thessaloniki (in Greek)
Papachristou A (2005) Manual of family, Athens/Komotini (in Greek)
Papadopoulou L (2009) National constitution and community law: the issue of the supremacy. Sakkoulas Publications, Athens/Thessaloniki (in Greek)
Papanikolaou P (2000) Methodology of private law and interpretation of legal acts. Ant. Sakkoulas Publications, Athens/Komotini (in Greek)
Papanikolaou P (2006) The constitution and the independence of civil law. Ant. Sakkoulas Publications, Athens/Komotini (in Greek)
Papanikolaou P, Roussos C, Christodoulou K, Karabatzos A (2003) The new law of sellers liability. Ant. Sakkoulas Publications, Athens/Komotini (in Greek)
Papantoniou N (1976) The private law of the Greek people during the 1821 revolution. Harmenopoulos 30:249 (in Greek)

Perakis E (2009) Article 1 of the Law 2251/1994, general provisions. In: Consumer protection law. Commentary of the Law 2251/1994 as it has been modified by the Law 3587/2008, ed. E. Alexandridou, pp 21–67. Nomiki Vivliothiki, Athens (in Greek)
Rokkas I (1999) Commercial law, general part, 4th edn. Nomiki Vivliothiki, Athens (in Greek)
Sachpekidou E (2011) European law. Sakkoulas Publications, Athens/Thessaloniki (in Greek)
Sakkelaropoulos A (1944) The friendly spirit of Greek labor law against workers. Epitheorisi Ergatikou Dikaiou 3:613 (in Greek)
Simantiras K (1967) Das griechische Zivilgesetzbuch und moderne Rechtsprobleme, Thessaloniki
Skouris B, Venizelos E (1985) The control of the constitutionality of laws. Ant Sakkoulas Publications, Athens/Komotini (in Greek)
Spiliotopoulos E (1983) Judicial review of legislative acts in Greece. Temple Law Q 56:463
Spyridakis I (1985) General principles of civil law, fasc. A'. Athens (in Greek)
Spyridakis I (1997) Adoption of minors. Ant Sakkoulas Publications, Athens/Komotini (in Greek)
Stamatis K (1999) The foundation of judicial reasoning: introduction into methodology of law, 4th edn. Sakkoulas Publications, Athens/Thessaloniki (in Greek)
Stathopoulos M (1992) Customs, Maurer and legislative policy in the field of civil law during the 19th century. Harmenopoulos 46:465
Stathopoulos M (2004) General law of obligations. Ant. Sakkoulas Publications, Athens/Komotini (in Greek)
Svolos A (1935) The first constitutions and the influence of the French revolution. Efimeris Hellinon Nomikon 2:737 (in Greek)
Tambacopoulos A (1940) The social content of the civil code. Themis 51:369 (in Greek)
Theocharides L (1971) The Greek national revival and the French enlightenment. Ph.D. Dissertation, University of Pittsburg
Triantaphyllopoulos K (1937) The history of the drafts of the Greek civil code. Archeio Idiotikou Dikaiou 4:433 (in Greek)
Triantaphyllopoulos K (1946) The problem of the two civil codes. Neon Dikeon 2:159 (in Greek)
Troianos S, Velissaropoulou-Karakosta I (1997) Legal history: from ancient to modern Greece. Ant. N. Sakkoulas Publications, Athens/Komotini
Valticos N (1947) Le nouveau Code civil hellénique, Bulletin Trimestriel de la Société de Législation. Comparée 70:54
Vassilakakis E (2010) Recent private international law codifications. Revue Hellénique de Droit International 62:103
Vegleris F (1977) The European convention of human rights and the constitution. ToSyntagma:211
Verschraegen B (2006) See Dutch civil code 1990–1992. In: Grundmann S, Shauer M (eds) The architecture of European codes and contract law. Kluwer International, p 106
Vlachos G (1991) La portée de la Révolution française sur la formation du droit grec moderne. In: NOMOS-Acta Legalia Quotannis Edita A Schola Jurisprudentiae, Charistia Ioanni Deliyanni, First Part, pp 81–94.Thessaloniki
Vrellis S (1990) Influences juridiques étrangères et droit comparé dans la Grèce du XIXe siècle. In: Institut Suisse de Droit Comparé (ed) Perméabilité des ordres juridiques. Schulthess, Zürich, pp 197–214
Yanopoulos A (2008) Historical development, Chapter 1. In: Kerameus K, Kozyris P (eds) Introduction to Greek law, 3rd edn. Kluwer Law International, Alphen aan den Rijn, pp 1–12
Zepos P (1946) The new Greek civil code of 1946. J Comp Legis Int'l L 28:22
Zepos P (1967) Twenty years of the Greek civil code: achievements and objectives, Balkan Studies 8, 2:395–406, Reprinted in Annals of the Faculty of Law and Economics of the Aristotle University of Thessaloniki, vol 2, farc.1, Memory P. Zeppos, 1988:923–933. Thessaloniki
Zepos P (1976) Jeremy Bentham and Greek independence. In: Proceedings of the Greek Akademy, pp 293–305. Reprinted in Annals of the Faculty of Law and Economics of the Aristotle University of Thessaloniki, vol 2, fasc.1, Memory P. Zeppos, 1988:729 (in Greek)
Zweigert K, Kötz H (1992) An introduction to comparative law, Translation by T. Weir, 2nd Edn. Oxford University Press, Oxford

Chapter 10
Private Law Codification in a Mixed Legal System – The Israeli Successful Experience

Eyal Zamir

Abstract Israel is a mixed legal system, profoundly influenced by both the Common Law and Civil Law traditions. Against the background of an unprincipled mixture of Ottoman, British, and religious legal norms, Israel embarked on the challenging project of crafting its own modern Civil Code, based primarily on Civil Law systems, but incorporating Common Law concepts and institutions as well. This process, which was carried out gradually from the 1960s, relied considerably on extant international attempts to harmonize Civil Law and Common Law, including the Uniform Law on International Sales 1964. This process resulted in 20-odd separate Laws, each comprehensively dealing with a certain field or transaction. In substance, Israel now enjoys a modern, codificatory legislation in most fields of private law. A Bill integrating the separate Laws into a unified Code is currently discussed in the parliament.

As a pioneer in legislatively harmonizing Common Law and Civil Law concepts and rules in all spheres of private law, Israel may serve as a laboratory for current attempts to unify and harmonize legal systems on the regional and even global levels.

Keywords Israel • Mixed legal systems • Comparative law • Codification • Harmonization

---

I thank Talia Ben Sasson-Gordis and Meirav Furth for their able research assistance.

E. Zamir (✉)
The Hebrew University of Jerusalem, Augusto Levi Professor of Commercial Law,
Director of the Aharon Barak Center for Interdisciplinary Legal studies, Jerusalem, Israel
e-mail: eyal.zamir@huji.ac.il

J.C. Rivera (ed.), *The Scope and Structure of Civil Codes*, Ius Gentium: Comparative Perspectives on Law and Justice 32, DOI 10.1007/978-94-007-7942-6_10,

10.1 General Overview of the Legislation in Private Law

Israel is a mixed legal system. When the State was established in 1948, its legal system was primarily comprised of Ottoman legislation that had been enacted during the four centuries when *Palestine-Eretz Yisrael* was part of the Ottoman Empire (until 1917) and British legislation and case law that had been introduced during the British Mandate Period (1917–1948). In specific areas, notably marriage and divorce, the religious communities—Muslims, Christians, and Jews—enjoyed autonomous jurisdiction that included separate tribunals, each applying its own religious law.

The two central Ottoman pieces of legislation in the field of private law were the Ottoman Land Law of 1878 and the *Mejelle*. The *Mejelle* was a 16-chapter civil code, enacted between 1867 and 1877. It was based on Muslim law, yet also inspired by European Civil Codes. During the British Mandate period, most of the Ottoman legislation, including the Land Law and the *Mejelle*, remained in force. Nevertheless, the legal system underwent a gradual, yet profound, process of Anglicization. This process was brought about in part by the enactment of Ordinances, including the Companies Ordinance 1929, the Bills of Exchange Ordinance 1929, the Bankruptcy Ordinance 1936, and the Civil Wrongs Ordinance 1944. Equally and perhaps more important, even in areas where there was no significant British legislation, such as contract law, the activity of the courts contributed to the Anglicization process. Many of the judges, whether imports from England or local, Jewish and Palestinian judges with an English orientation, had only limited familiarity with the Ottoman legislation. Hence they tended to read, interpret, and fill gaps in the local legislation using Common Law principles, concepts, and rules. This practice was based in part on Article 46 of the Palestine Order in Council, 1922–1947, which laid down the legal foundation for the British regime in *Palestine-Eretz Yisrael.* Article 46 instructed the courts to rule according to the Ottoman legislation and the Orders in Council, Ordinances, and Regulations enacted by the British Mandate. It added that subject to these sources, the jurisdiction of the courts "shall be exercised in conformity with the substance of the common law, and the doctrines of equity in force in England."[1] As a result, when the State of Israel was established in 1948, the overall orientation of the legal system was largely British.[2]

In and of itself, the establishment of the State of Israel did not cause a change in private law. While Israeli judges were less dependent on English sources and the Common Law tradition than their predecessors had been, the legal system remained Common Law oriented. A fundamental transformation of Israeli private law was brought about through legislation, primarily from the 1960s to the early 1980s. Like many other countries that became independent in the middle of the twentieth

[1] On the use—or, according to some, overuse or misuse—of this Article by the British mandatory and Israeli courts, see Guido Tedeschi, "The Problem of Lacunae in the Law and Art. 46 of the Palestine Order in Council, 1922", *Studies in Israel Law* 166 (1960).

[2] See generally Norman Bentwich, "The Legal System of Israel", 13 Int. & Comp. L.Q. 236 (1964).

century, Israel faced a pressing need to modernize its private law. Contrary to most, however, Israel did not meet this challenge by adopting and adapting an established European code, but instead embarked on a project of creating its own modern private law. This program was carried out against the backdrop of a controversy between three "camps": (1) those who believed that it would be more prudent to maintain the linkage of Israeli law to English Common Law, (2) those who argued that modern Israeli law should be based on Jewish law, and (3) those who advocated for a new system of Israeli law, inspired by both Civil Law and Common Law, but with greater emphasis on the former.[3] The third attitude prevailed in the Israeli legislative process.

The plan was to gradually replace the outdated Ottoman legislation and patchwork of Common Law doctrines with a systematic, comprehensive, code-like legislation that would eventually be integrated into a unified, Civil-Law-style code. In the absence of a developed and coherent Israeli legal tradition, this project was made possible thanks to the contribution of experienced jurists who immigrated to Israel from around the world before and after the establishment of the State of Israel. The leading figures in this process were excellent comparativists, well-versed in numerous legal systems, particularly German, Italian, and Anglo-American. Committees of experts were entrusted with the job of preparing original private-law legislation, drawing on the traditions of other legal systems.

This process of so-called "codification by installments" yielded more than 20 Laws, enacted from the 1960s to the early 1980s,[4] including the Legal Capacity and Guardianship Law 1962, the Standard Form Contracts 1964 (revised and reenacted in 1982), the Agency Law 1965, the Succession Law 1965, the Sales Law 1968, the Land Law 1969, the Contracts (Remedies) Law 1970, the Contracts (General Part) Law 1973, the Trust Law 1979, the Unjust Enrichment Law 1979, and the Insurance Contract Law 1981. These Laws replaced, chapter by chapter, the Ottoman *Megelle*. The *Mejelle* was ultimately abolished in 1984. However, even prior to its replacement by new legislation, its practical effect was limited due to the fact that most jurists in *Palestine-Eretz Yisrael* and then in the State of Israel had only limited acquaintance with this antiquated piece of legislation and its Muslim origins.

Despite the fact that these Laws were enacted one by one, and prepared by different expert committees over an extended period of time, they share certain features. Each was meant to comprehensively cover a certain field or transaction, taking into account the issues dealt with in other existing or planned Laws.

[3] See, e.g., Guido Tedeschi and Yaacov S. Zemach, "Codification and Case Law in Israel", *The Role of Judicial Decisions and Doctrine in Civil Law and Mixed Jurisdictions* 272 (Joseph Dainow ed. 1974).

[4] On this process, see Daniel Friedmann, "Independent Development of Israeli Law", 10 Isr. L. Rev. 515, 536–62 (1975); Aharon Barak, "Towards Codification of the Civil Law", 1 Tel Aviv U. Stud. in L. 9 (1975); Gabriela Shalev and Shael Herman, "A Source Study of Israel's Contract Codification", 35 La. L. Rev. 1091 (1975); Alfredo Mordechai Rabello and Pablo Lerner, "The Project of the Israeli Civil Code: The Dilemma of Enacting A Code in a Mixed Jurisdiction", *Liber Amicorum Guido Alpa*: *Private Law beyond the National Systems* 771, 772–74 (Mads Andenas et al. eds. 2007).

Thus, for example, the Sales Law 1968 did not deal with most of the questions regarding remedies for breach of contract, as it was expected that these issues would be governed by the provisions of the Contracts (Remedies) Law, enacted in 1970. These Laws were not designed to amend or complement extant law, but rather to replace it altogether.

The new private-law legislation is characterized by a high degree of abstraction and generality, and often establishes broad standards rather than detailed rules. This legislative style assumes and encourages an active role for the courts in shaping the details of the law and facilitates judicial adaptation of the law to changing economic and social conditions. The Laws reflect extensive comparative-law research, yet none closely follows any particular legal system.[5] The result was eclectic, functional, and pragmatic.[6]

Although the debate between continued reliance on the Common Law and the independent development of the Israeli system has yet to be resolved, it is clear (in my mind) that Israeli private-law legislation is an original, modern, and highly successful body of law. It differs substantially in form and substance from the Common Law tradition, yet is not patterned on any particular Civil Law system either. This legislation did not grow out of a developed and coherent legal tradition, but rather against the backdrop of a hodgepodge of Ottoman, British, and religious laws. As one of the key figures in the legislative project, Prof. Uri Yadin, put it in the early stages of the process: "[A]t present there exists a civil law in Israel, but there exists no Israeli civil law."[7] This void, which might have been seen as a serious shortcoming, actually proved to be an advantage. It enabled the drafters to adopt optimal solutions to any said legal problem—reflecting current liberal values of freedom and equality—regardless of whether they conformed to preexisting legislation or case law. A series of detailed Civil-Law-style commentaries on the various Laws, written by eminent scholars and edited by Prof. Guido Tedeschi, assisted the creative courts in developing a highly sophisticated, modern private law for the State of Israel.

Following the enactment of the separate Laws, in the mid-1980s, a committee of experts—informally known as "the Codification Committee"—was established to integrate the separate Laws into a unified Civil Code. Chaired by Chief Justice, Prof. Aharon Barak, the committee completed the first draft of a new Civil Code in 2004.[8]

---

[5] See Uri Yadin, "The Use of Comparative Law by the Legislator", *Israeli Reports to the XI International Congress of Comparative Law* 10 (Stephen Goldstein ed. 1982).

[6] Uri Yadin, "The Proposed Law of Succession for Israel", 2 Am. J. Comp. L. 143 (1952).

[7] Id. at 147.

[8] On the process and product of the work of the Codification Committee, see generally Aharon Barak, "Introduction to the Israeli Draft Civil Code", *The Draft Civil Code for Israel in Comparative Perspective* 1 (Kurt Siehr and Reinhard Zimmermann eds. 2008); Pablo Lerner and Alfredo Mordechai Rabello, "The (Re) Codification of Israeli Private Law: Support for, and Criticism of, the Israeli Draft Civil Law Code", 59 Am. J. Comp. L. 763 (2011); Rabello and Lerner, *supra* note 4, at 776–82; Tana Spanic, "Aspects of Israel's Private Law Codification Project", *Essays on European Law and Israel* 169 (Alfredo Mordechai Rabello ed. 1996).

While based on the existing Laws, the draft Civil Code introduced some significant changes and additions, including the harmonization of terms and concepts, reformulations of norms that had proved problematic, and the addition of new substantive provisions to fill gaps in extant legislation.[9] Notably, the draft Civil Code included a new chapter on tort liability to replace the Hebrew version of the British Civil Wrongs Ordinance 1944, which is still in force in Israel.[10] Another major change was the unification (or at least integration) of remedies for breach of contract and tort liability.[11]

The 2004 draft was revised following additional deliberations and preparatory work, with academics and practitioners offering comments and suggestions.[12] A legislative milestone occurred on June 20, 2011, when the Knesset, the Israeli parliament, approved the Bill of the Civil Code in its first reading. A parliamentary Committee is currently preparing the Bill for final approval—a process that will likely take several more years.

Thus, the answer to the question of whether there are Codes in Israeli private law is "no and yes." While the process of integrating the separate Laws into a unified, comprehensive Code has not yet been completed, the existing legislation—20-odd separate Laws—does resemble a Civil Code in style and substance. This codificatory legislation already covers most spheres of private law: property, contracts, unjust enrichment, and succession. Tort law is expected to be part of the Civil Code once the current legislative process is complete.[13] Israel does not have, and is not expected to have, a Contract Code or a Code of Obligations.

---

[9] For example, the current Contract for Services Law 1973 nominally applies to any contract for the performance of work or services (provided there are no employer-employee relationships between the parties), but its laconic provisions barely address most of the questions that arise in such contracts. In the draft Civil Code, this Law is replaced with three more elaborate chapters, which distinguish between contracts for the provision of professional services, contracts for the performance of a piece of work, and brokerage contracts. See Eyal Zamir, "Legislative Proposals Relating to Contracts for Services", 26 Mishpatim 97 (1995) (Hebrew); Eyal Zamir, "Toward Legislation of the Law of Brokerage", *Essays in Memory of Professor Guido Tedeschi* 225 (Aharon Barak et al. eds. 1996).

[10] See Izhak Englard, "The Israeli Draft Civil Code: Changes in Tort Law", *The Draft Civil Code*, *supra* note 8, at 133.

[11] See generally Yehuda Adar and Gabriela Shalev, "The Law of Remedies in a Mixed Jurisdiction: The Israeli Experience", 23 Tul. Eur. & Civ. L.F. 111 (2008); Nili Cohen, "The Four C's: Coherence, Clarification, Continuity, Change – Remedies for Breach of Contract in the Israeli Draft Civil Code", *The Draft Civil Code*, *supra* note 8, at 51. For different views on the desirability of this integration, see, e.g., Hanoch Dagan, "The Risks of Codification: On Over-Coherence and Multiplicity of Remedies", 36 Mishpatim 249 (2006) (Hebrew); Yehuda Adar, "Why Unify Tort and Contract Remedies? A Reply to Professor Dagan", 36 Mishpatim 357 (2006) (Hebrew).

[12] The main symposium on the draft Civil Code was held at the Hebrew University of Jerusalem: "The Draft Civil Code: A Critical Analysis", 36 Mishpatim 183–909 (2006) (Hebrew).

[13] For further details regarding the content of the Civil Code, see Section 4, below.

10.2 Socioeconomic and Political Background

The enactment of new private-law legislation is commonly perceived as one manifestation of the establishment of the independent State of Israel and its civil society. For two millennia, the Jewish people lived in the Diaspora, where they were often subject to discrimination, persecution, and violent attacks. Beginning in the late nineteenth century, the Zionist movement advanced the establishment of a sovereign state for the Jewish people in *Palestine-Eretz Yisrael*. In 1948, following the murder of six million Jews at the hands of the Nazis during the Holocaust (1939–1945), the State of Israel was established. The founders did not content themselves with providing shelter, but aspired to create an autonomous, liberal, and just society. Along with the private law legislation, an important step in the development of Israeli law into a mature, independent system was the annulment of Article 46 of the Palestine Order in Council, 1922–1947 in 1980.[14] Cutting the umbilical cord that linked Israeli law to the English Common Law and enacting new Laws in the field of private law were perceived at the time—and still are—as acts of independence and modernization.[15]

While Israel has always been a western democracy, it is rather socialist in orientation, although less so today than during its formative years. Even after privatization, the decline of workers' unions, the demise of communal forms of agricultural settlements (the *kibbutzim* and *moshavim*), and the like, the political atmosphere in Israel is far more socialist than in a country like the United States. While some of the jurists who led the private-law project were less socialist in outlook than the leading politicians of their time, the new Israeli legislation is sensitive to concerns of fairness and distributive justice while facilitating a market economy. It is no coincidence that Israel was the first country to enact a Standard Form Contracts Law (1964), aimed at regulating and invalidating harsh terms in contracts of adhesion.[16]

---

[14] *See* the Foundation of Law Statute 1980. Instead of the reference to English Common Law and doctrines of equity, section 1 of the Law states: "If the court sees a legal question requiring decision, and does not find the answer in the statute, in case law precedent, or by way of analogy, it shall decide it according to the principles of liberty, justice, equity, and peace of the heritage of Israel." This deliberately vague formulation was a compromise between those who called for replacing the reference to English law with a reference to Jewish law and those who saw no need for any external reference. In actuality, this section has had almost no impact on judicial practice, and the centerpiece of the 1980 Law has been the abolishment of Article 46, rather than the positive rule replacing it.

[15] See, e.g., Guido Tedeschi, "On the Technique of the Future Legislation of Israel", Studies in Israel Law, *supra* note 1, at 69, 79 ("It cannot, however, be denied that a people cannot have juridical independence if its legislature, its judiciary, and its science of law, are incapable of solving its legal problems in accordance with its own ideas and requirements"); Barak *supra* note 4; Aharon Barak, "The Independence of the New Civil Codification: Risks and Prospects", 7 Mishpatim 15 (1976) (Hebrew).

[16] On this pioneering Law, see generally Aubrey L. Diamond, "The Israeli Standard Contracts Law, 5724-1964", 14 Int'l & Comp. L.Q. 1410 (1965); Ariel Hecht, "The Israel Law on Standard Contracts", 3 Isr. L. Rev. 586 (1968); Kenneth Frederick Berg, "The Israeli Standard Contracts Law 1964: Judicial Controls of Standard Form Contracts", 28 Int'l & Comp. L.Q. 560 (1979). The new version of this Law from 1982 seems to be considerably more successful than the original. *See*, e.g., Varda Lusthaus and Tana Spanic, *Standard Contracts* (1994) (Hebrew).

10.3 Sources of Inspiration

Current Israeli legislation in the field of private law was influenced by both Civil Law and Common Law.[17] The drafters' catholic, integrative attitude was seen as yielding the best substantive solutions to legal problems and as particularly apt for a society of immigrants. The integration of foreign elements into the new legislation was described at the time as one of "the most important means towards the welding of the manifold and variegated immigrants from all over the globe into a unified, autonomous nation."[18]

More specifically, contemporary Israeli tort law is distinctively Common Law oriented, as the central piece of legislation is still the Hebrew version of the British Mandate Civil Wrongs Ordinance. This general orientation notwithstanding, there are important differences between the Israeli and English law of torts. These are the product of major legislative reforms—particularly the imposition of strict liability for defective products and the establishment of a no-fault liability regime coupled with mandatory insurance for bodily injuries in road accidents—and creative judicial law-making.[19] Once the unified Civil Code is enacted, the linkage to the Common Law tradition in this sphere will be further weakened, due to changes in the chapter on tort liability and the integration of remedies for tort liability and breach of contract—a distinctively Civil Law notion.[20]

Contract law in Israel is Civil Law oriented, yet it also bears some Common Law marks. Along with profound influence of Civil Law concepts, such as the principle of good faith, which plays a major role in Israeli private law (following the German tradition),[21] it also adopts certain rules and concepts distinct to Common Law, such as the foreseeability test in contract damages.[22] The functional attitude of the drafters

---

[17] See, e.g., Shalev and Herman, *supra* note 4; Pablo Lerner and Alfredo Mordechai Rabello, "A Civil Code for a Mixed Jurisdiction: Some Remarks about the Israeli Approach to Codification", *Legal Culture and Legal Transplants* (Reports to the XVIIth International Congress of Comparative Law, Washington, D.C., 2010), available at http://isaidat.di.unito.it/index.php/isaidat/article/viewFile/45/51.

[18] Yadin, *supra* note 6, at 147.

[19] See the Liability for Defective Products Law 1980; the Road Accident Victims Compensation Law 1975. For a detailed overview of Israeli tort law, *see* Israel Gilead, Israel (part of Tort Law, in *the International Encyclopaedia of Law*, 2003).

[20] See supra notes 10–11 and accompanying text.

[21] Sections 12 and 39 of the Contracts (General Part) Law 1973 impose the duties to negotiate contracts "in customary manner and in good faith" and to fulfill contractual obligations and exercise contractual rights "in customary manner and in good faith." Section 61(b) of the same Law extends the application of these norms *mutatis mutandis* to legal acts other than contracts and to obligations not arising out of a contract. On the central role of the principle of good faith in Israeli private law, see Gabriela Shalev, *The Law of Contract: General Part – Towards Codification of the Civil Law* 85–127 (2005) (Hebrew); Alfredo Mordechai Rabello, "Culpa in Contrahendo" and "Good Faith in the Formation of Contract: Pre-contractual Liability in Israeli Law", *Essays on European Law and Israel*, *supra* note 8, at 245.

[22] See section 10 of the Contracts (Remedies for Breach of Contract) Law 1970.

is manifest, for example, in the rules of contract formation. Following the international sales conventions, the Israeli law of contract formation manages without either the English "consideration" or the Civil Law "causa."

The legislation in the sphere of Property law is slightly more oriented to Civil Law than to Common Law. The Land Law 1969 neither retains the Ottoman classification of lands, nor adopts the complex Anglo-American categorization of interests in land.[23] The Trust Law 1979 expressly adopts the institution of Trust, yet the extent to which the Israeli concept is akin to the Anglo-American one is a subject of debate.[24]

The effect of Jewish law on the private law legislation differs from one Law to another. Jewish law seems to have inspired the Bailees Law 1967 and the Restoration of Lost Property Law 1973, but on the whole its impact is rather limited. Jewish law has mostly served as a source for Hebrew terms, often redefined for modern purposes. Issues of marriage and divorce are governed by religious laws, which are not an integral part of Israeli private law. Finally, the drafters of the new legislation took into account the local legal experience, as manifested in commercial practice and case law. For instance, an empirical survey of standard form contracts used in Israel was conducted before the Standard Form Contracts Law 1964[25] was legislated, and the Hire and Loan Law 1971 reflects the local experience regarding supervening circumstances precluding the use of leased property.[26]

One particular source of inspiration in the sphere of contract law was the two Hague Conventions of 1964: that relating to a Uniform Law on International Sale of Goods (ULIS) and that relating to a Uniform Law on the Formation of Contracts for the International Sale of Goods. These Conventions—themselves a product of integration of rules and concepts from different legal systems—directly inspired the Sales Law 1968 and the provisions on contract formation in the Contracts (General Part) Law 1973, as well as, to a lesser extent, the Contracts (Remedies for Breach of Contract) Law 1970. Indirectly, ULIS also affected the Hire and Loan Law 1971 and the Contract for Services Law 1973, both of which integrated some notions from the Sales Law.[27] The two Hague Conventions were not very successful on the international level, as only a handful of countries incorporated them into their local legal system. Hence they were replaced by the United Nations Convention on Contracts

[23] See generally Joshua Weisman, "The Land Law: A Critical Analysis", 5 Isr. L. Rev. 379 (1970).

[24] See, e.g., Joshua Weisman, "Shortcomings in the Trust Law", *1979*, 15 Isr. L. Rev. 372 (1980); Adam S. Hofri-Winogradow, "Shapeless Trusts and Settlor Title Retention: An Asian Morality Play" (unpublished manuscript, on file with author). Contrary to the existing Law, section 563 of the Bill of the Civil Code seems to adopt the Anglo-American concept by indicating that the trustee is the owner of the trust asset.

[25] See Guido Tedeschi and Ariel Hecht, "The Problem of Standard Contracts", 2 HaPraklit 3, 5–9 (1960) (Hebrew).

[26] See section 15 of the Hire and Loan Law 1971; Eyal Zamir, "*The Conformity Rule in the Performance of Contracts* 216–17 (1990) (Hebrew).

[27] See generally Eyal Zamir, "European Traditions, the Conventions on International Sales and Israeli Contract Law", *European Legal Traditions and Israel* 499 (Alfredo Mordechai Rabello ed. 1994).

for the International Sale of Goods, CISG (Vienna 1980), which enjoyed far more success internationally. Interestingly, the Israeli Laws enacted between 1964 and 1980 bear more of a resemblance to the Vienna Convention than to the earlier Hague Conventions. This is true regarding the organization of remedial rules, the principle of good faith, the concept of delivery in sales, and some other improvements in the 1980 Convention. The drafters of the Israeli Laws identified and avoided the shortcomings of the Hague Conventions without waiting for the drafters of the Vienna Convention to recognize the same.[28]

10.4 Relationship Between the Civil Code, the National Constitution and Public International Law

The very basic question of whether Israel has a constitution has been controversial for many years (and still is to a certain extent). Since the establishment of the State, the Israeli parliament has enacted a series of "Basic Laws," dealing with most of the institutional and human-rights issues that are ordinarily governed by a constitution. Only in the 1990s, however, with the enactment of the Basic Law: Human Dignity and Liberty (1992) and the Basic Law: Freedom of Occupation (1992, substituted with a new Basic Law in 1994), and the ruling of the Israeli Supreme Court in *United Mizrachi Bank v. Midgal Coop. Vill.*,[29] did it become clear that Basic Laws constitute supra-statutory constitutional norms, authorizing the courts to conduct judicial review of the constitutionality of ordinary Laws of parliament.[30]

While there are complex issues regarding the effect of the Basic Laws on preexisting legislation, as a practical matter it is unlikely that the constitutionality of any of the provisions of private-law legislation would ever be challenged as unconstitutional; and if there were such a challenge, it would be extremely unlikely to succeed. This will also be true, I believe, for the unified Civil Code (as it will be subject to the constitutional norms in force at the time of its enactment).

A more significant question relates to the effect of constitutional norms about human rights on the interpretation and application (as opposed to the validity) of extant private-law legislation. Shortly after the enactment of the two Basic Laws authorizing the courts to scrutinize the constitutionality of Laws, Chief Justice Aharon Barak published an influential article in which he called for the "constitutionalization of private law."[31] Pointing to the unity of the entire legal system, he argued that the elevation of certain rights to the status of constitutional, supra-statutory norms (which he dubbed "the constitutional revolution") should bear on

[28] *Id.*, at 503–08.

[29] 49(4) P.D. 221 (1995).

[30] Suzie Navot, *Constitutional Law of Israel* 40–48 (2007).

[31] Aharon Barak, "Protected Human Rights and the Private Law", *Klinghoffer Book on Public Law* 163 (Itzhak Zamir ed. 1993) (Hebrew). For a revised English version of the article, see Aharon Barak, "Constitutional Human Rights and Private Law", 3 Rev. Const. Stud. 218 (1996).

private law as well. Analyzing a number of models of possible relationships between constitutional and private law in other legal systems, he argued that the constitutional norms should affect the interpretation of private-law norms, the application and concretization of general standards such as good faith and public policy, and the judicial development of private law.

A central example for the (admittedly controversial) use of the new constitutional norms as a tool for judicial reform of private law had to do with the duty of contracting parties (primarily but not exclusively firms) to treat potential contracting partners equally. Although the Basic Law: Human Dignity and Liberty does not explicitly mention a right for equality or equal treatment, there is a good deal of support for the view that this right is part of the fundamental right to "human dignity" hailed by the Basic Law.[32] Assuming that the norms and standards of private law, and specifically the duty of good faith in negotiation, should be understood and applied in light of the constitutional norms, including the implied right to equality, it arguably follows that (at least in some circumstances) there is a duty to treat potential contracting parties equally. Such a duty likely prohibits firms from discriminating against clients on grounds such as gender, sexual orientation, and ethnic origin.[33] Less obviously, it has been argued that the constitutionalization of private law implies that a commercial firm conducting a tender must treat the bidders on equal terms both procedurally and substantively. It must not, for example, conduct separate negotiations with some bidders only.[34]

One could plausibly argue that in every case in which the court made reference to constitutional rights to justify its ruling in a matter of private law, it could have reached the same conclusion without the reference. Be that as it may, it is undeniable that in recent years constitutional rights have played a role in shaping Israeli private law in several contexts. These include equating the pension rights of widowers and widows under the contractual arrangements of pension funds,[35] striking a balance between freedom of contract and freedom of occupation in determining the validity of contracts in restraint of trade,[36] and expanding the remedy of specific performance to reinstatement of employees who had been fired for organizing their coworkers to engage in collective bargaining (thus infringing their constitutional freedom of association).[37]

As regards international law, the rules of international *customary* law are automatically incorporated into the Israeli legal system, unless they are unambiguously

[32] Navot, supra note 30, at 210, 217–20.

[33] The question of whether a prohibition on discrimination in market transactions can be derived from the constitutional norms through the principle of good faith in negotiation lost much of its practical importance after the Knesset enacted the Prohibition of Discrimination in Products, Services, and Entry into Entertainment and Public Places Law 2000.

[34] Barak (Hebrew), *supra* note 31, at 201–05.

[35] HCJ 2911/05 Elhanati v. Minister of the Treasury (unpublished, June 15, 2008).

[36] See, e.g., AES Systems Inc. v. Sa'ar, 54(3) P.D. 850 (2000); Ben Yishai v. Weingarten, 55(1) P.D. 939 (1999).

[37] See, e.g., HCJ 4485/08 Elisha v. Tel Aviv University (unpublished, October 5, 2009).

inconsistent with Laws enacted by the Knesset. Non-customary treaties are only accepted into the local legal system if they are incorporated by legislation.[38] Where Israeli legislation is open to alternative interpretations, domestic courts apply a presumption of compatibility between Israeli and international law, and prefer the interpretation that is consistent with the state's obligations under international law (both treaty and customary law).[39] As a matter of fact, I am not aware of any substantive judicial discussion of these principles in the context of private-law legislation.

10.5 Contents of the Civil Code

The new codificatory legislation in private law covers contracts, property, unjust enrichment, and succession law. It does not yet cover tort law (currently governed by the Hebrew version of a British Mandate Ordinance), but tort law will be included in the Civil Code according to the Bill that was recently approved in its first reading.[40] The current Bill does not deal with issues of private international law, but such provisions might be added before its final approval. The current Bill does not deal with marriage or divorce, and there is no plan to include these issues within the ambit of the Code, as they are governed in Israel by religious laws.

The Bill of the Civil Code currently under discussion in the Parliament consists of six main Parts: (1) Principles of the Civil Code, (2) Legal Acts, (3) Obligations, (4) Property, (5) Succession, and (6) Limitation of Civil Actions. The first Part consists of only six sections and establishes the general goals and underlying policies of the code in very broad terms. The second Part (sections 7–47) deals with legal capacity and agency. The third, Obligations (sections 48–498), is divided into six Sub-Parts: (1) General Provisions, (2) Contracts, (3) Specific Contracts, (4) Non-Voluntary Obligations (including torts and unjust enrichment), (5) Other Obligations (including bailment and fiduciary duties, whether contractual or not), and (6) Remedies for Breach of Obligations. The fourth (sections 499–692) deals with both immovable and movable property, the various proprietary rights in assets, and condominiums (the technicalities of land registration are left in a separate statute). The fifth Part (sections 693–821) deals with the law of succession and the Sixth (sections 822–859) with limitation of civil actions.

As further detailed below, the proposed Civil Code does not deal with commercial-law issues such as corporation law, the law of bankruptcy, and negotiable instruments. Similarly, most of the consumer legislation is not expected to be integrated into the Civil Code. Given the current stage of the codification process, it is too early to predict future additions to or omissions from the Civil Code.

---

38 Ruth Lapidoth, "International Law within the Israel Legal System", 24 Isr. L. Rev. 451 (1990); Navot, *supra* note 30, at 33–34.

39 See, e.g., John Doe et al. v. Minister of Defense 54(1) P.D. 721, 742–743 (2000); Michael Frudenthal v. State of Israel 57(6) P.D. 40, 46–47 (2003).

40 See supra notes 10–11, 19–20 and accompanying text.

10.6 The Civil Code and Commercial Law

There is no general commercial code in Israel. The Companies Law 1999, which replaced the British Mandate Companies Ordinance 1929, is a comprehensive, code-like statute. The Hebrew versions of two major Ordinances enacted during the British Mandate Period, the Bankruptcy Ordinance [New Version] 1980 and the Bills of Exchange Ordinance [New Version], are still in force. Specific Statutes deal with other types of legal entities.[41]

Issues subject to specific commercial legislation, such as the Companies Law, are also subject to the general private-law legislation. The commercial legislation is considered *lex specialis*. When there is no contradiction between the different bodies of legislation, both will apply to any specific case. The judicial development of commercial law in recent decades has often been based on the principles embodied in the general private-law legislation, rather than on the specific provisions of the commercial legislation.[42]

10.7 The Civil Code and Consumer Law

Along with the general private law legislation enacted since the 1960s, a considerable number of Laws have also been enacted in the sphere of consumer law. These include the Standard Form Contracts 1964 (later replaced by the Standard Form Contracts 1982), the Sales (Apartments) Law 1973, the Sales (Apartments) (Assurance of Purchasers Investments) Law 1974, the Consumer Protection Law 1981, the Regulation of Nonbank Loans Law 1993, and the Debit Cards Law 1986.[43] Sometimes, as with the Insurance Contract Law 1981 and the Debit Cards Law 1986, the legislation is both part of private law and consumer law. At other times, as in the case of the Guarantee Law 1967, the Law contains both general provisions applicable to any contract and specific chapters (added in subsequent reforms) that apply to consumer contracts. Consumer concerns play different roles in different Laws. There is no sharp divide between general, private-law legislation and consumer legislation, but rather a continuum between the two.

The Israeli consumer legislation reflects an amalgam of different values and policies. These include concerns about the lack of free will in consumer contracts, information problems, cartels and other market failures, redistribution of power and wealth, and (often undeclared) paternalism.

[41] See the Cooperative Societies Ordinance 1933; the Partnerships Ordinance [New Version] 1975; the Non-Profit Societies (*Amutot*) Law 1980.

[42] See Uriel Procaccia, "The Contribution of Barak to Company Law", *The Judicial Legacy of Aharon Barak* 625 (Celia W. Fassberg, Barak Medina and Eyal Zamir eds. 2009) (Hebrew).

[43] See generally Allen A. Zysblat, "Consumer Protection Legislation in Israeli", Essays on European Law and Israel, *supra* note 8, at 643.

As long as the new Israeli legislation consisted of separate Laws, the question of whether the consumer Laws were part of this body of legislation was inconsequential. However, this issue has become significant in preparing the unified Civil Code. The question of which, if any, consumer Laws should be included in the future Israeli Civil Code continues to be debated.[44] Some argue that if this legislation is not included, it might create the false impression that consumer legislation and its underlying policies are peripheral and transient compared to the primary and permanent rules and values of the Civil Code. Leaving the consumer legislation outside of the Civil Code might also adversely affect the interpretation of the other parts of the Civil Code, as it might be thought to imply that equivalence of exchange, fairness, distributive concerns, and protecting people from their own fallibilities are not legitimate considerations in interpreting and applying the nonconsumer provisions of the Code. Some opponents of the inclusion of consumer legislation in the Code believe that it is indeed less important and more peripheral; others object for the opposite reason, namely that consumer legislation is sui generis and too important to be integrated into the general Civil Code. They call for the enactment of a separate Consumer Code (an unlikely prospect given the various challenges facing the Israeli legislature). Opponents also point out that this legislation is often overly specific, requiring frequent amendments, and containing criminal and administrative sanctions.

The current Bill reflects an uneasy, ad hoc compromise between these two positions: It includes some but not all of the consumer legislation, and there is no discernable substantive inclusion/exclusion criterion.[45] Thus, the Bill contains a chapter on standard form contracts and consumer-oriented provisions applying to insurance and guarantee contracts, but does not include the provisions currently included in the Sales (Apartments) Law, despite the fact that these equally apply to the sale of residential and commercial units.

Similar to the relationship between private- and commercial-law legislation, both bodies of legislation ordinarily apply to any consumer contract, and often deal with different aspects of the same transaction. The consumer legislation is ordinarily perceived as *lex specialis*. As a matter of fact, much of the protection of consumer rights is attained through the general rules and doctrines of private law, rather than through the particular provisions of consumer legislation.[46]

---

[44] See Sinai Deutch, "Consumer Legislation and the Proposed Civil Code", 36 Mishpatim 499 (2006) (Hebrew); Eyal Zamir, "The Regulation of Specific Contracts in the Draft Civil Code", 36 Mishpatim 531, 542–47 (2006) (Hebrew); Ofer Grosskopf, Consumer Protection under the Israeli Draft Civil Code", *The Draft Civil Code*, *supra* note 8, at 15.

[45] Zamir, *supra* note 44, at 542–47.

[46] See Grosskopf, *supra* note 44, at 26 (concluding that "consumer protection in Israel is a hybrid of detailed regulation of specific markets by the legislator and tailored application of general contract legislation by the courts"); Deutch, *supra* note 44, at 523 (stating that consumer protection in Israel is based not only on the consumer legislation, but primarily on the general private-law legislation).

10.8 The Civil Code and Family Law

When the State of Israel was established, the entire field of personal status and family law was governed by religious law and subject to the exclusive jurisdiction of religious courts. Today, considerable parts of family law are subject to the general, secular Laws enacted by the Knesset.[47] Basically, matters of marriage and divorce are still governed in Israel by the religious law of the parties and subject to the jurisdiction of religious courts.[48] However, the broad recognition of civil marriages conducted abroad (even when both spouses are Israeli citizens and residents) limits the practical effect of the religious laws in this sphere.[49] This effect is further limited as a result of the very liberal, secular common-law marriage law, which largely equates the privileges and duties of unmarried cohabitants (including, following rulings of the Supreme Court, same-sex couples) to those of married ones.[50]

Child support is subject to a hybrid of religious and secular norms. A child is entitled to support according to religious law, yet in the absence of such an entitlement, he or she is entitled to support according to a general, secular Law.[51] Other family law issues, including guardianship, adoption, and succession, are governed by specific Laws (rather than by Muslim, Christian, or Jewish religious law).[52] Similarly, the proprietary aspects of marriage and divorce are governed by specific secular laws as well as the general Israeli law of property.[53] However, these issues are sometimes adjudicated before the religious courts, which do not always apply the general law, but instead adhere to religious law. The fact that certain aspects of spousal relationships are sometimes subject to competing jurisdiction of religious and secular courts is a constant source of institutional conflict and adjudication.[54] The current Bill of the Civil Code deals with guardianship and succession; adoption may be added in the future.

---

[47] See generally Talia Einhorn, *Private International Law in Israel* 165–269 (2009).

[48] See, e.g., Pinhas Shifman, "Family Law in Israel: The Struggle Between Religious and Secular Law", 24 Isr. L. Rev. 57 (1990); Ariel Rosen-Zvi, "Family and Inheritance Law", *Introduction to the Law of Israel* 75 (Amos Shapira and Keren C. DeWitt-Arar eds. 1995); Ruth Halperin-Kaddari, *Women in Israel: A State of their Own* 233–44 (2004). There is a special mechanism for determining court jurisdiction when each spouse belongs to a different religious denomination. *See* the Jurisdiction in Matters of Dissolution of Marriage (Special Cases and International Jurisdiction) 1969.

[49] Einhorn, *supra* note 47, at 180–83; Halperin-Kaddari, *supra* note 48, at 244–45.

[50] Einhorn, *supra* note 47, at 183–85; Halperin-Kaddari, *supra* note 48, at 245–49.

[51] See the Family Law Amendment (Maintenance) Law 1959; Einhorn, *supra* note 47, at 240–46.

[52] See the Legal Capacity and Guardianship Law 1962; the Adoption of Children Law 1981; the Succession Law 1965.

[53] See, in particular, the Spouses (Property Relations) Law 1973; Einhorn, *supra* note 47, at 201–12.

[54] See, e.g., Halperin-Kaddari, *supra* note 48, at 252–54.

10.9 The Civil Code and Private International Law

Subject to significant exceptions, private international law is governed in Israel by judge-made law, heavily influenced by the English Common Law.[55] The two main exceptions are the Foreign Judgments Enforcement Law 1958, which regulates certain aspects of recognition and enforcement of foreign judgments, and Chapter 7 of the Succession Law 1965, which comprehensively regulates choice-of-law issues in the area of succession.

Additional provisions dealing with private international law issues are included, *inter alia*, in the Spouses (Property Relations) law 1973, the Matters of Dissolution of Marriage (Jurisdiction in Special Cases) Law 1969, and the Capacity and Guardianship Law 1962.[56]

In 1987, upon the request of the Israeli Ministry of Justice, Prof. Avigdor Levontin of the Hebrew University of Jerusalem prepared a model statute of choice of law.[57] While not legally binding, the Israeli courts have sometimes referred to it as a source of inspiration. The Bill of the Civil Code, which was approved in first reading in 2011 and is currently prepared for final approval by a committee of the parliament, does not contain a chapter on private international law. However, the Bill's introduction indicates that such a chapter should be integrated into the Civil Code at a later stage.

10.10 A Civil Code in a Mixed Legal System: Concluding Remarks

The legal culture in Israel reflects its diverse sources of inspiration. In some respects Israeli legal culture is closer to the Civil Law tradition; in others it is closer to Common Law. In keeping with the Civil Law tradition, statutory law is the foundation of most legal spheres in Israel (with a number of exceptions, including private international law and administrative law, which are largely governed by case law). As in continental Europe, scholarly writing plays a major role in Israeli law, as it does in continental Europe. Contrary to the English tradition, the courts regularly cite and rely on academic scholarship. On the other hand, following the English tradition, Israel recognizes the principle of *stare decisis*. Related to this, court judgments are often very elaborate, and the courts engage in active and conscious law-making by setting new precedents. The 'division of labor' between the Israeli legislature and the judiciary therefore falls between the Civil Law and Common

[55] Einhorn, *supra* note 47, at 30.

[56] *Id.*, at 41.

[57] For an English version of this proposal, see Avigdor V. Levontin, *Choice of Law: A Model Statute with Section-by-Section Commentary* (2004).

Law paradigms (perhaps more so than in other legal systems).[58] The laconic style of the private-law legislation and its frequent use of broad standards of reasonableness, justice, and good faith serve to further encourage active law-making by the courts.

Against this background, it is clear that the new Israeli legislation is the backbone of Israel's private, commercial, and consumer law. It allowed for the independent development of Israeli law, as part of the process of severing ties to the English legal system. While the Israeli legal system often looks to comparative law—as a relatively young, mixed legal system would be expected to do—foreign systems are essentially sources for ideas and possible solutions. The new private-law legislation is therefore important not only in itself, but also for its immense contribution to the development of an independent and mature legal system in Israel.[59]

As a pioneer in legislatively harmonizing Common Law and Civil Law concepts and rules in all spheres of private law, Israel may serve as a laboratory for current attempts to unify and harmonize legal systems on the regional and even global levels.[60]

[58] On the Israeli legal culture, see generally Aharon Barak, "The Tradition and Culture of the Israeli Legal System", *European Legal Traditions and Israel*, *supra* note 27, at 473.

[59] For a different view, highlighting the importance of judge-made law in Israel even in areas covered by the private-law legislation (and to my mind, reflecting somewhat unrealistic assumptions regarding the self-sufficiency of Codes and the limited role of courts in Civil Law countries), see Daphne Barak-Erez, "Codification and Legal Culture: In Comparative Perspective", 13 Tul. Eur. & Civ. L.F. 125 (1998).

[60] Cf. Alfredo Mordechai Rabello and Pablo Lerner, "Israeli Contract Law: A Laboratory for Europe?", *Bases of European Contract Law: The Good Faith Principle and Precontractual Liability* 698 (Santiago Espiau Espiaui and Antoni Vaquer eds. 2003).

Chapter 11
A Civil Code Originated During the War (The Italian *Codice Civile*)

Rodolfo Sacco

Abstract The *Codice Civile* was drafted during Mussolini's dictatorial time and under the apparent total power of the fascist party. However, in 1942, Italy was no longer a sovereign country and had turned into a kind of German protectorate. And those with authority imposed the incorporation of a number of rules to the code which were unknown to the national tradition: marriage between "Arians" and "Semites" was forbidden, parents were under the obligation of giving a fascist education to their children, etc. Such political contributions damaged the code, but only superficially. Upon the fall of the fascist regime, a simple ordinance was enough to abolish them.

The draft of the civil code was commissioned to law professors. At that time, in Italy, nobody could have thought of another solution.

The code in force in Italy was a copy of the Napoleon's Code, which guaranteed protection to proprietors, employers, and the contractual intent. In 1942, history (even the political ideas of the fascist party) guaranteed a system of protection to the interests of communities, employees, the weak contracting party. The code makes reference to this situation. Anyway, it is a code aimed at private property and freedom to contract.

Keywords History of codification • Private law • Italy decodification • Current status of codification • Relation with other branches of law • 1942 Civil Code • Italian constitution 1948 • Commercial law • Common law • Family law • Consumer law • Labor law • International private law • Special laws • French legal models • Sources of law

R. Sacco (✉)
Dipartimento di Scienze Giuridiche, Università di Torino, Torino, Italy
e-mail: segretaria@sirdcomp.it

J.C. Rivera (ed.), *The Scope and Structure of Civil Codes*, Ius Gentium: Comparative Perspectives on Law and Justice 32, DOI 10.1007/978-94-007-7942-6_11,

11.1 History of Codification of Private Law in Italy

The *Codice Civile* was drafted during Mussolini's dictatorial time and under the apparent total power of the fascist party. However, in 1942, Italy was no longer a sovereign country and had turned into a kind of German protectorate. And those with authority imposed the incorporation of a number of rules to the code which were unknown to the national tradition: marriage between "Arians" and "Semites" was forbidden, parents were under the obligation of giving a fascist education to their children, etc. Such political contributions damaged the code, but only superficially. Upon the fall of the fascist regime, a simple ordinance was enough to abolish them.

The draft of the civil code was commissioned to law professors. At that time, in Italy, nobody could have thought of another solution.

The code in force in Italy was a copy of the Napoleon's Code, which guaranteed protection to proprietors, employers, and the contractual intent. In 1942, history (even the political ideas of the fascist party) guaranteed a system of protection to the interests of communities, employees, the weak contracting party. The code makes reference to this situation. Anyway, it is a code aimed at private property and freedom to contract.

The 1942 *Codice Civile* was not created from scratch.

It took over the 1865 *Codice Civile* (the unification code) and the 1882 *Codice di Commercio* which had superseded the 1865 *Codice di Commercio* (the unification code).

Formerly, there had been a civil code and a commercial code (of a French model), the Piedmont-Sardinian, in the south in Sicily, in the Duchies of Parma and Modena. The ABGB (Austrian Civil Code) was in force in Lombardy, the law of the eighteenth century was in force in the Pontifical States (Bologna and Perugia) and the Grand Duchy of Tuscany. In 1865, Rome, Venice, Trent and Trieste did not belong to Italy.

As a whole, Italy was, with its 1865 *Codice*, a country indebted to France as to its legislation. At the time of the unification, imitation of French law was absolute. University courses started to appear as well as French conceptualizations. However, there existed two exceptions: the law was conservative and was inspired in tradition (related to canon law) and the 1882 commercial code adopted autochthonous solutions distant from the French model.

But, to the end of the century, in Italy, as well as in Russia, Scandinavia, Poland, Hungary and Austria the German Begriffsjurisprudenz was created and imitated, that is to say, the conceptualist, systematic and dogmatic method exercised by German science on the educational basis of Savigny, Putcha, and the Pandectists following them.

The *Codice Civile* is the product of Italy's adhesion to the German categories and concepts. The practical rules are always French (consent transfers property, the succession contract is unknown, etc.), but the concepts are German. The *Codice* does not include the category of the Rechtsgeschäft (in Italian: negozio giuridico) (*legal transaction*) but the university teaches students that the contract is a negozio (business transaction), that is to say, an exchange of *declarations* (it is no longer the meeting of two minds). And the code develops the rules related to such declarations.

Partial disability is no longer a nullity, and from then on it has been called *annullabilità*. The 1942 code stems from a Romano-Germanic system. However, should we compare the systems of the French models with the German scientific model, we should conclude that the Italian *Codice* follows the French legal model and integrates it to the German scientific model, at a time when the Italian doctrine was closely related to the German Education.

11.2 The Process of Decodification

11.2.1 The Process of Decodification: Causes

Following the decodification process, the enactment of laws in the realm of the civil law was intense and sometimes even frenetic. This was probably due to the Italian legislator, an international convention or European institutions. On some occasions, the new law was incorporated to the code (though the Italians do not give such incorporations to the code the relevance the French do).

To begin with, in 1942, the code was defascised (laws related to race and prohibition of strikes were abolished as well as the "corporative" order, etc.).

In 1848, the new Italian constitution modified the civil law, in that it ensured an additional guarantee to some rights (freedoms, among which there was the freedom of strike, the rights of children with respect to their parents, property, etc.) and certain institutions (family, unions). But – with the exception of the right of work- it did not alter the content of civil law rules.

A number of changes were enforced later.

International private law, which is ruled under the provisions of the civil code, was modified by Law 975/84 (which ratifies an international convention) and it was later completely modified by Law 218/95, and updated once again by two EC regulations, related to contractual obligations (593/2008) and extracontractual obligations (864/2007).

A decree of the President of the Republic (396/2000) granted a new regulation to the civil state.

Law 91/1992 modernized the rules regarding the acquisition and loss of the Italian citizenship.

A Decree Law in 2003 (n. 196) created a system for the protection of personal data.

The law of persons and family was completely modified. Indeed, there existed a comprehensive reform of the family law, which included the equality between spouses (as to their authority in the marital life and with respect to their children).

Other texts were introduced, but were not incorporated.

Law 898/1970 incorporated the divorce (remedy).

Law 184/1983 ("Right of the minor to a family") introduced the full adoption (by the initiative of the European Council).

Decree 361/2000 issued by the President of the Republic simplified the procedure for the recognition of legal persons (associations and foundations).

Regarding assets, property and other real estate rights, we could see interesting changes.

Law 346/1976 creates the fast- track special adverse possession of small rural property.

Legislation (of administrative law other than civil law) on the construction right (Law 346/1976; Law 10/1977; Law 47/1985), followed by a *Testo Unico*, rules the provisions of all this subject matter (Decree of the President of the Republic 380/2001).

Legislative Decree 42/2004, ("Code of cultural property and landscape") was issued.

Multiple property was ruled under the "*codice del consumo*", which will be dealt with below.

The legislator was particularly focused on the law of acts, contracts and obligations.

As regards acts, digital procedures (condition for the validity of documents, its value, etc.) were ruled by the Decree of the President of the Ministers' Council 13-1-2004, the Decree of the President of the Republic 68/2005 and mainly by the "*Codice Dell'Amministrazione Digitale*" and Decree Law 82/2005, related to the act of the public power and, indirectly, to pertaining public relations.

Conversely, in relation to private law, Decree Law 70/2003 (of European origin) on electronic commerce was passed.

Within the scope of obligations, Law 52/1991 on the assignment of creditors in the enterprise; Law 130/1999 on the *cartolarizzazione* of creditors and Decree Law (of European origin) on the delay in payment in commercial contracts were enacted.

The Law of contracts was reshaped following the fundamental regulations of European law. The coming into effect of European principles in the Italian legislation (Law 287/1990; Law. 52/1996; Decree Law. 7/2007) paved the way to the transformation of the Italian national legislation. And, particularly, the law of contracts was amended with the creation of the "consumer" contractor, who is granted protection as the weak contracting party; Decree Law 206/2005 (*Codice del Consumo*), Decree Law 145/2007 (deceptive advertising).

A number of special contracts caught the attention of the legislator (supranational, conventional or national).

The international sale of products was ruled by the Vienna Convention (Law 765/1985).

The right of the purchaser of real property to build was ruled under Decree Law 122/1985.

Various measures modified the provisions of the lease agreement granting the tenant the right to renew the lease or to ensure the tenant a favorable rental payment. I will not make reference to the provisions of the first 12 of years following the war, regarded as exceptional and then temporary. However, I will refer to Law. 392/1978; Decree Laws 9/1982; 12/1985; 832/1986; 393/1987; 26/1988; 551/1988; Law 431/1998; Decree Law 32/2000; Law 21/2001; Decree Laws 450/2001; 122/2002; 147/2003;240/2004; 86/2005; 23/2006; Law 9/2007; Decree Laws 248/2007; 158/2008.

Such new laws had impact on the system of agricultural contracts. The old contracts of emphyteusis, of agricultural lease or the contract implying ownership rights over a fraction of the benefits were converted into a lease agreement. The amount of the lease and the duration of the contract are set forth by the law; e.g. Laws 567/1962; 756/1964; 590/1965; 606/1966; 11/1971; 814/1973; 176/1978; 203/1982; 29/1990; 97/1994.

Insurance contracts raised the attention of the legislator. The proprietor of a vehicle must insure his liability when driving a vehicle; the insurer must pay the debt with no delay; a number of remedies were created applicable to the event the proprietor failed to contract insurance: Law. 990/1969; Decree Law 209/2005, *codice delle assicurazioni prívate*; Decree of the President of the Republic 254/2006.

For the first time, a law (Law 364/1989) acknowledged the trust.

Commercial law was also in the interest of the legislator who acted after the codification.

Commerce is subjected to well-known fundamental rules, which form the basis of the European Union legislation in the matter of competition law.

As regards companies, the new laws structured the regime of corporations. Decree Law 6/2003 incorporated the new law to the *codice civile*.

Other specific rules which were not incorporated refer to balance sheets and their certification (Decree Law 332/1994 and Decree of the President of the Republic 136/1975), international accounting principles (Decree Law 38/2005), call to shareholders' meetings (Decree of Minister 437/1998), and the cross-border merger of corporations (Decree Law 108/2008).

The legislator also focused his attention on the cooperative associations which became subjected to more efficient controls. Laws 59/1992; 266/1997; 448/1998; Decree Law 220/2002.

The provisions of the code as to negotiable instruments are still in force. Additionally, a number of rules issued after the code relate to negotiable instruments which had been under the scope of special laws for many years, prior to the coming into effect of the code (bill of exchange, check).

The next topic is the enterprise. The chambers of commerce and the companies' registry were reorganized by Law 580/1993; Decrees of the President of the Republic 581/1995; 558/1999; 247/2004.

Intangible rights also posed a challenge to the legislator. In 1942, the code set forth the essential rules; the details were laid down in organic laws (one directed to the literary and artistic property and another to the industrial property).

Subsequent legislators focused on satellite transmission (Law 52/1996), databases (Decree Law 169/1999); extension of the term for the protection of the author (Law 1421/1956), and broadened the scope of the subject matter of law (Law 52/1996, of European origin, and Law 248/2000); and issued a number of specific measures resulting from a necessity posed by the new means of communication.

With reference to the industrial property, the *Codice Della Proprietà Industrial* (Decree Law 30/2005) replaced the 1939 law. And Decree Law 3/2006 ruled biotechnical inventions.

Naturally, the legislator also dealt with the subordinated labor contract. Cardinal regulations are comprised in the "Statuto dei lavoratori" (Law 300/1970). More specific rules related to the dismissal were adopted (Law. 604/1966; Law. 108/1990), as well as rules related to the rights of the employees upon the termination of the labor relation (Law 297/1982), and to the employee's right to certain information (Decree Law 152/1997).

11.2.2 The Process of Decodification: Effects

The civil code has lost its monopoly.

My friend Natalino Irti invites us to talk about the process of decodification.

Which is the setting he refers to?

The civil code has lost its central place to the constitution, administrative law, and labor law and shares its role with a number of small laws that speak a language and adopt their concepts.

All these facts are true.

The constitution has a central position, in the view of the Italian legal scholar.

The administrative law restricts the power of the owner of constructible land.

Labor law is cold with respect to the contractual freedom.

After the codification, six laws called "codes" ruled the ownership right which had been up to then under the scope of the *Codice Civile*.

The legislator does not work alone. He is requested to ratify conventions aimed at the creation of a unified law. Indeed, the European Union also gets involved by modifying categories, concepts and Italian traditions. So, should we talk about a process of decodification?

No.

The comparison will help.

Instead of saying that the law "is", we should say that it "derives from". In between the existing code and the next code new laws appear. The second code will absorb them. And after that, the new laws will endlessly multiply.

The civil code does not have a central place in the system.

The existence of constitutional texts which are rather detailed and rich in provisions of civil law has not been an obstacle to the flourishing of civil codes which characterized socialist countries at that time.

The constitution has never asphyxiated the civil code to death. Irti talks as if, during the golden era of the codes, countries in Europe did not have constitutions.

The codes translate the provisions of the constitutional texts into applicable rules. This is the reason to explain the stability of their rules, the formality of the procedures they instruct, the conclusive language of their articles or paragraphs setting forth their general rules.

The development of administrative law, labor law and fiscal law does not pose a threat to the civil code. The two main characters of the civil law of the socialist countries were at that time the socialist property of the State and the socialist contract. Both forms needed an administrative body which had no precedent in history. And, at a certain time and place, the property in the civil law became an empty shell and only the administrative law could fill its content. The framework within which the proprietor exercises his powers is fixed by administrative laws and regulations which deal with the activities of the human being (the rules on construction are the most studied example). The extracontractual liability needs a road circulation code and rules on the prevention of work accidents.

In Italy, the code is surrounded by special rules. But, we could find the same case in socialist countries, and nowadays in the African countries which have recently codified their legislation. The civil codes of the socialist countries set forth the rules common to all contracts, in addition to a limited number of rules on the different contractual relations. All the other rules – including the price of goods and services- were the matter of special laws or ministerial or bureaucratic provisions.

Additionally, at all times, the codes have included, other than the general rules on contracts, the rules on each of the contracts listed; the 1942 code recognized special rules to the different types of ownership rights, which the code distinguished one from another. The code is general and abstract; but it is possible to observe different degrees of abstraction. In addition to the law of contracts, the Italian code rules the sale, then the sale of real estate property and after the sale of real estate property consisting of a certain and limited body.

We can also observe that in the last decades certain special rules (provisions related to children born out of wedlock or regarding the capacity of women) have disappeared. Therefore, we could draft today codes more succinct than past models.

To conclude, the system of sources which is strongly embedded in Italy – and deemed by some Italian jurists as responsible for the death of the code- does not exist and does not succeed more in those countries which have recently codified or which are codifying now.

The accusers point out that the special laws speak a language which differs from the language of the *codice civile*: they draw legal forms which do not belong to the system, out of which the codifier has taken his models. The jurist who thinks this way believes that he will find in the code a unity that has never existed. In the first book of the code, the system of nullities is in French (the general category is the *nullità*, according to which, in some cases, any interested party could prevail, section 117, and in other cases only the subject protected by law, section 120, section 122), and in the fourth book the German system is adopted (the general category is the *invalidità*, which is called *nullità* if it is ipso jure and *annullabilità* if it is relative). A number of special laws, which emerged at the time of the *Codice Civile*, use the category *negozio giuridico* (*Rechtsgeschäft*) (legal transaction), which is rejected by the Civil Code. The language of the bankruptcy law – which is supplementary to the code- is not the language of the code (for example, *dazione in pagamento*, and *dazione in luogo di adempimento*, cf *dación en pago* and *Leistung an Erfüllungsstatt.*). Dissonance is the rule in a code which was written and published in separate books which, faithful to the practical French solutions, are frequently systematized on the basis of dogmatic German categories.

Irti considers that the Italian law, everyday more presidential, needs the legislator even less, and that its laws, each time more negotiated and less suggested by the reason or logic lack the qualities needed in a code.

As regards the negotiated rules, they only exist in Italy and nowhere else. But, all these rules which are directed to the granting of privileges or advantages, all this market of favors and rewards driven by the corruptive spirit of political parties, converge in a mass of rules which, everywhere and always, surround the code without having access to it. Generally, these rules exist outside the civil law, they more frequently trespass the fiscal law, the administrative law of the economy and the labor law. Should they cross the borders of civil law, they fail to modify the few relevant rules comprised in the Code which deal with family, inheritance, obligations and property.

The message to be given is another one here, and has to do with the acknowledgment of the Pretorian rule. For the first time in history, the Italian legislator finds in practice a law created by the judge – ordinary or constitutional.-.

Was the Napoleon's Code always surrounded by judges who are simply the "voice of the law"?

As from the coming into effect of this Code, the situation has changed.

The Code subjects the donation to the necessity of the form. The interpreter discovers the on hand donation.

Each and every payment implies a debt. The interpreter discovers that the repetition of a wrongdoing is subject to the condition of mistake.

Any act carried out by men which causes damage is a civil offence. The interpreter seeks the causes for its justification.

It is only the owner who is entitled to dispose of his assets. The interpreter finds the putative heir.

The owner has the exclusive right of possession. The interpreter discovers possessory actions.

And, I could continue with examples.

11.3 Actual Status of Codification

11.3.1 Actual Status of Codification: The Contents of the Civil Code Today

Italy is typically a codified law country.

It has a *Codice Civile*, in force from 1942.

In its origin, the 1942 code ruled the sources and the application of the law (even of the international private law); natural and legal persons; parental rights and duties, marriage and the patrimonial regime of the family, filiation; the incapacitated, civil status acts; succession in the case of death, the division, donation, ownership and other real estate rights on material assets, possession, obligations, contracts (in general and the contracts mentioned), promises, negotiable instruments (general rules), quasi contracts, illegal acts; the enterprise, the contractor and his employees, the rural enterprise, the commercial enterprise; the employment relation and the self-employed; companies (the general rules and the different types of companies); the going concern, immaterial rights (the principles), competition, publicity, the proof of acts, privileges, the pledge and mortgage; the obligation; the statutes of limitation and decadence.

We clearly see that the subject matter is comprised by the C*odice*, which sets forth the principles, and it is ruled in its details by an organic law, exhaustive, adopted at the time of codification and coordinated together with the code. This also applies to copyrights, industrial property, some negotiable instruments and labor legislation.

Having said this, there exist, naturally, as in other countries, other codes which bear no relation with the civil code: a criminal code, and civil and criminal procedural codes.

Certain laws, relevant to the civil law, and not included in the code are also referred to as codes: *Codice Della Strada* (traffic code), the *Codice Dei Beni el Culturali*, the *Codice Della Proprietà Industriale*, the *Codice Delle Assicurazioni*, the *Codice Dell'Amministrazione Digitale*, the *Codice de Consumo*. Each of these codes is a matter of concern not only to the civil law but also to other branches of the law. Each of such codes, except for the first one, began to exist when the *Codice Civile* was already in force.

11.3.2 Actual Status of Codification. The Legislation of Commercial Law

I have already pointed out that the *Codice Civile* rules the merchant (in a broader sense the "*imprenditore*"), the commercial contracts, the negotiable instruments, the companies – generally speaking all commercial matters. It excludes bankruptcy which is ruled by a special law enacted when the code first came into effect and in coordination with it, comprising substantive and procedural law. It also excludes all issues related to navigation (including air navigation): property, contracts, transfer of rights, publicity, public controls, public and private functions. All these matters (private substantive law, procedure and administrative law) are ruled by a law adopted to the Civil Code and passed in coordination with the code: el *Codice Della Navigazionel*.

The solution taken by the 1942 *Codice* was the continuation to what had existed up to then.

In 1865, Italy enacted a commercial code. In 1882, it was replaced by another code.

Which was the place of the commercial law in 1865? Which was the place in 1942?

The most relevant civil codes of the nineteenth century (the Napoleon's Code, ABGB, BGB) were based on the beliefs of *doctors* educated in the *jus commune*.

The commercial law, which involved habits natural in the commercial practice, had no access to the *jus commune*, and was neglected by the *doctors*; it would not have been natural to mix them with the Civil Code.

In Europe, the traditional civil law was Roman. The commercial law was subjected to German law (joint hands property, importance of the judicial appearance, and trust, the rule "possession is worth title", formalism of certain new documents (bill of Exchange, check), guarantees of oriental origin (sureties)).

The *doctor* did not teach such law, which he called "ius asininum". The student – I was told- learnt the concepts of commercial law he needed from an instructor who spoke the same language and dressed in plain clothes, without a toga.

The courts of justice were not the same for the practice of both civil and commercial law. Practitioners decided the controversies among the merchants.

At a certain time, the *jus commune* gave rise to a new model illustrated by the reason. The wise man reduced this model to concepts and dogmas; he organized it into a system. But, the bill of exchange could not adapt to the great rational ideas, such as the consensualism, and the de facto association did not suit the definition of legal act.

The Empires codified. They enacted civil codes, systematic, dogmatic and Roman. They drafted commercial law texts, in which the main character is the merchant or the act of commerce.

When Italy codified in 1942, the atmosphere was different.

The professors were the ones who codified. Of course, they were the professors in 1942.

In 1942, the civil law professor did not believe in Roman law, he did not believe in rational law, he debated between the French government and the German concept, I don't completely believe in one or the other.

The method (many committees to draft the different books of the code) prevents abstractions and generalizations, which forces a kind of empiricism.

There is still more. The new commercial law professor has the same educational background as his civil colleague, he can discuss with him and formulate the rules of law on the very same basis.

And at that time, the jurist who had a master in law and who was introduced to the career in court was conversant in the same way and to the same extent with the civil and commercial law. Therefore, commercial courts could be eliminated. And having reached this point, why drafting two codes?

11.4 Consumer Law

And then?

New provisions are possible. An area of private law seems to have a better tendency to uniformity. This is the law related to contracts and competition. And this area of private law seems to be prone to being subjected to conventional uniform sources (Vienna Convention, for example, the Geneva Convention on checks and bills of Exchange) or supranational sources (consumer protection enforced by the European Union). Statutes with persuasive strength (Principles of UNILAW), drafts (PECL, a draft of an European Code) illustrate the existing atmosphere.

This is not a feature which could broaden the gap between civil and commercial law even more. This is, in fact, a distinction which will isolate private law from exchange law. To a certain extent, the new category recalls the old distinction.

In all cases, there exists protection to the consumers.

In Italy, the statutes related to consumer law were gathered in a text called *Codice de Consumo* (Decree Law 206/2005).

As soon as consumer statutes appeared, Italian authors enthusiastically got down to working on the subject to construe the laws and to give them a place in the system.

The Italian jurist was familiar with the mechanism that, in the event of abusive clauses, protects the weak contracting party by subjecting the validity of the provision to the compliance of certain rules related to the termination of the contract.

To such effect, section 1341 of the *Codice Civile* sets forth:

> The general conditions of the contract, pre-stated by one of the contracting parties, are effective with respect to the other party if at the time the parties entered into the contract such party was aware of them or should have been aware by exercising due care.

In any case, the following clauses are not enforceable if they have not been agreed upon by the parties in writing: such are clauses which set forth in favor of the party pre-stating such provisions limitations to liability, the power to terminate the contract or interrupt its execution, or clauses which impose on the other party maturity dates, limitations to the power to raise exceptions, restrictions to the freedom to contract in relation to third parties or the implied extension or the renewal of the contract or arbitration clauses or waiver of the jurisdiction of judicial authorities.

Section 1341 has undoubtedly been one of the models which inspired the European legislator in the protection of the consumer.

The *Codice del Consumo* offers the jurist the answer to the difficult question of how to protect the weak contracting party without affecting the freedom to contract. The *Codice de Consumo* respects the contractual freedom, provided that the consent of the weak contracting party was the result of the exercise of freedom, enough information and adequate deliberation. For example, the code opposes to the abuse of dominant position (incompatible to the freedom to contract), deceptive commercial practices (incompatible to right to information) and the surprise (incompatible to the right to deliberate).

In a cognitive level, the Italian jurist focuses on the psychological research related to the process of decision making of the contracting party and the reasons behind it.

The *Codice de Consumo* is not alone. Section 1469 bis of the *Codice Civil* states that the protection set forth by the same code in favor of the consumer is still applicable if it is more favorable than the European regulation.

11.5 Family Law

Family law was ruled under the *Codice Civiel*, first book. The same solution had been adopted in all previous codifications in Italy.

We find the same situation in all Christian-occidental, catholic or protestant countries, which were catholic when their family law was systematized by scholars.

In these countries, family law was inspired by canon law, which had been introduced as a second component to the *jus commune*. That is why family law needs its own code in the orthodox occidental countries where canon law has no authority.

Civil law and family law could coexist in the *Svod Zakonov* of the Russian Empire of 1825, due to the fact that the *Svod* was a mixture of things, not a code. However, in 1908; when the Czar decided on a new legislative proposal, his *Proiect grajdanskoe ulojenia* had the BGB as a model, but in the matter of family law, the national tradition was pursued. Lenin and then his successors codified the civil law on the basis of the *proiect ulojenia* (Soviet basis and republican codes of civil law) and the family law on other basis (basis and codes of family law).

Civil law and family may also coexist in the Civil Code of an orthodox or muslin country if the writers of the Code have copied the code from a protestant or catholic country.

In Italy, family law was recorded in the *Codice Civile*.

The statutes enacted after the code have turned family law unrecognizable.

Let's see some examples. The code provided that the marriage celebrated before a catholic Minister would be effective with respect to the State, that its validity would be ruled by canon law, that it would be applied by an ecclesiastic court. Nowadays, this statute has been extended to the marriage celebrated in accordance with the rules of other religions, but the validity of the religious marriage (even catholic) is evaluated by a judge of the State who exercises his authority on the basis of the Italian public order.

The code pursued the principle of the indissoluble marriage. A statute enacted in 1970 permitted the divorce (divorce-remedy).

Under the code, the husband was the head of the family and the children were subjected to the father's parental authority. A law in 1975 set forth the equality between the spouses and between parents.

A statute introduced in Italy the full adoption, which was new to the code but existing in other countries.

Current statutes of family law are deemed by Italians as a coherent set of rules. They have been incorporated to the code.

11.6 Private International Law

Real ordinance of March 16th 1942 n. 262 which promulgates the *Codice Civile* authorises "… the text of the Civil Code … preceded by … the Provisions over the law in general".

Such Provisions, commonly referred to as *Preleggi* (31 articles) are separately numbered, but they should be deemed as a chapter of the code for all purposes. They make reference to the sources of the law, the interpretation (articles 1–15) and Private International Law (articles 16–31).

On October 9th 1980, Italy and other members of the European Community signed the Rome Convention on the law applicable to the contractual obligations.

Recently, Law n. 218 on 31st March 1995 ("Reform of the Italian system of Private International Law", 74 articles) derogated articles 17–31 of the "Preleggi", and ruled the matter on its entirety (including all the European statutes of 1980).

According to the Italian jurist, private international law is a chapter of the civil law because it governs private legal relations. But, the professor of civil law knows that the teaching of private international law is under the responsibility of the international law professor and adapts to this situation.

11.7 Labor Law

Labor law is not a chapter of the civil law, as it is not a continuation of the *jus commune*, erudite law focused on Roman and Canon law. But, on the other hand, if the people who were in charge of drafting the *Codice Civile* put together in one text the civil, commercial and family law, they were obviously willing to open their code to the matter of labor law.

This law had a special feature. During his dictatorship (1922–1943), Mussolini created a labor law according to this own views, which was a legal work most typical of the fascist trend of thought.

Governmental bodies put a lot of attention to labor controversies. Administrative bodies, called *Corporazioni*, systematically controlled the activities of unions and the relations between employers and employees.

Under each category, there existed only one union (the fascist union); each and every employer and employee was compulsorily recorded in the union which corresponded to their activity. Compensation and other employee's rights could be inferior to the levels established for each category in the collective bargain agreement signed by the corresponding unions.

All controversies were subjected to a *magistratura del lavoro*, with authority to create new rules of law enforceable to all the interested parties.

Conflict in the economic organization was thus eliminated. The strike was deemed as a criminal offence.

There existed assistance to all employees in the areas of social assistance, health, housing and holidays, etc.

A law in 1927, the "Carta del Lavoro"set down all such rules with special solemnity.

The 1942 code referred to the special sources of labor legislation (*norme corpoartive*: decisions of the *magistratura del lavoro*, collective bargain agreements, ordenanze corporative), and all employees' rights.

Upon the fall of the fascist power and the adoption of the Constitution in 1948, the *magistratura del lavoro*, the corporazioni and, together with them, the corporative ordinances were eliminated.

Additionally, this constitution safeguarded the basic rights of the workers and, as regards collective bargain agreements, it acknowledged their validity *erga omnes* (with respect to all the operators of the category in question) provided they were signed by representatives freely chosen by the corresponding union.

The "defascisation" of the labor legislation has eliminated some exceptional features: non-typical sources, the existence of administrative bodies which were in charge of observing the relation between employers and employees, etc. Now, the labor legislation is more clearly private law than it used to be at the time of the code; the rules pertaining to it are in the code and have no other exceptional character.

The labor contract is subject to the law of contracts. Undoubtedly, the protection of the worker brings about certain restrictions to the contractual freedom. However, such protection is similar to the protection of the weak contracting party under the *Codice Civile* (art. 1341), the protection of the tenant (also the weak contracting party) laid down in numerous special laws aimed at the protection of the consumer that the European Union has introduced in Italy as well as in the other member countries.

From the point of view of the system, the labor legislation is not civil law. The controversies are subjected to the ordinary judicial authority, but they are entrusted to special judges. The gap between labor law and civil law is perhaps wider than the gap between civil and commercial law. However, such difference should not be exaggerated.

After the codification, new laws have been adopted in the area of labor law (especially to rule the stability of the employment relation). The most remarkable statute is the *Statuto dei Lavoratori*, Law May 20th 1970, n. 300, which was devised to give certain individual or collective freedoms to the workplace. But, in general, the legislation of the period 1945–2012 has transformed family law and some areas of commercial law more than the labor law.

11.8 Relationship Between the Civil Code with the Constitution and Treaties

The code triggered a system of sources.

Article 1 set forth that the *disposizioni sulla legge in generale* (commonly referred to as *preleggi*) were sources of the law, as follows:

- Statutes;
- Regulations (passed by administrative authorities);
- The *norme corporative*;
- Uses and customs.

The corporative norms (collective bargain agreements, decisions of the *magistratura del Lavoro*, etc.) were connected to a fascist labor legislation and disappeared with the fall of the fascist power. The collective bargain agreements were later introduced in the 1948 Constitution.

Uses are effective only if the law makes reference to them. But, the Italian jurist makes a distinction between the *usi* (uses) and *consuetudini* (customs) and article 1 does not make reference to customs, which has led the interpreter to think that, at first sight, custom and use were the same, and later to the conclusion that the custom was not the use and that it could be applied without the aid of the law.

Now, the issue of the unwritten law (the latency of the law, the mute law) is under the study of Italian lawyers. And, the Constitutional Court generally uses two categories of *diritto Vigente* (legislation in force) and *diritto vivente* (living law), both of which are deemed as legitimate.

Italian regions have a legislative power which is not different.

To begin with, they are not empowered to legislate civil law. However, there exist two exceptions. In the Alto Adige-South Tyrol, succession *mortis causa* in the property of the *geschlossener Hof* (similar to a "closed farm") follows local tradition, which makes the real estate property indivisible. And, in the provinces of Bolzano, Trent, Trieste, Gorizia property is transferred by virtue of its public record. Both cases survive from the Austrian legislation, better inspired than the Italian tradition.

Other than the sources, if we pay attention to the relationship between the constitution and the civil code, the Italian case is rather special.

What can we find in the 1948 Italian Constitution agreed upon by the political parties of that time (*Christian Democracy, Communist Party, Socialist Party, Liberal Party and Partito de Azione*)? There existed certain rules in the "*Statuto Albertino*", first Piemontese constitution and then Italian, which were inspired in the Belgium constitution of 1831: division of powers, independency of the judge, human rights, etc. Naturally, the new Charter adds to such concepts the fact that the government needs the confidence of Parliament and that a constitutional court should be in charge of controlling the consistency between the laws enacted and the constitution. Furthermore, the Weimar Constitution gave Italians the model of the Region and the example of the social state. Finally, the Constitution is filled with vague proposals (article 1: "Italy is a Democratic Republic founded on the basis of work"), which seems to promise everything to everyone. The Italian Constitution is regarded, in the view and even more in the rhetoric of the Italian politician and jurist, as the political conquest, born out of the Resistance to the Hitler's invasion, as the summary of all the political and legal values, as the new natural law.

So as to be politically correct, the civilist should always base his conclusions on the Constitution. This concept does not imply a burden as he easily finds in the flexible and contradictory texts of the constitution what is convenient to him: the grounds for the market freedom and planned economy, for the power of the proprietor and obligations pertaining to him, for the individualism and solidarity.

The Italian is disciplined and inquisitive in the relationship with his co-citizens, but he deems international rules and authority as normal and necessary. He found the creation of the European Union as a normal issue, he considers that belonging to Europe is a promotion, he would have accepted as "natural" the political unification of his European Nation, he considers that the international authority is legitimate and that the freedom of the Italian State finishes where the jurisdiction of the international authority begins. The Italian judge has never posed difficulties if the European norm or international convention exceeds the national statute. Italian fears to be "provincial".

11.9 Conclusions About the Importance of the Civil Codification Today; and the Future of Codification

The Civil Code is not the only source in the field of private law.

In fact, it has never been the only source. But, between 1942 and now the other sources and their relevance have duplicated.

In spite of this, in Italy, the code has not lost its central and privileged place.

To the average Italian, the code is based on tradition, knowledge, an idea of justice. The special law may be the result of a political pressure or passion, or a mistaken compromise.

The Italian saw the code at home, he does not want to be liberated from it.

Some areas of the law (for example, administrative law) are not codified. In the instinctive feeling of the Italian, the administrative law is more empirical, less related to the principles of private law; the rules of administrative law lack the permanent feature of the civil law statutes.

The jurist encourages this conception, which deems the code as the basis of the positive law. It is in the code where the jurist finds the concepts and rules, without which the special laws could not be effective or understood.

However, the Italian does not worship the 1942 *Codice Civile*. He would not be surprised if another code (Italian or European) were to supersede the 1942 code.

But, it is not probable that in the near future the *Codice Civile* will be replaced. Italians would not be pleased with the idea that another code be adopted without the general consent of the citizens, inspired by the general consent of the jurists. And, for the time being, we do not see a general willingness on the part of the jurists in favor of one or another replacement of the code. Better the old code of 1942 with all its defects than adventure.

Bibliography

Aa Vv (2004) Le Code Civil, 1804–2004, Livre du Bicentenaire. Dalloz-Litec, Paris

Accademia dei Lincei (2006) Convegno Il Bicentenario del codice napoleonico. Atti:221

Baudouin JL (1982) XI Congrès int. de droit comparé. Textes présentés par l'Association québécoise pour l'étude comparé du droit, Montréal p. 1 ff (offset)

Bergel (2003) Les phénomènes de codification, de décodification et de recodification. In: Perret-Bisson (dir.), Évolution des systèmes juridiques, bijuridisme et commerce international, p 31

Bodenheimer (1982) Law in the USA for the 1980's reports from the USA f. the XI congress. Supp Am J Comp Law p. 15 ff

Coing (1982) Zeitschrift f. Vergleichende Rechtswissenschaft. (81 B), p. 1 ff

Crépeau (1977) La révision du code civil. In: Cours de perfect. de la Ch. des Notaires, p 339

Crespi Reghizzi, De Nova, Sacco (1983) Il Zivilgesetzbuch della DDR. Rivista di Diritto Civile I:117

De Cupis (1979) A proposito di codice e di codificazione. Rivista di Diritto Civile II:47

De Los Mozos (2001) Codificación y recodificacion: Reflexiones con motivo de la reforma del Código civil peruano. Rev Gen Legis y Jurisprud 91

Delnoy (1982) Rapports belges au XI Congrès intern. de droit comparé, Bruxelles

Frontera (2007) La descodificación come sintoma de la historicidad del derecho. In: Rev. electronica del Instituto Ambrosio Gioja
Guadagni (1976) La riforma del diritto privato nel Sudan. In: Raccolta per anguontesimo anniversario dell Univ. Trieste (1924–1974), EUT, p 183
Hondius (1982) Recodification of the Law in the Netherlands, in Netherlands reports to t. XI Int. Congress of Comp. Law, Deventer, (offset)
ID (1982) La codification, forme dépassée de législation?. In: Associazione italiana di diritto comparato, Rapports nationaux italiens au XI Congrès International de Droit Comparé, Caracas 1982, Milan, p 67
ID (1991) Reflexions on the process of recodification of the Québec civil code. Tulane Civ LF. p. 283
ID Il nostro codice civile ed i codici civili dell'ultimo cinquantennio. In: Accademia nazionale dei Lincei, Il codice civile. Congresso del cinquantenario, Roma, 15–16 dicembre 1992, Roma, 1994. Le rapport est paru également sous forme d'article: ID., I codici civili dell'ultimo cinquantennio, in Rivista di diritto
Ioriatti (1992) Il nuovo codice civile dei Paesi Bassi fra soluzioni originali e circolazione dei modelli. Rivista di Diritto Civile I:117
Irti (1979) L'età della decodificazione. Giuffrè, Milano
Jalfina (en translittération standard, HALFINA) (1982) Codificatión: necesidad e importancia, in El derecho en el socialismo desarrollado, Moscou
Kübler (1969) Kodification und Democratie. In: Juristenzeitung, p 645
Mc Auley (2003) Proposal for a theory and a method of recodification. Loyola L Rev 49:274
Moréteau-Parise (2009) Recodification in Louisiana and Latin America. Tulane Law Rev 83:1103
Rebuffa (1981) Servono ancora i codici? Sociol dir
Rémy (1997) La recodification civile. Droits:3
Rescigno (1994) Il "codigo civil" di Cuba, ultimo codice socialista. In: Scritti in on. Sacco, Milan, p I
ROT (1982) Les critères d'appréciacion d'une codification du droit. In: Rapports polonais présentés à l'XI Congrès int. de droit comparé, Varsovie
Sacco (1969) Il substrato romanistico del diritto civile dei Paesi socialisti. Rivista di Diritto Civile I:115
Suárez L (1982) El derecho venezolano en 1982. Caracas, p 11 ff

Chapter 12
Codification, Decodification, and Recodification of the Japanese Civil Code

Hiroyasu Ishikawa

Abstract The Japanese Civil Code was a product of the mixed reception of various foreign civil codes in the late nineteenth century, and thus deserves to be seen as the "fruit of comparative law." In Japan, while the Commercial Code is subject to decodification to a large degree, as company law and insurance law have been shifted from the Commercial Code to special laws, the Civil Code has escaped such direct decodification until now, retaining its original components. However, due to the emergence of numerous special laws, the Civil Code has been hollowed-out and decodified in an indirect manner. In particular, the rules of consumer law exist completely outside the Civil Code, so that the concept of consumer or business operator has been never incorporated within the Civil Code. However, to integrate the special rules for consumers and so forth into the Civil Code would not fit the vertically-segmented structure of the law-making and law-enforcing process in the ministries, which is a characteristic of Japanese bureaucracy. Such multilateral constraints on the basis of Japanese legal history and the political configuration form a certain image of the forthcoming recodification of the Civil Code.

Keywords Japanese law • Civil law • Judicial passivism • Law-making process • Bureaucracy

12.1 Introduction

The Civil Code and many other codes in contemporary Japan have origins in the transplantation of Western codes in the late nineteenth century. On the other hand, for over a century, an enormous number of cases, legal practices, and new special

H. Ishikawa (✉)
University of Tokyo, Tokyo, Japan
e-mail: hiroyasu@iss.u-tokyo.ac.jp

J.C. Rivera (ed.), *The Scope and Structure of Civil Codes*, Ius Gentium: Comparative Perspectives on Law and Justice 32, DOI 10.1007/978-94-007-7942-6_12,

laws have accumulated, reflecting the characteristics of Japanese law and the social system, and showing some divergence from the original content of the codes. In this report, I overview the history of the codification of the Civil Code and survey the concrete circumstances of the "decodification". Following this, a prospect for "recodification" of the Civil Code will be noted in light of the characteristics of the law-making process and the multilateral bureaucracy in Japan.

12.2 Codification of the Japanese Civil Code

12.2.1 Previous Stage of Codification of the Japanese Civil Code

The Japanese legal system, irrespective of the field of law in question, is primarily a statute-based system. The Civil Code of Japan is the most general and fundamental code in Japanese private law and covers the law of obligations, property law, and family law. As we shall see later, though the hollowing-out of the Civil Code has reached an advanced stage due to the emergence of numerous special laws, the Civil Code in itself retains the characteristics of general law in that the code is applicable to all citizens.

The present Civil Code of Japan was enacted in 1896, but before this enactment, a code generally applicable to all citizens did not exist. Though there were *Ritsu-ryō* codes, which were enacted during the seventh and the eighth centuries based on Chinese legalism, they contained mostly only criminal and administrative rules, and became invalid after the governance regime shifted to the feudal system in the twelfth century.[1]

The codification of the present Civil Code is considered a major step toward the modernization of the Japanese society. The modernization of Japan, which began in the middle of the nineteenth century, was primarily driven by foreign pressure to open Japanese borders for the purpose of international trade. In 1853, Commodore Matthew Calbraith Perry reached Japan's Uraga Harbor and asked Japan to renounce its policy of seclusion. In 1858, Japan concluded commercial treaties with the United States, England, France, the Netherlands, and Russia. However, these treaties contained several unbalanced provisions, including those on extraterritoriality and the renunciation of the tariff autonomy. To amend the treaties in order to remove such provisions, it was necessary for Japan to drive modernization and Westernization forward. In this sense, the Japanese Civil Code was the result of the acceptance of Western civilization.

[1] Yosiyuki Noda, *Introduction to Japanese Law*, trans. and ed. Anthony H. Angelo (Tokyo: University of Tokyo Press, 1976), 22–26.

12.2.2 The Japanese Civil Code as the "Fruit of Comparative Law"

The process of codification of the Japanese Civil Code in the late nineteenth century was divided into two stages. The first stage was the drafting of the Boissonade Civil Code. In 1873, the Japanese government invited Gustave Boissonade, a French legal scholar, to assist it in drafting new codes. After drafting a penal code and a code of criminal procedure, Boissonade started drafting a civil code. Approximately 10 years later, in 1890, he drew up what is called the "Boissonade Draft" of the Civil Code,[2] and the government promulgated the civil code based on this draft, which is now called the Old Civil Code. However, the Old Civil Code was predominantly based on the Napoleonic Code and was criticized for its lack of harmonization with the traditional customs and morality of Japan, such that the Old Civil Code never came into force.

Yatsuka Hozumi,[3] professor of constitutional law at Imperial University of Tokyo (the predecessor of University of Tokyo), is still known today as one of the jurists most opposed to the enactment of the Old Civil Code. Criticizing the Old Civil Code, Hozumi asserted a conservative and totalitarian vision; once the Old Civil Code came into force, respect for the power of a head of family, defense of imperialistic national polity, and devotion to traditional morality would become extinct. Hozumi's assertion was often seen as representative of the view of those who hoped the prevention of the enactment of the Old Civil Code but that interpretation is inaccurate in several respects. First, the first movement for preventing the enactment of the Old Civil Code was made by the alumni association of the faculty of law at Tokyo Imperial University in May 1889, while the Hozumi's article for objection to the Old Civil Code was published in August 1891. It is said that the fact that the association was composed of many members of the English law sect influenced the hostility towards the supporters of the Old Civil Code, many of whom belonged to the French law sect. Second, the present Civil Code hardly reflected Hozumi's assertion, as shown by the fact that the present Civil Code was drafted not in the direction of totalitarianism or absolutism, but rather could partly be seen as more individualistic than the Old Civil Code. For the same reason, one should be careful to avoid the exaggerated conclusion that the strengthened absolutist tendency of government policy or the shift of governmental model from France to Prussia drove the postponement of the enactment of the Civil Code. Thus, the postponement of the enactment of the Old Civil Code was influenced by multiple factors, political, ideological, academic, and sectarian.

---

[2]Gustave Boissonade, *Projet de code civil pour l'Empire du Japon,Tomes 1–4, Nouvelle éd.* (Tokyo: Kokubunsha, 1890–1891).

[3]For the antecedents and the thought of Yatsuka Hozumi, see Richard H. Minear, *Japanese Tradition and Western Law: Emperor, State, and Law in the Thought of Hozumi Yatsuka.* (Cambridge, MA: Harvard University Press, 1970).

The second stage of the process of codification was the revision of the Old Civil Code and the codification of the present Civil Code. The present Civil Code was formed by the revision of the Old Civil Code, but with fundamental changes and renewals made by the drafting commission under the Cabinet. The drafting commission consisted of three professors at the Imperial University of Tokyo: Nobushige Hozumi, Masaakira Tomii, and Kenjiro Ume. The drafting commission consulted many foreign codes and drafts, especially the first and second drafts of the German Civil Code, though the provisions of the Old Civil Code under the influence of French law also remained to some extent. In this way, the Japanese Civil Code was codified under the strong influence of both German law and French law, and is classified as part of the Romano-Germanic law family.

The Japanese Civil Code was a product of the mixed reception of various foreign civil codes in the late nineteenth century,[4] and thus deserves to be seen as the "fruit of comparative law." No matter how much attention was given to the traditional customs and morality in Japan, the Western character of the Civil Code cannot be denied. Each member of the drafting commission had studied in France, Germany, and England during their twenties, and, on the basis of their high level of scholarly acquaintance through experience and comparative legal studies with sensitive deliberations, they could persuasively transplant Western civil codes onto Japanese society. As a matter of course, the persuasiveness and fruitfulness of the transplant would eventually be attributable to Western legal tradition itself as the origin of the civil codes. Through practice and experience over 100 years, the Japanese Civil Code as the fruit of comparative law has taken root on the soil of the Japanese society and still retains the entity of the civil code as a whole.

12.3 Contents of the Civil Code Then and Now

When it comes to the structure of civil code, the Japanese Civil Code was determinately influenced by the drafts of the German Civil Code and compiled according to the German Pandekten system. The Civil Code is divided into five books, the same as the Saxonian Civil Code: General Part (Book I), Property (Book II), Obligations (Book III), Family (Book IV), and Succession (Book V). As will become apparent below, though the rules for family and succession were substantially revised as a result of the post-war reform, as for the rest, the original contents and structures were almost preserved. The hollowing-out and decodification of the Civil Code arose through matters outside the Code itself.

---

[4] Zentaro Kitagawa, "Japanese Civil Law and German Law: From the viewpoint of Comparative Law," in *The Identity of German and Japanese Civil Law in Comparative Perspectives: Die Identitat des Deutschen und des Japanischen Zivilrechts in Vergleichender Betrachtung*, eds. Zentaro Kitagawa and Karl Riesenhuber (Berlin: De Gruyter Recht, 2007), 28–30.

12.3.1 General Part

Placing the General Part at the beginning of the Civil Code is characteristic of the Pandekten structure. The General Part of the Japanese Civil Code contains general principles and rules that are common to all the other parts of the Civil Code, including rules of legal capacity, juridical persons, juridical acts, agency, and prescription. Major reforms were made to the General Part in the fields of adult guardianship and juridical persons.

12.3.1.1 Reform of Adult Guardianship System

The adult guardianship system was revised in 1999 and the new system entered into force in 2000, along with the Long-Term Care Insurance Act (1997).[5] For handling the progressively aging society, both institutional care and at-home care should be enhanced, supported by the renewal of the social security and guardianship systems. Under the new at-home care insurance system, the insured person's physical and mental conditions are classified into seven phases through public certification of long-term care need, and social security payment is made in proportion to the phase of long-term care need. The new system of adult guardianship also seeks proportionality, suitability, and practicality of legal support for adults in need of care. Incompetence and quasi-incompetence were the categories for guardianship under the old system of adult guardianship, but the system was so restrictive that almost nothing could be done by the principal alone (without supervision) once incompetence was adjudicated. The new system is based on the ideology of "normalization," which aims at maximum respect for the autonomy of a principal and encourages his or her self-determination with support from the guardianship system; it offers three categories of supported persons: guardianship, curatorship, and assistance. While census registration for adjudication of incompetence was indispensable under the old system and social discrimination was occasionally invoked on the basis of such stigma, there is no need for census registration under the new system. Additionally, in order to enable a principal to design the way their guardianship and property are managed before their decision-making ability is impaired, a voluntary guardianship system was introduced by the Act on Voluntary Guardianship Contract (1999). Though contracts for voluntary guardianship must be concluded through notarized documents, various arrangements of guardianship were made possible by the voluntary guardianship system.

Except for the Act on Voluntary Guardianship Contract, the reform of adult guardianship was executed within the Civil Code. As a result of the new legislation

[5] For the reform of adult guardianship system in 2000, see Makoto Arai and Akira Homma, "Guardianship for Adults in Japan: Legal Reforms and Advances in Practice," *Australasian Journal on Ageing* 24, Supplement S1 (2005): S19.

for the adult guardianship system, the old provisions in the Civil Code were overwritten and new ones introduced, so that the structure of the Civil Code remained almost unchanged.

12.3.1.2 Reform of the System of Juridical Persons

In contrast to the process of reforming the adult guardianship system, the reform of the system of juridical persons took place by creating new special laws and deleting relevant old rules from the Civil Code, with a hollowing-out the Civil Code to some degree. In 2006, the following laws were enacted for the purpose of rationalizing the system of juridical persons with public interest: the Act on General Incorporated Associations and General Incorporated Foundations (2006) and the Act on Authorization of Public Interest Incorporated Associations and Public Interest Incorporated Foundations (2006).[6]

Under the old system, the Civil Code provided for associations and foundations as two types of juridical persons and the rules in the Civil Code applied to associations and foundations with a public interest. However, the old system for public-interest juridical persons was often seen as inconvenient in terms of obtaining approval of the competent government agency at the establishment; also, after founding, public-interest juridical persons had to be strictly supervised by administrative agencies so that the status was not abused as a loophole in the tax system, though the supervision was practically ineffective. Especially, the fact that approval of establishment was entrusted to the direction of the competent government agency left the requirements for the establishment of public-interest juridical persons unpredictable and uncertain.

In order to improve the system for public-interest juridical persons, the new acts in 2006 replaced administrative control and supervision with internal control such as an operating or accounting audit. Under the new system, acquisition of juridical personality for non-profit juridical persons is divided from authorization as "public interest incorporated" juridical persons. As for non-profit juridical persons, whose purpose does not involve distribution of surplus earnings, the establishment approval of the competent government agency becomes unnecessary and the process of establishment is completed *ipso jure* once the requirements are satisfied. The requirements for establishment of non-profit juridical persons are notarial authentication of articles of incorporation and registration of establishment of juridical person, without any involvement of an administrative agency. When it is intended that the non-profit juridical persons obtain authorization as a public-interest juridical person, based on its application for the authorization and review by administrative agency in accordance with a reply by advisory panel, the administrative agency grants the

[6] For the reform of the system of juridical persons in 2006, see Hiroshi Oda, *Japanese Law*, *3rd ed.* (New York: Oxford University Press, 2009): 123–126; Tadatsune Mizuno, "Reform of the System for Charitable Corporations and Tax System Revision," *Hitotsubashi Journal of Law and Politics* 37 (2009): 1–10.

authorization under a kind of approval regime. The separation between acquisition of juridical personality and authorization as a public-interest juridical person has brought substantive transparency and convenience to the system of non-profit or public-interest juridical persons.

The new legislation for non-profit or public-interest juridical persons replaced the rules in the Civil Code via special laws, so that most of the rules for juridical persons were transferred away from the Civil Code. However, such an outflow of a major part of the rules contained in the Civil Code has been unusual until now. Even though new special laws were enacted, in most cases, the relevant rules in the Civil Code remain as rules of general law, with necessary modifications.

12.3.2 Property

Book II of the Civil Code is reserved for property law and contains rules for real rights and real securities. Real rights are allowed only when they are provided by statutory or customary law, and the content of a real right must not be changed.[7] This principle is derived from the absoluteness of real rights in that they can be claimed as against everyone, so as not to prejudice the predictability of the existence and content of such real rights. Thus, in the field of property law, legislative origination is imperative and statutory law is of great importance.

Most of the Property Law reforms were carried out in the field of real securities, as financial schemes developed and changed. Originally, the real securities section in the Civil Code contained four types of real security rights: the right of retention, statutory lien, pledge, and hypothec. The Civil Code still contains only these four types, adding provisions on revolving hypothec, which secures unspecified claims of a certain scope up to the limit of a maximum amount, which were added to the Civil Code in 1971 as one of the subcategories of hypothec. Mortgage by transfer has been utilized quite often in practice, but it remains an atypical (non-statutory) real security right. Atypical real security rights are only allowed by customary law or as a variant of ownership, that is, by making transfer of ownership subject to a condition.

After the enactment of the Civil Code, many special laws introduced new real security rights, especially movable hypothec. Because hypothec in the Civil Code was allowed only for immovable property, for the purpose of the creation of movable hypothec and floating hypothec, special legislation was needed. For movable hypothec, the Automobile Mortgage Act (1933), the Automobile Mortgage Act (1951), the Aircraft Mortgage Act (1953), and the Construction Machinery Mortgage Act (1954); for floating hypothec, the Railway Mortgage Act (1905), the Factory Mortgage Act (1905), the Mining Mortgage Act (1905), the Fishery Estate Mortgage Act (1913), the Fishery Estate Mortgage Act (1925), and so on.

---

[7] Article 175 of the Civil Code, "No real rights can be established other than those prescribed by laws including this Code." (Translations of Japanese laws in this essay are cited from the website of Ministry of Justice. http://www.japaneselawtranslation.go.jp/).

More recently, by the Act on Special Provisions of the Civil Code Concerning the Perfection Requirements for the Assignment of Movables and Claims (2004), a new form of publication for assignment of movables was introduced in order to enable asset-based lending and inventory financing. For assertion against a third party, transfer of possession was the perfection requirement for assignment of movables in the Civil Code (Article 178[8]), and the Act on Special Provisions additionally admitted a registration of assignment to a movables assignment registration file as another form of perfection. Because the new registration system is intended for business-financial use, it is required that the assignor of movables is a juridical person, while it does not matter whether the assigned movables are collective or individual or whether the legal nature is true assignment or assignment for security. Considering that Article 178 of the Civil Code concerns very fundamental and important principles for the publication of real rights, the fact that the exception to the rule was raised can be critical for the unity and coherence of the civil law system.

Property law in the Civil Code itself has been almost free from fundamental structural changes until now, but exceptional or complementary rules in the form of special laws have been made outside the Civil Code. Property law must especially meet a need for availability of various financial schemes such as asset based lending, and in the future, expeditious support by special laws would be strongly expected.

12.3.3 Obligations

The Law of Obligations, Book III of the Civil Code, is the most unchanged section in the Code. Though many reforms have been made to the rules on contracts or torts, they were carried out through the enactment of new special laws, leaving the rules in the Civil Code almost as untouched as the rules of general law. Thus, the original contents of Book III of the Civil Code remain as they were, but have lost substance through a flood of special laws. Though in the past Japanese contracting was often characterized as extrajudicial or informal behavior,[9] more recently, it is said that legal institutions that are based on a contractual structure and principles of classical contract theory prevail in many fields, such as labor law, consumer law, electronic commerce, and family law.[10] Considering the context, statutory contract law seems to be of increasing importance, even in Japanese society.

---

[8] Article 178 of the Civil Code, "The transfers of real rights concerning movables may not be asserted against third party, unless the movables are delivered."

[9] Takeyoshi Kawashima, "Dispute Resolution in Contemporary Japan," in *Law in Japan: The Legal Order in a Changing Society*, ed. Arthur Taylor von Mehren (Cambridge, MA: Harvard University Press, 1963), 41–72.

[10] Takashi Uchida and Veronica L. Taylor, "Japan's 'Era of Contract'," in *Law in Japan: A Turning Point*, ed. Daniel H. Foote, (Seatle, WA: University of Washington Press, 2007), 454–482.

In the field of contract law, the Act on Land and Building Leases (1991) and the Labor Contract Act (2007) provide special rules from the standpoint of social legislation, superior to the rules in the Civil Code. For the purpose of consumer protection, the Act on Specified Commercial Transactions (1976), which covers door-to-door sales, mail order sales, telemarketing sales, multilevel marketing transactions, specified continuous service offers, and business opportunity related sales transactions, provides the rules for the right of the customer to rescind a contract, and the duties of business operators, such as delivery of documents. Furthermore, the Consumer Contract Act (2000) presents comprehensive and fundamental rules for consumer contracts.

In the field of tort law, the Civil Code adopts the fault liability principle, but many special laws impose no-fault liability or strict liability, including the Automobile Accident Compensation Security Act (1955), the Act on Compensation for Nuclear Damage (1961), the Water Pollution Control (1970), the Air Pollution Control Act (1978), the Product Liability Act (1994), and so forth. Besides, the rules of tort law in the Civil Code are so brief and abstract that they are fundamentally supplemented by case law. For example, for the conditions of tort liability, Article 709 of the Civil Code states only that it is necessary "to have intentionally or negligently infringed any right of others, or legally protected interest of others" in order to incur such liability.[11] The meaning of negligence, the rule of causation, and the scope of damages are defined by case law.

As for the rules for assignment of claims, while, in the Civil Code, notification from assignor to obligor or consent for assignment from obligor was the perfection requirement for assertion against a third party (Article 467, paragraph 1[12]), the Act on Special Provisions of the Civil Code Concerning the Perfection Requirements for the Assignment of Claims (1998) introduced the new form of perfection, intended to facilitate a securitization scheme: a registration of assignment to a claims assignment registration file as another form of perfection. In the Act of 1998, assignment of a claim to an unspecified obligor that would arise in the future could not be registered, and the Act on Special Provisions of the Civil Code Concerning the Perfection Requirements for the Assignment of Movables and Claims (2004) amended the Act of 1998 and enabled assignment of a future claim to an unspecified obligor, in addition to newly introducing registration system for assignment of movables. The perfection requirement for the assignment of claims is concurrently provided in the Civil Code and in the Act of 2004, but the function and structure of each system is highly disparate. Any future reform of the Law of Obligations would aspire to integration of the perfection rules and recovery of coherence.

[11] Article 709 of the Civil Code, "A person who has intentionally or negligently infringed any right of others, or legally protected interest of others, shall be liable to compensate any damages resulting in consequence."

[12] Article 467, paragraph 1 of the Civil Code, "The assignment of a nominative claim may not be asserted against the applicable obligor or any other third party, unless the assignor gives a notice thereof to the obligor or the obligor has acknowledged the same."

It follows that the contents of Book III (the Law of Obligation) of the Civil Code have remained almost unchanged until now, but have become stale and hollowed by the flood of special laws, the accumulation of judicial decisions, and the social and economic changes that have occurred over the last hundred years. Therefore, it is necessary to fill the gap between law and practice by drastically reforming the Law of Obligation. As will be mentioned later, since 2009, the Ministry of Justice has been in the process of reforming the Law of Obligation.

12.3.4 Family

Books IV and V of the Civil Code cover the law of family and succession. These areas of law experienced an overall revision in the course of post-war reform. The old provisions of Books IV and V were strongly characterized by the patriarchal system, which was based on the great power of a head of family (*patria potestas*) and presupposed the large scale of the family. Under the old provisions, a head of family was obliged to support the members of the family and possessed the power to control the family register, such as the right of consent to marriages of family members. During the Allied occupation following the Second World War, the Meiji Constitution of 1889 was completely amended to the post-war Constitution in 1946, while Books IV and V of the Civil Code underwent a total revision in 1947. As a result of the post-war revision of the Family Law, the patriarchal system was abolished and equality between the sexes in the matter of family affairs was established.

In this way, the contents of the family law section of the Civil Code are more modernized than the other parts of the Civil Code, but it is often pointed out that even the present family law fails to conform or adapt to various new developments, such as the diversification of relationships or the remarkable progress of assisted reproductive technology. Family Law, along with the Law of Obligations, is expected to be reformed yet again.

12.4 The Civil Code and Commercial Law

The process towards codification of the Japanese Commercial Code was similar to that of the Civil Code. In 1884, by request of the Japanese government, Hermann Roesler, a German legal scholar, drew up a draft of the Commercial Code, the "Roesler Draft," and the Old Commercial Code was completed and promulgated in 1890, based on this draft. Like the Old Civil Code, the Old Commercial Code was fiercely criticized, especially for the indifference toward consuetudinary law and the customs of merchants in Japan. Though the parts of the Old Commercial Code on company law and bankruptcy law provisionally came into force in 1893, followed by the entire Code coming into force in 1898, in parallel with this process, a new draft was prepared by the drafting commission under the Cabinet. The new draft was completed in 1893, and the new and present Commercial Code was enacted in1899, replacing the Old Commercial Code.

The original Commercial Code was composed of five books: the General Part (Book I), Company (Book II), Commercial Acts (Book III), Commercial Paper (Book IV), and Maritime Commerce (Book V). In contrast to the Civil Code, whose original components remain unchanged, some books of the Commercial Code have been transferred to special laws, corresponding to the rapid changes in the rules and orders of commercial transactions. The law of commercial paper (Book IV) was transferred to the Act on Bills (1932) and to the Act on Check (1933); the company law (Book II) to the Companies Act of 2005; and the insurance law (Chapter 10 of the Book III) to the Insurance Act of 2008. The Commercial Code has substantially lost its original content, with matters of great importance instead being addressed through special laws.

The Commercial Code, especially the law of commercial acts in Book III, contains the rules for commercial contracts and transactions, which may conflict with the rules in the Civil Code. The relationship between the Civil and Commercial Codes is that between general law and special law, so the rules in the Commercial Code take priority over the ones in the Civil Code. For example, the statutory interest rate for commercial acts is 6 % per annum (article 514 of the Commercial Code), while the statutory interest rate in the Civil Code is 5 % per annum (article 404 of the Civil Code). When a merchant acts for the benefit of another person within the scope of business, appropriate remuneration can be claimed *ipso jure* (article 512 of the Commercial Code), while, in the Civil Code, a mandatary may not claim remuneration in the absence of any special agreements (article 648 of the Civil Code). A claim arising from commercial acts is barred by prescription after 5 years (article 522 of the Commercial Code), while the general period of extinctive prescription of a claim in the Civil Code is 10 years (article 167 of the Civil Code).

Thus, the Commercial Code provides the special rules for merchants or commercial acts, but nowadays it seems doubtful whether the concepts of merchants and commercial acts are significant enough to implement special regulations. For example, according to case law, a credit association cannot be a merchant, but a bank is. In the recent argument in favor of reforming the Law of Obligations, it is often argued that the concept of "merchant" should be replaced with "business operator," which is used in the Consumer Contract Act of 2000 and so forth, and that the special rules for this should be integrated into the Civil Code.

On the other hand, most of the original contents of the Commercial Code were already lost and transferred to special laws, and they would never be recovered in the Commercial Code. The Companies Act is too huge to bring into the Commercial Code and is expected to be revised promptly along with a transition of economic conditions and legal circumstances. As the insurance law in the Commercial Code (Chapter 10 of the Book III) was transferred to the Insurance Act of 2008, major portions of the law of commercial Acts in Book III would be replaced by special laws because the rules for particular commercial contracts and transactions, such as secret partnership (chapter 4), brokerage (chapter 5), factor (chapter 6), and carriage (chapters 7 and 8) would come to be expected to include regulatory and administrative rules as a hybrid entity of various business law rules, being not limited to private law rules. As for commercial law, decodification of the Commercial Code has already progressed a fair bit, and the lost contents of the Commercial Code will remain in special laws as it stands now.

12.5 The Civil Code and Consumer Law

In the Japanese legal system, consumer law exists outside of the Civil Code, as do special laws. The principle that the Civil Code is general law in the field of private law that equally applies to all the citizens still holds true. The Civil Code never uses the terms "consumer," "business operator," or "merchant," all of which presuppose subcategories of citizens.

The system of consumer law is composed of a number of special laws covering private law and administrative law.[13] Fundamental consumer rights and the general duties of businesses are provided in the Consumer Fundamental Act (2004), which was initially enacted as the Consumer Protection Fundamental Act (1968). For the general regulation of consumer contracts, the Consumer Contract Act (2000) governs the rules regulating unfair contract terms and behavior on contracting of business operators, and enables qualified consumer organizations to demand injunctions. As for the specific marketing practices that include some peculiar risks derived from their transaction structures, the Act on Specified Commercial Transactions (1976) regulates door-to-door sales, mail order sales, telemarketing sales, multilevel marketing transactions, and the like. The Act on Specified Commercial Transactions provided the rules for the right of withdrawal, the duty to provide information when concluding contracts, and the duty to deliver documents relating to the contents of contract. Moreover, as the special law of product liability, the Product Liability Act (1994) imposes no-fault liability on the manufacturer of the product with the defect.

Among them, the right of withdrawal in the Act on Specified Commercial Transactions is one of the most significant special laws for consumer protection. However, this rule is closely connected with administrative requirements for business operators, such as the duty to provide information about the right of withdrawal and other contents of contract. A violation of the requirements leads to administrative sanction and criminal punishment, but not to civil liability. Considering the

[13] For the details of the development of consumer law in Japan, see Masahiko Takizawa, "Consumer Protection in Japanese Contract Law," *Hitotsubashi Journal of Law and Politics* 37 (2009): 31–39; Masami Okino, "Recent Developments in Consumer Protection in Japan," *UT Soft Law Review* 4 (2012): 10–18.

nature of the rules, as a set of administrative rules, they reinforce and supplement the rules of civil law from the outside, and it would be difficult to incorporate them in the Civil Code.

In contrast, the Consumer Contract Act, except for the rules for collective action for injunction by qualified consumer organizations additionally introduced in 2006, contains solely civil law rules. Article 4 of the Consumer Contract Act allows consumers to rescind their manifestations of intention to offer or accept a consumer contract when business operators make improper solicitation for concluding a contract, such as misrepresentation (paragraph 1, section 1), provision of conclusive evaluations for uncertain facts (paragraph 1, section 2), failure to represent disadvantageous facts (paragraph 2), or failure to leave a residence of a consumer or to allow a consumer to leave a business place (paragraph 3). Article 10 of the Consumer Contract Act nullifies unfair consumer contract terms that grossly restrict the rights of consumers or expand the duties of consumers, and article 8 and 9 expressly prohibit consumer contract terms that exempt a business operator from liability for damages (article 8) and that stipulate the amount of liquidated damages in case of a cancellation or fix the penalty that exceed the normal amount of damages to be caused to a business operator (article 9). These rules expand the remedies of the consumer further than the correspondent rules in the Civil Code, that is, the article 4 of the Consumer Contract Act is the special rule for fraud and duress in the Civil Code (article 96 of the Civil Code,) and articles 8, 9, and 10 are the special rules for public order (article 90 of the Civil Code). Of course, these rules in the Consumer Contract Act are based on the disparity in bargaining or information power between consumers and business operators, so that they surely have a differing basis from the civil law rules to some extent. Nevertheless, if the Civil Code could accept the concept of consumer and the rules based on the disparity between consumers and business operators, the rules of consumer contracts in the Consumer Contract Act could be integrated into the Civil Code *mutatis mutandis*. It can be said that the fact that such rules for consumer contracts are provided outside the Civil Code as matters now stand results in the serious hollowing-out of the Civil Code, and some sort of recodification of the consumer contract law and the corresponding reform of the Civil Code must be executed in the near future, even though the concept of and rules related to "consumer" could not easily be included in the Civil Code.

Until now, the Civil Code has never known the concept of consumer or business operator, but the recent argument in favor of reforming of the law of obligations argues that the concepts and the rules in consumer law should be integrated into the Civil Code, insofar as the nature of the rules would permit the integration. Regarding the Consumer Contract Act, it is said that the requirements for business operators before or at the conclusion of the contract, and the rules for the regulation of unfair contract terms should be integrated into the Civil Code, but the rule of injunctions by a qualified consumer organizations should not. Through the reform of the law of obligation, recodification of the law of consumer contracts is expected to a significant degree.

12.6 Characteristics of the Process of Legislation and Constitutional Review

12.6.1 Relationship Between the Civil Code, the Treaties, and the Constitution

The Japanese Constitution provides that it has supremacy over other laws (Article 98, paragraph 1 of the Constitution). However, the relationship between the Constitution and ratified treaties is not stipulated in the Constitution. The majority of scholars think that the Constitution has priority over the treaties because the procedure for the amendment to the Constitution is more difficult than that for the ratification of treaties. Whether the Constitution takes priority over the treaties or not, both the Constitution and the treaties are superior to other laws, including the Civil Code. Therefore, if a treaty that contradicts the Civil Code is ratified, the provisions of the treaty are superior to that of the Civil Code.

Here, the reality of constitutional order is more important than such formal hierarchy of laws is. Judges in Japan retain the power of constitutional review but it is extremely rare to actually be sentenced for violation of the Constitution. Since the enactment of the Constitution of 1947, the Supreme Court has declared a statute unconstitutional only eight times. Though the extreme judicial passivism, avoiding declaration of unconstitutionality, is based on multiple and complicated factors,[14] one conclusive ground may be that there has been a bureaucratic influence on constitutional adjudication and constitution-abiding legislation, which is mainly undertaken by the General Secretariat of the Supreme Court and the Cabinet Legislation Bureau.

12.6.2 Bureaucratic Influence on Constitutional Adjudication and Constitution-Abiding Legislation

The first factor underlying extreme judicial passivism is related to the great authority of the General Secretariat of the Supreme Court. Article 13 of the Court Act (1947) only provides that the General Secretariat handles administrative affairs of the Supreme Court, but, in actuality, the General Secretariat is in almost complete control of judicial administration.[15] Especially through the exclusive power to decide

---

[14] For the various reasons of a very conservative constitutional jurisprudence, see Shigenori Matsui, "Why Is the Japanese Supreme Court So Conservative?" *Washington University Law Review* 88 (2011): 1400–1416.

[15] According to Hiroshi Itoh, *The Supreme Court and Benign Elite Democracy in Japan* (Burlington, VT: Ashgate, 2010), 26–27, it was described that "the top echelon of the Supreme Court General Secretariat forms the hard core of the elitist judicial administration."

personnel issues such as advancement or relocation, judges are urged to conform to the inclination of the General Secretariat as far as possible. Management posts of the General Secretariat are held by judges, but they only engage in administrative work, not in actual trial. Justices of the Supreme Court are appointed from a variety of legal professionals, such as judges, lawyers, attorneys, administrators, and professors, but almost all justices of the Supreme Court who are descended from judges have the experience of the members of the General Secretariat. As of 2013, while six justices of the Supreme Court are descended from judges, the five of them have belonged to the General Secretariat and the remaining one has worked at the Ministry of Justice for several decades instead of passing judgment on a case. Thus, the General Secretariat of the Supreme Court typically exemplifies bureaucratic elitism in the judicial branch of the government, and it has high control over not only administration of justice but also inclination of judicial decisions. Furthermore, in the process of legislation, the General Secretariat plays an important role. Under the bureaucratic legislative system in Japan, most bills are drafted by the legislative council in the each Ministry and submitted to the Diet by the Cabinet, and the General Secretariat consistently delivers several members to the legislative councils. In this way, the General Secretariat is directly taking part in the legislative process, let alone being in a close relationship with ministries and agencies, as part of bureaucratic structures. As a corollary of the participation in the legislative process or the cooperative relationship with bureaucrats in the Ministries, the Supreme Court distinctly shows a conservative tendency and refrains from declaring the unconstitutionality of a law.

The second factor behind the judicial passivism is concerned with the role of the Cabinet Legislation Bureau in the process of legislation. The Cabinet Legislation Bureau is called as the Prime Minister's "in-house lawyer[16]", and the cabinet bills, which amount to about 80 % of the bills passed by the Diet, must be minutely scrutinized by the Cabinet Legislation Bureau before submission to the Diet. Screening by the Cabinet Legislation Bureau broadly extends to the legality and rationality of the contents, legislative facts, wordings, and all other points of the bills. Of course, the constitutionality of the cabinet bills is founded on strict screening by the Cabinet Legislation Bureau. Thus, the cabinet bills acquire a strong estimation of constitutionality and the Supreme Court respects the results of the screening by the Cabinet Legislation Bureau.[17] In this way, it is thought that the Cabinet Legislation Bureau practically monopolizes the authority of official interpretation of the Constitution, and the extreme judicial passivism strongly depends on the bureaucratic power and capability of the Cabinet Legislation Bureau.

---

[16] Richard J. Samuels, "Politics, Security Policy, and Japan's Cabinet Legislation Bureau: Who Elected These Guys, Anyway?" *Japan Policy Research Institute (JPRI) Working Paper* 99 (March 2004).

[17] Matsui, "Why Is the Japanese Supreme Court So Conservative?" 1421.

12.6.3 Characteristics of Law-Making Process in Japan

As stated above, the roles of the General Secretariat of the Supreme Court and the Cabinet Legislation Bureau encourage judicial passivism in Japan, and this mechanism typically describes the characteristics of the Japanese bureaucracy: the homogeneous cluster of bureaucratic elites who share academic backgrounds and a sense of public or private interests that has structural and institutional influence on legislation and justice. Furthermore, it is remarkable that the General Secretariat of the Supreme Court and the Cabinet Legislation Bureau play a certain part already in the process of drafting cabinet bills in the government ministries. Namely, the Legislative Council (*Hosei-shingikai*) of the relevant ministry assumes the task of making a draft of the relatively important bills on the basis of a consultation of the minister, and about half of the members of the Legislative Council are academic experts, with the rest being counselors of the relevant ministry, representatives of interests in the private sectors, and other administrators, including counselors or division managers of the General Secretariat of the Supreme Court and the Cabinet Legislation Bureau.

It is an outstanding feature of the law-making process in Japan that the Legislative Councils of the ministries actually hold the authority to determine the concrete content of the bills. Conferences of the Legislative Council are a forum for coordinating various interests and opinions, and political maneuvers or compromises are often made in order to obtain a consensus of the members of the Legislative Council. In other words, practical and meticulous coordination through deliberations in the Legislative Council enables the ministries to propose balanced drafts that are acceptable to most concerned. It is said that the law-making process in the Legislative Council plays the role of "ex ante monitoring" for legislation and administrative rulemaking, which results in the suppression of ex post administrative adjudication.[18] Concerning the characteristics of legal governance in Japan, it is said that ex ante consensus building and respect for community norms are seen as crucial to governing and ruling in Japanese society,[19] and this explanation also applies to the process of rule-making in Japan. The Legislative Council is organized in each relevant ministry in a manner corresponding to the nature of the legal issues, reflecting the vertically divided administrative system in Japan, so that the form and content of a statute also become vertically segmented. Thus, while the unity of bureaucratic elites in every branch of government facilitates administrative and legislative coordination, it is not easy to draft a statute with multiple purposes that bestrides more than one presiding ministry due to the organizational configuration of the Legislative Council. In this respect, the special laws different in nature from the Civil Code, such as the laws for consumers or merchants, could not easily be integrated into the Civil Code, even by a major reform of the Civil Code.

---

[18] Hideki Kanda, "Finance Bureaucracy and the Regulation of Financial Markets in Japan" in *Japan: Economic Success and Legal System*, ed. Harald Baum (Berlin: De Gruyter, 1997), 312–315.

[19] John Owen Haley, *Authority without Power: Law and the Japanese Paradox* (New York: Oxford University Press, 1991), 198–200; John Owen Haley, *The Spirit of Japanese Law* (Georgia: The University of Georgia Press, 1998), 210–212.

12.7 Forthcoming Major Reform of the Civil Code (Reform of the Law of Obligations)

Concerning the Civil Code reforms, the largest reform was the total revision of family law in 1947. The reform of the system of juridical persons was also fundamental and substantial, as it deleted the provisions in the Civil Code related to juridical persons and, as a result, hollowed out the Civil Code to a certain extent. However, especially for the Property Law and the Law of Obligations, the major modifications and additions to the rules have been implemented outside of the Civil Code, through the enactment of special laws. "Decodification" of the Civil Code has taken place in only very limited cases up until now.

The next major reform being anticipated concerns the Law of Obligations. The Minister of Justice, on October 28, 2009, consulted with the Legislative Council of the Ministry of Justice about the reform of the Civil Code (the Law of Obligations). The contents of the consultation are as follows: "The Minister of Justice considers that provisions of law of obligations in the Civil Code, the basic code of private law, need to be reformed especially focusing on those provisions governing contract which are deeply relate to people's daily life and economic activities. This comes from the viewpoint that the Civil Code provisions need to correspond to the changes of social economy since its legislation so that they become more understandable to the public. Accordingly, the Minister of Justice requests the Legislative Council to present the basic policy of the reform.[20]" As a result, the Legislative Council established the Working Group on the Civil Code (the Law of Obligations) and entrusted them with material investigation and deliberation on the matter. The subject of the reform project extends to the Law of Obligations as a whole, and also to the provisions of juridical acts in the General Part of the Civil Code. If the reform project is successful, it will be one of the most fundamental reforms of the Civil Code, along with the reform of family law in 1947. In fact, this very large-scale "recodification" of the Civil Code in the field of the law of obligations is currently taking place. The details of the project, including the development of events, materials, and the summary of minutes are available on the Ministry of Justice's website.[21]

12.8 Conclusion

In Japan, while the Commercial Code is subject to decodification to a large degree, as the company law and the insurance law were transferred out of the Commercial Code to the special laws, the Civil Code has escaped such direct decodification until now and retains its original components. However, due to the emergence of numerous special laws, the hollowing-out and decodification of the Civil Code has been

[20] Consultation No. 88, at the 160th meeting.

[21] http://www.moj.go.jp/ENGLISH/ccr/CCR_00001.html

caused in an indirect manner. Especially, the rules of consumer law exist completely outside the Civil Code, so that the concept of a consumer or business operator has been never known within the Civil Code.

As the reform of the Law of Obligations in the Civil Code is now in progress in the Legislative Council of the Ministry of Justice, recodification of the Civil Code through a major reform is anticipated in the near future. However, even though such recodification of the Civil Code could be achieved, the character of the Civil Code that it is generally applied to all citizens would not be lost. To integrate the special rules for consumers and so forth into the Civil Code would not fit the vertically-segmented structure of the law-making and law-enforcing process in the ministries. The characteristics of Japanese bureaucracy extending to legislative and judicial operations not only support the high stability of laws, but also often define the nature of the law itself. Though the forthcoming recodification of the Civil Code, especially for the Law of Obligations, would effectuate the modernization of the Civil Code, it could be done only within the framework of the traditional bureaucracy. In this sense, it can be said that the structure of a law rather than its contents is strongly influenced by the characteristics of the political system.

The present situation is far removed from the situation in the late nineteenth century in which the Civil Code and the other codes were codified together on the forceful initiative of the government. The transplanted western codes have taken root on Japanese soil with over 100 years' practice and have accomplished the peculiar development as the Japanese law. Therefore, recodification of the Civil Code must be carried out with full respect for practical experience and the accumulation of extensive case law, and must adapt to the present bureaucracy, which has been established in post-war Japanese politics. The multilateral constraints on the basis of the history of law and the political configuration form a certain image of the forthcoming recodification of the Civil Code: law is the fruit of the history and spirit of the people[22] also in the twenty-first century.

Bibliography

Arai M, Homma A (2005) Guardianship for adults in Japan: legal reforms and advances in practice. Australas J Ageing 24(Supplement S1):S19–S24.

Boissonade G (1890–1891) Projet de code civil pour l'Empire du Japon, Tomes 1–4, Nouvelle éd. Kokubunsha, Tokyo

Haley JO (1991) Authority without power: law and the Japanese paradox. Oxford University Press, New York

Haley JO (1998) The spirit of Japanese law. The University of Georgia Press, Georgia

Itoh H (2010) The Supreme Court and benign elite democracy in Japan. Ashgate, Burlington

[22] In this regard, the concept of "*Volksgeist* as the basis of law" in the sense used by Savigny (Friedrich Carl von Savigny, *Vom Beruf unserer Zeit für Gesetzgebung und Rechtswissenschaft*. (Heidelberg: Mohr und Zimmer, 1814)) remains one of the most important guidelines for modern recodification of the Civil Code.

Kanda H (1997) Finance bureaucracy and the regulation of financial markets in Japan. In: Baum H (ed) Japan: economic success and legal system. De Gruyter, Berlin, pp 305–19

Kawashima T (1963) Dispute resolution in contemporary Japan. In: von Mehren AT (ed) Law in Japan: the legal order in a changing society. Harvard University Press, Cambridge, pp 41–72

Kitagawa Z (2007) Japanese civil law and German law: from the viewpoint of comparative law. In: Kitagawa Z, Riesenhuber K (eds) The identity of German and Japanese civil law in comparative perspectives: Die Identitat des Deutschen und des Japanischen Zivilrechts in Vergleichender Betrachtung. De Gruyter Recht, Berlin, pp 11–56

Matsui S (2011) Why is the Japanese Supreme Court so conservative? Wash Law Rev 88:1375–1423

Minear RH (1970) Japanese tradition and western law: emperor, state, and law in the thought of Hozumi Yatsuka. Harvard University Press, Cambridge

Noda Y (1976) Introduction to Japanese law. Translated and edited by H. Angelo AH. University of Tokyo Press, Tokyo

Oda H (2009) Japanese law, 3rd edn. Oxford University Press, New York

Okino M (2012) Recent developments in consumer protection in Japan. UT Soft Law Rev 4:10–18

Samuels RJ (2004) Politics, security policy, and Japan's cabinet legislation bureau: who elected these guys, anyway? Japan Policy Research Institute (JPRI) Working Paper 99

Takizawa M (2009) Consumer protection in Japanese contract law. Hitotsubashi J Law Politics 37:31–39

Uchida T, Taylor VL (2007) Japan's 'era of contract'. In: Foote DH (ed) Law in Japan: a turning point. University of Washington Press, Seatle, pp 454–482

Von Savigny FC (1814) Vom Beruf unserer Zeit für Gesetzgebung und Rechtswissenschaft. Mohr und Zimmer, Heidelberg

Chapter 13
A Matter of Honour, in Which a Small People Can Be Great – The Dutch Codification Efforts in Brief

Anna Berlee

Abstract The Dutch codification efforts in relation to Private Law started out in France and have since moved to Brussels. Codification started from a will to break free from the French and their *Code civil*, but soon after enacted a Dutch Civil Code not very dissimilar to its French counterpart in 1838. It would be another 110 years before Prof. Meijers would officially start with drafting a new Civil Code for the Netherlands. While from 1970 onwards the Books of the Civil Code saw gradual introduction, with the largest part entering into force in 1992, the Civil Code is not finished yet. Its most recent addition has been Book 10 on Private International Law which entered into force on 1 January 2012. The Dutch Civil Code is therefore a mixture of old and new provisions. Another type of mix is also notable. The growing influence of European and international legislation cannot be underestimated. It has led to a mix of provisions that have their origin from within as well as beyond the country borders. A cross-border Code, if you will. The influence of European and international legislation is for some areas however so great, that national codification efforts have stopped altogether, the prime example being Intellectual Property Law. From France to Brussels indeed. Other areas of the law are highlighted to show the aforementioned mixtures that exist in the Dutch Civil Code. These areas are Family Law, Labour Law and Consumer Law.

Keywords The Netherlands • Dutch codification • Private law • Dutch Civil Code • European legislation recodification • The Civil Code and Private International Law

A. Berlee (✉)
Private Law Department, Faculty of Law, Maastricht University (UM),
Maastricht, The Netherlands
e-mail: anna.berlee@maastrichtuniversity.nl

J.C. Rivera (ed.), *The Scope and Structure of Civil Codes*, Ius Gentium: Comparative Perspectives on Law and Justice 32, DOI 10.1007/978-94-007-7942-6_13,

13.1 Introduction

The codification efforts in the Netherlands, started outside of the (at that time) Dutch borders, and while for a brief period they were pulled back in, a trend in European and international legislative efforts have shown in recent years that the domain for codification is slowly crossing borders again. The peculiar case of the Netherlands codification started with a will to break free from the French and their *Code civil*, but soon after a Dutch Civil Code not very dissimilar to its French counterpart was nevertheless introduced. A Code that would remain almost untouched until Prof. Eduard Meijers, an eminent Dutch professor at Leyden University (again) suggested making a truly Dutch Civil Code, calling it a matter of honour in which a small people can be great.[1] Soon after he was given the task of drafting what would become the Civil Code the Netherlands has today.

In this Chapter the codification efforts of the Netherlands are looked at from three different perspectives: the past; the present and the cross-border. What will become clear is that the Dutch codification of private law cannot be seen separately from developments on the European and international level. In particular the influence of the European Union cannot be underestimated. The Chapter starts with a brief visit into the history of Dutch codification of private law after which the Civil Code as it stands today will be outlined and discussed, in particular the phased introduction of the Code and the peculiar case of Intellectual Property Law in Dutch Private Law codification will feature. Some areas such as Consumer Law, Family Law, Private International Law and Labour Law will be given some more specific attention. This is done as their development is a wonderful illustration of codification, European influence and international attention being paid to matters that were formerly within the (exclusive) realm of national law. Before concluding this Chapter a brief introduction as to relationship between the Civil Code and the Constitution is provided for.

13.2 From French to German Influences; A Brief History of the Dutch Codification of Private Law

In 1797 the southern part of the Netherlands, until the French occupation in 1794 governed by Austria, began to apply the *Code civil*, or French Civil Code, as it was annexed to France. The northern part of the Netherlands (the Republic of the United Provinces) had also come under French control, but had retained its sovereignty (so-called "constitutional independence") under the name of Batavian Republic (*Bataafsche Republiek*) that had been proclaimed that year. By doing so the Batavian Republic had waned off the influence of the *Code civil* and could set up its own national committee (*staatscommissie*) tasked with drafting a Civil Code for the Republic. The 'Committee of Twelve' as they were called made little progress in the

[1] 'Een eerezaak… waarin ook een klein volk groot kan zijn'. P. Scholten and E.M. Meijers, *Gedenkboek Burgerlijk Wetboek 1838–1939* (Zwolle: W.E.J. Tjeenk Willink 1990), p. 63.

area of private law. One of the pitfalls was that the president of the private law committee tasked with drafting the private law part wanted a code that would have a solution to all and any disagreements that might occur in private law relationships.[2] Not being able to finish their work (in time), the Batavian Civil Code never came into being, and the *ancient regime* was still in place.

Progress, however, was made when in 1804 the Republic became a Monarchy under the reign of King Louis Napoléon. Rather than simply adopting the French Civil Code as the Civil Code for the new Kingdom as his brother, then emperor Napoleon Bonaparte thought and wanted to happen,[3] Louis Napoléon refused. He would rather have a civil code that suited the new Kingdom. And so it was that in 1809 he enacted the 'Code Napoleon, designed for the Kingdom Holland' (*Wetboek Napoleon, ingerigt voor het Koningrijk Holland*). Although it was in force for only a brief period, it nevertheless signalled the end of all old law, specifically Roman Law.[4]

On 1 March 1811 the *French* Civil Code (*Code Napoléon*) entered into force in the entire Netherlands[5] after Napoleon Bonaparte had dethroned his brother and annexed the former Kingdom to France. Even though a mere 2 years later sovereignty was restored, the *Code Napoléon* would remain in force for as long as the efforts for a new Dutch Civil Code had not yielded any results. It would be another 25 years before this happened and the *Dutch* Civil Code, still largely based on the French equivalent, would be enacted.

The reason for this long delay was due to the somewhat tumultuous period of the United Kingdom of the Netherlands, after the defeat of Napoleon uniting the Southern and Northern Netherlands as a "guardian state" north of France. This period lasted from 1815 to 1830, at which time the Southern Netherlands became the independent Kingdom of Belgium. During this time several drafts of a new civil code had been made, though all were extensively revised or outright rejected. In 1830 Parliament took over the drafting process and finally finished the project. On 1 October 1838 the Dutch Civil Code was enacted.[6] While it was still largely based on the 1804 French Civil Code there were notable differences as well. The division of the 1838 Dutch Civil Code was very different from its French counter-

[2] J.H.A. Lokin and W.J. Zwalve, *Hoofdstukken uit de Europese Codificatiegeschiedenis*, (Deventer: Kluwer 2001), p. 295.

[3] Napoleon Bonaparte wrote his brother on 31 October 1807 a letter stating: 'Je désirerais que vous ordonnassiez qu'à dater du 1er janvrier prochain le code Napoléon sera la loi de vos peuples'. *See Correspondance de Napoléon Ier, publiée par ordre de l'empreur Napoléon III, XVI, Paris 1864, p. 131. See further*: Lokin, J.H.A., and Zwalve, W.J. 2001, p. 297.

[4] Article 3 of the Royal Decree that enacted the Civil Code: "Bij de invoering van dit Wetboek zullen zijn afgeschaft het Roomsche Regt, mitsgaders alle Wetten en Ordonnantiën, tot het Burgerlijk Regt betrekking hebbende, en welke tot nu toe in het Koningrijk, of eenig gedeelte van hetzelve in vigeur zijn geweest, het zij dezelve zijn bekend geweest onder de benaming van Plakkaten, Publicatiën, Ordonnantiën, Landregt, Reglementen, Keuren, Statuten, Octrooijen, Costumen, of onder welke benaming zulks zoude mogen zijn; zonder dat aan eenige van dezelve, voor het vervolg, eenige kracht van Wet zal mogen worden toegekend, ten zij dezelve uitdrukkelijk dit Wetboek zijn uitgezonderd."

[5] Left of the bank of the river Rhine from 1 January 1811 already and 1 March 1811 onwards for the rest of the Netherlands.

[6] For the province of Limburg this would be only on 1 January 1842.

part, a difference largely due to the (strong) divide between property law and the law of obligations that existed in the Dutch but not the French Civil Code.[7]

Soon after its enactment there was much criticism on the sloppy drafting of the code. This criticism was not turned into any fundamental revision efforts over the years to come, although the code underwent many small changes[8] and amendments. Attempts at a complete overhaul of Dutch private law had been made, but all without result.[9] Partial revision has also been attempted, but again, without much result.[10] It was not until 1938, on the occasion of the centennial celebration of the Civil Code, there appeared to be only one strong critical voice left, that of Prof. E.M. Meijers.[11] He again proposed a complete revision of the Civil Code, calling it a matter of honour in which a small people can be great.[12]

On 25 April 1947 it was requested of Eduard Maurits Meijers,[13] then professor of Law at Leyden University, to draft a design for a 'New Civil Code'. This would be a major revision of the then Civil Code that had been in force since 1838. It was the intention of all parties involved that this process of (re)drafting a (New) Civil Code would last no longer than 10 years.[14] However, it would be another 20 years before the first part of the Code had been enacted (Book 1 on Family Law) and a further 20 before the majority of the Code would be in force (1992) and the Netherlands would have its new Civil Code. Prof. Meijers was unable to finish the project due to his death, however, his influence is still notable today. By looking at the German Civil Code that had been in force since the beginning of the century, he took elements from the French and German Civil Code, and drafted a Code that was a mix between the two.

13.2.1 Timeframe

Each Book of the Civil Code that is currently in force, has been enacted at a different stage. These dates are (Table 13.1):

[7] Luijten, E.A.A. 1989, p. 9.

[8] Already in 1843 the first amendment was enacted, which did away with overly formalistic *Code civil* provisions. *See further*: E.A.A. Luijten, "146 jaar Burgerlijk Wetboek: Inleiding," in *146 jaar Burgerlijk Wetboek – Het jubileum van het 150-jarig Wetboek en zijn invoering in het Hertogdom Limburg op 1 januari 1842*, ed. E.A.A. Luijten (Deventer: Kluwer 1989), p. 10.

[9] In 1880 there was a committee Van Meerbeke which resigned 18 years later with nothing more to show than a draft that never became more than a draft for a revision of Books 1 and 2 of the DCC.

[10] After an overwhelming majority at the Dutch Lawyers Association (*Nederlandse Juristenvereniging*) requested such partial revision of the Civil Code, a new committee was constituted.

[11] See extensively on the 1838–1938 period: E.O.H.P Florijn, *Ontstaan en ontwikkeling van het nieuwe Burgerlijk Wetboek*, (Maastricht: Maastricht University Press 1994).

[12] 'een eerezaak… waarin ook een klein volk groot kan zijn'. Scholten and Meijers, *Gedenkboek*, 63.

[13] Due to his death in 1954 the work was not finished, after which Drion, Eggens and De Jong continued it.

[14] Florijn, *Ontstaan en ontwikkeling van het nieuwe Burgerlijk Wetboek*, 1.

Table 13.1 Entry into force Civil Code Books

Book	On	Entry into force
Book 1	Family Law and the Law of Persons	1 January 1970
Book 2	Legal Persons	1 July 1976
Book 3	Patrimonial Law in General	1 January 1992
Book 4	Inheritance Law	1 January 2003
Book 5	Property Rights in Respect to Objects	1 January 1992
Book 6	General Part on the Law of Obligations	1 January 1992
Book 7	Specific Contracts	1 January 1992
Book 7A	Specific Contracts, continued	1 January 1992
Book 8	The Law of Carriage and Means of Transportation	1 April 1991
Book 10	Private International Law	1 January 2012

13.3 Decodification or Recodification?

The Netherlands has not experienced a process of 'decodification'. If anything, it has experienced the opposite. As article 107 Const. requires that private law is regulated in general codes, there has been a movement towards recodification rather than decodification. The most recent example is Book 10 of the Civil Code which entered into force on 1 January 2012, absorbing several different laws.[15]

Nevertheless what is evidenced by the apparent halt to the development of Book 9, dealing with intellectual property law, is that while there is no real decodification going on, codification efforts have been suspended in certain areas of the law. Largely due to the codification efforts on the European and International level. On account of the monistic nature of the Dutch legal system, rather than having to transpose these provisions into national law, they become as such part of the legal order. In relation to EU legislation such as Directives which *do* require implementation, this has generally been done by adding provisions (or adapting existing provisions) as much as possible within the Civil Code, if these directives cover private law areas.

13.4 The Civil Code Today

The Civil Code of the Netherlands (*Burgerlijk Wetboek*), comprises of 10 Books. The most recent addition is Book 10 on Private International Law, which entered into force on 1 January 2012.[16] Each of the Books holds several titles (*titels*) which

[15] They were repealed at the same moment the new Book entered into force, *see* Article IV on the Act of 19 May 2011 on the determination and entry into force of Book 10 (Private International Law) of the Civil Code (*Wet van 19 mei 2011 tot vaststelling en invoering van Boek 10 (Internationaal privaatrecht) van het Burgerlijk Wetboek* (*Vaststellings- en Invoeringswet Boek 10 Burgerlijk Wetboek*), Stb. 2011, 272.

[16] Stb. 2011, 340 "Besluit van 28 juni 2011 tot vaststelling van het tijdstip van inwerkingtreding van de Vaststellings- en Invoeringswet Boek 10 Burgerlijk Wetboek".

in turn are subdivided into different sections (*afdelingen*). Combined these Books are an attempt to create a full overview of the legal relationships that may exist between (natural or legal) persons.

The structure of the Dutch Civil Code (DCC) is based on the underlying vision that private law deals with legal relationships between subjects (natural or legal persons), which for a considerable part concern objects (non-physical, such as performance of a contract, or physical such as land). The Civil Code is, therefore, divided into the laws of persons (Books 1 and 2 DCC) and patrimonial law (Books 3–8 DCC), while Book 10 CC (Private International Law) deals with both subjects and objects of civil law. Book 9 DCC on Intellectual Property Law has not yet been enacted. This division between, on the hand, the law of persons and, on the other hand, patrimonial law is continued in the layered structure of the Code. While there is no overarching general part that is applicable to both the law of persons (natural or legal) and that of patrimonial law, the general part on patrimonial law with for example the rules on the legality of legal acts also finds its application in non-patrimonial relationships governed by Books 1 and 2 by virtue of special provisions, which connect a particular part of the CC to parts not directly regulated by that part (*schakelbepalingen*). The layered structure is continued in the patrimonial law part where Book 3 holds general laws and principles of patrimonial law which are further elaborated on, supplemented by, and specified in the following Books (4–8 and 10) of the Code.

The Civil Code is arranged as follows[17]:

- Book 1: Family Law and the Law of Persons (*Personen- en familierecht*)
  - Title 1: General Provisions
  - Title 2: The Right to a Name
  - Title 3: Residency
  - Title 4: Registry of Births, Deaths, Marriages and Registered Partnerships
  - Title 5: Marriage
  - Title 5A: Registered Partnerships
  - Title 6: Rights and Duties of the Spouses
  - Title 7: The Statutory Community of Property
  - Title 8: Marriage Contracts
  - Title 9: Dissolution of a Marriage
  - Title 10: Judicial Separation and Dissolution of the Marriage after a Judicial Separation
  - Title 11: Parentage
  - Title 12: Adoption
  - Title 13: Minority
  - Title 14: Custody over Minor Children
  - Title 15: Right to Contact and Information
  - Title 16: Appointment of a Curator
  - Title 17: Maintenance

[17] Translation by: H. Warendorf, R. Thomas, and I. Curry-Sumner, *The civil code of the Netherlands* (Alphen aan den Rijn: Kluwer Law International 2009). This translation has not always been followed, where it is considered a different translation more accurate.

  - Title 18: Absence, Missing Persons and the Determination of Death in Specific Instances
  - Title 19: Fiduciary Administration for the Protection of Adults
  - Title 20: Protection Orders on behalf of Adults

- Book 2: Legal Persons (*Rechtspersonen*)
  - Title 1: General Provisions
  - Title 2: Associations
  - Title 3: Cooperatives and Mutual Insurance Society
  - Title 4: Companies Limited by Shares
  - Title 5: Private companies with Limited Liability
  - Title 6: Foundations
  - Title 7: Mergers and Divisions
  - Title 8: Regulation of Disputes and the Right of Inquiry
  - Title 9: Annual Accounts and Annual Report

- Book 3: Patrimonial Law in General (*Vermogensrechten in het algemeen*)
  - Title 1: General Provision
  - Title 2: Juridical Acts
  - Title 3: Power of Attorney
  - Title 4: Acquisition and Loss of Property
  - Title 5: Possession and Detention
  - Title 6: Fiduciary Administration of the Property of Another
  - Title 7: Community
  - Title 8: Usufruct
  - Title 9: Rights of Pledge and Hypothec
  - Title 10: The Right of Recourse against Property
  - Title 11: Rights of Action

- Book 4: Inheritance Law (*Erfrecht*)
  - Title 1: General Provisions
  - Title 2: Intestate Succession
  - Title 3: Intestate Succession of a Spouse Who Is Not Juridically Separated, of the Children and Other Statutory Rights
  - Title 4: Last Wills
  - Title 5: Various Types of Testamentary Disposition
  - Title 6: Consequences of the Succession

- Book 5: Property Rights in Respect to Objects (*Zakelijke rechten*)
  - Title 1: Ownership in General
  - Title 2: Ownership of Movables
  - Title 3: Ownership of Immovables
  - Title 4: Rights and Obligations of Owners of Neighbouring Properties
  - Title 5: Ownership in Common
  - Title 6: Servitudes
  - Title 7: Emphytheusis

  - Title 8: The Right of Superficies
  - Title 9: Appartment Rights

- Book 6: General Part on the Law of Obligations (*Algemeen gedeelte van het verbintenissenrecht*)

  - Title 1: Obligations in General
  - Title 2: Transmission of Claims and Obligations and Renunciation of Claims
  - Title 3: Torts
  - Title 4: Obligations Arising from Sources other than Torts and Contracts
  - Title 5: Contracts in General

- Book 7: Specific Contracts (*Bijzondere overeenkomsten*)

  - Title 1: Sale and Exchange
  - Title 2: Financial Collateral Arrangements
  - Title 3: Donation
  - Title 4: Lease and Hire
  - Title 5: Agricultural Tenancies
  - Title 7: Services
  - Titel 7A: Travel Contracts
  - Title 9: Deposit
  - Title 10: Contracts of Employment
  - Title 12: Contracts for Works
  - Title 14: Suretyship
  - Title 15: Contract of Settlement
  - Title 17: Insurance
  - Title 18: Annuities

- Book 7A: Specific Contracts; continued (*Bijzondere overeenkomsten*; *vervolg*)

  - Title 5A: Instalment Sales
  - Title 7: Leasing and Letting
  - Title 7A: [lapsed]
  - Title 9: Partnerships
  - Title 11: [lapsed]
  - Title 13: Loans for Use
  - Title 14: Loans of Consumables
  - Title 15: Vested or Perpetual Annuities
  - Title 16: Contracts of Chance
  - Title 17: [lapsed]
  - Title 19: [lapsed]
  - General Final Provisions

- Book 8: The Law of Carriage and Means of Transportation (*Verkeersmiddelen en vervoer*)

  - Title 1: General Provisions
  - Title 2: General Provisions Regarding Carriage

Maritime Law
- Title 3: Sea-Going Vessels and the Things on Board
- Title 4: The Crew of Sea-Going Vessels
- Title 5: Operations
- Title 6: Accidents
- Title 7: Limitations of Liability In Respect of Maritime Claims

Inland Waterway
- Title 8: Inland Waterway Vessels and the Things on Board
- Title 9: The Crew of Inlands Waterway Vessels
- Title 10: Operations
- Title 11: Accidents
- Title 12: Limitations of Liability in Respect of Owners

Carriage by Road
- Title 13: Carriage by Road
- Title 14: Accidents

Air Law
- Title 15: The Aircraft
- Title 16: Operations

Rail Law
- Title 18: Contracts of Carriage of Goods by Rail
- Title 19: Accidents

- Title 20: Prescription and Lapse of Time
- General Final Provisions

- Book 10: Private International Law (*Internationaal Privaatrecht*)[18]
  - Title 1: General Provisions
  - Title 2: Name
  - Title 3: Marriage
  - Title 4: Registered Partnerships
  - Title 5: Parentage
  - Title 6: Adoption
  - Title 7: Other Family Law Subject Matters
  - Title 8: Corporations
  - Title 9: Agency
  - Title 10: Law of Property
  - Title 11: Law of Trusts
  - Title 12: Inheritance Law
  - Title 13: Contractual Obligations
  - Title 14: Obligations from a Source other than Contracts
  - Title 15: Some Provisions with Regard to Maritime Law, the Law of Inland Shipping and Aviation Law

[18] Translation by: H. Warendorf, R. Thomas, and I. Curry-Sumner, *Burgerlijk wetboek Boek 10=Civil code book 10* (Deventer: Kluwer 2011).

13.4.1 The Peculiar Case of Intellectual Property Law

As is evident from the list of Books above, there is no Book 9 in the Civil Code. The first drafter of the (New) Civil Code, Prof. dr. E.M. Meijers, stated that 'the rights of the creating man' ('*de rechten van de scheppende mens*'), later referred to by him as 'rights to the productions of the mind' ('*rechten op de voortbrengselen van de geest*') would be in a Book 9.[19] This Book 9 would hold the rules on intellectual property law. These have never been finalised and the rules on intellectual property law are still the subject of separate Acts. The most recent reference to Book 9 in the official documentation was in 2011 when the (then) Minister of Security and Justice Opstelten was asked by the Dutch Senate (*Eerste Kamer*) what the plans were for Book 9. His answer was that the codification efforts on a Book 9 on Intellectual Property Rights have been dormant for a while[20] and that there were no current plans to take it up again. (Recent) EU legislation in this area has led to significant changes in patent, trade mark and copyright law, all of which would have been subject to codification in Book 9, had it ever been enacted. Next to this, according to the Minister, there appears to be no strong desire for codification in practice, which had led the Minister to conclude that he would rather prioritise other projects.[21]

This means that intellectual property still falls squarely outside the Civil Code and is governed by separate Acts as well as (international) treaties and regulations.

A more general list of areas of private law areas outside of the Civil Code is provided for below:

- Intellectual Property Rights
  - Copyright Act (*Auteurswet*)
  - Related Rights Act (*Wet op de naburige rechten*)
  - Patent Act (*Rijksoctrooiwet*)
  - Databases Act (*Databankenrecht*)
  - Trade Mark Act (*Handelsnaamwet*)
  - Sewing Seed and Young Plants Act (*Zaaizaad- en Plantgoedwet*)
- Code of Commerce (*Wetboek van Koophandel*)
- Insolvency Act (*Faillissementswet*)
- Code of Civil Procedure (Wetboek van Burgerlijke Rechtsvordering)

[19] At the time Book 8. However, due to the shuffle of inheritance law to Book 4, it was given its place as a Book 9. *See further* on the history of Book 9, N. Hagemans, "Boek 9 BW – 'Dat uitzonderlijk stuk privaatrecht'", *Maandblad voor Vermogensrecht* (2008): 142–147.

[20] The last person commissioned with preparing (a part of) the new Civil code, Prof. J.J. Brinkhof, laid down his work on Book 9 in 1997, after which there was little movement on the project, despite the desire by the then Minister of Justice W. Sorgdrager, *see* Parliamentary Documentation [1996–1997], 25 000 VI, nr. 44.

[21] Parliamentary Documentation [2010–2011], 32 137, C, p. 14.

13.4.2 Phased Introduction of New Civil Code

As the Civil Code of the Netherlands is rather recent, there have not been general reforms to the Code itself since its enactments in phases. That does not mean there have not been voices to suggest that a complete revision might be a good idea.[22]

The oldest of the Books in the Civil Code that is considered "complete"[23] is Book 1 dealing comprehensively with Family Law has undergone so many revisions and changes that commentators have stated that "(i)n the current Book 1 Civil Code, Book 1 of the 1970 Civil Code can hardly be recognised. Not just because the national and international legislation reflects the rapid changing societal changes in the area of human relations, also by means of case law these changes are apparent."[24] Shortly after the enactment of Book 1 in the 1970s there have already been proposals for revision of the law on family and persons that have, albeit to a limited extent, led to legislation in this area. From 1980 onwards there has been a surge of new legislation, in recent years mostly concerned with the rights of the child.[25] Furthermore, reference should be made in particular to the impact of the European Convention on Human Rights (ECHR), especially Article 8 on the right to respect for private and family life and Article 12, concerning the right to marry, often taken in combination with Article 14's prohibition of discrimination.[26] Also, the Convention on the Rights of the Child is of increased importance.[27]

Change in views in Dutch society on matters such as marriage and family, the much larger acceptance of living together without being married, the unwed mother, divorce and striving for equality between men and women as well as heterosexual and homosexual relationships can also help explain the powerful movement that is going on in family law.[28]

There are currently 60 proposals for a revision of the Civil Code. They range from family law to patrimonial law and partially deal with changes flowing from EU legislation. The status of some of these proposals is that they have not been discussed in Parliament since 1995. In the area of company law, there has been a proposal aiming at a complete overhaul of the current law on (company) partnerships that seemed to be so close to adoption that several law faculties in the Netherlands already taught their students the new law rather than the current law. However, in September 2011 the Minister of Security and Justice informed Parliament of his decision to start the

---

[22] De Ruiter in 1990 for Family Law. J. de Ruiter, "Drie treden in het familierecht," RM Themis (1990): 194–209.

[23] Book 7A on 'Specific contacts; continued' is older in time, this is the temporary Book that will disappear once Book 7 is complete.

[24] S.F.M Wortmann et al., *Groene Serie Personen- en Familierecht* (Deventer: Kluwer 2010).

[25] *idem.*

[26] Also, the International Covenant on Civil and Political Rights (ICCPR).

[27] S.F.M Wortmann and J. Van Duijvendijk-Brand, *Compendium van het personen- en familierecht* (Deventer: Kluwer 2009), pp. 1–2.

[28] *Ibdi, p. 1–2.* Reference can be made to the acceptance of homosexual marriages (article 1:39 CC) and of registered partnerships (art. 1:80a ff.).

withdraw procedure on the proposal, making an end (for now) on the revision of Book 2 in relation to company forms.[29] With this proposal being withdrawn and the efforts for a Book 9 on intellectual property law being halted,[30] there are no significant reforms in important areas of the Civil Code scheduled at this moment.

In relation to company law, a new law has very recently been enacted with great consequences for starting entrepreneurs and liability of limited companies. The Law on Simplification and Flexibilisation of the Law of Private Limited Companies (*Wet vereenvoudiging en flexibilisering bv-recht*),[31] has only been in force since 1 October 2012, so its effects cannot be described at this point. Nevertheless, the Act changed Book 2 of the Civil Code so as to relax the rules on starting up a private limited company.[32]

13.4.3 The End of the Code of Commerce

The Code of Commerce (*Wetboek van Koophandel*) is a special code, as it will be completely incorporated in the Civil Code, once Books 7 & 8 have been completed. This also explains the tremendous amounts of lapsed provisions in the Code of Commerce and the empty titles in the current Civil Code. Book 7 holds the provisions on Specific Contracts. This Book is however not finished and is therefore to be read in conjunction with Book 7A, which is a reflection of the old rules (pre-1992, i.e. prior to the enactment of Book 7) on Specific Contracts. Until Book 7 is finished, Book 7A will remain in force and see to matters that have not yet been dealt with in Book 7. The same holds true for the relationship between the Civil Code Books 7 & 8 and the Code of Commerce. Once the Civil Code is completed, there will be no separate Code of Commerce. The Commercial Code the Netherlands nowadays has entered into force on 1 October 1838.[33]

Currently the Code of Commerce has the following contents[34]:

- General Provisions
- Book 1 On Commerce in General (*Van den koophandel in het algemeen*)
  - Title 1: On Merchants and Acts of Commerce
  - Title 2: [lapsed]

---

[29] The letter of the Minister can be found at: https://zoek.officielebekendmakingen.nl/kst-31065-C-n1.html. Accessed 1 Dec 2012.

[30] Parliamentary Documentation [2010–2011], 32 137, C, p. 14.

[31] Wet van 18 juni 2012 tot wijziging van Boek 2 van het Burgerlijk Wetboek in verband met de aanpassing van de regeling voor besloten vennootschappen met beperkte aansprakelijkheid. Stb. 2012, 209.

[32] Starting capital is decreased, relaxed or not necessary at all, depending on the circumstances, for example.

[33] Stb. 1838, 12.

[34] Unofficial translation by Anna Berlee.

- Title 3: On the Partnership (*vennootschap*) in a Firm (*onder firma*) and that by Means of Financing (*bij wijze van geldschieting*) or "en commandite"
- Title 4: On the Stock Market of Commerce and Brokers
- Title 5: [lapsed]
- Title 6: On Bills of Exchange (*wisselbrieven*) and Promissory Notes to Order (*orderbriefjes*)
- Title 7: On Cheques, and Bearer Notes and Receipts (*Van cheques, en van promessen en quitantiën aan toonder*)
- Title 8: [lapsed]
- Title 9: [lapsed]

• Book 2: On the Rights and Obligations flowing from Shipping
  - General provisions
  - Title 1: On Sea Ships
  - Title 2: [*No title*: lapsed]
  - Title 3: On the Captain
  - Title 4: On the Crew
  - Title 5: [lapsed]
  - Title 5A: [lapsed]
  - Title 5B: [lapsed]
  - Title 6: [lapsed]
  - Title 7: [lapsed]
  - Title 8: [lapsed]
  - Title 9: [lapsed]
  - Title 10: [lapsed]
  - Title 11: [lapsed]
  - Title 11A: [lapsed]
  - Title 12: [lapsed]
  - Title 13: On Inland Waterway
  - General Final Provisions

Next to the Civil Code, the Code of Commerce and the Treaties to which the Netherlands are a party, there are also separate national Acts dealing with private law matters. Such as the Insolvency Act (*Faillissementswet*) which deals with the insolvency of both a natural as well as a legal persons.

However, most commercial matters are arranged in either the Civil Code or the Code of Commerce. The Code of Commerce and the Civil Code are closely linked, a relationship reflected in the first Article of the Commerce Code which reads: "The Civil Code is, insofar as this Code does not deviate from it in a particular case, also applicable to matters which are governed by this Code." Therefore, the current relationship between the Civil Code and Commerce Code may be described as being one of *genus* and *species* respectively. General principles of patrimonial law (in the Civil Code) are also applicable to the patrimonial relationships that are dealt with in the Commerce Code, and reference to the Civil Code and its particular Books is made on numerous occasions.[35]

As the Commerce Code will be completely absorbed by the Civil Code, during this integration process certain areas of the law require a close look at both codes. For example, maritime law is now to be found in both Book 8 CC and Book 2 Com.C.[36]

13.5 Consumer Law

The 'consumer' in Dutch law is a relatively new. So new in fact that when Prof. Meijers, the drafter of the (new) Civil Code was working on the Civil Code, there was no trace of any specific consumer protection.[37] It was not until the 1950s and 1960s that in line with international developments, a movement also termed 'consumerism' (*consumentisme*) appears in the legal lexicon.[38] This movement found its fundaments in the idea that the consumer should have an increased influence on the quality of goods and services as well as on the contracts they conclude in relation to these goods and services.[39] Consumers found strength in numbers, and consumer organisations were founded. Nowadays the most famous consumer organisation, *De Consumentenbond*, was founded in 1953 as an organisation that focused on factories and suppliers. Later it expanded its scope and its members,[40] and also its influence. The introduction of specific consumer law in the Netherlands was advanced by the lobbying efforts of the *Consumentenbond*.[41]

Consumer law vastly expanded when European efforts to strengthen the position of the consumer were undertaken.[42] When the Treaty of Rome entered into force in 1958 there were only five explicit mentions to the consumer.[43] None of these however represents an attempt to develop a sophisticated structure of consumer rights or interests.[44] At the time it was assumed that European integration itself would

[35] Articles 15 & 309 to name but a few.

[36] Cf. article 309(1) Com.C." Definitions in Book 8 Civil Code, with the exception of those in articles 5, 6, 7 and 10, also apply in this code."

[37] E.H. Hondius, "De rechtspositie van de consument naar nieuw burgerlijk recht," *Tijdschrift voor Consumentenrecht* 5 (1991):324–338, p. 324.

[38] G.J. Rijken, "Ontstaan en positie van het consumentenrecht," in *Handboek Consumentenrecht*, eds. E.H. Hondius and G.J. Rijken (Zutphen: Uitgeverij Paris 2006), p. 21.

[39] Rijken, *Onstaan en positive van het consumentenrecht*, p. 21.

[40] The latest numbers in relation to members is from 2010, in which there was a total of 482,813 members (NB> significantly lower than in previous years. *See* annual report of the *Consumentenbond*: http://www.consumentenbond.nl/morello-bestanden/algemeen-2012/CB-jaarverslag_2011-uitgave-2012.pdf, p. 15. Accessed 12 Dec 2012.

[41] Hondius, *de rechtspositie van de consument naar nieuw burgerlijk recht*, p. 324.

[42] Rijken calls the European Union 'the powerful engine of consumer regulation', *see* Rijken, *Ontstaan en positive van het consumentenrecht*, p. 24.

[43] Articles 39, 40, 85, 86 and 92 Treaty of Rome.

[44] S. Weatherill, *EU Consumer Law and Policy* (Cheltenham: Edward Elgar 2005), p. 4.

improve the consumer's position. Substantive provisions of the Rome Treaty dealing with the removal of barriers to the circulation of goods, persons and services were designed indirectly to improve the position of the consumer.[45] In this sense, the substantive provisions on free movement were considered in themselves instruments of consumer policy, albeit of the hidden type.[46]

The lack of a legal basis (which is required for Community legislation to be enacted) made legislative efforts in Brussels mute. However, by means of 'soft law' initiatives and approximation of laws some EU (then EC) policy did take shape. Political commitment to the establishment of a consumer protection programme for the EC had grown over the following years.[47] Thus when at the 'Paris Summit' in 1972 the Member States expressed their desire to broaden the appeal of the Community beyond economic affairs into the social sphere, the backing for consumer protection legislation was profoundly present. Inspired by initiatives in the USA,[48] the Council of Ministers adopted a Preliminary programme of the European Economic Community for a consumer protection and information policy as early as 1975, in which five fundamental rights of consumers[49] are singled out, among which the right to protection of health and safety as well as compensation.[50] The First was followed in 1981 by the Second Programme which repeats the five basic rights and expresses a priority call for action in the field of the quality of goods and services, the conditions affecting their supply and the provisions of information about them.[51] These programmes while still 'soft law' on their own led to an EU-widespread boost in legislation dealing with matters of consumers, one of such countries being the Netherlands.[52] In particular in the 1980s the amount of consumer legislation in the Netherlands significantly increased.

With the introduction of the (new) Civil Code of the Netherlands, consumer law became codified in the Civil Code. Books 6 and 7 DCC deal in selected parts with rights of consumers. By including it in these Books, the status of consumer law is no longer one of exception. The codification in the DCC also meant that the new term and concept 'consumer' was introduced in the Civil Code, and specific provisions as to contracts concluded with consumers were enacted. These inclusions were seen as a welcoming addition to strengthen the position of the consumer.[53]

Consumer law is currently codified in Books 6 and 7 DCC. There are no provisions of consumer law in the Commercial Code, which in itself will slowly disappear. Consumer law is therefore only codified in the Civil Code. These books of the Civil

---

[45] Weatherill, *EU Consumer Law and Policy*, p. 4.

[46] Weatherill, *EU Consumer Law and Policy*, p. 4.

[47] Weatherill, *EU Consumer Law and Policy*, p. 6.

[48] US President Kennedy's similar declaration in March of 1962.

[49] Right to protection of health and safety, right to protection of economic interests, right of redress, right to information and education, right of representation (the right to be heard).

[50] OJ C 92, 25.4.1975, p. 2–16.

[51] Weatherill, *EU Consumer Law and Policy*, p. 7.

[52] Rijken, *Ontstaan en positive van het consumentenrecht*, p. 22.

[53] Hondius, *de rechtspositie van de consument naar nieuw burgerlijk recht*, p. 337.

Code deal with the general part on the law of obligations and specific contracts. While general contract theory also applies to consumer transactions and party autonomy still is the cornerstone of Dutch contract law, it is now accepted that certain parties to contracts, e.g. consumers, require special protection, given the existence of inequality of bargaining power. For example[54] in the area of general terms and conditions,[55] problems of sale[56] and problems one may encounter in travel contracts.[57] This, however, does not mean that the initial paradigm of contract law has changed, but that the principle of weaker party protection is considered to be on an equal footing with the principle of freedom of contract.[58] Such is also prevalent in other areas of the law, such as, labour law.

In 1993 when the Maastricht Treaty entered into force, the European Union was established and with it a legal basis for consumer protection was created. This led to a decrease in longer soft law initiatives coming from Europe, yet a start and expansion of legally binding Regulations and Directives. This means that while the Civil Code contains most provisions on consumer Law. If consumer law is to be found in an EU regulation, which, unlike a directive, does not require implementation, it is EU law which governs the matter directly.

Current EU law in relation to consumer rights (by means of Directive or Regulation), extends to legislation in the area of unfair commercial practice,[59] General contractual rights,[60] E-Shopping,[61] Timeshare and travel,[62] Financial services,[63]

[54] This is not an exhaustive list.

[55] Book 6, Title 5, Articles 231–248 DCC.

[56] Book 7, Title 1, Articles 1–48 g DCC.

[57] Book 7, Title 7a, Articles 500–514 DCC.

[58] E.H. Hondius, "De innoverende functie van het consumentenrecht," *Maandblad voor Vermogensrecht* 7/8 (2011): 181–185, p. 182.

[59] Directive 2005/29/EC of the European Parliament and of the Council of 11 May 2005 concerning unfair business-to-consumer commercial practices in the internal market and amending Council Directive 84/450/EEC, Directives 97/7/EC, 98/27/EC and 2002/65/EC of the European Parliament and of the Council and Regulation (EC) No 2006/2004 of the European Parliament and of the Council ('Unfair Commercial Practices Directive'), OJ L 149, 11.6.2005, p. 22.

[60] Directive 1999/44/EC of the European Parliament and of the Council of 25 May 1999 on certain aspects of the sale of consumer goods and associated guarantees. OJ L 171, 7.7.1999, p. 12–16. Directive 97/7/EC of the European Parliament and of the Council of 20 May 1997 on the Protection of Consumers in respect of Distance Contracts. OJ L 144, 4.6.1997, p. 19–27.

[61] Directive 97/7/EC of the European Parliament and of the Council of 20 May 1997 on the Protection of Consumers in respect of Distance Contracts. OJ L 144, 4.6.1997, p. 19–27. Directive 2002/65/EC of the European Parliament and of the Council of 23 September 2002 concerning the distance marketing of consumer financial services and amending Council Directive 90/619/EEC and Directives 97/7/EC and 98/27/EC.

[62] Council Directive 90/314/EEC of 13 June 1990 on package travel, package holidays and package tours, OJ L 158, 23.6.1990, p. 59–64.

[63] Directive 2002/65/EC of the European Parliament and of the Council of 23 September 2002 concerning the distance marketing of consumer financial services and amending Council Directive 90/619/EEC and Directives 97/7/EC and 98/27/EC. OJ L 271, 9.10.2002, p. 16–24. Directive 2008/48/EC of the European Parliament and of the Council of 23 April 2008 on credit agreements for consumers and repealing Council Directive 87/102/EEC, OJ L 133, 22.5.2008, p. 66–92.

and many more of which are targeted at one particular issue. Next to these specified areas in which the EU handles consumer rights, there is also a general proposal for a Directive on Consumer Rights, which centralises these efforts, which is expected to enter into force as of 13 June 2014.[64] European legislative efforts in the area of private law are to a large extend reserved for contract law in general and consumer law in particular, to a much lesser extend are tort and property law governed by legislation with a European origin.[65]

It therefore comes as no surprise that most consumer legislation has an EU legislative background and the provisions in the Civil Code dealing with consumer law are often implementations from EU Directives. A small inventory in 2006 showed that of the some 650 Articles in Books 3, 6 and Title 7.1 Civil Code, 65 of them, were the result of an implementation of EU Directives.[66] That makes up for 10 % of the total amount of provisions, an amount that has only increased since then. Consumer law in the Netherlands looked at from a codification standpoint is therefore not a national affair, but a European one.

13.6 Family Law

Family law in the Netherlands is comprehensively arranged in Book 1 of the Civil Code. This includes, provisions on the right to a name, residency, registry of births, deaths, marriages and registered partnerships; marriage; registered partnerships; rights and duties of the spouses; the statutory community of property; marriage contracts; dissolution of a marriage; judicial separation and dissolution of the marriage after a judicial separation; parentage; adoption; minority; custody over minor children; right to contact and information; appointment of a curator; maintenance; absence, missing persons and the determination of death in specific instances; fiduciary administration for the protection of adults and protection orders on behalf of adults.

If family relations have an international character, in the sense that there is a conflict of laws, Book 10 should also be taken into account. As will be explained below this book deals with private international law issues on names; marriage; registered partnerships; parentage; adoption and other family law subject matters in titles 2–7.

---

[64] Directive 2011/83/EU of the European Parliament and of the Council of 25 October 2011 on consumer rights, amending Council Directive 93/13/EEC and Directive 1999/44/EC of the European Parliament and of the Council and repealing Council Directive 85/577/EEC and Directive 97/7/EC of the European Parliament and of the Council. OJ L 304, 22/11/2011, pp. 64–88.

[65] C. Asser and A.S. Hartkamp, *Mr. C. Assers handleiding tot de beoefening van het Nederlands Burgerlijk Recht. 3: Vermogensrecht algemeen*; *Dl. I: Europees recht en Nederlands vermogensrecht* (Deventer: Kluwer 2011), no. 160 Richtlijnen houdende privaatrecht.

[66] J.M. Smits, "Consumentenrecht: een zaak voor de Europese Unie? Een kritische beschouwing over het ontwerp voor een Europese richtlijn consumentenrechten," *Ars Aequi* 6 (2009): 367–373, p. 367.

13.6.1 The Development of Family Law from 1838 Onwards

Apart from some exceptions (refusal of adoption and martial age) family law in its early days was completely based on the French *Code Civil*. Characteristic of the law of that time was the law's close connection with 'nature' and (therefore) with marriage, which was considered to be the natural coming together of man and woman.[67] Marriage, the lasting life commitment a man and a woman made was considered to be a societal duty, and all the legal effects such as lineage and succession had all the attention of the legislator, where it concerns family law. On the other hand was very tough on the unwed mother and her child.[68] In line with the rest of society, family law was very patriarchal, focussing on the power of the man and viewing all the other family relationship in relation to the head of the family.[69]

The emphasis on the societal means of marriage and family life was very different from how it played out in reality. The Industrial Revolution highlighted the dire social, economic and hygienic circumstances in which many people lived.[70] The devastating effects of the Industrial Revolution with its inhumane long working hours for men, women and children made it so that one could not say there was anything close to a well-ordered family life for many people.[71] At the time, taking care of children (in need) and any other state interference in economic and social life was not considered to be part of the Government's 'core tasks' and was left to private initiatives such as charity.[72] Children were only interesting to the law if they could be prosecuted.

Arguably one of the main family law developments in the nineteenth century was that of allowing for divorce by mutual consent. Codification here was lagging, as it was not until the very late in the twentieth century that the legislator codified the Supreme Court's ruling decades earlier which allowed for divorce even if there were no adultery and relaxed the very stringent rules of evidence that came with such a claim.[73] The subjective guilt principle that had played a large part in the earlier legislation was replaced with a more objective disruption principle (*ontwrichtingsbeginsel*).

The development of family law in the second half of the twentieth-century was marked by the introduction of Book 1 on family law, which in itself however did not impede the legislator from enacting several individual Acts as well. The position of children was significantly improved, in child protection rules and parentage rules.

---

[67] C. Asser and J. de Boer, *Mr. C. Assers handleiding tot de beoefening van het Nederlands Burgerlijk Recht*; *1*: *Personen- en familierecht* (Deventer: Kluwer 2010), no. 3.

[68] Asser and de Boer, *Asser Personen- en familierecht*, no. 3.

[69] Asser and de Boer, *Asser Personen- en familierecht*, no. 3. Women were long considered to have no power to act or dispose.

[70] Asser and de Boer, *Asser Personen- en familierecht*, no. 4.

[71] Asser and de Boer, *Asser Personen- en familierecht*, no. 4.

[72] Asser and de Boer, *Asser Personen- en familierecht*, no. 5.

[73] Divorce was not accepted if the party accused of adultery either did not contest or confessed. The adultery itself had to be proven, that was, until this Supreme court Ruling of 22 June 1883, W 4929. *See further* Asser and de Boer, *Asser Personen- en familierecht*, no. 6.

Though here it should be noted that Dutch private law in general, but perhaps family law in particular was forced to develop at a much quicker pace due to external pressure to reform rules. Pressure imposed by for example the ECtHR. This mean that slowly but surely the differences between men and women were made smaller by law and the protection of children got more attention.

In the final years of the twentieth century, the focus was on partners of the same sex. As of 1 January 1998 the registered partnership (*geregistreerd partnerschap*), a partnership which for all intents and purposes is equal in law to marriage, was created for partners of the same sex.[74] Interesting to note is that while registered partnership was created for same-sex partners, the majority of couples that entered into this formalised partnership are couples consisting of people from a different gender.[75] Since 1 April 2001, (civil) marriage is also available to partners of the same sex, which led to a decrease of registered partnerships between partners of the same-sex and an increase in marriages.[76]

Overall, until the second half of the twentieth century Dutch family law was strongly oriented towards the monogamous marriage as an instrument of order in the relationships between man and woman and as the fundament of a family. A very moralistic period in the sense that the law explicitly considers marriage as an institute of a 'higher order' and will protect it even if this means that individual interests are sometimes sacrificed.[77] After this period there can be a gradual shift observed which takes into account these individual interests a bit more.[78]

13.6.2 European Influence on Family Law

While there are other treaties which influenced the development of family law in the Netherlands, the ECHR merits particular attention. Since 31 August 1954 the provisions of the ECHR have been applicable in the Netherlands. However, where it concerned family law, the influence of the ECHR was non-existent in the early days after its enactment. For a long time it was generally assumed that Dutch law would be

---

[74] Notable exceptions to this equality is that the father of a child born within such a partnership does have to legally recognise the child, as not paternity is assumed, but rather a 'familial relationship' to the child. Furthermore, the dissolution of such a partnership does not, unlike marriage, require the intervention of a court.

[75] Of the total amount of *new* registered partnerships in 2011, over 95 % was concluded between a man and a woman. A significant drop of same-sex registered partnerships can be seen since the opening up of marriage to same-sex couples. *See for specific numbers*: http://statline.cbs.nl/StatWeb/publication/?VW=T&DM=SLNL&PA=37772ned&D1=35-47&D2=48-l&HD=121205-1438&HDR=G1&STB=T Accessed 5 Dec 2012.

[76] For the precise numbers, *see* http://statline.cbs.nl/StatWeb/publication/?VW=T&DM=SLNL&PA=37772ned&D1=3-4&D2=20,48-61&HD=121205-1450&HDR=G1&STB=T Accessed 5 Dec 2012.

[77] Asser and de Boer, *Asser Personen- en familierecht*, no. 10.

[78] Asser and de Boer, *Asser Personen- en familierecht*, no. 10.

in conformity with the ECHR.[79] This notion of being in conformity would however soon disappear as there was an increase of types of familial relationships that constituted a 'factual' family life, which was also protected under article 8 ECHR.[80] As the ECtHR considered the ECHR to be 'a living instrument which, (…), must be interpreted in the light of present-day conditions',[81] the ECtHR made itself a very important institution. This interpretation method was given a boost by the Marckx-case.[82] The Marckx-case was the beginning of the extension of the notion of 'family life' which significantly influenced Dutch family law. This led to Prof. De Boer stating that not 'the law' selects relationships with legal effects, but familial relationships created in fact have to be recognised by the law and given legal effect.[83] This case of Marckx, and following case law coming from the ECtHR brought with it a realisation that the early on presumed conformity, might not always be a correct presumption. This led to an increased focus on the ECtHR's case law, which gave a strong impetus to family law development in the last 40 years.

Due to increased (international) mobility of people Dutch society had to adapt to people and families with different cultural backgrounds. This raised and raises questions on whether family law should adjust itself and to what extent to accommodate these differences. Of course, in particular countries cultural elements are intertwined with parts of its family law but that in itself does not necessarily mean that one cannot look for an approximation of family law in the different legal systems.[84]

As of yet one cannot speak of real harmonisation or unification of family law itself, although there has been tremendous progress in the area of international collaboration in the area of family law by means of conflicts of law instruments.[85] The Netherlands is a party to a large number of the treaties established by the Hague Conference on Private International Law (HCCH), ranging from determining the applicable law in respect of the protection of infants,[86] applicable law to maintenance obligations,[87] and more recently international recovery of child support.[88]

---

[79] Asser and de Boer, *Asser Personen- en familierecht*, no. 11.

[80] Asser and de Boer, *Asser Personen- en familierecht*, no. 12.

[81] ECtHR Case of Tyrer v. The United Kingdom 25/04/1978, Application number 5856/72.

[82] ECtHR Case of Marckx v. Belgium 13/06/1979, Application number 6833/74.

[83] Asser and de Boer, *Asser Personen- en familierecht*, no. 13.

[84] P. Vlaardingerbroek and M.J.C. Koens, "Personen- en familierecht in ontwikkeling; een introductie," in *Het hedendaagse personen- en familierecht*, ed. P. Vlaardingerbroek (Deventer: Kluwer 2004), p. 18.

[85] Vlaardingerbroek and Koens, *Personen- en familierecht in ontwikkeling*, p. 18.

[86] Convention of 5 October 1961 concerning the powers of authorities and the law applicable in respect of the protection of infants.

[87] Convention of 2 October 1973 on the Law Applicable to Maintenance Obligations. And Protocol of 23 November 2007 on the Law Applicable to Maintenance Obligations.

[88] Convention of 23 November 2007 on the International Recovery of Child Support and Other Forms of Family Maintenance.

These Treaties are an outcome of international collaboration of governments that take heed of the necessary protection of the child in cross-border situations such as international kidnapping and adoption.[89] Initiatives on the European level, rather than international, come from the Council of Europe where approximation also takes place in matters of family law.[90]

All in all, family law in the Netherlands is shaped by developments on multiple levels, on a national level in Book 1 Civil Code which is the result of the legislator's codification of society at that time, which is also influenced by the case law of the ECtHR. On a European level by the aforementioned case law of the ECtHR and legislation efforts in the Council of Europe and to some extent also the European Union in its approximation of laws efforts. Lastly the approximation efforts of the International Hague Conferences should not be underestimated, an international influence is further exercised by numerous initiatives by the United Nations and its treaties that deal with or provide additional inspiration for the national legislation.

13.7 Private International Law

The most recent addition to the Dutch Civil Code is Book 10 on private international law. It has only been in force since 1 January 2012. Its rich history dates back, not to the classical Roman times or the Greeks, but rather to the Medieval Northern-Italy, when Norther-Italy freed itself from the feudal structures in place, which opened up the northern city-states for a lively economic trade.[91] As each of these city-states created its own statute law (*Statuta*), legal diversity in such a relatively small geographical area pressed on the trade in these areas which led to the recognition of the collision of legislation (*collision statutorum*) and Private International Law was devised.[92]

Private international law (PIL) in the Netherlands was largely influenced by the French, and in particular Bertrand d'Argentré who made the distinction between *statuta personalia* (regulations dealing with persons generally governed by the principle of domicile), *statuta realia* (regulations in relation to immovable property and governed by principle of territoriality) and *statuta mixta* (residual group, also governed by the territoriality principle).[93]

---

[89] Vlaardingerbroek and Koens, *Personen- en familierecht in ontwikkeling*, p. 19.

[90] Think of for example the European Convention on the Adoption of Children, CETS No.: 058; or the recently signed (by the Netherlands) Council of Europe Convention on preventing and combating violence against women and domestic violence, CETS No.: 210.

[91] L. Strikwerda, *Inleiding tot het Nederlands Internationaal Privaatrecht* (Deventer: Kluwer 2012), p. 15.

[92] Strikwerda, *Inleiding*, p. 15.

[93] Strikwerda, *Inleiding*, p. 16–17.

The Dutch legal scholars[94] at the time took the reasoning of d'Argentré and made a study into the foundations and sought to connect this with d'Argentré's territoriality principle and Jean Bodin's sovereignty principle.[95] Territoriality was in d'Argentré's view leading for the *statuta mixta* and *realia* as everything within the borders of the land is subjected to the legislator, as the power of the State and consequently the law stops at the border. The Dutch scholars however took the development one step further and asked the question why this should not then also be true for the *statuta personalia*. They too realised that this would mean the end of conflicts of law and private international law as a whole as everything would stop at the border. A way out was found in the concept of *comitas*. Out of benevolence States allow for the application of foreign law within their own borders.[96]

These ideas (of the division into three *statuta*) remained in the old codification of Dutch law in matters of private international law in 1829, which is still in effect, save for many of the PIL rules which have been repealed over time.[97]

A new view on Private International Law was introduced by Friedrich Carl von Savigny and Carl Georg von Wächter.[98] In 1849 Von Savigny published his Systematics of Current Roman Law (*System des heutigen Römischen Rechts*) in which he developed a set of conflict rules which has stood the test of time.[99] Not the legal rule, but the legal *relationship* is the starting point of finding the applicable law. He therefore did not look at the geographical scope of the rule as was done before but rather Von Savigny focused on the international legal relationship from which the applicable law has to be found. Therefore, the somewhat dubious way in which the earlier Dutch scholars introduced the *comitas* principle in order to avoid problems with their own theory of private international law, is not at all present in Von Savigny's theorem. As the focus is on the legal relationship, borders are no longer that important, and accepting a foreign law within the courts of a particular legal system follows directly from adhering to such an approach.[100]

Von Savigny left his mark on modern-day PIL-rules. While the development continued, it did so within the proposed system by Von Savigny rather than contrary to it.[101]

---

[94] Some of Dutch's most famous legal scholars devoted time to this; Christiaan Rodenburg; Paulus Voet; Ulrik Huber and Johannes Voet.

[95] Jean Bodin, known for Six Livres de la République, 1576.

[96] The precise nature of the comitas concept is never been made really clear. *See* Strikwerda, *Inleiding*, p. 17–18.

[97] Law of 15 May 1829 dealing with general provisions in relation to the law of the Kingdom (*Wet van 15 mei 1829, houdende algemeene bepalingen der wetgeving van het Koningrijk*).

[98] The latter heavily criticised the old ideas and the former took it upon himself to propose an alternative.

[99] Strikwerda, *Inleiding*, p. 18.

[100] See in similar vein: Strikwerda, L. 2012, p. 19.

[101] Strikwerda, *Inleiding*, p. 19–20.

Nonetheless, in the second half of the twentieth century a heavy legal debate in terms of methods and foundations of PIL has taken place, which left some traces in the current PIL-rules.[102]

13.7.1 European Influences on Dutch Private International Law

International treaties and European Regulations are the most important source of Dutch private international law. Such should come as no surprise given the nature of private international law. Some of these international rules aim at unification of conflict laws, whereas others, especially the numerous bilateral treaties, hold regulations in matters of mutual recognition and enforcement of judgments. The types of rules are far and wide. The amount equally so.

The most important international organisation that deals with PIL-treaties is the Hague Conference on Private International Law, which has been established by one of the Netherlands' most famous legal scholars, T.M.C. Asser. At the time of writing, the Netherlands is part of 26 treaties, and has signed but not ratified a further four Treaties by the Hague Conference. These treaties range from approximation of laws in the area of family law to civil procedure,[103] but also matters of tort law[104] and trust law.[105] The International Commission on Civil Status (*Commission Internationale de l'Etat Civil*) also has copious amounts of legislation in place where it concerns family law.[106] The Council of Europe also has Treaties that directly and indirectly influenced Dutch private international law.[107]

Perhaps one of the most influential sources of Dutch private international law is the European Union. Leading to such an amount of PIL-rules stemming from EU-regulation that some scholars speak of an 'Europeanization' of PIL.[108] Where it concerns determining a hierarchy amongst all these international and European

---

[102] Strikwerda, *Inleiding*, p. 20.

[103] Convention of 15 November 1965 on the Service Abroad of Judicial and Extrajudicial Documents in Civil or Commercial Matters.

[104] Convention of 4 May 1971 on the Law Applicable to Traffic Accidents.

[105] Convention of 1 July 1985 on the Law Applicable to Trusts and on their Recognition.

[106] For example Convention No. 14 on the recording of surnames and forenames in civil status registers from 13 September 1973, (Convention relative à l'indication des noms et prénoms dans les registres de l'état civil, signee à Berne le 13.09.1973).

[107] Such as the European Convention on Information on Foreign Law, CETS No. 62; European Convention on Recognition and Enforcement of Decisions concerning Custody of Children and on Restoration of Custody of Children, CETS No. 105.

[108] Strikwerda, *Inleiding*, p. 12.

rules the treaties and Regulations themselves already deal with this, and if not, the Vienna Convention on the Law of Treaties solves it.[109] Where an international rule conflicts with *national* private international rule, the former will prevail. This is formalised in the Dutch Constitution in Articles 93 and 94.

It is striking that the advancing ‘Europeanization’ of private international law, has not led to a new debate on the method and foundations of PIL rules.[110] The European PIL rules still reflect the ideas of Von Savigny, yet these are not without criticism. For example, the Neostatutists zoom in on the changing function of legislation in the modern social welfare state. According to them law is ‘made’ and not ‘found’ and this instrumental aspect of law, denied since Von Savigny, should be given a new place in PIL-rules, if not be its premise.[111] The influence of the Neostatutists is seen in the existence of priority rules and its legacy is found in the idea that conflict rules should take into account of policy aspects (mainly of protecting the weaker party) of the substantive law.[112]

In conclusion, private international law has come a long way from the early statutists in Northern-Italy. Modern Dutch PIL-rules are largely based on Von Savigny’s characterisation of the field of law. Whereas the origin of the applicable PIL-rules is generally to be found on the European and international level, which should come as no surprise given the nature of the rules.

---

[109] Article 30 of the Vienna Convention states:

1. Subject to Article 103 of the Charter of the United Nations, the rights and obligations of States. Parties to successive treaties relating to the same subject matter shall be determined in accordance with the following paragraphs.
2. When a treaty specifies that it is subject to, or that it is not to be considered as incompatible with, an earlier or later treaty, the provisions of that other treaty prevail.
3. When all the parties to the earlier treaty are parties also to the later treaty but the earlier treaty is not terminated or suspended in operation under article 59, the earlier treaty applies only to the extent that its provisions are compatible with those of the later treaty.
4. When the parties to the later treaty do not include all the parties to the earlier one:
   (a) as between States Parties to both treaties the same rule applies as in paragraph 3;
   (b) as between a State party to both treaties and a State party to only one of the treaties, the treaty to which both States are parties governs their mutual rights and obligations.
5. Paragraph 4 is without prejudice to article 41, or to any question of the termination or suspension of the operation of a treaty under article 60 or to any question of responsibility which may arise for a State from the conclusion or application of a treaty the provisions of which are incompatible with its obligations towards another State under another treaty.

[110] Strikwerda, *Inleiding*, pp. 20–21.

[111] Strikwerda, *Inleiding*, p. 21.

[112] In particular seen in relation to PIL-rules in labour relations; consumer transactions; child protection and the like.

13.8 Labour Law

Modern labour law as we have it now has been developed in the past 125 years. Its roots however, date back all the way to Roman law, in which the labour contract was considered a particular type of hire-agreement (*huurcontract*).[113] The French Revolution was however the birth of the modern labour law and contract. The '*Liberté, Égalité and Fraternité*' principles had a strong influence on the 1804 Civil Code of France which in turn had a substantial impact on the design of the 1838 (old) Dutch Civil Code. In particular, contractual freedom extended to the employer-employee labour relationship. There were hardly any limitations imposed on this contractual freedom by the two provisions in the (old) Civil Code that dealt with 'hire and rent of services, labour and industry' (*huur en verhuur van diensten, werk en nijverheid*).[114] Neither was contractual freedom curtailed[115] by the three provisions concerning 'rent of servants and workmen' (*huur van dienstboden en werklieden*).[116]

At the time there were no unions yet on account of the coalition-prohibition in criminal law. When this prohibition was repealed in 1872, unions and employers' associations had the opportunity to flourish.[117] One does need to take heed of the fact that in the first half of the nineteenth century the amount of non-freelancers (*onzelfstandigen*) was relatively small. Overall, the labour force of the Netherlands consisted of farmers with next to these a limited amount of small industrial companies which were run by patrons that had little to none labourers under contract and who had paid the necessary capital from their own pockets.[118] More often than not, producers delivered the goods themselves to the end-user and there were hardly (large) chains of production-units.[119]

13.8.1 The Industrial Revolution and Labour Law

These small production chains soon vanished, as the Industrial Revolution came to pass in the Netherlands, roughly 100 years after it had started in England. New technological inventions and advances made it possible to start large scale production.

[113] C. Asser and G.J.J. Heerma van Voss, *Mr. C. Assers handleiding tot de beoefening van het Nederlands Burgerlijk Recht. 7: Bijzondere overeenkomsten; Dl. V: Arbeidsovereenkomst, collectieve arbeidsovereenkomst en ondernemingsovereenkomst* (Deventer: Kluwer 2008), 1 Invloed van het Romeinse recht.

[114] Articles 1583 and 1585 DCC (1838).

[115] Save for ship's officers and apprentices. Which had been covered extensively in the Commercial Code.

[116] Articles 1637–1639 DCC (1838).

[117] H.L. Bakels et al., *Schets van het Nederlandse arbeidsrecht* (Deventer: Kluwer 2011), p. 4–5.

[118] Bakels et al., *Schets van het Nederlandse arbeidsrecht*, p. 5.

[119] Bakels et al., *Schets van het Nederlandse arbeidsrecht*, p. 5.

Small businesses were threatened by these large factories and companies that started using the labour contracts and taking in large numbers of workers. This had two major effects. Small businesses slowly disappeared, and large groups of labourers were grouped together in dismal working environments that were insanitary, unhealthy and downright dangerous. In light of the developments in family law, which had not gotten to the level we are accustomed to nowadays, women and children were employed in great numbers.[120] Working condition were exacerbated by poor living conditions, low wages (which generally were spent by the men in bars, owned by their boss) leaving generally only half for food and water. These times were therefore also called 'The social problem' ('*de sociale quaestie*'[121]).[122] Resistance against this enfolding situation as noted earlier, did not come from the Unions, as they were only allowed when the social problem was already well under way and they had to start up from scratch, which mean that the organisations had to get organised first. No, resistance came from a committee of young liberals in 1870–1880 called the 'Committee to discuss the social problem' (*Comité ter bespreking der sociale quaestie*), which played a role in voicing the problems of industrialisation.[123] This led to some action on behalf of the legislator.

13.8.2 First Labour Laws

The first labour law that was enacted was the so-called 'Childlaw-Van Houten' (*Kinderwet-Van Houten*). Child labour at the time was one of the biggest concerns and the legislator was mute on the topic for some years. Then when government informed Parliament that it was not going to take any action, Member of Parliament Samuel van Houten initiated the Child Law. This did not however spark legislative action further, initially.[124] These developments did however lay bare the need to revisit the labour contract using only freedom of contract. This led to the most important law enacted in early labour law: The 1907 Act of the Labour Contract (*De Wet op de Arbeidsovereenkomst*). This was the first law that arranged matters such as wages; security within the establishment; the dissolution of the labour contract and held provisions on the collective labour agreement (*collectieve arbeidsovereenkomst*). While the 1907 Labour Law is very limited in scope compared to the current labour laws in place, it was of pronounced importance at the time, as these provisions were introduced in the Civil Code, and limited contractual freedoms in favour

[120] Largely because of small hands and thin fingers which were better suited for the work in the factory than.

[121] Spelling from that time, now it would be called 'De sociale kwestie'.

[122] Bakels et al., *Schets van het Nederlandse arbeidsrecht*, p. 6.

[123] F.J.L. Pennings, *Nederlands arbeidsrecht in een internationale context* (Deventer: Kluwer 2007), p. 4–5.

[124] Limited action was taken with the labour law of 1889, which further limited child labour. Further legislation concerned the prohibition on night labour, also in 1889.

of the employee.[125] The enactment of the law did not have an immediate effect in relation to the working conditions, but its effect was nevertheless radical on the longer term as it sparked a tremendous amount of new legislation, such as the Law on the Collective Labour Agreement (*De Wet op de Collectieve Arbeidsovereenkomst*) in 1927, to compensate the unequal relationship between employer-employee.[126] It can be seen as the spark to a radical change based on societal evolution.[127]

13.8.3 International and European Influence

Until the end of the WWI, labour law was in the exclusive domain of national law. There were parallels in different legal systems, but no supranational norms. The desire for these international norms did rise at the end of the nineteenth century as the threat of unfair competition deepened.[128] While it started with the Conference in Bern in 1905 dealing with white phosphor and night labour by women, it was not until the establishment of the International Labour Organization that legislation truly started to have an impact on the development of labour law post WWII.[129]

In the 1970s and 1980s European law developed much more than it the previous two decades and Council Directive 75/117/EEC of 10 February 1975 on the approximation of the laws of the Member States relating to the application of the principle of equal pay for men and women[130] was enacted and a year later Council Directive 76/207/EEC of 9 February 1976 on the implementation of the principle of equal treatment for men and women as regards access to employment, vocational training and promotion, and working conditions.[131] The implementation of these Directives demanded that nation law would be changed, and so the amount of prohibitions of grounds for dismissal were extended (you could no longer be 'let go' if you were getting married, were pregnant or had given birth), and men and women were to be treated equally.[132] The (now) Court of Justice of the European Union (CJEU) also strongly influenced Dutch labour law by its case law, such as *Defrenne II*.[133]

---

[125] Pennings, *Nederlands arbeidsrecht in een international context*, p. 10.

[126] Pennings, *Nederlands arbeidsrecht in een international context*, p. 10.

[127] Luijten, *146 jaar Burgerlijk Wetboek*, p. 11.

[128] When one legal system protects its employees more than in another system, a competition disadvantage may arise. *See* Pennings, *Nederlands arbeidsrecht in een international context*, p. 13.

[129] Think of for example the influence of the ILO during the oil crisis of 1974 and the influence. *See further*: Pennings, *Nederlands arbeidsrecht in een international context*, p. 13–18.

[130] OJ L 045, 19/02/1975 P. 0019–0020.

[131] OJ L 039, 14/02/1976 P. 0040–0042.

[132] Pennings, *Nederlands arbeidsrecht in een international context*, p. 20.

[133] Judgment of the Court of 8 April 1976. – Gabrielle Defrenne v Société anonyme belge de navigation aérienne Sabena. – Reference for a preliminary ruling: Cour du travail de Bruxelles – Belgium. – The principle that men and women should receive equal pay for equal work. – Case 43–75. ECR [1976] 455.

Furthermore, Regulations and Directives accumulated to such an extent that labour law in the Netherlands cannot be fully considered by only merely at domestic law. The influence of the ILO on the international level and the European Union on the European level cannot be disregarded.

13.8.4 The (New) Dutch Civil Code and Labour Law

The (new) Dutch Civil Code of 1992 brought about an important formal change to the legal regime of labour law, by introducing it (now in) Book 7 (on specific contracts), Title 10 (on the labour agreement). This setting of the labour agreement in this particular Book 7, did not bring about substantial changes, but is to be considered a technical revision of the labour agreement. As it is placed in Book 7, as a *species* of the *genus* 'contracts', books 3, 5 and 6 of the Civil Code on patrimonial law in general, property rights in respect to objects and the general part on the law of obligations respectively are also applicable and the labour contract fits within the system of the Civil Code. Next to this, some outdated provisions were repealed and overall the readability of the text was improved.[134]

In conclusion, the development of Dutch labour law has led to a considerable improvement of the working conditions of the employee. As a consequence however, this development has meant that employers are curtailed in their power to dismiss an employee or redeploy them elsewhere. This has led to some criticism over time on Dutch labour law. Arguments that have been put forth are that it would be too oppressive for employers who are increasingly confronted with international competition.[135] European developments have had an influence on these developments as well.[136]

13.9 The Civil Code and the Constitution

The place of the Civil Code within the Dutch legal order can be determined better by looking at the Constitution. The Constitution of the Netherlands provides in Article 107 a duty to enact general codes of law, dating back to the revolution that led to the Batavian Republic in 1798.[137] It came from the Revolution and the desire to have a Code for the 'resurrected Netherlands'.[138] The article reads: "(1) Private law, criminal law and civil and criminal procedural law are regulated by statute in general

134 Pennings, *Nederlands arbeidsrecht in een international context*, p. 21.

135 Pennings, *Nederlands arbeidsrecht in een international context*, p. 21.

136 See extensively Pennings, *Nederlands arbeidsrecht in een international context*, p. 55 *et seq.*

137 Lokin and Zwalve, *Hoofdstukken uit de Europese Codificatiegeschiedenis*, p. 293.

138 Lokin and Zwalve, *Hoofdstukken uit de Europese Codificatiegeschiedenis*, p. 300.

codes, save for the power to regulate certain subject-matters in separate statutes. (2) A statute will provide general rules of administrative law."

There has never been a discussion regarding the *desirability* of a general code of law (*algemeen wetboek*), as can be found in Germany between Savigny and Thibaut in 1814, because we already had general and definite (*stellige*) legislation in the shape of the *Code Civil* from France, and there was no intention to simply abolish the latter and restore the state of affairs prior to the enactment of the *Code Civil*. Rather, the intention was to replace the *Code Civil* with more national legislation.[139]

What makes the Netherlands particular regarding the question whether the Constitution prevails over the Civil Code is Article 120 of the Constitution which reads: "The judge does not enter into a review of the constitutionality of statutes and treaties." Of extreme relevance, however, is also Article 94 Const., which reads: "Statutory regulations in force within the Kingdom are not applicable if such application is incompatible with provisions of treaties and decisions of international organizations that are binding on everyone." Article 120 Const. should only be interpreted as meaning that a judge cannot declare a particular (provision of a) law invalid because of a conflict with the Constitution. However, if the law or a particular provision is incompatible with a Treaty provision that creates rights upon which citizens may rely, then Article 94 Const. requires that the national provision(s) are to be set aside in this particular instance. Thus, a treaty obligation can have the effect that a particular law (provision) is to be set aside, whereas similar effect cannot be drawn from the Constitution. Dutch courts will, therefore, not apply Dutch national law if it violates the European Convention on Human Rights or European Union law (EU Directives and Regulations and the free movement of persons, services, goods and capital, creating the EU internal market). This also clarifies the relationship between the Civil Code (as well as other national laws) and treaties. The Netherlands is a so-called monist country, meaning that provisions of treaties and of decisions of international organizations, which by virtue of their content can be binding upon everyone, become binding after they have been published, without any transposition into national legislation.[140]

13.10 Conclusions

13.10.1 Codification Is No Longer a National Affair

The importance of the Civil Code in private law relationships is still very prevalent. The Civil Code is (still) the starting point for determining the legal consequences of private law relationships. However, it is not the *sole* source of

[139] Florijn, *Ontstaan en ontwikkeling van het nieuwe Burgerlijk Wetboek*, p. 12–13.

[140] Article 93 Const.

legislation that provides answers to private law issues. As the Netherlands is a monist legal system also directly binding provisions of treaties and decisions by international organisations have to be taken into account. Furthermore, the impact of EU law should not be underestimated. Company law is one example.[141] Family law is another perfect example of the influence legislation enacted beyond the Dutch borders influences the Civil Code. Judges adjudicating over cases that involve children, for example, have increasingly made reference to the Convention on the Rights of the Child.[142] Furthermore, the approximation of laws in the area of family law on both the European and international level has been significant, and the influence of the European Court of Human Rights in Strasbourg is profound. Leading to the first conclusion that areas of the law that used to be the sole domain of the national legislature and the Civil Code, have increasingly been adapted according to standards and rules emanating from external sources and supranational institutions.[143] We must however not forget, that developments from 'within' also influence legislation abroad. Here too, family law is a wonderful example. Introducing same-sex marriage well before most other Member States within the European Union, and indeed the world, is but one example.[144]

13.10.2 Dutch Codification Is a Continuing Process That Is Not Yet Over

The phased introduction of the (new) Civil Code, a process which saw its first success with the enactment of Book 1 in 1970, still has not finished. This means that codification in the Netherlands is still going on. The most recent addition to the Civil Code has been Book 10 on Private International Law, a Book which entered into force 42 years after the introduction of the First Book, on 1st January 2012. The tremendous time gap between earlier and later Books of the Civil Code makes it difficult to give a singular assertion as to the status of the Dutch Civil Code. If anything, one could say that the Civil Code of the Netherlands is a continuing

---

[141] Many provisions and adaptations to Book 2 dealing with Company Law were established by European Directives. Such as the, up until that point unfamiliar, company with limited liability.

[142] Study carried out by Centre for Children's Rights Amsterdam looking at jurisprudence from 2002 to 2011. J.H. de Graaf et al., *De toepassing van het IVRK in de Nederlandse rechtspraak* (Nijmegen: Ars Aequi Juridische Uitgeverij 2012).

[143] In 2006 already 10 % of the Books on patrimonial rights in the Civil Code had a European origin.

[144] *For a more extensive overviews*: M. Antokolskaia and K. Boele-Woelki, "Dutch Family Law in the 21st Century: Trend-setting and Straggling behind at the Same Time," *Electronic Journal of Comparative Law*, vol. 6.4 (2002).

work-in-progress whereby the introduction of a new Book brings to the forefront questions about the validity of older Books of the Civil Code[145] and with it the need for a complete (re)codification.[146]

13.10.3 A Look to the Future

Indeed, the fact that the Civil Code is somewhere between 1 and 42 years old, raises questions of compatibility with current society. Certain topics and matters that are current, were not on the minds of the drafters at the time. The development of consumer law shows this for the earlier drafts of the Civil Code. Another is the internet and its rapid development and influence on the law. Virtually the entire Civil Code was not prepared to deal with particular questions arising out of the (ab)use of the Internet.[147] However, according to some the Civil Code turned out to be flexible enough to handle certain aspects of the influence internet has had on private law legal relationships.[148] Nevertheless, technological advances and law in relation to 'bits&bytes' is more and more in focus. It requires a new way of thinking about classical distinctions such as (intellectual) property and contract law.[149] Will this new way of thinking also influence the structure of the Civil Code? Indubitably. When and in which way and perhaps most importantly at which level of legislation be it national or European, is yet to be seen.

[145] W. Snijders, "Twintig jaar nieuw BW," *Ars Aequi* 12 (2012): 946–954, p. 947. .M. Schrama, "Ontwikkelingen in het familierecht," *Ars Aequi* 2 (2012): 144–150. In particular Family Law was already ready for recodification in the eyes of De Ruiter in 1990, *see* Ruiter, *Drie treden in het familierecht*.

[146] *For instance*: T.F.E. Tjong Tjin Tai, "Twintig jaar nieuw BW: bijzondere overeenkomsten," *Ars Aequi* 11(2012): 859–868 who states that by the formal requirements to the introduction of new Titles to Book 7 on Specific Contracts, the codification efforts have been weakened significantly. Ruiter, *Drie treden in het familierecht*.

[147] See also Snijders, *Twintig jaar nieuw BW*.

[148] Snijders, *Twintig jaar nieuw BW*, p. 952.

[149] *See for example*: D. van Engelen, "UsedSoft v Oracle: the ECJ quietly reveals a new European property right in 'bits & bytes'," *European Property Law Journal* 2(2012): 317–329.

Chapter 14
The Scope and Structure of the Portuguese Civil Code

Dário Moura Vicente

Abstract The current Portuguese Civil Code was enacted in 1967 and subsequently amended a number of times. It covers the basic categories of civil law relationships (obligations, real rights, family relationships and successions *mortis causa*) and contains a general part with provisions governing issues common to all these kinds of legal relationships, as well as rules on the sources of the law, the efficacy, interpretation and application of laws, conflict of laws and personality rights. Commercial, labour and consumer relationships are left to specific codes and statutes, although the Civil Code, which is the common core of Portuguese Private Law, subsidiarily applies to such relationships. Thanks to its enactment in the former Overseas Provinces of Portugal, the Code also applies in several African and Asian Portuguese-speaking countries, and it has influenced the Brazilian Civil Code. It is therefore the basis of a Portuguese legal community covering four continents and comprising over 250 million people.

Keywords Portugal • Civil Code • Codification • Decodification • Recodification • Expansion of codification

14.1 General Overview of Legislation on Private Law in Portugal

Private law has for a long time been codified in Portugal. The first efforts aimed at assembling an official collection of Private Law provisions in this country resulted in the enactment, in 1446, by King Afonso V, of the so-called *Ordenações Afonsinas*. This collection of laws was subsequently replaced by the *Ordenações Manuelinas,* enacted in 1521 by King Manuel I, and by the *Ordenações Filipinas,* enacted in 1603 by King Philip II.

D. Moura Vicente (✉)
University of Lisbon, School of Law, Lisbon, Portugal
e-mail: dmouravicente@fd.ul.pt

J.C. Rivera (ed.), *The Scope and Structure of Civil Codes*, Ius Gentium: Comparative Perspectives on Law and Justice 32, DOI 10.1007/978-94-007-7942-6_14,

Taken as texts containing the fundamental rules that govern a given category of legal relationships, organized according to a scientific criterion, codes only emerged in Portugal, however, in the nineteenth century, the first one being the Commercial Code of 1833, which was replaced by a new Commercial Code in 1888.

The first Portuguese Civil Code dates back to 1867. It ceased to apply in the Portuguese mainland on the 1st of June of 1967, when a new Civil Code entered into force, which still applies in this country. This Code sets out the fundamental rules that govern obligations, real rights, family relationships and successions *mortis causa.* It also contains rules relating to the sources of the law, the interpretation and application of the law, conflict of laws and personality rights. As will be explained hereafter, the Civil Code is currently supplemented by several special statutes concerning specific topics. Other codes also govern Private Law relationships in this country, such as the Commercial Code, the Companies' Code, the Copyright and Related Rights Code, the Industrial Property Code and the Labour Code.

14.2 The Civil Codes

14.2.1 The Civil Code of 1867

The Civil Code of 1867 was drafted by António Luiz de Seabra, a judge at the Oporto Court of Appeal, whom the Queen of Portugal had entrusted with that task in 1850. His draft code, originally submitted to the Government in 1858 and subsequently revised by a committee of experts, was approved by a Law of 1 July 1867 and entered into force on 23 March 1868.

The code was preceded by very important doctrinal works, among which those of Borges Carneiro, Correia Teles and Coelho da Rocha, which Seabra used widely when he prepared the code.[1]

Although inspired in the French Civil Code, the Portuguese Civil Code of 1867 follows a different system. It is divided into four parts, dealing respectively with civil capacity, the acquisition of rights, the right of property and the breach of rights and its remedies.

The Code embodies an *individualistic vision* of the law: it puts the emphasis on the individual holder of the rights, not on social institutions. Party autonomy knows very few limits. The consequences of the lawful exercise of individual rights are not relevant.[2] The influence of the German philosopher Immanuel Kant on the author of the code is visible throughout its provisions.[3]

[1] See António Pedro Barbas Homem, *O movimento de codificação do Direito em Portugal no século XIX*, Lisboa, 2007.

[2] See article 13 of the Code, according to which: «He who exercises a right in conformity with the law shall not be not liable for the damages that may arise from such exercise».

[3] See Francisco José Velozo, «Orientações Filosóficas do Código de 1867 e do futuro Código», *Scientia Iuridica*, 1967, pp. 155 ff.; and António Braz Teixeira, «Sobre os pressupostos filosóficos do código civil português de 1867», *Fides. Direito e Humanidades,* 1994, pp. 137 ff.

Nevertheless, the Portuguese code didn't share the secularism that characterized its French counterpart: catholic marriage, for example, was awarded civil effects in Portugal, which was not the case in France.

By a Decree of 18 November 1869, the Civil Code of 1867 was extended to the Overseas Provinces of Portugal.

Thus, in 1961, when Goa, Daman and Diu (which constituted the former Portuguese State of India – *Estado da Índia*) were integrated in the Indian Union, as territories thereof, the Civil Code of 1867 was fully applicable there.

By virtue of the *Goa, Daman and Diu (Administration) Act 1962*, enacted by the Indian Parliament, all laws in force in these former Portuguese territories, including the Civil Code, were kept in force «until amended or repealed by a competent Legislature or other competent authority». Accordingly, they became internal laws of the new Union Territories (as they then were).[4]

Several provisions of the 1867 Civil Code, notably those concerning Family and Succession Law,[5] Property Law (except its transfer) and Tort Law, are thus still in force in Goa, Daman and Diu. They apply not only to Christians born there during Portuguese administration and to their descendants, but also to non-Christians in all matters not regulated in their Codes of Usages and Customs.[6] In this sense, the Civil Code in force in Goa, Daman and Diu should be characterised as a *uniform code*, not as a personal law.[7] In these territories of India, the aspiration to a uniform Civil

[4] See, on the status of Portuguese Law in Goa, Daman and Diu, Dirk Otto, «Das Weiterleben des portugiesischen Rechts in Goa», *in* Erik Jayme (ed.), *2. Deutsch-Lusitanische Rechtstage. Seminar in Heidelberg 20.-21.11.1992,* Baden-Baden, 1994, pp. 124 ff.; Carmo D'Souza, *Legal System in Goa*, vol. II, *Laws and Legal Trends (1510–1969),* Panaji, 1995, pp. 253 ff.; *idem,* «Evolução do Direito português em Goa», *Revista da Faculdade de Direito da Universidade de Lisboa*, 1999, pp. 275 ff.; Manohar Sinai Usgãocar, «Bird's Eye View of the Portuguese Civil Code of 1867 and of the Portuguese Civil [Procedure] Code of 1939», *Revista da Ordem dos Advogados,* 1998, pp. 19 ff.; *idem,* «Civil Code as a Source of Civil Rights», *Goa Law Times,* 2001, vol. 1, pp. 1 ff.; F. E. Noronha, *Understanding the Common Civil Code. An Introduction to Civil Law,* Nagpur, 2008, pp. 95 ff. and 111 ff.; and Ave Cleto Afonso, *The "Portuguese Law of Goa (Succession and Inventory)/O Direito "Português" de Goa (Sucessão e Inventário),* Goa, 2009.

[5] See, for an English translation of those provisions, Manohar Sinai Usgãocar, *Family Laws of Goa, Daman and Diu,* 2 vols., Goa, 1979/1988; Dário Moura Vicente *et al.* (eds.), *O Direito da Família e das Sucessões no Código Civil português de 1867: uma perspectiva do século XXI – Family and Succession Law in the Portuguese Civil Code of 1867: a XXIst Century Approach,* Lisbon, 2008; and Ave Cleto Afonso, *The "Portuguese Law of Goa" (Succession and Inventory)/O Direito "Português" de Goa (Sucessão e Inventário),* Goa, 2009.

[6] *I.e.,* the *Code of the Usages and Customs of the Non-Christian Inhabitants of Daman,* of 31 August 1854; the *Code of Usages and Customs of Gentile Hindus of Goa,* compiled in the Decree of 16 December 1880; and the *Code of Usages and Customs of Non-Christian Inhabitants of Diu,* approved on 10 January 1894. See on the second of these codes Luís da Cunha Gonçalves, *Direito hindú e mahometano. Comentário ao Decreto de 16 de Dezembro de 1880 que ressalvou os usos e costumes dos habitantes não cristãos do distrito de Goa na Índia Portuguesa,* Coimbra, 1923.

[7] See, in this sense, Y. V. Chandrachud, «Inaugural Speech on the Goa Lawyers' Symposium on "Family Laws in Goa"», *in Glimpses of Family Laws of Goa, Daman and Diu,* Margão, Goa, 1982, pp. 1 ff. (at p. 3); and Manohar Sinai Usgaocar, «Family Laws in Goa, Daman and Diu: Are they uniform?», *in ibidem,* pp. 85 ff. (at p. 89).

Code, as expressed in article 44 of the Indian Constitution,[8] has thus become a reality.[9]

14.2.2 *The Civil Code of 1966*

A very different notion of Civil Law inspired the Portuguese Civil Code of 1966. Its preparatory works began in 1944 and were undertaken by a commission composed mostly by law professors of the Universities of Coimbra and Lisboa, chaired by Adriano Vaz Serra, a former Minister of Justice. Once concluded, those preparatory works underwent a comprehensive revision, in which a major role was played by Antunes Varela, a distinguished professor of the University of Coimbra who at the time held the office of Minister of Justice. The code was approved by a Decree-Law of 25 November 1966 and entered into force on the 1st of June 1967.

The system of this code is very similar to the German Civil Code (BGB). It is divided into five books: a General Part comprising the provisions that are common to all categories of civil law relationships; the Law of Obligations; the Law of Things; Family Law; and the Law of Successions. The style of the code's provisions, which are highly abstract and technical, is similar to those of the BGB.

The code was preceded by a long doctrinal evolution in which the writings of Guilherme Moreira and Manuel de Andrade, both law professors of the University of Coimbra, played a significant role. It reflects the evolution of Portugal towards a Welfare State and a higher concern with the protection of the weaker party and the compliance with ethical standards in civil law relationships. Several important restrictions are thus imposed on the free will of the parties, which the previous Code did not provide for. The principle of good faith (*boa fé)* in the formation and performance of contracts, the prohibition of the abuse of rights (*abuso de direito)* and a certain *favor debitoris* are hallmarks of the new code, which thus overcame the liberal ideology that inspired the 1867 Civil Code.[10]

It what concerns Family Law, the new code reinstated adoption as a source of family relationships and established the communion of acquired assets (*comunhão de adquiridos)* as the default matrimonial regime, instead of the general communion of assets provided for in the previous code.

In Succession Law, the code provides that the portion of the testator's property that he or she cannot dispose of (*legítima)* varies according to the heirs at stake and thus no longer consists, in all cases, of ½ of that property, as was the case under the Civil Code of 1867.

---

[8] Which provides that: «The State shall endeavour to secure for the citizens a uniform civil code throughout the territory of India».

[9] See Gustavo Filipe Couto, *in Glimpses of Family Laws of Goa, Daman and Diu*, p. VII.

[10] See Antunes Varela, «Do projecto ao Código Civil», *Boletim do Ministério da Justiça*, vol. 161 (1966), pp. 5 ff.

By widely adopting general clauses, in particular good faith, the code also gives judges a much wider discretion than its predecessor when deciding cases.[11]

Owing *inter alia* to the characteristics of the Civil Code, Portuguese Law clearly pertains to the Roman-German, or Civil Law, Legal Family.[12]

14.3 Relationship Between the Civil Code, the Constitution and Public International Law

According to Article 8 of the Portuguese Constitution, which governs the effect of International Law within the national legal system, the rules and principles of general or common international law are an integral part of Portuguese law. Rules set out in duly ratified or approved international agreements come into force in Portuguese internal law once they have been officially published, and remain so as long as they are internationally binding on the Portuguese state. By virtue of this provision, International Law prevails over Portuguese internal law and is directly applicable by Portuguese courts, provided that, in the case of international treaties, these have been duly ratified or approved and published in the official journal of the Portuguese Republic.

Article 204 of the Constitution further states that in matters that are brought to trial, courts may not apply rules that contravene the provisions of the Constitution or the principles enshrined therein. Hence, the provisions of the Civil Code must abide by the Constitution and are not applicable insofar as they are deemed to contravene it. This is why on 25 November 1977 a major reform of the Civil Code was enacted, aimed at adapting it to the 1976 Constitution, which ensued from the Revolution of 25 April 1974. We shall return to this topic hereafter.

14.4 Contents of the Civil Code

As mentioned above, the Civil Code governs the fundamental categories of legal relationships according to the Germanic classification, i.e.: obligations (which is the subject-matter of Book II); real rights (regulated in Book III); family relationships (governed by Book IV); and successions *mortis causa* (to which Book V is dedicated).

This classification somehow leaves in the dark a category of legal relationships that does not constitute the object of an autonomous part of the code: those stemming

[11] See, on this, António Menezes Cordeiro, *Da boa fé no Direito Civil,* Coimbra, 1985.

[12] See Dário Moura Vicente, *Direito Comparado,* vol. I, 2nd ed., Coimbra, 2012, pp. 93 ff.

from the exercise of *personality rights*, which are regulated in the general part of the Portuguese Civil Code.[13]

A number of provisions common to all these kinds of legal relationships (concerning e.g. legal capacity, legal persons, things, legal acts and the exercise and protection of subjective rights) are to be found in Book I (General Part) of the Code, which also governs the sources of the law; the efficacy, interpretation and application of laws; foreigners' rights and conflict of laws (including the general problems raised by the application of conflict rules, such as characterization, renvoi, *fraus legis* and public policy, as well as the law applicable to the different types of legal relationships).[14]

The general part of the Portuguese Civil Code has thus been more broadly conceived than its German counterpart.

The growing intervention of the State in social life, in particular through the regulation of economic activities, has led to the adoption, in recent years, of a large number of special statutes on Civil Law matters, many of which are the result of the transposition of European Union Directives. This is the case, *inter alia*, of statutes on unfair contract clauses (Decree-Law no. 446/85, of 25 October 1985), product liability (Decree-Law no. 383/89, of 6 November 1989), time-sharing contracts (Decree-Law no. 275/93, of 5 August 1993), electronic signature (Decree-Law no. 290-D/99, of 2 August, 1999); distance contracts (Decree-Law no. 143/2001, of 26 April 2001), delays in payments (Decree-Law no. 32/2003, of 17 February 2003), and e-commerce (Decree-Law no. 7/2004, of 7 January 2004).

Certain issues pertaining to the personal status of individuals are also governed by special statutes. This is the case notably of the protection of persons living in a common economy (*economia comum*) (Law no. 6/2001, of 11 May, 2001), the protection of *de facto* unions (*união de facto*) (Law no. 7/2001, of 11 May, 2001), and civil sponsorship (*apadrinhamento civil*) (Law no. 103/2009, of 11 September 2009).

To a certain extent, a phenomenon of *de-codification* has thus also occurred in Portugal, by virtue of which Civil Law now comprises many rules not included in the Civil Code.

14.5 The Civil Code and Commercial Law

In Portugal, Commercial Law has been, as mentioned earlier, the subject-matter of specific codes: first, the Commercial Code of 1833 (named, after its main author, *Código Ferreira Borges*); thereafter, the Commercial Code in 1888 (named *Código Veiga Beirão*).

[13] It should also be mentioned in this regard that articles 24 ff. of the Portuguese Constitution contain a detailed regulation of fundamental rights, some of which are also deemed to be personality rights and are thus equally a subject matter of Civil Law.

[14] Several provisions governing these issues have been replaced, in their specific field of application, by conflict of laws rules stemming from the European Union origin; but they still form the basis of Portuguese Private International Law. See Dário Moura Vicente, *Direito Internacional Privado. Textos normativos fundamentais,* Coimbra, 2012.

A *code unique* approach, such as the one that prevailed in the Swiss, Italian, Dutch and Brazilian Civil Codes (which also comprise rules on several Commercial Law issues),[15] has thus been rejected by the Portuguese legislators.

The basic reason for this is that, according to the traditional view prevailing in Portugal, Civil Law is the *common core* of Private Law, whilst Commercial Law is seen as a special branch of Private Law, dealing with relationships arising from acts of trade and with the specific needs of trade. The latter should accordingly remain outside the scope of the Civil Code.[16]

Some Portuguese authors have nevertheless noted that many acts of trade are nowadays performed by ordinary people in order to satisfy their personal needs; and that many rules that were formerly only to be found in Commercial Law, such as those aiming at the protection of reliance, have also flourished in Civil Law, which to a certain extent takes into consideration commercial interests as well.[17]

The fact, however, is that even in countries that follow the *code unique* approach, some matters have always remained outside the scope of the Civil Code: such is the case, for example, of industrial property, which is regulated autonomously in Switzerland, Italy, Holland and Brazil.

In Portugal, many Commercial Law issues are regulated by special statutes. This is the case, for example, of corporations (which are the subject-matter of the Code of Corporations – *Código das Sociedades Comerciais* – approved by Decree-Law no. 262/86, of 2 September 1986), securities (a Code of Securities – *Código dos Valores Mobiliários* – was adopted by Decree-Law no. 486/99, of 13 November 1999), industrial property (which is governed by the Code of Industrial Property – *Código da Propriedade Industrial* – approved by Decree-Law no. 36/2003, of 5 March 2003), and insolvency (a Code of Insolvency – *Código da Insolvência* – was approved by Decree-Law no. 53/2004, of 18 March 2004).

The Civil Code provides the legal background against which these codes operate. Any problems not specifically dealt with by them are thus to be referred to the provisions of the Civil Code.

14.6 Consumer Law

In Portugal, Consumer Law issues are currently regulated by a number of special statutes, the most important of which is Law no. 24/96, of 31 July 1996 (Consumer Protection Law).

---

[15] In Brazil, however, the Commercial Code of 1850 is still in force in what concerns Maritime Law matters, covering articles 457–913 of that code.

[16] See, in this line of reasoning, Rabindranath Capelo de Sousa, *Teoria geral do Direito Civil,* vol. I, Coimbra, 2003, pp. 28 f.; José de Oliveira Ascensão, *O Direito. Introdução e teoria geral,* 13th ed., Coimbra, 2005, pp. 348 ff.; Carlos da Mota Pinto, *Teoria geral do Direito Civil,* 4th ed. (by António Pinto Monteiro e Paulo Mota Pinto), Coimbra, 2005, p. 49.

[17] See Menezes Cordeiro, *Tratado de Direito Civil Português,* I, *Parte geral,* tome I, 3rd ed., Coimbra, 2005, pp. 169 ff.

A *Draft Consumer Code*, which to some extent reflected the influence of the Brazilian Consumer Code, was published in Portugal in 2006[18]; but it has so far not been enacted.

Among the reasons for this, the fact has been pointed out that, as a source of «common rules applicable to common persons», the Civil Code should also regulate consumer relationships.[19]

To this, one may add that one of the most relevant purposes of Consumer Law – the protection of the weaker party in relationships entered into between professionals and consumers – has also become a major concern of the Portuguese Civil Code, many provisions of which nowadays reflect that concern.

14.7 The Civil Code and Family Law

As mentioned above, Family Law is the subject-matter of Book IV of the Civil Code, which deals extensively with marriage, divorce and legal separation, the relationship between parents and children, adoption and alimony. The registration of family relationships is governed by the Code of Civil Registry, approved by Decree-Law no. 131/95, of 6 June 1995.

Notwithstanding its codification, Family Law has proven to be a highly unstable area of Civil Law in Portugal, where it has been the subject-matter of frequent legislative amendments, often allegedly aimed at keeping abreast with sociological changes, but in fact sometimes also preceding them. The traditional patriarchal family was still the model envisaged by the drafters of the Civil Code in 1966; but, as will be seen hereunder, in the mid-70s it gave way to a new one, based on the equality of spouses and the dissolubility of marriage. *De facto* unions, which became much more common, were legally recognized in 2001, albeit on the basis of special statutory provisions; and same-sex marriages have been allowed since 2010.

14.8 Reforms of the Civil Code

As already mentioned, the 1966 Civil Code underwent some substantial changes after the 1974 Revolution.

The first one ensued from the Additional Protocol to the Concordat between Portugal and the Holy See, concluded in 1975, by virtue of which divorce became applicable to persons married under the Catholic rite.

---

[18] See Comissão do Código do Consumidor (ed.), *Código do Consumidor. Anteprojecto,* Lisboa, 2006.

[19] See, on the issue of whether a Consumer Code should be adopted, with very different opinions, José de Oliveira Ascensão, «O Anteprojecto do Código do Consumidor e a publicidade», *in Estudos do Instituto de Direito do Consumo,* vol. III, Coimbra, 2006, pp. 7 ff.; and António Pinto Monteiro, «Sobre o Direito do Consumidor em Portugal e o Anteprojecto do Código do Consumidor», *in ibidem,* pp. 37 ff.

On 25 November 1977, a major reform of the code was enacted, aimed at adapting it to the 1976 Constitution. It affected mostly Family and Succession Law.[20]

By virtue of that reform, the principle of equality between spouses in what concerns their rights and duties towards each other and in exercising parental authority was introduced in the code. Also, parents must now take into account children's opinions and recognize them autonomy in organizing their lives. Nubile age was set at 16 for both genders. The dotal regime was abolished.

As for Succession Law, the 1977 reform awarded spouses the status of mandatory heirs (*herdeiros legitimários*), along with the children and parents of the deceased. In intestate succession, the spouse is now in the first succession group, competing with descendants. He or she may never receive less than one fourth of the inheritance. He or she is also in the second group, competing with ascendants. Finally, he or she cumulates his or her capacity as heir with his or her rights to one half of the goods eventually corresponding to the communion. Discrimination against children born outside wedlock (*filhos ilegítimos*) for succession or other purposes was also abolished in 1977.

Other amendments of the Code, related *inter alia* to Family Law, have taken place since 1977.[21] This was the case of the 2003 reform of the rules on adoption. Also, a law enacted in 2010 allowed same-sex marriages, thus abolishing the centuries-old requirement of diversity of genders for matrimony and the definition of marriage contained in article 1577 of the Civil Code, which is now deemed to be «the contract entered into by two persons wishing to constitute a family by means of a full communion of life, under the provisions of this code».

In 2002, the Portuguese Government announced an ambitious plan to reform the Civil Code. This plan was not continued by subsequent Governments, which gave priority to procedural law reforms; but in 2006 a new law on urban leases re-inserted many rules previously contained in special statutes into the Civil Code. *Re-codification* of Civil Law is therefore, as in other countries, taking place in Portugal.[22]

14.9 Current Importance and Domain of the Civil Code

Notwithstanding the abovementioned phenomenon of *decodification* of Civil Law, as well as the fact that Commercial Law and Consumer Law issues are largely dealt with by special statutes and Codes, the Portuguese Civil Code of 1966 still stands as

[20] See, on the impact of the 1977 reform in Family Law, Antunes Varela, *Direito da Família,* vol. I, 5th ed., Lisbon, 1999, pp. 58 ff.; and Jorge Duarte Pinheiro, *O Direito da Família Contemporâneo,* 3rd. ed., Lisbon, 2010, pp. 88 ff.

[21] See Heinrich Hörster, «Evoluções legislativas no Direito da Família depois da reforma de 1977», *in Comemorações dos 35 anos do Código Civil e dos 25 anos da reforma de 1977,* vol. I, *Direito da Família e das Sucessões,* Coimbra, 2004, pp. 63 ff.

[22] See António Menezes Cordeiro, *Da modernização do Direito Civil,* I, *Aspectos gerais,* Coimbra, 2004; and Paulo Mota Pinto, «O Código Civil Português: "de uma possível tendência para o esvaziamento a uma também possível necessidade de reforma"? Algumas reflexões», *Themis,* 2008, pp. 25 ff.

the cornerstone of Private Law in this country. It is also a major achievement of Portuguese legal science, unsurpassed by any subsequent piece of legislation.

The current importance of this Code must also be assessed in the light of its geographical scope of application.

A Decree of 4 September 1967 extended the new Civil Code to the Portuguese Overseas Provinces, where it entered into force on the 1st of January, 1968.

When these Provinces became independent,[23] the Civil Code was therefore applicable there.

The new States thus constituted expressly kept Portuguese laws in force until amended or repealed and insofar as they are not contrary to their Constitutions.

Thus, the Portuguese Civil Code of 1966 became the Civil Code of five new African countries. To be sure, these countries have in the meantime extensively modified or revoked certain parts of that code, notably that on Family Law (which is no longer in force in Angola and Mozambique); but in their essential traits their Civil Codes are still identical to the Portuguese.

A different process took place in Macau. The administration of this territory was formally handed over by Portugal to the People's Republic of China on 20 December, 1999, 2 years after Hong Kong took the same course. By virtue of the *Joint Declaration of the Government of the Portuguese Republic and of the Government of the People's Republic of China on the Question of Macau* entered into by the two countries in Beijing on 13 April, 1987, the Portuguese legislation in force in that territory at the moment of handing over the administration to China should remain «basically unchanged» for 50 years thereafter. This is why the Civil Code is still applicable in Macau, albeit in a reformed version enacted on 3 August, 1999.[24]

Still another case is that of East Timor. This former province of Portugal was annexed by Indonesia in 1975, after its independence was unilaterally proclaimed on 28 November of that year; as a consequence of that, Portuguese laws *de facto* ceased to apply.[25] However, in a referendum held on 30 August 1999, the East

[23] In Guinea-Bissao, independence was unilaterally declared by the People's National Assembly on 24 September 1973; in Mozambique, Cape Verde, São Tomé e Príncipe and Angola, it was a consequence of the agreements negotiated between Portugal and the liberation movements of those territories and took place on 25 June, 5 July, 12 July and 11 November 1975, respectively.

[24] See Teresa Vieira da Silva/Carlos Dias (coords.), *Direito e Justiça em Macau,* Macau, 1999; Luís Miguel Urbano, «Breve nota justificativa», *in Código Civil. Versão portuguesa*, Macau, 1999, pp. VII ff.; Alexandre Dias Pereira, *Business Law: A Code Study. The Commercial Code of Macau,* Coimbra, 2004; Rute Saraiva, «Ventos de Este, Ventos de Oeste. A "questão de Macau" nas relações internacionais», *in Estudos em honra de Ruy de Albuquerque*, vol. II, Lisboa, 2006, pp. 707 ff.; José de Oliveira Ascensão, *A legislação de Macau no termo da administração portuguesa*, available at http://www.fd.ul.pt/ICJ.

[25] See Paulo Otero, «A lei aplicável às relações jurídico-privadas envolvendo timorenses e constituídas em Timor-Leste entre 1975 e 199», *in* Jorge Miranda (org.), *Timor e o Direito,* Lisboa, 2000, pp. 37 ff.; António Marques dos Santos, «O sistema jurídico de Timor-Leste – Evolução e perspetivas», *in Estudos de Direito Internacional Privado e de Direito Público*, Coimbra, 2004, pp. 595 ff.; and Florbela Pires, «Fontes do direito e procedimento legislativo na República Democrática de Timor-Leste – alguns problemas», *in Estudos em memória do Professor Doutor António Marques dos Santos*, vol. II, Coimbra, 2005, pp. 101 ff.

Timorese people voted to become independent from Indonesia. The independence of the Democratic Republic of East Timor was accordingly restored on 20 May, 2002. The new country has in the meantime adopted its own laws. A Civil Code, which is highly based on the Portuguese Civil Code of 1966, was enacted in 2011.

In Brazil, which became independent in 1822, a Law of 20 October 1823 provided that the ordinances, laws and regulations of the King of Portugal would remain in force there until a new Code was adopted and insofar as they were not amended. By virtue of this law, the Ordinances of King Philip applied in Brazil until January the 1st, 1917, when the Brazilian Civil Code came into force. This code, notwithstanding its original traits, reflected to a large extent Portuguese legal tradition (according to some authors, even more faithfully so than the Portuguese Civil Code of 1867).[26]

In 2002, a new Civil Code was adopted in Brazil. It had been drafted in 1975 by Professor Miguel Reale, of the University of São Paulo. One of its major inspirations was, unsurprisingly, the Portuguese Civil Code of 1966, from which it took several of its innovations, such as the protection granted to personality rights, the rules on legal acts (*negócios jurídicos*) and on agency (*representação*), as well as the relevance awarded to good faith (*boa fé*), the prohibition of the abuse of rights (*abuso de direito*) and unjust enrichment (*enriquecimento sem causa*) as a source of obligations.[27]

From this brief outline one may conclude that a reception of the Portuguese Civil Code of 1966 has taken place in several Portuguese-speaking countries and territories, by virtue of which this code has either become a part of the law of these countries and territories, or has at least highly influenced it. A *legal community* comprising these countries and territories has thus emerged, within which jurists share many fundamental legal values and concepts, and can therefore easily understand each other.[28] The centrepiece of this legal community is the Portuguese Civil Code of 1966.

---

[26] In this sense, see Guilherme Braga da Cruz, «Formação histórica do moderno direito privado português e brasileiro», *in Obras esparsas,* vol. II, *Estudos de História do Direito e Direito moderno,* Coimbra, 1981, pp. 25 ff. (pp. 66 f.); Sílvio Meira, *Clóvis Beviláqua. Sua vida. Sua obra,* Fortaleza, 1990, pp. 174 s. See also Orlando Gomes, «Historical and Sociological Roots of the Brazilian Civil Code», *Inter-American Law Review,* 1959, pp. 331 ff.; and António Santos Justo, «A base romanista do Direito Luso-Brasileiro das Coisas (Algumas figuras jurídicas)», *Revista da Ordem dos Advogados,* 2009, pp. 73 ff.

[27] See António Santos Justo, «O Direito luso-brasileiro: codificação civil», *Boletim da Faculdade de Direito da Universidade de Coimbra,* 2003, pp. 1 ss.; Francisco Amaral, «A parte geral do novo Código Civil brasileiro. Influência do Código Civil português», *in* Faculdade de Direito da Universidade de Coimbra (org.), *Comemorações dos 35 anos do Código Civil e dos 25 anos da Reforma de 1977,* vol. II, *A parte geral do Código e a teoria geral do Direito Civil,* Coimbra, 2006, pp. 43 ss.; and Judith Martins-Costa, «A contribuição do Código Civil Português ao Código Civil Brasileiro e o abuso de direito. Um caso exemplar de transversalidade cultural», *Themis,* 2008, pp. 107 ff.

[28] See, on this, Dário Moura Vicente, «O lugar dos sistemas jurídicos lusófonos entre as famílias jurídicas», *in* AAVV, *Estudos em homenagem ao Professor Doutor Martim de Albuquerque,* Coimbra, 2010, pp. 401 ff.

Chapter 15
Some Personal Observations on Codification in Puerto Rico

Luis Muñiz Argüelles

Abstract Puerto Rico, a Spanish colony from 1493 to 1898, received most Spanish Codes and shared the Continental European Romano-Germanic legal culture to the turn of the twentieth century. The Island was ceded to the United States as a result of the Spanish defeat in the 1898 Spanish American War and has since received American Public (Constitutional, Administrative and Procedural Law) and Commercial Law and adopted many American legal methodologies (the role of precedent, inductive analysis, legal education methods). Since the 1970s the country, which has suffered many economic and social changes, has debated the so-called process of decodification and recodification, has examined the increasing codification of American Law, has debated its legal future and reaffirmed, at least somewhat, its Romano-Germanic tradition but, despite efforts, has not yet revised its main Private Law codes or adapted many American Common Law rules to its Civil Law tradition. It is, given its tradition, its economic and political ties with the United States and its goal to reaffirm itself as a cultural distinct country, to paraphrase a Canadian's observation of her own country, *as codified as possible under the current conditions*.

Keywords Puerto Rico • Mixed legal system • Codification • Private law • Civil Code

---

In these comments I will omit most of the data included in the report submitted to the Taiwan Congress organizers, which will be made available together with these comments. For this reason these comments will be scant in footnotes. More than a research paper, I want to provide my readers with the basic facts with which to follow my ideas regarding codification in general and in Puerto Rico in particular. Other notes can be found in my report to the Thematic Congress; in my chapter on Puerto Rico in Vernon V. Palmer, ed, *Mixed Jurisdictions Worldwide*: *The Third Legal Family* (Cambridge University Press, Cambridge, 2nd Ed., 2012, and in a presentation I made to the McGill Law School Faculty published as "Some Thoughts on Conditions Favoring Recodification", *Ateliers de droit civil*, McGill University Law School, 2010, in which I cite additional sources.

L. Muñiz Argüelles (✉)
University of Puerto Rico School of Law, San Juan, Puerto Rico
e-mail: luismunizarguelles@yahoo.com

J.C. Rivera (ed.), *The Scope and Structure of Civil Codes*, Ius Gentium: Comparative Perspectives on Law and Justice 32, DOI 10.1007/978-94-007-7942-6_15,

Puerto Rico, as many other countries with codified laws, is today, to paraphrase an almost half century old Canadian student's description of her people, *as codified as possible under the circumstances.*[1]

15.1 The Background

Puerto Rico lived almost exclusively with a Continental European legal culture[2] until the Island was ceded to the United States following the 1898 Treaty of Paris, which put an end to what has been variously called the *Spanish-American War* and the *Hispano-American-Cuban War.*[3] Prior to that war we had a French style Civil Code, in force in Spain since 1889 and in the Spanish overseas colonies of Cuba, the Philippines and Puerto Rico since 1890[4]; complementary laws dealing with Mortgages,[5] the secured transactions statute of the time, when immovable were the

[1] The original phrase comes from a 1971 Canadian Broadcasting System radio contest, organized by the then well-known animator Peter Gzowski as part of his This Country in the Morning broadcast. He asked listeners to complete a phrase similar to the American phrase *As American as apple pie*. The winning entry was submitted by a young music student, Heather Scott, who said the phrase should read: *As Canadian as possible, under the circumstances.*

[2] Alfonso García-Gallo, *Manual de historia del Derecho español*, Vol. I, Madrid, 3ra ed., 1967, pages 126 and 173 et seq. Many last names of Spanish speaking authors appear hyphenated because in Spanish last names include, first, what in most other Western countries are called family names and, second, what in these countries are called the mother's maiden names. To use only one of these will prevent readers from finding the sources, particularly if the only name used is the second last name or mother's maiden name. For a summary of the Spanish codes and statutes in force just prior to the U.S.: invasion, see José Trías-Monge, *El choque de dos culturas* (Equity., Hato Rey, 1991), pages 86 et. seq.; Pedro F. Silva-Ruiz, "Desarrollos recientes y tendencias del Derecho civil para el Siglo XXI en Puerto Rico", *Rev. Acad. Puertorriqueña Jurisp y Legisl* 85 (1989) pages 85–88 and Luis E. González-Vale, "Apuntes para una historia del proceso de adopción del Código Penal luego del cambio de soberanía", *Rev. Acad. Puertorriqueña Jurisp. y Legis.* 141 (1989) pages 142–143.

[3] See http://avalon.law.yale.edu/19th_century/sp1898.asp

[4] The Spanish Code was adopted in 24 July 1889 and was made applicable to Puerto Rico, Cuba and the Philippines by the Royal Decree of 31 July 1889 and was in force as of 1 January 1890. For a more detailed account see the annotations under 1 L.P.R.A. §1 (L.P.R.A. stands for *Leyes de Puerto Rico Anotadas*); Ochoteco, Félix, *Código Civil de Puerto Rico*: *Estudio Preliminar*, Madrid, 1960. See also: José Antonio Escudero, *Curso de Historia del Derecho* (Madrid, 2nd ed., 1995), pages 817 et seq.; Juan Francisco Lasso-Gaite, *Crónica de la codificación española* (To. 4, Vol. I, Ministerio de Justicia, Madrid, 1970), pages 41 and 151; Luis Muñoz-Morales, *Reseña histórica y anotaciones al Código Civil de Puerto Rico*, (Ed. Univ. de Puerto Rico, Río Piedras, 1947), pages 23 and 68.

[5] The first comprehensive Spanish Mortgage Law (*Ley Hipotecaria*) came into force in 1861. Escudero, *supra*, Lasso-Gaite, *supra*, pages 322–337. The Spanish Mortgage Law in force in Puerto Rico at the time of its conquest by the United States was that of 1893. The current Puerto Rican law is that voted by Law no. 198 of August 8, 1979, patterned after the 1944/1946 Spanish statute. For more details see the annotations under 30 L.P.R.A. §1.

main guarantee, and Notary Law[6]; a Commercial Code[7]; a Penal Code[8]; and civil and criminal procedure statutes.[9] There were some complementary statutes, such as the Intellectual and Industrial property laws,[10] but codified laws were the heart of the judicial world.

As of then, and as a direct result of the American takeover, the country had to deal with a multitude of forces which have at times led to Civil Code modifications, but which more than that led to the substitution of Spanish public (constitutional and administrative law and organization) with American rules and statutes, the virtual suppression of the Commercial Code given the adoption of many special commercial statutes copied from the United States,[11] and the adoption of United States models

---

[6] The Spanish Notary Law (*Ley Notarial*) was put in force in 1862, just a year after the first comprehensive Mortgage Law. Escudero, supra, Lasso-Gaite, *supra*, pages 320–321. The current Puerto Rican Notary Law is that of Law no. 75, of July 2, 1987. For more details see the annotations prior to 4 L.P.R.A. §1.

[7] The Commercial Code (*Código de Comercio*) was the first of the modern Spanish Private Law Codes. It was originally enacted in 1829, revised in 1861 and revised again in 1885. Escudero, *supra*. The Code was made applicable to the overseas territories, like Puerto Rico, the following year. It was readopted in Puerto Rico in 1932. For more details see the annotations under 10 L.P.R.A. §1.

[8] The Penal Code (*Código Penal*) was first voted into law in 1821 and revised in 1848 and 1870. Escudero, *supra*. The 1870 Code was in force in Puerto Rico as of 1879 and was in force 1902, when it was replaced by a version of the 1873 California Penal Code. Several other codes replaced this one. The current Penal Code dates from the approval of Law no. 149, of June 18, 2004. For a detailed explanation of the approval of the U.S. inspired code see González-Vale, *supra*, pages 159–173.

[9] The civil procedure law (*Ley de Enjuiciamiento Civil*) was first adopted in 1855 and followed a prior Commercial Procedure Law (*Ley de Enjuiciamiento de Comercio*) of 1830 and a Judicial Administration Regulation (*Reglamento para la Administración de la Justicia*) of 1838. The criminal procedure statute (*Ley de Enjuiciamiento Criminal*) was first voted into law in 1872 and revised in 1882. Escudero, *supra*. The Spanish statutes were in force in Puerto Rico from 1886 to 1889, respectively, but were replaced by procedural statutes patterned after those of California and Idaho early in the twentieth century. The current heart of procedural regulations is now in rules patterned after the federal procedural rules and date from 2004 (Civil), 1963 (Criminal) and 2009 (Evidence). For more details see the annotations under 32 L.P.R.A. Apendix V and VI and under 34 L.P.R.A. Apendix II.

[10] The intellectual property law dates from 1847 and the industrial property law from 1878, Lasso Gaite, *supra*, page 320. Puerto Rico kept the Moral Rights part of the Spanish Intellectual Property Law, *Reynal v. Tribunal Superior*, 102 D.P.R. 260 (1974) (D.P.R. stands for the Spanish version of the Puerto Rican Supreme Courts Reports, the only version published as of volume 101) and voted two laws to update it, Law no. 96, of July 15, 1988, and the current statute, Law no. 55, of March 9, 2012.

[11] Some of these Spanish laws ceased to have legal value given the U.S. Constitution's supremacy in matters such as maritime and bankruptcy matters. See the annotations under 10 L.P.R.A. §1. Others replaced the insurance articles of the Commercial Code. A new insurance law, eventually called a Code, was voted in 1921. This was replaced by the Code of 1957, which has suffered several amendments. For more details see the annotations under 26 L.P.R.A. §1. The *sociedades*, both civil and commercial, are today governed by the Corporations statute, originally from 1911 and replaced by 1956, 1995 and 2009 statutes, the last voted is Law no. 164, of December 16, 2009, which may be consulted in 14 L.P.R.A. §3501. For more details see the annotations under 14 L.P.R.A. §1, 1101, 2601, 3501 and 4061.

of judicial administration and procedure.[12] American case law crept in quickly and by 1938, legal studies became U.S. patterned, with students entering law schools after completion of any one of a series of university studies and learning the law, at least the public, procedural and commercial law through the case method.[13]

Private noncommercial law, however, remained codified and since the early 1970s a renewed source of pride and revival,[14] although efforts to adopt a new, modernized Civil Code have proved fruitless. The Civil Code has been modernized through special statutes, especially in matters of Family Law, which at times have amended the Code[15] and at times complemented it.[16] Other modernizations have also come through jurisprudence,[17] which for decades has been recognized as a valid source of law, the most notable of which was a 1963 decision, based on the 1952 local Constitution, which declares null and void all distinctions of children based on the marital status of their parents.[18] Another notable case reforming Family

[12] See note 12, *supra*.

[13] Escuela de Derecho, Universidad de Puerto Rico, *Boletín Informativo, 1988–1990* (Río Piedras, 1988), pages 2–4.

[14] Trías-Monge, *supra*, *El choque de dos culturas*, describes the process of defense of cultural traditions from 1952 to 1973, pages 245 et. seq., and of revitalizations, from 1973 onward, 297 et. seq. A strongly pro U.S. government, elected in 2008, approved several U.S. patterned statutes and packed the Supreme Court with active pro American judges insisting on drawing mainly from U.S. sources. The government lost the 2012 elections, which may mark a return to the revival of the more codified tradition.

[15] Three cases in point are the Trust statute, based on a Panamanian statute, the Alfaro Law, which in Puerto Rico dates from the approval of Law no. 21 of April 23, 1928 and which may be found in articles 834 et seq. of the Civil Code, 31 L.P.R.A. §2541 et. seq, a series of law establishing equality amongst marriage partners, the product of several 1976 amendments, and the Time Sharing statute, also a part of the Code as the result of Law no. 252 of December 26, 1995, 31 L.P.R.A. §1251 et. seq.

[16] A case in point is the adoption statute, which has amended articles 130 et. seq. of the Civil Code, 31 L.P.R.A. §531 et. seq., last amended by Law no. 248 of September 14, 2012. We can also point to the Condominium Law, Law number 104, of June 25, 1958, since amended several times, the last of which was when Law 103 of April 5, 2003, and the rules dealing with urban planning, a series of somewhat complex set of statutes and regulations, the last of which dates from approval of Law no. 161 of December 1, 2009, 23 L.P.R.A. §9011 et. seq. Consumer regulations have been adopted by a new Executive Branch department, that of Consumer Affairs, created in 1973 through Law number 5, of April 23, 1973 upgrading agencies created since 1942. The Department has issued a series of regulations regarding commercial sales and offers, weights and measures and the like and adjudicates, through administrative judges, state and U.S. federal consumer protection statues and regulations, but efforts to have a consumer code approved have proved fruitless.

[17] A 1980 case, *Méndez Purcell v. A.F.F.*, 110 DPR 130, 136 (1980) ruled, however, that precedents will not bind if they are based on clear doctrinal errors. Given that the courts bound are the lower courts, it is they who must pass judgment as to if the decision is or not doctrinally correct, which opens the door for a deviation from the rule of precedent, not too different from what occurs in more traditional Civil Law countries.

[18] *Ocasio v. Díaz*, 88 D.P.R. 673 (1963). See also Migdalia Fraticelli-Torres, "Relevancia actual y secuela jurisprudencial de Ocasio v. Diaz", available in: http://www.fundacionsupremo.org/proyectos/2010-foro-ocasio-vs-diaz/, accepted for publication in 51 *Rev. Der. Puertorriqueño* ___, (2012).

law was a 1978 case stating mutual consent was a constitutionally valid reason for divorce, despite the then standing statutory prohibitions to the contrary.[19]

On the other hand, codification crept into the law of the new metropolis. Since the mid-nineteenth century there was a move to codify the law outside the former French Louisiana, starting with the Field Code of Civil Procedure, promoted by David Dudley Field, adopted in New York in 1850. Federal Procedural Law, both civil and criminal, are in practice codified norms and have been the inspiration for procedure in most states since the first third of the twentieth century. Later that century, Commercial Law was in effect codified thanks to the work of jurists like Karl Llewellyn. The first edition of the Uniform Commercial Code, now the main statute in all the states in the U.S., first appeared in 1952. True, a myriad of other special statutes exist outside these basic ones and case law is often cited as the controlling source, but many decisions simply paraphrase the statute, which they also cite, and the codified end results of the procedural and commercial process do not seem so foreign to a country with a Civil Law tradition like our own, who adopts them. The main difficulty is that of coordinating legal terms, not that of adopting many of the substantive rules advanced by the statutes themselves.

15.2 Decodification and Recodification

To say this is not to deny that, as in many other Western countries, Puerto Rico has lived a process known as *decodification* and has experienced legal fragmentation and specialization for the past century.[20] Some have, in our country, asked if it is possible to carry out a new codification, be it of civil or of other codes.[21]

---

[19] *Figueroa Ferrer v. E.L.A.*, 107 D.P.R. 250 (1978). In 2011 Law No. 192, of August 18, 2011, added mutual consent and irreparable rupture of marriage as new causes for divorce.

[20] As regards other countries, writings on decodification have been abundant. See, for example, in Italy, Natalino Intri, *La edad de la descodificación* (Ed. Bosch, Barcelona, 1992); in Spain, Miguel Pascua-Liano, *Código Civil y Ordenamiento Jurídico* (*Otra reflexión sobre el devenir del Derecho Civil*) (Ed. Comares, Granada, 1994), especially pages 62–76; Luis Diez-Picazo, *Codificación, descodificación y recodificación*, 45 *A.D.C.* 473 (1992) y Jacinto Gil-Rodríguez, *Acotaciones para un concepto de Derecho Civil*, 42 *A.D.C.* 317 (1989); in Holland, Arthurs Hartkamp, in P.P.C. Haanppel, and Ejan Mackaay, *Nieuw Nederlands Burgerlijk Wetboek*: *Het vermogensrecht* (Kluwer,Deventer, 1990), page XIV; in France *Répertoire de Droit civil*, Dalloz, Paris, under *Code civil*, numbers 104–160; in Costa Rica, Ricardo Zeledón-Zeledón, "Bases económicas y sociales para la modernización del Código Civil con miras al siglo XXI", 52 *Rev. Col. Abog.* (*PR*) 81 (1991); in Quebec, Paul André Crepeau, "La Reforme du Code Civil du Quebec", 31 *Revue International de Droit Comparé* 269, 271 (1979); in Puerto Rico, Luis Rivera-Rivera, "Reflexiones en torno a la proyectada revisión y reforma del Código civil", 32 *Rev. Jur. U.I.A.* 355, 356 (1998) and Trías-Monge, *El choque de dos culturas jurídicas en Puerto Rico*, *supra*, *in passim*.

[21] See Mirjan Damaska, "On circumstances favoring codification", 52 *Rev. Jur. U.P.R.* 355 (1983), and Michel J. Godreau-Robles, in his presentation to the Code Revision Commission on April 17, 1998, published as "Notas sobre una posible revisión del Código Civil de Puerto Rico", 32 *Rev. Jur. U.I.A.* 323 (1998).

Our belief, which we share with others who have studied the law reform process, even in jurisdictions like the United States where codification grew somewhat but did not fall on such fertile grounds as in Europe or Latin America, is that the revision and recodification process is valid as a means to purge statutes of inconsistencies and modernize the law.[22] This modernization does not mean, as it has never meant, that absolutely all rules having something to do with a specific topic be included in a new code or that the result be faultless,[23] but it does mean that a serious effort should be made to polish the existing law and update it so that the basic rules be made a part of it and serve as a guide for future statutes and rules, even if in the absence of these, the existing codes can be reinterpreted and renewed so as to not loose relevance.

Recodification today requires a huge effort given the large number of court rulings, the number of specialized statutes adopted, and the huge number of existing regulations to put the statutes in practice, but since the 1991 adoption of the new Quebec Civil Code, a number of countries have regained hope in the process. Some, like Peru, had done it before. Others, like Mexico,[24] Germany[25] or France,[26] have reformed important parts of their codes to update them. Revision does not mean rejection. It means, as French jurist André Tunc once said, taking another look at what we have and making important decisions about what we wish to keep and wish to change.[27]

15.3 Success and Failure

The question one must ask is why the comprehensive revision efforts to integrate many of these special statutes and decisions into a new code as has occurred in Quebec, in good part in Catalonia and, perhaps to a lesser but still notable degree,

---

[22] John Hazard, "Modernization and Codification", in "Etudes juridiques en l'honneur du Prof. Trajan Ionesco", 12 *Rev. roumaine des sciences sociales* 63 (1968).

[23] Reinhard Zimmerman, "The Civilian Experience Reconsidered on the Eve of a Common European Sales Law", opening lecture of the Thematic Congress of the International Academy of Comparative Law in Taiwan on 24 May 2012, page 15.

[24] Most recent reforms took place between the mid-1990s and the year 200. The current text can be examined in the Internet, in: http://www.ordenjuridico.gob.mx/Documentos/Estatal/Distrito%20 Federal/wo29081.pdf

[25] See, for example, Horst Ehmann, and Holger Sutschet, *La reforma del BGB*, trans. by Claudia López-Días and Ute Salach-de-Sánchez (Univ. del Externado de Colombia, Bogotá, 2006).

[26] See, for example, Ministère de la Justice, *Del contrato, de las obligaciones y de la prescripción* (Univ. del Externado de Colombia, Bogotá, 2006).

[27] See his comments in Genviève Viney, *Le déclin de la responsabilité individuelle* (L.G.D.J., Paris, 1965), page ii. See also Jean Louis Baudouin, who was vice president of the Quebec Code Revision Office, in *Quelques perspectives historiques et politiques sur le processus de codification*, en *Conférences sur le nouveau Code civil du Québec* (Ed. Yvon Blais, Cowansville, Quebec, 1992), pages 17–18; Jean Louis Baudouin, "The Reform of the Civil Code of Quebec: Objectives, Methodology and Implementation", 52 *Rev. Jur. U.P.R.* 149, 166 (1983)., and Gérard Cornu, *La lettre du Code à l'épreuve du temps*, en *Mélanges offerts à Réné Savatier* (Dalloz, Paris, 1965), pages 157–181.

in Holland, but not in countries such as Argentina or my own, Puerto Rico, and what does this failure mean for the future of codification in these countries. Why is it that we, among others, who through the adoption of special legislation and legal interpretations in the case law have implicitly admitted our codes do not solve all twenty-first century problems, have not yet adopted a new set of codes, more attune to our needs?

The answer, I think, is complex. Code revision or the revival of a codified system *à la française* of 1804–1810, requires various things, which I discussed in a 2012 McGill publication,[28] but it does not mean the outright rejection of all or even most of the prior rules, which explains why the old codes are till useful. The needed perception that legal rules are in need, even in urgent need of revision does not imply that all the prior rules should be discarded, but only reexamined. Not doing so in a comprehensive and coordinated statute, in effect, in a code, may prove frustrating, but this failure to reform does not mean the rejection of the rules contained in the code as a valid starting point and as the source of many basic rules of law we still cherish and use.

15.4 Symbols of Nationhood and Modernity

What I have seen, in the Western countries I have studied where recodification has been carried out, is that the new codes are seen as a symbol of either nationhood or change and has come in societies where codification has a long history and has been accepted, perhaps even unconsciously, as an efficient instrument or problem solving. Societies with a similar long codification history who have failed to undertake or complete code revisions are not, for that sole reason, uncodified or losing their legal tradition. They have a problem of legal adaptation, but by itself this does not mean they are moving irrevocably away from their tradition.

Codification, for example, has been a symbol in countries like Quebec. Louisiana and Puerto Rico, where legal traditions were threatened by conquering societies such as England and the United States, where codification has not been a historical landmark. The conquered, thus, have embarked in some measure of code revision as part of an effort to save their national souls and not only to modernize their legal rules. Obviously the prior symbols that have been the object of study and/or revision have been perceived as inadequate and in need of change, but that alone has not been sufficient for recodification to take hold.

Codification today serves various roles not present when statutes like the *Code Napoléon* were adopted. The situation today differs from that of the early nineteenth century, when newly independent nations of the Western Hemisphere adopted their

[28] See Muñiz-Argüelles, "Some Thoughts on Conditions Favoring Recodification" *supra*, note 2. Of course, as always happens, there are exceptions. Israeli codification might be a case in point, for there codification occurred as part of a process to clarify the law, without much prior debate as to whether other models could do the job just as well.

various codes. True, nation building can still play a role in some places, but generally countries who have chosen to take on the difficult task of modernizing their nineteenth century statutes have done so for reasons other than those that inspired France, Italy, Germany, Spain, Argentina, Brazil and Chile, for example, to either adopt or attempt to adopt comprehensive statutes to regulate most private, commercial, penal and procedural problems. This new role, however, does not necessarily mean that codification does not still play a symbolic role.

True, also, liberalism has adapted and humanized to make it less abrasive than it was 200 years ago. Liberalism, however, is still today dominant and laissez faire ideas need not be imposed through legal instruments. Courts are in the hands of the descendants of those who triumphed in the internal political struggles of the past and the need to guard the political ideas of the French styled code from pervasive judicial influences are no longer a deep-felt need, so stonewalling for the Code is no longer seen as necessary.

Today codification seeks, yes, to bring about change, but that change, although at times very important, is often tied more to adapting accepted principles to changing family values or patterns of manufacture and national or international commerce. Paternal authority has given way to parental supervision; divorce is an accepted notion; estates are today an important means of protecting heirs, but share that role with insurance policies and retirement systems; legal emancipation is now almost universally recognized at ages far below what it was two centuries ago; fault is no longer the exclusive basis of liability; punitive damages are beginning to be considered in many Civil Code countries and economic principles, such as freedom of contract and freedom of property have given way to governmental regulation and protection of the working class, small business, consumers and urban communities, regulations that hose now in power claim are for the general good or the common wealth, regardless of how debatable the precise results may be.

Code revision sometimes seeks harmonizing rules on a global or regional scale, for the countries private law rules were harmonized decades or centuries ago. This harmonization is the result, for example, of greater international commerce and integration, but is based on principles shared by various nations. The debate over the adoption of common Conflict of Law rules, known now as Rome I and Rome II accords, the now not so recent entry into force of treaties concerning international sale of goods and, in Family Law, international adoptions or recognition of diverse matrimonial decrees are certainly important, but they are more fine tuning than was the adoption of the French Code Civil rules in most of the Western World in the first decades of the nineteenth century.[29] Fine tuning requires a lot of hard work and profound knowledge of the inconsistencies of new statutes and court decisions we wish to iron out, but the political debate surrounding it is less violent that it was 200 years before.

Legal reform today only at times raises questions regarding revised values, as occurs with the debate over abortion, surrogate motherhood, same sex marriages and changed

[29] See, for example, Juan Roca-Guillamón, *Codificación y Crisis del Derecho Civil*, en *Centenario del Código Civil* (E. Centro de Estudios Ramón Areces, Madrid, 1990), Vol. II, pages 1767–1775.

rules of inheritance. The political battle regarding these topics has at times not yet been won by any of the conflicting groups and until that happens, in democratic societies, the legal changes will probably not occur, or will only find a slight entry passage. Private Law is political, as is evidenced by the Greek tragedies Oedipus Rex and Antigone, which dealt with family rules, by not so distant tensions regarding the maintenance of democracy in Uruguay,[30] or by the French, Russian and Cuban revolutions, which dealt with the control and exchange of the principal means of production, but most of the Western World, at least, has reached consensus about most of the Private Law topics, which leaves jurists with the task of iron out problems related to these.

Politics still does play an important role in the attempt to recodify, but often that role is not of adopting totally new values but of telling the World the country is willing to play by the rules of the more industrialized and often economically envied nations, who would be reluctant to engage in trade and investment, were it otherwise. This could very well be the case of formerly socialist countries of Eastern Europe, now wanting to integrate into the European Union or, on less traditional grounds, of emerging economies that have had to accept international commercial arbitration and intellectual property rules as a condition for foreign aid and international trade and investment.

Politics are also at play when a country ties to send out, or at time to tell itself that it wishes to keep some traditional values without adopting others that would bring it in conflict with international interplay. This is the case for countries such as my own, Quebec and Catalonia, who have tried, with varying success, to modernize their old codes in order to preserve one of the important symbols of what it meant to be Puerto Rican, Quebecker or Catalonian.[31] In these places legal reform means more than just

---

[30] In the early 2000s, after restoration of democracy in Uruguay, it's president left a Mercosur meeting in Northeastern Brazil and threatened an Army colonel with the most severe punishment if he refused to testify in a case where a mother was seeking to confirm the identity of a son torn away from her by the military dictatorship. The story can be seen in the Internet by inserting the son's name, Simon Riquelo, in the browser.

[31] In commenting the Quebec Civil Code reform, the Vice President of the Code Revision Commission, later Judge Jean Louis Baudouin stated that Quebec's inability to revise its Civil Code, the Civil Code of Lower Canada, for most of the Twentieth Century stemmed from the fact the Code was a symbol: A symbol of the Quebecker's resistance to Anglo Canadian control. "One, of course," he added, "does not touch on symbols." Judge Baudouin's remarks remind us of what another jurist, Prof. Harold Berman, wrote regarding Western Law in general. In the Preface of his first book on the origins of Western legal tradition, *Law and Revolution* (Harvard University Press, Cambridge, 1983), page v, Prof. Berman also reminded his readers of the difficulty of dealing with symbols. In doing so, he quoted American poet Archibald MacLeish, a Harvard Law School graduate and one time lawyer, who, in his 1955 poem, *The Metaphor*, wrote:

A world ends when its metaphor has died.
An age becomes an age, all else beside,
When sensuous poets in their pride invent
Emblems for the soul's consent
That speak the meanings men will never know
But man-imagined images can show:
It perishes when those images, though seen,
No longer mean.

adapting trusts or Anglo-American secured transactions to Civil Law structures and carrying out the many other tasks fine tuning requires. It means carrying out these tasks within a structure of one or a series of codes which can be easily identified with those of the former cultural communities be they the old metropolitan powers of Paris and Madrid or the autonomous regions of the eastern extreme of the Iberian Peninsula. In these cases the Code, as a symbol, can be a formula for its revision.

Recodification, successful in Quebec since the 1991 adoption of its new Code Civil, and to a large degree in Catalonia, where several statutes dealing with varying parts of that which is typically found in the Civil Codes have been adopted, is still a living dream in Puerto Rico. This is closely tied to the fact the codes there are symbols and that symbols can't be done away with without ripping out as important a rallying post as is language itself. Local codes, and certainly it would be better if they were modernized local codes, mean almost as much as the Spanish language to Puerto Ricans, as French to the Quebeckers and as Catalan to the Catalonians.

The legal symbol of nationhood in Catalonia is so strong that the regional government has adopted a series of wide ranging private laws dealing with Property, Family, Successions and Contracts, amongst other topics,[32] and this despite the fact that section 149 (1), subsections viii and xviii of the Spanish Constitution of 1978 states that basic contractual legislation is the exclusive province of the central government with its seat in Madrid. Even prior to claiming more autonomy or outright independence, the Catalonians decided they would risk confrontation to have their legal symbol in place. I believe they did this to tell themselves that they are governed by their own and not by Madrid laws. The adoption of a contracts statute was important, for changes to other areas of Private Law meant little when they were not forbidden by the Constitution. Adopting the obligations statutes meant, among other things, making the point that Catalonia rules itself. These statutes, like their own Catalonian language, which like in Quebec is protected by special legislation, is a powerful symbol that they, like Quebec, are not only a *société distincte*, but one that is willing to risk confrontation, if that is what is needed, to emphasize the point.

True, codification in these places has occurred also because jurists there have had a life-long experience with codes, be it in their own countries or in others where they have lived or studied, but this alone has not been enough. Recodification is hard and requires a moving force that will push a society and the team of experts charged with carrying it out with the energy and resources to complete the job, but it also requires the backing of a society that for whatever reason, and cultural identity is a common one, feels that the new code is worth the effort.

15.5 The Future

Perhaps the failure of Puerto Rico to adopt new rules is only a temporary one, due to the inability to bring together a group of workaholics with sufficient standing to push the idea through. I believe that in the not so distant future we will finally revise

[32] These may be consulted in the Internet at: http://civil.udg.es/normacivil/catalunya.htm

our basic laws and integrate legal instruments so that special statutes and court created rules will be in harmony.[33]

I personally dream of this not because of cultural identity reasons, although cultural identity is to me very important, but because, in my eyes, codes allow for a relatively quick solution for many legal problems, which attacks one of the most formidable problems of today's legal systems, that of judicial delay and thus of the effective denial of justice for a very large sector of the population that has neither the time nor the money to spend on prolonged and seemingly never ending trials. This problem, one that worries me even more than legal reform,[34] raises serious doubts about the legitimacy of the judicial system.

But saying that I favor reform also implies that I do not believe codified systems *freeze* the law in time and inhibit development,[35] for if I did I would not back it. I think that expressions to the contrary are really the product of chauvinism and not of true analysis.[36] I believe this perhaps because I come from a system where case law has in fact contributed to legal updating, as was stated by one of our excellent Supreme Court justices, Marcos Rigau.[37]

The so-called basic difference between a Civil Law and a Common Law system, the doctrine of *stare decisis*, is in my eyes less marked than it is portrayed to be. I say this from what I see in other systems – France, with its notions of *jurisprudence constant* and Spain, with that of *doctrina legal*, to name but those two countries – and I have no doubt that this is also the situation elsewhere. How can one explain the fact so many legal publishers – Dalloz, in France, La Ley in Argentina, Aranzadi, now Westlaw.es, in Spain – make a handsome amount of money printing and selling court decisions if it were not that these are so important that lawyers read and quote them? I propose that lawyers are as rational as all other human beings and that they spend money and time reading what are, for the most part, boring court decisions only because these help explain how the statutes are adapted to new situations, as Jean-Étienne Marie Portalis suggested would be the case in his *Discours préliminaire au projet de code civil* before the French National Assembly, when presenting the final version of the *Code*. This, I believe, amply proves that codified systems are

[33] Luis Muñiz-Argüelles, "Some Thoughts on Conditions Favoring Recodification": *supra* note 2; Luis Muñiz-Argüelles, Luis "La Revisión y Reforma del Código Civil de Puerto Rico, (The Revision and Reform of the Puerto Rican Civil Code)", 59 (3–4) *Rev. Col. Abog.* (*P.R.*) 149 (1998), Luis Muñiz-Argüelles, "Propuesta para un mecanismo de revisión del Código civil de Puerto Rico (Proposal for a Revision Mechanism for the Puerto Rican Civil Code)", 54 *Rev. Jur. U.P.R.* 159, 160 (1985). See also the *Guiding* Principles prepared for the Permanent Joint Commission for the Revision and Reform of the Puerto Rican Civil Code, 1998 Annual Report (Informe annual, 1998), Vol. I, pages 68–99, once available in http://www.codigocivilpr.net/, under Documents.

[34] "Legitimidad y Justicia, (Legitimacy and Justice)", 73 *Rev. Jur. U.P.R.* 255 (2004).

[35] Zimmerman, *supra*, states: *The codifications neither (as was sometimes feared) ossified the law, nor did they constitute a "prison cell" for legal scholarship*. page 15, footnotes omitted.

[36] I am also aware there are chauvinists in both sides of the fence and that some defend codification as if anything else means chaos, ignoring the non-chaotic reality of a good number of Common Law countries who, in varying degrees and in certain areas, have decided against codification.

[37] See *Borges v. Registrador*, 91 DPR 112 (1964).

not fossilized systems but develop, through court rulings as well as legislation, as other systems similarly develop.

For the moment, however, Puerto Ricans have learned to live with the fragmented rules for, as so many have so often stated, life is a bit messy and learning to live means learning to cope with some inconsistencies. Also, despite the decodification, many rules are not all that fragmented (insurance is based and analyzed as a contract and not as something foreign to it, zoning is seen as a restriction on the owner's bundle of rights and not as a new concept of property, condominium is perceived as a variant of co-ownership, regulations to pinpoint parental obligations of child support are viewed as complementary to Family Law rules in this field). The fragmentation has been, at least in part, a result of modernization, even if it came in a Common Law costume, one worn by the new metropolis with which some felt the need and others the desire to dance with and adapt to, and as so it has been understood and incorporated, more or less adequately. And let us not forget that much of the inconsistent and uncodified law had never been codified before. Codification, as was stated in the opening lecture in the Taiwan Thematic Conference, is a matter of Private Law.[38]

15.6 Concluding Remarks

We are, yes, only *as codified as possible under the current conditions*, but that in no ways means we are not codified in the Western sense, for the main private law solutions are found or based on the Civil Code rules and because many of the special statutes are in accordance with the Code's principles. Yes, there are many special statutes, but some of these are sufficiently complex to warrant their being out of the code (insurance, banking, labor, zoning, welfare legislation, even adoption rules being cases in point). Other statutes deal with special areas which need pinpoint rules and do not require codes (traffic, education, tourism promotion). Still others deal with areas that were never part of traditional codified systems (Constitutional Law, public agency organization, municipal or local government organization, electoral law, taxation, and public security being some examples). Codification, let us not forget, was never that all-encompassing as has sometimes been said and stating that we will be more codified because we have *traffic codes*, *tax codes*, *public security codes tourism codes* or the like or because we cease to call procedural rules by that name and call them *procedural codes* will not make much of a difference, either practically or historically.

[38] See Zimmermann, *supra*, *in passim* and especially at pages 2–5.

Chapter 16
Mixed but Not Codified: The Case of Scotland

Elspeth Reid

Abstract In this collection of studies on codification Scotland is an obvious outsider. The Scottish legal system has no Codes – at least not in the sense of comprehensive legislation providing the fundamental structure for the entire legal system. Nonetheless, the civil law survives alongside the common law tradition in Scotland's mixed legal system. The essential question considered by this essay is therefore how Scotland preserves its civil law as well as its common law character without the support of a civil code. First of all, however, some explanation is required of the nature of the Scottish mix and its historical origins.

Keywords Scotland • Mixed legal system • Not codified • Civil law and common law traditions • 1998 Scotland Act

16.1 Introduction: The Scottish Mix

The distinctiveness of mixed legal systems has long been recognised,[1] but this "extended family",[2] sharing the dual legacy of civil law and common law, has in recent years acquired a new self-awareness, marked by the publication of numerous volumes of comparative scholarship.[3] Rejoicing in a rediscovered sense of common identity, the family members have formed a World Society of Mixed Jurisdiction

[1] For a history see K. Reid "The idea of mixed legal systems" *Tulane Law Review* 78 (2003) 5.

[2] *Mixed Jurisdictions Worldwide*, 2nd edn. ed. V.V. Palmer (Cambridge: Cambridge University Press, 2012) 3. The family includes South Africa, Scotland, Louisiana, Quebec, Puerto Rico, The Philippines, Botswana, Malta, Sri Lanka, Israel and others around the world.

[3] Notably Palmer *Mixed Jurisdictions*, note 2 supra, as well as the first edition of this work, *Mixed Jurisdictions Worldwide* ed. V.V. Palmer (Cambridge: Cambridge University Press, 2001); see also *Mixed Legal Systems at New Frontiers*, ed. E Örücü (London: Wildy, Simmonds and Hill, 2010).

E. Reid (✉)
School of Law, University of Edinburgh, Edinburgh, Scotland, UK
e-mail: elspeth.reid@ed.ac.uk

J.C. Rivera (ed.), *The Scope and Structure of Civil Codes*, Ius Gentium: Comparative Perspectives on Law and Justice 32, DOI 10.1007/978-94-007-7942-6_16,

Jurists,[4] and have celebrated with numerous international conferences.[5] It would be churlish to dwell on suggestions that in the modern world all legal systems are to an extent becoming mixed in character.[6] Nonetheless, the notion of a "family" requires qualification to the extent that the composition of the mix differs hugely as between different mixed systems. So what exactly makes up the Scots law mix?

As observed by Reinhard Zimmermann, the Scottish legal system is one where "legal history and modern legal doctrine have not categorically been 'thought apart' and where the 'vital connection' between the past and the present is thus particularly evident."[7] Although private law has not been codified, the jurists of the seventeenth to the early nineteenth centuries (who are recognised as "Institutional" and whose writings follow the civilian tradition) have had considerable influence on the shaping of private law.[8] At the same time, common law influences have been central to the development of the legal system, at least since the Union of the Scots and English Parliaments in 1707, if not from before. Civil and criminal procedure is much closer to the English than the continental European models, judicial decisions are regarded as a source of law, and the doctrine of precedent is applied. Civilian principle remains important, but to the extent that it is embedded in case law, it is increasingly developed by applying common-law forms of reasoning. At the same time, statutory regulation, as in all common law systems, is gaining in volume, and increasingly codifying statutes are promulgated for whole subject areas such as Company Law, Tax Law or Insurance.

16.2 Historical Background

Unlike in many other mixed jurisdictions, the Scots law mix was not the product of a mixed colonial history, but rather of a consensual union with a common law jurisdiction and a complex interweaving of legal traditions over several centuries. Indeed it is arguable that the character of the Scottish legal system has been mixed "from the very beginning", although the exact ingredients in that mix have been the subject of constant debate.[9] During the political upheavals of the Middle Ages,

---

[4] Founded in 2002: see http://www.mixedjurisdiction.org/.

[5] E.g. the World Society of Mixed Jurisdictions Jurists has held major conferences in New Orleans (2002), Edinburgh (2005), Stellenbosch (2009), Jerusalem (2011) and Valetta (2012).

[6] See review of *Mixed Jurisdictions Worldwide,* 1st edn, note 3 supra, by A. Rahmatian, *Edinburgh Law Review* 8 (2004) 427.

[7] R. Zimmermann, "'Double Cross': Comparing Scots and South African Law", in *Mixed Legal Systems in Comparative Perspective: Property and Obligations in Scotland and South Africa*, ed. R. Zimmermann, D. Visser and K. Reid (Oxford: Oxford University Press, 2004), 1 at 4.

[8] See T.D. Fergus and G. Maher "Sources of law" in *The Laws of Scotland: Stair Memorial Encyclopaedia*, ed. T.B. Smith et al., Vol 22 (Edinburgh: Butterworths, 1987) paras 532–538.

[9] See W.D.H. Sellar, "Scots Law – Mixed from the Very Beginning? A Tale of Two Receptions" *Edinburgh Law Review* 4 (2000) 3; also N.R. Whitty, "The Civilian Tradition and Debates on Scots Law", in two parts, *Tydskrif vir die Suid-Afrikaanse Reg* 1996 227 and 442; H.L. MacQueen, "Mixture or Muddle?: Teaching and Research in Scottish Legal History" *Zeitschrift für Europäisches Privatrecht* 5 (1997) 69.

and in its subsequent development, Scots law had acquired a significantly different character from that of English law. In Scotland a central civil court structure was established much later than in England. This meant that, as compared with England, a class of secular professional lawyers was slow to develop. It has been suggested that this absence of a secular legal profession, and the rise of academically qualified ecclesiastical lawyers, rendered Scots customs and practice open to influence from the *ius commune* of the Continental European legal systems.[10] Certainly when the Court of Session, became established at the centre of Scotland's court structure in 1532,[11] (where it remains to this day), canon lawyers held sway,[12] and Romano-canonical procedure was applied.[13] A secular legal profession did establish itself in Scotland by the end of the sixteenth century,[14] but unlike in England, where legal education was based in the Inns of Court, it did not itself organise a formal training structure. Before the Law Faculties became properly established in the Scottish Universities in the eighteenth century, aspiring lawyers commonly studied the canon law and the civil law at universities in Continental Europe, commonly in France prior to the seventeenth century,[15] and increasingly in the Low Countries thereafter[16] (and indeed many still travelled to the German universities in the eighteenth and nineteenth centuries).[17] The traditions brought home to Scotland by these early students were not only those of the European *ius commune*,[18] but also, to a lesser extent, the *ius proprium* of the countries in which they had studied.

---

[10] J.W. Cairns, "Historical Introduction", in *A History of Private Law in Scotland*, ed. K. Reid and R. Zimmermannn (Oxford: Oxford University Press, 2000) 14 at 44–47; see also P. Stein, "The influence of Roman law on the law of Scotland" *Juridical Review* (1963) 205, reprinted in P.G. Stein, *The Character and Influence of the Roman Civil Law: Historical Essays* (London: Hambledon Press, 1988).

[11] *APS* ii 335, c.2 (available at http://www.rps.ac.uk/). See also J.W. Cairns, "Revisiting the Foundation of the College of Justice", in *Miscellany Five*, ed. H.L. MacQueen (Edinburgh: Stair Society, Vol 52, 2006) 27.

[12] Cairns, "Historical Introduction", supra note 10, at 70.

[13] J.W. Cairns, "Codification and Scottish Legislation", *Tulane European and Civil Law Forum* 22 (2007) 1 at 5; J. Finlay, *Men of Law in Pre-Reformation Scotland* (East Linton: Tuckwell Press, 2000), 87–122.

[14] Finlay, *Men of Law in Pre-Reformation Scotland*, 228.

[15] Of 60 applicants between the years 1574 and 1608 for the status of advocate in the Court of Session, 20 had studied in French universities, most commonly Poitier, but also Bordeaux, Toulouse, and Paris. (R. Hannay, *The College of Justice: Essays on the Institution and Development of the Court of Session* (1933, reprinted Edinburgh: Stair Society, 1990) 146).

[16] R. Feenstra, "Scottish-Dutch legal relations", first published in *Academic Relations between the Law Countries and the British Isles 1450–1700. First proceedings of the First Conference of Belgian, British and Dutch Historians of Universities held in Ghent, Sept 30–Oct 2 1987*, and reprinted (as part XVI) in *Legal Scholarship and Doctrines of Private Law, 13th–18th Centuries* (Aldershot: Variorum Press, 1996) On the failure of legal education to take root in the Scottish Universities prior to 1700 see J.W. Cairns, "Academic feud, bloodfeud, and William Welwood: legal education in St Andrews, 1560–1611" (in two parts) *Edinburgh Law Review* 2 (1998)158 and 255.

[17] A. Rodger, "Scottish advocates in the nineteenth century: the German connection" *Law Quarterly Review* 110 (1994) 563.

[18] See P. Stein "Influence of Roman Law on the Law of Scotland", supra note 10.

After the Scots King James VI ascended to the English throne, in succession to Elizabeth I, in 1603, a century before the Union of the Parliaments, various plans were considered to harmonise the laws of the two kingdoms. These schemes led to nothing, not least because the English were unconvinced that the differences between the legal systems were marginal[19] and feared the imposition of the civil law south of the border.[20] Within Scotland, however, the significant body of legal literature that already existed by the beginning of the eighteenth century[21] indicated an already mixed legal system in which an important, but not the only, element was the Civil Law tradition of the *ius commune*, but in which English influence had also played its part. Of course the balance of different elements was not to remain static thereafter, nor indeed uncontentious. For some, the "soul" of modern Scots law has remained Civilian.[22] Others, however, have counselled against making "Scots law into some kind of civil law theme park".[23] Some legal historians have suggested that the importance of other elements, the customary law as well as the Canon law, has been underestimated[24] – that the "resilience" of the *Scottish* common law has been overlooked, and that earlier English influences survived the reception of Roman law in the later middle ages.[25] Nevertheless, few would deny the importance of the civil law tradition in the shaping of Scots law,[26] or that the civilian element is a "deep and powerful"[27] one in the Scottish legal tradition.

An interesting parallel in relation to the survival of the civilian tradition may be drawn between Scotland and South Africa. Roman-Dutch law was largely obliterated in the Netherlands by the introduction of a Civil Code on the French model, but it survived in the Cape of Good Hope, where it developed, under English influence and without a Code, into a mixed system. Hence the links between Scottish and

[19] See Thomas Craig's comparative analysis of the laws of Scotland and England, concluding that "There is not that difference between the laws of the two countries that is popularly supposed to exist": *De Unione Regnorum Britanniae Tractatus* (1605, The Scottish History Society, 1909) 328.

[20] B. Levack, *The Formation of the British State: England, Scotland and the Union, 1603–1707* (Oxford, Clarendon Press, 1987), 68–101.

[21] For a comprehensive survey of the development of the law in the seventeenth century see J.D. Ford, *Law and Opinion in Scotland during the Seventeenth Century* (Oxford: Hart, 2007).

[22] J. Blackie and N. Whitty, "Scots Law and the New Ius Commune", in *Scots Law into the 21st Century* ed. H.L. MacQueen (Edinburgh: W. Green, 1996) 65–81. See also Whitty, "The Civilian Tradition and Debates on Scots law", note 9 supra.

[23] A. Rodger, "The Use of the Civil Law in Scottish Courts", in *The Civilian Tradition and Scots Law*, ed. D. Carey Miller and R. Zimmermann (Berlin: Duncker and Humblot, 1997), 225 at 231.

[24] E.g. MacQueen, "Mixture or Muddle?", supra note 9, at 380–381.

[25] W.D.H. Sellar, "The Resilience of the Scottish Common Law" *The Civilian Tradition and Scots Law* ed. Carey Miller and Zimmermann, note 23 supra, 149; Sellar "Scots Law – Mixed From The Very Beginning?", note 9 supra. See also Stair, *Institutions* 1.1.16 (note 76 infra) on the importance of *Scots* common law.

[26] Sellar "Resilience of the Scottish Common Law", supra note 24, at 164.

[27] MacQueen, "Mixture or Muddle?", supra note 9, at 380.

South African lawyers that have flourished in the post-Apartheid era and have developed into various successful collaborative projects.[28]

The Parliaments of Scotland and of England and Wales united in a single Westminster Parliament in 1707 by virtue of a Treaty of Union, supported by a majority in both parliaments. The Treaty of Union made express provision for the continuing distinctiveness of the Scots legal system and its separate institutions including the courts, and to this day Scotland has retained a separate, Scottish-administered, court system, rules of procedure and legal profession. The Treaty required laws concerning trade, customs and excises to be harmonised with those of England, but all other laws were to remain in force in Scotland as previously. Such laws might be amended by the Westminster Parliament, but a distinction was made between public and private law. The former could be made the same throughout the whole United Kingdom, but the latter could not be altered "except for evident utility of the subjects within Scotland".[29] Whether or not all subsequent alterations have indeed been for the "utility" of the Scots, it was inevitable that private law should become anglicised to a significant degree from the time of the Union onwards.

16.2.1 The Impact of the Common Law

In contrast with England, where the study of law traditionally remained within the control of the professional bodies, Law Faculties were established and prospered in the Scottish Universities from the eighteenth century onwards, with prestigious chairs in Civil and Scots Law instituted at Edinburgh and Glasgow Universities.[30] The continuing influence of the *ius commune* in legal literature continued well into the eighteenth century and even nineteenth century. Yet Scots law became increasingly penetrated by common law influence during the nineteenth century and use of civil law sources declined sharply.[31] There were various reasons for this, even leaving aside the decline of the *ius commune* throughout those European countries in which it had previously flourished and the spread of codification in the nineteenth century.[32] The most obvious was the simple fact that all legislation relating to Scotland, whether in the form of statutes applicable to Britain as a whole or to Scotland separately, was

[28] For an example of the fruits of one such project see the collection of essays in *Mixed Legal Systems in Comparative Perspective: Property and Obligations in Scotland and South Africa*, ed. R. Zimmermann, D. Visser and K. Reid (Oxford: Oxford University Press, 2004).

[29] See Treat of Union, Article XVIII, and see also Lord Dervaird, "Afterword: Prospects for the Future", in M.C. Meston, W.D.H. Sellar and Lord Cooper, *The Scottish Legal Tradition*, revised edn. by S.C. Styles (Edinburgh: Saltire Society, 1991) 91–93.

[30] See Cairns, "Historical Introduction", supra note 10, 129–130.

[31] Whitty, "The Civilian Tradition and Debates on Scots Law", supra note 9, at 231.

[32] A. Rodger "Thinking about Scots Law" *Edinburgh Law Review* 1 (1996) 3 at 14–15.

made until 1999 by the English-dominated legislature in London. The second was the position of the House of Lords in London as the supreme court of appeal for Scots civil cases.[33] But a third, highly significant, consideration was the growth inside Scotland itself of legal unionism paralleling the growth of British nationalism.

16.2.2 An English-Based Legislature

The anglicising influence of legislation made by the British legislature in London was most readily apparent in regard to commercial law, which developed rapidly after the Union.[34] Statutes common to both England and Scotland were often enacted in areas that developed in parallel in each jurisdiction, such as company law, intellectual property,[35] or bills of exchange.[36] The Sale of Goods Act 1893, for example, introduced a British law of sale that was largely English and represented at least a partial "surrender on the part of Scots law".[37] English influence also penetrated through some statutes applicable only in Scotland. Sometimes for the purposes of such legislation the draftsmen "put the kilt on" English models with little adaptation.[38] A relatively recent example of this tendency is the importation of the Floating Charge (form of security over company assets) into Scots law by the Companies (Floating Charges) (Scotland) Act 1961. It should be added, however, that harmonisation was often welcomed by the Scots as being to their commercial advantage, that English doctrines could sometimes be assimilated to advantage "in the best eclectic tradition of the Scottish common law", and that the process has worked both ways, in that the English have on occasion been amenable to using Scots models.[39]

---

[33] A full treatment of this subject can be found in A. Dewar Gibb, *Law from over the Border* (Edinburgh: W. Green, 1950).

[34] See G.C.H. Paton, "The Eighteenth Century and Later", in *Introduction to Scottish Legal History* ed. G.C.H. Paton, (Edinburgh: Stair Society, vol 20, 1958) 50 at 56–58.

[35] E.g. the Copyright Act of 1709 (8 Anne c 19) was common to Scotland and England, as was subsequent legislation on copyright and performing rights.

[36] Bills of Exchange Act 1892.

[37] See W.M. Gordon, "Sale", in *History of Private Law in Scotland,* ed. Reid and Zimmermann, note 10 supra, Vol. 2, 305 at 328–321.

[38] An instance of this is the Lands Consolidation (Scotland) Act 1845 of which Lord Dunedin spared no criticism in *Governors of George Heriot's Trust v Caledonian Railway Company* 1915 SC (HL) 52 at 65, and which Lord Johnston spoke of in *Fraser v Caledonian Railway Co.* 1911 SC 145 at 154 as "a very inartistic, if not careless, adaptation of an English Act to a totally different system of law and tenure".

[39] W.D.H. Sellar, "A historical perspective", in M.C. Meston, W.D.H. Sellar and Lord Cooper, *The Scottish Legal Tradition*, revised edn. by S.C. Styles (Edinburgh: Saltire Society, 1991) 29 at 55–56.

16.2.3 The House of Lords as the Supreme Court of Appeal in Scots Civil Cases

A feature of Scottish procedure before the Union of the Parliaments in 1707 was that litigants in the Court of Session had the right to protest to the Parliament of Scotland "for remeid of law", and soon after the Union jurisdiction in civil matters was accepted by the House of Lords as the upper chamber of the Parliament of Great Britain.[40] From the start appeals to London were numerous, and still number only a handful per year, but the impact of these cases cannot be ignored. The presence of Scots lawyers in the Judicial Committee of the House of Lords was not secured until the Appellate Jurisdiction Act 1876. Thereafter it became customary to have two Scots lawyers as Lords of Appeal in Ordinary,[41] and as a convention, not a rule, those two sat in Scots cases. (Given that their Lordships normally sat in committees of five, this still did not constitute a majority.) That practice was still in place when the Judicial Committee of the House of Lords ceased to sit in 2009[42] and it has been replicated in the new Supreme Court of the United Kingdom,[43] to which jurisdiction has been transferred. In effect therefore, binding precedent in matters of Scots law has since the eighteenth century been generated by a court of which, at best, only the minority of members are qualified to practice in the Scots courts.

Initially, notwithstanding the imbalance of English and Scots judges, the essential differences between the two systems were largely respected.[44] However, citation of English cases progressively increased from the second half of the nineteenth century, with their greater accessibility in the official English law reports from the 1870s onwards,[45] leading increasingly to convergence in some areas. By the same token, however, the availability of the reports of Scots decisions meant that Scots case law was likewise being cited more often in English cases. An obvious example of this is *Donoghue* v *Stevenson*,[46] the celebrated Scots House of Lords case in the

[40] See A.J. MacLean, "The 1707 Union: Scots Law and the House of Lords", in *New Perspectives in Scottish Legal History*, ed. A. Kiralfy and H.L. MacQueen, (London: Cass, 1984), 50.

[41] Lord Gordon was appointed to the House in 1876, although the Lord President, Lord Colonsay, had been sent to the House of Lords to assist with Scottish appeals some years earlier, in 1867.

[42] See Constitutional Reform Act 2005.

[43] The Supreme Court website is at http://www.supremecourt.gov.uk/.

[44] See, e.g., *Collins v Collins* 1884 11 R (HL) 19, a House of Lords case in which the English counsel for one party was roundly criticised for citing English authorities and neglecting a clear line of Scots authorities to the opposite effect; or *Glasgow Corporation v Barclay, Curle & Company Ltd* 1923 SC (HL) 78, in which the Earl of Birkenhead refrained from arguing the English law, commenting: "In a Scotch appeal, raising some matters at least which are peculiar to the practice and law of Scotland, I am not prepared to set myself against so great a weight of authority [as that of the Scots Law Lords]. I do not, therefore, great as is the doubt which I have entertained, record a dissenting opinion".

[45] See Rodger, "Thinking about Scots Law", note 32 supra, at 16–17; Dewar Gibb, *Law from over the Border*, note 33 supra.

[46] 1932 SC (HL) 31.

1930s which became the starting point for the analysis of negligence in tort liability not just in England but in all Common Law jurisdictions.

An easily-overlooked feature of the anglicisation of Scots law in the late nineteenth century was the contribution made by Scots judges themselves, both at home and on elevation to the House of Lords, towards the assimilation English law.[47] As one of Scotland's most prominent legal nationalists, the late Sir Thomas Smith, once reflected, "The main subverters of Scots law in modern times have been the Scots."[48]

16.2.4 Legal Unionism

One important explanation for the readiness of those within the Scottish legal system to welcome assimilation of Scots to English law was the force of British nationalism in the late nineteenth and early twentieth centuries. As in any small country, Scots lawyers have been used to looking outwards in order to supplement relatively scant native resources. John Blackie, writing on attitudes towards comparative material, has pointed to the Scots tendency in the sixteenth and seventeenth centuries to cite modern continental European literature: "The reason was that the world of the *ius commune* at that period was decidedly forward looking. Accordingly, what mattered was to engage with the latest material."[49] Blackie identifies a shifting focus towards English material during the eighteenth century to the extent that by the mid-nineteenth century, the Common Law had become the "new 'foreign'". This was an obvious resource to assist Scots lawyers in dealing with the demands that the changing economic and social environment was placing upon the legal system. It was not only linguistically completely accessible, but it also derived from a culture that was in many ways extremely similar. However, the notion of law as a unifying force of Empire is almost certainly an additional factor in this process.[50] The aspiration to align Scots law with the law of the British Empire is perhaps unsurprising, even leaving aside the obvious lack of linguistic barriers. For Scots looking to the future the obvious path for the development of the legal system would have been harmonisation with the law of the Empire in which they had so enthusiastically participated as administrators and entrepreneurs as well as lawyers.[51] Indeed, a tentative comparison may be drawn with those who today seek harmonisation with the law of other European jurisdictions.

---

[47] E.g. in *Dumbreck v Addie's Collieries* 1929 SC (HL) 51, the case that "anglicised" occupiers' liability, the speeches of the two Scots on the Committee, Lords Dunedin and Shaw, were central in assuring their brethren in the House of Lords that English and Scots law were already at one in this area.

[48] *British Justice: The Scottish Contribution* (London: Stevens, 1961), 227.

[49] "History, historiography and comparative law", in *The State of Scots Law*, ed. L. Farmer and S. Veitch, (Edinburgh: Butterworths, 2001) 75 at 87ff.

[50] See Lord Shaw of Dunfermline, "Law as the link of Empire", reproduced in *Law of the Kinsmen* (London: Hodder and Stoughton, 1923, reprinted 1996), at 133. See esp 155–156.

[51] On the willing participation of the Scots in the codification of commercial law see A Rodger, "The codification of commercial law in Victorian Britain" *Law Quarterly Review* 108 (1992) 570.

16.2.5 The Modern Scots Mix

There is no clear consensus as to the relative importance of common law and civil law sources in modern Scots law, or as to the character of its "mixedness". For Zweigert and Kotz, Scots law represented a "symbiosis" of the civil and common law traditions,[52] while others have asked whether it is truly a "mixture" or merely a "muddle".[53] Whatever the respective contributions of the different legal traditions, the Scots law mix is certainly not perfectly homogenised. It offers an example of how civil law and common law traditions may develop side-by-side without one being obliterated by the other, but its substantive content does not indicate a Darwinian blend of the best elements of each, as demonstrated by the examination of specific subject areas in Sect. 16.3 below.

However, a further feature is that a degree of mixedness is evident not only in sources of law, but also in style. Patterns of legal reasoning are strongly rooted in the Common law, in that they are for the most part inductive, moving from the specific case to general principle, rather than deductive, starting from general principle and moving to the specific case. At the same time, a conceptualist tradition can also be discerned. If there is no obvious answer in statute or in case-law, the writings of the classic civil law jurists, the Scots "Institutional" writers discussed in Sect. 16.3.3 below, may be used to build a principled solution to the given problem, and in turn this solution is developed through, and embedded within subsequent case law. Mixedness is thus deep-rooted, and Scots law has reached a stage where[54]

> ...no purpose is served by distinguishing between rules derived from Rome and rules derived from England. Regardless of provenance, the rules today work in the same way and rely on the same types of sources. In short, they are part of the modern law of Scotland. It is possible that, in this respect, Scotland is a special case among mixed jurisdictions, due to the long and unbroken development of its law. For the most part, the civil law in Scotland is mediated through native authority by means of case law and juristic writing. Today, direct recourse to Roman law, in any form, is unusual. By contrast, mixed systems which take their civil law from a foreign source – Quebec, for example, or, to a lesser extent, South Africa – must first characterize a rule before choosing the appropriate source

The beginning of the twenty-first century has marked a new era for the Scottish legal system, with a devolved parliament. Following a popular referendum held in September 1997, legislation was passed in 1998, providing for the establishment of a Scottish Parliament, which was duly opened on 1 July 1999. The Scotland Act 1998, with its express incorporation of the European Convention of Human Rights, is tantamount to a form of constitution for Scotland and sets out the framework for

---

[52] *Introduction to Comparative Law*, 3rd edn tr T. Weir (Oxford: Oxford University Press, 1998) at 204; see also J. Smits, "Scotland as a mixed jurisdiction and the development of European private law: is there something to learn from evolutionary theory?" *Electronic Journal of Comparative Law* 7(5) (2003) at http://www.ejcl.org/ejcl/75/art75-1.html.

[53] MacQueen, "Mixture or Muddle?", supra note 9; see also R Evans-Jones, "Receptions of law, mixed legal systems and the myth of the genius of Scots private law" *Law Quarterly Review* 114 (1998) 228.

[54] Reid, "The idea of mixed legal systems", note 1 supra, at 24.

the legislature to make law on a wide range of matters, as discussed further below. For present purposes it is important to note that matters of private law were devolved, and so new legislation in these areas has become a matter for the legislature in Edinburgh.[55]

Devolution has brought a new era of self-confidence to the Scottish legal system. Academic legal literature is flourishing and its authors, once "not read till dead" are now cited without embarrassment in the courts.[56] Civilian sources are seldom used directly, but the importance of the civilian tradition in the evolution of the legal system is acknowledged, alongside that of English law. Secure now in its unique identity, Scots law no longer requires to define itself by reference to similarities with, or dissimilarities from, either the civil law or the common law.

As far as codification is concerned, however, the Scottish Parliament has shown little more enthusiasm than its Westminster neighbour. It has embarked upon an energetic programme of legislative reform over the last decade, but this has resulted in a series of discrete statutes rather than comprehensive codes. Land law, for example, was identified as being in urgent need of reform, since in 1999 a feudal system of land tenure still operated across Scotland (with owners answerable to their feudal superiors if they did not adhere to the conditions created in the original feudal grant). The dismantling of the feudal system also entailed that much of the framework of landownership should be reconfigured, but all this was achieved not at once by a comprehensive land code, but progressively by a series of statutes: the Abolition of Feudal Tenure etc. (Scotland) Act 2000, Title Conditions (Scotland) Act 2003, the Tenements (Scotland) Act 2004, and the Land Reform (Scotland) Act 2003.

Mistrust of codification is illustrated even more tellingly in relation to criminal law. Much of Scotland's substantive criminal law is to be found in the common law, and not in statute. In 2003, following a collaborative research project lasting several years, a group of distinguished Scots academic lawyers published their draft *Criminal Code for Scotland* with extensive accompanying commentary.[57] But while this document had been produced under the auspices of the Scottish Law Commission, and had drawn support in the academic press,[58] it failed to capture the enthusiasm of the general public, the legal profession or the Scottish government.[59]

---

[55] Scotland Act 1998s. 29. For further discussion see C. Himsworth, "Devolution and the mixed legal system of Scotland" 2002 *Juridical Review* (2002) 115. For an assessment of the first 10 years, see *Law Making and the Scottish Parliament*, ed. E Sutherland et al., (Edinburgh: Edinburgh University Press, 2011).

[56] See K.G.C. Reid, "The third profession: the rise of the academic lawyer in Scotland", in *Scots law into the 21st Century*, ed. MacQueen, note 22 supra, 39.

[57] Available at www.scotlawcom.gov.uk/download_file/view/521/. The authors were Eric Clive, Pamela Ferguson, Christopher Gane, and Alexander McCall Smith. The history of the project and the fate of the draft is narrated in E. Clive, "Codification of Scottish criminal law" *Scottish Criminal Law* (2008) 747.

[58] A listing of that academic literature can be found in the article by Clive, "Codification", note 57 supra.

[59] See E Clive, "Thoughts from a Scottish perspective on the bicentenary of the French Civil Code" *Edinburgh Law Review* 8 (2004) 415 at 418.

Various obstacles were perceived: the complexity and volume of private law legislation to be included; the increasing difficulties of drawing boundaries between private and public law spheres; and the difficulty of composing such a document in a jurisdiction accustomed to the common law style of legislative drafting.[60] In any event it now looks increasingly improbable, a decade on, that the Code will ever be enacted, and it is hardly surprising therefore that no further projects of this nature are in preparation.

16.3 Sources of Law

16.3.1 Legislation of the UK and Scottish Parliaments

Statutes of the UK Parliament in Westminster and statutes of the Scottish Parliament at Holyrood (Edinburgh) are primary sources as the "principal means of change and innovation" in Scots law.[61] Between 1707 and 1999 all primary legislation relevant to Scotland was enacted by the Parliament in Westminster, as discussed in Sect. 16.2 above, whether by means of statutes applicable to the whole of the UK, or by means of statutes extending only to Scotland. Following the creation of the Scottish Parliament by means of the Scotland Act 1998, the London parliament reserved for itself power to legislate for Scotland in relation to areas including the constitution; foreign affairs; defence; the civil service; certain financial and economic matters; national security; immigration and nationality; misuse of drugs; trade and industry, energy, social security; employment; and broadcasting.[62]

Thus the Scottish parliament was granted legislative competence in health; education; local government; social work; housing; planning; economic development; tourism; transport; most aspects of criminal and civil law and criminal justice; the courts; police and fire services; environment; agriculture; forestry; fisheries; sport; the arts; and public records.[63] In particular, most areas of private law are within the competence of the Scottish Parliament, including the law of persons, obligations, property, and the law relating to court procedure.[64]

Additionally, there is a very considerable body of "delegated" legislation on matters of detail, made directly or indirectly under powers delegated by an Act of either the UK or Scottish Parliament, typically to Government Ministers, public

[60] See commentary in A Rahmatian, "Codification of private law in Scotland: observations by a civil lawyer" *Edinburgh Law Review* 8 (2004) 31; A Rodger, "The Bell of Law Reform" *Scots Law Times (News)* (1993) 339.

[61] See *Stair Memorial Encyclopaedia*, vol 22, note 8 supra, para 523.

[62] Scotland Act 1998, Sch 5.

[63] Scotland Act 1998 s 29.

[64] Scotland Act 1998 s 126(4). For proposals for further devolution of power to the Scottish Parliament in fiscal matters see the Scotland Bill before the UK Parliament at the time of writing (text at http://services.parliament.uk/bills/2010-11/scotland.html).

authorities, or the courts.[65] And of course the accession of the United Kingdom to the European Union has bound Scotland, as part of the United Kingdom, to comply with EU legislation.

16.3.2 Judicial Precedent

Judicial precedent – the reasons or principles of law embodied in the decisions of the courts – is an important source of law in Scotland alongside legislation. A brief word is required here to explain the hierarchy of the courts for the purposes of ascertaining the binding force of precedent. The status of the United Kingdom Supreme Court as the final court of appeal in private law matters has been noted above in Sect. 16.3. Within Scotland the highest court in Scotland is the Court of Session in Edinburgh, which has an appellate as well as a first-instance jurisdiction. The judiciary in the local courts (the "sheriff courts" and other specialised tribunals), as well as judges sitting at first instance in the Court of Session, are bound not only by the decisions issued by Supreme Court, but only by those of the Court of Session in its appellate jurisdiction. Of course Scotland as a small jurisdiction has a correspondingly restricted case law, and much use is therefore made of comparative law sources, particularly decisions from England and the Commonwealth, which may be persuasive but are not binding upon the Scots courts.[66] (A decision by the House of Lords or Supreme Court in an English case is not and has never been binding upon the Scottish courts. The exception is where the point at issue is based on legislation which has equal applicability in both countries, or has been decided by an authoritative and binding court to be exactly the same and have the same legal significance in both countries.[67] In cases where provisions are merely similar, English authority may be persuasive but differences between Scots and English law must be respected).[68]

For some there is little perceptible difference in the Scots evaluation of precedent as compared with that of other common law jurisdictions.[69] Others concede the growing influence of precedent since the mid-nineteenth and over the course of the twentieth centuries, but argue that Scottish courts nonetheless exhibit a greater tendency to seek out the principle underlying a particular legal problem rather than "isolated instances" of its occurrence, and that the Scottish interpretation of prec-

---

[65] See http://www.parliament.uk/about/how/laws/delegated/.

[66] See H.L. MacQueen, "Mixing it? Comparative law in the Scottish courts" *European Review of Private Law* 11 (2003) 735.

[67] *Dalgleish v Glasgow Corporation* 1976 SC 32.

[68] *Glasgow Corporation v Central Land Board* 1956 SC (HL) 1.

[69] See, e.g., *Interpreting Precedents: A Comparative Study*, ed. D.N. MacCormick and R.S. Summers (Aldershot: Dartmouth, 1997) containing a single chapter on the UK, by Z. Bankowski, D.N. MacCormick and G. Marshall at 315, which had little to say on Scottish difference.

edent has "a broader basis than in the South".[70] Various illustrations of this trend in Scots case law could be instanced, but one example which brings the contrast into clear focus can be found in the case of *Sharp v Thompson*. This case involved the sale of land in which the contract of sale had been concluded, the full purchase price had been paid, and entry to the property had been given. There was, however, a delay in registering title to the property in the Property Register, and in the meantime the sellers, a company, had become insolvent. The question for the court to decide, in essence, was whether title had passed to the purchasers, or whether the receivers appointed to wind up the company's affairs could lay claim to it. The basis for the decision at first instance in the Court of Session in Edinburgh[71] (in favour of the receivers) was the fundamental framework of real and personal rights, backed up by reference to case law and the Institutional writers. This decision was affirmed on appeal to the Inner House of the Court of Session in Edinburgh.[72] However, it was overturned on final appeal to the House of Lords in London,[73] where English judges were in the majority, and where the fundamental principles of property law were set aside in favour of an approach that was regarded as more "practical and realistic".[74]

The interaction of statute and case law will be discussed further below in relation to specific subject areas. Some parts of the law, such as Family Law, are governed primarily by statute, while in others, such as Delict, there is relatively little statutory provision, so that the very framework of principle is embedded in case law and custom. And of course case law may also, of course, be important with regard to areas that are largely statutory, in that judicial authority may be invoked where there is controversy or uncertainty in the application of statutory provisions.

16.3.3 Institutional Writings

Major significance is still attached to the work of jurists writing in the seventeenth, eighteenth, and nineteenth centuries presenting comprehensive and systematic accounts of Scots law in the form of "Institutes", following the Roman law model. These "Institutional" writers include, on civil matters, Thomas Craig (*Jus Feudale*, 1655),[75] James Dalrymple, Viscount Stair (*Institutions of the Law of*

[70] T.B. Smith, *Judicial Precedent in Scots Law* (Edinburgh: W. Green, 1952) 17 and 107–108.

[71] 1994 SC 503.

[72] 1995 SC 455.

[73] 1997 SC (HL) 66.

[74] It should be added that this decision was much criticized at the time, and has now been deemed, by the House of Lords, to be restricted in authority to certain situations involving floating charges – securities granted by companies. See *Burnett's Trustee v Grainger* 2004 SC (HL) 19.

[75] A translation from the Latin by Lord Clyde was published under the title *The Jus Feudale* (Edinburgh: W. Hodge, 1934).

Scotland, 1681);[76] Andrew MacDouall, Lord Bankton (*Institute of the Laws of Scotland*, 1751–53);[77] John Erskine of Carnock (*Institute of the Law of Scotland*, 1773);[78] and George Joseph Bell (*Commentaries on the Law of Scotland and the Principles of Mercantile Jurisprudence*, 1804[79] and *Principles of the Law of Scotland*, 1829[80]).[81]

Whereas the literature of the *ius commune* continued to inform Scots legal literature and the reasoning of the courts up until the eighteenth century, by the nineteenth century such references had receded, and, in their place, attention was turned to these "Institutional" writings. The authority of such writings increased over the course of the nineteenth century, so that the principles expounded there have in many instance been mediated and developed over time through the case law. However, the Institutional writings themselves continue to be cited regularly in the Scots courts to the present day, commanding "special authority"[82] as a formal source of law, especially where there is no modern case law or statute in point. To take a recent example, *Morris v Rae*[83] was a case appealed to the Supreme Court in London on an issue regarding the nature of "warrandice" (the guarantee of title provided by the seller of land to the buyer). This is an area of law governed almost entirely by custom and case law, but there was no case law specifically relevant to the problem at issue in this case. Lord Reed therefore prefaced his survey of the authorities with the reflection that "as there does not appear to be any judicial authority directly in point, it is appropriate to begin by considering the relevant principles. Stair states in his *Institutions of the Law of Scotland* ..." The analysis which follows also made reference to Bell's *Principles of the Law of Scotland*, as well as Pothier's *Traité du Contrat de Vente*.

[76] The edition most often used is the second, as revised by D.M. Walker (Edinburgh: University Presses of Edinburgh and Glasgow, 1981).

[77] As reprinted by the Stair Society, Edinburgh, Vols. 41–43, 1993–1995.

[78] 8th edn. by J.B. Nicholson (Edinburgh: Bell and Bradfute, 1871).

[79] 7th edn. by J. McLaren (Edinburgh: T. and T. Clark, 1870).

[80] The last edition by Bell himself was the 4th, although a further six followed at the hand of different editors. The 4th has recently been reprinted (Edinburgh: Edinburgh Legal Education Trust, 2010).

[81] *Baron David Hume's Lectures 1786–1822*, ed. G.C.H. Paton (Edinburgh: Stair Society Vols. 5, 13, 15–19, 1939–1958) and Henry Home, Lord Kames' *Principles of Equity* (Edinburgh: A. Kincaid and J. Bell, 1760), have not been universally recognised as Institutional in status, but in practice are accorded similar respect.

[82] For overview, see Cairns, "Historical Introduction", note 10 supra, 170–171, and for more detailed treatment see J.W. Cairns, "Institutional Writings in Scotland Reconsidered" *Journal of Legal History* 4 (1983) 76. Indeed one twentieth century writer maintained that "the authority of an institutional writer is approximately equal to that of a decision by a Division of the Inner House of the Court of Session" (T.B. Smith, *A Short Commentary on the Law of Scotland* (Edinburgh: W. Green, 1962) 32).

[83] [2012] UKSC 50.

16.4 Sources of Law in Specific Subject Areas

16.4.1 Property Law

Until recently the main source of property law was in case law and custom, and the Institutional writings have continued to inform the development of the law.[84] However, the transfer, mortgaging and registration of land ownership has been the subject of detailed legislation in recent years, including the Conveyancing and Feudal Reform (Scotland) Act 1970, the Land Registration (Scotland) Act 1979, and the Requirements of Writing (Scotland) Act 1995. Since devolution, as noted in Sect. 16.2 above, the Scottish parliament has enacted a further raft of statutory provisions in relation to land law, many of which have followed on from the abolition of feudal tenure by the Abolition of Feudal Tenure etc. (Scotland) Act 2000, including the Title Conditions (Scotland) Act 2003, the Tenements (Scotland) Act 2004, and the Land Reform (Scotland) Act 2003.

The framework of Scots property law is civilian, as is indicated by the Roman law origins of its fundamental concepts: dominium, real rights, *traditio*, possession, *accessio*.[85] Like the systems of Continental Europe (and following Roman law), but unlike England, Scots law makes a fundamental distinction between rights against a person, or personal rights, and rights in things, or real rights. Scotland follows the civilian pattern of having a fixed list of real rights, the main items on which are: ownership; liferent (or usufruct); lease; servitude; and rights in security.

On the other hand, the civilian basis of property law has not prevented Scotland from developing the institution of the trust. Its rules contained part in custom and case law and part in statute,[86] The trust has existed in Scots law since earliest times as an arrangement by which one person manages assets for another. However, its basic structure is fundamentally different from that of the English trust. Scots law does not recognise the division between law and equity, and so cannot divide ownership into legal and equitable categories as is done in English trust law: "in a Scottish trust there is separation of patrimony without separation of personality; and from this fundamental idea many of the consequences of trust flow".[87] The Scots trustee has the right of ownership over trust assets. The trustee's estate is therefore divided into an ordinary patrimony and a trust patrimony, and the latter is immune to the claims of the trustee's personal creditors. The trustee stands in a fiduciary relationship towards the beneficiaries, who, in turn, have a personal right against the trustee. The origins of the Scots trust are not clear. English trust law has been influential,

---

[84] For detailed treatment see K. Reid, "Property Law: Sources and Doctrine", *History of Private Law in Scotland,* ed. Reid and Zimmermann, note 10 supra, vol 1, 185.

[85] K.G.C. Reid, *The Law of Property* (Edinburgh: Butterworths, 1996) para 2.

[86] Notably the Trusts (Scotland) Act 1921, Trusts (Scotland) Act 1961, For a full account see W.A. Wilson and A.G.M. Duncan, *Trusts, Trustees and Executors*, 2nd edn. (Edinburgh: W Green, 1995).

[87] K.G.C. Reid, "National Report for Scotland", in *Principles of European Trust Law*, ed. DJ Hayton et al., (The Hague: Kluwer, 1999) 67 at 68.

but mainly after the mid-nineteenth century, by which time the basic framework of the Scots trust was already settled.[88] A few Scottish authorities recognise the existence of the constructive trust and the associated technique of tracing in Scots law, but the nature, extent and policy justification of the reception are uncertain and controversial.[89]

16.4.2 Succession Law

The law on testate succession (where there is a will) remains specific to Scotland and is largely based on the common law, in the sense of custom and precedent, rather than statute. The law of intestate succession (where there is no will) is for the most part contained in a statute specific to Scotland, the Succession (Scotland) Act 1964. As in most civilian systems, Scots law retains a fixed share of the moveable estate for children and spouses and same-sex partners in testate succession irrespective of the Will,[90] contrasting with the English principle of freedom of testation as qualified by the Inheritance (Provision for Family and Dependants) Act 1975. However, a recent statutory reform has also introduced a discretionary entitlement, similar to that provided under the English legislation, for the unmarried cohabitants of deceased persons.[91]

16.4.3 Contract Law

In contract law similarly (and in the law of unjustified enrichment), the main source is case law and custom. Increasingly in recent years, however, statute has been introduced, often to mitigate difficulties of inequalities of bargaining power in consumer law, as discussed further below, for instance in the Consumer Credit Act 1974, the Unfair Contract Terms Act 1977, and the Equality Act 2010 (outlawing discrimination in contract). The Contract (Scotland) Act 1997 deals with certain matters of interpretation. The Sale of Goods has also been substantially codified by

---

[88] See G. Gretton "Trusts", in *History of Private Law in Scotland,* ed. Reid and Zimmermann, note 10 supra, vol 1, 480; Scottish Law Commission, Discussion Paper on *The Nature and Constitution of Trusts* (Scot Law Com DP No 133, 2006) (available at http://www.scotlawcom.gov.uk/law-reform-projects/trusts/)

[89] See G. Gretton "Constructive Trusts" (in two parts) *Edinburgh Law Review* 1 (1997) 281 and 408.

[90] For discussion of the Scots rules on *legitim*, and their *ius commune* origins see the judgment of the Lord Ordinary, Lord Fraser, in *Earl of Kintore v Countess Dowager of Kintore* (1884) 11 Rettie 1013 (affirmed (1886) 13 Rettie (HL) 93). For extension of "legal rights" to same-sex civil partners see Civil Partnership Act 2004, s 131.

[91] Family Law (Scotland) Act 2006, s 29.

the Sale of Goods Act 1979 (a UK statute succeeding the Sale of Goods Act 1893).[92] And matters relating to electronic commerce are governed by the Electronic Commerce Act 2000 implementing the Directive on Electronic Signatures 1999/93/ EC.

English influence on the law of contract has been substantial, particularly from the nineteenth century onwards, and English authorities have been used extensively.[93] However, the main feature of Scots contract law by which it is distinguished from English law is the absence of the doctrine of consideration.[94] Thus Scots law recognises and enforces gratuitous unilateral promises, provided that their existence can be proved in the proper way,[95] and offers may be recognised as irrevocable in certain circumstances. Like European systems,[96] Scotland accords to third parties substantial rights of enforcement in relation to contracts entered into by others (the important of the doctrine of "privity" in English contract law has meant that limited third party rights have only relatively recently been recognised).[97] Finally, in Scots law, unlike in English or American law but like in European systems, "specific implement" (i.e. a court order ordaining the other party to fulfill its contractual obligations) is the primary remedy in contract.[98] The rules on contractual capacity and on formal validity also remain distinct.

As noted above, these rules are largely embodied in precedent rather than in codifying statute, and there is no statutory embodiment of a general theory of contract. However, certain limited areas of the law of contract have been the subject of more or less comprehensive statutory provision.

As noted above, the law governing sale of goods is to a large extent contained in the Sale of Goods Act 1979. (Sale of immovables is still governed to a large extent by case law and custom, although specific statutory provisions govern the execution of deeds in relation thereto,[99] some matters of conveyancing practice, and registration of title).[100]

One of the oldest "codifying" statutes was the Leases Act 1449, a statute of the pre-Union Parliament of Scotland, and indeed this remains the source which sets

---

[92] As amended by the Sale and Supply of Goods Act 1994 and the Sale and Supply of Goods to Consumers Regulations 2002, with additional consumer protection contained in the Unfair Contract Terms Act 1977, and the Consumer Credit Act 1974 as amended by the Consumer Credit Act 2006.

[93] See W.W. McBryde, *The Law of Contract in Scotland*, 3rd edn (Edinburgh: W. Green, 2007) paras 1–21 – 1–27. For detailed treatment see in *History of Private Law in Scotland,* ed. Reid and Zimmermann, note 10 supra, vol 2, containing chapters on formation of contract, interpretation, error, force and fear, pacta illicita, unfair contract terms, breach, specific implement, third party rights, and restrictive covenants.

[94] For a comparative law discussion see K. Zweigert and H. Kötz, *Introduction to Comparative Law*, 3rd edn, tr T. Weir (Oxford: Oxford University Press, 1998) 389–99.

[95] See Requirements of Writing (Scotland) Act s 2.

[96] See Zweigert and Kötz, *Introduction to Comparative Law*, note 94 supra, 456–469.

[97] Contracts (Rights of Third Parties) Act 1999.

[98] See, e.g. *Highland and Universal Properties Ltd v Safeway Properties Ltd* 2000 SC 297.

[99] Requirements of Writing (Scotland) Act 1995.

[100] Land Registration (Scotland) Act 1979.

out the fundamental principles underlying the contract of lease. Needless to say, much of the detail has been added by case law and custom over the years, and precedent is an important source of the law in relation to modern leases.[101] However, statute has taken over in relation to certain specific types of lease. The law relating to agricultural holdings, for example, is governed by the Agricultural Holdings (Scotland) Act 2003.[102] Residential leases are governed a series of enactments, including the Housing (Scotland) Acts 1987, 1988, 2001, and 2006.

Contracts relating to consumer borrowing are subject to the Consumer Credit Act 1974, as amended by the Consumer Credit Act 2006. The procedure for the creation of a mortgage or hypothec over immovables (the "standard security") is provided by the Conveyancing and Feudal Reform (Scotland) Act 1970. There is no codifying statute in relation to guarantees ("caution" in Scots law), another area governed by custom and case law.

16.4.4 Consumer Law

There is no general theory of consumer contracts, or single document embodying consumer law in Scotland. However, there is a very considerable body of legislation modifying the general principles of contract law in relation to consumer contracts, protecting the consumer in the light of inequalities of bargaining power as compared with commercial contracting parties. This will be outlined only briefly, as consumer law is an area which has not been devolved to the Scottish Parliament in terms of the Scotland Act, and is therefore common more or less throughout the UK.[103]

Consumer law has a long history,[104] but the modern era in consumer law is commonly traced to the publication of the Molony Report[105] in 1962, reviewing the legislative provision for consumer issues across the UK and proposing reform in various areas. The Trade Descriptions Act 1968, a UK statute providing for criminal liability in relation to misdescription of goods, is one of the most notable products of the Molony Report's recommendations, although many others followed directly or indirectly. In the intervening half century, specific legislation has followed, in the

[101] See A. McAllister, *Scottish Law of Leases* 4th edn (Edinburgh: Bloomsbury Professional, 2010).

[102] With additional provision made in relation to "crofts" – small holdings in rural areas – by the Crofting Acts, most recently the Crofting Reform (Scotland) Act 2010.

[103] As discussed above. See Scotland Act 1998, Sch. 5. For the initial "Concordat" outlining the working arrangements between the Scottish Government and the UK Department of Trade and Industry, now the Department for Business, Innovation and Skills, see http://www.bis.gov.uk/files/file33008.doc

[104] The standard Scots textbook, W.C.H. Ervine, *Consumer Law in Scotland* 4th edn (Edinburgh: W. Green, 2008) narrates the historical background in chapter 1, pointing out that some of the earliest statutes of the Parliament of Scotland regulated matters such as weights and measures, and the policing of standards of safety for food and drugs has been the subject of legislation since the mid-nineteenth century.

[105] Final Report of the Committee on Consumer Protection (Cmnd 1781) (1962).

form of statutes on consumer safety,[106] consumer credit,[107] contractual clauses restricting liability,[108] and unfair marketing and advertising practices.[109]

In the latter part of the twentieth century various institutional structures have been provided to support the consumer, in the form of the Office of Fair Trading, set up in London for the whole of the UK but with a Scottish office, by virtue of the Fair Trading Act of 1973, as well as the National Consumer Council, with an affiliated Scottish Consumer Council, now replaced by Consumer Focus and Consumer Focus Scotland. There has also been a rise in self-regulation in relation to provision of various areas of consumer services. Codes of practice, with related complaints procedures have been set up by the relevant industries, again usually on a UK-wide basis. These include a wide range of different spheres, from the Association of British Travel Agents' Code of Practice, to the Credit Services Association Code of Practice and even the Private Investigators UK Code of Conduct.

16.4.5 Delict

The main source of the law of Delict is likewise case law and custom. Over the course of the twentieth century, however, statute has been used increasingly to codify specific discrete areas of liability, such as the Animals (Scotland) Act 1987, and the Occupiers' Liability (Scotland) Act 1960. There has also been legislation to rationalise the law of damages, recently reenacted in the Damages (Scotland) Act 2011. At UK level there been a number of enactments concerning safety in the workplace; the Workman's Compensation Acts of 1897 onwards and subsequent legislation regarding industrial injuries have applied to England and Wales also, as did, for example, the Employer's Liability (Defective Equipment) Act 1969, and the Manual Handling Operations Regulations 1992. A number of general UK statutes provide for strict liability in relation to well-defined hazards, such as the Civil Aviation Act 1982 or the Nuclear Installations Act 1965. European law has provided a further impetus for statutory reform, most notably in Part I of the Consumer Protection Act 1987, a UK statute which implements the Product Liability Directive 85/374/EEC.

---

[106] Consumer Protection Act 1987, Part 1, (UK statute) implementing the Product Liability Directive 85/374/EEC (reinforced in terms of public law regulation by the General Product Safety Regulations 2005/1803).

[107] Consumer Credit Act 1974, (UK statute) a lengthy statute supplemented by numerous items of delegated legislation with regard to specific areas of control.

[108] Unfair Contract Terms Act 1977 (UK statute).

[109] The Trade Descriptions Act 1968, providing for criminal liability in relation to misdescription of goods has been supplemented by a variety of enactments, in some cases providing for criminal liability in specific circumstances (e.g., the Consumer Protection Act 1987, s 20, on misleading prices, and the Property Misdecriptions Act 1991), others providing for private law remedies (e.g., the Consumer Protection (Distance Selling) Regulations 2000/2334 provide that it is an offence to demand payment for unsolicited goods). See also the Enterprise Act 2002, Part 8, which gives various public bodies power to obtain orders restricting the activities of traders.

As far as the relationship between Scots and English law is concerned, the "intellectual superstructure" of the law of delict remains distinct from that of the law of tort.[110] Nonetheless, there has been very substantial interaction between Scots and English law. In the hugely important area of the law of negligence (liability for accidental, non-intentional harm) there has been convergence to the point where the foundation for the modern law of negligence in the English and other common law systems is the 1932 Scots case of *Donoghue v Stevenson*,[111] and there are now few areas of significant cross-border difference. It is open to question whether English or Scots law was the more influential in this process,[112] but in practice Scots and English authorities are used more or less interchangeably in the law of negligence. However, the intentional delicts have been far less susceptible to common law influence and interaction. The "delinquences" or injuries identified by the Institutional writers as giving rise to a claim for reparation[113] still form the basis for the modern Scots law on assault, deprivation of liberty, and defamation and have retained a framework and a terminology strongly influenced by their civilian origins.[114]

16.4.6 Commercial Law

There is no Commercial Code as such in Scots law. However, as indicated above in Sect. 16.2, over the second half of the nineteenth century, a considerable body of the Commercial law of Scotland underwent a revision process in order both to modernise it and to align it with English law. Economic and political partnership with England in the nineteenth century meant that there was a natural tendency to draw on English law as a source of legal models, as well as a desire on the part of many Scots businessmen to harmonise commercial laws with those of England and the Empire, so that "so far from there being any plot by English lawyers to impose their law on Scots law, if it had been left to the English lawyers, this commercial legislation would almost certainly have applied to England and Wales only."[115]

In 1814 a committee of London businessmen was formed to report on a Bill that would reform Scots bankruptcy laws.[116] The focus broadened from bankruptcy to

[110] See H.L. MacQueen and W.D.H. Sellar "Negligence", in *History of Private Law in Scotland,* ed. Reid and Zimmermann, note 10 supra, vol 2, 515 at 547.

[111] 1932 SC (HL) 31; [1932] A.C. 562.

[112] See A. Rodger, "Lord MacMillan's speech in *Donoghue v Stevenson*" *Law Quarterly Review* 108 (1992) 236, also R Evans-Jones, "Roman Law in Scotland and England and the development of one law for Britain" *Law Quarterly Review* 115 (1999) 605 at 618–628.

[113] See, e.g., Stair, *Institutions*, 1.9.4 (note 76 supra).

[114] See J Blackie, "Unity in diversity: the history of personality rights in Scots law", in *Rights of Personality in Scots Law: A Comparative Perspective*, ed. N R Whitty and R Zimmermann, (Dundee: Dundee University Press, 2009), 31.

[115] Rodger, "The Codification of Commercial Law", note 51 supra, at 572.

[116] *Report of the London Committee on the Scotch Bankrupt Bill* (London: W. and S. Graves, 1814).

other areas of mercantile law and a Royal Commission was set up in 1853 in order to investigate which of the Mercantile Laws of Great Britain and Ireland could be assimilated.[117] This led to the enactment of the Mercantile Law Amendment Act 1856 in England and Wales and the Mercantile Law Amendment (Scotland) Act 1856, which introduced limited reform with regard to sale, cautionary obligations (sureties), bills of exchange, and liability of carriers. These Acts changed English law and Scots law without making them the same. Though witnesses could give the Commission few actual examples of inconveniences caused to businessmen by national differences, further assimilation was favoured not only by the business community but also by legal practitioners and academics.[118] Generally speaking, new areas of regulation which had a clear cross-border dimension, such as company law, developed on a mainly British basis during the nineteenth century.

Later, some of the important legislation drafted for England was also applied to Scotland, including statutes which effectively "codified" much of commercial law in the late nineteenth century. Most of the provisions of the Bills of Exchange Act 1882, presented by its draftsman as "An Experiment in Codification",[119] applied both to Scotland and to England. Similarly, the Sale of Goods Bill drafted by Chalmers and introduced to Parliament in 1889 was extended to Scotland before its enactment in 1893. The Partnership Act 1890, drafted by Sir Frederick Pollock, was also applied to Scotland, although certain fundamental Scots principles were left intact, such as the partnership having a personality separate from its partners. In more recent times, the floating charge was imported into Scots law by the Companies (Floating Charges) (Scotland) Act 1961.

The assimilation of English law was not without problems, in so far as the imported commercial laws interacted with the Scots framework of property and obligations.[120] However, this raft of commercial law reform has provided the basis for modern commercial law. The Bills of Exchange Act 1882 and the Partnership Act 1890 remain in force. The Sale of Goods Act 1893 has been replaced by the Sale of Goods Act 1979, another statute common to the UK. Company law has been in effect codified for the whole of the UK, the current legislation being the Companies Act 2006, a comprehensive statute comprised of 1297 sections and 16 Schedules. The insurance industry is regulated by a series of modern statutes common to the UK, including the Insurance Companies Act 1982, the Financial Services Act 1986, the Policyholders Protection Act 1975, and the Insurance Brokers (Registration) Act 1977, as well as having submitted itself to various extra-statutory

---

[117] *First Report of the Commissioners Appointed to Inquire and Ascertain how far the Mercantile Laws in the Different Parts of the United Kingdom of Great Britain and Ireland may be Advantageously Assimilated* (London: Her Majesty's Stationery Office, 1854).

[118] See Rodger "The Codification of Commercial Law", note 51 supra, at 576–7.

[119] M. Chalmers, "An Experiment in Codification" *Law Quarterly Review* 2 (1886) 125.

[120] Thus, for example, the appropriateness of the some of the changes made to the Scots law of sale by the introduction of the 1893 statute has been questioned, e.g., the Act applied the English rule that ownership passed with the contract, as distinct from the Scots rule by which ownership passed on delivery. There is a large literature on this subject, but see e.g. T.B. Smith, *Property Problems in Sale* (London: Sweet and Maxwell, 1978).

codes of practice.[121] Much of modern commercial law thus rests on statute common to the UK as a whole, but there is little sign of any initiative to draw this now vast body of legislation together into a single Commercial Code.

16.4.7 Family Law

Although there is no Code as such, Family Law is in effect codified by a series of interconnected modern statutes, mostly specific to Scotland.[122] While case law is of course regularly cited in family law litigation, this is for the most part in order to elucidate the rules contained in statute, rather than as a source of fundamental principle. Legislation is the primary source in this area of the law, but in the form of discrete enactments, rather than a comprehensive code.

The basic rules relating to the ceremony of marriage are contained in the Marriage (Scotland) Act 1977, and rules relating to Civil Partnerships (for same-sex couples) in the Civil Partnership Act 2004 (a UK statute in which provisions relating to Scotland were included, although, as noted above, the Scottish Government has recently consulted on the possible enactment of legislation specific to Scotland enabling same-sex marriage).[123] The consequences of marriage or Civil Partnership in terms of property relationships are provided for in the Family Law (Scotland) Act 1985, Where the matrimonial home is owned by one partner only, occupancy rights are created by the Matrimonial Homes (Family Protection) (Scotland) Act 1981. Procedure on divorce (or dissolution of a civil partnership) is set out in the Divorce (Scotland) Act 1976 (or Civil Partnership Act 2004), with details rules on the division of property contained in the Family Law (Scotland) Act 1985.

Cohabitation gives only limited legal rights to the parties, perhaps the most important of which is a right to seek financial provision from the other partner on the breakdown of the relationship, as provided for in the Family Law (Scotland) Act 2006, s 28. On the death of the first partner without a will, there is also a right to the surviving partner to seek financial provision at the discretion of the court, as set out in the Family Law (Scotland) Act 2006, s 29.

The detail of parental rights and responsibilities is set out in the Children (Scotland) Act 1995, with the child's right to aliment (material support) set out in the Family Law (Scotland) Act 1985 s 1. The law relating to adoption has recently been reenacted in the Adoption and Children (Scotland) Act 2007. The age at which children are deemed to have capacity to enter into legal relationships is set out in the Age of Legal Capacity (Scotland) Act 1991.

---

[121] See Association of British Insurers' Codes of Practice (available at http://www.abi.org.uk/information/codes_and_guidance_notes/codes_and_guidance_notes.aspx).

[122] For an assessment of the first decade of law making by the Scottish Parliament in matters of Family Law see E Sutherland, "Child and Family Law", in *Law Making and the Scottish Parliament*, ed. E. Sutherland, note 55 supra, 58.

[123] See http://scotland.gov.uk/Publications/2011/09/05153328/0

16.5 The Impact of Human Rights upon Private Law

Much of the constitutional framework for the devolved, post-1999 Scotland is set out in the Scotland Act 1998. This legislation limits the competence of the Scottish Parliament so that it may not make legislation incompatible with the Convention (s. 29(1)(d)), and also requires the Scottish Government to act compatibly with the Convention. In addition, the Human Rights Act 1998, a statute binding the whole of the UK, "brought home"[124] the rights enshrined in the European Convention on Human Rights into UK domestic law as of 2 October 2000.[125] The assimilation of Convention rights into domestic law has important consequences primarily as a check on the powers of public authorities, so that the content of Convention rights may be relevant in determining, for example, the circumstances in which a public authority may interfere with a person's right to property in terms of Article 1 of the First Protocol ECHR, or the scope of a public authority's duty of care where it is alleged that its negligence in fulfilling statutory obligations has resulted in injury to the individual.[126]

However, Convention rights may also be relevant to disputes between private entities. The Articles of the Convention cannot be directly invoked as the sole basis of a claim between private parties, but it is accepted that the courts are themselves public authorities for the purposes of the Human Rights Act 1998, and are thus required to act compatibly with Convention rights not only in deciding cases brought against public bodies but also in resolving disputes between private parties.[127] The courts' duty is to develop the common law in a manner which takes account of ECHR standards. Thus the values embodied in the Convention may in practice be "as much applicable in disputes between individuals or between an individual and a non-governmental body such as a newspaper as they are in disputes between individuals and a public authority".[128] Indeed in certain areas where the common law and the Convention alike are concerned to protect the individual's "autonomy, dignity and self-esteem"[129] it has been said that the Articles of the Convention,

---

[124] According to Lord Irvine of Lairg, the then Lord Chancellor, House of Lords Debates, 3 Nov 1997, col 1228, echoing the Labour Party's 1997 manifesto pledge. See also the UK Government White Paper, *Rights Brought Home: The Human Rights Bill* Cm 3782 (London: H.M.S.O., 1997).

[125] For general discussion see A. O'Neill, "Human Rights and People and Society", in *Law Making and the Scottish Parliament*, ed. E. Sutherland, note 55 supra, 35.

[126] For recent discussion see *Mitchell v Glasgow City Council* 2009 SC (HL) 21; [2009] 1 AC 874, although there was held to be no duty in that case.

[127] For a more detailed introduction to the application of Convention rights in domestic law, see R. Reed and J. Murdoch, *A Guide to Human Rights Law in Scotland*, 3rd edn (Haywards Heath: Bloomsbury, 2011) ch 1; see also *Attorney General's Reference No 3 of 1999* [2009] UKHL 34; [2010] 1 AC 145 per Lord Hope at para. 18–19, Lord Brown at para 54.

[128] *Campbell v MGN* [2004] 2 AC 457 at para 17 per Lord Nicholls.

[129] *Mosley v News Group Newspapers Ltd* [2008] EWHC 1777 (QB) at para 7 per Eady J.

have ceased to be "merely of persuasive or parallel effect" but have become "the very content" of the common law.[130]

Of course, many rights now enshrined in the Convention had long been the subject of statutory and common-law protection in any event. The right not to be wrongfully imprisoned or detained is an obvious example.[131] Indeed it has been suggested by one senior English judge that "the values to which the Convention gives effect are very much the same values that have been recognised by the common law for hundreds of years".[132] Nonetheless, significant areas of private law have been affected. It is suggested that Convention rights are relevant in deciding what terms might be implied in a contract, particularly a contract related to employment.[133] Reference to Article 1 of the First Protocol may be made in connection with the proposed exercise of contractual remedies that are disproportionate,[134] or with the use of oppressive measures to recover debt.[135] Delictual remedies for the misuse of private information have been shaped partly upon the common law, and partly upon the balancing of ECHR Article 8, protecting private life and reputation, and Article 10 protecting freedom of expression.[136] A similar balancing exercise between Articles 8 and 10 is performed in the law of defamation, where the defender claims to have spoken in a privileged context on a matter of public interest.[137]

16.6 Attitudes Towards Codification

Although Jeremy Bentham's *Codification Proposal* addressed, in 1822, to *All Nations Professing Liberal Opinions* went unanswered in England, nineteenth century codification was nonetheless to attract considerable attention in England

[130] *McKennitt v Ash* [2006] EWCA Civ 1714; [2008] QB 73 at para 11 per Buxton LJ, citing Lord Woolf CJ in *A v B plc* [2003] QB 195 at para 4.

[131] Stair observed, the right to personal liberty was "a most precious right" although it was "not absolute" (*Institutions*, I,2,5., note 76 supra). Although the harm inflicted by deprivation of liberty was said by Stair to be "inestimable" (*Institutions*, I,9,4), damages were awarded for infringement (*Institutions*, I,2,16). See also the Act of the Parliament of Scotland of 1701 "For preventing wrongous Imprisonments and against undue delayes in trials" (*Acts of the Parliament of Scotland*, X, 272–5 (c.6)).

[132] Lord Woolf, "European Court of Human Rights on the occasion of the opening of the judicial year" *European Human Rights Law Review* (2003) 257 at 258.

[133] McBryde, *Law of* Contract, note 93 supra, para 19–41.

[134] McBryde, *Law of* Contract, note 93 supra, para 19–42.

[135] See *Karl Construction Ltd v Palisade Properties Plc* 2002 SC 270. On the other hand one particular recommendation to reform trust law was discounted due to a possible conflict with Article 1 of the First Protocol: see Scottish Law Commission, Report on Variation and Termination of Trusts (Scot Law Com No 206, 2007) paras. 5.12–5.15, discussed at G. Gretton and A. Steven, *Property, Trusts and Succession* (Haywards Heath: Tottel, 2009), para 31.18.

[136] For more specific discussion see E. Reid, *Personality, Confidentiality and Privacy in Scots Law* (Edinburgh: W. Green, 2010) chapters 14 and 15.

[137] See *Adams v Guardian Newspapers Ltd* 2003 SC 425, endorsing the approach to qualified privilege adopted in *Reynolds v Times Newspapers Ltd* [2001] 2 AC 127.

and in Scotland. Many in the Scottish legal profession had taken a keen interest in codification projects not only in Europe but also in the British Empire, in particular in India. A volume of essays published in Edinburgh in 1893[138] reflected on the success of European codification as well as of the recent, more limited, codifications of British commercial law,[139] and presented codification as the practical "remedy" for a "chaotic state of matters" in Scotland and the United Kingdom as a whole, by which statute was heaped "upon state, case upon case – Pelion upon Ossa, and Ossa upon Olympus – till at length even the profession of lawyers becomes overwhelmed and unable to cope with the accumulated mass".[140] However, on both sides of the English border the legal community was divided on the viability of codification, and on the benefits of a Civil Code over the flexibility of the common law,[141] and in the end the proponents of codification failed to garner sufficient popular or political support to advance their project.

The issue of codification surfaced once again in the 1960s when a draft Code of contract law was drafted as a joint project for the English and Scottish Law Commissions, but although the draft itself was completed,[142] the Commissions failed to agree on a conclusion to the project. It is not clear why this project was not taken further, although it has been suggested that there was no firm intention to introduce a unitary law of contract at that stage. Rather this was a project undertaken in order to provide a starting point for negotiations on developing a common European law of contract.[143] Since that time both Scotland and England have participated in such European initiatives, but with separate representatives from north and south of the border.

As discussed in Sect. 16.2 above, the inauguration of the devolved Scottish Parliament in 1999 brought with it a flurry of legislative activity that has not yet abated, but it did not result in any new-found enthusiasm for codification, as illustrated by the fate of the draft Criminal Code for Scotland, completed in 2003 but never taken up by the Scottish legislature.[144] A project to prepare a Civil Code for Scotland has made even less progress and has not advanced beyond the drawing board.[145] Perhaps the codification project is now too complex, and therefore too

[138] H. Goudy, Ae. J.G. Mackay, and R. Vary Campbell, *Addresses on Codification of Law* (Edinburgh: Banks and Co, 1893); see also J. Dove Wilson, "Recent Progress of Codification" *Juridical Review* 3 (1891) 97.

[139] See Sect. 16.4.6. above.

[140] H. Goudy, "Codification: Its Meaning and History", in *Addresses on Codification*, note 138 supra, 7 at 12.

[141] See A. Craig, "Codification of the Law", in two parts, *Journal of Jurisprudence* 26 (1882) 281and 337.

[142] H. McGregor, *A Contract Code: Drawn up on behalf of the English Law Commission* (Milan: Giuffrè/Sweet and Maxwell, 1993).

[143] See comments in Lord Hope of Craighead, "The role of the Judge in developing Contract Law", speech to the Contract Law Conference, Jersey, 15 Oct 10, available at http://www.supremecourt.gov.uk/docs/speech_101015.pdf.

[144] See Sect. 16.2. above.

[145] See E. Clive, "Current Codification Projects in Scotland" *Edinburgh Law Review* 4 (2000) 341; E. Clive, "Thoughts from a Scottish perspective on the bicentenary of the French Civil Code" *Edinburgh Law Review* 8 (2004) 415.

ambitious, for any individual state to undertake successfully, especially when it is as small as Scotland, and especially when there is no obvious political imperative to carry it forward. But while the would-be codifiers have good reason for discouragement at home, their attention has now shifted from local initiatives to the possibility of a European Civil Code. There has been considerable Scottish interest and participation in the working groups which prepared the *Principles of European Contract Law*, the *Principles of European Trust Law*, the *European Civil Code Project*, and the *Draft Common Frame of Reference*.[146] The Scottish experience serves as a reminder there, if a reminder were needed, that characteristics thought to be unique to the common law or to the civil law can not only coexist within one legal system but also develop in a way which is positive and dynamic. The Scots presence in these European arenas also demonstrates that that a smaller legal system is inevitably altered, but need not sacrifice its identity, by joining a larger political unit.

[146] And for a Scottish Law Commission project to consider Scots contract law in light of the DCFR see http://www.scotlawcom.gov.uk/law-reform-projects/contract-law-in-light-of-the-draft-common-frame-of-reference-dcf/.

Chapter 17
Is It Possible for a Minor Code of the Nineteenth Century to Serve as a Model in the Twenty-First Century?

Gabriel García Cantero

Abstract The 1889 Spanish Civil Code, belonging to the *Civil Law* and of a clear French inspiration, is a minor code in the big continental Romano-Germanic family, late adopted owing to domestic political reasons, which failed to satisfactorily solve the so called *foral problem* (or Proper Civil Law, surviving for historical reasons in many territories), to which article 149.1.8 of the Constitution in force gives a generous solution. The Code was enacted after the 1885 Commercial Code, which was deemed as *special law*, compared to the common or general law of the Civil Code, and was based on the old-fashioned theory of the act of commerce. The Code included the provisions of Private International Law and was supplemented by a number of special laws. In 1973, the Preliminary Title was modernized by clearly outlining the role of case law and by developing legal interpretation techniques, as well as the private international law system. Family law and succession were deeply modified by the 1978 Constitution. Since 1985, it has become part of the European Union, and it has incorporated to its provisions the Communitarian Law, highly important in relation to the protection to consumers. Civil doctrine was originally inspired in the French and Italian doctrine of the nineteenth century, but it is through the Italian doctrine that it has received a strong influence of the German Dogmatic. As from the end of the twentieth century, it has also been sensitive to the *Common Law*, especially from the United States of America. It is also open to the unification movement in Europe and, in general, to the comparative law.

Keywords Civil law • Romano-Germanic family • Spanish sub-family or micro-systems • Decodification and recodification • 1978 Spanish Constitution: art. 149.1.8 • Civil Law of general application and Foral Law • Role of special laws • Autonomous regions and communities • Communitarian Law • Unification of the European Contractual Law • Consumer Law

G. García Cantero (✉)
University of Zaragoza, Departamento de Derecho Privado,
Private Law Department, Civil Law, Zaragoza, Spain
e-mail: ggarcia@unizar.es

J.C. Rivera (ed.), *The Scope and Structure of Civil Codes*, Ius Gentium: Comparative Perspectives on Law and Justice 32, DOI 10.1007/978-94-007-7942-6_17,

17.1 Overview of the Private Law Legislation in Spain

Spain belongs to the *Civil Law* system based on the existence of civil codes, which is in force in all the States of the European continent (excluding the special case of the Scandinavian countries,[1] due to the doubts arisen). Our Commercial Code was enacted in 1885 and has not been derogated yet, although its most relevant matters (companies, bills or Exchange, insolvency) are ruled outside the code by special laws; furthermore, it is important to point out that this code is the second Spanish code in the commercial area (the first was drafted by SAINZ DE ANDINO in 1829), and both codes originated in the provisions of article 258 of the 1812 Constitution: "The Civil and Criminal Codes as well as the Commercial Code shall be the same in all the Monarchy".

The Civil Code was enacted in 1889[2] and was regarded as the late product of the European codification movement of a French inspiration, because it chronologically followed all the Italian pre-unitarian codes (especially the codes of Piedmont and Naples) and also the first 1865 Italian Civil Code, the Rumanian Code of the same year, the 1867 Portuguese Civil Code and in the United States of America, the first Code of the French colony of Louisiana in 1825; and the Spanish legislator took also into account Ibero-American codes (especially the 1855 Chilean Code and the 1869 Argentinean Code), but did not forget to include certain isolated principles inspired in the 1811 Austrian General Civil Code.

The Spanish Civil Code is not at all a pure and simple copy of the French Civil Code. Specially in matters such as family law, it acknowledges the legal effects of the canonic marriage and it did not originally accept the divorce; regarding hereditary succession, it was directly inspired in Roman Law in the concepts *heres* and *successio in universum ius*; as to the acquisition of property, it accepts the theory of *titulus* and *modus acquirendi*, developed by the German school of the *Usus modernus pandectarum*. There are, of course, articles that directly reflect the Napoleon's Code (approximately, less than half), but sometimes it receives the French law through the 1865 Italian Civil Code. Having been trained in conservative political years, the legislator first undertakes to codify the Spanish traditional law mainly by making use of the Civil Code Draft introduced by García Goyena in 1851, and also by taking into account solutions found in the modern codes to the new problems arising in the Spanish society, but on the condition that they be accepted by the qualified doctrine. We should bear in mind that García Goyena had done a great job in Comparative Law[3] using in his last draft the recent codes in force at that time (in addition to the

---

[1] See my paper, "El Sistema Jurídico de los países nórdicos", *Revista Jurídica del Notariado (Madrid)*, núm. 72 October-December 2009, p. 489 ff.

[2] The Civil Doctrine uses the historical stages already established by De Castro (1949, pp. 185–210) in addition to the works of Laso Gayte (1970), Gacto Fernández (1979), and especially of Peña and Bernaldo De Quirós on the Bill of 1882–1888, which was restated with notes and a preliminary study in *Publicaciones del Centenario de la Ley del Notariado* (Madrid 1965).

[3] Modern doctrine attributes to García Goyena a relevant role in the civil codification process in Spain (despite the criticism he receives from the *foralists*) and is highly regarded in Ibero – America (De Los Mozos, 1977, p. 242).

French Civil Code and the Italian pre-unitarian codes, the codes of some Swiss Cantons, the 1825 Code of Louisiana and even the BGB Austrian Code and on some occasions the *Codex bavaricus civilis*, and the 1794 Prussian Civil Code).

The legislative process for the drafting of the 1889 Civil Code was very slow and sometimes eventful. Since the beginning of the nineteenth century, and in accordance with the provisions of the 1812 Constitution, the Government had written various drafts of the Civil Code (in 1821 and 1838, among others) which failed due to a number of reasons: the political instability, the absence of a civil doctrine qualified to draft a code and also because of the resistance of some territories which had their own civil law, partly encouraged by the doctrine of the School of SAVIGNY (this refers to what is generally known as the *problem of foral law*, which will be dealt with later).

The Spanish Civil Code was enacted too late for the new Ibero-American countries, which had gained political independence in the first years of the nineteenth century, to use as a precedent to draft their own codes. However, from the perspective of the twenty-first century, and the modesty of a second line of comparative importance, the 1889 Civil Code had certain influence outside Europe: it was in force in Cuba (Spanish colony emancipated in 1898) up to the enactment of the 1985 Civil Code of communist inspiration (which, however, on several occasions had the old Spanish law embedded or abstract); it is still in force in Puerto Rico (a free state associated to USA), with modifications, but in the external context of the *Common Law*, giving rise to a complex mixed legal system. Such is the case of the Philippines Islands with the 1949 Civil Code, which literally or partially restates the old 1889 Spanish Civil Code, in force during the occupation by the United States, in 80 % of its content. It could be argued that there exists a reduced legal sub-family – or micro system – of Spanish origin within the big Romano-Germanic family.[4]

Regarding its content, the Spanish Civil Code is inspired in the division of subjects instituted by the French Civil Code, but with some modifications: After the preliminary book devoted to the effects of the law and the conflict of laws, Book I deals with physical and legal persons and the personal relations in the family (marriage, paternity, maintenance, adoption, guardianship, age majority and emancipation). Book II deals with assets, property and the modifications pertaining to them. In addition to the classification of assets, it rules property, roman community property, possession, usufruct, right of use and habitation, easements, the Property Registry (making reference to the special law). Book III covers all the different ways to acquire property (occupancy, donation and *mortis causa* inheritance). As opposed to the French Code, this has a book IV on Obligations and Contracts. There is a Title dealing with the obligations in general and another on the general theory of contracts; and the subsequent titles cover the economic regime of marriage, the sales contract, the barter, the annuity contract, the company agreement, the agency, the loan agreement, the contract of deposit, the aleatory contract, the trust, the pledge, the mortgage and antichresis, the quasi contract, the extracontractual responsibility, the preferred credits and statutes of limitations. To sum up: 1976 articles, 13 temporary provisions and 4 additional provisions.

[4] I supported this idea in my paper "Significado del Cc cubano del 1987 en el proceso de codificación", *Estudios de Derecho comparado* (Zaragoza 2010) p. 153.

17.2 Other Than the Civil Code, There Exist Other Statutes or Codes in Many Spanish Territories (Aragon, Navarre, Basque Country, Catalonia, Balearic Islands, Galicia, Valencia). The Appearance of the "Foral Problem" and the Solution Given by the 1978 Constitution (Art. 149.1.8). The Autonomic Civil Law

In fact, in Spain, and together with the 1889 Civil Code, there exist other laws or even civil codes in force in certain territories (known as *territories of special civil law or foral law*). The Civil Code of Catalonia of 2004 and the Code of Foral Law of Aragon of 2011 (other codes could be enacted in the future) and also civil laws of the Basque Country, Balearic Islands, Galicia and Valencia. All this is due to historical reasons.[5]

Even when the civil law at the time of the Romans, when the Iberian Peninsula was divided into provinces of the Empire (*Tarraconensis*, *Betica*, *Lusitania*), was relatively uniform to all its inhabitants, the Visigoth conquest brought about the end of the legislative unit and the application of either Roman Law or German Law to the citizens (both generally opposed legal systems), by virtue of the principle of personality of the law. Thus, the judge asked the parties in controversy: *Sub qua leges vivis*?, even though the *Lex romana wisigothorun* had attempted to legislatively unify the kingdom. The Muslim invasion in Spain at the beginning of the eighth century contributed to the political fragmentation of the country, which required a long term effort to recover the political power (the Reconquista ended in 1492 with the surrender of the Arabic kingdom of Grenade). At the beginning, it was the territory of Asturias that belonged to the kingdom of Leon which took over the battle against the Muslim invader, and then it was joined by Castile, Aragon and Navarra, with many historical alternatives, to restore the independency of this country which was called in texts and documents *Hispania or Spain*. The marriage between Isabel of Castile and Ferdinand of Aragon created a personal bond in the kingdom which set the foundations for the modern Spain. Up to the beginning of the eighteenth century, there was not a unity in private law, because the law applicable to the old inhabitants of the kingdom of Castile and the kingdom of Aragon (and their territories: Catalonia, Mallorca, Valencia) and of Navarre was their proper law, though in practice the real courts were more conversant with Roman Law, Castile Law and real law than foral law. After the war of the Spanish dynastic succession (there was one Austrian candidate and one French candidate), the King Philip V, who had defeated his opponent, failed to recognize at first the proper civil

[5] Bibliography on the foral problem is extensive. A brief exposition is that by Lacruz, *Elementos*, I-1 ° (Madrid 2002) pp. 79–106, dealing with the origins of the problem, the situation at the time of the codification, the solution first taken by the Civil Code, the "Appendices" of the 1931 Constitution, the "Compilations" and the enactment of the new Preliminary Title in 1974, the 1978 Constitution and the Statutes of Autonomy, the matters reserved "in all cases" to the State and the Civil Law of the Communities with their proper Civil Law.

law to those territories that had resisted, but shortly after he enacted the "Nueva Planta Decrees" ("*Decretos de la Nueva Planta*") (the title makes reference to the new organization of the courts in all the Spanish territory) partially restoring the old charters (*Fueros*) to such territories. Did the "Decrees", with exception of Navarre and the Basque Country, imply that the foral law precluded the State at the moment they were enacted without the possibility of changing them in the future. This gave rise to the appearance of the *foral problem*, which has been the object of various alternatives (especially when the 1889 Civil Code was enacted), up to the coming into force of the 1978 Constitution in which article 149 provides that the State has the exclusive jurisdiction in the matter of commercial, criminal and procedural law (article 6) as well as in civil law (rule 8). But, following this rule there is an exception, not properly written, which aroused many controversies before the Constitutional Court:

> Notwithstanding the conservation, modification and development by the Autonomous Communities of their civil, foral or special law, where they exist. In all cases, the rules pertaining to the application and efficacy of the legal statutes, to civil relations related to the forms of marriage, organization of registries and public instruments, to the basis for the contractual obligations, norms to resolve the conflict of laws and the definition of the sources of the law, referring in this last case to foral or special law.

According to article 149,3: *State law shall be, in all cases, supplementary to the Autonomous Communities.*

Anyway, could the law of the State supplement the law of the Autonomous Communities.

The 1978 Constitution was eager to definitely solve the *foral problem*, and in order to do that it outlined clear points, but in doing so it left aside or created other less clear issues:

> In the general framework of the exclusive jurisdiction of the State in the civil legislation (as in the case of the commercial, criminal or procedural legislation), an exception was made with respect to foral law, according to which the power to legislate such law is granted to the Autonomous Communities in which such law was already in force in 1978. Before the enactment of the Constitution, it was the central power that legislated the matter. As a result, in the future, we will not be able to submit any complaint or bring any dispute against the State on this issue: it is their business! We will be answered. However, it is necessary that the Autonomous Communities record this authority in their Statutes of Autonomy and act accordingly. In fact, by the time all Autonomous Communities effectively assumed such power in their Statutes, they also exercised this power as well as other constitutional powers detailed in article 148 of the Spanish Constitution. (for example, *social assistance*, which gave rise to abundant autonomous legislation in the matter of the protection of minors and of adoption).

Furthermore, foral law is far from being *frozen or hibernating* due to the fact that the Autonomous Communities have the competence to modify and develop it. However, in the exercise of this authority, there seems to be no limits to the Autonomous Communities. So, will the competence to legislate foral law be limitless? The Constitution lists a number of matters under the category of *minimal competence of the* State, to which other provisions of article 149 should be added as they are reserved *in all* cases to the State: 1st the regulation of the fundamental conditions to guarantee the equality of all the Spanish people in the exercise of their constitutional rights and compliance of their obligations; 2nd the nationality and the status of foreigners 5th the administration of justice; 9th Legislation on the intellectual and industrial property,; 11th credit, banking and insurance; 13th the basis and coordination of the general organization of the economic activity 25th the basis of the mining and electricity regulations.

More than 30 years after the Constitution was enacted, we have witnessed that the Constitutional Court in various decisions has favored a broad interpretation of the foral jurisdiction of the Autonomous Communities, so in many territories there has been a race to demand as soon as possible from the central power competences which have been many times the price paid for the support given to the etatic parties that were a minority in the Parliament in Madrid. A very important sector of the Spanish civil doctrine calls for a period of reflection to properly interpret and consolidate the text of article 149,1,8 of the Spanish Constitution.[6]

Many civilists believe that if the State had enacted the Civil Code more quickly, the legislative union would have been possible in the Spain of the nineteenth century,[7] as it was possible in France with the Napoleon's Code in spite of the importance of customary law or in Italy when the 1865 and 1942 codes were enacted notwithstanding the number of pre-unitarian codes, or in the federal countries such as Switzerland (in fact, a confederation of states) with the 1911 Civil Code, or in the German empire or the Austrian BGB despite the diffuse and fragmented political power existing at that time. Therefore, there was in Spain in the nineteenth century a missed opportunity. One could wonder: was it definite? It is hard to reach a conclusion. In fact, the systems of foral law are constitutionally *sub-systems* that constitutionally form part of the Spanish global civil law system. Though, it would be deliberate to accurately predict what will happen in the future in this system. Anyway, we will see later that the majority of the civil doctrine gives the Spanish Civil Code a central role in private law.

17.3 The Relation Between the Civil Code, the 1978 Constitution, European Community Law and Public International Law

In the old Spanish civil doctrine, there existed a certain *constitutional value of the Civil* Code and case law still acknowledges this concept (judgments of the Supreme Court on April 5th 1981, April 7th, 1987 and November 20th 1989). However, after the 1978 Constitution, the general framework has changed a lot and the Constitution, in its Title I, details the rights and obligations of the citizens and acknowledges their right to file an appeal for legal protection on the grounds of unconstitutionality

[6] See recent critics of Ragel, "Las Competencias legislativas en materia de Derecho y su deseable reforma constitucional", RDP, julio-agosto, 2005, p. 5 ff.

[7] In this sense Lacruz and *altri*, cit. p. 79.

(*recurso de amparo*) against a court judgment or their entitlement to an administrative resolution of their fundamental rights.

The Constitution is the supreme law which is in the summit of the Spanish legal system. According to article 9 °. 2 of the Constitution "The citizens and the public powers are subjected to the Constitution". The Constitutional Court is empowered to declare the unconstitutionality of the laws inconsistent with its provisions. The Constitution outlines the criteria to which they are subject and that must inspire all the other legal norms, including the Code and other foral or special laws (principle of hierarchy of the law article 9.3 of the Constitution). The Constitution states that an organic law will authorize that international treaties be entered into which will grant an international organization or institution the authority to exercise the competence resulting from it. The Constitution details the parliamentary procedure to follow in order that the international treaties could be part of the Spanish legal system. A typical case: The law of the Spanish Parliament that authorized the adhesion of our country to the North Atlantic Treaty Organization (NATO) or to the European Union.

Following the doctrine of Prof. GARCÍA DE ENTERRÍA, and making a distinction with the former constitutions, the constitutional text was given a direct and immediate legal efficacy. Therefore, and after the coming into effect of the 1978 Constitution, family law and succession law in the Civil Code (and also in Foral Laws) had to be immediately modified so that they be in agreement with the new constitutional principles of equality between men and women and the children born in or out of wedlock. Abundant case law of the Constitutional Court consecutively annulled certain provisions of the Civil Code and other civil laws which violated the principle of equality.

The current Spanish civil doctrine, following in special the Italian legal doctrine and the Argentinian doctrine, has accepted the concept of *constitutional civil law*.[8]

The relation between Communitarian Law (that is to say, the civil law originated in the legislative bodies of the European Union) and the Spanish Civil Law is complex due to the originality of its sources (for example, when a non-founding member joins the European Union – such was the case of Spain in 1985 – should it accept the entire community acquis, then the most relevant difference lies in the *Rules and Directives*.) Despite some initial objections on the part of some countries, these provisions are generally accepted: (1) The autonomy of Communitarian Law with respect to national laws; (2) The Communitarian Law is to be inserted into the legal system of each member State; (3) The Communitarian Law is supreme with respect to the laws of each member State; and (4) The supplementary character of communitarian law and the law of each State should be taken into consideration. The Court of Justice of the European Community also confirmed the supreme character of Communitarian Law, even above the constitutions of each member State and this doctrine was finally accepted by the German Constitutional Court in 1986 and the French Council of the State in 1989.

[8] On the Spanish doctrine: Arce Florez-Valdés (Madrid 1986), in the Argentine doctrine, Julio César Rivera, "El Derecho Privado constitucional", *Estudios de Derecho Privado* (1984–2005) (Buenos Aires, Santa Fe, 2006), pp. 741–766.

In general, it is important to point out that the Spanish Constitution was drafted taking into account the successive adhesion of Spain to the Human Rights Declaration in 1948 and other similar international treaties. Article 10.2 of the Spanish Constitution states: "The statutes related to the fundamental rights and freedoms that the Constitution recognizes shall be construed in accordance with the Universal Declaration of Human Rights and the international treaties and agreements on the same matter ratified by Spain". In a more concrete matter, article 39.4 of the Constitution states that "minors[9] shall be granted the protection set forth in the international agreements that herald their rights". The Constitution also includes a detailed procedure in articles 93–96 for the ratification of the international Treaties (applied, for example, to the adhesion of Spain to the EU).

17.4 Content of the Civil Code

I have briefly described the content of the Spanish Civil Code in number 1. In this paragraph I will make reference to the different roles that the *special laws* have historically had in Spain in the civil matter.

In the first period, and upon the failure of the Civil Code Draft of GARCÍA GOYENA, the government changed its strategy to enact special laws of *general application in the entire national territory to anticipate to the legislative unification*. This is the case of the 1861 Mortgage Law, the 1870 Civil Registry Law or the Laws pertaining to what is referred to as special property (water, mining and intellectual property). Despite its name, the 1861 Mortgage Law not only guarantees the real estate right, but it also creates for the first time the modern Property Registry that has permitted that Spain could pursue its first economic and industrial development. Inspired in the principle of the *protection of bona fide third parties*, it set the basis of a system in between France and German or Switzerland, which is still in force in our country and has been ruled by consecutive special laws inspired in the 1861 Law.[10] The regulation of a new public official (the *Property Registrar, equivalent to the Mortgage Registrar*), and also the 1862 Notarial Law by means of which another public official was created, the *Notary*. Both, the *Registrar* and the *Notary* have become the two pillars of the real estate business. At the moment the Civil Code was enacted, the idea to reproduce such special laws in there was rejected, due to its civil nature, and they limited to the inclusion of simple references or to mentioning some principles or to introducing some partial reforms (art. 332 about the

[9] The text in Spanish refers to *niños*, literal translation from the French text (*enfants*), and English (*children*). I prefer the terms *minors* (*of age*) as it is more accurate.

[10] In fact, the relation between the Civil Code and the Mortgage Law has always been a matter of debate: see the work of De La Rica Y Arenal, "Dualidad legislativa de nuestro régimen inmobiliario", AAMN, VII (Madrid 1953) p. 642 ff. About the genesis of the Law and this issue: Lacruz and *altri*, *Elementos*, vol. IIIa (Madrid 2003) p. 29 y ff, p. 35 y ff.

Law of Civil Registry of 1870; arts. 426 and 427 related to the mining property ruled by Law of 1868; arts. 428 and 429 related to the intellectual property also ruled by Law of 1879; arts. 605–608 related to the Property Registry. However, the ownership of the water represents an exception since articles 407–425 modified the 1879 Law of Water, though art.425 refers to it as subsidiary law. To complete this information, we should bear in mind that the Mortgage Law has been partially changed on a number of occasions, though maintaining its primitive system (the last reform was in 1944) and its Regulations; the 1870 Civil Registry Law was replaced and reformed in 1957, and finally amended by Law 20/2011, on July 21st 2011 so as to incorporate the new technologies, law which suffered a 3 years' delay to come into effect; and finally, relevant reforms occurred in the matters of the ownership of the water (2001), mining property (1973–2007) and intellectual property (1996–2007).

Considering that the Civil Code was enacted in 1889, it would be sensible that this centenary Code should be amended to adapt to the political, economic and social changes. To do so, there exist two legislative methods: either replacing the entire text of the Code for another one maintaining its primitive structure and even the article number, or the enactment of a special law separated from the Code. In this last case, there are two possibilities, including in the Code an express referral to the special Law or keeping silence with respect to it.

In my view, it will not be relevant to detail all the relevant reforms (about 50) of the Civil Code which took place throughout this historical period. But, I would like to stop at the most significant changes. Before the Civil War (1936–1939), the amendments to the Civil Code fell on special details. But, in 1939 the regime of absence (arts. 181–198) was deeply modified to give a solution to the number of missing persons who were not known to be living or death. The destruction of a large number of houses as a consequence of the war also inspired a new property regime of joint tenancy in article 396. In 1960, a special law was passed, the Condominium Property Law (*Ley de Propiedad Horizontal*) which gave rise to a new article 396, and in 1999 a new law was sanctioned which permitted the construction of "private real estate apartment complexes", also known as "urbanizations", a system based on condominium property. A first family law reform – deemed as pale by the existing doctrine – took place in 1958 on a hundred of articles about the capacity of women, the marriage regime and the succession rights of the married woman. A second reform occurred in 1975 which eliminated the marital Licence and introduced the principle of equality between spouses in their personal relations. But, in this historical period, the major reform took place in 1973–1974 in the Preliminary Title of the Code which modernized the theory of the sources and the interpretation of the law and also dealt with the concept of analogy, fraud, abuse of process, and private international law. Without considering case law as a real source of the law, the statute attributes to case law the role of *complementing the legal system with the doctrine that the Supreme Court shall repeatedly render in the application and interpretation of the law, custom and general principles of the law (article 16 of the Spanish Civil Code).*

I will outline below the most significant reforms, many having modified the text of the Civil Code by the application of the principles set forth in the 1978 Spanish Constitution:

- Law of May 13th about filiation, parental rights and duties, matrimonial regime (articles 108–171, 1315–1444, and another on the matter of succession);
- Law of July 7th 1981 about marriage (articles. 42–107), which reintroduces the divorce and, on the other hand, it applies the legal agreement with the Vatican in 1979;
- Law of May 5th 1982 on the civil protection of the right to one's honor, personal and family intimacy and to one's image;
- Law of October 24th 1983 on the declaration of incapacity, guardianship and the introduction of the guardianship authority and the elimination of the supervising institution and the Family Council;
- Law of November 11th 1987 on adoption always regarded as a form of protection and assistance of minors closely supervised by the public Administration;
- Law of January 15th 1996 on the protection of minors, applying the UN 1989 Convention;
- Law of November 5th 1999 on family name and first name which modified article 109 of the Civil Code;
- Law 1/2000, of January 7th which deeply changed the content of the Law of Civil Procedure of 1881 and eliminated a number of articles of a procedural nature in the Civil Code (articles 127–130, 202–214, 294–296 and 298, 1214, 1215, 1226, 1231–1253, which content we can find with changes in the new 2000 Law of Civil Procedure);
- Law 41/2003, of November 18th, on the patrimonial protection of the disabled;
- Law 42/2003, of November 21st, on the amendment of the Civil Code in the matter of family relations between grandparents and grandchildren;
- Law 13/2005, of July 1st, which authorized the homosexual marriage and substantially modified article 44 of the Civil Code. Judgment rendered by the Constitutional Court on October 17th 2012 declared its constitutionality;
- Law 15/2005, of July 8th, which modified the system of separation and divorce.
- Law 14/2006, of May 26th, on assisted reproductive technology;
- Law 33/2006, of October 30th, about the equality between men and women in the succession of nobility titles;
- Law 39/2006, of December 14th, of the promotion of the personal autonomy and assistance to the persons in dependency;
- Law 3/2007, of March 22nd, on the effective equality between men and women;
- Law 54/2007, of December 28th, on the international adoption;
- Law 20/2011, of July 21st, on the Civil Status Registry, which will be in force as from July 23rd 2014.

Many of these reforms are already part of the Civil Code, having been inserted in its text, giving rise sometime to *bis articles* (for example article 289) or to *empty* articles, for example, articles 307–313, as a result of the 1983 Guardianship

Law or articles 1231–1253, derogated by Law 1/2000). It is possible to see that Spain has not been lately characterized by a good legislative method in the enactment of laws...

17.5 The Decodification and Recodification Process

There existed in Spain a process of decodification.[11] But, there was also an inverse movement. Let's take the example of the lease agreement or the rental contract, insufficiently regulated by the Civil Code, due to its liberal inspiration in the nineteenth century. On concrete circumstances, the legislator was forced to intervene throughout the twentieth century with laws which were originally rather of an exceptional nature and which later became special laws, to the margin or even inconsistent with the Civil Code. Therefore, the problems of the farmers during the Second Republic (1931–1939) prompted the enactment of the Law of Agricultural Rental in 1935, which was maintained and was even strengthened during the political regime of General Franco, and which included measures for the protection of farmers by means of the enactment of various statutes (for example, the 1973 Law of Agricultural Reform and Development, nowadays partially in force). Now, the Law of 2003, modified in 2005, significantly cut down this protection and the legislation is now half way in comparison with the liberal system of the Civil Code (of course, the recent Common Agricultural Policy of the European Union favors in part its return to the Civil Code). There is a certain parallelism with the legislation on lease agreements (Law of Urban Rentals) which had a broad practical application between 1950 and 1970, firstly, owing to the destructions of our civil war worsened by the economic crisis resulting from the international isolation of Spain at the end of the Second World War. All this gave rise to the compulsory renewal of the lease contracts and the State control over the leases (Acts of 1944, 1956 and 1964). But, as the economic and social situation of the Spanish society started to improve, these protection laws became unnecessary and the Law of Urban Rentals in force in 1994 also represented a clear return to the Civil Code.

Other laws are still outside the Civil Code. The Law of December 16th 1954 created *ex novo* the personal property mortgage (but the personal property mortgage is also ruled, in part, by a special law). The Law of July 13th 1998 on the sale of personal property on terms (a modification of the sales contract is under preparation and the content of this law could be inserted into it). It is important to point out that the Law 26/1984, of July 19th, general for the defense of the consumers and users, gave rise to abundant legislation which has been compiled in part in the Compilation Text (approved by Legislative Real Decree 1/2007). We will deal with this matter later.

[11] Irti's classical work, not only broadly spread in Spain, but also translated (Barcelona 1992). Cf. Also, Julio César Rivera, "La recodificación. Un Estudio de Derecho comparado", op. cit. pp. 275–378. Sacco, "Codificare: Modo superato di legiferare?", RDC, 1983; Busnelli, "El Derecho Civil entre el Código y las Leyes Especiales", RGLJ, 1975 p. 757.

17.6 The Civil Code and the Commercial Code

Following the French model, imitated by Portugal and Germany later, Spain has always had two separate Codes in the civil and commercial matters. The civil doctrine teaches that the Civil Law represents the general or common private law, whereas the Commercial Law is in a separate branch of a common tree.

Articles 2 and 50 of the Commercial Code do ratify this opinion:

> Article 2: "The acts of commerce, even though they may be performed by non- merchants and despite the fact they may be ruled in this Code, shall be governed by their own conditions, or in the absence of such conditions, by the uses of commerce generally observed in each place, and in any case, by the provisions of the common law."
>
> Article 50: "The commercial contracts, as to the conditions for their validity, amendment, exceptions, interpretation and termination and also in relation to the legal capacity of contractors shall be governed by this Code or by special laws and finally by the general rules of the common law."

The Spanish commercial doctrine abandoned long time ago the theory of the commercial transactions, however, as to the rest, the legal doctrine is clear when defining the relationship between these two branches of the private law. We should point out that in accordance with article 50 of the Commercial Code in the matter of commercial contracts, the commercial use or custom was eliminated as a source of the law.

The following provisions are the content of the 1885 Spanish Commercial Code: Book I, Of the merchants and the commerce in general. Book II, Of the special commercial contracts (companies, commercial agency, deposit, loan, sale, barter, transfer of credit, ground transportation, insurance, bonds, bills of exchange, cheques, letters of credit). Book III, Of the maritime commerce. Book IV, Of the Bankruptcy and Statutes of Limitations. The most important part of this code was derogated by special laws. But, we have seen in two recent laws a pale attempt on the part of the legislator towards the unification, because the Insurance Contract Law of 1980 simultaneously derogated the rules on this contract existing in both Codes which were replaced by the new Law. In addition, the 2003 Bankruptcy Law unified the judicial liquidation procedure against the commercial person and the non-commercial person in the event of bankruptcy.

As to the rest, and in relation to the unification of the civil and commercial texts, following the Swiss or Italian model, the discussion in our country seems to have ceased,[12] given the current orientation of the majority of the Spanish commercial doctrine towards the worldwide unification, or at least, regional, of the Commercial Law and even though there exist Spanish authors in favor of the unification of the civil and commercial obligations into one code. There could possible exist a constitutional obstacle derived from the existence of the foral law or special civil law in specific territories, but with a rule of constitutional competence not applicable at all to the Commercial Law.

---

[12] To this respect, see Lacruz *y altri*, I-1 ° (Madrid 2002, ed. Delgado) p. 30. The report submitted by Professor Roca Guillamon, in the XVI Jornadas de la Asociación de Profesores de Derecho Civil (Zaragoza 16–17 octubre 2012), pp. 48–58, was very interesting with original points of view.

17.7 Consumer Law

There is not a uniform doctrine or majority doctrine in Spain as regards Consumer Law. In fact, this subject is generally taught by civil law professors rather than commercial law professors. I myself, in the last editions of the Tratado de Derecho Civil of CASTÁN TOBEÑAS (Book of Civil Law), personally wrote a chapter on this issue,[13] in which I outlined that this modern branch of the Law is a transversal matter that comprises many other autonomous subjects (civil law, commercial law, administrative law, criminal law, fiscal law, and in Spain, the law of the Autonomous Communities, among others), and mainly because we are being subjected to the Consumer Code sanctioned by the European Union as this is a matter included in the EU Treaties. In Spain, the 2007 Compiled Text (*Texto Refundido*) on the consumer protection, following the example of France and Italy, and without the necessity of using the name Code, represents a defective attempt of a Consumer Code, which must coincide with the European Code if it is finally approved (the 2011 Directive and the Optional Proposal for the Regulation of the Right of Sale seem to be a dead-end and a change of criteria of the European Union). Thus, the countries that do not belong to the European Union have a broader freedom to legislate with respect to this matter than the other countries.

17.8 The Civil Code and the Family Law

In theory, we should say that in the Spanish civil doctrine, the ideas of the Italian Professor Antonio CICU on the nature of the public law applicable to the Family Law had some eco in the first years of the twentieth century. The author himself later clarified his ideas when he published an article in a Spanish magazine. In fact, this opinion was not accepted neither by doctrine, jurisprudence, or even the legislature. In Fidel Castro's Cuba, and following the inspiration of the socialists countries (that is to say, due to ideological reasons), a Family Code was enacted which is still in force even though the Civil Code was sanctioned 1985. But, it seems that the division of the Family Law into two different Codes (the personal relations and the patrimonial relations) poses a few problems in practice. Temporarily, Catalonia passed a Code of Family Law for Catalonia which was quickly derogated when the Civil Code appeared in which it was included. Owing to a number of reasons, other Ibero-American countries also enacted family codes during the last centuries, but this matter is of no concern to the Spanish doctrine.

[13] 17ª ed. de Castán, *Derecho Civil Español, Común y foral*, III, *Derecho de Obligaciones*, Madrid 2008, pp. 549–578.

17.9 The Reforms of the Civil Code

In four above, I pointed out the sense and the significance of the major reforms of the Spanish Civil Code. Now, I would like to focus on the current most important reforms of the Civil Code. If we leave aside various reforms of an ideological inspiration (for example, homosexual marriage), we should mention that the General Committee of Codification published in 2009 a draft for the modernization and amendment of Title I, Book IV, of the Civil Code, which took into account the evolution of doctrine and jurisprudence, communitarian law and compared law.[14] The German example of the 2002 Reform, which incorporated to the centennial German Code the major principles deriving from the communitarian law, and also the French draft of the Civil Code in the matters of obligations and prescription, which did not succeed, should make the Spanish civil doctrine reflect on the current situation of our Code. It seems that up to now we have allowed a *waiting period* so that the Autonomous Communities could exercise their competence under their Autonomy Statutes to modernize their civil law. Most of these Communities have done so, either in the form or structure of a Code, or by means of special autonomous laws. In any case, in my view, I think that the State should not have a passive role by waiving its competition in the matter of Civil law but, in fact, by modifying it to modernize our old civil Code.[15]

17.10 Current Importance of the Civil Code

Even though the reasons behind codification in Europe have changed in the twenty-first century, the *ultima ratio* of a civil code is still valid today and the reasons behind it, in my view, have not disappeared. The codes maintain the tradition of the Roman Law and of the *jus commune* which gave rise to many Schools of Law in the majority of European countries and which inspired the most recent creation of other branches of the law. The most representative Spanish civil doctrine objects to the central idea of the d*ecodification* and, on the other hand, suggests a new *recodification*. In my opinion, article 4 ° .3 of the Civil Code expressly recognizes the value of the permanent Civil Code: *The provisions of this Code shall supplementary apply in the matters governed by other statutes*. It is important to note that the legislator only focuses on private law matters, but this article also makes reference to public law.[16]

We should not forget we are members of the European Union and we should bear in mind the consequences of the creation of a Communitarian Law, every day more abundant (more than 20,000 Directives have been issued after the Rome

[14] "Propuesta de Modernización del Código civil en materia de Obligaciones Contratos (Proposal to Modernize the Civil Code in the matter of Obligations and Contracts)", *Boletín de Información del Ministerio de Justicia*, enero 2009, p. 5 ff.

[15] In this sense: Díez Picazo, "Codificación, descodificación y recodificación", ADC, 1992.

[16] Also Lacruz *and altri*, *Elementos*, I-1 ° cit., p. 78.

Treaty in 1957) and its superiority over domestic law. This has given rise to a number of communitarian attempts to enact a European Civil Code, or at least, a Code of obligations and contracts or at least a European Consumer Code. I myself participate in the activities of the Pavia Group which has already published a *draft* of the general part and of some contracts.[17] It is a private initiative, coordinated by Professor GANDOLFI who supervises the work of 150 professors, judges and jurists of Europe and America. The product of his research will join the work of other groups also carrying out their activities in the same direction (Lando Group, Von Bar Group, etc.)[18]

All such attempts to lengthen the state character of the Civil Code do not have a fixed date to accomplish their objectives, and, for the time being, I believe we should undertake to work and assist other countries in the enhancement and development of their codification techniques, which are generally applicable on a state level, and have extended to all continents, to all countries which are inspired in the *Civil Law* as well as beyond civil law.

17.11 Public International Law

The original draft of the Civil Code, in which provisions of Public International Law were laid down in articles 8–11, and which was inspired in the medieval theory of statutes, was described by doctrine at that time as inadequate and imperfect. The reform in 1973 improved this system by means of the introduction of Chapter IV of the Preliminary Title of the Civil Code under the title of "Norms of Private International Law", thus, articles 8–12 of the Civil Code were rewritten in a more modern terminology and by means of the use of a technique more refined and coherent to the modern doctrine, despite the rapid growth of the new phenomena of the frequent movement of people across the borders, which forced our country to complete the rules of the Civil Code for the Public International Law by signing bilateral or multilateral treaties with other States or even from the European Community.

In any case, the fact that the basic rules of the Public International Law are included in the Spanish Civil Code – a fact that does not give rise to serious doctrinal debate – does not prevent the recognition of the specific nature of the subject and the necessary scientific development and the need to adapt the legislation to the circumstances.[19] ROCA GUILLAMÓN[20] has just reminded us of the pioneer nature

[17] García Cantero, "La traducción española de la Parte General del Código Europeo de Contratos", RJNot, núm. 44 octubre-diciembre 2002, pp. 299–396, with bibliography in note 9, pp. 304–305.

[18] Regarding the recent information on these works, García Cantero, "Bibliographic Note of the Book "Derecho privado europeo: Estado actual y perspectivas de futuro"" (Jornadas de la Univ. Autónoma de Madrid, 13 a 14 diciembre, 2007.), RJNot, núm. 70 abril-junio 2009, pp. 311–329.

I have outlined my point of view on codification in the matter of obligations and contracts in Castán, op. y el robo. cit. pp. 600–605.

[19] De Los Mozos, op. cit. pp. 729–759, deals in depth with the current problems of the International Public Law.

[20] Roca Guillamon, loc. cit. p. 23, note 39.

of the Public International Law in the European judicial unification and of the fact that half of the rules applicable in countries belonging to the European Union are already common rules in the core of the European Union.

Furthermore, we should not forget that in Spain, international conflicts of law appear in the interior of the country due to the existence of various sub-systems of Civil Law in some territories of the State, which has prompted the passing of rules of interregional law to solve such regional controversies, inspired, in part, in the provisions of Public International Law itself (rules in the Preliminary Title articles 13–16).

In summary, we can conclude that a secondary Civil Code of the nineteenth century, belonging to the Romano-Germanic family, and which is still in force in different forms in the areas of America, Asia and Africa (Puerto Rico, Cuba, Philippines, Equatorial Guinea), giving rise in many cases to mixed systems of law and offering a solution to the problems appearing everywhere, may serve in some way as a model to other states in the twenty-first century.

Bibliography

In all the general works of Civil Law, there is a chapter on Codification and its effects. Among the more recent works, we can find

Lacruz and altri (2002) Elementos de Derecho Civil, I-1 (3me.ed. a los cuidados de Delgado Echeverria). Dykinson, Madrid, pp 53–106

VVAA (2008) Curso de Derecho Civil (I) Derecho Privado Derecho de la persona (Pablo Álvarez y Perex Contreras), 3 ed. Madrid, pp 47–130, both with plenty of updated bibliography, Colex. Editorial Constitucion y Ley

On the historical formation of the Spanish Civil law and the history of codification we find

De Castro (1949) Derecho civil de España, 2ª ed. Instituto de Estudios Politicos, Madrid, pp 137–210

Mozos L (1977) Derecho Civil español, I, Parte general. Kadmos, Salamanca, pp 157–258

Pazos B (1983) La codificación del Derecho civil de Espana – 1889 1808. Universidad de Cantabria, Santander

Other materials

On the 1851 Draft:

De Pablo Contreras (2004) Unidad constitucional y codificación del Derecho privado. In volume "La proliferación legislative: Un desafío para el Estado de derecho (dir. Menéndez y Pau Padrón). Thomson/Civitas, Madrid, p 499

Fernández G (1979) Temas de Historia del Derecho: Derecho del constitucionalismo y la codificación, II, Sevilla (1889) Código civil. Debates parlamentatios (1885–1889) (Estudio preliminary de De Los Mozos). Universidad de Sevilla, Madrid

Gaite L (1970) Crónica de la codifcación española. 4. Codificación civil (Génesis e Historia del Código). Ministerio de Justicia, Madrid

García G (1852) Concordancias, motivos y comentarios del Código civil español Madrid, there is a reprint, with a preliminary note in charge of Lacruz Berdejo (Zaragoza 1974). Sociededad Tipográfico-Editorial

Tomás y Valiente (1983) Offers a comprehensive version of the codification process between 1880 and 1889, in his Manual de Historia del Derecho español, 4e. ed. Tecnos, Madrid

On the current value of the Civil Code we find

Arce y Flórez-Valdés (1986) El Derecho civil constitucional. Cuadernos Gritas, Madrid

De Aguirre M (1991) El Derecho civil a finales del siglo XX. Tecnos, Madrid

Gil H (1943) El concepto de Derecho civil. Madrid: Revista del Derecho Privado (1950) s.v. Derecho civil, in Nejs. Barcelona; (1984) En defensa del Código civil. Escuda Social de Madrid, Madrid

Liaño P (1994) Código civil y ordenamiento jurídico. Comares, Granada

Martínez V (2011) Acerca del valor permanente del Derecho civil como Derecho de la persona en la era de la globalización, "Estudios Hom. Monté Penadés" II. Tirant lo Blanch, Valencia, p 2825 ss

Perera C (1988) El Derecho civil: Señas, imágenes y paradojas. Tecnos, Madrid

Rodriguez G (1989) Acotaciones para un concepto de Derecho civil, ADC

Soriano Torralba (1975) El Derecho civil desde la codificacióon hasta el tie mpo presente, RGLJ, 2, p 280 ff

On its relationship with commercial law we find

Bercovitz R (1990) Codificación mercantile, "Centenaro del Cc", I. Centro de Estudios Ramón Areces, Madrid, p 287 ff

Broseta (1965) La empresa la unificación del Derecho de obligaciones y el Derecho mercantile. Tecnos, Madrid

García-Mina R (1969) Introducción al Derecho mercantile. Barcelona, p 7 ff

Guillamón R (2012) Armonización, unificación y modernización del Derecho de Obligaciones y Contraos (Notas para una reflexión). Report submitted in the XVI Jornadas de los Profesores de Derecho civil (Civil Law Professors' Workshop) (Zaragoza, 16–17 November 2012)

Jordano, Derecho civil y Derecho mercantile, RDP (1964)

On the interpretation of article 149.1.8 of the 1978 Constitution: bibliography is abundant and Professor De Pablo Contreras points out in this respect three fundamental positions of doctrine: (1) Restrictive (Elizalde, Lasarte, Díez-Picazo); (2) Autonomous (Encarna Roca Trías, M Paz Sánchez González); (3) Historical (Delgado, R. Bercovitz). More in detail, Lasarte (1980) Autonomías y Derecho privado en la Constitución española. Arce, Madrid; Janáriz (1987) Constitución y Derechos civiles forales. Pena, Madrid; López (1995) Derecho civil, Derecho común, Derecho especial, AC

Special Civil Law: A general exposition, though more comprehensive, of special civil law or foral law and including autonomic civil laws: Bercovitz R et Martínez Simancas (directores) (2000) Derechos civiles de España, 9 tomos, Madrid

Chapter 18
The Scope and Structure of Civil Codes: The Turkish Experience

Ergun Özsunay

Abstract The Turkish Civil Code and Code of Obligations as well as other private law Codes of 1920s were modeled upon Swiss Codes as the result of a "voluntary global reception of foreign laws" for the purpose of westernization and secularisation. These Codes were revised in 2000s in the light of recent developments in several jurisdictions (e.g., Switzerland, Germany, Austria etc.) and international conventions. Recently new laws in Turkey in several fields of private law have been modeled upon EU legislation (regulations and directives) and Continental legal system.

Keywords Turkey • Civil Code • Occidentalization of the law • Swiss Code of Obligations • Renovation of private law • European Union

Abbreviations

Art	Article, article
EU	European Union
fSCC	Former Swiss Civil Code of 10 December 1907
p	Page
SCC	Swiss Civil Code in force
SCO	Swiss Code of Obligations of 30 March 1911 (as revised)
TCC	Turkish Civil Code
TCO	Turkish Code of Obligations
TComC	Turkish Commercial Code
TFEU	Treaty on the Functioning of the European Union

E. Özsunay (✉)
Comparative Law and EU Private Law, Istanbul University School of Law, Istanbul, Turkey
e-mail: ergun.ozsunay@ito.org.tr

J.C. Rivera (ed.), *The Scope and Structure of Civil Codes*, Ius Gentium: Comparative Perspectives on Law and Justice 32, DOI 10.1007/978-94-007-7942-6_18,

18.1 General Overview on Private Law in Turkey

In Turkish law under term of "private law" (droit privé, Privatrecht) it is understood the branch of law which deals with the relationships between persons. The main source of private law is the Turkish Civil Code, No. 4721 of 22 November 2001 including Turkish Code of Obligations, No. 6098 of 11 January 2011 and Turkish Commercial Code, No. 6102 of 13 January 2011.[1]

The new Turkish Commercial Code, No. 6102 (TComC) is also an integral part of the Turkish Civil Code (Article 1). This Code entered into force on 1 July 2012 with the exception of its provisions on supervision of stock-corporations (share corporations) which entered into force later on 1 January 2013 (Article 1534, No. 1 and No.3).

18.2 The Civil Codes

18.2.1 Adoption of Swiss Civil Code in Turkey

When the Republic of Turkey was founded on 29 October 1923 after the War of Independence, Mustafa Kemal Atatürk, leader of modern Turkey and the founders of the Republic decided to secularize and modernize Turkish law.[2]

For this purpose the Swiss Civil Code (SSC, Zivilgesetzbuch) of 10 December 1907 (entry into force on 1 January 1912) and Code of Obligations (SCO, Obligationenrecht) of 30 March 1911 (entry into force on 1 January 1912) were translated into Turkish from their French versions with some alterations and modifications because of the differences between the State structures and judicial systems in Switzerland and Turkey.

Turkish Civil Code, No. 743 of 17 February 1926 entered into force 4 October 1926. This Code was replaced by the new Turkish Civil Code, No. 4721 of 22 November 2001 which entered into force on 1 January 2002 (Article 1029).

Turkish Code of Obligations, No. 818 of 8 May 1926 which constituted the 5th Book of Turkish Civil Code, No. 743 entered into force on 4 October 1926. It was replaced by the new Turkish Code of Obligations which will enter into on 1 July 2012.

---

[1] The new Turkish Civil Code, No. 4721 (TCC) is composed of Four Books: Book 1. Law of Persons, Book 2. Family Law; Book 3. Law of Inheritance and Book 4. Law of Things (i.e. property law). The new Turkish Code of Obligations, No. 6098 (TCO) is the Book 5 of the Turkish Civil Code and an integral part of the Civil Code (Article 646). This Code will enter into force on 1 July 2012 (Article 648).

[2] For this purpose, some special Commissions were set up by the Ministry of Justice to draft modern codes which would be based on the new developments in the contemporary legal systems and satisfy the social needs of the nation. The Law Reform Commissions could not achieve these goals. Upon failure of the Commissions, it was decided to adopt foreign codes.

The new Turkish Code of Obligations (TCO) constitutes also the 5th Book of the new Turkish Civil Code.[3]

SCC and SCO were the newest codification in the first decade of the twentieth century. In spite of the influence of French Code civil on the lawyers' generation in those days in Turkey, Swiss Codes were preferred.[4]

With the voluntary adoption of western laws Turkey has changed the "legal sphere" or "legal family" to which it belonged by leaving the Islamic law sphere and adhering to the continental legal sphere.[5]

18.2.2 Alterations and Amendments in the Turkish Civil Code at the Time of Adoption

Several changes were made for "political, social, moral, geographical, economic grounds" when Turkey adopted the Swiss Civil Code by "voluntary reception".

---

[3]For details on the history of adoption of foreign laws during the Ottoman Empire and after the foundation of the Republic of Turkey see Ergun Özsunay, *Legal Science During the Last Century in Turkey*, Inchieste di diritto comparato "La Science du droit au cours du dernier siècle", Padova, 1976, pp. 695 et seq.; Ergun Özsunay, *The Total Adoption of Foreign Codes in Turkey and Ist Effect*, in "Le Nuove Frontiere del Diritto e Il Problema Dell'Unificazione", Università degli Studie di Bari, Milano, 1979, Vol. II, pp. 803 et seq.; Ergun Özsunay, *Some Remarks on the Amendments Proposed by the Preliminary Draft of the Turkish Civil Code*, "Liber Memorialis François Laurent 1810–1887", (Editors: J. Erauw/B. Bouckkaert/H. Bocken/H. Gaus/M. Storme), E. Strory-Scientia, Bruxelles, 1989, pp. 605 et seq.; Ergun Özsunay, *Religious Fundamentalism: Turkish Experience*, Universidade da Coruna, Nacionalismo en Europa-Nacionalismo en Galicia, La religion como elemento impulsar de la ideologia nacionalista, Simposio internacional celebrado en: Pazo de Marinan A Coruna, 4–6 Septiembre 1997, NINO Centro de Impresion Digital, 1997, pp. 116 et seq.; Ergun Özsunay, *Karşılaştırmalı Hukuka Giriş* (Introduction to Comparative Law), Istanbul, 1978, pp. 269 et seq.; Ergun Özsunay, *Türkiye'de Yabancı Hukukun Benimsenmesi Hareketi İçinde Türk Medeni Kanunu'nun Anlamı ve Önemi* (The Meaning and Importance of the Turkish Civil Code within the Movement of Adoption of Foreign Law in Turkey), Istanbul Üniversitesi, Mukayeseli Hukuk Enstitüsü, TMK'nun 50. Yıl Sempozyumu (Symposium for the 50th Anniversary of the TCC), Istanbul, 1976, pp. 399 et seq. Further see H.N. Kubalı, *Les facteurs determinants de la reception en turquie et leur portée perspective*, Annales de la Faculté de Droit d'Istanbul, 1956, No. 6, pp. 44–52.

[4]Regarding the relationships between Swiss Civil Code as "adopted law" or "mother law" (Mutterrecht) and Turkish Civil Code, No. 743 of 4 April 1926 as "daughter law" (Tochterrecht) (entry into force on 4 October 1926) from the time of adoption until the enactment of New Turkish Civil Code, No. 4721 of 22 November 2001 (entry into force on 1 January 2002) see Ergun Özsunay, *Relaties tussen Turks en Zwitsers recht: ervaringen met de toepassing van "geadopteerd recht" in een andere rechtscultuur* (Relations between Swiss and Turkish Laws: Experience on Application of "Adopted Law" in Another Climate), Ars Aequi Mei 2007 (AA 56 (2007) 5, pp. 430–437.

[5]For several types of "reception of foreign law" and particularly "total reception of foreign codes" see Ergun Özsunay, *Karşılaştırmalı Hukuka Giriş*, pp. 271 et seq.; Ergun Özsunay, *Türkiye'de Yabancı Hukukun Benimsenmesi Hareketi İçinde Türk Medeni Kanunu'nun Anlamı ve Önemi*, pp. 399 et seq.

(a) Some changes were due to the different "forms of the State" in Turkey (i.e. centralized State) and Switzerland (CH). Such provisions were not adopted.
(b) As the Turkish "judicial system" was different from Switzerland, some provisions of fSCC were adapted to the Turkish "judicial structure". In general the provisions related to the cantonal law were not received.
(c) Some provisions of SCC were altered on the ground of the "revolutionary character of the adoption" in Turkey. For instance, as Turkey secularized its law leaving the Islamic legal system, marriage could be solemnized only by a marriage officer (i.e. mayors or their representatives). Under TCC, only the "civil marriage" was valid. The so-called "imam marriage" was regarded as "non-existent". Only after obtaining the civil marriage certificate, religious ceremony could be done (TCC Article 110; fSCC Article 118).
(d) In the fields of family and inheritance laws, some provisions of SCC were altered on the ground of "social and moral structure" of the Turkish nation. A typical example deals with the age of legal majority: 18 years (TCC Article 11; fSCC Article 14). The age of majority by the decision of court (i.e. emancipation) was lowered to 15 years (TCC 12; fSCC 15). Likewise, the marriage age was also lessened: for male 17 years; for female 15 years; and in exceptional cases for male 15 years; female 14 years (TCC Article 88; fSCC Article 96).

For "social grounds", the "matrimonial regime" in Switzerland was not adopted. The traditional Swiss "marital system" (Güterverbindung) as "ordinary matrimonial regime" was not adopted. It was found not suitable for matrimonial property in the Turkish family life. Instead, "system of separate estates" (Gütertrennung) was adopted as "ordinary matrimonial regime" (TCC Article 170 et seq.; fSCC Article 178 et seq.).

Moreover, the provision of al. 3 of Article 137 of the fSCC on the "consent to the adultery" (loss of the right of action) was not adopted as it was not compatible with the conservative Turkish family life in 1920s. In case of "desertion" as a divorce ground, the "period of absence" was reduced to 3 months (TCC Article 132) by taking into account economic and social structure of the Turkish family whereas this period was 2 years in fSCC Article 140.

Likewise, the provision of SCC on judicial separation for an indefinite period (fSCC Article 147 al. 1) was not adopted in Turkey (TCC Article 139). A "period of 1–3 years" was found sufficient for "judicial separation" on the reason of the Turkish family relations.

Several provisions of fSCC were not adopted for they were not compatible to the Turkish family life relations. Therefore, "several periods" in the family law or law of inheritance was reduced by TCC: E.g. "1 month" for disavowal of child born in wedlock (TCC Article 242; in fSCC Article 253 "3 months").

For "moral grounds", "the proportions of property and usufruct of the surviving spouse" were reduced in order to protect father and mother and grandparents of the deceased, (TCC Article 444; fSCC Article 462).[6]

[6] For details on other modifications and alterations see Ergun Özsunay, *Some Remarks on the Amendments Proposed by the Preliminary Draft of the Turkish Civil Code*, p. 611.

18.2.3 Amendments of the SCC After Its Enactment and Amendments of TCC Between the Date of Adoption of the SCC and Enactment of the New Turkish Civil Code of 22 November 2001

18.2.3.1 Amendments in the Swiss Civil Code

(a) Grounds of amendments

The SCC has been amended several times after its entry into force on 1 January 1912. In the family law, the rearrangement of divorce and matrimonial regimes in the light of new developments, the need for a better protection of married women and children born out of wedlock, the reform of adoption and parental responsibility (parental authority) under the new concepts and understandings were the main reasons of amendments.

Moreover, the new issues related to co-ownership, arrangement of flat ownership and right of building (Baurecht, droit de superficie) needed of new regulations.

(b) Major amendments in the SCC

The amendments and rearrangements in SCC have been carried out by federal laws enacted on various dates. Following the system of SCC, the important reforms and rearrangements can be cited as follows:

(c) Law of persons

- Federal Law of 16 December 1983 on Amendment of SCC amended Article 28 on "protection of personality right" (Article 28) and added new Articles 28a-28l relating to lawsuit in case of infringement of personality right, interim measures, types of compensation etc.
- Some provisions relating to "foundations" (Article 89bis) were added by Federal Law of 21 March 1958. This Law provided the application of provisions on foundations when a "fund for assistance to the personnel" (Personalfürsorgeeinrichtungen) was established in the form of "foundation".

(d) Family law

- Federal Law of 5 October 1984 on the Amendments of Swiss Civil Code made amendments on the effects of marriage, matrimonial property and law of inheritance.
- Federal Law of 5 June 1974 amended the provisions of SCC on "recognition" and "action for paternity".[7]
- Federal Law of 30 June 1972 has reformed the "adoption" in the light of the new developments after the Second World War in this field.[8]
- Federal Law of 1976 on Child's Law revised the legal situation of children in SCC.

---

[7] See SCC Article 260 et seq.

[8] This Law added new Articles 264–269 to SCC on adoption.

- Federal Law of 26 June 1998 has rearranged the parental authority (die elterliche Gewalt) in the light of the new "Child's Law" in the neighboring countries for a better protection of child.[9]
- Federal Law of 5 June 1974 has amended duties of parents relating to the education and training of children and the child's property.[10]

(e) Law of inheritance

Federal Law of 5 October 1984 rearranged the "freedom of disposition" (Verfügungsfreiheit).[11]

(f) Property Law (Law of Things)

- Federal Law of 19 December 1963 on the Amendments of SCC rearranged co-ownership (Miteigentum) and provided provisions for flat ownership. It amended several Articles relating to property (Eigentum) and added new Articles to the Code on ordinary and important management transactions on property under co-ownership (647a–647e).
- The legal regime for "flat ownership" was established by this Law.[12]
- Federal Law of 19 March 1965 rearranged the provisions of SCC on "right of building" (Baurecht, droit de superficie) in the light of new developments in this field for a better use of land and premises.[13]

18.2.3.2 Amendments in the TCC After the Adoption of SCC (1926)

18.2.3.2.1 The Need of "Revision" of TCC in General

TCC has experienced several amendments after its coming into force in 4 October 1926 until the enactment of the New Turkish Civil Code of 2001.

Regarding the amendments of TCC of 1926, it should be noted that not only the problems encountered in the practice of the Code, but also the developments and amendments in the "adopted (mother) law" have been taken into account.

The need of revision of TCC has been felt in the early 1950s. For the revision of the Code, the Ministry of Justice has established several Revision Commissions. The first one was set up in 1951. After the work of 20 years, the Commission's "Preliminary Draft and Its Explanatory Memorandum" was published in 1971.[14]

---

[9] See SCC Article 296 et seq.

[10] See SCC Article 276 et seq. and 318 et seq.

[11] See SCC Articles 470 et seq.

[12] See SCC Articles 712a–712t.

[13] See SCC Articles 779, 779a–779 l.

[14] On the criticism of the Revised Draft see Haluk Tandoğan, *Türk Medeni Kanunu Ön Tasarısının Tüzel Kişilere İlişkin Hükümleri Üzerine Görüşler* (Remarks on the Provisions of the Preliminary Draft of the TCC on Legal Entities), Ankara Üniversitesi Hukuk Fakültesi Dergisi, Vol. XXX, 1973, No. 1–4, pp. 121 et seq.; İsmet Sungurbey, *MK Öntasarısının Nesneler Hukukunun Eleştirisi* (Criticism of the Law of Things of the Preliminary Draft of TCC), İstanbul, 1972.

Upon the serious criticism of the Revision Draft, the Ministry of Justice set up a second Revision Commission to reform particularly the "divorce law" that was interested by all people in those years. However, the members of this Commission objected such a limited assignment. Thereupon the Ministry of Justice never convened again the Commission.

The third Revision Commission was established by the Ministry of Justice in 1976. Despite the endeavors of this Commission for reforming the Code, its drafting activity was halted by the Ministry in 1978, probably for political reasons.[15]

The fourth Revision Commission was established by the Act on Establishment of a Commission for Revision of the Turkish Civil Code, No. 2647 on 1 June 1981. This Commission started to revise the Code on 3 July 1981 and finished its revision work on 7 October 1984. The Commission revised the whole Turkish Civil Code except the Vth Book on Code of Obligations. The Commission's "Preliminary Draft and Its Explanatory Memorandum" was published by the Ministry of Justice in the same year.[16]

Nevertheless, the coalition governments in 1980s and 1990s could not present, unfortunately, this Revised Code to the parliament. Thereupon, another Revision Commission was set up by the Minister of Justice in mid 1990s. The revision work of the Code was completed in 4 years. The Revised Turkish Civil Code was presented on 30 December 1999 to the Grand National Assembly. The new Turkish Civil Code, No. 4721 was enacted on 22 November 2001 and published at the Official Gazette, No. 24607 on 8 December 2001. It entered into force on 1 January 2002.[17]

18.2.3.3 Amendments in the TCC from 1926 Until 2001

After the entry into force of TCC on 4 October 1926 several amendments and additions have made to the Code in order to satisfy the requests of the practice and to arrange new social and economic needs until the New Turkish Civil Code of 22 November 2001 was passed by the Grand National Assembly.[18]

---

[15] See Ergun Özsunay, *Some Remarks on the Amendments Proposed by the Preliminary Draft of the Turkish Civil Code, p. 615.*

[16] See Ministry of Justice, *Türk Medeni Kanunu Öntasarısı ve Gerekçesi* (Preliminary Draft of Turkish Civil Code and Its Explanatory Memorandum), Ankara, 1984. For a detailed assessment of this Revised Code see Ergun Özsunay, *Some Remarks on the Amendments Proposed by the Preliminary Draft of the Turkish Civil Code*, p. 616 et seq.

[17] See Ministry of Justice, *Türk Medeni Kanunu Tasarısı* (Preliminary Draft of the Turkish Civil Code), Ankara, 1998.

[18] On this occasion it should be noted that several statutes have been enacted in order to arrange the field of civil law beside TCC. The following statutes are of importance regarding the application of TCC: Act on Associations, No. 2908 of 4 October 1983 repealed by Act on Associations, No. 5253 of 4 November 2004; Act on Flat Ownership, No. 634 of 23 June 1965 (amended); Act on Land Register, No. 2644 of 22 December 1934 (amended); Act on Rents of Real Estate, No. 6570 of 18 May 1955 (amended); Act on Family Name, No. 2525 of 21 June 1934; Act on Registration of Livings Together without a Formal Marriage as Valid Marriage and Correction of Legal Status of Children Born out of Wedlock as Children Born in Wedlock, No. 3716 of 8 May 1991; Act

The important amendments have been shown below following the system of TCC of 1926.

(a) Law of persons

- Law, No. 3444 of 4 May 1988 added Article 24/a relating to several kinds of lawsuits in case of infringement of personality rights. Later, Article 23 of TCC on "protection of personality" was amended by the Law, No. 3678 of 11 November 1990.
- Law, No. 3612 of 7 February 1990 added a new provision to Article 36 on Records for Personal Status Registry by granting the power for recording to diplomatic representatives of Turkey abroad.
- The provisions of TCC on "foundations" were amended essentially by the Law, No. 903 of 13 July 1960. This Law added also several Articles to the Code.[19]

(b) Family law

- Law, No. 3080 of 15 November 1984 amended Articles 97, 105 and 110 relating to the persons authorized to solemnization of marriage and religious solemnization after solemnization of civil marriage.
- Law, No. 3444 of 4 May 1988 reformed the ground of "incompatibility" for divorce (Article 134). An essential reform was realized with regard to "divorce" by this Law in Turkey. This solution was adopted by the new TCC (Article 166).[20]
- Law, No. 3678 of 14 November 1990 rearranged the legal status of divorced woman. The right to use the husband's family name was granted to divorced woman under some circumstances (Article 141). This solution was adopted by the new TCC (Article 173).[21]
- Article 144 related to "alimony for poverty" was rearranged and "request for alimony without time limit" was granted to divorced spouse under certain

on Prevention of Infringements upon Possession of Real Estate, 3091 of 4 December 1984; Act on Foundations (established before the enactment of TCC), No. 2762 of 5 June 1935 (repealed by the Law, No. 5555 of 9 November 2006); Act on Construction, No. 3194 of 3 May 1985; Act on Mortgage of Commercial Undertaking, No. 1447 of 21 July 1971; Act on Environment, No. 2872 of 9 August 1983; Act on Protection of Cultural and Natural Heritage, No. 2863 of 27 January 1983; Act on Land Surveying and Land Register, No. 2613 of 11 December 1934 repealed by the Act, No. 3402 of 21 June 1987; Regulation on Land Register, No. 94/5623 of 7 June 1994; Regulation on Application of the Provisions of TCC on Parental Authority, Guardianship and Inheritance, No. 6/5100 of 24 July 1965; Regulation on Foundations Established under TCC, No. 7/1066 of 25 July 1970.

[19] See Articles 73–77, 77/A, 78, 79, 80, 80/A, 81, 81/A, 81/B

[20] Cf SCC Article 142

[21] Cf SCC Article 149

circumstances by Law, No. 3444 of 4 May 1988. This rule was emphasized by the new TCC (Article 175).[22]

- Law, No. 4248 of 14 May 1997 granted to married woman the right to use her family name together with the husband's family name. This solution was adopted by the new TCC (Article 187).
- Article 159 TCC that required husband's approval for married woman's professional or trading activity was abolished by the decision, No. 30/31 of the Constitutional Court of 29 November 1990. This solution was adopted by the new TCC.
- Law, No. 2846 of 16 June 1983 changed the age for "adoption". The age was lowered from 40 to 35 (Article 253). The Law, No. 2846 rearranged also the effects of adoption (Article 257).
- Law, No. 3678 of 14 November 1990 added a provision to the Code concerning "non-request of parents' consent for adoption of a child" (Article 254/a). This Law amended also the "form requirement" for adoption (Article 256).

The decision, No. 67/23 of the Constitutional Court of 21 May 1981 found unconstitutional and cancelled the provision of Article 310 Al. 2 of TCC that prevented the court to render judgment for paternity if the defendant father was married at the time of sexual intercourse. This solution was adopted by the new TCC.

(c) Inheritance law

- In the field of law of inheritance, the Law, No. 3678 of 14 November 1990 amended Article 441 Al. 2 with regard the "rights of inheritance of grandparents as heir" and abolished Article 442 related to the rights of inheritance of "parents of grandparents".

  These solutions were adopted by the new TCC.
- Under TCC, if a child born out of wedlock was recognized by the father or bound to the father as a result of a paternity action, he or she could be heir of the father. Nevertheless, if children born in wedlock and out of wedlock were heirs of their father, children born out of wedlock were entitled to inherit the half of the inheritance shares of children born in wedlock (Article 443). This rule was found unconstitutional by the decision, No. 1/18 of the Constitutional Court of 11 September 1987 and cancelled. Later Law, No. 3678 of 14 November 1990 emphasized the "principle of equality" with regard to inheritance between children born in wedlock and out of wedlock by amending Article 443. This solution was adopted by the new TCC.
- Law, No. 3678 of 14 November 1990 rearranged the inheritance right of surviving spouse. It abolished the "right of usufruct" on the part of surviving spouses (Article 444). This solution was adopted by the new TCC.
- Law, No. 3678 amended also Article 448 related to the inheritance of Treasury (State) as the last statutory heir. When the Treasury was the last

[22] Cf SCC Article 152

heir, "the rights of usufruct of parents of grand fathers and grand mothers" were abolished.

– Article 453 TCC on "compulsory portion" was amended by Law, No. 3678 with regard to "foundations devoted for public benefit". The compulsory portions of heirs were reduced when the deceased established a foundation and if the half of its income was devoted to "public services". This solution was adopted by the new TCC.

(d) Property law (Law of Things)

– In the field of property law, Law, No. 3678 of 14 November 1990 provided the possibility for "exclusion of co-owner from the co-ownership status" by a court decision under certain circumstances (TCC Article 626/a). Likewise, other right holders (such as holder of usufruct right or holder of the right of tenancy that is entered as an immovable in the Land Register a permanent and independent right) could also be excluded like co-owner (Art. 626/b).
– Article 632 TCC deals with the subject-matter of land ownership. Ownership of land means ownership of all immovable property which includes (i) land; (ii) independent and permanent rights entered in the land register, and (iii) mines.[23]
– Another important amendment realized in TCC dealt with "right of building" (Baurecht, droit de superficies). According to Article 751, under the "right of building" the owner of a piece of land can create as servitude in favor of another by giving him the right to construct or retain a building or other construction on or under the land. In absence of a contrary agreement this right is alienable and transmissible to the heirs. If this purports to be a permanent and independent right it can be entered as an immovable in the Land Register Law, No. 3678 of 14 November 1990 amended Article 751 TCC and added Articles 751a–751j to the Code that were modeled upon the amendments realized by the Federal Law of 19 March 1965 in SCC (Articles 779a–779l).
– Law, No. 3678 of 14 November 1990 provided the possibility to establish mortgage to be based on foreign currency by adding Article 766/a to the Code.

18.2.4 New Turkish Civil Code, No. 4721 of 22 November 2001

As explained above (III 2 a) the new Turkish Civil Code is a work of a Revision Commission composed of law professors, judges, attorneys and bureaucrats of the Ministry of Justice.

[23] Regarding the mines a special Act on Mines, No. 3213 of 4 June 1985 was enacted. Under the new TCC mines are no more the subject-matter of ownership on immovable property (Article 704). Instead of mines, "independent parts entered in the register for flat ownership" has been cited as the subject-matter of immovable property.

During the work of revision, the Revision Commission has taken into account particularly the legal problems encountered in practice, the needs of the people, the recent understanding of Turkish family relations and values, latest developments for the protection of personality right and personality values and amendments realized in the SCC for during last decades of the twentieth century.

Revision Commission maintained, on the one hand, the amendments in TCC realized by several Laws during the last half of the twentieth century; and imported, on the other hand, the latest amendments in SCC. Further the developments in some neighboring jurisdictions (e.g., German amendments in BGB, French revisions in Code civil etc.) have also been taken into consideration.

Therefore, the amendments in TCC by several Laws, particularly by Law, No. 444 of 4 May 1988; Law, No. 3678 of 11 November 1990; Law, No. 4248 of 14 May 1997 that we have explained above III 2 b have been included to the new TCC.

On this occasion, it should be noted that one of the most important developments in new TCC is related to the "matrimonial regime". Regarding the reform of matrimonial regime, new TCC adopted the new solution of SCC (i.e. joint ownership of acquired property, regime of community of income and profits acquired during the marriage, Errungenschaftsbeteiligung). Therefore, if spouses do not make a "marriage contract" at a notary public for "separation of property" or "community of property" (Gütergemeinschaft) or "separate of estates to be shared" (paylaşmalı mal ayrılığı), the "legal matrimonial regime" would be the "regime of community of income and profits acquired during the marriage" (Errungenschaftsbeteiligung) (Article 205).

18.2.5 Impact of Swiss Law on Turkish Law: Major Consequences of the "Voluntary Global Reception" of Swiss Law in Turkey

18.2.5.1 In General

The voluntary global reception of Swiss Civil Code and Code of Obligations together with some other Swiss Codes in 1926 (e.g. Federal Code on Enforcement and Bankruptcy, Bundesgesetz betr. Schuldbetreibung-und Konkurs) was a "legal revolution" in Turkey.[24]

---

[24] See J.L. Constantinesco, *Rechtsvergleichung, Band II: Die rechtsvergleichende Methode,* Köln/Berlin/Bonn/München, 1972, p. 415. For details on "types of reception of foreign law" see Ergun Özsunay, *Karşılaştırmalı Hukuka Giriş*, pp. 270 et seq. Further see M. Rheinstein, *Types of Reception*, Annales de la Faculté de Droit d'Istanbul, 1956, No. 6, pp. 31–43; A.B. Schwarz, *Rezeption und Assimilation auslaendischer Rechte*, "Rechtsgeschichte und Gegenwart", Karlsruhe, 1960, pp.149–160; I. Zajtay, *La réception des droits étrangers et le droit comparé*, RIDC, 1957, No. 4, 686–713; Neumayer/Dopffel, *Ein Jahrhundert türkscher Rezeptiongeschichte-Versuch einer Würdigung*, Annales de la Faculté de Droit d'Istanbul, 1956, No. 56, pp. 53–62.

The most important consequences of "global reception of Swiss law" on Turkish law, legal practice and legal science can be summarized as follows:

(a) First of law, as the result of global reception of foreign law, Turkey left the religious legal system of Islam that dominated for centuries in the Ottoman Empire. The ties with Islam as a legal system were cut off voluntarily by reception of foreign law. Thus the law of modern Turkey became a part of the continental legal sphere.

In spite of maintenance of some traditions based on religion (e.g., Imam-marriages) by conservative circles, Islamic law today in Turkey constitutes only a part of the "history of national law".

(b) The second impact of global reception of foreign law was the termination of "legal plurality" that dominated in the last century of the Ottoman Empire, particularly after the "Tanzimat" (Reforms) movement (1839).

(c) Thirdly, prohibition of polygamy, introduction of compulsory civil marriage and divorce subject to certain grounds brought a radical change in Turkish family life and status of married woman.

(d) Fourthly, the voluntary global reception of foreign law has introduced new legal forms and concepts to Turkish law. The global reception of foreign law introduced "a new approach" to legal problems and a "new way of legal thinking".[25]

18.2.5.2 Influence of Swiss Law Regarding the Application of TCC

The adaptation of foreign law to "new legal climate" is not an easy task. In several cases, the application of the provisions of TCC has taken a different direction from the application of SCC despite the norms and solutions are similar in both Codes. In order to cope with such contradictions, Turkish lawyers tried to follow carefully the Swiss Civil Law doctrine and decisions of the Federal Court in several fields of civil law.

With regard to interpretation of several provisions and filling the legal gaps, Turkish doctrine and jurisprudence enjoyed usually the Swiss doctrine and practice.[26]

All generations at the Law Schools in Turkey since 1926 (particularly the teaching staffs at Istanbul and Ankara Universities Law Faculties) studied closely Swiss

[25] For details see Ergun Özsunay, *Some Remarks on the Amendments Proposed by the Preliminary Draft of the Turkish Civil Code*, pp. 638 et seq. Further see B. Davran, *Bericht über die Aenderung im türkischen ZGB gegenüber dem schweizerischen, verbunden mit einigen Bemerkungen über den Sinn der Rezeption*, Annales de la Faculté de Droit d'Istanbul, 1956, No. 6, pp. 131–143.

[26] In the Unification of Decisions of 28 November 1945, No. 13/15 of the all chambers of the Court of Cassation, the highest court makes the following statement: "Regarding interpretation of our laws, whereas we take into account our own texts in principle, we cannot give up to examine their origins on the ground of the doctrine (scientific opinions) is enjoyed in respect of interpretation". See Ergun Özsunay, *Medeni Hukuka Giriş* (Introduction to Civil Law), 5th Edition, Istanbul, 1986, p. 218.

law and some neighboring laws (e.g. German and French laws) regarding legal problems they examined in their dissertations and "Habilitationschrift"s.[27]

Translations of important Swiss "commentaries" (i.e. Bern and Zurich Commentaries) into Turkish played an important role in respect of the development of Turkish law.

Further, "Turkish-Swiss Lawyers' Meeting", organized each 4 years, in which Swiss and Turkish lawyers come together, contributed much to observe similarities and differences of the applications of Swiss and Turkish Civil Codes, to analyze the grounds of different applications. Thus, the papers submitted to these meetings (journees juridique) and discussions among Swiss and Turkish lawyers on the application of "adopted law" in the "receiving country" contributed also to the improvement of Turkish law.

18.3 Relationship Between the Civil Code, the National Constitution and Public International Law

It is possible to find several provisions in the current Turkish Constitution, No. 2709 of 18 October 1982 (as amended several dates and lastly on 12 September 2010) which directly or indirectly deal with the Turkish private law in general and Turkish civil law in particular.

The following principles and constitutional guarantees dominate the Turkish civil law as well as the whole Turkish law: the principle of equality (Article 10), the right of privacy and protection of private life (Article 20), inviolability of domicile (Article 22), freedom of communication (Article 22), freedom of religion and conscience (Article 24), freedom of thought and opinion (Article), freedom of expression and dissemination of thought (Article 26), freedom of science and arts (Article 27), right and freedom of assembly (Article 33), right to own and inherit property (Article 35), protection of family (Article 41), land ownership (Article 44), freedom to work and conclude contracts (Article 48), right and duty to work (Article 49), right to housing (Article 57), principle of conservation of historical, cultural and natural wealth (Article 63), protection of consumers (Article 172), principle of primacy of the international agreements and conventions duly ratified (Article 90 para. 5).

---

[27] Comparative law meant for a while in Turkey the "comparison of Turkish and Swiss laws" regarding examination of legal problems before the "comparative law" was developed as an autonomous branch of law. For details see Ergun Özsunay, *Karşılaştırmalı Hukuka Giriş*, pp. 4 et seq. Ergun Özsunay, *Legal Science During the Last Century in Turkey*, pp. 803 et seq.; Ergun Özsunay, *Some Remarks on the Amendments Proposed by the Preliminary Draft of the Turkish Civil Code*, pp. 638 et seq.

18.4 Contents of the Civil Code

The contents of the new Turkish Civil Code, No. 4721 of 2001 and the former Turkish Civil Code, No. 818 of 1926 are exactly the same: As explained above under I the Turkish Civil Code are composed of a Preliminary Part and four Books:

Preliminary Part (application and sources of law, subjective and objective good faith, discretion power of judge, burden of proof) (Articles 1–7);
Book 1. Law of Persons (physical persons and legal persons) (Articles 8–117);
Book 2. Family Law (Articles 118–494);
Book 3. Law of Inheritance (Articles 495–682);
Book 4. Law of Things (property law) (Articles 683–1030).

The Code contains 1030 Articles.

Family law in Turkey is a part of the Turkish Civil Code. A separate Family Law Act does not exist.

Turkish Code of Obligations, No. 6098 of 2011 (TCO) is the Book 5 of the Turkish Civil Code and its integral part (Article 646).

Turkish Code of Obligations is composed of two Parts. Each Part is divided into Chapters and each Chapter into Sections. The Code contains 649 articles.

Part I of the Code of Obligations deals with General Provisions. It covers the provisions on sources of obligation, contracts, torts, unjust enrichment, performance of obligation, legal consequences of non-performance of obligations, impacts of obligation relationships on third parties, prescription periods, obligations undertaken jointly and severally, solidarity, conditions, forfeit money, contractual penalty, assignment of receivables, undertaking of obligation (Articles 1–206).

Part II regulates Specific Contracts as sale contract, donation, lease contract, loan contract, service contract, work contract, publishing contract (der Verlagsvertrag), mandate (der Auftrag), letter of credit and credit order (mandatum crediti), brokerage contract (der Maeklervertrag), management of affairs without mandate (die Geschaeftsführung ohne Auftrag), contract for commercial agency (die Kommission), agent having full power of representation (commercial representation, die Prokura), persons having commercial power of attorney (die Handlungsvolmacht, der Handlungsbevollmaechtigte), other auxiliaries to a trader, remittance (die Anweisung), deposit contract, surety contract (die Bürgschaft), gamble and wagering (Spiel und Wette), life annuity contract (Leibrentenvertrag), contract for caring of one's lifetime (Verpfründungsvertrag), ordinary partnership (einfache Gesellschaft). (Articles 207–649).[28]

As seen contract law is a part of the Turkish Code of Obligations. A separate Law on Contracts does not exist in Turkish law.

---

[28] Regarding the revision works on the Code of Obligations the works "*A More Coherent European Contract Law – An Action Plan*" *and* "*European Contract Law and Revision of the Acquis*: *The Way Forward*" published by the EU Commission have been taken into account in general and "*Principles of European Contract Law*" and "*Principles of Tort Law*" have been examined for the formulation of several legal rules. The Revision Commission has benefited also from the German Commercial Code (HGB) particularly in respect of the "ordinary partnership". See Explanatory Report of the new Code of Obligations.

18.5 The Commercial Code

Turkish Commercial Code, No. 6762 enacted on 29 June 1956 and entered into force on 1 January 1957 is a separate Code, but at the same time an integral part of Turkish Civil Code, No. 4721 of 2001.

Turkish Commercial Code, No. 6762 of 29 June 1956 has been replaced by the new Turkish Commercial Code, No. 6102 of 13 January 2011. This Code would enter into force on 1 July 2012 (Article 1534 No. 1) with the exception of the provisions on supervision of the joint stock (share) corporations that will enter into force on 1 January 2013 (Article 1534, No. 4).

New Turkish Commercial Code has been inspired partly by the revised Swiss Code of Obligations, but various legal concepts and institutions in the Code are based on the EU legislation (i.e. regulations and directives in several fields of commercial law).

New Turkish Commercial Code is composed of an Introduction, 6 Books, and Final Provisions. Each Book is divided into Parts; each Part into Chapters, each Chapter into Sections.

Introductory Part of the Code lays down provisions on application of the Code, commercial custom and usage, commercial transactions, commercial proceedings and rules of proof, commercial courts, prescription periods, interest rate in commercial transactions (Articles 1–10).

Book I deals with "Commercial Enterprise" (undertaking). It contains provisions on trader, trade registries, trade name, unjust competition, commercial books, current account, agency contract (der Agenturvertrag) (Articles 11–123).

The EU legislation taken into account regarding Book I (Commercial Enterprise) (undertaking) is the following:

On unfair competition:

- Directive 84/450/EEC of 10 September 1984 relating to the approximation of the laws, regulations and administrative provisions of the Member States concerning misleading advertising;
- Directive 97/55/EC of European Parliament and of the Council of 6 October 1997 amending Directive 84/450/EEC concerning misleading advertising so as to include comparative advertising;
- Directive 2005/29/EC of the European Parliament and of the Council of 11 May 2005 concerning unfair business-to-consumer commercial practices in the internal market and amending Council Directive 84/450/EEC, Directives 97/7/EC, 98/27/EC and 2002/65/EC of the European Parliament and of the Council and Regulation (EC) No 2006/2004 of the European Parliament and of the Council ("Unfair Commercial Practices Directive");
- Directive 2002/58/EC of the European Parliament and of the Council of 12 July 2002 concerning the processing of personal data and the protection of privacy in the electronic communications sector ("Directive on privacy and electronic communications")[29]

[29] See the Explanatory Report of the new Turkish Commercial Code.

On commercial registry:

- First Council Directive 68/151/EEC of 9 March 1968 on co-ordination of safeguards which, for the protection of the interests of members and others, are required by Member States of companies within the meaning of the second paragraph of Article 58 of the Treaty, with a view to making such safeguards equivalent throughout the Community.[30]

On commercial agents:

- Council Directive 86/653/EEC of 18 December 1986 on the of the laws of the Member States relating to self-employed commercial agents[31];

Book II regulates "Commercial Companies". The provisions are laid down on general partnership (Kollektivegesellschaft, société en nom collectif); limited partnership (Kommanditgesellschaft, société en commandit), joint-stock (share) companies (corporations, Aktiengesellschaft, société anonyme), limited liability companies (Gesellschaft mit beschraenkter Haftung, société a responsabilité limitée) (Articles 124–644).

Regarding the "company law" the following EU legislation has been taken into account:

On mergers, divisions and conversions of companies:

- Third Council Directive78/855/EEC of 9 October 1978 based on Article 54 (3) (g) of the Treaty concerning mergers of public limited liability companies;
- Sixth Council Directive 82/891/EEC of 17 December 1982 based on Article 54 (3) (g) of the Treaty, concerning the division of public limited liability companies.[32]

On stock-corporations:

- First Council Directive 68/151/EEC of 9 March 1968 on co-ordination of safeguards which, for the protection of the interests of members and others, are required by Member States of companies within the meaning of the second paragraph of Article 58 of the Treaty, with a view to making such safeguards equivalent throughout the Community;
- Second Council Directive 77/91/EEC of 13 December 1976 on coordination of safeguards which, for the protection of the interests of members and others, are required by Member States of companies within the meaning of the second paragraph of Article 58 of the Treaty, in respect of the formation of public limited liability companies and the maintenance and alteration of their capital, with a view to making such safeguards equivalent;
- Fourth Council Directive 78/660/EEC of 25 July 1978 based on Article 54 (3) (g) of the Treaty on the annual accounts of certain types of companies;

---

[30] See the Explanatory Report of the new Turkish Commercial Code.

[31] See the Explanatory Report of the new Turkish Commercial Code.

[32] See the Explanatory Report of the new Turkish Commercial Code.

- Seventh Council Directive 83/349/EEC of 13 June 1983 based on the Article 54 (3) (g) of the Treaty on consolidated accounts;
- Eighth Council Directive 84/253/EEC of 10 April 1984 based on Article 54 (3) (g) of the Treaty on the approval of persons responsible for carrying out the statutory audits of accounting documents;
- Eleventh Council Directive 89/666/EEC of 21 December 1989 concerning disclosure requirements in respect of branches opened in a Member State by certain types of company governed by the law of another State;
- Twelfth Council Company Law Directive 89/667/EEC of 21 December 1989 on single-member private limited-liability companies;
- Council Directive 2001/86/EC of 8 October 2001 supplementing the Statute for a European company with regard to the involvement of employees;
- Regulation of the European Parliament and of the Council EC, No 1606/2002.of 19 July 2002 on the application of international accounting standards[33]

Moreover the following decisions of the European Court of Justice have been examined regarding the formulation of several rules:

- "Centros" case (ECJ Case C-212/97, Centros Ltd. v. Erhvervs- og Selskabsstyrelsen, decision of 3/9/1999);
- "Überseering" case (ECJ Case C-208/00, Überseering B.V. v. Nordic Construction Company Baumanagement GmbH (NCC), decision of 11/5/2002);
- "Inspire Art" case (ECJ Case C-167/01, Kamer van Koophandel en Fabrieken voor Amsterdam v. Inspire Art Ltd., decision of 9/30/2003).[34]

Book III covers "Negotiable Instruments". The provisions of Book III covers registered instruments (die Namenpapiere), bearer instruments (die Inhaberpapiere), bill of exchange, promissory note and checks (Articles 645–849).

Book IV deals with transactions for "Transportation" (Article 850–930).

Book V concerns "Maritime Law" (Sea Trade). Book V covers the provisions on ship (vessel), ship owner and association of ship owners, ship registry, secured transactions on ships, contracts for maritime trade, charter parties, liability of transporter, maritime accidents, collision, salvage, general average, ship creditors, etc. (Article 931–1400).

Regarding the revision of the "Maritime Law" the following EU legislation has been taken into account:

- Council Directive 79/116/EEC concerning minimum requirements for certain tankers entering or leaving Community ports;
- Council Directive 79/115/EEC of 21 December 1978 concerning pilotage of vessels by deep-sea pilots in the North Sea and English Channel;
- Council Recommendation 79/114/EEC of 21 December 1978 on the ratification of the 1978 International Convention on standards of training, certification and watch keeping for seafarers

[33] See the Explanatory Report of the new Turkish Commercial Code.

[34] See the Explanatory Report of the new Turkish Commercial Code.

- Council Decision 77/587/EEC of 13 September 1977 setting up a consultation procedure on relations between Member States and third countries in shipping matters and on action relating to such matters in international organizations;
- Council Decision 78/774/EEC of 19 September 1978 concerning the activities of certain third countries in the field of cargo shipping;
- Council Decision 79/4/EEC of 19 December 1978 on the collection of information concerning the activities of carriers participating in cargo liner traffic in certain areas of operation[35];

Book VI concerns "Insurance Law". The provisions on insurance contract, kinds of insurance, rights and obligations of insurer and insured have been laid down here (Articles 1401–1520).

Regarding the "Insurance Law" the following EU legislation has been taken into account:

- First Council Directive 79/267/EEC of 5 March 1979 on the coordination of laws, regulations and administrative provisions relating to the taking up and pursuit of the business of direct life assurance;
- First Council Directive 73/239/EEC of 24 July 1973 on the coordination of laws, regulations and administrative provisions relating to the taking-up and pursuit of the business of direct insurance other than life assurance;
- Council Directive 72/430/EEC of 19 December 1972 amending Council Directive 72/166/EEC of 24 April 1972 on the approximation of the laws of the Member States relating to insurance against civil liability in respect of the use of motor vehicles and to the enforcement of the obligation to insure against such liability;
- Second Council Directive 84/5/EEC of 30 December 1983 on the approximation of the laws of the Member States relating to insurance against civil liability in respect of the use of motor vehicles;
- Third Council Directive 90/232/EEC of 14 May 1990 on the approximation of the laws of the Member States relating to insurance against civil liability in respect of the use of motor vehicles;
- Council Directive 78/473/EEC of 30 May 1978 on the coordination of laws, regulations and administrative provisions relating to Community co-insurance;
- Council Directive 87/344/EEC of 22 June 1987 on the coordination of laws, regulations and administrative provisions relating to legal expenses insurance;
- Council Directive 87/343/EEC of 22 June 1987 amending, as regards credit insurance and suretyship insurance, First Directive 73/239/EEC on the coordination of laws, regulations and administrative provisions relating to the taking-up and pursuit of the business of direct insurance other than life assurance;
- Directive of the European Parliament and of the Council 2002/83/EC of 5 November 2002 concerning life assurance;
- Council Directive 64/225/EEC of 25 February 1964 on the abolition of restrictions on freedom of establishment and freedom to provide services in respect of reinsurance and retrocession;

[35] See the Explanatory Report of the new Turkish Commercial Code.

– Council Directive 84/641/EEC of 10 December 1984 amending, particularly as regards tourist assistance, the First Directive (73/239/EEC) on the coordination of laws, regulations and administrative provisions relating to the taking-up and pursuit of the business of direct insurance other than life assurance.[36]

Final Provisions deal with electronic transaction, electronic signature, electronic resolutions in companies etc. (Articles 1521–1535).

Bankruptcy is dealt with in Turkish law by a separate Code of Enforcement and Bankruptcy, No. 2004 of 1926 modeled upon the Swiss Federal Code on Enforcement and Bankruptcy (Bundesgesetz betreffend Schuldbetreibung und Konkurs) (as amended).

18.6 Consumer Law

Under Turkish Constitution, No. 2709 of 18 October 1982 (as amended several times and lastly 12 September 2010) Turkish State has the duty to take measures to protect and inform consumers and encourage their initiatives to protect themselves.

Consumer law is a separate branch of law in Turkey. The main source of Turkish consumer law is the Consumer Protection Act, No. 4077 (CPA) of 23 February 2003 (as amended) is based at a great extend on EU legislation. Many provisions of the Turkish Civil Code and Turkish Code of Obligations apply also to consumer transactions.

Consumer Protection Act is composed of Four Parts. The Act contains 34 Articles. CPA is structured as follows:

Part One deals with "Aims and Scope of the Act and Definitions" related to consumer protection (Article 1–3).

Part Two deals with "Protection and Information of Consumer". It regulates the following matters: Defective goods (including the product liability), defective services, failure to supply, unconscionable conditions in contract, credit sales, time-sharing contracts, package tours, campaign sales, doorstep sales, distance contracts, consumer credit, credit cards, contracts to finance housing, periodic publications, subscription contracts, indication of prices on labels, guarantee certificates, promotion and user's guide, after sales services, commercial advertising and notices, Board of Advertisement, hazardous goods and services, supervision of goods and services, consumer education, (Articles 4–20).

Part Three has been devoted to "Consumer Institutions". It deals with the Consumer Council, Arbitration Panel for Consumer Problems (Articles 21–22).

Part Four contains provisions on "Proceedings and Penalties". Consumer Courts, prevention of production and selling and collection of defective goods, and penal sanctions (i.e. fines) and relevant matters (jurisdiction for penal sanctions, objection against fine decisions and prescription periods) have been regulated in Part Four (Articles 23–26).

---

[36] See the Explanatory Report of the new Turkish Commercial Code.

Part Five lays down "Miscellaneous Provisions" relating to supervision of factories, commercial premises, warehouses, etc., and use of private or public laboratories (Articles 27–34).

In drafting of the Consumer Protection Act and its complementary amendments the following EU legislation has particularly been taken into account:

- Directive 93/13/EC of the Council of 5 April 1993 on unfair commercial practices in consumer contracts;
- Directive 97/7/EEC of 20 May 1997 on consumer protection in distance sales (Distance Selling Directive);
- Directive 2008/122/EC of 14 January 2008 on consumer protection with respect to certain aspects of contracts for timeshare on property for tourist use, acquisition of long-term holiday products, resale and exchange (Timeshare Directive);
- Directive 2009/22/EC of 23 April 2009 on injunctions for the protection of consumer interests;
- Directive 85/577/EC of 20 December 1985 on consumer protection concerning contracts executed out of the commercial premises (Doorstep Selling Directive);
- Directive 2008/48/EC of 23 April 2008 on consumer credit contracts by repealing Directive 87/102 (Consumer Credit Directive);
- Directive 1999/44 of 25 May 1999 on certain aspects of the sale of consumer goods and associated guarantees;
- Directive 2005/29/EC of 11 May 2005 on unfair commercial practices;
- Directive 98/6/EC of 16 February 1998 on consumer protection in the field of indication of prices of products offered to consumers;
- Directive 2006/114/EC of 12 December 2006 on deceptive advertising and comparative advertising;
- Directive 85/374/EC of 25 July 1985 on liability for damages for defective products (Product Liability Directive);
- Directive 90/314/EEC of 13 June 1990 on package travels, package holidays and package tours.

18.7 Concluding Remarks

1. As seen the former and new Turkish Civil Codes, Code of Obligations and Commercial Codes are the products of the movement and endeavors for westernization and secularization in Turkey since the foundation of the Turkish Republic. They are the outcomes of a "legal revolution" through which Turkish law left a "religious legal system or sphere" (i.e. Islamic law) and adhered to the Continental European legal sphere. Islam law is a kind of "droit ancient" in Turkey and a part of the "legal history" studies.
2. Secondly adoption of foreign codes for ideological and political purposes after the foundation of Republic in Turkey is a typical aspect of the voluntary adoption of foreign law. These codes were not imposed by foreign powers, but voluntarily

were adopted by the founders of the Republic. The aim of Atatürk, founder of the Republic and other founding fathers was to establish a secular and westernized state on the ashes of the Ottoman Empire.

3. Regarding the terminology related to "adoption of foreign law" the relationship between Swiss law and Turkish law is explained as a relationship between "mother law" and "daughter law". Swiss law is the "mother law" (Mutterrecht) as and Turkish law is the "daughter law" (Tochterrecht). After the adoption of major codes in the field of private law lawyers of the "daughter law" (i.e. Turkish lawyers) have carefully followed the developments in the "mother law". Further, they did their best to examine the developments in the other national laws (e.g., Austrian law) belonging to the same "legal sphere". In the early stages of the applications of adopted laws translations of major commentaries and works on Civil Law published in Switzerland, sending students and scholars to Switzerland, Germany and Austria for doctoral studies, and advanced legal researches and observing of new developments in these jurisdictions are the indications of this attitude. The "Swiss-Turkish Lawyers' Meetings" (Semain juridique turco-suisse) arranged each 4 years and "Austrian-Turkish Lawyers Meetings" (Österreichisch-türkische Juristentagen) organized each 2 years contribute at a remarkable extend to the development of modern Turkish law.
4. Nevertheless it should be noted that the recent endeavors for the revisions and modernizations of civil and commercial laws in Turkey are partly based on the Swiss law, but mostly inspired by the EU legislation. This situation derives from the EU-Turkey relationships and Copenhagen criteria for full membership of the Republic of Turkey to the EU. The new Turkish Civil Code, Turkish Code of Obligations, Turkish Commercial Code, Consumer Protection Act, No. 4077 and Act on the Protection of Competition (based on Articles 85 and 86 of Rome Treaty, 81 and 82 of the Amsterdam Treaty and 101–102 of the TFEU) are typical aspects of this trend. Likewise the same attitude can also be encountered in other fields of law, particularly in intellectual property law. The Turkish legislation (Governmental Decrees, No. 551, 556, 555 having the power of law) on protection of patent rights, trademarks, geographical indications are mostly based on the EU legislation.

Chapter 19
Costs of No Codes

James R. Maxeiner

Abstract It is well known that the United States does not have a national civil code. This article shows what is less well known about the lack of codes in American law: it is not because Americans did not want codes. Throughout much of the nineteenth century they expected that they would have them. They made many attempts to adopt civil codes at the state level. Only when their attempts failed, did Americans turn to the well-known alternatives of uniform state laws and restatements of the law. These alternatives have proven disappointing. The United States is drowning in sea of uncoordinated laws. It pays a heavy price for the lack of a national civil code.

Keywords United States of America • Lack of codes • Alternatives of codes • Restatements • Uniform laws • Privatization of America contract law • Costs of no codes

19.1 Introduction

The United States does not have true codes. It has not had codes for so long that Americans don't think about the cost of not having them. We are simply accustomed to it. We do not realize that the lack of codes contributes significantly to the high cost of legal services in the United States. Karl Llewellyn colorfully wrote: "The bar has grown up with the causes as part of its natural environment, has adjusted to them as one adjusts to the pressure of the atmosphere, and would read with amazement

J.R. Maxeiner (✉)
Center for International and Comparative Law, University of Baltimore
School of Law, Baltimore, MD, USA
e-mail: maxeinerj@optonline.net

J.C. Rivera (ed.), *The Scope and Structure of Civil Codes*, Ius Gentium: Comparative Perspectives on Law and Justice 32, DOI 10.1007/978-94-007-7942-6_19,

that legal services could be performed at a level of charge materially lower ....[1]" More recently, less colorfully, and more troubling, the Organisation for Economic Co-operation and Development ("OECD") concluded: "At the heart of the most severe regulatory problems in the United States is the quality of primary legislation."[2]

The purpose of this Article is to bring readers' attention to the lack of a civil code in the United States and its cost for the American legal system. Section 19.2 addresses the lack of codes. Section 19.3 considers American alternatives to codes. Section 19.4 looks at the history of civil codes. Section 19.5 reflects on the costs of no codes.

19.2 No Codes

For a century following adoption of their Constitution of 1787, Americans debated codification. In 1791, in Philadelphia, then the nation's capital, Americans launched "endeavors to improve the law by the legislature."[3] The Pennsylvania House of Representatives directed James Wilson, one of only six persons to have signed both the Declaration of Independence and the Constitution, to revise and digest the laws of that state. In beginning his work, Wilson explained to the legislature his intention to reduce statutes and common law "into a just and regular system." He would write codes as experiments in "justness and efficacy." His work would have "simplicity and plainness and precision." Since it would claim the "obedience" of all, it would be "at a level to the understanding of all."[4]

In the first hundred years, state codes were the topic of discussion; a national code was not considered. Then, in about 1887, Americans stopped talking of systematic codes. Instead, they debated *national* laws addressing particular problems. Today, these national laws take one of three principal forms: federal statutes, uniform laws, and restatements of law. We discuss these in Sect. 19.3. With rare exception, these national laws are not codes, although some of them have a similarity to codes.

The United States is a country without a national civil code and practically without national codes. Private law, including the topics of this Article, contract law, commercial law, consumer law, and family law are principally composed of

---

[1] Karl Llewellyn, "Bar's Troubles, and Poultices and Cures, The Unauthorized Practice of Law Controversy," 5 *Law & Contemp. Probs*. 114, 117–18 (1938).

[2] *Organisation for Economic Co-operation & Development, Regulatory Reform in the United States* 48 (1999).

[3] Hugh Henry Breckenridge, "Some View of the Endeavors to Improve the Law by the Legislature," *in Law Miscellanies* 27 (1814).

[4] James Wilson to Speaker of the House of Representatives of the Commonwealth of Pennsylvania (August 24, 1791), *reprinted in* Bird Wilson, "Introduction" to 1 *Works of the Honorable James Wilson* (1804), scholarly edition, 1 *Collected Works of James Wilson* 418–22 (Kermit L. Hall and Mark David Hall eds., 2007). Although Wilson made a good beginning on his work, the legislature failed to fund him and he died 7 years later with the task unfinished.

the law of the 50 separate states. State law, with the lone exception of Louisiana, is uncodified law. The relationship of state law to federal law is ad hoc.

Although there is no national *civil* code in the United States, arguably the Uniform Commercial Code ("UCC") is a national *commercial* code,[5] discussed below in Sect. 19.3. Among the legislation governing contract, commercial, consumer, and family law, it is the only American candidate for *national* code status. Among the states, only Louisiana arguably has a *state civil code*.

Although true codes are rare or nonexistent in the United States, many American laws are called codes. The name is a vestige of the attempts to codify law. We briefly examine that history below in Sect. 19.4. Already in the nineteenth century, Europeans held the appellation of "code" to American laws to be a misnomer because American codes are not systems of law.[6] They are laws without logical order: compilations of statutes arranged in alphabetical order of subject matter groupings.[7] Within these compilations, however, one can find individual laws, such as the UCC, which *might* qualify for code status outside the United States. Most of these possible codes are in public rather than in private law (e.g., criminal law and procedure).

Despite a dearth of true codes, there is no shortage of statutes in the United States. Today, American law principally takes the form of legislatively-adopted statutes. In day-to-day American life, statutes, more than precedents, prescribe what people shall do and proscribe what they shall not do. Statutes, and not court precedents, are the principal tool that Americans use to order society.

Most American statutes deal with some specific problem as it arises and do not seek comprehensive and systematic solutions. The result is a lot of laws, but little cohesion or "correlation" among them.[8] A leading German textbook on legislation says of American law that one cannot speak of a system of law in the way that a French or German jurist would.[9]

---

[5] *See, e.g.*, William D. Hawkland, "Uniform Commercial "Code" Methodology," 1962 *U. Ill. L.F.* 291, 293 (making that argument). *See also* William D. Hawkland, "The 23rd John M. Tucker, Jr., Lecture in Civil Law: The Uniform Commercial Code and the Civil Codes," 56 *La. L. Rev.* 231 (1995) [hereinafter *Lecture*]. *Accord* Richard Buxbaum, "Is the Uniform Commercial Code a Code?," *in Rechtsrealismus, multikulturelle Gesellschaft und Handelsrecht*: *Karl Llewellyn und seine Bedeutung Heute* 197, 220 (1994) ("the UCC is indeed a code, of course within the American frame of reference").

[6] *See, e.g.*, J.L. Tellkampf, "On Codification or the Systematizing of the Law," *in Essays on Law Reform, Commercial Policy, Banks, Penitentiaries*, etc. *in Great Britain and the United States* 3 (1859).

[7] For example, the *United States Code*, after setting out six initial "titles" related to government organization, goes alphabetically from Title 7 Agriculture to Title 50 War. Already in 1791, James Wilson found that for a digest, "an alphabetical order would be unnatural and unsatisfactory." Wilson, *supra* note 4, at 418.

[8] The term is that of Ernst Freund, *Standards of American Legislation*: *An Estimate of Restrictive and Constructive Factors* 225 (1917).

[9] Hans Schneider, *Gesetzgebung, Ein Lehr- und Handbuch* § 19, margin no. 728, page 401 (3rd ed. 2002).

19.3 American Alternatives to Codes

19.3.1 In General

Although the United States does not have a national civil code, it does have laws of national applicability that provide some of the benefits of a national civil code. These laws take three forms: federal statutes, uniform state statutes, and "restatements" of law. In areas of private law, state law eclipses federal statutes. So in this part, we focus on state laws of national applicability (i.e., uniform state laws and restatements) and leave federal law to a brief discussion in Sect. 19.4.

19.3.1.1 Uniform State Laws

American uniform state laws are statutes like other statutes. What makes them distinctive is that they are proposed by an extra-governmental body (usually the Uniform Law Commission) with two goals: that they will be adopted by all state legislatures and that they will be adopted with the same, identical text.

The first goal is rarely fulfilled. Few proposed uniform laws have been adopted by all or nearly all of the states. Most have been adopted by ten or fewer states.[10] The premier success of the Uniform Commercial Code has been overshadowed by a colossal failure to update it for the digital age. In 2011, after nearly two decades of work on revisions, the American Law Institute ("ALI") and the Uniform Law Commission ("ULC") abandoned their proposals. They could not get them enacted.[11]

The goal of uniformity of text among those few uniform laws that are adopted is more often achieved but with significant imperfections. Sometimes, the uniform laws themselves allow for variations. Other times, state legislatures introduce variations. Sometimes, variations arise because amendments to uniform laws are not concurrently adopted by all states; more than one version is in effect in different states. Perhaps the most serious of all imperfections in uniformity is that there is no provision for uniform interpretation of uniform laws. Each state's court system decides for itself what a uniform law means. No court sits above them all to interpret conclusively a uniform law's meaning. The United States Supreme Court is not such a court, since it has no competence to decide the meaning of state laws.

19.3.1.2 Restatements of the Law

Restatements of the law look like well-drafted statutes, or even like codes, but they are neither. Unlike uniform laws, they are not adopted by legislatures. As a result,

---

[10] The ULC lists at its website how many states have adopted its various proposals. *See* "Legislative Report by State 2012," Uniform Law Commission *available at* http://www.uniformlaws.org/shared/legreports/legrpt_state.pdf (last visited Oct. 1, 2012)

[11] *See infra* Sect. 19.4.

they are not law and do not have the force of law. They are not addressed to the public as binding rules. Restatements are intended to "guide and aid" courts in their decisions of individual disputes.[12]

Yet restatements have a similarity to codes that sets them apart from compilations of precedents: they are meant to "scan an entire legal field and render it intelligible by a precise use of legal terms . . . ."[13] Restatements seek to distill the existing common law of all the states into one set of rational rules. Those rules are not binding; they are guides to follow, unless there is some reason not to follow them. For appellate courts, they are never binding. For lower courts, they are binding only if an appellate court adopts them as law binding judicial decisions. They are intended to be like common law. Where restatements are used, they permit a common law to continue, but instead of a state common law, a kind of common law of national applicability.

Restatements—if one seeks uniformity of law—are third-best solutions.[14] In any given case, they may or may not provide a governing rule. In any given case, all possibly applicable statutes must still be consulted.[15] Yet, they *were* an ingenious, albeit partial and imperfect solution, to a peculiarly American problem: 50 separate systems of similar but non-uniform private law. Significantly, restatements are largely confined to private law. They have not been widely used for public law. There are no restatements of criminal law, administrative law, or procedural law.[16] Indeed, even in the private law area, they are not used in family law, where laws are not as similar as in other areas of private law.[17]

19.3.1.3 Common Challenge: Law Reform

The American Law Institute and the Uniform Law Commission are both organizations dedicated to law reform. They share a common challenge: how to bring about law reform consistent with their non-political institutional roles. In the case of the ALI, the problem is inherent in the concept of restatement—a restatement is supposed to restate law common to the states and not to create new law. The ALI is an unelected body; it has no authority to make changes in public policy.

---

[12] *Report of the Comm. on the establishment of a Permanent Org. for the Improvement of the Law Proposing the Establishment of an Am. Law Inst.* (1923), *reprinted in The American Law Institute*: *Seventy-fifth Anniversary* (1923–1998) 173, 198 (1998).

[13] *Capturing the Voice of the American Law Institute*: *A Handbook for ALI Reporters and Those Who Review Their Work* 5 (2005) [hereinafter *Capturing the Voice*].

[14] First best is a single law; second best is a uniform law universally adopted.

[15] *See, e.g., Restatement (Second) of Contracts* § 8 (1981).

[16] The principal exception is the Restatement (Third) of Foreign Relations Law of the United States.

[17] For further comparative reading on restatements, see J. Gordley, "European Codes and American Restatements: Some Difficulties," 81 *Colum. L. Rev.* 140 (1981). For further reading on the relationship of restatements to codification, see Nathan M. Crystal, "Codification and the Rise of the Restatement Movement," 54 *Wash. L. Rev.* 239 (1979).

Its authority and that of its restatements derive not from the ballot box, but from the Institute's "competence in drafting precise and internally consistent articulations of law."[18] Limited authority restricts the reforms that restatements can make: they are "necessarily modest and incremental, seamless extensions of the law as it presently exists."[19]

The problem for the Uniform Law Commission is analogous, but it is political rather than conceptual in origin. The Commission *could propose* far-reaching changes. But it could not count on all or even many state legislatures adopting them. Consequently, to get its uniform laws passed, it prefers to present the best among existing choices rather than to offer new departures. *Enactability* is a ULC guiding criterion.[20]

To continue their missions of law reform without compromise, both the American Law Institute and the Uniform Law Commission have added to their product lines a new offering: *model laws*. A model law makes no pretension of restating existing law, so it avoids the ALI's conceptual problem that restatements should not make major changes in law. Model laws may do that. Moreover, model laws make no claim to uniform and universal adoption, so they avoid the practical issues that afflict proposed uniform laws.[21]

The ALI alone has created a third type of product: *principles*. Principles state the law as the Institute thinks it "should be." The ALI uses principles when state law varies widely. It has in mind that it can create greater predictability through principles sufficiently general that they attain widespread assent while leaving details to local decision.

19.3.1.4 Common Concern: Private Legislatures Without Political Power

Both the Uniform Law Commission and the American Law Institute are private bodies. The Commission consists of about 300 commissioners chosen in various non-electoral ways by state governments. Commissioners do not represent state governments and are not politically responsible. The Institute consists of about 3,000 private individuals chosen by ALI itself based on the nominees' professional achievements. They are responsible only to themselves.[22] This raises several problems. The most-recognized problem is the political legitimacy of their proposals, but other less noted problems follow from the remoteness between their proposals and political power.

---

[18] *Capturing the Voice*, *supra* note 13, at 5.

[19] *Id.*

[20] *Unif. Law Comm'n, Comm. to Review the ULC Drafting Process*, *Final Report* 16 (June 29, 2011), *available at* http://www.uniformlaws.org/Shared/Docs/ULC%20DPC/Tab%202.G.2_ULC%20DPC_Final%20Report_062911.pdf [hereinafter *Final Report*].

[21] For the ALI and model laws, see *Capturing the Voice*, *supra* note 13, at 10. For the ULC and model laws, *Final Report*, *supra* note 20, at 20.

[22] The author is a member of the ALI. The views expressed here are his alone.

(a) Lack of democratic legitimacy of proposals

Legislation is normally subject to political compromise among democratically chosen legislators, but proposals for uniform laws, restatements, model laws, or principles do not share these characteristics. Ideally, the efforts of the ALI and the ULC are non-partisan, but when choices are difficult, it may not look that way. Drafting sessions are open to the public; the industries and individuals most concerned with the topic at issue are often represented. There is compromise, but comprise can consist of drafters acceding to the outspoken views of those participating. A perception of "capture" by those participating industries is common.

(b) Lack of public institutional support in drafting

Drafters of restatements and of uniform laws act without public institutional support. They write their own laws almost in a vacuum, and do not review laws proposed by the government offices in whose competencies legislation falls. They forego the knowledge of the very institutions that should know best the existing laws and the problems they address. The support they do get is likely to come from those motivated by private interest (e.g., from trade associations, businesses, and private persons).

(c) Lack of political investment in adoption

Once the ALI and the ULC propose new legislation, they have limited opportunity to bring about its enactment. In the case of restatements, this is inherent in the product's intended use only as a guide for judicial decision-making. In the cases of uniform and model laws, however, it is not a necessary characteristic of the products. Because neither state governments nor political parties participate in drafting, neither is invested in their enactment.[23] Yet state legislatures are the very institutions that must turn uniform and model laws into binding statutes.

19.3.2 Contents of Civil Code Counterparts

19.3.2.1 National "General Laws"—Restatements, Uniform Laws, and UN CISG

Although the United States has no national civil code, ALI Restatements combined with the Uniform Commercial Code provide something akin to a national law of contracts. There are no competing systems of contract law. Louisiana's Civil Code is a tolerated exception but is no competition. Much of that national contract law, other than the UCC and the United Nations Convention on the International Sale of

[23] That the fragmentation of American governments and political parties would present a major hurdle is not addressed in this Article.

Goods ("UN CISG"), is "soft" law. That is, it guides, but does not bind. This national law of contracts is formally state law (except for the little-used CISG) and leaves no place for the United States Supreme Court to interpret it.[24]

For contract law, because it is mostly default law, the lack of a national contract law is not felt acutely.[25] Parties that do not like the solution offered can choose the solution that they would prefer. Lack of national law is felt more acutely in the practice areas of consumer and family law, where more law is mandatory.

(a) **Restatements (ALI)**
The most important of the restatements for contract law is the *Restatement of the Law Second Contracts* (1981). Other restatements addressing contracts are *Restatement of the Law Third Agency* (2006), *Restatement of the Law Third Restitution and Unjust Enrichment* (2011), and *Restatement of the Law Third Suretyship and Guaranty* (1996).[26]

(b) **Uniform Laws (ULC)**
The principal uniform law for contracts is the UCC. It is not limited to transactions of merchants. It covers sales of goods, leases of goods, negotiable instruments, bank deposits and collections, funds transfers, letters of credit, documents of title, investment securities, and secured transactions. The Uniform Electronics Transactions Act (UETA) upholds electronic signatures. It works together with a federal law, the Electronic Signatures in Global and National Commerce Act (ESIGN). The Uniform Computer Information Act (UCITA) has been adopted by only two states. The UCC and UETA have been adopted generally.

---

[24] *Cf.* Erie R.R. Co. v. Tompkins, 304 U.S. 64 (1938), overruling *Swift v. Tyson* (1842), where the United States Supreme Court had authorized federal courts to create a federal commercial law independent of state law. Grant Gilmore asserted that it "worked extremely well in practice." Grant Gilmore, *The Death of Contract* 105 (2nd ed., 1995).

[25] *See* John Honnold, "American Experience under the Sales Article of the Uniform Commercial Code," *in Aspects of Comparative Commercial Law sales, consumer credit, and secured transactions: papers presented at a conference held at McGill University on Sept. 3–5, 1968* 3, 5 (J.S. Siegel and W.M. Foster, eds., 1969) ("When counsel for a business has been concerned about one of the rules of sales law, the remedy has usually been in his hands: he could put the rule he want in his sales agreement."). *Cf.* Symposium, "Contracting Out of the Uniform Commercial Code," 40 *Loy. L.A. L. Rev.* 1 (2006).

[26] There is now a *Principles of the Law of Software Contracts* (2010). In view of past failures in this area, its future is cloudy. It should not be assumed that it will find the same acceptance as the Restatements. Stephen J. Burton and Melvin A. Eisenberg, *Contract Law: Selected Source Materials Annotated* 338 (2012 ed.).

Relevant to a law of obligations are restatements of torts. These include the *Restatement (Second) of Torts* (1965), *Restatement (Third) of Torts: Products Liability* (1998), *Restatement (Third) of Torts: Apportionment of Liability* (2000), *Restatement (Third) of Torts: Liability for Physical and Emotional Harm* (2009), and the *Restatement of Unfair Competition* (1995).

Relevant to a civil code are several restatements of property law and of conflicts of law. There is no restatement of family law. There is only a *Principles of the Law of Family Dissolution: Analysis & Recommendations* (2002).

(c) International Treaties

The UN CISG applies in all states to international sales of goods. It is little noticed.

19.3.2.2 Special Laws Affecting Contracts

Were the national laws just discussed above all the laws to be considered, one might, with some confidence, say that the United States has something close to a national contracts code. These laws are what American law professors teach their students. Only later, when those unsuspecting students go into practice do they learn about special laws. The law professors should not, however, be blamed (as often they are by bench and bar) for overlooking the practical. The number and variety of such special laws is so great that their study would extend law school beyond limit. Because they are special statutes, the likelihood of any one student encountering any one statute in practice is low. Legal education is not directed to niche contract practices.

How does one convey to readers from code countries the labyrinth that American lawyers must navigate? Reciting the number of pages alone is not enough, for other systems have many pages too.[27] When non-American readers think of special laws, how many special laws do they think of? And when they think of special laws, are they not conveniently referenced or even reprinted in their code commentaries? American lawyers have a different course to run.

Seeing is believing. In 1859, J.L. Tellkampf, a German jurist and later member of the Prussian parliament, after several years visiting the United States as professor at Amherst College, reported to the Prussian Royal House that he saw in America law "a confused mass of materials, certainly of great value, but whose practical utility is much diminished by the incongruous manner in which they have been heaped together . . . [with] much crudeness and an almost total want of system."[28] Running the course is even more believing: Gustav L. Drebing, an immigrant American lawyer and contemporary of Tellkampf, acidly observed of American law: "Characteristic features of this law are an almost total lack of clear terms, of systematically applicable general principles, and a repulsive prolixity resulting from

[27] For example, the United States Code has more than 40,000 pages; a German compilation, Das Deutsche Bundesrecht, is comparable in size. The former, however, does not include regulations (about another 140,000 pages in the Code of Federal Regulations), while the latter does. Neither includes state law, although there are fewer German states and their laws are probably less extensive.

[28] Tellkampf, *supra* note 6, at 4–5. Other Europeans reach similar conclusions. *See, e.g.*, M.E. Lang, *Codification in the British Empire and America* 189 (1924) ("from a national standpoint, one gets a picture of a legal system abounding in diversity and dissension, amounting to nothing short of utter confusion . . . . [I]n carrying on business in the country as a whole, . . . [one] comes face to face with the most profound uncertainty and chaos that is to be found to-day in any legal system the civilized world over.").

interpretation of these statute . . . ."[29] Both Tellkampf and Drebing wrote when the battle over the adoption of a civil code in New York was just getting underway. Tellkampf was hopeful that the battle would be won. As we shall see in Sect. 19.4, it was lost. For readers who have not seen for themselves, we refer them to a partial list of federal, New York State, and New York City laws listed in the Annex to this article in its first publication (31 *Mississippi College Law Review* 363, at pages 381–396 (2013)).

19.3.3 Privatization of American Contract Law

Americans (and foreigners doing business in the United States) deal with the proliferation of special laws in a variety of ways. One way is to get your own special law. One of the charges levied against the unsuccessful information Article 2B for the UCC was that it was Microsoft's law. However, it does not take a Croesus or a Bill Gates to get a special law. An adept trade association or a few well-placed sympathetic legislators may do the trick. All that is needed are resources, a continuing interest in the issue, and an issue that lends itself to a special law. These requirements are often met.

For situations that do not lend themselves to special laws, the default nature of contract law and the universal ownership of electronic word processing permits everyone to have, through standard terms, their own law and courts. If you do not like the law—special or otherwise—choose your own. You do not have to limit yourself to choosing someone else's law; you can write your own. That is not a peculiarly American approach: it is sanctioned by the French Code Civil.[30] Perhaps, however, it gets more of a workout in the United States, where there may be less trust in written law and in its institutional application. It is said that American contracts are so long and detailed in order to avoid the vagaries of American juries finding facts and courts applying the law.[31]

If you are too hurried to write your own law, another popular approach is to choose your own court, or more commonly, to choose your own arbitrators. One need not be a cynic to recognize that directing disputes to an industry arbitrator can bring comfort to industry participants. Who is better to guide proceeding through the labyrinth of special laws?[32]

---

[29] Gustav L. Drebing, *Das Gemeine Recht, (Common Law) der Vereinigten Staaten von Amerika, nebst den Statuten der einzelnen Staaten* iii (1866) [author's translation].

[30] Code Civil [C. Civ.] art.1134 (Fr.) (John. H. Crabb trans. 1977) ["Contracts legally formed take the place of the statutory law for the parties to the contract"].

[31] *See* John H. Langbein, "Comparative Civil Procedure and the Style of *Complex Contracts*," 35 Am. J. Comp. L. 381, 386–87 (1987).

[32] *Cf.* Charles L. Knapp, "Taking Contracts Private: The Quiet Revolution in Contract Law," 71 Fordham L. Rev. 761, 798 (2002) ("So ultimately the choice is a political one, whether made by a legislature (state or federal), or by a court. Can powerful private interests, with the ability to control most of the terms of most of the contracts they make, deprive large segments of American society of their access to the courts for which all of us pay, and to which all of us have historically had

Today, perhaps owing to the inadequate state of civil justice in the United States, it is hard to imagine an arbitration, choice of law, or choice of forum clause that the United States Supreme Court would not approve.[33]

19.3.4 The Uniform Commercial Code

The Uniform Commercial Code is America's national commercial code. It comes as close as any American private law legislation both to being a code[34] and to being nationally adopted.

As a uniform law, it is not enacted, but is proposed for adoption. It was drafted in the 1940s as a joint product of the Uniform Law Commission and the American Law Institute.[35] The first Official Text was presented for adoption in 1951, but was adopted by only one state—Pennsylvania. It was then reformulated. The 1962 Official Text was the first that was widely adopted. Forty-nine of fifty states adopted the entire code with only a few variations. Louisiana eventually adopted all but Article 2 Sales, 2A Leases of Goods, and 6 Bulk Transfers and Bulk Sales.

The UCC today consists of ten articles: 1. General Provisions, 2. Sales of Goods, 2A. Leases of Goods, 3. Negotiable Instruments, 4. Bank Deposits, 4A. Funds Transfers, 5. Letters of Credit, 6. Bulk Transfers and Bulk Sales (repealed), 7. Warehouse Receipts, Bills of Lading and Other Documents of Title, 8. Investment Securities, and 9. Secured Transactions. It thus brings together all of the basic aspects of American commercial transactions.

The UCC is not limited in its application to merchants. It governs all persons. Occasionally, it does have special rules for merchants or for consumers. As a code of contract law, it influenced the drafting of the *Restatement of the Law Second Contracts* (1981) and continues to influence development of general contract law.

The Uniform Commercial Code was designed to be a code. It replaced several separate uniform laws that were not integrated into one code.[36] Its principal drafter, Karl N. Llewellyn, was familiar with the German Civil Code and drew inspiration from it. Like the German Civil Code, the UCC has a "general part" (albeit a small one). It incorporates important features of German law (e.g., good faith and control of

---

access? The answer, until now, is – sadly, to some of us – that apparently they can. And do. And will.").

[33] *See, e.g.*, *Carnival Cruise Lines*, Inc. v. Shute, 499 *U.S.* 585 (1991).

[34] *See* Jean Louis Bergel, "Principal Features and Methods of Codification," 48 *La. L. Rev* 1073, 1080 (1988); Buxbaum, *supra* note 5; Hawkland, *Lecture*, *supra* note 5; William D. Hawkland, "The Uniform Commercial Code and the Civil Codes," 56 La. L. Rev. 231 (1995) [hereinafter *UCC and the Civil Codes*].

[35] *See* Allen R. Kamp, "Uptown Act: A History of the Uniform Commercial Code: 1940–49," *51 SMU L. Rev. 275 (1998); Allen R. Kamp, "Downtown Code: A History of the Uniform Commercial Code 1949–1954," 49 Buff. L. Rev. 359 (2001).*

[36] Hawkland, *UCC and the Civil Codes*, *supra* note 34 at 233–34 (1995).

standard terms).[37] Perhaps owing to the political circumstances of the day (i.e., Hitler's Germany), Llewellyn did not disclose the German origin of these ideas.

Llewellyn designed the Uniform Commercial Code to be national. The Uniform Sales Act, which the UCC replaced, was not adopted by many important states. The catalysts for the UCC were multiple attempts to reach a national sales law through federal legislation.[38] The UCC headed off federal legislation.

Today, one might wish that the UCC had been adopted as federal law in the 1960s. Through the middle of the 1990s, the Uniform Law Commission and the American Law Institute had success in keeping the UCC up to date and in getting nationwide acceptance of amendments. The dawn of the digital age, however, made the need for extensive revision palpable. Prescient observers at the time doubted the ULC amendment process was up to the task.[39] They have been proven right. A new Article 2B governing information failed to get all approval. The ULC reissued it as a separate law, the Uniform Computer Information Transactions Act. It was adopted by only two states, Maryland and Virginia. After substantial disagreement, ULC and ALI did agree on extensive revisions to Article 2, but were unable to get any states to adopt it. In May 2011, they gave up and withdrew the revision from consideration.[40]

There are other uniform laws affecting commercial transactions. Foremost is the Uniform Electronic Transactions Act, which as its prefatory comment reminds readers, is no general contracting statute. Its purpose is more modest: "to remove barriers to electronic commerce by validating and effectuating electronic records and signatures."[41] With that modest purpose to be achieved, states moved quickly to adopt it. Twelve years later all but two have.

The UCC covers commercial paper and warranties for goods. These matters are, however, also covered in important separate legislation, including the Magnuson-Moss Warranty—Federal Trade Commission Act (1975), 15 U.S.C. §§ 2301 *et seq.* The UCC makes clear that it does not preempt the field. UCC section 1–103(b) states that "unless displaced" by particular provisions of the UCC, the "principles of law and equity . . . supplement" the Code.

There are other important commercial laws. There is a federal bankruptcy law called a code. Each state has its own laws (often called codes) that govern corporations, insurance companies, and trusts. These laws show substantial similarity. They typically rest on model codes, often prepared by ALI or ULC.

---

[37] *See* Michael Ansaldi, "The German Llewellyn," 58 *Brook. L. Rev.* 705 (1992); *Shael Herman, "The Fate and the Future of Codification in America,"* 40 *Am. J. Legal Hist.* 407, 427–28 (1996); Shael Herman, "Llewellyn the Civilian: Speculations on the Contribution of Continental Experience to the Uniform Commercial Code," 56 *Tul. L. Rev.* 1129 (1982); James R. Maxeiner, "Standard-Terms Contracting in the Global Electronic Age: European Alternatives," 28 *Yale J. Int'l L.* 109, 116–18 (2003); James Whitman, "Commercial Law and the American Volk: A Note on Llewellyn's German Sources for the Uniform Commercial Code," 97 *Yale L.J.* 156 (1987).

[38] *See* Karl N. Llewellyn, "The Needed Federal Sales Act," 26 *Va. L. Rev.* 558 (1940).

[39] Neil B. Cohen & Barry L. Zaretsky, "Drafting Commercial Law for the New Millennium: Will the Current Process Suffice?," 26 *Loy. L.A. L. Rev.* 551 (1993) (proposing a federal law).

[40] *See* Maxeiner, *supra* note 38 (while Vice President & Associate General Counsel of Dun & Bradstreet, Inc., the author testified in favor of UCITA in the Maryland legislature).

[41] *Uniform Electronic Transactions Act* prefatory note (1999).

19.4 American Code History

We distinguish four time periods relevant to American attempts to legislate in form of codes: (1) Colonial Era (1609–1776); (2) pre-Civil War Era (1776–1860); (3) Civil War and post-Civil War Era (1861–1887); and (4) National Era (1887 to present). Here, we only briefly review these attempts.

That today the United States does not have codes might surprise jurists of the nineteenth century. Both American and foreign jurists then expected that codes might come to America as a natural development of nation-building. Serendipity rather than conscious choice for uncodified law seems responsible for their absence today. Conditions favorable to codification in other countries were lacking in the United States. Unlike in France, private law codification in America was not identified with displacement of feudal law with modern law. Also unlike France, codes were not statements of political identity (except in Louisiana, where there is a civil code). Furthermore, unlike in France and in Germany, private law codification in America was not identified with national legal unity. To the contrary, in the United States, codification undercut national legal unity. And, unlike in France and in Germany, codification in the United States never had politically powerful sponsors.[42]

In the United States, the common thread of support for codification was the inconvenience and accompanying injustices of uncodified law. Reform-minded governors, legislators, judges, and lawyers proposed codification in the nineteenth century. That was not enough to overcome the inertia of other governors, legislators, judges and, above all, the practicing bar, who, were already invested in the law that currently was and were less interested in the law that might be.

19.4.1 Colonial Era (1609–1776)

Long before national independence in 1776 on a colony-by-colony basis, Americans made "codes" of written laws. In 1641, only a dozen years after the charter of Massachusetts, and more than 150 years before James Wilson began work on codes for Pennsylvania, the Massachusetts Colony adopted the *Body of Liberties* of 1641. In 1648, the Colony incorporated that text into the more extensive *Laws and Liberties of Massachusetts of 1648*, which is today commonly known as the Code of 1648. American historians judge it "a comprehensive legal code . . ., no mere collection of English laws and customs, but . . . a fresh and considered effort to order men's lives and conduct in accordance with the religious and

---

[42] *See* David Gruning, "La lettre d'Amérique: Vive la différence? Why No Codification of Private Law in the United States?," 39 *La Revue Juridique Thémis [rjt]* 153 (2005); John W. Head, "Codes, Cultures, Chaos, and Champions: Common Features or Legal Codification Experiences in China, Europe and North America," 13 *Duke J. Comp. & Int'l L.* 1 (2003).

political ideals of Puritanism."[43] The Massachusetts Code of 1648 is the best known, but is not the only example of such colonial legislation. In other colonies, similar legislation is found. It ceased in the first half of the 18th century. Cessation has been attributed to the politics of the colonial relationship to Britain and to the arrival in America of professionals trained in the English common law.[44]

19.4.2 Pre-Civil War (1776–1860)

The 1787 Constitution turned a confederation into a federal state, but it did not bring legal unity. So long as slavery was permitted in one part of country but prohibited in another, national private law legislation was rarely proposed and practically impossible.[45] Complicating adoption of national codes was then, and is to this day, the unresolved question of the extent to which federal power permits federal private law. Famously, in 1811, Jeremy Bentham extended an offer to President Madison to write a code for the United States.[46] President Madison politely declined the offer as one not within "the scope of my proper function."[47] So when Americans spoke of a civil code, it was of a state and not a national code. The hope was that all states might copy the civil code of one state—most likely, New York, Massachusetts or Pennsylvania.

American discussions of what Europeans might count codification did not get under way in earnest until the War of 1812 was concluded.[48] Louisiana's first efforts in 1808 were the work of a newly-installed territorial government seeking to preserve conditions that existed prior to American acquisition in 1804. In those early days, the state of American law did not permit systematic codification. State legal systems were too precarious. Jurists had their hands full struggling for a "learned law" different from a popular folk law of informal dispute resolution.[49]

---

[43] George Lee Haskins, *Law and Authority in Early Massachusetts* 2 (1960), *quoted with approval in* Thomas D. Barnes, "Introduction" to *The Laws and Liberties of Massachusetts*. Reprinted from the Copy of the 1648 Edition in The Henry E. Huntington Library xiii (1982).

[44] *See* Gruning, *supra* note 42; Robert Gerard Smith, Toward a System of Law: Law Revision and Codification in Colonial America (1977) (unpublished Ph.D. dissertation, Cornell University) (on file with author).

[45] But it was not inconceivable. *See*, e.g., James Sullivan, *The History of Land Titles in Massachusetts* 354 (1801).

[46] *The Collected Works of Jeremy Bentham, reprinted in 'Legislator of the World': Writings on Codification, Law and Education* 20, 21, 36 (Philip Schofield and Jonathan Harris eds., 1998).

[47] *Id.* at 36. (James Madison to Jeremy Bentham on May 8, 1816). Bentham extended his offer to write codes to state governors. They, too, did not take up the offer. *See* Peter J. King, *Utilitarian Jurisprudence in America: The Influence of Bentham and Austin on American Legal Thought in the Nineteenth Century* 109–11 (1986).

[48] *See* Charles M. Cook, *The American Codification Movement: A Study of Antebellum Legal Reform* x (on Louisiana), 69 *et seq.* (1981).

[49] *See* John H. Langbein, "Chancellor Kent and the History of Legal Literature," 93 *Colum. L. Rev.* 547, 566 (1993).

Yet, already then, states and the newly-formed federal government moved to create conditions conducive to codification (i.e., they published their statutes regularly and republished them in authoritative collections compiling and revising existing statutes). At the turn of the 18th century, private lawyers began publishing collections of precedents.

From the 1820s through the 1840s, codification was a topic of serious debate. Already in 1822, the newly-formed State of Louisiana (1812) began work on what was to become its Civil Code of 1825. While it and the Code Napoleon of 1804 provided inspiration to codification proponents, practical concerns flowing from the need to compile and revise existing laws seem to have been the driving force. These concerns led to extensive work particularly in New York, Massachusetts, and Pennsylvania.

It was in 1820s New York that the work first came into being and took its most concrete form: the *Revised Statutes of New York of 1828*.[50] The legislature spent 3 months considering the specific provisions proposed. Much discussed was whether the revisers had revised too much. The *Revised Statutes* governed New York for more than half a century. The Constitution of 1846 anticipated their replacement with codes. Already, before the Civil War, the private lawyer David Dudley Field, Jr., drafted a code of civil procedure adopted by the state in 1848. During the Civil War, Field and his colleagues drafted a civil code. Field's attempt to secure that code's adoption is the main topic of the next subsection.

In the 1830s, Massachusetts had the most learned discussion under Supreme Court Justice Joseph Story. Story was the nation's leading authority in private law. Scholars debate the extent to which he was a strong or only lukewarm advocate of codification. A key issue was the future relationship between contemplated civil code and continuation of common law.

Throughout the country, states followed the leads of New York and Massachusetts in compiling and revising their laws. Those efforts slowed in the 1850s as the nation slid into civil war over the continuation of slavery.

Developments in the western reaches of the country before the Civil War suggest that the tenor of the time favored codification. Indiana is an example. Made a state only in 1816, already in that year its constitution required adoption of a penal code.[51] Eleven years later, in 1827, the state's governor, in his annual message to the legislature, promised to draft a civil code to exclude common law from private law and to enable the people to understand "that system of jurisprudence which controls their actions." He praised the new Louisiana Civil Code, drafted by Edward Livingston, as being suitable for adoption with modification in any state, called for acceptance of good ideas wherever they might be found, whether in common law, the Code Napoleon, or the Livingston Code, and implored the bar not to condemn his anticipated proposal until they read it.[52] The governor's proposal did not reach

---

[50] *See generally* William D. Driscoll, *Benjamin F. Butler: Lawyer and Regency Politician* (1987).

[51] *Ind. Const. of* 1816, art. 9, § 4.

[52] James Brown Ray, "Message to the General Assembly (December 4, 1827)," *in Messages and Papers relating to the Administration of James Brown Ray, Governor of Indiana 1825–1831*, 271, 295–97 (Dorothy Riker and Gayle Thornbrough eds., 1954).

the state legislature in draft form. But throughout the nineteenth century, the western states were a ready market for completed eastern state drafts. When New York adopted Field's code of civil procedure, many western states, beginning with Missouri, followed suit. After the Civil War, California, the Dakota Territory, and Montana adopted Field's other draft codes.

19.4.3 Civil War and Immediate Post-Civil War (1861–1887)

The codification movement lost steam as the Civil War (1861–1865) approached. Only after the War did codification resume a place in legal discussion. In the late 1870s and through the 1880s, it was largely a struggle between two men: David Dudley Field, Jr., the proponent, and James Carter, the opponent. Both Field and Carter were practitioners of law. Neither held a government or academic position. The struggle played out mostly in New York and, to a lesser extent, in California, where Field's brother, Stephen J. Field, later a Supreme Court Justice, had achieved adoption of the Field draft codes.

The New York Constitution of 1846 provided for separate commissions to create procedural and substantive codes. Only in the mid-1850s did Field achieve a position on the substantive law commission. The commissions drafted two public law codes (the Political Code and the Code of Criminal Procedure) before turning to private law. During the Civil War, the substantive law commission prepared two drafts of a Civil Code (1862 and 1865). Although the commission presented its drafts to the legislature, they languished there unattended until after the post-war Reconstruction era ended in 1876. Field managed to get the legislature to take up the drafts in the late 1870s. In reasonably prompt order, New York adopted the Code of Criminal Procedure and a Penal Code.

Scholars debate the relative importance of jurisprudential, political, and personal considerations in the defeat of Field's Civil Code. That the opposition of the organized bar was central to the defeat is indisputable. Twice the New York State legislature passed the Civil Code, only to have the governor veto the legislation. The third time, the legislature's lower house passed it only to see it die in the upper house. If one can speak of a popular voice for such a technical and mundane issue as a code, the public should be counted as having endorsed codification.

19.4.4 The National Era (1887 to Present)

By 1887, codification had lost its appeal. It was replaced by the more urgent issue of uniform national law. Already in 1878, the American Bar Association ("ABA"), upon its founding as the first national association of lawyers, stated in its Constitution that its mission was to promote "uniformity of legislation throughout the Union." In 1887, Congress passed the first of the great federal laws regulating commerce, the

Interstate Commerce Commission Act. The Sherman Antitrust Act followed in 1890. Both of these laws regulated limited aspects of commerce among the states. These were not the first efforts at creating national law, but they were among the first to achieve public recognition as such.[53]

In 1889, New York reconstituted its law revision commission. It called for a national body to promote uniform national laws. That led, in 1892, to the foundation, in conjunction with the ABA, of the Uniform Law Commission discussed above.

Thereafter, codification no longer meant a civil code. Soon there was a proposed Federal Code, but it was successor of the Revised Statutes of 1874/1877 and predecessor of today's United States Code, that is, a compilation of federal laws. The next 50 years led to the patchwork of national laws that America has today: a combination of special federal laws applicable only to matters of special federal concern (including a limited segment of commerce among the states), a group of semi-uniform laws adopted by some states, and restatements of common law.

19.5 No Code as Global Mode? What Are the Costs?

The United States is the largest economy in the world; it gets along without a civil code. Without a code, it is the most potent power on the planet. Sans code, it is said to be the freest nation on earth. People from around the world come to the United States to study the American legal system. Americans go abroad, not to learn about code-systems, but to promote the benefits of their quasi-common law system. The World Bank—headquartered in the United States—seems convinced: it holds that common law systems have economic advantages over non-code systems.[54] Should not the world emulate the United States?

Comparativists—especially aspiring comparativists—often fall into this trap. How many foreign jurists come to the United States to study American law thinking that the country with the largest economy must have the best legal system? One can hardly blame them, for the American bar tells that story.

So what is life like in the United States without a national code? Is it an idyllic paradise of decentralized subsidiarity? Are there 50 laboratories where great new ideas are tested and then implemented nationwide? Do thousands of courts decide according to the best law, chosen specially for the case, to do justice and produce economic efficiency in every case?

[53] Prior efforts took three forms: (1) national legislation where the Constitution assigned Congress the lead role, principally bankruptcy and immigration; (2) development of a national common law for commercial matters in federal court in cases following Justice Story's decision in *Swift v. Tyson* in 1842; and (3) development of a national jurisprudence of private law, led again by Justice Story in his famous series of Commentaries.

[54] *See* Ralf Michaels, "Comparative Law by Numbers? Legal Origins Thesis, Doing Business Reports, and the Silence of Traditional Comparative Law," 57 *Am. J. Comp. L.* 765 (2009).

Not exactly.

The United States pays a heavy price for lack of a national civil code. Without a civil code, there is no foundation on which to build special law. There is no gap filler, and there is no tie-breaker. Without a code, there is no guide to fitting the special laws together. Priority among special laws can degenerate into a choice among hierarchies rather than a choice among solutions that work better for the system. Which law governs: the federal constitution, federal statutes, federal regulations, state constitutions, state statutes, state regulations, state common law, municipal charters, municipal ordinances, or municipal regulations?

Americans do not accept this unfortunate situation. Those with financial means escape. They lobby legislatures to pass special statutes written for them. They write their own choice of law into their contracts. They choose their preferred forums. They write standard terms that benefit themselves.

Although many Americans are resigned to this situation, not all limit themselves to simply working around what is. Some campaign for change. They seek a law that should be. Law reform organizations abound. No one, it seems, is happy with the performance of the U.S. legal system. Although there is no campaign for a civil code, reformers seek solutions to problems that elsewhere codes are intended to resolve.

The vision of one reform organization, the Common Good, is a modern day call for codes. The United States, it says, is drowning in law. So many laws are passed every year by Congress, state, and local legislatures, that they have "piled up like sediment in a harbor, bogging the country down."[55] Americans fail to distinguish the different types of laws, the timeless from the temporary.

That world of America in 2012 could be the world of 1789 that confronted the drafters of the French Civil Code, among them Portalis, who wrote:

> Facing us was only a confused and shapeless mass of foreign and French laws, of general and particular customs, of abrogated and non-abrogated ordinances, of contradictory regulations and conflicting decisions; one encountered nothing but a mysterious labyrinth, and at every moment, the guiding thread escaped us. We were always on the point of getting lost in an immense chaos.[56]

Common Good, in an aptly-named initiative, calls on Americans to *Start Over*. Its rallying cry is "Radically Simplify Law."[57] It reminds Americans that, "[i]t is beyond human capacity to foresee every possible circumstance or specify how to address or prevent every conceivable event."[58] Yet, it does not seek to eliminate law,

---

[55] "The Problem: Drowning in Law," *CommonGood*, http://www.commongood.org/pages/the-problem (last visited Nov. 25, 2012). The program of the Common Good is that of its *Start Over* initiative, available at its website, www.commongood.org. [hereinafter *Common Good*]

[56] *Quoted in* 1 P. Fenet, *Recueil complet des travaux prépartoires du Code Civil* xcii (1836), *translated in* Arthur Taylor von Mehren and James Russell Gordley, *The Civil Law System* 14 (2d ed. 1977).

[57] *Common Good*, *supra* note 57.

[58] *Id.*

but to rationalize it. "Law is supposed to be a framework for human judgment."[59] "Law should set outer boundaries of required conduct, not intercede in everyday disputes."[60]

Start Over seeks that which Portalis sought in the French codes:

> *To simplify everything*, that is an operation on which one needs to agree. *To foresee everything*, that is a goal impossible of attainment . . . . We have thus not felt that we were obliged to simplify the laws to the point of leaving the citizens without rules and without guarantees as to their most important interests. . . . The function of the law (*loi*) is to fix, in broad outline, the general maxims of justice (*droit*), to establish principles rich in suggestiveness (*conséquences*), and not to descend into the details of the questions that can arise in each subject.[61]

Amen.

[59] *Id.*

[60] *Id.*

[61] Portalis, Tronchet, Bigot-Préameneu and Maleville, "Discourse préliminair," *in* 1 J. Locré, *La Législation Civile, Commerciale et Criminelle de la France* 251, 255–72 (1827), *translated in* von Mehren & Gordley, *supra* note 56, at 54–55.

Chapter 20
Private Law in Louisiana: An Account of Civil Codes, Heritage, and Law Reform

Agustín Parise

Abstract The evolution of private law in the state of Louisiana (USA) provides a unique account of civil codes, heritage, and law reform. The resulting legal system in the state was significantly shaped by the enactment of civil codes. Evolving from a first precedent found in the Digest of 1808 and until the ongoing revision efforts, yet also through the enactment of the 1825 and 1870 civil codes, Louisiana can claim a strong connection with codification. That connection is also explained by the Spanish and French heritage that molded the private law of the state. The heritage was petrified by the incorporation of provisions of continental European origin within the text of the Louisiana civil codes. The heritage was also subject to interferences from sister common law states, resulting in a blend of its own. A natural consequence of law reform, that blend was also sensed as part of a decodification process, reflected in the contents of revised statutes and special legislation. This essay aims to help readers understand (i) the context for codification in Louisiana;

An abridged version of this paper was presented as the Report for the State of Louisiana for the *Second Thematic Congress of the International Academy of Comparative Law* (Taiwan), on May 24, 2012. It was drafted during a research stay at the *Max-Planck-Institut für europäische Rechtsgeschichte* (Germany).

The author is indebted to Julio Romañach, Jr. and Julieta Marotta de Parise for their suggestions and constructive criticisms. He is also indebted to James Maxeiner for his comments on earlier drafts and to Julio César Rivera for entrusting him with the drafting of the abovementioned report.

Part of the research needed for this paper was originally undertaken by the author when completing his doctoral dissertation entitled: *Historia de la Codificación Civil del Estado de la Luisiana y su Influencia en el Código Civil Argentino* (on file with the Universidad de Buenos Aires). The content of this paper was extracted for many sections *verbatim* from previous writings authored, and co-authored, in the period 2005–2012. General references to those works were intended at the beginning of sections. The author thanks Olivier Moréteau, who co-authored one of those previous works, and kindly granted permission for reproduction.

A. Parise (✉)
Faculty of Law, Maastricht University, Maastricht, The Netherlands
e-mail: pariseagustin@gmail.com

J.C. Rivera (ed.), *The Scope and Structure of Civil Codes*, Ius Gentium: Comparative Perspectives on Law and Justice 32, DOI 10.1007/978-94-007-7942-6_20,

(ii) the evolution of the civil code and its different changes, focusing mainly on the rich legal history of the state; (iii) the structure and content of the current civil code, highlighting its more recent changes; (iv) the interplay of the civil code with other areas of law, such as constitutional law; and finally, (v) the place of the civil code within the legal universe of Louisiana private law.

Keywords Codification • Comparative law • Law reform • Legal history • Louisiana private law

20.1 Context of the Code

20.1.1 Private Law[1]

The geographical location, historical background, and resulting legal culture of the state of Louisiana (USA) tend to attract comparative-law scholars. René David, when referring to Louisiana, indicated that it is "ruled by mixed laws, borrowing certain elements from the common law but, to a certain extent, retaining [its] membership in the Romano-Germanic family."[2] Louisiana is the only U.S. state that is considered to be a member of that family, and is the only state with a civil code that originally followed the tenets of nineteenth-century continental European codes. As a consequence of many of the events that will be developed in this paper (and other events that exceed its scope), scholars now consider Louisiana a traditional mixed jurisdiction, where the predominant legal system is no longer pure, and the influence of the common law is sensed.[3]

The state of Louisiana was no exception to the nineteenth-century codification movement that spread throughout the Western hemisphere. The legal culture of Louisiana was an isolated "civil law[4] island" partially surrounded by a "sea of common law," a status that had to be safeguarded to survive.[5] A look into the early

[1] See generally, Agustín Parise, "Codification of the Law in Louisiana: Early Nineteenth-Century oscillation between Continental European and Common Law Systems", 27 Tulane European & Civil Law Forum 133 (2012); and Agustín Parise, "Legal Transplants and Codification: Exploring the North American Sources of the Civil Code of Argentina (1871"), 1:2 ISAIDAT Law Review 1 (2011).

[2] René David & John E. Brierley, *Major Legal Systems in the World Today: An Introduction to the Comparative Study of Law* 59–60 (1968).

[3] William Wirt Howe, "Law in the Louisiana Purchase", 14 Yale L. J. 77, 79 (1904). See, Vernon Valentine Palmer, "Introduction", *Louisiana: Microcosm of a Mixed Jurisdiction* 3, 4 (Vernon Valentine Palmer ed., 1999).

[4] *n.b.*, in this paper, the terms Civil Law, Romano-Germanic, and Continental European will be used indistinctly to refer to the prevailing system of private law that applies in Louisiana.

[5] Agustín Parise, *Non-Pecuniary Damages in the Louisiana Civil Code Article 1928: Originality in the Early Nineteenth Century and Its Projected Use in Further Codification Endeavors* 14 (May 18th, 2006) (unpublished LL.M. thesis, Louisiana State University, Paul M. Hebert Law Center) (on file with the LSU Law Library).

American period in Louisiana (c. 1803–1830) provides an illustration of a clash of legal systems between continental European and common law principles.[6]

In Louisiana, during the early 1800s, the first decisions on the adoption of provisions from different systems were taken in criminal law and procedure, and in civil procedure. A group of inhabitants advocated for the implementation of the American law courts and another group advocated for the continuity of the continental European court system (*n.b.*, excluding criminal law).[7] In criminal law and criminal procedure the common law achieved a first bastion, and its principles prevailed. In civil procedure, at least during the first years, the bastion was shared between continental European and common law principles, although there was a pre-eminence of principles from the former.[8]

In the area of civil law the bastion was controlled by continental European ideas. Early, the inhabitants opted for those principles, perhaps due to cultural and economic interests,[9] and to protect the property rights they had received during the French and Spanish periods.[10] Some local inhabitants wanted to codify following continental European principles and in that way preserve the law and rights they previously had. Those continental European ideas, however, were not adopted blindly in Louisiana.[11]

Civil law codification endeavors in Louisiana had an early projection on other US states and territories. For example, David Dudley Field, who advocated for codification in the US during the nineteenth century,[12] presented a Project of a Civil Code for the State of New York before the legislature in 1865.[13] Many sections of the project had notes indicating references to, among others, the *Code Napoléon*,[14] and paramount for this paper, the Louisiana Civil Code of 1825.[15]

---

[6] See generally, George Dargo, "Jefferson's Louisiana: Politics and the Clash of Legal Traditions" (rev. ed. 2009).

[7] *Id.* at 222.

[8] Parise, "Codification of the Law in Louisiana", *supra* note 1.

[9] J.R. Trahan, "The Continuing Influence of le Droit Civil and el Derecho Civil in the Private Law of Louisiana", 63 La. L. Rev. 1019, 1024 (2003).

[10] Richard Holcombe Kilbourne, *A History of the Louisiana Civil Code: The Formative Years 1803–1839* 41 (1987).

[11] Parise, "Codification of the Law in Louisiana", *supra* note 1.

[12] See generally, Rodolfo Batiza, "Sources of the Field Civil Code: The Civil Law Influences on a Common Law Code", 60 Tul. L. Rev. 799 (1986).

[13] The Civil Code of the State of New York ix (1865). The project comprised 2034 sections, throughout four divisions: persons; property; obligations; and general provisions applicable to persons, property, and obligations, or to two of those subjects (*Id.* at 2 and 647). Even though the Project was never adopted in New York, its drafts were very influential. Henry M. Field, *The Life of David Dudley Field* 88 (1898); *Extracts from Notices of David Dudley Field* 39 (1894); and Shael Herman, "The Fate and the Future of Codification in America", 40 Am. J. Legal Hist. 407, 425 (1996).

[14] For example, the note to article 444 reads: "This and the four sections following are similar to those of the Code Napoleon, art. 559–563." Civil Code of New York, *supra* note 13, at 135.

[15] For example, the note to Chapter 2, Title 3, Part 4, Division reads: "The provisions of this chapter, except § 455, are similar to those of the Code Napoleon and the Code of Louisiana." *Id.* at 136.

Even when a commercial code was drafted in the 1820s, following to some extent continental European principles, the last bastion was won by general commercial practices also effective in other US states. In commercial law, local inhabitants seemed to prefer the flexibility that those practices provided. That flexibility would also grant the ability of locating local traders in a similar standing with the ones from other nations and US states.[16]

Louisiana and its legal system, however, kept evolving in the twentieth and twenty-first centuries. In 1935, the Louisiana State University Law School (LSU) appointed Gordon Ireland to teach law.[17] After 2 years of teaching in Louisiana, Ireland claimed that it should be admitted that Louisiana had become a common-law state.[18] Ireland understood that France and its legal texts had been left aside, that the Louisiana Civil Code was nothing other than a compilation that was applied whenever a local decision was not rendered in that area, and that the legal system of Louisiana resembled that of other states of the Union that at some point had been Spanish or French colonies.[19] A reaction to this statement was quick to come. In 1937, Paul M. Hébert, together with three other law professors, challenged Ireland's position,[20] and concluded that Louisiana continued to be a civil law jurisdiction.[21] This scholarly discussion, known as the Great Debate,[22] is considered positive for the civil law in Louisiana. It generated a movement towards the enhancement of the civil law; the creation of the Louisiana Law Review, which aimed to develop the civil and comparative law in Louisiana; the appointment of foreign civil law professors, mainly at the Tulane Law School and at LSU; and the creation of the Louisiana State Law Institute (LSLI), which was envisioned to be a tool for law reform in the state.[23] The Great Debate also resulted in further revisions in the text of the Louisiana Civil Code, which started in the 1970s and extended into the twenty-first century. There is an on-going revision process of the Louisiana Civil Code, and it was estimated, by 2003, that 72 % of the nineteenth-century text had been revised.[24]

---

[16] Parise, "Codification of the Law in Louisiana", *supra* note 1.

[17] Kenneth M. Murchison, "The Judicial Revival of Louisiana's Civilian Tradition: A Surprising Triumph for the American Influence", 49 La. L. Rev. 1, 3 (1988).

[18] Gordon Ireland, "Louisiana's Legal System Reappraised", 11 Tul. L. Rev. 585, 596 (1937). See also, Murchison, *supra* note 17, at 4.

[19] Ireland, *supra* note 18, at 595–597.

[20] Harriet Spiller Daggett et al., "A Reappraisal Appraised: A Brief for the Civil Law of Louisiana", 12 Tul. L. Rev. 12, 12 (1937).

[21] *Id.* at 41.

[22] See generally, Paul Brosman, "A Controversy and a Challenge", 12 Tul. L. Rev. 239 (1938); and Marta Figueroa-Torres, "Recodification of Civil Law in Puerto Rico: A Quixotic Pursuit of the Civil Code for the New Millennium", 23 Tul. Eur. & Civ. L.F. 143, 155–56 (2008).

[23] Murchison, *supra* note 17, at 4.

[24] Vernon Valentine Palmer, "The French Connection and The Spanish Perception: Historical Debates and Contemporary Evaluation of French Influence on Louisiana Civil Law", 63 La. L. Rev. 1067, 1112 (2003).

20.1.2 Revision Efforts[25]

The current Louisiana Civil Code resulted from a revision of the text of the civil code of 1870,[26] which had been a revision of the text of 1825.[27] The current Louisiana Civil Code is subject to the following division: Preliminary Title; Book I, of persons; Book II, of things and the different modifications of ownership; Book III, of the different modes of acquiring the ownership of things; and Book IV, of conflict of laws.[28] Each book is divided, when pertinent, into titles, chapters, sections, subsections, paragraphs, and articles. The numeration of the latter extends from 1 to 3,556.[29] The different revisions to the text of 1870 took place mainly during the second half of the twentieth century.[30]

---

[25] See generally, Olivier Moréteau & Agustín Parise, "Recodification in Louisiana and Latin America", 83 Tul. L. Rev. 1103, 1120 (2009).

[26] The text of 1870 had the following structure: Preliminary Title, of the general definitions of law and of the promulgation of the laws; Book I, of persons; Book II, of things, and of different modifications of ownership; and Book III, of the different modes of acquiring the ownership of things. The Revised Civil Code of the State of Louisiana (1870).

[27] The text of 1825 had the following structure: Preliminary Title, of the general definitions of rights and the promulgation of the laws; Book I, of persons; Book II, of things and of the different modifications of property; and Book III, of the different modes of acquiring the property of things. Civil Code of the State of Louisiana (1825).

[28] Louisiana Pocket Civil Code – 2010 Edition (Alain Levasseur ed. 2010).

[29] *Id. n.b.*, that numbering also includes blank and repealed articles.

[30] **Preliminary Title:** Chapters 1 and 2 (1987), Chapter 3 (1987 and 1991); **Book I:** *Title I*-Natural and Juridical Personas (1987), *Title II*-Domicile (2008), *Title III*-Absent Persons(1990), *Title IV*-Husband and Wife (1987), *Title V*-Divorce (1990, 1993, and 1997), *Title VI*-Of Master and Servant (repealed in part in 1993), *Title VII*-Parent and Child (1993), Chapters 1–3 (1976, 2005), Chapter 4 (2008), *Title VIII*-Minors, of their Tutorship and Emancipation, Chapter 2 (2008), *Title IX*-Persons Unable to Care for Their Persons or Property (2000), *Title X*-Of Corporations (repealed in part in 1993); **Book II:** *Title I*-Things, *Title II*-Ownership, *Title III*-Personal Servitudes, *Title IV*-Predial Servitudes, *Title V*-Building Restrictions, *Title VI*-Boundaries (all revised from 1976 to 1979), *Title VII*-Ownership in indivision (added in 1990); **Book III:** *Preliminary Title* (1981), *Title I*-Of Successions, Chapters 1–3 (1981), Chapters 4–6 and 13 (1997), *Title II*-Of Donations *Inter Vivos* and *Mortis Causa*, Chapter 1 (2008), Chapter 2 (1991), Chapter 3 (1996), Chapter 4 (2001), Chapter 5 (2008), Chapter 6 (1997 and 2001), Chapters 8 and 9 (2004), *Title III*-Obligations in General (1984), *Title IV*-Conventional Obligations or Contracts (1984), *Title V*-Obligations arising Without Agreement, Chapters 1 and 2 (1995), *Title VI*-Matrimonial Regimes (1979), *Title VII*-Sale (1993), *Title IX*-Of Lease, Chapters 1–4 (2004), *Title XI*-Partnership (1980), *Title XII*-Of Loan (2004), *Title XIII*-Deposit and Sequestration (2003), *Title XV*-Representation and Mandate (1997), *Title XVI*-Suretyship (1987), *Title XVII*-Compromise (2007), *Title XXII*-Mortgages (1991, 1992, and 2005), *Title XXII-A*-Of Registry (2005), *Title XXIII*-Occupancy and Possession (1982), *Title XXIV*-Prescription, Chapters 1–3 (1982), Chapter 4 (1983), *Title XXV*-Of the Signification of the Sundry Terms (1999); and **Book IV** (added in 1991). A. N. Yiannopoulos, "The Civil Codes of Louisiana", 1Louisiana *Civil Code 2010* Edition LIII, LXVI-LXIX (A. N. Yiannopoulos ed. 2010); and see William E. Crawford & Cordell H. Haymon, "Louisiana State Law Institute Recognizes 70-Year Milestone: Origin, History and Accomplishments", 56 La. B.J. 85, 91–92 (2008).

A very significant amount of legislation in Louisiana is to be found in a collection of revised statutes. The Louisiana Revised Statutes[31] are arranged in titles running by alphabetic order and extending from 1 to 56. Some of these titles are called codes, like Title 22 (*i.e.*, Insurance Code)[32] and Title 31 (*i.e.*, Mineral Code).[33] Title 9 contains the Civil Code Ancillaries. The structure of Title 9 runs parallel to that of the Louisiana Civil Code. It contains some laws that may be seen as a product of decodification, such as the Louisiana Trust Code.[34] Most provisions contained in Title 9 are ancillary to the articles of the Louisiana Civil Code, dealing for instance with procedural details that pertain to a topic dealt with in the Louisiana Civil Code (*v.gr.,* divorce).[35]

20.2 Evolution of the Code

20.2.1 Current Text[36]

In 1938, the Legislature created the Louisiana State Law Institute,[37] which should be the "official advisory law revision commission, law reform agency and legal research agency"[38] of Louisiana. Although some states (*v.gr*, New York, New Jersey) have law revision commissions, the LSLI has a clear charge and greater role than those commissions in sister states. Accordingly, law reform in Louisiana is many times gestated and proposed by LSLI experts in the different areas of law, who will then recommend their drafts to the legislative body.

In 1948, facing the need to update the civil law, the Legislature instructed the LSLI to prepare a comprehensive revision of the text of 1870.[39] With that same purpose in 1960, the LSLI created its civil-law section attempting to accomplish a revision and an advancement of the civil law.[40] The LSLI decided to

---

[31] Section 1, Title 1 of the Louisiana Revised Statutes reads:

> This Act shall be known as the Louisiana Revised Statutes of 1950 and shall be cited as R.S. followed by the number of the Title and the number of the Section in the Title, separated by a colon. Example: Section 1 of Title 20 shall be cited as R.S. 20:1.

La. Rev. Stat. Ann. § 1:1.

[32] La. Rev. Stat. Ann. § 22:1 *et seq.*

[33] La. Rev. Stat. Ann. § 31:1 *et seq.*

[34] La. Rev. Stat. Ann. § 9:1721 *et seq.*

[35] La. Rev. Stat. Ann. § 9:301 *et seq.*

[36] See generally, Agustín Parise, "A Constant Give and Take: Tracing Legal Borrowings in the Louisiana Civil Law Experience", 35 Seton Hall Legis. J. 1 (2010).

[37] 1938 La. Acts 429–433.

[38] *Id.* at 430.

[39] 1948 La. Acts 810.

[40] A.N. Yiannopoulos, "The Civil Law Program of the Louisiana State Law Institute", 12 La. B.J. 89, 90 (1964).

undertake a revision on a title-by-title basis,[41] which started in the 1970s,[42] and that is ongoing.[43]

Reporters occupy a key role in revisions by the LSLI. When the LSLI encounters a need for reform, a reporter is appointed. The reporter works with a group of researchers and a committee of experts who provide advice. Once the reporter completes the project, it is sent to the LSLI's council for discussion and revision.[44] Dozens of reporters and hundreds of attorneys, judges, and law professors have participated in the revision efforts.[45]

The sources of the revisions by the LSLI are diverse because they resulted from partial revisions undertaken by different reporters and researchers. For example, Saúl Litvinoff, acting as reporter of the titles on obligations,[46] indicated that they studied and consulted the texts of the codes of several countries (*v.gr.,* Germany, Argentina, and Ethiopia[47]) and local[48] and foreign jurisprudence.[49] The revision by the LSLI, however, was built strongly upon local jurisprudence, local acts, and local scholarly writings.

20.2.2 Previous Texts[50]

20.2.2.1 Towards Codification

The protection of the continental European system for the provisions dealing with private law in Louisiana may be traced to the first years of the territorial period. In 1804, the Legislative Council of the Territory of Orleans appointed a committee to draft a civil code for the territory.[51] The following year it was resolved that the committee was "authorized to employ two counselors at law, to assist them in drafting the said [civil and criminal] codes."[52] A new step towards codification was taken in 1806.

---

[41] Saúl Litvinoff, "Codificación en Louisiana", 2 *La Codificación: Raíces y Prospectivas* 127, 135 (2004).

[42] Crawford & Haymon, *supra* note 30, at 91.

[43] See, for example, *supra* note 30; and Moréteau & Parise, *supra* note 25, at 1118–1119.

[44] Ferdinand F. Stone, "The Louisiana State Law Institute", 4 Am. J. Comp. L. 85, 87–88 (1955).

[45] Crawford & Haymon, *supra* note 30, at 91.

[46] La. State Law Inst., "Exposé de motifs", *Revision of Book III, Titles III and IV of the Louisiana Civil Code* 1, 1–86 (1983).

[47] *Id.* at 57, 11, and 37 (respectively).

[48] *Id.* at 21.

[49] *v.gr.*, the work includes references to Argentine jurisprudence. *Id.* at 41.

[50] See generally, Parise, *supra* note 36; and Moréteau & Parise, *supra* note 25.

[51] Kate Wallach, *Research in Louisiana Law* 46 (2d ed. 1960); and "Orleans Legislative Council: Monday, December 10", *Louisiana Gazette*, Dec. 21, 1804, at 3.

[52] 1805 La. Acts 458–460.

The Legislature adopted a bill[53] by which the pre-existing Spanish and Roman laws would govern the Territory.[54] Governor William C. C. Claiborne vetoed the bill.[55] The bill did not prosper, even when the newspaper *Le Telegraphe*[56] published contemporaneously a manifesto in which members of the House of Representatives proposed the dissolution of the Legislature after the veto and explained why they preferred the continental European system.[57]

20.2.2.2 Digest of 1808

Another step was made towards codification again in 1806, when the Legislature appointed James Brown and Louis Moreau-Lislet to draft a civil code.[58] According to the resolution, the "two jurisconsults shall make the civil law by which this territory is now governed, the ground work of said code."[59] On March 31, 1808, the Legislature promulgated the *Digest of the Civil Laws now in force in the territory of Orleans* (Digest of 1808).[60] Claiborne did not veto the Digest of 1808.[61]

---

[53] See also Mitchell Franklin, "Introduction" to 1 *The Laws of las Siete Partidas Which are Still in Force in the State of Louisiana* 1, 8–11 (L. Moreau Lislet & Henry Carleton, trans., 1978) (1820); Mitchell Franklin, "Some Considerations on the Existential Force of Roman Law in the Early History of the United States", 22 Buff. L. Rev. 69, 69–70 (1972); Mitchell Franklin, The Eighteenth Brumaire in Louisiana: Talleyrand and the Spanish Medieval Legal System of 1806", 16 Tul. L. Rev. 514, 516 (1942); Mitchell Franklin, "The Place of Thomas Jefferson in the Expulsion of Spanish Medieval Law from Louisiana", 16 Tul. L. Rev. 319, 323–26 (1942).

[54] Yiannopoulos, *supra* note 30, at LVI.

[55] "Letter from W. C. C. Claiborne to the Legislative Council and the House of Representatives (May 26, 1806)", 3 *Official letter books of W. C. C. Claiborne, 1801–1816*, at 313 (Dunbar Rowland ed., 1917).

[56] "Letter from W. C. C. Claiborne to the Secretary of State (June 3, 1806)", 9 *The Territorial Papers of the United States: The Territory of Orleans, 1803–1812*, at 642–657 (Clarence Edwin Carter ed., 1940). See also, Elizabeth Gaspar Brown, "Legal Systems in Conflict: Orleans Territory 1804–1812", 1 Am. J. Legal Hist. 35, 49–53 (1957).

[57] 9 *The Territorial Papers*, *supra* note 56, at 650.

[58] 1806 La. Acts 214–219.

[59] *Id.* at 214.

[60] The complete French title is *Digeste des lois civiles actuellement en force dans le territoire d'Orléans, avec des changemens et améliorations adaptés à son présent système de gouvernement.* 1808 La. Acts 122–123. See generally, *A Digest of the Civil Laws Now in Force in the Territory of Orleans, with Alterations and Amendments Adapted to its Present System of Government* (Bradford & Anderson 1808).

[61] Claiborne informed the Legislature that he approved the Digest of 1808 by a letter dated March 31, 1808. "Letter from W. C. C. Claiborne to the Legislature (Mar. 31, 1808)", 9 *The Territorial Papers*, *supra* note 56, at 642–657. See also Vernon Valentine Palmer, "Two Worlds in One: The Genesis of Louisiana's Mixed Legal System, 1803–1812", *Louisiana: Microcosm of a Mixed Jurisdiction* 23, 34 (Vernon Valentine Palmer ed., 1999).

The Digest of 1808 did not include notes explaining its sources.[62] Some copies of the Digest of 1808 contain interleaves with manuscript notes that seem to have been dictated by Moreau-Lislet, or in some cases, even written by him.[63] One of these manuscripts, the de la Vergne copy,[64] includes facing the English text references to Roman and Spanish materials intended to be paired to each title of the Digest of 1808, and facing the French text references to Roman and Spanish materials intended to be paired to each article.[65] The manuscript also includes references to French texts of Roman grounding, such as the works of Pothier and Domat. In addition, 645 articles of the 2160 of the Digest of 1808 do not have corresponding notes or comments.[66]

The content of the de la Vergne copy was tested in the 1970s and is still unsettled. Rodolfo Batiza published his study on the textual sources of the Digest of 1808 in 1971.[67] Batiza concluded that approximately 85 % of the text of the articles of the Digest of 1808 had been extracted from French texts.[68] In 1972, Robert A. Pascal published a reply providing his reasons why he understood the Digest of 1808 to be comprised in its substance of Spanish, not French, law.[69] Pascal asserted that Spanish law, including Roman law and *derecho común*, were the law of Louisiana in 1806 and were not codified or easily accessible to those who intended to draft a digest.[70] In addition, Brown and Moreau-Lislet had been instructed to draft the Digest of 1808 in English and French.[71] According to Pascal, French law, composed of elements from Roman, Romanized Frankish, Burgundian, and Visigothic origin, habitually resembled the Spanish law that derived from Roman or Roman-Visigothic origins.[72] He understood that the *Code Napoléon* was a valuable model,[73] and the

[62] See Joseph Dainow, "Moreau Lislet's Notes On Sources of Louisiana Civil Code of 1808", 19 La. L. Rev. 43 (1958).

[63] John W. Cairns, "The de la Vergne Volume and the Digest of 1808", 24 Tul. Eur. & Civ. L.F. 31, 74 (2009).

[64] *The de la Vergne Copy – Bicentennial Edition of A Digest of the Civil Laws Now in Force in the Territory of Orleans* (2008). The most recent and perhaps most exhaustive study of the de la Vergne Copy was elaborated by Cairns (See Cairns, *supra* note 63).

[65] See "Foreword" to *The de la Vergne Copy*, *supra* note 64; Cairns, *supra* note 63, at 77; and Mitchell Franklin, "An Important Document in the History of American Roman and Civil Law: The de la Vergne Manuscript", 33 Tul. L. Rev. 35, 39–42 (1958).

[66] Vernon Valentine Palmer, "The Recent Discovery of Moreau Lislet's System of Omissions and Its Importance to the Debate Over the Sources of the Digest of 1808", 49 Loy. L. Rev. 301, 311 (2003).

[67] Rodolfo Batiza, "The Louisiana Civil Code of 1808: Its Actual Sources and Present Relevance", 46 Tul. L. Rev. 4 (1971).

[68] *Id.* at 12.

[69] Robert A. Pascal, "Sources of the Digest of 1808: A Reply to Professor Batiza", 46 Tul. L. Rev. 603, 605 (1972).

[70] *Id.* at 605.

[71] *Id.*

[72] *Id.*

[73] *Id.*

Projet of 1800 afforded greater attention to the Roman and Roman-Visigothic institutions that had been in force in the South of France.[74] He claimed that the Digest of 1808, although largely written with words from French texts, tried and largely succeeded in reflecting the substance of the Spanish law in Louisiana.[75]

20.2.2.3 Civil Code of 1825

Several factors contributed to a tendency in the legal community to deemphasize the Digest of 1808.[76] In 1817, it was decided in the case of *Cottin v. Cottin*[77] that the laws that were not contrary to the Digest of 1808 were not repealed with its enactment.[78] Therefore, the Digest of 1808 had not completely repealed the civil laws that had existed in Louisiana.[79]

The Legislature of Louisiana reacted accordingly by working towards a revision. In 1822, the Legislature appointed Pierre Derbigny, Edward Livingston, and Moreau-Lislet to draft what would be known as the Project of 1823.[80] The Project of 1823 included comments accompanying the text proposed for many of its articles.[81] The comments of the drafters cover 25 % of the proposed articles.[82] The comments include approximately 340 references to diverse codes, laws, and works of legal doctrine, which are spread very unevenly throughout the draft.[83] Most comments are found in Book I and in titles 1 and 2 of Book II. In contrast, titles 3 to 23 of Book III contain very few references.[84] A study by Batiza indicated that the drafters used, among others, the following texts: the *Corpus Iuris*, the *Partidas*, the *Projet* of 1800, the *Code Napoléon*, the Digest of 1808, and various acts of the Legislature of Louisiana. The study also indicated that the drafters consulted, among others, works by Blackstone, Domat, Febrero, Maleville, Merlin, Toullier, and Pothier.[85]

---

[74] *Id.* at 606.

[75] *Id.* at 604.

[76] Kilbourne, *supra* note 10, at 62; and Agustín Parise, "The Place of the Louisiana Civil Code in the Hispanic Civil Codifications: The Comments to the Spanish Civil Code Project of 1851", 68 La. L. Rev. 823, 833 (2008).

[77] "Cottin v. Cottin", 5 Mart. (o.s.) 93, 101–02 (La. 1819).

[78] *Id.*

[79] Kilbourne, *supra* note 10, at 62.

[80] H.R. Journal, 5th Leg., 2d Sess., at 73 (La. 1822); Ira Flory, "Edward Livingston's Place in Louisiana Law", 19 La. Hist. Q. 328, 346 (1936).

[81] See generally, *Additions and Amendments to the Civil Code of the State of Louisiana*, Proposed in Obedience to the Resolution of the Legislature of the 14th, March, 1822, by the Jurist Commissioned for that Purpose (1823).

[82] Rodolfo Batiza, "The Actual Sources of the Louisiana Projet of 1823: A General Analytical Survey", 47 Tul. L. Rev. 1, 3 (1972).

[83] *Id.*

[84] *Id.*

[85] *Id.* at 28–30.

The Project of 1823 was subject to discussion by the Legislature.[86] Derbigny, at that time Secretary of State of Louisiana,[87] issued a certificate of promulgation on May 20, 1825, indicating that the new text would take effect 1 month later.[88] The promulgated text would be known as the Civil Code of 1825.

The Spanish laws that had been applied in the state before the adoption of the Digest of 1808 kept generating a feeling of uncertainty about their application. The Civil Code of 1825 tried to terminate the debate on the application of Spanish laws and to give a sense of originality and a new starting point. Therefore, the Civil Code of 1825 included article 3521, which could be read as not repealing all previous laws but only those "for which it has been especially provided in this Code."[89] That language opened the door to different interpretations, and allowed a limit to the express repeal: when faced with silence in the Civil Code of 1825, it would have been admissible to look for solutions in the previous laws.[90] The Louisiana Supreme Court applied this interpretation,[91] and in 1827, decided that Spanish law that was not contrary to the Civil Code of 1825 continued in effect, while the articles of the Digest of 1808 that had been omitted in the Civil Code of 1825 were still in force.[92] To end that uncertainty, the Legislature of Louisiana enacted two acts[93] aiming towards a great repeal.[94] Debate outlived the acts, especially since the higher court claimed that the acts only repealed the previous positive law and not the principles that derived from them, which had been acquired by the practice of the courts.[95]

---

[86] "Bank of Louisiana v. Farrar", 1 La. Ann. 49, 60 (1847). See also, John H. Tucker, "Source Books of Louisiana Law I", 6 Tul. L. Rev. 280, 287 (1931).

[87] 1 *A Dictionary of Louisiana Biography* 239 (Glenn R. Conrad ed., 1988).

[88] Tucker, *supra* note 86, at 288. See also, *Civil Code of the State of Louisiana*; With Annotations by Wheelock S. Upton, LL.B., and Needler R. Jennings 9 (1838).

Nevertheless, the Louisiana Supreme Court stated that the code had been promulgated on different dates in different parts of the state; New Orleans on May 20 and West Feliciana Parish on June 15. Tucker, *supra* note 86, at 288–289. See also, Yiannopoulos, *supra* note 30, at LX; and Wallach, *supra* note 51, at 48.

[89] Article 3521 of the Civil Code of 1825 reads:

> From and after the promulgation of this Code [of 1825], the Spanish, Roman and French laws, which were in force in this State, when Louisiana was ceded to the United States, and the acts of the Legislative Council, of the Legislature of the Territory of Orleans, and of the Legislature of the State of Louisiana, be and are hereby repealed in every case, for which it has been especially provided in this Code, and that they shall not be invoked as laws, even under the pretence that their provisions are not contrary or repugnant to those of this Code.

Civil Code, *supra* note 27, at 1112.

[90] Vernon Valentine Palmer, "The Death of a Code–The Birth of a Digest", 63 Tul. L. Rev. 221, 246 (1988).

[91] "Cole's Widow v. His Executors", 7 Mart. (n.s.) 41, 46 (La. 1828).

[92] "Flower v. Griffith", 6 Mart. (n.s.) 89, 92–93 (La. 1827).

[93] 1828 La. Acts 66; and 1828 La. Acts 160.

[94] Palmer, *supra* note 24, at 1077.

[95] "Reynolds v. Swain", 13 La. 193, 198 (1839). See also, John T. Hood, "The History and Development of the Louisiana Civil Code", 33 Tul. L. Rev. 7, 18 (1958).

20.2.2.4 Revision of 1870

The Civil Code of 1825 survived without significant alterations for approximately half a century.[96] Nevertheless, at that time, the new social context (*v.gr.*, abolition of slavery[97]) and the needs of the legal community created a need for change through revision. John Ray was appointed to undertake the needed work. Ray claimed in his report that his revision had "required much labor and a thorough acquaintance with the Civil Code [of 1825], the Statutes of the State, and the Decisions of the Supreme Court."[98] In 1870, the Legislature of Louisiana adopted Ray's revision.[99] The act of adoption reads in part "that the Civil Code of the State of Louisiana be amended and re-enacted so as to read as follows..."[100] The wording seems to indicate that the Legislature did not intend to clearly repeal the Civil Code of 1825, and that on the contrary, they intended to reflect continuity.[101] In addition, the revision of 1870 did not include a repealing clause.[102] Finally, this interpretation was also favored by the Louisiana Supreme Court, which has consistently rendered decisions in accordance therewith.[103]

[96] Moréteau & Parise, *supra* note 25, at 1116.

[97] Abolition in the US motivated the elimination of all provisions on slavery that existed in the Louisiana Civil Code at that time. Provisions on slavery had been previously incorporated in the Digest of 1808 and in the Civil Code of 1825. This paper does not cover the drafting, enactment, and application of the Black Code of 1806. That text was adopted by the Legislature on June 7, 1806, and applied to the enslaved inhabitants in the region (1807 La. Acts 150). For further readings on the Black Code see, amongst the abundant literature, Francis P. Burns, "The Black Code", 5 Loyola Law Journal 15 (1923); Wallach, *supra* note 51, at 45–46; Hans W. Baade, "The Law of Slavery in Spanish Louisiana", *Louisiana's Legal Heritage* at 43 (Edward F. Haas and Robert R. Macdonald ed., 1983); Thomas N. Ingersoll, "Slave Codes and Judicial Practice in New Orleans, 1718–1807", 13 Law & Hist. Rev. 23 (1995); and Vernon Valentine Palmer, "The Origins and Authors of the Code Noir", 56 La. L. Rev. 363 (1996).

[98] "Letter from Ray to Joint Committee on the Revision of the Statutes and Codes (Dec. 27, 1869)", John Ray, *The Civil Code of the State of Louisiana*, revised, arranged and amended vii (1869).

[99] The complete title in English reads: "An Act to amend and re-enact the Civil Code of the State of Louisiana, including, besides all other matters embraced in said Code, the several objects set forth in the Table of Contents here annexed and made part of this title." Revised Civil Code, *supra* note 26, at iii.

[100] Ray, *supra* note 98, at xxi.

[101] Palmer, *supra* note 90, at 248.

[102] Palmer, *supra* note 90, at 248–249.

[103] The cases are collected in the US Fifth Circuit decision in Mary H. Shelp v. Nat'l Surety Corp., 333 F.2d 431, 439 (5th Cir. 1964); and Palmer, *supra* note 90, at 249.

20.3 Structure and Content of the Code[104]

Codification, as understood today, finds its origins in Europe, where it experienced a significant development during the eighteenth and nineteenth centuries.[105] A scientific revolution led the way for codification, originated in Enlightened and Humanistic ideas, and followed by Rationalistic Natural Law Theorizing.[106] This revolution advocated for a new presentation and form of laws which would replace the existing provisions,[107] while grouping different areas in an organic, systematic,[108] clear, accurate, and complete way.[109] In addition, codification suggested the laying out of a plan with terminology and phraseology.[110] Codification spread throughout the Western hemisphere. Europe experienced two seminal codifications in the area of civil law: the drafting of the French Civil Code of 1804 (later called *Code Napoléon*) and the coming into effect in 1900 of the *Bürgerliches Gesetzbuch*. Nineteenth-century codification also developed in the Americas, many times building on European sources. In Latin America and in the US comprehensive attempts towards codification were made.[111] Structure and content of nineteenth-century civil codes in Louisiana was pretty much in harmony with that of other contemporaneous codification endeavors. The structure in Louisiana followed the model provided by the *Code Napoléon,* and a similar situation took place with other civil codes in the Latin American countries.[112]

The structure and content of the current Louisiana Civil Code have been previously addressed.[113] It has been stated, in addition, that there is an ongoing revision and a sensible decodification process. Pascal provided the most exquisite

[104] See generally, Parise, "Codification of the Law in Louisiana", *supra* note 1; and Parise, *supra* note 36.

[105] See generally, Alain Levasseur, "On the Structure of a Civil Code", 44 Tul. L. Rev. 693 (1970); and Jean Louis Bergel, "Principal Features and Methods of Codification", 48 La. L. Rev. 1073 (1988). For a very complete study of the previous period, see Jacques Vanderlinden, *Le Concept de Code en Europe Occidentale du XIII au XIX Siècle*, Essais de Définition (1967).

[106] 1 Abelardo Levaggi, *Manual de Historia del Derecho Argentino* 185 (2001).

[107] 1 Luis Diez-Picazo & Antonio Gullon, *Sistema de Derecho Civil* 51 (1982).

[108] 1 Arturo Alessandri Rodriguez & Manuel Somarriva Undurraga, *Curso de Derecho Civil* 49 (1945).

[109] Genaro R. Carrió, "Judge Made Law Under a Civil Code", 41 La. L. Rev. 993, 993 (1981).

[110] Bergel, *supra* note 105, at 1084–1085.

[111] Parise, *supra* note 76, at 831.

[112] For additional reading on the influence of the *Code Napoléon*, see: Université Panthéon-Assas (Paris II), 1804–2004—*Le Code Civil: Un Passé, Un Présent, Un Avenir* (2004); M.C. Mirow, "The C. Napoleon: Buried but Ruling in Latin America", 33 Denv. J. Int'l L. & Pol'y 179 (2005); and Roscoe Pound, "The French Civil Code and the Spirit of Nineteenth Century Law", 35 B.U. L. Rev. 77 (1955).

[113] See *supra* Sects. 20.1.2 and 20.2.1; and regarding sources see Sect. 20.2.2, and especially Sect. 20.2.2.2.

and precise description and assessment of the structure and content of the current Louisiana Civil Code.[114] The following passage captures a summary of his understanding:

> [...] after a Preliminary Title on Law in General, the entire subject matter of the civil law is divided into three main parts. [...] Book I treats of persons, the subjects of the law; Book II, of permissible interests in things, or patrimonial goods, the objects of the law; and Book III, of the acquisition, transfer, and loss of rights to things. Today, a Book IV, on the Conflict of Laws, has been added, asserting Louisiana's understanding of its jurisdiction and that of other states and nations to have their laws apply to particular persons, things, and events.[115]

The content of the Louisiana Civil Code presents interesting features: it is applicable in a mixed jurisdiction, and it is drafted in English language. Louisiana, considered by many a mixed jurisdiction, combines aspects of common- and civil-law. This interaction of systems may be valued by jurists and businessmen who intend to implement continental European principles while undertaking their practices in the common law and vice versa. In addition, the *lingua franca* now is English. Scholars both of continental European and common law systems may reach to Louisiana for civil-law terminology in English. For example, the co-author of one of the English translations of the *Catala Avant-Projet of the French Law Obligations and the French Law of Prescriptions* stated that civilian concepts such as *solidarity* and *confusion* should not be translated or interpreted with common-law terminology, because they could easily generate misunderstandings.[116] It must be acknowledged that there is a valuable know-how in Louisiana civil-law scholars.[117] The more than 200-year old tradition of English language civil-law codification in Louisiana should be valued.[118] For example, the European Union is exploring the adoption of a civil code.[119] In the revision of civil codes of Member states (or in the drafting of a uniform text) the European Union should benefit from the Louisiana experience.[120]

---

[114] Robert A. Pascal, "Of the Civil Code and Us", 59 La. L. Rev. 301, 302–307 (1998).

[115] *Id.* at 303.

[116] Alain Levasseur & Vicenc Feliu, "The English Fox in the Louisiana Civil Law Chausse-Trappe: Civil Law Concepts in the English Language; Comparativists Beware", 69 La. L. Rev. 715, 735–739 (2009).

[117] See generally, *id.*

[118] See generally, Olivier Moréteau, "Les frontières de la langue et du droit", Revue internationale de droit comparé 695 (2009).

[119] Agustín Parise, "Derrotero hacia un código civil europeo", La Ley 6 (Feb. 14, 2011) (Arg.).

[120] *n.b.*, a similar legal borrowing, though from opposite direction, was welcomed by Louisiana in 1910. A member of the Louisiana Bar Association then said, while assessing the merits of a Louisiana revision project, that:

> It is generally understood that the Civil Codes of Germany, Holland, Italy, Belgium and other European States under the regime of the Civil Law represents the highest point of development of that system of law. There is no reason why the State of Louisiana in the revision of its Code should not receive the benefit of the learning and the experience of the great European jurisconsults.

20.4 Interplay of the Code

20.4.1 Constitutional Law[121]

The US Constitution enables state legislatures to dictate their own provisions as long as they do not conflict with federal enactments or ratifications vested in the US Congress.[122] The supremacy clause states that the supreme law of the land is to be found in the US Constitution and federal statutes, and treaties entered into by the US.[123] The plenary powers granted by the US Constitution to the state legislature assure the autonomy of private law in Louisiana by Louisianans, however with a need to "accommodate a superior national principle that may intrude from outside and above state law."[124]

In 1812, on the ninth anniversary of the Louisiana Purchase, Louisiana was admitted as the eighteenth state of the Union.[125] In November of the previous year, a Constitutional Convention had met, presided by Julien Poydras, with the objective of drafting a constitution for the state of Louisiana.[126] The first Louisiana Constitution was approved by the US Congress in April of 1812.[127] That first Louisiana Constitution would be then modified on numerous occasions.[128] The current Louisiana Constitution dates from 1974.[129]

Ernest T. Florence, *Report of Special Committee Revision Civil Code*, 14 Rep. La. B. Ass'n 345, 347–348 (1913). See also, A.N. Yiannopoulos, *Two Critical Years in the Life of the Louisiana Civil Code: 1870 and 1913*, 53 La. L. Rev. 5, 27 (1992).

[121] See generally, Parise, "Codification of the Law in Louisiana", *supra* note 1.

[122] Compare the scenario in Louisiana with that of other civil law jurisdictions, such as Argentina. See Santiago Legarre, "Common Law, Civil Law, and the Challenge from Federalism", 3 Journal of Civil Law Studies 167, 173 (2010).

[123] Article VI, Clause 2, of the US Constitution states that:

> This Constitution, and the Laws of the United States which shall be made in Pursuance thereof; and all Treaties made, or which shall be made, under the Authority of the United States, shall be the supreme Law of the Land; and the Judges in every State shall be bound thereby, any Thing in the Constitution or Laws of any State to the Contrary notwithstanding.

[124] Shael Herman, "Book Review", 80 Tul. L. Rev. 1491, 1541 (2006).

[125] Edwin Adams Davis, Louisiana: *The Pelican State* 136 (1978).

[126] See the letter of remission of the constitutional draft to the US President. "Letter from Julien Poydras to the President (January 28, 1812)", 9 *The Territorial Papers*, *supra* note 56, at 998.

[127] Davis, *supra* note 125, at 135. Additional information on the Louisiana Constitution of 1812 is available at Warren M. Billings, "From this Seed: The Constitution of 1812", *In Search of Fundamental Law: Louisiana's Constitutions, 1812–1974* 6 (Billings & Haas eds. 1993).

[128] The text of the constitution was modified in 1845, 1852, 1861, 1864, 1868, 1879, 1898, 1913, 1921 and 1974. Additional information on the history of the different constitutions of Louisiana is available at Alden L. Powell, "A History of Louisiana Constitutions", 1:1 *Projet of a Constitution for the State of Louisiana* with Notes and Studies 271 (1954).

[129] The text of the current Louisiana Constitution is available at: http://senate.legis.state.la.us/documents/Constitution/ (last visited August 20, 2011).

Incorporation of a system or code of laws *in totum* by general reference was not, and still is not, welcomed in Louisiana. The first Louisiana Constitution, of 1812,[130] read in part: "the Legislature shall never adopt any system or code of laws, by a general reference to the said system or code, but in all cases, shall specify the several provisions of the laws it may enact."[131] Scholars claim that the provision was incorporated to prevent the encroachment of the common law system in Louisiana.[132] Louisianans, however, had already taken isolated steps towards the adoption of codes, though not *in totum* by general reference, with the Digest of 1808 being the best exponent. The current Louisiana Constitution (1974) still does not welcome incorporation *in totum* by general reference. Article III, Section 15, Paragraph B, of the current Louisiana Constitution[133] reads that "no system or code of laws shall be adopted by general reference to it."[134]

The current Louisiana Constitution includes other provisions with effects on civil-law codification. For example, Article III, Section 12, states the limitations and prohibitions regarding local and special laws[135]; and Article III, Section 15,

---

[130] Additional information on the Louisiana Constitution of 1812 is available at Warren M. Billings, "From this Seed: The Constitution of 1812", *In Search of Fundamental Law: Louisiana's Constitutions*, 1812–1974 6 (Billings & Haas eds. 1993).

[131] Article IV, Section 11, Louisiana Constitution (1812). See The First Constitution of the State of Louisiana 19 (Cecil Morgan ed., facsimile edition 1975); and Dale E. Bennett, "Louisiana Criminal Procedure–A Critical Appraisal", 14 La. L. Rev. 11, 11 (1953).

[132] Louisiana Constitution (1812), supra note 131, at 12.

[133] The text of the current Louisiana Constitution, of 1974, is available at: http://senate.legis.state.la.us/documents/Constitution/ (last visited September 07, 2011).

[134] Article III, Section 15, Paragraph B, Louisiana Constitution (1974).

[135] Article III, Section 12, reads:

> (A) Except as otherwise provided in this constitution, the legislature shall not pass a local or special law: [...]
>
> (2) Changing the names of persons; authorizing the adoption or legitimation of children or the emancipation of minors; affecting the estates of minors or persons under disabilities; granting divorces; changing the law of descent or succession; giving effect to informal or invalid wills or deeds or to any illegal disposition of property.
>
> (3) Concerning any civil or criminal actions, including changing the venue in civil or criminal cases, or regulating the practice or jurisdiction of any court, or changing the rules of evidence in any judicial proceeding or inquiry before courts, or providing or changing methods for the collection of debts or the enforcement of judgments, or prescribing the effects of judicial sales. [...]
>
> (6) Regulating labor, trade, manufacturing, or agriculture; fixing the rate of interest.
>
> (7) Creating private corporations, or amending, renewing, extending, or explaining the charters thereof; granting to any private corporation, association, or individual any special or exclusive right, privilege, or immunity.
>
> (B) The legislature shall not indirectly enact special or local laws by the partial repeal or suspension of a general law.

Article III, Section 12, Louisiana Constitution (1974).

Paragraph A, states the object of bills.[136] Finally, relating to language, and relevant for understating the legal history of civil-law codification in Louisiana, the first Louisiana Constitution stated that the laws be enacted in the language of the US Constitution.[137] The Louisiana Constitution of 1845 instructed the bilingual publication in French and English[138]; while the Louisiana Constitution of 1868 finally returned to mandatory promulgation in the English language.[139]

20.4.2 Commercial Law

20.4.2.1 Codification Attempt[140]

A codification attempt of commercial laws in Louisiana was made in the early 1820s. According to a resolution of 1822, Moreau-Lislet, Derbigny, and Livingston[141] had to "add to their [codification] work a complete system of the commercial laws in force in this state together with the alterations they will deem proper."[142] A draft was completed by February 1825.[143] The draft, however, was never adopted by the local legislature, which abandoned the project without a formal rejection.[144] In 1826, the legislature omitted to decide on the fate of the work.[145] On the one hand, this omission could have been motivated because of a concern about the authority of the local legislature to elaborate in that area or because they recognized conflicts between state and federal provisions.[146] In addition, if the legislature would have rejected the work, they would have contradicted previous interpretations of applicable commercial law.[147] On the other hand, the omission could have been motivated, as a statement before a court in 1848 indicates, because "the commercial law

---

[136] Article III, Section 15, Paragraph A, reads in its relevant part:

> Every bill, except the general appropriation bill and bills for the enactment, rearrangement, codification, or revision of a system of laws, shall be confined to one object. Every bill shall contain a brief title indicative of its object.

Article III, Section 15, Paragraph A, Louisiana Constitution (1974).

[137] Article VI, Section 15, Louisiana Constitution (1812) cited by Wallach, *supra* note 51, at 10.

[138] Article 132, Louisiana Constitution (1845) cited by Wallach, *supra* note 51, at 10.

[139] Article 109, Louisiana Constitution (1868). *n.b.*, article 154 also allowed, yet not required, publication in French language. Both articles cited in Wallach, *supra* note 51, at 10.

[140] See generally, Parise, "Codification of the Law in Louisiana", *supra* note 1.

[141] Richard Holcombe Kilbourne, *Louisiana Commercial Law: The Antebellum Period* 29 (1980).

[142] 1822 La. Acts 108. See also Kilbourne, *supra* note 141, at 28.

[143] Kilbourne, *supra* note 141, at 30. References are made to the payment to Livingston for the drafting of the Commercial Code in the case of "Flower v. Arnaud", 1825, 4 Mart. (n.s.) 73.

[144] Kilbourne, *supra* note 141, at 33.

[145] *Id.*

[146] *Id.*

[147] *Id.*

of England and of the sister States of the Union was thought better adapted to the habits and commercial relations of our people."[148]

Livingston is generally identified as the one who completed the commercial law project.[149] It can not be claimed, however, that he was the only author, but that Moreau-Lislet or Derbigny also participated in the endeavor.[150] The commercial law project had 1,963 articles,[151] and was entitled *Commercial Code for the State of Louisiana*[152] (Commercial Code). The Commercial Code used the French *Code de commerce* as a model.[153] The format of both texts is similar and several articles are identical.[154] It was said before a local court that the Commercial Code "was mainly taken from the French Code on the same subject."[155] The Commercial Code, however, has several original elaborations, while it rejected some French dispositions, such as the establishment of commercial courts and the system of registers.[156] Common law influences are recurrent in the Commercial Code.[157] For example, the majority of the 584 articles on commercial paper are derived from the treatise of Joseph Chitty entitled *A Practical Treatise on Bills of Exchange*.[158] It must be noted that some common law provisions encroached uncomfortably upon the continental European provisions.[159]

Louisiana neglected the adoption of the Commercial Code, and together with other US states adopted the *lex mercatoria*,[160] which started to govern commerce in

[148] "U.S. v. U.S. Bank", 1844, 8 Rob. (La) 262.

[149] Kilbourne, *supra* note 141, at 34.

[150] *Id.*

[151] It also included a selection of "articles to be added in the body of the code of commerce," resulting in 1987 articles for the entire code. See Commercial Code for the State of Louisiana 248–249 (1825).

[152] *Id.* The Commercial Code was divided into two books. Book I, of commerce in general, had five titles (i.e., of merchants in general; of the books they are bound to keep; of commercial partnerships; of commercial agents; and of bills of exchange, promissory notes, checks and bank notes), which were subdivided into chapters and sections. Book II, of maritime commerce, was divided into seven titles (i.e., of ships and other vessels; of ship owners; of ship masters; of masters of boats and other crafts employed in the inland navigation; of the hiring and wages of sailors; of the carriages of goods in ships; and of insurance), and also contained a subdivision into chapters and sections. The text was also drafted both in French and English.

[153] Max Nathan, "In Search of a Missing Link: Edward Livingston and the Proposed Code of Commerce for Louisiana", 48 Tul. L. Rev. 43, 48 (1973). See also Isaac Smith Homans, *A cyclopedia of commerce and commercial navigation*, with maps and engraving 394 (2d ed. 1859).

[154] Nathan, *supra* note 153, at 48.

[155] "U.S. v. U.S. Bank", 1844, 8 Rob. (La) 262.

[156] Nathan, *supra* note 153, at 48.

[157] Kilbourne, *supra* note 141, at 67.

[158] *Id.* at 68.

[159] *Id.* at 68–69.

[160] Dargo, *supra* note 6, at 297.

the region.[161] Hence, the commercial provisions of other US states slowly started to percolate into the law of Louisiana.[162] Activities of local courts and the decisions they rendered provided a guideline for entrepreneurs, and identified local commercial practices to those of other US states. Eventually, commercial law in Louisiana would continue developing, however with fair and elastic means.[163]

20.4.2.2 Louisiana and the UCC[164]

Louisiana never enacted a commercial code.[165] Other states of the Union have largely adopted provisions of the Uniform Commercial Code (UCC).[166] Louisiana, therefore, was surrounded by the text of the UCC,[167] and a claim for its adoption from common-law trained lawyers was somehow felt. The adoption of the text of the UCC has been gradual in Louisiana during the past 30 years. The resulting gradual adoption of the UCC in Louisiana found exceptions in articles 2 (sales) and 6 (bulk sales). Title 10 of the Louisiana Revised Statutes, however, may now be referred to as the "Uniform Commercial Code."[168]

Even though Articles 2 and 6 of the UCC are not applied directly in Louisiana, some of their dispositions have entered into the legal framework of the state. For example, the revision of Title 7 on Sale, Book III of the Louisiana Civil Code, includes a new Chapter 13, which incorporates some of the ideas that exist in the UCC, such as the battle of the forms, and the buyer's rights of inspection and of rejection of nonconforming goods.[169] Commentaries on the revision by the LSLI indicate that those provisions are new and are in accordance with the provisions and spirit of the text of 1870; therefore, the continental European background of Louisiana prevails when articles on sale are analyzed or applied.[170]

---

[161] Samuel B. Groner, "Louisiana Law: Its Development in the First Quarter-Century of American Rule", 8 La. L. Rev. 350, 377 (1947).

[162] See the illustration of early court decisions provided by Thomas Jones Cross, "The Eclecticism of the Law of Louisiana: A Charcoal Sketch of the Legal System of that State", 55 Am L. Rev. 405, 414 (1921).

[163] Robert Feikema Karachuk, "A Workman's Tools: The Law Library of Henry Adams Bullard", 42 Am. J. Legal Hist. 160, 165 (1998).

[164] See generally, Parise, *supra* note 36.

[165] See generally, Kilbourne, *supra* note 141.

[166] The text of the UCC is available at *Uniform Commercial Code*, Legal Info. Inst., http://www.law.cornell.edu/ucc/ (last visited October 07, 2012).

[167] Litvinoff, *supra* note 41, at 137.

[168] La. Rev. Stat. Ann. § 10:1–101. See also, Parise, *supra* note 36, at 29.

[169] David Gruning, "Bayou State Bijuralism: Common Law and Civil Law in Louisiana", 81 U. Det. Mercy L. Rev. 437, 458 (2004).

[170] *Id.* at 458–459.

Preservation of civil-law principles had to be considered during the revision process of the Louisiana Civil Code and during the incorporation of provisions from the UCC. That preservation may have slowed the adoption of provisions from the UCC in Louisiana, because the potential operability of new provisions before Louisiana courts had to be considered. That sense of preservation is reflected in an act adopting the revision on sales, which states that the revision adopted "whatever provisions were thought useful, regardless of the source, yet to adapt the language of those provisions to fit the civilian mould and the plan of the Louisiana Civil Code. The result is a modern sales scheme that fits well in Louisiana's civil law tradition while at the same time adequately serving the personal and commercial needs of Louisiana citizens."[171]

20.4.3 Consumer Law

Amendments and developments in consumer protection and family law[172] reflect a decodification process. In Louisiana, many reforms in those areas have taken place by the enactment of special laws. This phenomenon, however, is not limited to Louisiana. Other civil-law jurisdictions, such as France and several Latin-American countries, have enacted family codes and consumer protection special laws.[173] Changes in practices and needs relating to those areas have been dramatic in recent decades and forced a growth of provisions out-side of civil codes. Those new provisions aimed and found flexibility in special laws or autonomous codes, even when potentially sacrificing the systematic approach and phraseology unity that civil codes provide.

Protection of consumer rights is welcomed in the Louisiana Civil Code. For example,[174] consumers can seek for protection in the warranty against redhibitory defects that is included in Chapter 9, Title 7, Book III of the Louisiana Civil Code.[175] Defects are redhibitory when the buyer would have not bought the thing had he known of the defect or paid a lesser price for it.[176] Additional codified tools for

[171] 1993 La. Sess. Law Serv. Act 841 (H.B. 106).

[172] See *infra* Sect. 20.4.4.

[173] See generally, Moréteau & Parise, *supra* note 25, at 1109 and 1155.

[174] An additional example may be found in the approach to performance of obligations in good faith. See Ronald L. Hersbergen, "Consumer Protection", 43 La. L. Rev. 343 (1982).

[175] Louisiana Pocket Civil Code, *supra* note 28, at article 2520.

[176] Article 2520 of the Louisiana Civil Code reads:

> The seller warrants the buyer against redhibitory defects, or vices, in the thing sold.
>
> A defect is redhibitory when it renders the thing useless, or its use so inconvenient that it must be presumed that a buyer would not have bought the thing had he known of the defect. The existence of such a defect gives a buyer the right to obtain rescission of the sale.
>
> A defect is redhibitory also when, without rendering the thing totally useless, it diminishes its usefulness or its value so that it must be presumed that a buyer would still have bought it but for a lesser price. The existence of such a defect limits the right of a buyer to a reduction of the price.
>
> *Id.*

consumer protection can be found in the law of obligations (*i.e.*, article 1758)[177] and in the law of torts (*i.e.*, article 2315) of the Louisiana Civil Code.[178]

Consumer protection, however, has grown significantly in the Louisiana Revised Statutes, resulting in an example of decodification.[179] For example, in 1972, Louisiana adopted the Unfair Trade Practices and Consumer Protection Law,[180] which was modelled after the Federal Trade Commission Act of 1914.[181] The Louisiana act was incorporated as Chapter 13, Title 51, Louisiana Revised Statutes.[182] That title comprises the main sources for dealing at state level with harms caused by business practices.[183] On the other hand, the main source at federal level is Title 15, United States Code.[184] As a result of the Louisiana act, the Louisiana

---

[177] Article 1758 of the Louisiana Civil Code reads:

A. An obligation may give the obligee the right to:

(1) Enforce the performance that the obligor is bound to render;
(2) Enforce performance by causing it to be rendered by another at the obligor's expense;
(3) Recover damages for the obligor's failure to perform, or his defective or delayed performance.

B. An obligation may give the obligor the right to:

(1) Obtain the proper discharge when he has performed in full;
(2) Contest the obligee's actions when the obligation has been extinguished or modified by a legal cause.

Id. at article 1758.

[178] Article 2315 of the Louisiana Civil Code reads:

A. Every act whatever of man that causes damage to another obliges him by whose fault it happened to repair it.
B. Damages may include loss of consortium, service, and society, and shall be recoverable by the same respective categories of persons who would have had a cause of action for wrongful death of an injured person. Damages do not include costs for future medical treatment, services, surveillance, or procedures of any kind unless such treatment, services, surveillance, or procedures are directly related to a manifest physical or mental injury or disease. Damages shall include any sales taxes paid by the owner on the repair or replacement of the property damaged.

Id. at article 2315.

[179] In addition to Louisiana positive law, business practice in Louisiana requires the attention to applicable federal law, often resulting in the application or guidance provided by common-law principles followed in other states. William E. Crawford, 12 *La. Civ. L. Treatise*, Tort Law § 26:1 (2d ed.).

[180] See the early works on the act by Paul L. Zimmering, "Louisiana's Consumer Protection Law-Three Years of Operation", 50 Tul. L. Rev. 375 (1976); and Keith E. Andrews, "Louisiana Unfair Trade Practices Act: Broad Language and Generous Remedies Supplemented by a Confusing Body of Case Law", 41 Loy. L. Rev. 759 (1996).

[181] Andrews, *supra* note 180, at 759.

[182] La. Rev. Stat. Ann. § 51:1401

[183] Crawford, *supra* note 179, at § 26:1.

[184] *Id.*

Attorney General's Office has a Public Protection Division with a Consumer Protection Section.[185] That section aims mainly "to investigate, conduct studies and research, to conduct public or private hearings into commercial and trade practices in the distribution, financing and furnishing of goods and services to or for the use of consumers"[186] that are not included in the exceptions of the act.[187] Through that section the Attorney General may investigate complaints with respect to unlawful consumer practices[188] and even impulse class actions.[189] Provisions of the act are not preempted by federal legislation[190]; and the protection of the act has been recently interpreted broadly by the Louisiana Supreme Court,[191] extending to plaintiffs other than consumers and business competitors.[192]

Two additional acts, though not being the only examples, clearly reflect decodification in Louisiana. These acts have been incorporated to Title 9 of the Louisiana Revised Statutes. A first act that provides an example of protection for consumers is the Louisiana Consumer Credit Law of 1972.[193] According to the title of the act, it aims to, amongst others, provide a system of laws relating to consumer transactions, "collection of time-price differential, service, finance and other similar charges thereon and for insurance thereon; to amend the laws relating to interest and usury; to provide for civil and criminal penalties; [and] to prohibit certain collection practices."[194] The act limits interest rates, and states that the interest in a loan granted to consumers may be charged at rates above the legal limitation, according to the amounts financed.[195] A second example of consumer protection is to be found in the Louisiana Products Liability Act of 1988.[196] This act states the liability of manufacturers for the damages their products may produce,[197] and its purpose is to protect consumers.[198] The act states the liability theories to be pursued by consumers and

---

[185] See http://www.ag.state.la.us/Article.aspx?articleID=2&catID=0 (last visited October 07, 2012).

[186] La. Rev. Stat. Ann. § 51:1404.

[187] La. Rev. Stat. Ann. § 51:1406. See also, Crawford, *supra* note 179, at § 26:5.

[188] La. Rev. Stat. Ann. § 51:1404.

[189] "State ex rel. Guste v. General Motors Corp.", Sup.1978, 370 So.2d 477, cited by Crawford, *supra* note 179, at § 26:5. See also, Kelly Mangum, "The Class Action as a Consumer Protection Device: State v. General Motors Corp.", 40 La. L. Rev. 497, 498 (1980).

[190] Crawford, *supra* note 179, at § 26:5.

[191] Zachary I. Rosenberg, "Consensus at Last: The Broadening of LUTPA Standing", *Cheramie v. Shell Deepwater Production*, 85 Tul. L. Rev. 1121 (2011).

[192] Andrews, *supra* note 180, at 763.

[193] La. Rev. Stat. Ann. § 9:3510 *et seq.* See the early work on the act by Alonzo P. Wilson, "Symposium: Louisiana's New Consumer Protection Legislation", 34 La. L. Rev. 597 (1974).

[194] La. Rev. Stat. Ann. § 9:3510.

[195] Saúl Litvinoff, 6 La. Civ. L. Treatise, Law Of Obligations § 9.8 (2d ed.).

[196] La. Rev. Stat. Ann. § 9:2800.51 *et seq.*

[197] *Id.*

[198] "Kampmann v. Mason", 921 So.2d 1093.

generally precludes recovery in cases of ordinary negligence or redhibition action.[199] Actions against manufacturers fall within the category of fault and belong to the scope of torts law (*i.e.*, article 2315 *et seq*).[200]

20.4.4 Family Law

Family law provisions, being a fundamental element of private law, fall within the legislative scope of the Louisiana state legislature.[201] In Louisiana, family law provisions were predominantly found in the Louisiana Civil Code. Specificity and developments both in the civil law of Louisiana and in the common law of neighboring states generated the need to elaborate provisions outside of the Louisiana Civil Code. Louisiana family law underwent a decodification process, where now many specific acts included in the Louisiana Revised Statutes help to deal with the ever-evolving aspects of family law.

Family law, since the enactment of the Digest of 1808, has occupied a paramount position in Book I of the civil codes of Louisiana. Together with the law of persons[202] and domicile,[203] which are not to be considered elements of family law exclusively, the Louisiana Civil Code addresses family law predominantly in Book I: Title 4, deals with marriage; Title 5, addresses divorce and its effects (*v.gr.*, spousal support,[204] child custody,[205] child support[206]); Title 7, provides on filiation and parental authority[207]; and Title 8, addresses tutorship.[208] Matrimonial regimes, however, found its place in Title 6, Book III.[209]

Special enactments provide many and important regulations on family law. Louisiana has adopted a Children's Code[210] that took effect in 1992. In addition,

---

199 Crawford, *supra* note 179, at § 16:23.

200 *Id.*

201 *n.b.*, the US Congress may also regulate when the scope extends federally, aiming to avoid conflicts between states. An example of such regulation is found in the Defense of Marriage Act. See, 28 U.S.C.A. § 1738C; Sheldon A. Vincenti, "The Defense of Marriage Act and the Recognition of Judgments", 3 Ave Maria L. Rev. 669 (2005); and David B. Cruz, "The Defense of Marriage Act and Uncategorical Federalism", 19 Wm. & Mary Bill Rts. J. 805 (2011).

202 Louisiana Pocket Civil Code, *supra* note 28, at Title 1, Book I.

203 *Id.* at Title 2, Book I.

204 *Id.* at Section 1, Chapter 2, Title 5, Book I.

205 *Id.* at Section 3, Chapter 2, Title 5, Book I.

206 *Id.* at Section 4, Chapter 2, Title 5, Book I.

207 *Id.* at Chapters 1–5, Title 7, Book I. See generally, Katherine Shaw Spaht, "Who's Your Momma, Who Are Your Daddies? Louisiana's New Law of Filiation", 67 La. L. Rev. 307 (2007); and J.R. Trahan, "Glossae on the New Law of Filiation", 67 La. L. Rev. 387 (2007).

208 Louisiana Pocket Civil Code, *supra* note 28, at Chapter 1, Title 8, Book I.

209 *Id.* at Chapters 1–4, Title 6, Book III.

210 The code took effect on January 1, 1992. 1991 La. Acts 235, § 1 *et seq.*

Title 9 of the Louisiana Revised Statutes also contain fundamental provisions (*v.gr.*, human embryos,[211] covenant marriage,[212] child support,[213] post-separation family violence,[214] and removal of personal property).[215] Special enactments within the ancillaries replicate the structure of the Louisiana Civil Code.[216]

Same-sex marriage is currently occupying legislative agendas in many jurisdictions. Some states of the Union (*v.gr.,* Massachusetts, Connecticut, and New Hampshire) have introduced same-sex marriage,[217] while other civil law jurisdictions have also legalized same-sex marriage (*v.gr.,* Argentina).[218] In Louisiana, same-sex marriages can not be celebrated,[219] and same-sex marriages from other states of the Union can not be recognized as valid.[220]

---

[211] La. Rev. Stat. Ann. § 9:121 *et seq.*

[212] Covenant marriages, pioneered by Louisiana, have been addressed in the Louisiana Civil Code (arts.102 and 103), yet also being developed outside of the code as part of the ancillaries (La. Rev. Stat. Ann. § 9:272). See, Katherine Shaw Spaht, "What's become of Louisiana Covenant Marriage through the Eyes of Social Scientists", 47 Loy. L. Rev. 709 (2001).

[213] La. Rev. Stat. Ann. § 9:315 *et seq.*

[214] La. Rev. Stat. Ann. § 9:361 *et seq.*

[215] La. Rev. Stat. Ann. § 9:373.

[216] *v.gr.*, there is an amended and re-enacted Chapter 1, Title 4, Book I of Title 9 of the Louisiana Revised Statutes, which contains, similarly to Chapter 1, Title 4, Book I of the Louisiana Civil Code, relevant legislation dealing with the general principles of marriage. See La. Rev. Stat. Ann. T. 9, Cdbk. I, Cdtl. IV, Ch. 1.

[217] Cruz, *supra* note 201, at 805.

[218] Law 26,618, promulgated on July 21, 2010, available at: http://infoleg.gov.ar/infolegInternet/anexos/165000-169999/169608/norma.htm (last visited September 07, 2011).

[219] Article XII, Section 15 of the current Louisiana Constitution reads:

> Marriage in the state of Louisiana shall consist only of the union of one man and one woman. No official or court of the state of Louisiana shall construe this constitution or any state law to require that marriage or the legal incidents thereof be conferred upon any member of a union other than the union of one man and one woman. A legal status identical or substantially similar to that of marriage for unmarried individuals shall not be valid or recognized. No official or court of the state of Louisiana shall recognize any marriage contracted in any other jurisdiction which is not the union of one man and one woman.
>
> Article XII, Section 15, Louisiana Constitution (1974).

[220] Article 3520 of the Louisiana Civil Code reads:

> A. A marriage that is valid in the state where contracted, or in the state where the parties were first domiciled as husband and wife, shall be treated as a valid marriage unless to do so would violate a strong public policy of the state whose law is applicable to the particular issue under Article 3519.
> B. A purported marriage between persons of the same sex violates a strong public policy of the state of Louisiana and such a marriage contracted in another state shall not be recognized in this state for any purpose, including the assertion of any right or claim as a result of the purported marriage.
>
> Louisiana Pocket Civil Code, *supra* note 28, at article 3520.

20.5 Position of the Code[221]

The state of Louisiana used codification of its private law provisions as a way of preserving its continental European roots. Early inhabitants opted for those principles, perhaps due to cultural and economic interests, and to protect property rights they had received during the pre-American period. That preservation attitude in Louisiana, above all, has to do with identity, with the defensive attitude of those who feel threatened by external elements. Since the early 1800s, Louisiana has been an isolated "Civil Law island" partially surrounded by a "sea of Common Law." This motivated Louisianans to opt for revision and decodification instead of recodification, as ways of modernizing the Louisiana Civil Code, in order to match current standards and remain competitive with regards to other states of the Union. A recodification might have been perceived as a complete and drastic break with the past, and therefore a threat to a fragile collective identity.

Louisianans are currently familiarized with a codified system that states their seminal private law needs. Lay people are aware that the core of private law dispositions is dealt with in the Louisiana Civil Code.[222] Louisiana-law practitioners, though knowing that private law provisions are also dealt with outside of the code, are well trained in seeking for solutions in the codified text.[223] A generalized familiarity with the code is a result of this scenario: a scenario that, however, has not prevented the development of new codes or special legislation outside the Louisiana Civil Code. Some provisions incorporated by Louisiana law have a common-law origin or have been generated as practices in the other states of the Union. As a result, Louisiana is sensed to some extent as a mixed jurisdiction, especially with regards to practice before courts. This paper, however, showed that the state enacted laws that spin around what is still in Louisiana the centre of private law: the Louisiana Civil Code.

[221] See generally, Moréteau & Parise, *supra* note 25, at 1161–1162.

[222] See the example found in popular culture as reflected by Stanley Kowalski (though incorrectly referring to the *Code Napoléon*), in Tennessee Williams, *A Streetcar Named Desire* (Methuen Drama 2009) (1947).

[223] For example, the Louisiana state bar examination differs from that of other US states. Candidates are not tested on the Multistate Bar Exam, and are tested in, amongst others, civil code subjects. The first three subjects that are listed (out of nine) as tested in Louisiana are entitled *Civil Code I, II*, and *III*. See James R. Maxeiner, "Uniform Law and Its Impact on National Laws Limits and Possibilities", *Reports to the Intermediary Congress of the International Academy of Comparative Law* 34; and Section 7 Rule XVII, available at http://www.lasc.org/rules/supreme/RuleXVII.asp (last visited October 07, 2012).

Chapter 21
Codification in Venezuela

Eugenio Hernández-Bretón and Claudia Madrid Martínez

Abstract The codification of Civil Law in Venezuela is an ongoing process dating back to the first half of the nineteenth century. However, the first Venezuelan Civil Code was only passed in the second half on that century. The main structure of the Civil Code, amended as of 1982, remains very much the same as the earlier codes. However, a significant process of decodification has taken place particularly on family law matters. Obligations, contracts, torts, property, wills and estates continue to be subject to the Civil Code. Commercial laws are mostly reunited in the Commercial Code, although significant parts thereof are now governed by special legislation. Private International Law is codified in a special law, but the Civil Code still contains some scattered provisions on the matter. True to its origins, the Venezuelan Civil Code continues to be the main pillar of Private Law legislation. All Private Law still revolves around the provisions of the Civil Code; it constitutes the glue that keeps the unity of the system of Venezuelan Private Law legislation.

Keywords Venezuelan laws • Codification • Civil Code • Comparative law • Decodification

21.1 History of Codification of Private Law[1]

The first Venezuelan Civil Code was enacted in 1862. It is also known as the *Páez* Code, named after the then incumbent President of Venezuela. It was based on a draft code prepared by the Venezuelan scholar *Julián Viso*, and was heavily

[1] Luciano Lupini, "La influencia del Código Napoleón en la codificación civil y en la doctrina venezolana", in *El Código Civil venezolano en los inicios del siglo XXI: en conmemoración del bicentenario del Código Civil fránces de 1804*, ed. Irene de Valera, (Caracas: Academia de

E. Hernández-Bretón (✉) • C. Madrid Martínez
Derecho Internacional Privado y Comparado, Universidad Central de Venezuela, Caracas, Venezuela
e-mail: Eugenio.Hernandez-Breton@bakermckenzie.com; cmadridmartinez@yahoo.es

J.C. Rivera (ed.), *The Scope and Structure of Civil Codes*, Ius Gentium: Comparative Perspectives on Law and Justice 32, DOI 10.1007/978-94-007-7942-6_21,

influenced by the 1855 Chilean Civil Code authored by *Andrés Bello*, and the 1851 draft Spanish Civil Code prepared by *Florencio García Goyena*. The Venezuelan Code was enacted in October of 1862 and was to come into force on 1 January 1863, but that date was postponed until 19 April 1863. Nonetheless, the Code was repealed on 8 August 1863, as a result of general legislative measures adopted by then-President *Falcón* during the Venezuelan Federal War.

The next Civil Code was enacted in 1867. Its contents deviated from the Chilean Civil Code and came closer to the *García Goyena* draft. Venezuelan commentators considered both the 1862 and 1867 Codes as impracticable.

The first Civil Code with actual substance and practical application was enacted in 1873 by President *Antonio Guzmán Blanco*. This Code was the result of the works of the most distinguished practitioners of that time. The main source of inspiration was the 1865 Italian Civil Code, but rather than merely translating it into Spanish, the drafters adapted it to the Venezuelan realities of that time.

The Civil Code of 1873 was amended three times. The first amendment took place in 1880, introducing several modifications regarding matrimonial impediments, council of tutelage and possession. The second amendment took place in 1896, in which the home (*hogar*) was regulated, formal requirements of celebration of marriage were made more flexible, and marriage by operation of law was eliminated. The third amendment was made in 1904 for the purpose of introducing divorce and judicial separation. Further, the right of debtors to impute payments to capital with preference over interests was introduced, and the right to petition the rescission of sub-retro sales in order to suppress usury abuses was allowed.

In 1916 a new Civil Code was approved. This Code leans toward Italian scholarship and improves legal terminology. It introduced the *actio pauliana* and the petition of simulation of legal transactions. In family matters, it allowed for the investigation of out-of-wedlock paternity, provided more flexibility in the celebration of marriage of concubines, increased the number of officers entitled to authorize marriages, and granted identical inheritance rights *vis-à-vis* their mother to children born to a married couple as well as to children born out-of-wedlock.

This Code was amended in 1922 for the sole purpose of eliminating the *posesión de estado* as evidence of filial relationship (*filiación*) *vis-à-vis* the father, and allowing the free investigation of out-of-wedlock paternity, which had been introduced in 1916.

In 1936 the National Commission on Codification was created and entrusted with the task of preparing a draft Civil Code finally approved in 1942. In 1942 Venezuela was in the process of building a modern democracy, General Isaías Medina Angarita was the then incumbent President, designated by Congress in 1941. In 1943 the Hydrocarbons Law was enacted, and the first Income Tax Law came into force. These two laws allowed for more government resources and

Ciencias Políticas y Sociales; Embajada de Francia en Venezuela; Asociación Franco Venezolana de Juristas, 2005), p. 70. See also: Eloy Maduro Luyando, *Curso de obligaciones. Derecho civil III*, (Caracas, Universidad Católica Andrés Bello, Manuales de Derecho, 8ª edic., 1993), p. 20. See also: José Mélich Orsini, "Trabajo de incorporación a la Academia de Ciencia Políticas y Sociales", (Caracas: Academia de Ciencias Políticas y Sociales, 1986).

limited the participation of multinational companies in the profits from the oil industry. During his administration the direct election of deputies, women'-s suffrage and the legalization of all political parties allowed for the return of all political exiles and the liberation of all political prisoners. By that time the first Venezuelan national identification system was implemented, and a comprehensive plan for the modernization of the major cities was launched.

The main changes introduced by the 1942 Code were in the field of obligations, following the French-Italian Draft Code on Obligations and Contracts. The 1942 Code regulates in detail offer and acceptance as the contract formation mechanism, introduces unjust enrichment and abuse of rights as sources of obligations, expressly establishes the tort liability of the guardian of things without fault, and the right to indemnification of moral damages. In family matters it introduced the presumption of joint ownership between concubines provided that the woman has contributed to the formation or increase of the man's wealth. Additionally, it allowed the free investigation of out-of-wedlock paternity during the life of the father, and if there was *posesión de estado* then even in respect of the heirs of the father, out-of-wedlock children acquired the status of forced heirs of their father, being entitled to a quota equivalent to one-half of the quota of a matrimonial child. Finally, the State assumed in fact the tutelage of abandoned children.

The 1942 Code was amended in 1982, currently in force,[2] particularly on Family Law matters. This major amendment was aimed at the equal legal treatment of mothers and fathers in respect of title and exercise of parental authority, equality of men and women regarding personal and patrimonial effects of marriage, and the adoption of the principle of unity of filial relationship (*filiación*), granting thus equal treatment to matrimonial and out-of-wedlock children.

To the best of our knowledge, currently there are no Civil Code reform drafts.

21.2 The Process of Decodification: Causes and Effects

Decodification is the proliferation of special civil legislation outside the Civil Codes. Currently, the civil law is mainly outside the Civil Code, which creates a new order dispersed and confused.[3]

During the twentieth century, in response to social and economic changes, civil codes faced decodification when special legislation removed large areas of law from the coverage of the civil codes creating new areas of law or "microsystems" that differed ideologically and methodologically from the original structure of the civil

[2] Published in Special Official Gazette 2,990 of 26 July 1982.

[3] See: Alfredo de Jesús O., Notas generales sobre el bicentenario del Código Civil y el proceso de codificación, descodificación y eventual recodificación de su Derecho civil, in *El Código Civil venezolano en los inicios del siglo XXI: en conmemoración del bicentenario del Código Civil fránces de 1804*, ed. Irene de Valera, (Caracas: Academia de Ciencias Políticas y Sociales; Embajada de Francia en Venezuela; Asociación Franco Venezolana de Juristas, 2005), p. 32.

codes. Consequently, areas of heterogeneous statutory law have increased on a variety of civil code topics such as, employment law, urban and agrarian leases, intellectual property, insurance, contracts of carriage, competition, monopoly, and consumer protection law. These laws are not merely a supplement to the code to complete or clarify its provisions, but rather, they break up the original unity of the civil system creating a plurality of microsystems with different principles.[4]

In Venezuela, several subjects have been eliminated from the Civil Code, and in such a way it has experienced a "decodification" process. As will be more fully explained below, this process is particularly notorious in matters of Family Law.

21.3 Actual Status of Codification

21.3.1 The Contents of the Civil Code Today[5]

The original structure of the first Venezuelan Civil Code deviated from the Italian and French codifications of the Nineteenth Century, because the Code of 1862 was composed of four books and a preliminary title. The first book dealt with individuals; the second one referred to goods, possession, use and enjoyment of goods; the third book regulated wills and donations. The last one referred to obligations and contracts. The Civil Code of 1873 adopted the structure that is still kept today, thus dividing the Code into three books and a preliminary title.

The preliminary title contains rules about the effects of the Law and its application. Book One, entitled "On the individuals" contains rules relating to individuals in general, domicile, marriage, parenthood, adoption, custody, education and support of children, parental authority, interdiction and disablement/disqualification, absence and non-presence, and the civil registry. The Book Two, "On Ownership and its modifications", governs ownership of goods and the limitations thereto, joint property and ownership. The Book Three is entitled "On the manner to acquire and transfer ownership and other rights" and it regulates occupation, wills and estates, contractual and non-contractual obligations, donation, sales, swapping, leases, work contracts, association agreements, mandates, loans, bailment, deposit agreements, gambling and betting, bonds, pledges, antichresis, privileges and mortgages, foreclosure of assets and civil restructuring of debts (*beneficio de competencia*) and statutes of limitations.

With a few specific exceptions, the Code structure adopted in late Nineteenth Century is still kept, thus it cannot be affirmed that new contents have been incorporated into the Civil Code. Its structure reflects traditional European civil

[4] María Luisa Morillo, "The evolution of codification in the civil law legal systems: towards decodification and recodification", *Journal of Transnational Law & Policy*, Vol. 11, Issue 1 (Fall 2001), p. 173.

[5] José Luis Aguilar Gorrondona, "Derecho Civil I. Personas", (Caracas, Universidad Católica Andrés Bello, Manuales de Derecho, 18th. edition., 2005), pp. 20–24.

codification. Currently, in addition to a preliminary section covering general rules on the application of laws, the Civil Code is divided into three books. Each Book, in turn, is divided into Titles and Chapters.

Book One On Persons deals with the general regime of individuals and legal entities, marriage and its legal consequences, kinship, parental authority, and protection of persons. Book Two On Goods, Property and Modifications deals with Property Law, either real estate or movable property. Book Three On the Ways to Acquire and Transfer Ownership and other Rights, the most extensive Book, deals with wills and estates, obligations, civil liability, evidence, torts and contracts, guarantees, and statutes of limitation.

Family Law is partially regulated in Book One and also in the Organic Law on Boys, Girls and Adolescents, the contents of which will be described below. Commercial relations are regulated by the Commercial Code.[6] This Code is based on the notion of merchant and commercial acts, either objective or subjective. It contains rules on the application of commercial legislation, merchants, commercial registry, accounting, commercial contracts, commercial companies, negotiable papers, reorganization and bankruptcy, commercial courts and proceedings. Insurance contracts and maritime trade have been taken out of the Commercial Code and are now regulated by special legislation.

21.3.2 The Legislation of Commercial Law: What Commercial Law Is; The Commercial Code; The Microsystems (Corporate Law, Bankruptcy Law, etc.)

The current Commercial Code was enacted in 1919, and was amended in 1955. Subsequently, it has suffered significant amendments by way of special legislation that has excluded matters, which originally were under the scope of the Commercial Code, such as the insurance contract,[7] and water navigation and maritime trade.[8]

The Venezuelan Commercial Code has three books. The first one regulates trade in general and contains rules on traders, commercial contracts, commercial companies, negotiable instruments and insurance. The second book regulates maritime commerce and the third refers to default and bankruptcy.

As mentioned above there is special legislation governing insurance contracts, water navigation and maritime trade. Insurance and reinsurance companies are subject to the Law on Insurance Activity; financial institutions are subject to the Organic Law on the National Financial System[9]; cooperative associations are

[6] Published in Special Official Gazette 475 of 21 December 1955.

[7] Law on the Insurance Contract, published in Special Official Gazette 5,553 of 12 November 2001 and Law on the Insurance Activity, published in Special Official Gazette 5,990 of 29 July 2010.

[8] Currently regulated in the Law on Maritime Trade, published in Official Gazette 38,351 of 5 January 2006.

[9] Published in Official Gazette 39,447 of 16 June 2010.

governed by the Special Law on Cooperative Associations.[10] There is special legislation dealing with trusts, i.e., the Law on Trusts (*Fideicomisos*).[11]

The Commercial Code contains special legislation *vis-à-vis* the Civil Code. The Commercial Code applies to merchants and commercial transactions as defined in the Commercial Code (Article 1 of the Commercial Code). The Commercial Code is of preferential application on commercial matters (Article 14 of the Civil Code). In turn, the provisions of the Civil Code will apply to commercial matters not regulated in the Commercial Code, laws or by commercial customs and usages. (Article 8 of the Commercial Code). In almost all cases commercial transactions will be regulated simultaneously by a combination of Commercial and Civil Code provisions. This is because of the special nature of commercial legislation, which must be supplemented by general Civil Code provisions.

21.4 Consumer Law: Relationship with the Civil and Commercial Codes

Consumer Law has never been regulated in the Civil Code. Rules on consumer protection appeared in 1974 for the first time, as rules directed to correct market inefficiencies, particularly in respect of uneven sharing of information and negative external influences in a consumer society. However, in Venezuela consumer law reflects a state policy pointing at traders and merchants as responsible parties for economic ills, i.e., inflation, scarcity of goods, defects in quality, etc.), which in most cases are actually caused by state intervention precluding the free interplay between market forces.

The 1974 Consumer Protection Law was amended in 1992 and 1995, and finally repealed in 2004 by the Law for the Protection of the Consumer and the User. In 2008, the President of the Republic issued a Decree with the Rank, Value and Force of Law for the Defense of Persons in the Access to Goods and Services, which was amended by Parliament in 2009 and 2010.[12] The current Law is aimed to the defense, protection and safekeeping of the rights of persons, as well as their individual and collective interests in the access to goods and services, the establishment of administrative sanctions and procedures, crimes, and compensation for damages. The Law also provides for application by state entities together with the active participation of the local communities for the protection of social peace, justice, right to life and the people's health.

It is also worth mentioning that Article 117 of the Constitution[13] grants special status to consumer protection. This provision acknowledges the right of all persons

[10] Published in Official Gazette 37,285 of 18 September 2001.

[11] Published in Special Official Gazette 496 of 17 August 1956.

[12] Published in Official Gazette 39,358 of 1 February 2010.

[13] Published in Official Gazette 36,860 of 30 December 1999.

to access quality goods and services, to have access to adequate and non-misleading information regarding the contents and characteristics of consumer goods and services, to freedom of choice and a fair and equitable treatment. Furthermore, it mandates the legislature to establish the mechanisms necessary to guarantee those rights, to establish the quality and quantity control rules on goods and services, to establish the procedures for consumer defense, the compensation of damages and the sanctions for the breach of those rights.

There is no general theory of consumer contracts in Venezuela. Consumer Law legislation is mostly directed to regulate the formation of consumer contracts, particularly regarding the pre-contractual duty to inform the consumer. Additionally, there are certain rules regarding standard form and electronic contracts. Besides that, consumer law legislation is composed of norms governing administrative proceedings aimed to secure protection of consumer rights.

While Civil Code scholars have not devoted much consideration to this matter, administrative law scholars have made significant contributions particularly regarding the analysis of the applicable proceedings. In practice consumer contracting has been distorted even more because of the state intervention through the Constitutional Chamber of the Supreme Court of Justice, which, invoking the principle of the social state of law and justice (*Estado Social de Derecho y de Justicia*) embodied in the Constitution, has had a major impact on the contracting dynamics between private individuals and entities.

On the other hand, the Institute for the Defense of Persons in the Access to Goods and Services (INDEPABIS), the consumer protection agency, has limited itself to imposing fines and closing commercial establishments in application of the law.

In summary, it is a rather disorganized legal structure, and thus it is impossible to speak of a general theory of consumer contracts.

The relationship between the Civil Code and the rules on consumer law is not entirely clear, to say the least. Nonetheless, in light of Article 3 of the Law for the Defense of Persons in the Access to Goods and Services, that Law will apply to all juridical acts between suppliers of goods and services and persons, whether organized or not, as well as between the latter, pertaining to the acquisition or leasing of goods, the hiring of services to be rendered by private or public entities, and any other legal transaction of economic interest, as well as to hoarding, speculation, boycott and any other act affecting the access to food or goods declared essential or not, by any of the economic subjects of the chain of distribution, production and consumption of goods and services, whether it be the importer, warehouser, transporter or manufacturer, supplier, merchandiser, retailer or wholesaler.

Thus, in these matters consumer legislation is of preferential application *vis-à-vis* the Civil Code. In turn, the latter will supplement the former. For example, there is an express provision establishing that consumer laws do not preclude the application of the Civil Code with respect to civil liability matters (Article 151 of the Law for the Defense of Persons in the Access to Goods and Services).

21.5 Family Law

Throughout Venezuela's history, Family Law, including, among others, marriage, divorce, separation of spouses, matrimonial property, kinship and parenthood, children's rights, parental authority and adoption, was traditionally regulated in the Civil Code only. In the early 1970s the first Adoption Law was enacted, thus derogating the provisions of the Civil Code on that matter. In the late 1990s the Civil Code's section on Family Law experienced a significant modification when the Organic Law for the Protection of Children and Adolescents ("LOPNA") was approved. The LOPNA had a major impact on domestic and international adoption, children's rights, parental authority, including guardianship and custody, visitation rights and child support payments, for example. The LOPNA now in force, under the name of Organic Law for the Protection of Boys, Girls and Adolescents or LOPNA.[14] Most of the provisions of the Civil Code on registration of family matters were derogated by the Organic Law on Civil Registry.[15]

21.6 Private International Law

Most of the rules on private international law have been removed from the Civil Code. Up until the coming into effect of the Act on Private International Law,[16] the main rules of Private International Law were spread out in the Civil Code, the Commercial Code and the Code of Civil Procedure. This was the trend since the first Venezuelan Codes of the Nineteenth Century. The basic rules of Private International Law contained in the Civil Code were mainly of statutarian nature, which were antagonistic with Article 8 of the same Code mandating the territorial application of Venezuelan law. The Act on Private International Law came into effect on 6 February 1999 (Article 64), and replaced almost all rules of private international law contained in the Civil Code and other codes (Article 63). Nowadays, the Act on Private International Law is unquestionably the main source of private international law in Venezuela. However, a few specific provisions of private international law contained in the Civil Code, the Commercial Code and the Code of Civil Procedure as well as in other special laws continue to apply.

21.7 Labor Law

Since 1936 labor contracts are regulated by special legislation. Until then, the rights and obligations of employers and employees arising from a labor relationship were regulated in the Civil Code. Currently, the Civil Code acknowledges the preferential

[14] Published in Special Official Gazette 5,859 of 10 December 2007.

[15] Published in Official Gazette 39,264 of 15 September 2009.

[16] Published in Official Gazette 36,511 of 6 August 1998.

application of labor legislation to labor contracts (Article 1,629 of the Civil Code). Labor relationships are regulated in the Organic Labor and Workers' Law ("OLWL"), which came into effect on 7 May 2012.[17] Because of its over 550 articles, the OLWL can be well named as the Labor Code. It applies to individual labor contracts and to collective bargaining agreements. In some case it also applies to workers that are not under an employment relationship. These are defined as persons that habitually get a living from their work without being under an employment relationship with one or several employers. The principle of preference of substance over form of the labor relationship/contract has been incorporated in the OLWL, and is routinely applied by labor courts.

The OLWL regulates in detail all stages of the labor relationship/contract, from its inception to termination, including performance, labor benefits and suspension of the relationship, as well as the consequences of termination independently from the causes of termination. Most of its rules are of a mandatory nature and can only be modified for the benefit of the employee. A vast sector of workers is protected against dismissals whether for cause or not. Under certain circumstances and formalities, settlement agreements are allowed upon termination of the labor relationship. Labor laws are applicable to labor relationships performed in Venezuela or contracted in Venezuela, either for local performance or abroad. There is a considerable and important case law that must be taken into consideration when dealing with labor law issues.

21.8 Relationships Between the Civil Code with the Constitution and Treaties

The Constitution is the highest law of the land and the base of the entire legal order (Article 7 of the Constitution). Treaties have the rank and force of a law of Parliament, i.e., the National Assembly, because they are executed and ratified in direct execution of the Constitution by the President of the Republic or his designee (Article 236.4 of the Constitution). The treaty-making power of the President extends to all matters under the authority of the National Power (Article 156.32 of the Constitution *in fine*). The subject matters regulated in the Civil Code correspond to the legislative powers of the National Power (Article 156.32 of the Constitution). Technically, the Civil Code is an ordinary law of Parliament (Article 202 of the Constitution), hierarchically subordinated to the Constitution. Generally, treaties require a formal approval by way of a formal law of Parliament before ratification by the President of the Republic takes place (Articles 154 and 187.18 of the Constitution). Ratification of treaties is discretionary upon the President of the Republic (Article 217 of the Constitution).

As a general rule, treaties and laws have the same rank and force, and both are subordinated to the Constitution. Treaties are of preferential application vis-à-vis

[17] Published in Special Official Gazette 6,076 of 7 May 2012.

the Civil Code on their specific subject matters. This is the result of the special legislative authority exclusively entrusted to the President of the Republic on international matters, which cannot be overstepped by the National Assembly. Treaties, thus, do not derogate domestic legislation. They merely have a different scope of application.

The treatment of treaties on human rights deserves special mention. Such treaties in force in Venezuela have constitutional status and are of preferential application to the extent that they provide more favorable rules than those contained in the Constitution and other domestic legislation. Those treaties are of immediate and direct application by courts and other state bodies (Article 23 of the Constitution). In practice, however, this rule has been dead letter. The generosity of Article 23 of the Constitution coupled with Article 30 of the Constitution, which allows for protection of human rights by international entities, the Supreme Court of Justice, as supreme constitutional guardian (Article 335 of the Constitution), has opposed strict constitutional public policy control, therefore denying actual force of law and constitutional status to treaties on human rights.[18]

In recent years the Constitutional Chamber of the Supreme Court of Justice has issued relevant case law on subjects regulated by the Civil Code, thus affecting the text and current interpretation of the Code's rules in light of constitutional provision. For example, it has ruled on the scope of the autonomy of the will of contracting parties in contract matters,[19] on the scope of reparation of damages,[20] on the applicability of contract clauses dealing with unilateral termination for cause,[21] on indivisible obligations,[22] just to name a few. Accordingly, the Civil Code has suffered significant transformations as a result of judicial decisions, irrespective and beyond any action of the Legislative Power.

21.9 Conclusions About the Importance of Civil Codification Today; And the Future of Codification

True to its origins, the Venezuelan Civil Code continues to be the main pillar of Private Law legislation. All Private Law still revolves around the provisions of the Civil Code; it constitutes the glue that keeps the unity of the system of Venezuelan

[18] See Supreme Court of Justice, Constitutional Chamber, decision of 17 October 2011, *Leopoldo López* case, denying effect to a decision of the Inter American Court on Human Rights.

[19] See Supreme Court of Justice, Constitutional Chamber, decision of 24 January 2002, *ASODEVIPRILARA* et al. v. *Superintendencia de Bancos y otras Instituciones Financieras* (*SUDEBAN*) and *Consejo Directivo del Instituto para la Defensa y Educación del Consumidor y el Usuario* (*INDECU*) case.

[20] See *Teodoro de Jesús Colasante Segovia* case of 20 March 2006.

[21] See Supreme Court of Justice, Constitutional Chamber, decision of 4 March 2005, *IMEL* case.

[22] See Supreme Court of Justice, Constitutional Chamber, decision of 14 May 2004, *Transportes Saet* case.

Private Law legislation. The Civil Code is by far the most carefully drafted piece of Venezuelan legislation. Legal developments over the last 50 years show that Public Law legislation, particularly on Constitutional and Administrative Law matters, has severely limited the scope of application of the Civil Code. This is especially evidenced in Family Law matters where state intervention is notorious and where regulations have been removed from the Civil Code.

Regardless of growing state intervention on economic matters, to a very large extent all contracts, whether named or unnamed, are subject to the Civil Code. The same applies to the general system of civil liability. Likewise, the Civil Code governs Property Law regarding movable and immovable assets. While a couple of years ago the President of Venezuela announced the death of the Commercial Code, nothing similar has been said in respect of the Civil Code. The future role of the Civil Code will largely depend on the use that commentators and courts give to the Code's provisions, particularly its general provisions, most of which remain unexplored. Inasmuch as the human being is considered the *alfa* and *omega* of any legal system, a Civil Code will be a necessary legal tool. In Venezuela, transactions between private individuals and entities are subject and will continue to be subject to the Civil Code.

About the Authors

Editor

Prof. **Julio César Rivera** is a regular member of the *Academia Nacional de Derecho de Buenos Aires* as of November 1999; correspondent member of the *Academia Peruana de Derecho*; president of the *Argentine Comparative Law Association*; president of the *Capítulo Rioplatense del Club Español del Arbitraje* and member of the *ICC Latin America Group*; Vice-president at *Centro de Mediación y Arbitraje Comercial* (CEMARC) – (Commercial Arbitration Centre); correspondent member of the *International Institute for the Unification of Private Law* (UNIDROIT, Rome) and member of the *Asociación Internacional de Juristas Andrés Bello* (París).

Argentina

Prof. **Graciela Medina** graduated Summa Cum Laude from the University of Mendoza, Argentina. She obtained her Ph.D. in Judicial and Social Sciences from the University of Mendoza. She is currently Judge at the Federal Appeals Court in Civil and Commercial Matters and Chair Professor of Civil Law at the University of Buenos Aires.

Belgium

Prof. **Dirk Heirbaut** studied law and history and is currently Professor of legal history at the Universiteit Gent. He is the president of the Scientific Committee for Legal History of the Royal Flemish Academy of Belgium for Arts and Science, founding vice-president of the European Society for Comparative Legal History,

J.C. Rivera (ed.), *The Scope and Structure of Civil Codes*, Ius Gentium: Comparative Perspectives on Law and Justice 32, DOI 10.1007/978-94-007-7942-6,

member of the board of editors of the Tijdschrift voor rechtsgeschiedenis/Legal History Review and co-editor of the series *Studies in the History of Private Law*.

Prof. **Matthias E. Storme** is Professor of contract, commercial and insolvency law and legal philosophy at the Katholieke Universiteit Leuven and Guest Professor of international business law at the CUPL Beijing. He studied law in Antwerpen, Leuven (Dr.iur. 1989), Bologna and Hamburg and philosophy in Antwerpen, Leuven and Yale (M.A. 1982). He was a member of the Commission on European Contract Law (1992–2002) and the Study group on a European Civil Code (1999–2009) and founding member of the European Law Institute (2011) and is joint editor in chief of the European Review of Private law and editor of the Tijdschrift voor Privaatrecht.

China

Prof. **Augusto Teixeira Garcia** is Associate Professor and Associate Dean of the Faculty of Law of the University of Macau. He is Arbitrator of Arbitration Center of World Trade Center of Macau. He is also an associate member of the International Academy of Comparative Law and a founding member of the Macau Association for Comparative Law. He coordinated the reform of the Commercial Code and the Commercial Registry Code. His research interests are Commercial Law, Company Law and Intellectual Property Law.

Prof. **Dan Wei** is Associate Professor, Director of the Institute for Advanced Legal Studies of the Faculty of Law of the University of Macau and Editor-in-Chief of *Macau Law Review*. She is Arbitrator of Arbitration Center of World Trade Center of Macau, elected member of the International Law Association, being also member of the Committee of International Trade Law and member and Rapporteur of the Committee of International Protection of Consumers. Wei is elected associate member of the International Academy of Comparative Law and Secretary-General of the Macau Association for Comparative Law.

Paula Nunes Correia is Assistant Professor, Coordinator of the Bachelor of Law in Portuguese Language programme and former Director of the Centre for Law Studies of the Faculty of Law of the University of Macau. She teaches Civil Law and Comparative Law. Paula is a former member of the Lawyers' Superior Council of the Macau Lawyers' Association. She is also an associate member of the International Academy of Comparative Law, a member of the International Society of Family Law and a founding member of the Macau Association for Comparative Law.

Prof. **Tong Io Cheng** is a Professor and Associate Dean of the Faculty of Law, University of Macau. In this same University, he serves also as the member of Senate and member of University Council. In terms of professional participation, Tong is qualified as lawyer, private notary and arbitrator; he is frequently invited as the examiner for the Lawyers Qualification Examinations since 2005, and appointed a member of the Lawyers' Superior Council since 2009. He was admitted as an associate member of the International Academy of Comparative Law, and currently appointed as the Visiting Professor of the Centre for Macau Study. He is also a Deputy of the Macau Legislative Assembly, as well as a counselor of the Macau Legal Reform Consultative Committee.

Czech Republic

JUDr. PhDr. **David Elischer**, Ph.D. (Parts IV, VI and VIII), Department of Civil Law, Faculty of Law, Charles University Prague. His dissertation thesis focused on wrongfulness and damage as prerequisites of civil responsibility in European legal context. As an Assistant Professor, he deals with the law of obligations, particularly with its general part, contracts and civil responsibility (torts). In 2008–2009, member of a working group on new Czech civil code, Legislation Council of the Czech Government, member of Common Core Group.

JUDr. **Ondřej Frinta**, Ph.D. (Parts I, II, VII and IX), Department of Civil Law, Faculty of Law, Charles University Prague. As a postgraduate student, he focused on issues concerning the legal regulation of subjects, namely of those with artificial nature. As an Assistant Professor he continues in his research activities. From 2006, member of Commission for Recodification of Private Law of the Ministry of Justice of the Czech Republic.

Prof. JUDr. **Monika Pauknerová**, CSc., DSc. (Brief Introduction and Parts III and V), Professor of private international law and international commercial law, Department of Commercial Law, Faculty of Law, Charles University Prague, member of the European Group for Private International Law, member of the International Academy of Comparative Law (IACL) and President of the Czech National Committee of the IACL, Vice-President of the International Association of Legal Science, arbitrator at the Arbitration Court in Prague.

Estonia

Irene Kull (born on 6 May 1961) graduated from the Faculty of Law of the University of Tartu in 1984. Professor Kull obtained her doctoral degree in 2002 from the University of Tartu and was appointed Professor of Civil Law in 2006 at the Faculty of Law. She is holding the position of the Head of the Chair of Commercial Law and Intellectual Property. She has been a member of drafting group of Estonian Civil Code Acts, author of the Commentaries to the Estonian Law of Obligations Act and Commentaries to the General Part of the Civil Code Act and text books in civil law. Professor Kull was a member of the Study Group on European Civil Code and a member of the Expert Group on a Common Frame of Reference in the area of European Contract Law. She lectures on contract law, law of obligations and European contract and commercial law. Professor Kull is a founding member of the Academy for European Private Law and a member of European Law Institute. She is also an advisor at the Civil Chamber of the Estonian Supreme Court of Estonia and member of the Supervisory Board of the Bank of Estonia.

Finland

Teemu Juutilainen is a doctoral candidate and researcher at the University of Helsinki, Faculty of Law. He is a member of the Centre of Excellence in Foundations of European Law and Polity, funded by the Academy of Finland.

France

Prof. **Jean-Sébastien Borghetti** graduated in management (HEC Paris) and in law (université Paris I). He wrote his Ph.D. on product liability in a comparative perspective (*La responsabilité du fait des produits. Étude de droit comparé*, Paris: LGDJ, 2004). He became first a Professor in Nantes (2005–2009) and is now Professor of Private Law at université Panthéon-Assas (Paris II). His main fields of research are tort and contract law.

Greece

Christina Deliyanni-Dimitrakou is a graduate of the Law School of the Aristotle University of Thessaloniki. Following her postgraduate studies in International Private Law and International Social Law at the Law Faculty of the University of Geneva (Switzerland), she received her Ph.D. diploma from the same University. She is an Associate Professor at the Law School of the Aristotle University of Thessaloniki, where she teaches Comparative Law and European Social Law at undergraduate and postgraduate level. A Visiting Professor at the Law Schools of Dijon and Toulouse (France), she is a member of the International Academy of Comparative Law, of the French Society of Comparative Legislation and of the Greek Society of Labor Law and Social Security. Except for Comparative Law and European Social Law, her areas of interest include Trust Law, European Tort Law, Human Rights and Comparative Non-Discrimination. Among her most recent publications are "Comparative Law and Legal Pluralism (in Greek) Sakkoula Publ. 2008, Trust and Fiducia" (in Greek), Sakkoula Publ. 1998, "Comparative Law and the Problem of the Recoverability of Pure Economic Loss" Sakkoula Publ. 2008, (in English) as well as selected articles in Law Reviews [e.g. *«Mutations des prémisses philosophiques du droit comparé»*, in, Mélanges X. Blanc-Jouvan, Paris 2005, p. 25

et seq (in French); «*Négociation collective et règles communautaires de la concurrence*», Revue Internationale de Droit Comparé, 3-2006, p. 785 et seq (in French); «*Le droit social de l'Union européenne façe aux nouvelles formes de famille*», "Mélanges à l'honneur de Yota Kravaritou: a trilingual tribute", I. Schömann (éd), ETUI, 2011, p. 49 et s (in French); *"Medical Confidentiality and Interfamily Conflicts Regarding the Medical Care of Adolescents: Legal Framework and Comparative Observations"*, Hellenic Review of International Law, 2011, p. 886 et s (in English); *"Multiple Discriminations in Europe : A Comparative Approach"* Labor Law Review (in Greek).

Israel

Prof. **Eyal Zamir** is Augusto Levi Professor of Commercial Law at the Hebrew University of Jerusalem, Israel. He served as Dean of the Faculty of Law and is currently Director of the Aharon Barak Center for Interdisciplinary Legal Research. Professor Zamir was a visiting scholar or Visiting Professor at Harvard, Yale, NYU, Georgetown, and UCLA Law Schools. He authored or edited 11 books and published more than 30 articles in American and Israeli law reviews, including the *Journal of Legal Studies, Columbia Law Review, California Law Review, Virginia Law Review*, and the *American Journal of International Law.*

Italy

Prof. **Rodolfo Sacco**. Born in 1923. Doctor in law, 1946. Professor of Civil Law (1946–1971), Private Comparative Law (1971–1994) and later in Legal Anthropology in Trieste, Pavia, Turin. Dean at the Faculty of Law of the Somali National University (1969–1970). Professor at the International Faculty of Comparative Law in Strasbourg (1960–1994). Doctor honoris causa at Paris II, Genève, Mc Gill, Toulon. President of the International Association of Legal Science, of the Associazione Italiana di Diritto. Comparato, and the Società Italiana per la Ricerca nel Diritto Comparato. National member of the Accademia dei Lincei, member of the Academia Europaea, Correspondant de l'Institut de France, member of the International Academy of Comparative Law.

Japan

Prof. **Hiroyasu Ishikawa**, Associate Professor of Institute of Social Science at the University of Tokyo, was born in1974, received an LL.B. from Waseda University in 1998, an LL.M. from the University of Tokyo (Graduate School of Law and

Politics) in 2000, and was appointed as Research Associate of the University of Tokyo (2000–2003), Associate Professor of Law of Gakushuin University (2004–2008), the present position since 2008.

Netherlands

Anna Berlee (1986) is a Ph.D. candidate in Comparative and European Private Law, with a particular interest in Property Law at Maastricht University. She is working under the supervision of Prof. J. H. M. van Erp and Dr. Bram Akkermans, LL.M (Maastricht University). She took both her LL.B European Law School [English Track] (cum laude) and subsequent LL.M in Dutch law (cum laude) from Maastricht University. During her studies, she was also a participant of the bachelor honours programme and held several student-assistantships in the areas of criminal procedural law and (Islamic) family law. She is currently the Ph.D. representative within the Faculty of Law, and sits in the faculty's Science Committee in that capacity. She is also an editorial assistant for the *European Property Law Journal* (EPLJ).

Portugal

Prof. **Dário Moura Vicente** was born in Lisbon in 1962. He obtained his Ph.D. in Law from the University of Lisbon, in which he is a Full Professor (*Catedrático*). He teaches Civil Law, Comparative Law, Intellectual Property Law and Private International Law. He is also an Adjunct Professor at the Faculty of Law of the University of Macau, China, and was formerly a Visiting Professor at The Hague Academy of International Law, Holland, and at several African, Asian, European and South-American Universities. He is an Associate Member of the International Academy of Comparative Law.

Puerto Rico

Prof. **Luis Muñiz Argüelles** is Member, International Academy of Comparative Law; member, World Society of Mixed Jurisdiction Jurists; Professor, University of Puerto Rico School of Law, 1979 to present; B.A., Cornell University, 1968; M.S. Columbia University, 1970; J.D., Universidad de Puerto Rico, 1975; Visiting Scholar, Harvard University, 1986; Doctorat de l'Université de droit, d'économie et des sciences sociales de Paris (Paris II), 1989; Fulbright Scholar, Universidad Nacional del Uruguay, 1994, Universidad de Buenos Aires, 2000.

Scotland

Prof. **Elspeth Reid** is Professor of Scottish Private Law at the University of Edinburgh. Author of *Personality, Confidentiality and Privacy in Scots Law* (2010), *Personal Bar* (2006, with John Blackie) and various edited collections, she is currently preparing a monograph on *The Scots Law of Delict*. Her list of publications ranges across comparative private law, and extends also to Russian legal matters. She was previously editor of the *Edinburgh Law Review* (2002–2006), and is Editor of the *Edinburgh Studies in Law* monograph series. She is a Fellow of the Royal Society of Edinburgh, an Associate Member of the International Academy of Comparative Law and also a qualified solicitor in Scotland.

Spain

Prof. **Gabriel García Cantero**, Chair Professor of Civil Law, Professor Emeritus at the Universidad de Zaragoza (Spain). President of the Spanish Association of Comparative Law. Member of the International Academy of Comparative Law (París).

Turkey

Prof. Dr. **Ergun Özsunay**, Civil Law, Comparative Law and EU Private Law, Istanbul University School of Law (Em.) and Istanbul Culture University School of Law, President of the International Association of Legal Science, Titular member of the International Academy of Comparative Law, corresponding member of the Deutsche Gesellschaft für Rechtsvergleichung, Turkish delegate in the UNCITRAL Working Groups II (Arbitration) and VI (Secured Transactions).

USA

Prof. **James R. Maxeiner**, J.D., Cornell; LL.M., Georgetown; Ph.D. in Law (Dr. jur.), Ludwig Maximilian University (Munich, Germany). Associate Professor of Law and Associate Director, Center for International and Comparative Law, University of Baltimore School of Law. His chapter is a somewhat revised version of one of three United States National Reports of the American Society of Comparative Law to the *Codification* Congress of the International Academy of Comparative Law held in Taiwan, May 24–28, 2012. See http://www.law.ntu.edu.tw/iacl/law.html. This is the report on "The Scope and Structure of Civil Codes: The

Inclusion of Commercial Law, Family Law, Labor Law, Consumer Law." It has been published in the Mississippi College Law Review and appears here by permission. Work on his chapter was supported by a sabbatical leave and a summer research stipend of the University of Baltimore School of Law and by the Common Good Institute. Participation in the Congress was facilitated by the American Society of Comparative Law and the University of Baltimore School of Law. Views expressed are the author's.

Agustín Parise is Researcher at the Faculty of Law, Maastricht University; LL.B., Facultad de Derecho, Universidad de Buenos Aires; LL.M., Louisiana State University Law Center; LL.D. Facultad de Derecho, Universidad de Buenos Aires; Member, Asociación Argentina de Derecho Comparado; Member, Instituto de Investigaciones de Historia del Derecho; Fellow, Maastricht European Private Law Institute.

Venezuela

Prof. **Eugenio Hernández-Bretón** is Professor and Chairman of the Master's Program on Private International and Comparative Law at Universidad Central de Venezuela; Member and Vice President of the Venezuelan Academy of Political and Social Sciences; Associé of the International Academy of Comparative Law; Doctor of Laws, University of Heidelberg; Master of Laws, University of Tubingen; Master of Laws, Columbia University, New York; Abogado, Universidad Católica Andrés Bello, Caracas.

Claudia Madrid Martínez is Professor at Universidad Central de Venezuela; Vice President of the Venezuelan Association of Private Law; Doctor of Laws, Master of Private International and Comparative Law, Abogado, Universidad Central de Venezuela; Post Doctoral Researcher, University of Cologne.

Index

J.C. Rivera (ed.), *The Scope and Structure of Civil Codes*, Ius Gentium: Comparative Perspectives on Law and Justice 32, DOI 10.1007/978-94-007-7942-6,

D

The manufacturer's authorised representative in the EU is Springer
Nature Customer Service Centre GmbH, Europaplatz 3, 69115 Heidelberg,
Germany. If you have any concerns regarding our products, please
contact ProductSafety@springernature.com

Printed and bound by CPI Group (UK) Ltd, Croydon, CR0 4YY
30/09/2026
02225444-0016